A READER IN C
PHILOSOPHICAL THEOLOGY

A READER IN CONTEMPORARY PHILOSOPHICAL THEOLOGY

Edited and with
an Introduction by

OLIVER D. CRISP

t&t clark

Published by T&T Clark
A Continuum Imprint
The Tower Building, 11 York Road, London SE1 7NX
80 Maiden Lane, Suite 704, New York, NY 10038

www.continuumbooks.com

British Library Cataloguing-in-Publication Data
A catalogue record for this book is available from the British Library

ISBN: HB: 978-0-567-03145-7
ISBN: PB: 978-0-567-03146-4

Typeset by Newgen Imaging Systems Pvt Ltd, Chennai, India

To my theological and philosophical teachers, especially:
David Fergusson
Trevor Hart
Paul Helm
W. P. Stephens
Iain Torrance

A disciple is not above his teacher, but everyone who is perfectly trained will be like his teacher.

Luke 6.40

CONTENTS

ACKNOWLEDGEMENTS

I am grateful to the following individuals who have given their time and expertise, or have answered my queries along the way: Marilyn McCord Adams, Michael Rea, Richard Swinburne, Alan Torrance, Nicholas Wolterstorff and Mark Wynn. Gavin D'Costa and Paul Helm deserve special thanks for reading through drafts of the introduction and offering numerous helpful comments. Naturally, none of these scholars is responsible for the errors of commission or omission that remain.

I am also grateful to the committee for the Read–Tuckwell Fund in the Faculty of Arts at the University of Bristol, which provided a generous grant towards the costs of reproducing the essays contained in this volume.

Finally, thanks are also due to the following journals and publishing houses for their kind permission to reprint the following items (in order of their appearance in this volume):

- Plantinga, Alvin, 'Sheehan's Shenanigans: How Theology Becomes Tomfoolery' in James F. Sennett (ed.), *The Analytic Theist: An Alvin Plantinga Reader* (Grand Rapids: Eerdmans, 1998), ch. 12, pp. 316–327. Copyright W. B. Eerdmans Publishing Company.
- Davis, Stephen T., 'The Bible Is True' in *Christian Philosophical Theology* (Oxford: Oxford University Press, 2006), ch. 16, pp. 284–299. Copyright Oxford University Press.
- Wolterstorff, Nicholas, 'True Words' in Alan G. Padgett and Patrick R. Keifert (eds), *But is it all True? The Bible and the Question of Truth* (Grand Rapids: Eerdmans, 2006), pp. 34–43. Copyright W. B. Eerdmans Publishing Company.
- Helm, Paul, 'Infallibility' in *The Divine Revelation* (Vancouver, BC.: Regent College Publishing, 2004 [1986]), ch. 4, pp. 75–91. Copyright Paul Helm.
- Plantinga Jr, Cornelius, 'Social Trinity and Tritheism' in Cornelius Plantinga Jr and Ronald Feenstra (eds), *Trinity, Incarnation and Atonement* (Notre Dame: University of Notre Dame Press, 1989), pp. 21–47. Copyright University of Notre Dame Press.
- Leftow, Brian, 'A Latin Trinity' in *Faith and Philosophy* 21, 3 (2004): 304–333. Copyright *Faith and Philosophy*.
- Van Inwagen, Peter, 'Three Persons in One Being: On Attempts to Show that the Doctrine of the Trinity is Self-Contradictory' in Melville Y. Stewart (ed.), *The Trinity*, (Dordrecht: Kluwer Academic Publishers, 2003), pp. 83–97. Copyright Springer Science and Business Media.
- Forrest, Peter, 'The Incarnation: A Philosophical Case for Kenosis' in *Religious Studies* 36 (2000): 127–140. Copyright Cambridge University Press.

- Stump, Eleonore, 'Aquinas' Metaphysics of the Incarnation' in Stephen T. Davis, Daniel Kendall and Gerald O'Collins (eds), *The Incarnation* (Oxford: Oxford University Press, 2002), pp. 197–218. Copyright Oxford University Press.
- Flint, Thomas P., 'The Possibilities of Incarnation: Some Radical Molinist Suggestions' in *Religious Studies* 37 (2001): 307–320. Copyright Cambridge University Press.
- Morris, Thomas V., 'Rationality and the Christian Revelation' in *Anselmian Explorations, Essays in Philosophical Theology* (Notre Dame: University of Notre Dame Press, 1986), pp. 213–241, 253. Copyright University of Notre Dame Press.
- Adams, Robert Merrihew, 'Original Sin: A Study in the Interaction of Philosophy and Theology', in F. J. Ambrosio (ed.), *The Question of Christian Philosophy Today* (New York: Fordham University Press, 1999), ch. 4, pp. 80–110. Copyright Fordham University Press.
- Adams, Marilyn McCord, 'Sin as Uncleanness' in James Tomberlin, (ed.), *Philosophical Perspectives 5, Philosophy of Religion* (Atascadero, CA.: Ridgeview Publishing, 1991), pp. 1–27. Copyright Ridgeview Publishing Company.
- Wyma, Keith D., 'Innocent Sinfulness, Guilty Sin: Original Sin and Divine Justice' in Peter van Inwagen (ed.), *Christian Faith and the Problem of Evil* (Grand Rapids: Eerdmans, 2004), pp. 263–276. Copyright W. B. Eerdmans Publishing Company.
- Crisp, Oliver D., 'Penal Non-substitution' in *Journal of Theological Studies* 59, 1 (2008), pp. 140–168. Copyright of the author.
- Lewis, David, 'Do We Believe in Penal Substitution?' in *Philosophical Papers* 26 (1997): 203–209. Copyright *Philosophical Papers.*
- Quinn, Philip L. 'Abelard on Atonement: "Nothing Unintelligible, Arbitrary, Illogical, or Immoral about it"' in Eleonore Stump (ed.), *Reasoned Faith: Essays in Philosophical Theology* (Ithaca: Cornell University Press, 1993), pp. 281–300. Copyright Cornell University Press.
- Swinburne, Richard, 'The Christian Scheme of Salvation' in Thomas V. Morris (ed.), *Philosophy and the Christian Faith* (Notre Dame: University of Notre Dame Press, 1988). Copyright University of Notre Dame Press.

INTRODUCTION

> *[P]hilosophical theology . . . is a matter of thinking about central doctrines of the Christian faith from a philosophical perspective; it is a matter of employing the resources of philosophy to deepen our grasp and understanding of them.*
>
> *Alvin Plantinga[1]*

In this introduction I set out a brief *résumé* of the relatively recent resurgence of philosophical theology in the analytic tradition. I then consider the relationship this new strain of philosophical theology bears to systematic theology. My contention is that this is an important development for theologians as much as for philosophers that has a great deal in common with certain traditional styles of doing theology, and has much to commend it to theologians willing to consider its merits.

From philosophy of religion to philosophical theology

One of the most remarkable changes that have taken place in theology in the last quarter century is the way in which philosophical theology has been revitalized through the work of analytic philosophers. In the late 1970s and early 1980s Christian philosophers in the analytic tradition began to turn their attention to making sense of particular Christian doctrines, instead of restricting themselves to the more general topics that fall under the generic rubric 'classical theism', such as the concept of God, arguments for the existence of God and the problem of evil. In part, this was due to a desire to tackle concrete issues in Christian theology that seemed ripe for analytic scrutiny. But another factor was that analytic philosophy itself was changing. Whereas in the middle third of the twentieth century logical positivism and then ordinary language philosophy held sway in departments of philosophy in the Anglophone world, by the end of the 1960s these ways of thinking had run into the sand. In the 1970s analytic philosophers began to turn back to the subject matter of metaphysics, one of the central concerns of the Western philosophical tradition that had been eschewed, even maligned, by representatives of logical positivism and a number of the ordinary language philosophers.[2] One important component in this change was the development of modal logic and its applications to *de re* necessity and a return to essentialism in the work of philosophers like Saul Kripke, David Lewis and (importantly for philosophy of religion), Alvin Plantinga.[3] The concern for intellectual virtues like clarity, logical rigour in argument, the importance of carefully expounding and rebutting potential objections to lines of reasoning, all remain hallmarks of analytic philosophy. However, although epistemological issues continue to be important intellectual considerations for analytic philosophers (and philosophical theologians), it is no longer the case that the *central* concerns of analytic philosophers are narrowly linguistic concerns – as if complex philosophical (even theological) problems could be 'solved' by isolating and analysing certain linguistic units of a given language. In light of such developments in analytic philosophy since the 1970s Richard Swinburne points out, 'the goal' of contemporary analytic philosophy 'is now metaphysical: to give a correct account of what are the ultimate constituents of the world and how they interact. "Analytic" is merely a title for this kind of philosophy inherited from its ancestry'.[4] Much of the interest in philosophy of religion, and, latterly philosophical theology, has been spurred on by this metaphysical turn in the latter third of the twentieth century, since much – though not all – of the subject matter of these two subdisciplines is what we might call theistic, and theological, metaphysics.[5]

This new interest in philosophical theology precipitated a number of interesting essays and monographs in the area, which gradually multiplied in number. Today there is a thriving literature dealing with Christian doctrines from an analytic perspective. Yet until now there has been no single volume that gives the student and scholar a sample of this literature. This book is an attempt to remedy that lacuna.

By its very nature a reader cannot hope to cover everything, nor every important paper written on a particular topic. The primary objective of this book is to give a sample of a range of different views taken on five central theological topics or *loci* in contemporary Christian philosophical theology. The papers reprinted here have been chosen because they make important contributions to the literature, with an eye to bringing under the covers of one volume as many of the best-known thinkers in this burgeoning field as possible. The five parts of the book comprise Revelation and Scripture; the Trinity; the Incarnation; Sin and Original Sin; and the Atonement. All of these doctrines yield particular problems for the Christian theologian, which do not arise for theologians in other religious traditions, even those religious traditions most closely related to Christianity. Hence, they are all properly *Christian* theological doctrines, not merely theistic doctrines which are in some important respects shared in common with other, non-Christian theists, such as the doctrine of creation, or providence. For, clearly, the Jewish or Muslim theologian does not have to wrestle with the doctrines of the Trinity,

Incarnation, original sin, or atonement in the way that a Christian theologian must.[6] And although what we might call 'plain-and-simple monotheists' in the Judaeo-Islamic traditions may offer arguments for the inspiration and authority of their scriptures, such arguments will differ in important respects from those proffered by Christian thinkers.[7]

There are other issues not included here that have also been the subject of considerable scrutiny in recent Christian philosophical theology of the analytic variety. The most important of these are the concept of prayer, particularly, petitionary prayer or impetration and problems with eschatology, including discussion of heaven, hell, purgatory and universalism. It is hoped that in time philosophical theologians will begin to tackle other topics of traditional systematic theology too, including the *ordo salutis* (order of salvation, e.g. regeneration, justification, sanctification); ecclesiology; and sacramental theology. There are encouraging signs that such discussions are beginning in some of these areas,[8] and every chance that further reflection will uncover exciting new avenues of research.

The relationship between philosophical theology and systematic theology

It is a fact often noted and sometimes regretted that philosophers, particularly those in the analytic tradition, do not really speak to theologians. Nor, for that matter, do theologians often speak to analytic philosophers. Thus, Dean Zimmerman observes, 'Unfortunately, there is very little dialogue between Christian philosophers in the analytic tradition and Christian theologians.' He goes on to explain, 'there are vast differences between the philosophical canons and methods of analytic philosophers with theological interests, on the one hand, and most Christian theologians with philosophical interests, on the other. When the groups do interact, terminological and methodological differences (and sometimes, sadly, prejudice and mistrust) hinder fruitful exchange.'[9]

This is not to say that theologians talk to *no* philosophers. It is just that analytic philosophers are treated with a certain suspicion by theologians, and, for their part, some analytic philosophers seem to have a rather sneering view of the content and place of theology. As I have pointed out elsewhere,[10] part of the reason for this mutual animosity has to do with the perception theologians have about the analytic 'tradition' of philosophy. Too often it is identified with that mid-twentieth century phase of its life that was largely inhospitable to theology (and metaphysics and ethics). But, as has already been mentioned, analytic philosophy is not synonymous with logical positivism. A number of the founders of analytic philosophy (e.g. Bertrand Russell or G. E. Moore) were interested in metaphysics and ethics, even if they were not so keen on theology.

But these are not the only reasons for hostility. Many academic theologians are deeply indebted, either personally, or through the (Western) theological tradition to which they belong, to a cluster of post-Enlightenment thinkers whose work is usually thought to be the preserve of what is now referred to as 'continental' philosophy.[11] This tradition of thought, and especially those thinkers whose point of departure is Kant's Copernican Revolution in philosophy, eschew large metaphysical schemes of thought because (following Kant) they are deeply sceptical that any such schemes are possible.[12] All we can conceive of in our theology and philosophy is that which is phenomenal, a part of this world of sensation in which we live, not the realm of the noumenal, the eternal and unchanging, that is forever beyond us.[13] Moreover, many (though by no means all) theologians, taking their cue from this continental tradition of philosophy, think that matters metaphysical, such as they may be understood or apprehended, are seldom as amenable to the cut-and-dried 'logic-chopping' of analytic philosophy.[14]

This is not to say there are no theologians who look to the 'continental' philosophical tradition, whose work is deeply influenced by metaphysics. Karl Rahner's Heidegger-imbued theology is one influential example; contemporary Radical Orthodoxy's penchant for French philosophy might be another. In cases such as these, the differences with analytic philosophical theology may well be less clearly defined, having more to do with differing views about the nature and scope of theology (and philosophy), as well as which intellectual virtues one privileges, or thinks appropriate for theological discourse, e.g. clarity, brevity and simplicity of argument, or a more allusive, complex and referential way of approaching matters theological and philosophical.

Consequently, for a variety of reasons, those theologians who are committed to what we might call a 'continental' philosophical project – or at least, are indebted to this philosophical tradition – may find the essays herein somewhat baffling, even off-putting. But it would be a mistake to think that the analytic tradition has nothing to offer the theologian. In fact, in many ways, one could think of current analytic philosophical theology as a return to the sort of careful theologic-philosophical contributions that characterized by far the largest part of the Christian theological tradition. Thinkers as diverse as Origen, Irenaeus, Augustine, John of Damascus, Anselm, Duns Scotus, William Ockham, Thomas Aquinas, Martin Luther, John Calvin, Francis Turretin, John Owen, Jonathan Edwards and a host of others, were all, in various ways, involved in such positive theological-philosophical projects even if they did not all write formal systems of theology. Nor are modern systematic theologians immune from this fondness for grand schemes, even when they claim to reject the hold of philosophy over theology, as with the work of Karl Barth, or, more recently, Colin Gunton or Robert Jenson. Indeed, some contemporary systematicians have welcomed analytic work alongside the more continental streams of thought. Wolfhart Pannenberg's theology is a case in point; Bruce Marshall's is another.[15]

Still, some theologians will remain suspicious of analytic philosophers doing philosophical theology, or theologians indebted to this philosophical tradition, rather than the continental one, because they think that an analytical approach tends towards ahistoricism. There is a mistaken historicism, of course. As Alvin Plantinga points out, 'some theologians seem to harbour the impression that philosophical theology as pursued by contemporary philosophers is often unduly ahistorical and uncontextual. Sometimes this arises from the thought that any concern with [these] topics is ahistorical; those topics belong to another age and can't be properly discussed now. That seems to me to be historicism run amok; but no doubt some of this work could profit from closer contact with what theologians know.'[16] Yet too often analytic philosophers have tended to create and demolish theological straw men that bear little resemblance to historic developments in the Christian tradition. Moreover, some analytic philosophers seem to think that removing the historical husk to get at the conceptual kernel of a particular theological issue is what is important. But such a procedure often fails to take seriously enough the fact that the Church has adopted certain positions for reasons that are rooted in complex historical discussions, where issues other than conceptual clarity were considered crucial factors in the outcome of such theological debate. Nevertheless, such ahistoricism is not a reason for rejecting the insights analytical discussions of Christian doctrine may provide, although it is a reason for pursuing a more historically informed approach to these issues. And, as a number of the essays in this volume demonstrate, much of the recent work in analytical Christian philosophical theology has been at pains to address this shortcoming, with some impressive results.

According to William Hasker, the most interesting criticism of analytic philosophy of religion is its preoccupation with a generic 'theism' rather than concrete issues in particular religious traditions. Here the concern is that 'theism as discussed by philosophers is but a pale, skeletal abstraction, far removed from the rich complex of beliefs and practices of a living religion.'[17] There is some truth in this criticism. But it cuts very little ice as an objection to contemporary analytic philosophical theology, which is all about discussion of the concrete doctrinal problems.

So, it seems, matters are somewhat more complicated than a simple cameo of the analytical–theological divide might suggest. There is even some evidence of theologians beginning to engage with such philosophers to fruitful theological ends. This volume is offered in the hope that by bringing together a selection of some of the best recent analytic philosophical theology, students and teachers alike might be stimulated to engage with analytic philosophers, not necessarily in order to further a particular kind of philosophical project, but perhaps in order to use what is helpful in this tradition for properly theological ends. Theologians are faced with an opportunity. Not to make theology in the image of philosophy (i.e. *ontotheology*), but to countenance an *analytic theology*, where philosophy plays the subordinate role of handmaid to her theological mistress. Such an engagement would be a most useful and potentially fruitful arrangement, and one that theologians may welcome.

Oliver D. Crisp
August 2008

Notes

1. Alvin Plantinga, 'Christian Philosophy at the End of the Twentieth Century' in James F. Sennett (ed.), *The Analytical Theist, An Alvin Plantinga Reader* (Grand Rapids: Eerdmans, 1998), p. 340.
2. This is true of much ordinary language philosophy, though not all. For instance, P. F. Strawson's essay *Individuals, An Essay in Descriptive Metaphysics* (London: Methuen, 1959) is a powerful piece of metaphysics from someone often associated with the ordinary language philosophy. Nor is it true to say no metaphysics was done, even during the heyday of logical positivism. R. G. Collingwood wrote on metaphysics from the idealist tradition in this period. But there were others like Bruce Aune, Arthur Prior and Richard Taylor who wrote on metaphysical issues from within the analytical tradition in the immediate post-War period. For useful, if slightly dated, historical discussion of the development of analytical philosophy up to the mid-twentieth century, see John Passmore, *A Hundred Years of Philosophy* (London: Duckworth, 1957).
3. See, for example, Saul Kripke, *Naming and Necessity* (Oxford: Blackwell, 1980), David Lewis, *Counterfactuals* (Cambridge, MA.: Harvard University Press, 1973), idem, *On The Plurality of Worlds* (Oxford: Blackwell, 1986), and Alvin Plantinga, *The Nature of Necessity* (Oxford: Oxford University Press, 1974). *De re* necessity has to do with objects that possess certain properties essentially, and essentialism has to do with certain sorts of objects being substances that have properties. Thus a dog is a substance that has the contingent property, 'being shaggy' and the essential property 'being doggish'. The dog may cease to be shaggy, if it is shaved. But it cannot cease to be 'doggish'.

4. Richard Swinburne, 'The Value and Christian Roots of Analytical Philosophy of Religion' in Harriet A. Harris and Christopher J. Insole (eds), *Faith and Philosophical Analysis, The Impact of Analytical Philosophy on the Philosophy of Religion* (Aldershot: Ashgate, 2005), p. 35.

5. Religious epistemology has also been a central plank in the recovery of philosophy of religion and remains an important area for philosophical theologians, as the essays in Part I of this reader and that of Thomas Morris on the Incarnation, demonstrate. But not all religious epistemology is exclusively concerned with analytic philosophical theology. Reformed Epistemology, associated with William Alston, Alvin Plantinga and Nicholas Wolterstorff might be thought of as a species of Christian philosophy. But it is not quite philosophical theology in the restricted sense of being concerned with making sense of Christian doctrines, which is the way in which I am using the term 'philosophical theology' here. Instead, such Christian Philosophy has a broader concern to explain how the Christian belief in God is not irrational. An answer to this question must be given if philosophical theology is to be credible; but an answer to such questions is not a matter of philosophical theology, strictly speaking. This is an example of the distinct, but overlapping concerns of philosophy of religion and philosophical theology.

6. This is not to deny that Jewish or Islamic theologians have some account of distinctive Christian doctrines, sometimes even incorporating aspects of such doctrines into their own theologies, such as the Islamic account of the crucifixion of Isa (Jesus). In the case of the doctrine of sin, both Jewish and Islamic theologians may well have a robust account of how it is that human beings are sinful, but the doctrine of *original* sin, having to do with how it is that the sin of the first human being affected the rest of humanity that can only be atoned for through the work of Christ, is a peculiarly Christian preoccupation, as set forth in places like Rom. 5.12-19.

7. This is true even though Christians share the scriptures of Judaism. But even if Jewish theologians regarded their own scriptures in a way parallel to a Christian understanding of scripture as the inspired Word of God, this would not mean that such Jewish theologians shared the same view of their scriptures as Christians do. For one thing, Christians view the Jewish scripture as the Old Testament, which is fulfilled and understood in light of the New Testament. For this reason, as Richard Swinburne has recently pointed out, Christian theologians cannot speak of a *Hebrew* Bible, since there can be no Hebrew Bible (i.e. Old Testament) that is not 'completed' by the New Testament canon. See Swinburne, *Revelation, From Metaphor to Analogy* (Oxford: Oxford University Press, 1992), ch. 10.

8. See, for example, Marilyn McCord Adams, *Christ and Horrors, The Coherence of Christology* (Cambridge: Cambridge University Press, 2006), ch. 10, entitled 'Christ in the Sacrament of the Altar: Christ in the Meantime', and Brian Hebblethwaite *Philosophical Theology and Christian Doctrine* (Oxford: Blackwell, 2005), ch. 8.

9. Dean W. Zimmerman, 'Three Introductory Questions: Is Analytic Philosophical Theology an Oxymoron? Is Substance Dualism Incoherent? What's in

this Book, Anyway?' in Peter van Inwagen and Dean Zimmerman (eds), *Persons, Human and Divine*, (Oxford: Oxford University Press, 2006). pp. 5–6.

10. Oliver D. Crisp, 'On Analytic Theology' in Oliver D. Crisp and Michael C. Rea (eds), *Analytic Theology: New Essays in The Philosophy of Theology* (Oxford: Oxford University Press, 2009), ch. 1.

11. For a careful, nuanced overview of 'continental' philosophy of religion, see Merold Westphal, 'Continental Philosophy of Religion' in William J. Wainwright (ed.), *The Oxford Handbook to Philosophy of Religion*, (Oxford: Oxford University Press, 2005), pp. 472–493.

12. Here I think of classical liberal theologians and their intellectual progeny. Thus, Albrecht Ritschl says 'Logically, the rejection of natural religion [viz. natural theology] means, at the same time, a rejection of all universal concepts which one might possess prior to the particular structures of revealed religion or apart from the actuality of those structures in the founder and in the community.' From 'Theology and Metaphysics', in *Albrecht Ritschl, Three Essays*, trans. Philip Hefner (Eugene, OR: Wipf and Stock, 2005 [1972]), p. 210. Many 'postmoderns' are also sceptical of a certain sort of metaphysical system building in theology, as they are sceptical of all 'metanarratives', and of any theological hegemony which might be a thinly disguised 'will-to-power', to borrow Nietzsche's famous phrase. Indeed, for some such theologians, the very idea that God is a supreme being whose character can be delineated by philosophical reflection is tantamount to 'ontotheology' – the making of God in a particular philosophical image. For discussion of this, see, for example, Thomas A. Carlson 'Postmetaphysical Theology' in Kevin J. (ed.), *The Cambridge Companion to Postmodern Theology*, Vanhoozer (Cambridge: Cambridge University Press, 2003), pp. 58–75.

13. In this regard, see Nicholas Wolterstorff 'Is it Possible and Desirable for Theologians to Recover from Kant?' in *Modern Theology* 14 (1998): 1–18 and the symposium on *Kant and the New Philosophy of Religion* in *Philosophia Christi* 9, 1 (2007).

14. The essay by Swinburne in *Faith and Philosophical Analysis* and Zimmerman in *Persons, Human and Divine*, cited earlier, give detailed attention to these issues. Another valuable resource is the editorial introduction to Gijsbert van den Brink and Marcel Sarot (eds), *Understanding the Divine Attributes* (Frankfurt am Main: Peter Lang, 1999).

15. There are other names we could mention in this connection including David Brown, Sarah Coakley, Ingolf Dalferth, Christoph Schwöbel and Alan Torrance.

16. Plantinga, 'Christian Philosophy at the End of the Twentieth Century', p. 341.

17. William Hasker, 'Analytic Philosophy of Religion' in *The Oxford Handbook to Philosophy of Religion*, pp. 442–443.

PART I

REVELATION AND SCRIPTURE

INTRODUCTION

The inspiration and authority of Scripture have long been theologically contentious issues. Advances in historical biblical criticism since the seventeenth century, and in particular, the so-called quests for the historical Jesus, have undermined the faith of many Christians in the authority of Scripture as the normative source of divine revelation, and, hence of Christian doctrine. Yet in recent times the methods and conclusions of historical biblical critics have been the subject of critical scrutiny.[1] In the same period, there have been several important treatments of divine revelation and the authority of Scripture by philosophical theologians, although more work is needed. This part begins with an essay by arguably the most important philosopher of religion at work today, Alvin Plantinga. While his work has been directed to central problems in metaphysics and epistemology, as well as philosophy of religion, he has also written on topics that fall within the purview of philosophical theology. Perhaps his most important contribution in this regard has been the discussion about the place of historical biblical criticism as a tool for understanding the form and content of Scripture. In the essay reprinted here, Plantinga takes issue with the work of fellow philosopher, Thomas Sheehan. Sheehan has a rather expansive view of what historical biblical criticism can show us about the compilation and content of Scripture, and what this means for the inspiration and authority of the biblical (especially New Testament) documents. Plantinga is less sanguine about the deliverances of historical biblical criticism, and offers several lines of criticism directed against this more optimistic approach.

Stephen Davis has made an important contribution to the resurgence of contemporary Christian philosophical theology, with work on the doctrines of the Incarnation and Resurrection. In his essay reproduced here, Davis argues that there are several ways one could construe the phrase 'The Bible is true', at least one of which is intellectually defensible.

Nicholas Wolterstorff is widely recognized as one of the most important and wide-ranging contemporary philosophers of religion. He has made ground breaking contributions to religious epistemology, being one of the original triumvirate of Reformed Epistemologists. He has also made an important contribution to the doctrine of divine revelation in his monograph, *Divine Discourse*.[2] Wolterstorff's essay in this volume is something of a follow-up piece to *Divine Discourse*, which takes issue with the claim, often associated with biblical fundamentalists, that every word of the Bible 'is true'. Wolterstorff maintains that such a claim simply does not do justice to the complexity of material in scripture. Although there are many assertions in Scripture that can be analysed in terms of the truth or falsity of what is being asserted, there is much else besides which is not clearly asserting anything, such as questions, commands, blessings.

Finally in this part, there is an essay by the British philosopher of religion, Paul Helm, drawn from his book on divine revelation. Helm argues that the notion of infallibility can be delineated clearly enough for it to be of use in philosophical theology. And this has particular reference to the doctrine of revelation, and Scripture (Bibliology).

Notes

1. See, for example, the essays in Eleonore Stump and Thomas P. Flint (eds), *Hermes and Athena* (Notre Dame: University of Notre Dame Press, 1993).
2. (Cambridge: Cambridge University Press, 1995).

Suggested further reading

- Davis, Stephen T., *Christian Philosophical Theology* (Oxford: Oxford University Press, 2006).
- Helm, Paul, *The Divine Revelation: The Basic Issues* (Vancouver, BC: Regent College Publishing 2004 [1986]).
- Plantinga, Alvin, *Warranted Christian Belief* (New York: Oxford University Press, 2000), ch. 12.
- Stump, Eleonore and Flint, Thomas P. (eds), *Hermes and Athena* (Notre Dame: University of Notre Dame Press, 1993).
- Swinburne, Richard, *Revelation: From Metaphor to Analogy, Revised Edition* (Oxford: Oxford University Press, 2007 [1992]).
- Wolterstorff, Nicholas, *Divine Discourse* (Cambridge: Cambridge University Press, 1995).

CHAPTER 1

SHEEHAN'S SHENANIGANS: HOW THEOLOGY BECOMES TOMFOOLERY

Alvin Plantinga

I

Higher criticism – source criticism, form criticism, redaction criticism, various contemporary amalgams – has been with us now for at least a century and a half. To the layman it can easily seem that higher critics disparage what they see as the naiveté of the ordinary Christian's belief in the events reported in the New Testament: Christ's virgin birth, his miracles, his death, his (literal and physical) resurrection, his being seen by "more than five hundred of the brethren," his ascension into heaven, and the like. Thus David Strauss, in his *Life of Jesus, Critically Examined,* published in 1835: "Nay, if we would be candid with ourselves, that which was once sacred history for the Christian believer is, for the enlightened portion of our contemporaries, only fable." To the layman it can also seem that the grounds for this disparagement are sometimes extremely slender – so gossamer thin as to be nearly nonexistent. There is much confident assertion but little compelling evidence, abundant speculation but next to nothing of real solidity.

Protestants have had to deal with "higher criticism" for a good long time; but Catholic scholars have been discovering (or at any rate employing) it only over the last quarter-century or so. The result has been a spate of books of biblical criticism by Catholic scholars, some of them, I am sorry to say, running to sizeable excess. Thomas Sheehan's much publicized *The First Coming: How the Kingdom of God Became Christianity* (New York: Random House, 1986) is a case in point. Sheehan is professor of philosophy at Loyola University in Chicago.

Sheehan begins his book by claiming that the Christian church is undergoing a crisis in what she thinks and believes about Jesus: "The crisis grows out of the fact now freely admitted by both Protestant and Catholic theologians and exegetes: that as far as can be discerned from the available historical data, Jesus of Nazareth did not think he was divine [and] did not assert any of the messianic claims that the New Testament attributes to him . . ." (p. 9). Sheehan's project is apparently fourfold:

(a) to try once more to determine the actual content of Jesus' preaching (as opposed to what Christians have thought it was); (b) to determine how the idea that Jesus arose from the dead developed in the early church; (c) to do the same for the idea that Jesus was the Christ, the Messiah, and the divine Son of God; and (d) to discover what is the *actual* significance of the preaching and life and death of Jesus. The project is to try to accomplish (a), (b), and (c) "from below": without making such theological assumptions as, for example, that Jesus is the incarnate Son of God, or that the Bible is in any special sense the word of God, or that there is such a thing as the testimony of the Holy Spirit, enabling us to grasp scriptural truths we would otherwise miss. Sheehan hopes to accomplish (a)-(c) by using the sorts of methods that would be employed by a historian confronting any ancient text: "I adopt the viewpoint of the historian, not that of the believer. I take the word 'history' in the context of the original Greek verb that underlies it: *historein,* to search and inquire, using only the light of natural, empirical reason" (p. 9). So the idea is to try to discover what Jesus preached, and how the belief in the resurrection developed, and how the early Christologies developed "using only the light of the natural, empirical reason."

On (b) and (c) Sheehan adopts what is by now a very familiar line: none of the apparent testimony to Jesus' resurrection from the dead and his being literally and physically seen by his disciples ("by more than five hundred of the brothers at the same time"; 1 Cor. 15:6) is to be taken seriously. The nature miracles are

> simply legends which arose among early Christians and which were projected backward, under the impact of faith, into the life of the historical Jesus. (p. 74)

> The reason for the patent inconsistencies and the physical unrecordability of these miraculous "events" comes down to one thing: The gospel stories about Easter are not historical accounts but religious myths. (p. 97)

> To counter the climate of doubt aroused by Jesus' failure to return, some gospel accounts embellished the Easter experience with elaborate apocalyptic stories that concretized the "resurrection" of Jesus by providing him with a preternatural body that was physically seen, touched and elevated into heaven. (p. 293)

The addition of mythical elements was due to a sort of failure of nerve on the part of Peter and others; as a result of this failure there developed in the early church these myths about angels at the tomb, Jesus' being literally seen by many, and the like. Similarly for the development of Christology culminating in the Prologue to the Gospel of John, the Philippians hymn, and Paul's letter to the Colossians: Jesus himself made none of these claims for himself; they were invented later on by a church intent on buttressing a theological point.

Now taken in its own terms Sheehan's case for these claims is at best tenuous, speculative, and fanciful. However, I shall mostly neglect what he says about (b) and (c) and concentrate on what he says under rubrics (a) and (d); then I'll turn to a brief examination of the sorts of reasons scholars sometimes give for supposing that Christology "from below" – attempting to understand the relevant texts without recourse to theological beliefs about Christ or the Bible – is in fact correct and *de rigueur* for Scripture scholarship.

Well then, what does "natural, empirical reason" reveal about what Jesus actually preached? Sheehan's answer may strike an ordinary Christian as indeed amazing, not to say preposterous. Jesus, for example, did not claim to be the Messiah or even a messiah, let alone the divine Son of God:

> What then have the post-Bultmannian critics discovered about the historical Jesus . . . ? Negatively, they have established that Jesus did not express his self-understanding in any Christo- logical titles – certainly not in the so-called higher titles (such as "God" or "Lord") in the full divine sense and not even in the so-called lower titles (for example "messiah," . . . and "Son of Man"). (p. 25)

What did he claim then? What was his positive message? It isn't easy to understand Sheehan's answer. It all began, however, when Jesus came under the spell of John the Baptist; upon hearing the latter, says Sheehan, "Jesus, we may imagine, was pierced to the heart. He repented and was baptized" (p. 53). "Jesus was impressed by the fact that John, unlike the apocalyptic preachers so popular in those days, preached no messiah, proclaimed no end of the world, and promised no future aeon of bliss" (p. 52). Following suit, Jesus too proclaimed no end of the world, preached neither that he nor some other was the messiah. He followed John in "the reduction of apocalypse to its existential core" (p. 55); this means, as far as I can make out, that Jesus had no apocalyptic message, but did enjoin justice and mercy. Further:

> The immediate presence of God as a loving Father is what Jesus meant by the "kingdom. . . ." As Jesus preached it, the kingdom of God had nothing to do with the fanciful geopol- itics of the apocalyptists and messianists – a kingdom up above

or up ahead. . . . Rather, it meant God's act of reigning, and this meant – here lay the revolutionary force of Jesus' message – that God, as God, had *identified himself without remainder with his people* [Sheehan's italics]. The reign of God meant the *incarnation* of God. (p. 60)

That is, Jesus destroyed the notion of "God-in-Himself" and put in its place the experience of "God-with-mankind." Henceforth, according to the prophet from Galilee, the Father was not to be found in a distant heaven but was entirely identified with the cause of men and women. Jesus' doctrine of the kingdom meant that God had become incarnate: He had poured himself out, had disappeared into mankind and could be found nowhere else but there. . . . The doctrine of the kingdom meant that henceforth and forever God was present only in and as one's neighbor. Jesus dissolved the fanciful speculations of apocalyptic eschatology into the call to justice and charity. (p. 61)

[Jesus'] proclamation marked the death of religion and religion's God and heralded the beginning of the post-religious experience: the abdication of "God" in favor of his hidden presence, among human beings. (pp. 61-62)

So Jesus did not proclaim that he was the Messiah, let alone the Son of God; what he preached is not "Believe on me and thou shalt be saved," but something quite different: "God has disappeared into mankind." But what could *that* mean? "God, as God, had *identified himself without remainder with his people*"; "God has disappeared into mankind"; "the abdication of 'God' in favor of his hidden presence among human beings": how are we to understand these dark sayings?

It isn't easy to tell, but I *think* what Sheehan means here is that according to Jesus, there simply *is* no all-powerful being who has, say, created the world and to whom we owe worship and obedience. There is nothing at all like the sort of being Christians and other theists believe in: a transcendent, all-powerful, all-knowing person who has created the heavens and the earth and sustains them in being. And although Sheehan speaks of God's *disappearing into* mankind, *becoming* incarnate without remainder, and the like, the idea is not, I gather, that previously there was such a being, but then later on he somehow disappeared into humanity: the idea is that there never was any such person at all. All there had ever been to God, we might say, was his incarnation in his people: "All Jesus did was bring to light in a fresh way what had always been the case, but what had been forgotten or obscured by religion. His role was simply to end religion – that temporary governess who had turned into a tyrant . . ." (p. 68). So Jesus' message, according to Sheehan, was that theism is false and there is no God. It isn't that theism is at best *approximately* true (as with the nineteenth-century liberals with leanings towards absolute idealism); it isn't true *at all*. Jesus was really an atheist; he preached the end of religion and religion's God, dissolving all this into the recommendation of justice and mercy.

Among liberal theologians of a certain stripe there appears to be a kind of desperate quest for novelty; those who take part in this derby seem to vie with each other to see who can make the most outrageous pronouncements. To understand Sheehan and his claims about Jesus, we must see him and them in their historical context. Twenty years ago when "Death of God Theology" burst (or perhaps dribbled) upon the scene, many of us thought that heights of theological tomfoolery had been achieved that could never be exceeded. One of their number, Paul Van Buren, suggested that logical positivism with its Verifiability Criterion of Meaning – according to which most of what Christians say about God is literally nonsense – was really the proper foundation of Christian theology. Another, Thomas Altizer, seems to have claimed that God died when Christ was born, that he died again in the nineteenth century, and that he has also died in human history generally. He then went on to say that atheism is in fact the final flower and purest form of Christianity (neglecting to add the obvious corollary that bigotry is the final flower and purest form of chastity).

What we had here, many thought, was theological foolishness than which none greater could be conceived. And indeed, Altizer's achievement along these lines is truly formidable. But credit where credit is due: Sheehan, it seems, has topped it. According to Altizer, the real Christian recognizes that atheism is the truth; and now Sheehan adds, in a spectacular burst of insight, that this is the gospel Jesus Christ himself brought! Colossal! There is only one way to go beyond this: to hold that God himself, eternal, omnipotent, and omniscient as he is, was an atheist even before Jesus, and has suffered from a distressing inability to get the message across. (Using terminology in the confusing, vaguely dishonest way characteristic of such theology, one could support this view by pointing out that God worships no one and does not acknowledge a superior being, both of which are characteristic of the atheist.) But even this suggestion, logically impossible though it is, doesn't have quite the sheer bite and panache of Sheehan's preposterous claim.

Sheehan's own message – what *he* sees as the real meaning of the empty tomb, as opposed to the meaning ascribed to it by Christians – is of apiece with the message he puts in the mouth of Jesus. (The tailless fox, as R. G. Collingwood says, preaches taillessness.) According to Sheehan, the real meaning:

> As we peer into that emptiness [of the tomb, with no resurrection], the absence of the living Jesus and even of his dead body allows us to identify a unique form of seeking: the desire for that which can never be had. This unique kind of seeking is the experience that makes human beings different from any other kind of entity, and we see it exemplified in the women who actually found the tomb empty on that first Easter Sunday. Such seeking is not something we occasionally get caught up in; rather, it is what makes us human, constitutes us as the futile passion, the unfulfilled and presumably unfulfillable desire that we are. (p. 172)

> Taking Jesus *as (sic)* his word means understanding that he is what everyone else is: a finite fallible, mortal act of interpretation. Every human being is just that and no more: a hermeneusis, a lived interpretation (in action, in play, in language and thought) of what one's existence is and is about. (p. 225)

> All of us, including Jesus, are inevitably and forever a question to which there is no answer. Taking Jesus *as* his word means understanding and accepting that. (p. 226)

Taking Jesus *as* his word? This is already enough to make one a bit nervous; how are we to do a thing like that? Would it be to believe that Jesus (contrary to what we have always thought) was really a *proposition* or an assertion? As I say, this is enough to make one a bit nervous; but it is only the tip of the iceberg. Easter, for the Christian, is a time of joy and celebration, a time of profound gratitude for the unthinkable splendor of God's gift of salvation through the death and resurrection of his Son. But according to Sheehan, the *real* meaning of Easter, the real meaning of the empty tomb, is not the glad Easter cry "He is risen" with the declaration that Christ is the firstfruits and the earnest of our own resurrection, so that death has been swallowed up in victory. Not at all; what it really means, he says, is that we are all futile and unfulfillable passions, questions to which there are no answers.

Being a question without an answer certainly sounds like a depressing condition, and no doubt something of a comedown; but what could it *mean?* What is it to be a futile passion, or a question without an answer? You meet some unusual people nowadays, but hardly ever anyone who is a question, let alone a question without an answer. Shorn of excessive pathetic rhetoric, what Sheehan means, I think, is that it is very hard to be sure of anything; no matter what you believe there are always equally satisfactory alternatives. This fits in with Sheehan's claim earlier on in the introduction that

> Christianity is a "hermeneusis," or interpretation. Its beliefs and doctrines are but one of many possible and equally valid ways of understanding the universally available empirical data about Jesus of Nazareth. Christians may claim that their faith is based on revelation, but as far as one can tell empirically, such revelation is a name for the historically relative and culturally determined hermeneutical process in which Christians, confronting the humanly available information about Jesus of Nazareth, choose to interpret him as their savior who reigns with God in heaven. (p. 7)

There is much to be said about this (most of it not flattering), but I won't take the time to say it. The basic idea here seems to be the notion, familiar in some varieties of continental philosophy, that whatever we think or believe is only a hermeneusis or interpretation, to which there are equally satisfactory alternatives. No matter what you believe on any important matter, there are alternatives to your belief that are quite as valid and acceptable. Indeed, for any belief you hold, its *denial* will be just as valid or satisfactory as it is.

Of course if this is true, then Christianity, despite Sheehan's confident pronouncements, is as good an interpretation as any other. Thus Sheehan winds up (p. 223) having to concede that Christianity is as acceptable an interpretation or hermeneusis as any other, and, indeed, as *true* as any other – Sheehan's own interpretation, for example. (How we are to understand that is a bit puzzling, since Christianity and what Sheehan proposes are clearly inconsistent; but then Sheehan neither says nor suggests that ordinary logic is part of *his* interpretation.) Self-referential problems loom here. The fundamental claim seems to be that all we can ever have are equally acceptable if conflicting interpretations. But then, of course, if this claim is true, then it is itself just one more interpretation, and it is no better or closer to the truth than alternatives – for example, its denial. If all is interpretation, then this idea itself has no more to be said for it than the contrary idea that some interpretations are vastly preferable and vastly closer to the truth than others. If all is interpretation to which there are equally satisfactory alternatives, then this very claim is an interpretation to which there are equally satisfactory alternatives: one can take it or leave it. As for me and my house, I think we'll leave it.

II

How does Sheehan reach these starting claims as to what Jesus taught? By starting from what he sees as the agreed-upon results of New Testament scholarship and extrapolating: "I depend upon (and hope that I am faithful to) the scientifically controllable results of modem biblical scholarship; but then I go beyond that scholarship, by using its scientific results as data for my own theories" (p. 9). Sheehan draws upon source criticism, form criticism, redaction criticism, and some hitherto unclassified similar criticisms; and his introduction contains a clear and readable account of some of these developments.

To the uninitiated, it can easily seem that much that is tenuous lies at the very foundations of some of these methods. Thus, for example, Sheehan reports that the post-Bultmannian form critics

> make use of at least four criteria for determining whether elements of the gospel material are authentically historical, that is, traceable to Jesus himself. First, the criterion of dissimilarity allows the exegete to attribute to Jesus at least those sayings which can be shown to be probably unique to him insofar as they are notably dissimilar from sayings that are provably typical either of the early church or ancient Judaism. Secondly, the criterion of coherence allows these exegetes to attribute to Jesus those sayings that are coherent with the material that has already been established to be "unique because dissimilar." Thirdly, the criterion of multiple attestation permits the exegete, within limits, to attribute to Jesus those deeds or kinds of behavior which are attested in all or many of the distinct gospel sources (for example, Mark and Q). Finally, according to the criterion of language and environment, any authentic saying of Jesus would have to reflect Aramaic speech and, in general, the cultural patterns of early Palestine – although it is possible that such characteristics might reflect only the earliest Palestinian churches. (p. 25)

But there is a clear tension here between the first and the fourth criterion: only those sayings that are dissimilar from what was current will be certified by the first criterion, while if the saying does not reflect the cultural patterns of early Palestine then it will be decertified by the fourth. (And of course if you think that Jesus is indeed the divine Son of God, you will no doubt hesitate to assume that any authentic saying of Jesus would have to reflect the cultural patterns of early Palestine.) Further, these methods seem to display an alarming degree of flexibility or flaccidity, permitting an astoundingly wide range of conclusions. Sheehan's own conclusions require, as you can imagine, a good bit of picking and choosing among texts. Using these methods, this is always easy enough: you simply demote any text that doesn't fit your interpretation; you claim that it is a later addition by the Christian community intent on making a theological point. Does Mark 14 or Matthew 26 say Jesus says he is the Son of God and will return in glory? No problem: simply declare that it was added later on and is not a report of anything Jesus actually said.

I shall leave it to the experts to decide how much of value there is in these methods; what concerns me here is Sheehan's tendentious use of them. For example, he regularly speaks of what has been *confirmed* by these methods, or *shown* (p. 12) by them, or *discovered* by them (p. 13), or *established* by them (p. 15); in nearly all of these cases there is scholarly opinion on both sides of the question. (Of course there is also the fact that, from Sheehan's perspective, nothing can really be shown or established; all we have are interpretations to which there are always equally acceptable alternatives.) Further, there is a great deal of dogmatic and unsupported assertion. For example, speaking of John's "leaping in the womb" when his mother Elizabeth met Mary: "But that legend, like the inspiring but unhistorical story about the miraculous virginal conception of Jesus, is a theological interpretation created some decades after the death of Jesus to express Christianity's faith in his special status" (p. 55). Again: "And in any case the words the Gospels put into Jesus' mouth at his [Sanhedrin] hearing (for example, his claim to being the Messiah; Mark 14:62) are later theological interpolations of the early church and cannot be credited as historical statements" (p. 86). And: ". . . it is not true that the Jewish crowds shouted out that Jesus should be crucified (Mark 15:12) or that they took his blood upon themselves and their children (Matt. 27:25). . . . These sentences, which were later written into the accounts of Jesus' passion, are the product of a bitter polemic between early Christianity and Judaism . . ." (p. 87). Here one wonders at the source of Sheehan's information, and here, as in many other places, the footnotes reveal that the matter in question is very much a topic of scholarly debate.

Frequently the text contains a bland assertion to the effect that such and such is the case, and a footnote contradicting the assertion. Thus Sheehan claims that "There is no evidence that Jesus himself forgave sinners in his own name"; in a footnote he gives the evidence, adding that while some take the saying in question to be authentic, others do not. Again, "Jesus had not fainted. He was dead. And in the spirit of the New Testament we may add: He never came back to life" (p. 101). Here there is a footnote, directing us, not as you might expect, to the New Testament, but to Thomas Aquinas – who, of course, does not say that Jesus never came back to life: what he does say is that upon his resurrection Jesus entered a life that was immortal and Godlike.

Sheehan also displays a certain distressing inability to distinguish the assertion that not-p from the failure to assert p. Thus, for example, he says that according to Matthew, "He does not ascend into heaven" (p. 97), giving as a reference Matthew 28:16-20. But of course Matthew 28: 16-20 does not say that Jesus did not ascend into heaven; it simply doesn't say that he did. Again, there is often a certain lack of balance between the plausibility of a claim and the weight of its documentation. For example: "For Simon and the others," he says, "'resurrection' was simply one way of articulating their conviction that God had vindicated Jesus and was coming soon to dwell among his people. And this interpretation would have held true for the early believers, even if an exhumation of Jesus' grave had discovered his rotting flesh and bones" (p. 109). The evidence for this astonishing claim is the fact that there is at least one Scripture scholar who says so. Finally, as Sheehan interprets 1 Corinthians 15:3-8, Paul did not mean to say that Christ had physically risen from the dead: "The raising of Jesus has nothing to do with a spatio-temporal resuscitation, a coming back to life . . ." (p. 112). But here he completely neglects the remainder of the chapter, where Paul relates Jesus' resurrection to our own coming resurrection, which he clearly sees as literal, physical, and spatio-temporal.

III

The most interesting issues raised by this book, I think, have less to do with Sheehan's dubious claims than with the enterprises of Christology "from below" and "objective" biblical scholarship – i.e., scholarship in which one does not assume or take for granted what one knows or believes by faith about (say) Jesus, but instead treats the Bible as one would any ancient text and Jesus as any character in such a text. The idea is to see what can be established (or at least made plausible) using only the light of "natural, empirical reason," ignoring anything one may know by faith. The idea is that a proper Scripture scholar will be "objective." Objectivity is sometimes represented as a matter of sticking to the objective facts, not bringing in any theological interpretation. What is really meant in this context, however, is that the objective scholar will not use any theological assumptions or knowledge in the attempt to determine what the objective facts are. Thus, for example, Barnabas Lindars, a well-known New Testament scholar, seems to suggest that it is somehow wrong or improper to rely upon what one knows or believes by faith in biblical interpretation:

> There are in fact two reasons why many scholars are very cautious about miracle stories. . . . The second reason is historical. The religious literature of the ancient world is full of miracle stories, and we cannot believe them all. It is not open to a scholar to decide that, just because he is a believing Christian, he will accept all the Gospel miracles at their face value, but at the same time he will repudiate miracles attributed to Isis. All such accounts have to be scrutinized with equal detachment. (*Theology,* March 1986, p. 91)

Why think this? Why *isn't* it open to a scholar to accept the Gospel accounts of miracles, but reject others? Because, thinks Lindars, proceeding that way wouldn't be properly detached or objective; there would be something merely arbitrary about it. The real question here is this: is it legitimate for a Christian scholar – a Christian Scripture scholar, for example – to employ assumptions or beliefs the source of which is her Christian faith? Can one properly employ, in scholarship, assumptions that aren't shared by all members of the scholarly community? Can you properly employ what you know by faith? Thus, for example, the Christian, thinking that Jesus is indeed the divine Son of God, might be inclined to credit certain miracle stories as sober historical accounts of what Jesus did (the raising of Lazarus, e.g., or his own resurrection). If you don't think Jesus was divine, however, you would plausibly think it very unlikely that these are accounts of what actually happened; it might be more plausible to see them as added by the early church to make a theological point of one sort or another. So whether you think Christ was (is) in fact divine could certainly make a big difference to how you proceed in Scripture scholarship.

And isn't it simple common sense to think that a Christian scholar (or the Christian scholarly community) should use everything she knows in pursuing her discipline? Suppose you (or the Christian community) do in fact believe that Jesus was divine. If what you want, in scholarship, is to reach the truth about the matters at hand, then why not use all that you know, regardless of its particular source? Isn't it merely perverse to limit yourself to only *some* of what you know, or only *some* sources of knowledge, if your aim is to reach the truth about the phenomenon in question? That would be like trying to do physics, say, without in any way relying upon your own memory or the memory of anyone else. (Any proposition accepted in part by virtue of reliance upon memory, you declare, is not to be taken as part of the evidence.) You might be able to do a bit of physics that way, but it would be pretty limited, a poor, paltry, truncated thing. And why would you want to do it? (Perhaps I could climb Devil's Tower with my feet tied together, but why would I want to?) If your aim is to reach as much as you can of the full-fledged, full-orbed truth about the matter at hand, then presumably the right way to proceed is to use all of your resources, everything you know, including what you know by faith.

But, says Lindars, isn't it just arbitrary to treat miracle stories about Jesus differently from miracle stories about Isis? Well, no; for you think that Jesus was divine but Isis was not – or perhaps you think that "Isis," in this use, doesn't name anything at all, so that there simply wasn't any such person or thing as Isis. So there is a great difference between the two, a difference which requires that they be treated differently. (Objectivity requires that we treat similar things similarly; it doesn't require that we ignore important differences.)

But then isn't it arbitrary to have *that* belief – that Jesus was Christ, and the Son of God, and hence special? What makes you think that is true? How could you sensibly come to *that* belief, except upon the basis of historical investigation – investigation that does not start by presupposing the truth of the belief in question? The suggestion is that any appropriately justified belief about Jesus must be based entirely upon ordinary historical investigation. But why should we believe a thing like that? Christians don't typically come to their beliefs about Jesus in that way; and I know of no good reason to think that this is the way they *would* do it, if they did it properly. This claim – that one ought not to employ the view that Jesus was (is) divine in scholarship – rests on the assumption that the only way in which we could properly come to characteristically Christian beliefs is by way of ordinary scientific or historical investigation. But this assumption is dubious *in excelsis;* it is part and parcel of classical Foundationalism and shares its liabilities (see, for example, my "Reason and Belief in God").[1] Further, it fits poorly with Christian ideas as to the sources of our Christian belief. Reformed Christians, for example, will be likely to follow John Calvin in holding that there is such a thing as the internal testimony of the Holy Spirit; and they will add that this testimony is a source of reliable and perfectly acceptable beliefs about what is communicated in Scripture. Other Christian traditions have other suggestions for sources of belief that play the same role; but nearly all the major Christian traditions unite in rejecting the idea that the only acceptable source of beliefs about Jesus is ordinary scientific investigation. So why should we accept it in Scripture scholarship?

What is really at issue here is a philosophical (epistemological) view about what constitutes correct or reasonable belief, about what constitutes proper or real knowledge. The objectivist thinks that the only sources of knowledge or acceptable scholarly belief are perception, memory, mathematico-Iogical intuition, and the like – i.e., "natural empirical reason"; he rejects any such alleged sources of belief as the testimony of the Holy Spirit. But there is no good reason for the Christian to join him here; and of course objectivism is an entirely unnatural position for a Christian to adopt. A more natural position is that if we employ all that we know (not just natural empirical reason), we stand a much better chance of getting close to the actual full-orbed truth. And isn't that what we are after in scholarship? So why should we handicap ourselves in the fashion suggested by the objectivist?

Note

1. See Alvin Plantinga and Nicholas Wolterstorff, eds. *Faith and Rationality* (Notre Dame: University of Notre Dame Press), pp. 17–93.

CHAPTER 2

THE BIBLE IS TRUE

Stephen T. Davis

I

Suppose we wanted to capture part of our attitude towards the Bible via the sentence, 'The Bible is true.' What might we mean by this statement?

Let me begin with what I take to be three *desiderata* for a theory of 'the Bible is true,' that is, three things that such a theory must accomplish. First, such a theory must take note of our special human status as 'verbivores'.[1] Every living organism has certain needs that must be met in order for it to survive and thrive – food, shelter, a method of reproduction, and so on. But human beings are special among all the creatures in that we have an additional need, a need for words, particularly *words from God*. Thus in Deuteronomy 8: 3, Moses, speaking for God, says to the children of Israel, 'one does not live by bread alone, but by every word that comes from the mouth of the Lord'.[2] Secondly, such a theory must explain why Christians read the Bible as opposed to any other book. Why do we Christians hold the Bible to be unique among such classics as *The Iliad* or *The Koran* or *The Critique of Pure Reason?* Thirdly, such a theory must explain why Christians take the Bible to be normative or authoritative. Why is the Bible such that it is not only appropriate, but also mandatory for Christians to allow themselves to be formed as persons by it?

To tip my hand, I believe it will turn out that a strong factor in satisfying all three *desiderata* is the notion that in some important sense, *God speaks to us in the Bible*.

II

Now let us return to the statement, 'The Bible is true.' What might this statement mean? Well, for a philosopher this formulation presents some difficulties. Although we are well aware that there are several uses of the word *true*, philosophers normally think that the only sorts of things that can be true (or false) in the paradigmatic or realist sense of *true* are things like assertions, claims, statements, or propositions. This sense of *true* means 'having the truth-value true', that is, being in accord with what is the case. Thus Aquinas' justly famous claim that 'truth is the agreement between the idea and the thing.'[3]

Accordingly, rocks, trees, numbers, galaxies, quarks, and books (like the Bible) do not have truth-values and accordingly are neither true nor false. Of course if a given statement can be true, then surely a set of statements can be true, presumably if all the statements in the set are true. Thus we might speak of someone's testimony about a certain event being true, if all the statements made by the witness are true. Then perhaps even a book could be true if all the statements in it were true.

But this does not seem a helpful route to follow in trying to decide what we might mean by 'The Bible is true.' For one thing, to say that the Bible is true in *this* sense – all the statements in it are true – does not seem nearly enough to capture what orthodox Christians want to say about the Bible. To illustrate this point, imagine the following scenario: for a lark, I decide to write a book that contains nothing but true statements. It contains sentences whose truth I know by experience like, *Grass is green* and *San Francisco is north of Los Angeles.* It also contains mathematical or logical truths like, *7+5=12* and *All triangles have three sides.* It also contains true statements about the past like, *Lincoln was shot at Ford's Theatre* and *The Pirates were world champions in 1960.* Imagine that the book is three hundred pages long and consists of nothing but one true statement after another. Notice that we could call such a book 'true'. We might even call it 'inerrant'. But it would be a banal, pointless, virtually incoherent, religiously useless book – in other words, quite unlike the Bible.

Indeed, the Bible consists of far more than assertions. (I emphasize this point because those who hold conservative views of the Bible are sometimes caricatured as holding that the Bible consists only of a set of propositions.) Everybody knows that the Bible contains all sorts of genres and linguistic elements – law codes, poetry, parables, songs, commands, questions, expressions of praise, exhortations, and many others – which seem incapable of being, in the paradigmatic sense, true (or false).

None of this is meant to deny the importance of there being true statements in the Bible. There are obviously many narrative sections in the Bible in which historical assertions are made; there are also many theological and moral assertions. Doubtless it is important that most or even all of these assertions be true. It does seem difficult to grasp how a book replete with false claims could be considered authoritative. Yet surely those Christians who want to express their attitude towards the Bible by the statement, 'The Bible is true,' must mean a great deal more than just, 'its assertions are all true'.

Of course the word *true* can be used in ways other than 'having the truth-value of true'. We sometimes use expressions like 'true to oneself', 'true blue', 'true north', 'true feelings', 'a true copy', and 'to come true', and such expressions seem not to have much to do with 'having the truth-value of true'. 'True' can mean things like loyal, sincere, trustworthy, having fidelity, giving helpful guidance, or proving accurate. And some of these usages are surely relevant to what we might mean by saying, 'The Bible is true.'

Still, I want to see whether we can make progress by sticking to something like the paradigmatic sense of true. Suppose we ask this question: What psychological attitude do we have towards assertions that we regard as true, statements such as

San Francisco is north of Los Angeles;
7 + 5 = 12;
My mother loves me;

and (if we are theists)

God exists?

And what psychological attitude do we have towards assertions that we regard as false? Part of the answer, as I suppose, is that with regard to statements which we take to be true, we commit ourselves to believe them (together with all propositions entailed by them), we accept their propositional content, we 'trust' them, we 'lay ourselves open' to them. That is, we allow our noetic structures and behaviour to be influenced by them. And we do not do any of that with statements that we regard as false.

Let me suggest that we mean something like this when we say, 'The Bible is true.' We mean that our attitude towards the Bible is such that we believe what it says, we trust it, we lay ourselves open to it. We allow our noetic structures and beliefs to be influenced by it. Such an attitude will include, but not by any means be limited to, accepting the truth (in the paradigmatic sense) of the assertions that we find in it. (What they are, obviously, will have to be interpreted.[4]) It also means taking questions in the Bible ('Should we sin the more that grace may abound?') as legitimate and probing questions addressed to us. It also means taking biblical exhortations ('Give thanks to the Lord, for He is good') as exhortations addressed to us that we must heed. It also means taking poetic sections from the Bible ('We are his people, and the sheep of his pasture') as powerful affective expressions of the way reality is.

If we take the Bible to be true, we trust it to guide our lives. We allow our lives to be influenced by it. We intend to listen where it speaks. We consider it normative. We look to it for comfort, encouragement, challenge, warning, guidance, and instruction. In short, we *submit to* the Bible. We place ourselves under its theological authority.

III

Notice that some of the things I believe to be true I believe more firmly than other things that I believe to be true. I believe the statement, *The dean of the faculty respects me.* After all, he and I have been friends and colleagues for years, and I think I know him and his opinions quite well. But I believe the statement, *My mother loves me,* much more firmly than I believe the statement, *The dean of the faculty respects me.* Now in fact I believe both statements; but I believe the one with a great deal more certainty than I believe the other. It will be much more difficult to convince me that my mother does not love me than to convince me that the dean does not respect me. Much more powerful defeaters will be needed.

Clearly, those who hold the Bible to be true in the sense we are considering – they trust it, listen to it, look to it, submit to it, consider it normative – believe the Bible to be true with a great deal of firmness or certainty. Their belief in it is not tentative. Their submission to it is not halting. The Bible is allowed to guide their lives, influence their behaviour, and form them as persons.

In one sense, this submission is quite voluntary. It is not as if somebody coerces Christians to submit to the Bible, like the way most people obey rather quickly when a policeman says, 'Put your hands behind your back!' But I do not want to give the impression that those folk who in some strong sense submit their lives to the Bible do so randomly or capriciously. It is not like flipping a coin or choosing one flavour of ice cream over another. It is not like one person saying to another, 'My holy book speaks to me but, somehow, yours leaves me cold.' Those who place themselves under the authority of the Bible do so precisely because they hold that the Bible is true. That is, they hold that the Bible is objectively authoritative. It is, as we might say, *worth* submitting to.

If I submit myself to the Bible, it has authority over me in one sense only because I take it as authoritative. (Note that it is possible for people to reject a given law – say, the law forbidding exceeding the speed limit – to regard it as having no authority over them.) But in another sense I take the Bible as authoritative over my life precisely because I regard it as objectively authoritative. (Similarly, even those who choose to ignore it are under the authority of the law forbidding speeding and can be ticketed and fined.) The Bible is objectively authoritative, then, in that people *ought* to accept its authority, whether they do so or not.

In philosophy we say that every assertion or proposition has certain truth-conditions, that is, the conditions that must be satisfied in order for the proposition to be true. The truth condition of 'San Francisco is north of Los Angeles' is simply San Francisco's being located north of Los Angeles. Maybe the linguistic utterances from the Bible that are not assertions (e.g. 'Honour your father and your mother', 'Pray without ceasing', 'Praise God in the sanctuary') also have (in an extended sense) truth conditions. Reality must be in a certain way, and not in other ways, in order for them to be objectively authoritative. It must be the case that it is morally obligatory to honour one's mother and father; it must be the case that God commands us to pray without ceasing; it must be the case that God deserves our praise and that the sanctuary is an appropriate place to express that praise.

IV

There is nothing in the theory of 'the Bible is true' that I am espousing that requires a defender of it to reject the theory known as biblical inerrancy. This is the theory that every properly interpreted assertion in the Bible – whether about theology, history, science, logic, sociology, geography, mathematics, or whatever – is true. Still, it is also perfectly possible to hold the theory without embracing inerrancy. To some folk, that indeed might amount to one of its strong points. Early in my career, I wrote a brief critique of biblical inerrancy in favour of what I called biblical infallibility.[5] Although I still embrace its overall approach, I now regard some of the arguments used in that book as unconvincing, and I am now familiar with more nuanced ways of understanding the concept of 'biblical inerrancy' than were available in 1977. Still, my basic problem with the doctrine of inerrancy, and the reason that I do not defend it, is that commitment to it seems to drive interpreters of the Bible at various points towards forced, awkward, and even ridiculous interpretations of the Bible in order to make problematic assertions come out true.

It is clear that a great many people do *not* regard the Bible as true in the sense just explained. (1) Some of them – atheists, religious sceptics, enemies of Christianity – explicitly disbelieve what the Bible says, or at least much of it. Certainly they reject the crucial bits. (2) Others in effect suspend judgement on what the Bible says until there exists a scholarly consensus. This latter seems to be the attitude of many Scripture scholars today; they consider the Bible to be no different in principle from any other ancient text – Plato's *Republic*, for example, or the Gospel of Peter. They believe what the Bible says only if historical-critical research substantiates what it says. In other words, their view is that it is a wholly human book, like any other book. (3) Many other people today have no idea what the Bible says, and don't seem to care. Anybody who has taught undergraduates in secular colleges or universities in recent years is familiar with such attitudes.

Those who hold that the Bible is true are in effect distancing themselves from all such views as this. They approach the Bible with a hermeneutic of trust. As Anselm said, 'I am sure that, if I say anything which
plainly opposes the Holy Scriptures, it is false; and if I am aware of it,
I will no longer hold it.'[6] Such folk take Scripture to be the source of
religious truth above all other sources, the norm or guide to religious
truth above all other norms or guides. The idea is that all sources of
religious truth are subordinate to Scripture and should be tested by
Scripture; Scripture has the last word or final say; whatever Scripture
says (when it is correctly interpreted) goes. I take it that this is what
the Westminster Divines were affirming when they wrote: 'The Supreme
Judge, by whom all controversies of religion are to be determined,
and all decrees of councils, opinions of ancient writers, doctrines of
men, and private spirits, are to be examined, and in whose sentence we
are to rest, can be no other but the Holy Spirit speaking to us in the
Scriptures.'[7]

The opinion that the Bible is true depends on a certain view of its
character, so to speak. It is not just that *we take it* to be Scripture (although
we do). (As if we could also take *Thus Spoke Zarathustra* or *The History of
the Synoptic Tradition* to be Scripture if we wanted.) It depends on the
view that the Bible is a special book, a book unlike all other books,
a book in which in some strong sense *God speaks to us.* Those who hold
that the Bible is true can never regard it as merely or simply a human
product like the *Iliad* or the *Phaedo* or the works of Nietzsche or the
works of Bultmann. They hold it to be the word of God. Despite their
status as cultural or academic classics, God does not speak to us in the
words of the *Iliad* or the *Phaedo* or *Thus Spoke Zarathustra* or *The History
of the Synoptic Tradition.* Or at least, God does not do so in anything like
the same way.

V

In this connection, it will be helpful to refer to the writings of two of
my fellow philosophers who have recently written about the status of
the Bible. Explaining what troubles me about their arguments – especially what they say about the various discrepancies and difficulties in the
Bible – will help me develop my own view.

The first is Nicholas Wolterstorff's excellent and ground-breaking
book, *Divine Discourse.*[8] I fully accept and presuppose much of his argument; the item I will mention constitutes the only major point where
I demur. Wolterstorff wants to argue that the Bible constitutes, or can
constitute, divinely appropriated human discourse (or that it can be
rational to hold that it does). That is, in the Bible, God can be taken

as speaking. Wolterstorff notes that there are discrepancies between different narrative accounts of the same events in the Bible. But since God cannot speak falsehoods, how can this be?[9]

One of Wolterstorff's strategies for dealing with this problem amounts to a suggestion that the Gospels can be seen as analogous in genre and intent to Simon Schama's book, *Dead Certainties*.[10] (I have not read this book and so will accept at face value everything Wolterstorff says about it.) Ostensibly a book of history – it is about the controversial death of British General James Wolfe in the battle of the Plains of Abraham near Quebec in 1759 – it is actually a work of what might be called imaginative history. Schama offers several quite different and even mutually inconsistent perspectives on this event, some from wholly invented characters writing wholly imaginary accounts, but which are plausible given one way or another of looking at the actual historical evidence. Schama also makes invented, but again (according to him) plausible, claims about the inner thoughts and feelings of Wolfe at various points. Wolterstorff sees Schama as asserting not actuality but *plausibility*. In effect, Schama says that things might well have actually gone this way in 1759. Schama never suggests anything *contrary* to the available historical evidence, but he goes far beyond it at points. He offers something like artistic portraits of Wolfe.

Wolterstorff wants to suggest that the Gospels are something like this. They are *portraits* of Jesus. In places they suggest not what certainly happened, but what might well have happened. The evangelists agree on 'the identity and significance of Jesus', but they disagree, for example, on whether the cleansing of the temple occurred early or late in his ministry. In places the evangelists were claiming to report what actually happened, but in other places they were only claiming 'illuminating plausibility' for their accounts. This viewpoint, Wolterstorff suggests, explains why the early church, aware as it was of the discrepancies, was so little troubled by them.

Now perhaps I have misunderstood Wolterstorff, but, if I have caught his meaning, I cannot agree. I too am aware of, and to a certain extent troubled by, the discrepancies between various narrative accounts of the same events in the Gospels. But if the Gospels are viewed as similar in genre and intent to *Dead Certainties,* then I think that the Christian church faces an immense problem. Unlike Schama's book, almost nothing in the Gospels as individual texts makes us want to think of them in this way. (I say 'almost nothing' because I agree with Wolterstorff, Eusebius, and Papias that Mark was not much concerned with issues of chronology.) Indeed, I think it is about as clear as anything can be that the evangelists believed, and wanted us to believe, that *this is how things actually happened.* That is, they all seem to be making factual assertions about what Jesus said and did and what happened to him.

I suspect Wolterstorff feels moved to make his proposal not by looking at the individual Gospels or their pericopes, but by comparing the several Gospels. And of course there is nothing in the world wrong with doing that. But perhaps there are other and better responses to the discrepancies than this. One is to deny that they are there, that is, to try to harmonize the discrepant accounts. In the case of many of the discrepancies, I believe this enterprise can succeed. Another response is to deny that the discrepancies much matter, since none (or none of the discrepancies that cannot sensibly be harmonized) seems to affect any crucial area of Christian belief or practice. Another response is to affirm inspiration, infallibility, and maybe even inerrancy, but arrive at a way of understanding those notions that is not undermined by occasional discrepancies. Another response is to claim that the discrepant accounts mean different things, which is what Philo did with discrepancies in the Hebrew Bible, and certain Church Fathers of the Alexandrian school did with discrepancies in the New Testament.

I said that adopting Wolterstorff's proposal would present the Christian church with a big problem: his proposal requires a hermeneutic for distinguishing between those texts in the Gospels that are meant as actualities and those that are meant only as likely plausibilities. But surely radical interpreters of Christianity – to whom I, for one, want to give little ground – will claim, for example, that the resurrection of Jesus from the dead was not meant to be an actuality. How will we refute such people? I suppose by showing them that the chapters at the end of the Gospels simply do not read that way; the evangelists thought of themselves as reporting sober fact. But surely that is true of just about everything we find in the Gospels (again, with the possible exception of Mark's chronology, Luke's grouping together of episodes with similar themes, etc.). I do not see how the job can possibly be done.

Rather than offering a useful interpretive tool, Wolterstorff's distinction between those accounts that the Gospel writers intended as true and those that they intended only as plausible seems almost impossible to apply to individual texts. How will we be able to tell where a given text fits? Moreover, the distinction can easily play into the hands of those interpreters who deny the literal truth of points that I at least consider crucial to the Christian faith, for example, that Jesus really was God incarnate and really was raised from the dead.

VI

The second scholar whose views I want to explore briefly is Mark Wallace.[11] So far as I can tell, he and I are miles apart on several important philosophical issues. I am much more inclined to embrace realist notions of truth than he is. And although I would never want to de-emphasize the interaction between the Bible and its reader, I see the act of interpretation primarily (not entirely) as the discovery of something that is there in the text, rather than the creation of something new.

To put the point crudely, Wallace is concerned that there is both good content and bad content in the Bible. The good content is constituted, presumably, by the teachings and example of Jesus and the high ethical teachings found elsewhere. The bad content consists of passages that picture God as capricious, taunting, violent, malicious, malevolent, and vengeful, for example, the stories of Job, the Passover, and Ananias and Sapphira. Wallace's sensitivity to this issue leads him to see 'truth' in relation to the Bible as something that is made or created (by the Bible *and* its reader), rather than something that is found in the Bible.

Wallace says: 'biblical truth is the ethical performance of what the Spirit's interior testimony is prompting the reader to do in the light of her encounter with the scriptural texts.' And: 'biblical truth consists in performing the Spirit's promptings to love God and neighbor.'[12] So it seems that according to Wallace, biblical truth exists (presumably exists *for* someone; let's eschew originality and call her Jones) when four conditions are satisfied:

(1) Jones reads biblical passage P.
(2) In reading P, Jones is prompted by the Spirit to do action A.
(3) Jones does A.

and

(4) A is ethical, that is, loving towards God and neighbour.

Notice that the definition of biblical truth that Wallace provides is not a characteristic of the Bible, but rather a result of interaction between the Bible and a reader. Accordingly, my central difficulty with Wallace's proposal is that it does little to preserve any sense of the Bible's uniqueness.[13] Notice that almost any other piece of writing can be true in this sense, for example, *The Republic* or *War and Peace* or the *Bhagavad-Gita*. As such, Wallace's notion is insufficient to preserve what I think the Christian community wants to say about the Bible. His definition of biblical truth leads him to a larger, but closely related, notion of theological truth. In theology, he says, a belief is true 'just insofar as it fosters a life of benevolent regard toward the "other"'. A theological judgement is valid, he says, 'whenever it enables compassionate engagement with the world in a manner that is enriching and transformative for self and other.'[14]

Here I only want to point out the real possibility that false theological statements (false in the sense of not corresponding to reality) might be true in Wallace's sense. Indeed, two logically inconsistent theological statements might *both* be true in his sense. Indeed, it is entirely possible that some true (true in a realist sense) theological statements may be false in Wallace's sense because they never foster 'a life of benevolent regard for the "other"'. Take some abstruse and long-forgotten statement from, say, eighteenth-century Reformed theological anthropology, for example, *Adam was the federal head of the human race.* Now assuming, as I do, that the statement is coherent, it follows that either it or its negation must be true in a realist sense. But it is quite possible that the true one – whichever it is – has never fostered any particular ethical attitude in anyone and thus is false in Wallace's sense.

In short, even if we adopt Wallace's notion of truth and apply it to some biblical text, it is still an open question whether the claims made in that text (if any are made) are true in Aquinas' sense. In many cases, this is a question in which many Christians will be deeply interested. For example, I genuinely want to know whether Jesus' claim, 'I and the Father are one' (John 10: 30), is true in a realist sense, quite apart from whether the Spirit has ever used that text to induce anyone to act lovingly and non-violently.

What are the other available options for someone who wants to claim that the Bible is true but is as aware of and sensitive to the troubling texts in the Bible as Wallace is? Well, it seems that there are lots of possibilities. One has been mentioned already: (1) harmonization. Here the effort would be to try to show that the character of God as apparently presented in the 'bad content' texts is not really God's character; when properly understood, the bad content passages do not teach that God is violent or malevolent. Here are some others: (2) Two of my Claremont colleagues, John Roth and Frederick Sontag, simply grasp the nettle and embrace both the bad content and the good content; their view is that God is both evil and good; God has a demonic side.[15] (3) One might try to find a theological principle that allows one to subordinate the bad content to the good content, for example, some such notion as 'the progress of revelation'. The idea would be to argue that the bad content texts represent a lower or more primitive understanding of the character of God than the good content texts do; the good content texts accordingly are allowed to criticize and supersede the bad content texts. (4) One might engage in what might be called theodicy – argue that the bad content texts are not as bad as they look, argue that God was morally justified in killing Ananais and Sapphira, for example.

Most of us who are committed to some version of what Wallace calls 'the infallibilist model' engage in all three of (1), (3), and (4). We try to find a hermeneutic that allows us to emphasize the good content over the bad content (which in his own way is of course exactly what

Wallace does). And I see no reason for his worry that people who follow that path will fail to listen to the voices of suffering people or fail to allow them space to struggle with God or express their anger with God.

The central point is that not all texts of Scripture are of equal theological importance or relevance to various religious issues. I believe that virtually all Christians – even those who believe in biblical inerrancy – at least implicitly recognize this fact. If proper hermeneutical principles simply entailed lining up various biblical texts and treating them all equally, there would be no sense in talking (as Wallace apparently does want to talk, given his notion of the 'supreme christological plot line' of the Bible[16]) about a unified theme or message in the Bible. More ominously, if we were simply to line up texts and treat them equally, then the Bible could fairly be said to teach things like the legitimacy of slavery, or the subordination of women, or the need to sacrifice animals at the altar of the temple in Jerusalem. Christians have always sensed that certain texts take hermeneutical and theological priority over others.

It is clear that there are places in the Bible where the Christian community has found it difficult to hear God's voice. What is needed, in the light of the murkier nooks and crannies of the Bible (among which I would include the divine command to slaughter all the Canaanites (Deut. 2: 31–5; 3: 1–8; 7: 2; Josh. 6:15–21; 8:25–6; 11:12), as well as the conclusion of Psalm 137) is what I will call *theological exegesis.* This is exegesis in the light of what the early Fathers called 'the rule of faith', that is, the church's view of the overall message of the Bible. Any given text must be interpreted in the light of the Christian community's vision of the witness of the whole of Scripture. Of course such a vision must always be viewed as fallible and amendable by future exegesis. Otherwise, the Spirit's freedom to speak to us in Scripture is curtailed. Moreover, theological exegesis ought never amount to simply disregarding the clear and obvious sense of a text in favour of a reading that we like better. Nevertheless, that overall vision of the macro-meaning of Scripture can be seen as a canon against which to test various interpretations of various texts. In the end, Christians need to be open hearers of the word, expecting that even the less promising parts of Scripture will have something or even much to say to us.

Three hermeneutical principles help clarify (although they do not exhaust) what I mean by theological exegesis: (1) the Old Testament should be interpreted in terms of the New Testament; (2) obscure passages are to be interpreted in terms of clear passages; and (3) everything is to be interpreted christologically. Many of the psalms, the four Gospels, and certain of the Pauline epistles (especially Romans and Galatians) are taken to be hermeneutically foundational.[17] Are they 'more inspired' or 'more truly God's word' or even 'more true' than others texts? No.

The claim is merely that they are more hermeneutically foundational to Christian belief and practice. Nor is this an attempt to find something helpful or authoritative in a book which one largely rejects. I disassociate myself entirely from any view such as that (nor am I accusing Wallace of holding it).

I take it that Wallace thinks that some such procedure is acceptable as long as it is recognized that it is merely an act of interpretation, rather than a discovery of the Bible's 'original meaning'. Well, certainly discovering what one takes to be the rule of faith is an act of interpretation, one that in the early church involved strenuous effort, vigorous debate, and careful discernment. However, I do not accept the idea that any proposal as to the macro-meaning of the Bible must be imposed on the Bible. It is entirely possible that it is really there.

My own Reformed theological tradition has always placed great emphasis on the sovereignty of God. One aspect of this sovereignty is that, throughout redemptive history, God makes choices that are free, even (so far as we can tell) arbitrary. God chooses Abel over Cain, Jacob over Esau, the children of Israel over the Moabites or the Philistines. And God is not required to account for those choices. My fear is that the parts of the Bible that are *true* in Wallace's sense reveal a God that is too tame, too much under our control, not sovereign, not mysterious or 'wholly other'.

Moreover, as I argued in Chapter 12, the biblical concept of the wrath of God – an embarrassment to theology in the last century or more – is in my view, an essential part of the Bible's message. Indeed, I would go so far as to say that the wrath of God is *our only hope* as human beings. (The grace of God is also our only hope, but that is another story.) Once when I was a child, the foreman of our family's ranch was showing me how to do something with a horse. He said, 'There are lots of wrong ways, and one right way, to do this.' I proceeded to do it in one of the wrong ways, and I had to pay for it with bruises, cuts, hurt pride, and some colourful language directed my way by the foreman. Similarly, there are lots of wrong ways and one right way to live a life, and if we live our lives in any of the wrong ways, we will have to pay for it. The wrath of God shows us clearly that it matters deeply how we live our lives. Our contemporary folk wisdom is not true, for example, when it says that any way you choose to live your life is okay, as long as you are sincere and try hard not to hurt anybody.

My conclusion, then, is that we need a stronger notion of biblical truth than Wallace provides. We need to know why anybody should read the Bible as opposed to any other book. One has the feeling that Wallace thinks the Bible is a worthwhile book to read because we can take good things from it, or (more fairly) because the Spirit can use it to make us act compassionately. But can't the Spirit use other books too? Again, why then the Bible?

In the end, I need to admit quite frankly that not all biblical problems can be solved, at least not by me. No matter what moves are made or arguments are presented, we will still be deeply troubled by some of them. In places, our belief that the Bible is true will amount to an act of *trust*. There are texts that we will have to believe are true despite our inability to show that or how they are true. We may just have to *wait*. And perhaps that is not altogether a bad thing. As it says in one of the most troubling books in the Bible, 'It is good that one should wait quietly for the salvation of the Lord' (Lam. 3: 26).[18]

VII

I now return to my main argument. Discerning readers will have noticed that I have been saying two quite different things about the sentence, 'The Bible is true.' Let us summarize the trusting attitude towards the Bible that I have been discussing (submitting to it, considering it authoritative, holding it higher than all other sources or norms of religious truth, etc.) as 'submitting'. Now it is clear that I have been claiming both (1) when I say the sentence 'The Bible is true' I *mean* 'I submit to the Bible'; and (2) my belief that 'The Bible is true' is *caused by* my belief that 'The Bible is worthy of submission' (which ultimately is caused by the Holy Spirit). There is no inconsistency here. I am indeed saying both.

I have said little in this chapter until now about *how one comes to know or believe* that 'The Bible is true.' Some theologians have claimed that the Bible is 'self-authenticating'. I would prefer not to use this expression, primarily because, following Calvin, I think some things *do* authenticate the words of Scripture. Calvin lists, as I would, the testimony of the church (which he mentions but de-emphasizes), the admirable properties of the Bible itself, and (far and away the most important) the inward testimony of the Holy Spirit.[19] As noted in Chapter 1, I would define the inward testimony as that influence of the Holy Spirit on the minds of believers that they reach certainty that in the Bible God speaks to them and that, accordingly, they must submit to it.

What do we mean when we say, 'The Bible is true'? It is vital to note that the question is in the first person plural – 'What do *we* mean?' I take the 'we' in this question to range over the whole of the Christian community, past and present. That is why I want to stress a notion of the Bible's truth that honours what the Fathers call the rule of faith, one that includes as many Christians as possible and as much of the past as possible. There are, of course, Christians with whom I cannot agree at various points, nor am I recommending slavish obedience to the Christian past.

But as a Christian academic who has spent his entire full-time career at secular institutions of higher education, this 'we' has always been important and comforting to me. In the face of opposition or, more often, indifference from my colleagues, I frequently need to remind myself that my affirmation that the Bible is true is not an affirmation made by me alone. It is an affirmation made by the community of which I am part, the Christian community, the Body of Christ.

We human beings are 'verbivores'. We live by the words that come from the mouth of the Lord. I have not committed myself to any particular theory of Biblical inspiration in this chapter. I have, however, affirmed that in the Bible we hear God speaking to us. We read the Scriptures expecting them to give us light and life. As we hear God's voice in them, the proper response is submission, wonder, and praise. That God speaks to us in the Bible and that we faithfully submit to those words is what we mean when we say 'The Bible is true.'[20]

Notes

1. I did not invent this term; so far as I know it was coined by Robert C. Roberts, 'Parameters of a Christian Psychology', in Robert C. Roberts (ed.), *Limning the Psyche: Explorations in Christian Psychology* (Grand Rapids, MI: Eerdmans, 1998).
2. Notice also *Phaedo* 85d, where Plato has Simmias say: 'It is our duty to do one of two things, either to ascertain the facts, whether by seeking instruction or by personal discovery, or, if this is impossible, to select the best and most dependable theory which human intelligence can supply, and use it as a raft to ride the seas of life – that is, assuming that we cannot make our journey with greater confidence and security by the surer means of a divine revelation.' *The Collected Dialogues of Plato,* Edith Hamilton and Huntington Cairns (eds.) (New York: Pantheon Books, 1963), p. 68.
3. *De Veritate,* 1, 3. See also William P. Alston's magisterial defence of realism on truth in his *A Realist Conception of Truth* (Ithaca, NY: Cornell University Press, 1996).
4. Indeed, I should point out that in the present chapter I am abstracting away from all hermeneutical questions in a quite arbitrary way. I know well that judgements about the truth of an utterance – whatever notion of 'true' is envisaged – are parasitical on judgements about the meaning of that utterance. Although I do make a few hermeneutical comments in Section VI of the chapter, for the most part I am simply assuming that we know what various biblical utterances mean.
5. Stephen T. Davis, *The Debate About the Bible: Inerrancy Versus Infallibility* (Philadelphia: Westminster Press, 1977).

6. Anselm, *St Anselm: Basic Writings* (trans. S. N. Deane) (La Salle, IL: Open Court, 1962), p. 220 (*Cur Deus Homo,* I, xviii).

7. The Westminster Confession, I, 10. See *The Constitution of the Presbyterian Church (USA),* Part I (New York: Office of the General Assembly, 1983), 6.010.

8. Nicholas Wolterstorff, *Divine Discourse: Philosophical Reflections on the Claim that God Speaks* (Cambridge: Cambridge University Press, 1995) (hereinafter *Divine Discourse*).

9. *Divine Discourse* (n. 8 above), pp. 252–60.

10. New York: Knopf, 1991.

11. See his essay, 'The Rule of Love and the Testimony of the Spirit in Contemporary Biblical Hermeneutics', in A. Wiercinski (ed.), *Between the Human and the Divine: Philosophical and Theological Hermeneutics* (Toronto: The Hermeneutic Press, 2002), pp. 280–91.

12. Wallace, ibid., pp. 283, 284.

13. Indeed, he denies that the Bible is unique in this regard. See p. 286.

14. Wallace (n. 11 above), p. 286.

15. See their respective essays in Stephen T. Davis, *Encountering Evil: Live Options in Theodicy,* 2nd edn. (Louisville KY: Westminster John Knox Press, 2001).

16. Wallace (n. 11 above), p. 289.

17. Several of these points were suggested years ago by E. J. Carnell in his *The Case for Orthodox Theology* (Philadelphia: Westminster Press, 1959), pp. 51–65.

18. There is a version of biblical inerrancy, which I cannot honestly say that I hold, but which I have no desire whatsoever to oppose. We might call it 'eschatological inerrancy'. This would be the claim that in the eschaton, when we will 'know as we are known' (1 Cor. 13: 12), it will turn out that, properly interpreted, every claim that the Bible makes will turn out to have been true. But this theory is a long way from the here-and-now inerrancy that is widely defended in some circles today.

19. See *The Institutes of the Christian Religion* (Philadelphia: Westminster Press, 1960), I, vii, 4; III, ii, 34.

20. I would like to thank Dale Tuggy for his helpful comments on an earlier version of this chapter.

CHAPTER 3

TRUE WORDS

Nicholas Wolterstorff

In the first part of this chapter I will argue that truth is not the main issue when we are dealing with Scripture; in the second part I will suggest that truth *is* the main issue.

I

Many of those who accept the Bible as canonical, and do not study it just for its scholarly interest or literary merit, are fixated on whether what it says is true. Consider Harold Lindsell's *Battle for the Bible,* a book that I take to offer a paradigmatic presentation of that way of thinking about the Bible characteristic of American fundamentalism. The battle for the Bible, in Lindsell's account, is all about the truth of what's said. Lindsell understands liberals to be of the view that only some of what the Bible says is true; Lindsell himself holds that everything it says is true. From the very beginnings of fundamentalism in the early twentieth century, biblical inerrancy has been a central plank in its credo; and what fundamentalism means when it says that the Bible is inerrant is that all that's said is true.

It is also characteristic of my fellow philosophers in the Society of Christian Philosophers to take the truth of what's said as the central issue to be raised when we reflect philosophically on the Bible's canonical status in the Christian community. That is part of what leads some of those outside the society to characterize its members as fundamentalists. Very few are in fact fundamentalists. They do, however, resemble fundamentalists in that the bulk of them – or at least the bulk of the vocal ones among them – regard the central issue concerning the Bible to be the truth of what's said.

Mainline and liberal Christians are different. For them the central category in reflecting on the role of the Bible in the Christian community is not the category of truth but the category of revelation: the Bible is revelation, or it effects revelation. But revelation, whatever else it may be, is perforce revelation of what is the case. What is not the case cannot be revealed: I cannot, for example, reveal that I am twenty-five years old, since I am not. What is the case is not the same as the truth of what's said; but the two are obviously closely connected. So whatever may be their differences on other matters, in this respect the difference between fundamentalists and conservatives, on the one hand, and liberals and mainliners, on the other, comes to very little.

One of the aims I had in mind in writing my book *Divine Discourse* was to break the grip of these categories – the truth of what's said and what is the case – when reflecting on the Bible and its role as canonical in the Christian community. "Oh, the depth of the riches both of the wisdom and knowledge of God!" exclaims Paul in Romans 11. "To him be glory forever." Is this true? Is it the case? The question misfires because exclamations are neither true nor false. "Blessed are those who hunger and thirst for justice," says Jesus in Matthew's report of his Sermon on the Mount. Is this true? Again, the question misfires: to bless someone is not to say something true or false.

To fixate on the question "Is what's said true or false?" when dealing with Scripture is to distort profoundly what is actually there. When an assertion is made, it is appropriate to ask whether what was said is true or false. There are a great many assertions in Scripture, and I am all for raising the question of truth about those. But we also find in Scripture an abundance of questions, commands, optatives, blessings – you name it. If we approach any of these with the question "Is what's said true?" we are trying to force square pegs into round holes. "Sell all that you have and give to the poor," said Jesus to the rich young ruler. The issue this saying presented to him – and presents to us – is not truth or falsehood but obedience or disobedience.

My own proposal in *Divine Discourse* was that, instead of thinking of the Bible in terms of revelation, we think of it in terms of speech; second, that instead of giving priority to speech as symbol-system, we give priority to speech as action, as discourse; third, that within discourse we distinguish between locutionary acts and illocutionary acts; and fourth, that we introduce the concept of double-agency discourse, thereby enabling us to understand how it might be that God speaks – that is, performs illocutionary acts – by way of the writing and speaking of the biblical writers.

Assertions are a type of illocutionary act, but only one among many. If it is God's speech that we are reading and interpreting on a given occasion, and if we determine that God is issuing a command by way of the passage in question, then it makes no sense to ask whether what's said is true. And we evade the point of the discourse if we ask what the issuance of this command reveals about God. The point is to obey. I am standing on a ladder, holding the board, ready to nail it in place, and I ask you to hand me the hammer. Instead of handing it to me, you ask yourself, "I wonder what his asking that question reveals about Wolterstorff?" Infuriating! Hand me the hammer!

In the course of my discussion in *Divine Discourse,* I made the point that, though the issue I was discussing in the book was how God could speak by way of the human words of Scripture, it was by no means my view that the only thing the Christian community should do with Scripture is ask what God says thereby. We take the Psalms on our lips to speak our own praise, lament, and dismay; so too we take on our own lips the doxological passages of the New Testament. We allow the metaphors of Scripture to shape the way we see reality. And so forth.

I trust that my point is clear: we distort and abuse what the biblical writers say, and distort and abuse what God says by way of what the biblical writers say, if we fixate on the question of whether what's said is true. Don't get me wrong: that question is usually important when relevant. But often it is not relevant. We have to get over our monomaniacal fixation on truth and on what's the case when dealing with the Bible.

II

Now for the second part of my essay. Every now and then one hears biblical scholars, theologians, and others – perhaps sensing intuitively that there is something wrong with our preoccupation with the truth of what's said or the what's-the-case of what is revealed – suggesting that we need a new concept of truth. Or suggesting, alternatively, that we ought to use the biblical concept of truth. In my experience there is nothing so effective in straightening and stiffening the back of an analytic philosopher as this sort of suggestion. If the suggestion made is the former, that we need a new concept of truth, the philosopher replies that such talk is all confused. You can make up whatever new concept you want and call it "truth"; but that does not give you a new concept of truth. It just gives you a new concept to which, since you made it up, you can attach any word you wish, old or new. I do not get a new concept of duck by making up the concept, say, of a small hairy animal with a bill and a tail and webbed feet and announcing that this is a new and improved concept of duck. And if the suggestion we make is the latter – that we should use the biblical concept of truth – the philosopher first asks why exactly it is that we should do that; and she then points to the very large number of passages in the Bible – and it is a very large number indeed – in which the word "true" appears for all the world to be used in the very same way that the philosopher uses it, namely, as expressing a property that propositions have when they bear the requisite relation to what is the case.

But perhaps my fellow philosophers are too quickly dismissive here. Not that either of the two points they make is incorrect. But maybe these points do not settle the issue; maybe there is more to be said. And just maybe, when that more is said, the possibility of a mediating position opens up before us. In the New Testament we rather often find a speaker saying that he is telling the truth and not lying (three examples: John 8:44-45; Rom. 9;1; 1 Tim. 2:7). Similarly, it is rather often said about some testimony that it is true (two examples: John 19:35; John 21:24). These are the passages that the philosopher latches onto: truth is ascribed to something asserted. (I have come to suspect that something more is being said, or at least suggested, in some of these passages than just that the content of what is asserted bears the relation that makes for truth to what is the case. But let that pass.)

Let us now look at a small sampling of the many passages in which something other than conformity to the facts is ascribed to an assertion by the predicate "true," or in which the predicate is ascribed to something other than assertions. Let us start with what is closest to that and move to what is farthest away. I will confine myself on this occasion to the writings ascribed to John; and from among these, my examples will be drawn almost exclusively from John's Gospel. Given the prominence of the word *alêtheia* and its grammatical variants in these writings, that is not a severe limitation.

In John 5:31, Jesus says, "If I bear witness to myself, my testimony is not true; there is another who bears witness to me, and I know that the testimony which he bears to me is true." Testimony is, of course, expressed with the illocutionary act of assertion, and it can accordingly be judged as true or false – in the sense of being in accord with, or out of accord with, what is the case. It is most unlikely, however, that that is what Jesus had in mind here in saying that testimony to himself would not be true if he spoke it. Why would his speaking it make a difference as to whether it was or was not in accord with what is the case? Add to this Jesus' remark in John 8:17: "In your law it is written that the testimony of two men is true." Here, too, it seems unlikely that he is using the philosopher's standard sense of "true" (cf. 8:13-14).

In the first letter of John we find the writer saying: "I am writing you a new commandment, which is true in him and in you. . ." (2:8). Here that of which truth is predicated is no longer an assertion. Though it is still predicated of something that is said, the something said is now a commandment rather than an assertion. In John 3:21, Jesus says that "he who does the truth comes to the light.. . .." Here it is no longer even one or another sort of illocutionary act that is said to be true but an action of some other kind. Moving on, we get phrases such as "true worshipers" (4:23), "true vine" (15:1), "true God" (17:3). In these expressions it is no longer even actions that are said to be true. Closely related, we find it said that God is true (3:33, 7:28, 8:26). And lastly, we get Jesus' well-known saying: "I am the way, the truth, and the life" (14:6; closely related to 17:17: "thy word is truth").

What are we to make of all this? Is the writer just speaking loosely over and over – so that we are to make nothing of it at all? Alternatively, is the writer perhaps using a number of distinct concepts, and it just so happens that all these distinct concepts are expressed with the same Greek word *(alêtheia)* and its grammatical variants (and with our word "truth" and its grammatical variants)? Or again, is the writer perhaps using a distinctly biblical (Hebraic, Semitic) concept, which coincides only in part with the concept attached to our word "truth"? If this last were the case, it would seem that our translators are to be charged with seriously misleading us in translating all the occurrences of the Greek *alêtheia* with the English "truth."

Let me approach my own suggestion, distinct from all the above, by calling attention to what is rarely if ever noted by philosophers, namely, that you and I also regularly predicate the word "true" of things other than assertions. We regularly say such things as these: "he's a true friend," "she's a true leader," "he's a true Dutchman," "she's a true scholar," "he's a true student," "that's true north," "this is true coffee," "that was a true wish," "here's a true copy," "that was a true aim," "the daylily is not a true lily," and "that tractor over there is not a true John Deere B anymore because it has been modified." We speak of "being true to the facts" and of "being true to life." We may say of a portrait, "It's just not true to her." And we confess that Jesus was "true God and true human being." In the face of all this, the suggestion that there is some peculiarly biblical – or Hebraic or Semitic – concept of truth has no plausibility whatsoever. Our English word "truth," along with its grammatical variants, maps the Greek word *alêtheia* and its grammatical variants, as they are used in the New Testament, about as closely as one could wish.

But is the force of the words "true" and "truth" constant amid all these different uses? That is surely the assumption that we should begin with, acknowledging that we may be forced to give it up. So on that assumption, let's see whether it is possible to state that force. Some will want to introduce Heidegger into the discussion at this point. Heidegger and his followers claim that he has achieved the purportedly remarkable feat of recovering the deeply buried root of our concept of truth. I think he has done nothing of the sort. At least in *Being and Time,* Heidegger is merely as fixated on the truth of assertions as is your average analytic philosopher. His argument is that, rather than understanding the truth of assertions in terms of correspondence between propositional content (Frege's *Gedanke*) and a fact, we get rid of the idea of propositional content and think, in ontologically reductionist fashion, of a true assertion as involving nothing more than an exercise of our linguistic practice whereby some fact is disclosed, unveiled, uncovered, or revealed. Disclosedness, he says, is "the ontological condition for the possibility that assertions can be either true or false."[1]

Another suggestion that is rather often made, one to which I was myself previously attracted, is that the root content of the biblical concept of "truth" is that of keeping faith with someone or something, of being faithful to someone or something. The truth of a proposition would then consist in its being faithful to the facts. The old English word "troth" has this sense of being faithful to someone or something: for me to pledge you my troth is to pledge you my fidelity. But this will not do either, and for this simple reason: "true" is often used in Scripture, and in ordinary speech, when the idea of keeping troth or being faithful is simply not in view. A true vine is not a faithful vine: what would a faithful vine be? And a true Dutchman is not a faithful Dutchman. Whatever constitutes a true Dutchman is both more than that and different from that.

A third suggestion to be considered is what Anselm proposes in the opening eleven sections of his *De Veritate* ("On Truth"). *De Veritate* is structured as a dialogue between a teacher and his student: the teacher and the student together take note of a wide range of applications of the predicate "true" – pretty much as wide as what I've pointed to above. And in each case they explore what "true" means in the application under consideration. The conclusion they reach is that in each case truth amounts to rectitude. And to say that something has rectitude is to say that, in the respect under consideration, it is as it ought to be. Here, from section 7, is a nice statement of that line of thought:

> Teacher: But tell me if anything ought to be otherwise than it is in the highest truth.
> Student: No.
> T: Therefore, if all things are what they are there, they are without doubt what they ought to be.
> S: They are truly what they ought to be.
> T: And whatever is what it ought to be, exists rightly.
> S: It cannot be otherwise.
> T: Therefore, whatever is, exists rightly.
> S: Nothing is more obvious.
> T: Therefore, if truth and rectitude are in the essence of things because they are that which they are in the highest truth, it is certain that the truth of things is rectitude.
> S: Nothing is plainer than the consequence of the argument.

And here is another passage making the same point, this from section 10, when teacher and student are beginning to draw the discussion to a conclusion:

> T: You will not deny that the highest truth is rectitude.
> S: There is nothing else that I can say it is.

T: Consider . . . all the foregoing rectitudes are such because
they are in things which are or do what they ought. . . .[2]

From the course of the discussion it is clear that, in arriving at and
stating his general thesis, Anselm is employing the "ought" of proper
formation and functioning rather than the "ought" of obligation; he
thinks of obligation as a special case of proper functioning. After servic-
ing one's car, the mechanic claims that it ought to run much more
quietly now; this is the "ought" of proper functioning, not the "ought"
of obligation. Two of Anselm's own examples of oughtness, or rectitude,
are that sentences ought to be grammatically well-formed, and that
sentences, when used assertively, ought to be true. Anselm's suggestion
comes close to accounting for the examples I have put on the table,
much closer than either of the other two suggestions I have considered.
But there are still a few examples that escape its net. When I say that the
daylily is not a true lily, I do not mean that it is a malformed lily – that
it is not what it ought to be. And when I say that a story is true to life,
I do not mean that it is properly formed.

So let me now offer my own suggestion, which comes rather close to
Anselm's. I suggest that the root notion of truth is that of something's
measuring up – that is, measuring up in being or excellence. A true
friend is one who measures up with respect to the quality of his friendship; true coffee is coffee that measures up with respect to its flavor or
composition. When we speak of "a true so-and-so," we are implicitly
drawing a contrast between this so-and-so that measures up and other
so-and-so's that do not, or would not, measure up. What exactly that
contrast is, will differ from case to case. A daylily is not a true lily because,
though its flowers are definitely lily-like, it does not belong to the family
Lilium and thus is not a lily at all. By contrast, a person who is not a true
student is still a student – or then again, she may not be. One has to gather
from the context what contrast it is that the speaker had in mind, and
hence what sort of failure to measure up he meant to call attention to.

It is striking how often, in the New Testament writings ascribed to
John, the contrast with what does not measure up is made explicit: there
is a contest going on between the true and the not true – the true God
versus all the false gods, and so forth. The exception to the point I made
above about context determining meaning is that some phrases of
the kind "a true so-and-so" have acquired a standard sense, so that, in the
absence of contrary indications, the listener naturally takes the speaker
to have in mind that way of measuring up that has become part of the
sense of the phrase. This strikes me as being the case, for example, for
the phrases "a true copy" and "a true [carpenter's] square."

Back to where we began, namely, with assertions. True assertions take
their place along with true Dutchmen, true lilies, true coffee, and so

forth, as things that measure up, in being or excellence, to whatever way is operative in the context, with this qualification: "true assertions," like "true copies" and "true squares," have long ago acquired a standard sense, with a particular way of measuring up built into that standard sense. That standard sense is this: a true assertion is one whose propositional content fits, or corresponds to, the facts. Or on the Heideggerian analysis: a true assertion is one that discloses the facts – one that is, as we say, true to the facts. In the absence of counter-indications, the listener assumes that the way of measuring up built into that standard sense is the way of measuring up that the speaker has in mind.

But a speaker need not use "true assertion" in the standard sense. I suggested that when Jesus said that, were he to testify to himself, it would not be a true testimony, he had something else in mind than the standard sense for "true testimony." He had in mind some other way in which a testimony given by himself concerning himself would not measure up. What that other way was, he did not say; we have to gather what it was from context. I once heard a sermon on the Massacre of the Innocents that began thus: the massacre of the innocents was a case of child abuse; in our society there is also child abuse; let us then talk about child abuse this morning. I submit that, though each assertion the preacher made was true in the standard sense, nonetheless the totality of what he said was profoundly false.

Truth is the fundamental issue to be raised concerning Scripture. Do the words of Scripture measure up? Are they true words? "Oh, the depth of the riches both of the wisdom and knowledge of God. . . . To him be glory forever." Is that exclamation a true exclamation? Does it measure up? "The Lord is my shepherd; I shall not want." Is that expression of confidence a true expression of confidence? Does it measure up?

Notes

1. Martin Heidegger, *Being and Time* (New York: Harper and Row, 1962), p. 269.
2. I am quoting from the translation by Ralph McInerny in Brian Davies and G. R. Evans, eds., *Anselm of Canterbury: The Major Works* (Oxford: Oxford University Press, 1998).

CHAPTER 4

INFALLIBILITY

Paul Helm

God is by definition infallible and totally trustworthy. It would seem to follow from this that any special revelation from God, any disclosure of propositions not otherwise knowable, will reflect God's character. If he is infallible, the special revelation will be infallible, for it is inconceivable that what God says should not fully reflect his character. But what does 'infallible' mean, and what does it mean to say that any special revelation is infallible? When we have paid attention to these matters, and made some suggestions about them, we shall begin to investigate how someone might argue that some document, such as the Bible, is the Word of God. Finally, in this chapter, we shall look at the two distinct senses of 'reveal' that it is necessary to employ when it is argued that the Bible is God's special revelation.

The meaning of 'Infallible'

'Infallible' is a modal term. That is, it expresses the manner in which something is known or is true. If something is infallibly true then (in some sense yet to become clear) it could not fail to be true. Since the point of saying that a special revelation is infallible is to ascribe to it something of the character of God himself, it might help to get clearer about infallibility by first considering the proposition *God is infallible.* To say that God is infallible is to say that whatever God believes is true or that God's believing a proposition guarantees the truth of that proposition. Unlike fallible human beings, God cannot believe what is false. Further, of course, God is omniscient; that is, with respect to any proposition whatever, God either believes that proposition (if it is a true proposition) or believes the denial of that proposition (if it is false). And to say that some particular proposition or set of propositions is infallibly true is, presumably, to say that anyone who believed such a proposition could not be in error.

It is important, however, to see what this account of infallibility does *not* commit us to. There are a number of possible misunderstandings

which we must avoid. After we have considered some of these we shall
return to the question of what it means to say that some special revelation is infallible.

Some may think that from our definition it follows that whatever is
infallibly known must be necessarily true, that it could not, as a matter of
logic, be false. A moment or two's reflection will show, I hope, that this
would be ludicrous.

What sorts of thing could not conceivably be false? Such propositions
as *A triangle has three sides, My red scarf is coloured* and *Everything is identical
with itself.* Such propositions are necessary truths in that their denials
are self-contradictory. To say that a triangle has or may have more than
three sides is not simply to say something that is false. It is to say something that could not be true. Such propositions are respectable enough,
and no doubt God, who knows everything, knows all necessary truths.
But such propositions are not typical of those that, it is claimed, occur in
special revelation. If, begging no questions about whether or not the
Bible is God's special revelation, we take some examples from the Bible,
we find such expressions as:. 'Paul left Trophimus at Miletum because he
was sick' (2 Tim. 4:20). But it is not a necessary truth that Trophimus was
sick. It is quite conceivable that Trophimus was not sick during this
period.

It may be said that this is a rather trivial example. What about a more
central, theologically important case, such as 'God was in Christ reconciling the world unto himself (2 Cor. 5:19)? No doubt this proposition
has a certain appropriateness to it, given the truth of other propositions,
but even those theologians who have gone so far as to say that the incarnation would have taken place had there been no sin have not said that
the incarnation would have taken place even if there had been no human
race. Many people think that it is false that God was in Christ reconciling the world. In so thinking they may be mistaken but they are not
thinking self-contradictory thoughts.

So, many *contingent* propositions are among the propositions that many
have claimed to be a part of God's infallible revelation. In order to free
ourselves of the temptation of thinking that whatever is infallibly known
must be logically necessary, we need to distinguish between the idea
of a necessary truth, such as *My red scarf is coloured,* and the idea of a necessary consequence of some truth. It follows that *if* God knows a certain
proposition (say, *The Eiffel Tower is taller than the Tower of London*) *then* that
proposition is true. But it does not follow that that proposition, considered by itself, is necessarily true.

Earlier we discussed briefly the relationship between God's infallibility and his omniscience. But it does not follow that to know a proposition infallibly one has to be omniscient. This would be to confuse
'Whatever someone believes is true' with 'Someone believes whatever

is true'. It is at least possible that someone should know some proposition infallibly but be ignorant or in error about other propositions.

A rather more complicated confusion is the following. There is a class of propositions which many philosophers have called *incorrigible*. These are propositions which if a person believes any of them then his belief could not fail to be true. He is infallible with respect to them. Clearly this is not true of *all* the propositions that I believe, even all the propositions about me that I believe. From the fact that I believe that I am the life and soul of the party it does not follow that I *am*. Further, there are multitudes of true propositions which no one knows, and multitudes of false beliefs. Yet it has been claimed that there are some propositions about which, if I believe them, I could not be mistaken. For example, *I seem to see a shape, I feel tired* and *I think I remember locking the door before I left home.* Whenever they are believed they are true and they cannot be corrected by a second person.

They are, however rather peculiar propositions. They are all expressed in the first person, and are all about the utterer's own mental or emotional or cognitive state. Such propositions are true *just because* they are about a person's own states, reported by that person at the time when he is in that state, and are not about the states of the world at large.

We can ignore the philosophical dispute about the exact nature and importance of such propositions. But it is clear that the propositions for which infallibility is often claimed are not propositions of that kind. The proposition that Paul left Trophimus at Miletum because he was sick, or that God was in Christ reconciling the world, are not statements about the utterer's own state of mind, but are statements about matters that are external to his mind.

To say that a given proposition or set of propositions is infallible is presumably to say that this set represents a published sub-set of all the propositions believed by God. It would follow that the propositions of this subset could not be discovered to be false by any observer or investigator. If God reveals a particular proposition then for that reason that proposition could not turn out to be false.

At this point we come up against a difficulty that we rarely find discussed in the literature about revelation. What more is added by the word 'infallible' to 'true'? Obviously if the revealed propositions are true they cannot be false, for no proposition or set of propositions can be both true and false. If some proposition turned out to be false then it could not have been true. If this is so in the case of *true* propositions, and of *infallibly true* propositions, what is the point in insisting that the special revelation is infallibly true? Is anything gained, beyond a certain theological hyperbole by the addition of the adverb 'infallibly'?

Perhaps the adverb can be justified in the following way. The point of saying of a set of propositions that it is infallible is that (unlike most or perhaps all other sets) it is wholly true. But more than this. It is not simply that the assertions of the special revelation happen to be wholly true, but that there is a guarantee of the wholly-true character of the set of propositions. It is not sufficient, then, to say sets of propositions are infallible because they are all true, otherwise an accurately, drawn up telephone directory would be infallible. It is rather that an infallible special revelation is one the truth of whose propositions is somehow guaranteed or endorsed.

But how guaranteed or endorsed? Here I want to explore two possibilities. The first way is to take 'infallible' as a term of knowledge. To know that some proposition is infallibly true is to know without the shadow of a doubt that it is true. 'Infallibly' there refers to the way we know or the grounds for knowledge. To suppose that a proposition is known infallibly is to attribute to it a unique or peculiar kind of basic-ness. It is to say that the evidence for it is such that no amount of new evidence could overthrow or modify it.

The idea that there are such infallible propositions has exerted an enormous influence not only in theology but in the whole structure of western thought. For the classical exponents of both rationalism and empiricism held the view that all human knowledge rests upon foundations which are infallible, which have a self-certifying or self-guaranteeing quality. To regard the special revelation as infallible in *this* sense would be to think within this tradition, though someone who took this view would not be saying that the special revelation was the sole foundation for all knowledge (as Descartes thought that 'clear and distinct ideas' were, or Locke thought that 'simple ideas' were) but that it is foundational for all those matters which it specially reveals. Thus to say that it is foundational in *this* sense is to say that with regard to such matters nothing is more basic than it. What the *marks* of infallibility might be, and what are the problems raised by the relation between an infallible revelation and other knowledge, are matters that we shall take up later.

A second way of taking the claim that the special revelation is infallible (because it is the Word of God who is infallible) would be to regard the infallibility as a *normative* or *regulative* matter. To affirm that some special revelation is infallible would be to express a resolve to treat the revelation as theologically basic, to refer controversies to it, to take what it teaches unreservedly, and so on. This would mean that it is not strictly true that the special revelation is infallible, but nor is it false. Rather it is that the special revelation plays the role of a supreme adjudicator. It functions theologically like the House of Lords in the UK or the Supreme Court of the USA function in their respective political systems. To say that the verdicts of such courts are true would be to misunderstand their function.

Rather they represent *rulings* which, unlike the rulings of lower courts, cannot be appealed against since in each case the ruling is *final*.

Two things ought to be noticed about such a view. In the first place it is considerably weaker than the first view, that the special revelation can be taken to be unfailingly true because God endorses the matters which it contains. While it is the case that if the special revelation is infallibly true then it also has a basic, regulative function (since there can be no higher appeal than to infallible truth), the opposite does not follow. Something can be supremely regulative because it has a certain recognized constitutional position. The second thing to note is that if this view were adopted then there would be an equivocation over 'infallible' in the propositions *God is infallible* and *The special revelation is infallible*. For to say that God is infallible is (as we noted earlier) to say something about truth, namely that God is unable to err. But on the regulative view of infallibility to say that the revelation is infallible is not to say that what it says is true but that what it says is to be regarded as final and binding. So that 'infallible' would mean one thing when applied to God and another when applied to the special revelation. But this would be unfortunate since it would break the bond between God's infallibility and the infallibility of his revelation.

However, it may be possible to overcome this, and to combine the two views just expressed in the following way. It may be possible to argue that to regard 'infallible' as a regulative term is justifiable when it modifies 'true'. To say that the special revelation is infallibly true would be *ipso facto* to say that it is true. The addition of 'infallibly' expresses the commitment never to regard any other proposition from another source, however well-attested, to overrule any proposition of the special revelation and never to equate one's own understanding of the propositions of the special revelation with what those propositions actually mean but to be willing to test currently-held views of what the propositions mean against the propositions themselves.

Special revelation and the Bible

So far in our study we have employed the idea of 'special revelation' in a deliberately abstract way. This has been necessary in order to try to think clearly about the *concept* of special revelation. We have outlined a concept which might be defined as follows: a special revelation is a body of propositions revealed by God of matters not otherwise discoverable by the human mind. But for our discussion to have religious or theological interest it must descend from these abstract heights. For what is important is whether in fact there is a special revelation in this sense, and how it might be known that there is, if there is. In particular, what problems are raised by saying that the Bible is God's special revelation? What are, or would be, good reasons for making that identification? Again, as befits a study of this kind, we shall not be concerned, in detail, with the actual reasons people have and give for this identification but with the types of approach exemplified.

Before we proceed, however, we need to distinguish between the sorts of reasons that people have given for identifying God's special revelation with the Bible, and the question of how we can be certain that some proposed candidate for special revelation is in fact a case of special revelation. In what immediately follows we shall be concerned with the first of these questions, the problem of *identification*. In the next chapter we shall come to the central question of our study: given that men wish to identify the Bible as God's special revelation, what reasons can be given for knowing that this is in fact the case, the problem of *justification*. Often in practice these two questions have been considered together but they are separable and we shall consider them separately. So from this point onwards our study becomes much less abstract, and focusses on the character of the Bible and claims made on its behalf.

There seem to be two main approaches to the problem of identification, of why men have thought that the Bible is not in some vague way the source of special revelation, but that it is to be identified with that special revelation. Some have argued as follows: there are good reasons for thinking that the Bible is the Word of God and therefore, since the Word of God is infallible (since God is infallible) there are good reasons for thinking that the Bible is infallible. Others have argued: there are good reasons for thinking that the Bible is infallible and hence good reasons for thinking that it is the Word of God, since whatever is infallible must be the Word of God. For the first position the identification is a theological matter, for the second it is empirical.

Sometimes this difference of approach is said to be the difference between a deductive and an inductive approach to the Bible. But this is misleading for two reasons. In the first place, any approach to the Bible is going to be inductive, discovering what the facts about it are, including facts about the Bible's own attitude to itself, or more precisely the attitude of the various biblical writers to the Old Testament and to themselves, as well as facts about the phenomena of the Bible – its style and subject matter.

Secondly, if one wants to arrive at an understanding of the Bible as a whole, it is necessary to allow the phenomena to throw light upon the explicit statements, to show us more precisely what these statements imply.

A question has arisen over which of these sets of data, the explicit statements of the Bible or the 'phenomena' ought to have priority. For instance,

B. B. Warfield has argued[1] that in constructing a doctrine of divine inspiration (and therefore of infallibility) the explicit statements of the Bible about itself should have priority, just as they would have priority in the construction of any Christian doctrine. The phenomena can, on occasion, correct exegetical processes and so modify exegetical conclusions,[2] but this is not the same as modifying the teaching of the Bible itself, as exegetically ascertained.

So Warfield draws a fine line between the exegetical conclusions which may be modified, and the teaching of the Bible, which may not. What does he mean? Presumably that no evidence from the phenomena can be allowed to overturn the fact that the Scriptures are inspired (and so are infallible) if the Scriptures assert that they are inspired, since as a trustworthy teacher of doctrine the Bible must be held to be a trustworthy teacher of *this* doctrine. What the phenomenal facts do, as Warfield allows, is to modify the conclusions to be drawn about the exact nature of this inspiration, and so about the exact nature of the infallibility, by correcting any prior assumptions we may have had about it.

Let us look at some of these arguments in more detail. In the case of the so-called deductive approach, one typical argument proceeds as follows:

(1) It is true as a matter of fact that Jesus teaches that the Old Testament (and also implies that the New Testament) is the Word of God.
(2) Jesus, the Son of God, speaks with divine authority.
(3) Therefore, God says that the two Testaments are the Word of God.
(4) Therefore, they are the Word of God.

The argument is inductive to the extent that it appeals to what the teaching of Jesus actually is. There are no prior assumptions about this and it is at least possible, as far as the argument is concerned, that Jesus did *not* teach the infallibility of the Testaments. The idea of an infallible written special revelation is not regarded as being *logically* necessary for Christianity. But though the approach is inductive to the extent that it is based on what Jesus actually taught, the identification that Jesus is said to make is not the result of an inductive examination by him.

Further, the view is the outcome of a religious commitment to Jesus. It is a Christian view of the Bible, though this is not to say that all committed to Jesus believe that Jesus taught this, nor that all that believe that Jesus taught this believe that he was correct to do so. But as the outcome of a religious commitment to Jesus, this argument already depends on the Bible for one of its premisses, as a historical source for what Jesus as a matter of fact taught. And it also depends on a particular interpretation of the historical documents.

Given that the argument proceeds directly from the (inductively established) teaching of Jesus to the status of the Bible, the only factors that could count against it would be factors throwing doubt on what Jesus actually taught, since Jesus' teaching is necessary and sufficient for the conclusion. Facts or theories which are discrepent with the view that the Bible is God's special revelation will be discounted *unless* they are thought to affect the trustworthiness of Jesus' testimony. In terms of the argument difficulties such as historical inaccuracies, apparent contradictions, apparently outdated science will have the status of problems which ultimately need adjusting to the theory. But, since the conclusion is not inductively established it cannot be inductively overthrown except by considerations throwing doubt on the trustworthiness of Jesus.

A second main way of making the identification would be in a straightforwardly inductive way. The Bible is examined to see if it has those features which might be expected of a body of propositions constituting a divinely-given special revelation. Only when and insofar as the actual documents which make up the Bible meet such tests would it be proper for the identification between the Bible and special revelation to be made. So that the proposition *The Bible is God's special revelation* is on this view an empirical hypothesis confirmable or disconfirmable by the relevant data. The existence of factual errors, inconsistencies and the like would presumably decisively count against the view that the Bible is God's special revelation, and perhaps lead to the view that the Bible *contained* God's special revelation or was in some looser way related to it.

How good arguments of these two types are, and whether they provide a *justification* for the conclusion that the Bible is God's special revelation, is beyond the scope of the present chapter.

Some other arguments

Although the arguments just given are the *main* arguments for the identification of the Bible with God's special revelation they are by no means the *only* ones. Naturally we cannot consider every argument but we shall now look at two other popular arguments for the identification, and one argument against it.

The first argument might be put as follows: there is a logically necessary connection between believing that the Bible is God's special revelation (and so is infallible) and believing the Christian gospel. No one can justifiably believe, let us say, that Jesus Christ rose from the dead unless he believes this because it is contained in the infallible revelation.

Presumably, to justifiably believe that the Bible is infallible is sufficient for justifiably believing that Jesus Christ rose from the dead (unless one was adopting principles of interpretation of a rather special kind which we cannot go into here). But the converse of this is not the case, surely. It is quite possible to believe that Jesus rose from the dead without ever having heard of the Bible much less having read it and accepted it as infallible. Belief in the one is only accidentally or contingently related to the other. For the information might have come in other ways, or have come through the documents of the New Testament regarded merely as reliable historical data.

To this it might be said that although belief in an infallible book is not absolutely or abstractly necessary, it is necessary *for us*. But even this does not seem in the least to be plausible, for it is conceivable that we should have received the knowledge of the gospel through oral tradition. Even such a stalwart defender of the infallibility of the Bible as B. B. Warfield has remarked that 'We may say that without a Bible we might have had Christ and all that he stands for to our souls. Let us not say that this might not have been possible.'[3]

It might be conceded that there is only a contingent connection between the body of Christian belief and the identification of the Bible with God's special revelation, and yet it might be said that Christian belief is only fully *justifiable* if it is based upon belief in the Bible as God's special revelation. But this would be a piece of special pleading, and nothing more. Who says that this is so? There is sometimes a subtle but crucial shift in arguing about infallibility which it is necessary to guard against. A shift from 'Jones believes that the Bible is infallible' to 'Jones infallibly believes that the Bible is true'. These are very different, one saying that a *document* is infallible, the other that the *believing* is infallible. It by no means follows that only if I am infallibly sure that the Bible is true do I really believe that it is true, nor is it obviously true that I am only justified in believing what I infallibly believe. Indeed it seems false, otherwise I would be justified in believing very little.

A second argument is related to the one just discussed, and is often dubbed the 'slippery slope' argument. We have just seen that there is only a contingent or accidental connection between biblical infallibility and those doctrines which together make up the central core of the Christian faith. It is true that for most of us who believe these doctrines they are believed because they are found in the Bible in the sense that the Bible is the source of them. We may even give as a *reason* for believing them that they are found in the Bible. But clearly this is not *the only* reason.

One form of 'slippery slope' argument is: whoever, having once held that the Bible is identical with God's special revelation, gives this up, will inevitably give up the central doctrines of the Christian faith. The causal factors that are sufficient to bring about a change of mind with respect to the status of the Bible are also sufficient to bring about a change of mind with respect to other matters. But this contention seems to be plainly false, for there have been many in the history of the Christian church who have held to the central Christian doctrines and yet have not held to the infallibility of the Bible. The most that can be said for this position is that it expresses an hypothesis which cannot be decided *a priori* but which must be either confirmed or disconfirmed by the facts.

Another form of the 'slippery slope' argument can be expressed in some words of Augustine: 'If you grant any untruth to obtain in such a crowning height of authority (and this is done by doubting Scripture or not holding it to be absolutely sure), then not the smallest portion of these books will remain that cannot be called into question.' What Augustine appears to be saying here is that if the only reason for accepting the identification of the Bible with God's special revelation is the direct authority of God himself (as Augustine believed), then that recognition calls for absolute commitment to the whole of the special revelation. One cannot consistently have a reason for doubting some of the special revelation but no reason for doubting the remainder.

The first form of the 'slippery slope' argument we considered was *causal*. It said that giving up belief in the infallibility of the Bible would inevitably cause other things to happen. This form of the argument is *logical*, that one cannot consistently hold that some of the Scripture is true and some not true *if* the only reason for holding it to be true in the first place is on the direct authority of God. And what Augustine says seems to be correct, *if* his view of how the identification is justified is accepted.

There is one rather unwelcome assumption behind the *causal* 'slippery slope' argument. It is that a theological belief such as the belief that the Bible is identical with God's special revelation ought to be held because otherwise unfortunate consequences will follow. But surely something ought to be believed because it is true and not because the consequences of not believing would be unfortunate or unwelcome.

The final argument to be examined says that there are good grounds for not regarding the Bible as identical with special revelation in any sense which would make it the infallible foundation of theological knowledge. A version of this argument is to be found in Nicholas Wolterstorff's book *Reason within the Bounds of Religion*.[4] In this study Wolterstorff attacks the philosophical position known as *foundationalism*, the doctrine that all knowledge rests upon indubitable, non-inferential foundations. Wolterstorff shows that there are difficulties over the idea that knowledge is justified with reference to such foundations. If it is said, for example, that anything that we call knowledge must be entailed by the foundational propositions, this seems impossibly strong, for there are many propositions which we seem warranted in believing which are not deductively related to the foundations, for example, universal propositions about physical objects such as *All metals expand when heated*. If, on the other hand, we say that the foundational propositions must render probable any proposition we are warranted in believing, this stumbles over the notorious argument of *David Hume* (1711–1776), that only if we *assume* that nature is uniform can we properly employ proba-bilistic arguments. But we can only justifiably assume this either if we know indubitably that nature is uniform (and we do not), or if we regard it as probable. But as we need the uniformity of nature to make any proposition about the world probable, this is not much help.

Wolterstorff claims that similar questions can be raised about the view that the Bible is the infallible foundation of (perhaps some, perhaps all) knowledge. We cannot by reading and interpreting the Bible come to have indubitable knowledge of the propositions that it contains. Referring to the writers of the various books of the Bible, such as Amos, Wolterstorff says:

> How could Amos, say, have had the indubitable knowledge that what he was hearing and what he was writing was what God was saying? Perhaps, indeed, he knew. But did he know *indubitably* in the foundationalist's sense of the term? Would it have been *impossible* that he should have had a reason which would have warranted him in disbelieving? Suppose he had discovered that some clever enemies of his had deceived him by whispering things from behind the rocks while he was tending his sheep. Would that not be a reason to warrant disbelief that he was hearing what God was saying?[5]

Let us suppose that Wolterstorff is correct in his critique of founda-tionalism. It will follow that none of us can know indubitably what the Bible means or that what it says is correct. It will also follow that none of us can know indubitably that there is a Bible or indeed that there is a single book in the universe.

Someone might be tempted to use such arguments against classical foundationalism to show that since we cannot know indubitably that the Bible is infallible there is no good reason for identifying God's special revelation with the Bible, but that regarding the Bible as God's special revelation is a matter of basic personal *commitment,* and nothing more. But there are a number of reasons why we ought not to take this view.

In the first place, although it may not be the case that a man knows indubitably that the Bible is God's special revelation, he may still have good reasons for believing this. At least we cannot rule this out *a priori.* We shall examine in more detail in the next chapter what this position amounts to. But if we can rule this out *a priori* it would seem to follow that no one can have good reasons for believing anything.

Further, let us suppose that Wolterstorff is correct and that no one can be indubitably certain of anything with that degree of certainty required by classical foundationalism, except certain things about his own states of consciousness. Then we could express this as: no one can *know* anything except about his own states of consciousness. He cannot know that he has a body, that there is an external world of bodies other than his, that there are other minds, that there is a God, and hosts of similar propositions.

Faced with this line of argument the best response is to surrender the use of the word 'know'. We might then say that we do not *know* any of these things, but with respect to many of them we can be very *certain* indeed. For instance, I can be very certain that there are five digits on my right hand. It *might* be the case that my hand consists of four natural digits and a cunningly devised artificial thumb. It *might* be that 'my right hand' is really a cat's paw or a crab's claw. But I can be very certain that it is not, and indeed perhaps I can be as certain as anyone can be of any physical object that my right hand has five digits. If you ask me how I can be so sure, I have no difficulty in answering, though the answer will be a long one in terms of repeated use and observation, the coherence, simplicity and economy of the belief, and so on. If you say, but you *may* be mistaken, you do not *know*, the point is granted.

It may be the case that some people are as certain that the Bible is God's special revelation as I am that there are five digits on my right hand. Such people will not *know indubitably* that the Bible is God's special revelation but then (as we have already granted) in the nature of things such knowledge is impossible. Note that I am not saying that anyone *is* as certain that the Bible is God's special revelation as I am that I have five digits on my right hand. But such a view cannot be dismissed *a priori* on the grounds that no indubitable knowledge of anything physical is possible. (In fact it seems highly unlikely that such a degree of certainty can be achieved in the case of the Bible since the Bible is a complex book and I may make many mistakes about its meaning. But even then such a view cannot be ruled out, for I could know for certain that something was true even though I was not sure what it meant. I am pretty sure that I am genetically related to my physical father even though I know next to nothing about the meaning of 'gene'. A fuller consideration of such matters must be left for later.)

Two senses of 'Reveal'

The main thrust of this chapter so far has been to give a sense to words such as 'infallible', and to suggest what types of argument might be deployed to show how it can be argued that the Bible is identical with God's special revelation. Now, I want to glance briefly at one consequence of making the identification.

In order to safeguard misunderstanding, it is necessary to distinguish two senses of 'reveal'. This has been done before, either in terms of the distinction between revelation and inspiration or between a wider and a narrower sense of 'revelation', but often this has not been done with sufficient clarity and emphasis to avoid misunderstanding.

The first sense of 'reveal' we shall call the *recording* or *reporting* sense. Revelation in this sense is simply the accurate recording of the often mistaken and wicked beliefs and opinions of men. It is revelation to us in that without these opinions and views being recorded it is highly probable that we would be ignorant of them. This is probably the case also with the recording of certain historical events.

The second sense of 'reveal' we shall call the *disclosing* or *endorsing* sense. If God reveals in this sense then his disclosure of whatever the matter is is a necessary and sufficient condition for that matter being true or right.

This distinction has two important consequences. The first is that since the Bible contains beliefs, opinions and the like that are false, it does not count against the identification of the Bible with God's special revelation that it contains falsehoods of *this* kind. For example, when David expressed the belief that Saul would one day kill him (1 Sam. 27:1) this belief was false, for Saul died before David. But the fact that this incident is recorded in the Bible does not count decisively against identifying the Bible with God's special revelation, since the incident forms part of a narrative the whole of which is recorded as a history of God's dealings with his people for certain instructional purposes.

The second important consequence is that the existence of this distinction imposes a considerable hermeneutical burden on any would-be interpreter of the special revelation. For he has to determine the exact limits of each kind of revelation, otherwise it may happen that the mistaken beliefs of men would be equated the special revelation of God's will.

So phrases such as 'the Bible in its entirety is revelation from God,' have to be treated with some caution. If the Bible in its entirety is God's revelation it does not follow that every sentence of the Bible is God's revelation, any more than it follows that because a poem rhymes every word in the poem rhymes. Because of this a phrase such as 'the Bible in its entirety' must be understood as referring to the total 'message' of the Bible.

Sometimes the distinction that we are making has been put in terms of the distinction between *revelation* and *inspiration*. Charles Hodge, for example, says:

> The object of revelation is the communication of knowledge.
> The object or design of inspiration is to secure infallibility in

teaching. Consequently, they differ in their effects. The effect of revelation was to render its recipient wiser. The effect of inspiration was to preserve him from error in teaching.[6]

But this terminology could be misleading in that many of the matters which Hodge says the biblical writers were inspired in writing about, but which were not revealed to them (but learned through ordinary processes of discovery), are revelation *to us*.

In the recording of reporting sense of 'reveal' what is revealed does not correspond to what God himself regards as being true, and is therefore false. Consequently such revelation must be of the form 'God reveals that B did X, said X, thought X.' This is clearly connected with the distinction between God's *voluntas beneplaciti*, the will of God's good pleasure, what in his wisdom he determines to bring to pass, and God's *voluntas signi*, that will of God which is to form the duty of man.

Perhaps we can go as far as to say that the distinction we are drawing between different senses of 'reveal' cannot be an accidental one, purely fortuitous, but that some such distinction as this *must* be made given that God's revelation is redemptive, addressing a situation of revolt, hostility, or indifference.

Notes

1. Cf. B. B. Warfield, 'The Real Problem of Inspiration' in *Revelation and Inspiration*, 1927.
2. 2. Cf. ibid., p. 206.
3. Ibid., p. 72.
4. N. Wolterstorff, *Reason Within the Bounds of Religion Alone*, Grand Rapids, 1976.
5. Ibid., pp. 56–57.
6. C. Hodge, *Systematic Theology Vol. 1*, p. 155.

PART II

THE TRINITY

INTRODUCTION

From earliest times Christians have affirmed the Trinitarian form of the baptismal formula found in Mt. 28.19. The great ecumenical creeds of the catholic Church, forged in the midst of great spiritual and intellectual ferment as the very language of theological discourse was thrashed out, yield a robustly Trinitarian account of the divine nature. God is not merely the one and only true God. He is also a Trinity of divine persons. This doctrine is distinctively Christian and notoriously problematic, with some anti-Trinitarians decrying it as 'an error in counting'.[1] Recent philosophical-theological work in this area has focussed on the so-called *threeness–oneness problem*, that is, how it is that God can be said to be both one and three at one-and-the-same time. Some philosophical theologians have opted for a social model of the Trinity, which can be traced back to the patristic period. Exactly how one should characterize the social account of the Trinity is disputed. But according to one influential way of thinking about this view, the Trinity is a community of divine individuals that share together in one divine essence. In this part Cornelius Plantinga Jr expounds the social account of the Trinity. His irenic work at the interface between philosophy and theology has sought to bring representatives of both disciplines into dialogue on central topics in Christian theology. In his essay he marshals an impressive theological argument in favour of this model as a superior account of the divine life.

The alternative 'model' of the Trinity is the Latin, or psychological view, often associated with the 'Trinitarian Law' that states, '*In God all is one where there is no opposition of relations*'.[2] According to Latin Trinitarians, it is the relations had by one or at most two of the divine persons that distinguishes the Triune God from the God of classical theism. These include predicates like 'being the Son' or 'being spirated by the Father and the Son' (for most Western Christians, at least), which refer to the Second and Third persons of the Trinity, respectively. On the Latin view it is the fact that we can predicate things like 'being the Son' of the Second Person of the Trinity that distinguishes him from, say, the First Person of the Trinity, to whom such appellations cannot apply. Whereas the danger of a social view of the Trinity is that, at least as it has sometimes been formulated, it may be indistinguishable from tritheism (the notion that there are three gods, not one Triune God), the opposite problem is often said to apply to the Latin view, namely, that some versions of the Latin account are modalist (the heresy according to which the differing divine 'persons' are no more than masks worn by the one

God for different tasks in the economy of salvation). In this part, the Latin view is set forth with characteristic rigour by Brian Leftow, well-known for his work in retrieving metaphysical theology from medieval theologians like Thomas Aquinas, in order to make use of their ideas for contemporary philosophy and theology. Leftow maintains that the Latin view is perfectly defensible and does not entail modalism.

The logical objections to the Trinity that depend upon the threeness–oneness problem are addressed head-on in the third essay of this part, written by Peter van Inwagen, one of the most important and original metaphysicians and philosophers of religion at work today. It is his contention that the most serious of such objections can be turned back, if the notion of relative identity is employed. The heart of this doctrine depends on the idea that one object may be identical with more than one sort of thing, rather like, in recent discussion of the problems of material constitution, it might be said that the statue and the lump of clay are distinct things somehow composed by the same matter. The conceptual pay-off for Christian theology in avoiding at least some of the nastier 'problems of counting' with the traditional Trinity, may offer some motivation for taking seriously van Inwagen's interesting but controversial proposal.

Notes

1. As one Unitarian put it, 'this [doctrine of the Trinity] is an error in counting or numbering; which, when stood in, is of all others the most brutal and inexcusable; and not to discern it is not to be a man', Anon (John Biddle?), cited by Keith Yandell in 'The Most Brutal and Inexcusable Error in Counting?: Trinity and Consistency' *Religious Studies* 30 (1994): 201.
2. From the canons of the Council of Florence, AD 1441, cited in Ludwig Ott, *Fundamentals of Catholic Dogma* (Rockford: Pan Books, 1960), p. 70.

Suggested further reading

- Davis, Stephen, *Christian Philosophical Theology* (Oxford: Oxford University Press, 2007), ch. 4.
- Merricks, Trenton, 'Split Brains and the Godhead,' in Thomas Crisp, Matthew Davidson and David Vander Laan (eds), *Knowledge and Reality: Essays in Honor of Alvin Plantinga* (New York: Springer-Verlag, 2006), pp. 299–326.
- Rea, Michael and Brower, Jeffrey, 'Understanding the Trinity', in *Logos* 8 (2005), pp. 145–157.
- Swinburne, Richard, *The Christian God* (Oxford: Oxford University Press, 1994), ch. 8.

CHAPTER 5

SOCIAL TRINITY AND TRITHEISM

Cornelius Plantinga Jr.

In the Creed of the (Eleventh) Council of Toledo (675) we find the following statement of the doctrine of the Trinity:

> Although we profess three persons we do not profess three substances, but *one substance* and three persons . . . If we are asked about the individual Person, we must answer that he is God. Therefore we may say God the Father, God the Son, and God the Holy Spirit; but they are not three gods, he is one God . . . Each single Person is wholly God in himself and . . . all three persons together are one God.[1]

This typically Latin formulation, like others of its kind, possesses great puzzling power. Of course the main problem or puzzlement here is that of threeness and oneness. Suppose the divine life includes both a three and a one. What are the referents of these numbers? Three what? One what? And, especially, how are these three and this one related?

The section of the Toledo Creed just quoted tells us, expectably, that there are three persons and one God. Or, alternatively, three persons and one substance. But, at least initially, the relation of the three and one is by no means wholly clear. Indeed, one who reads that each of Father, Son, and Spirit is a "single person," and "wholly God in himself," and yet that "they are not three gods, he is one God," may be reminded of the seventeenth-century antitrinitarian complaint that trinitarians are people who do not know how to *count*. A similar response often greets a reading of what is doubtless the classic statement of Western trinitarianism, namely, the fifteenth and sixteenth verses of the Athanasian Creed: "(15) So the Father is God, the Son is God, and the Holy Spirit is God; (16) And yet they are not [or, there are not] three Gods, but one God."

This, as Boethius says in *De sancta trinitate,* is "a point that deserves a moment's consideration."

In any case, the definition and relation of threeness and oneness in the doctrine of the Trinity are obviously its central problem or mystery. Not surprisingly, particular understandings of the three and the one, and of their relation, serve to classify traditional trinitarian theories both between orthodoxy and heresy, and also within them.

In what follows I want to state a strong or social theory of the Trinity and defend it against the usual objection that theories of this kind are tritheistic. By strong or social trinitarianism, I mean a theory that meets at least the following three conditions: (1) The theory must have Father, Son, and Spirit as distinct centers of knowledge, will, love, and action. Since each of these capacities requires consciousness, it follows that, on this sort of theory, Father, Son, and Spirit would be viewed as distinct centers of consciousness or, in short, as *persons* in some full sense of that term. (2) Any accompanying sub-theory of divine simplicity must be modest enough to be consistent with condition (1), that is, with the real distinctness of trinitarian persons. This second condition is not idle. From Augustine to such twentieth-century trinitarians as R. C. Moberly and Taymans d'Eypernon,[2] one finds statements in which Father, Son, and Spirit appear to be full persons, but are also said to be each identical with the divine essence, thus making the *de facto* number of persons in God hard to estimate. (3) Father, Son, and Spirit must be regarded as tightly enough related to each other so as to render plausible the judgment that they constitute a particular social unit. In such social monotheism, it will be appropriate to use the designator *God* to refer to the whole Trinity, where the Trinity is understood to be one thing, even if it is a complex thing consisting of persons, essences, and relations.

Before stating a theory of this kind, I want to sketch briefly the Pauline and Johannine materials that generate it. Along with the epistle to the Hebrews, these are the fullest deposits of biblical witness to Father, Son, and Spirit, and to their relation.

I should add that I do this in part because I believe theological theories ought to be drawn and elaborated from Scripture, and I do it in part because some prominent contemporary social trinity statements sit loose to Scripture – statements of Bracken and Moltmann,[3] for instance. In this way such statements tend to become individualistic and oblique to the interests and traditions of the Christian church.

Biblical considerations

In 1 Corinthians 8, in the midst of addressing a problem of conscience, Paul says this:

> We know that an idol is nothing at all in the world and that there is no God but one. For even if there are so-called gods, [even if there are] many 'gods' and many 'lords,' yet for us there is but one God, the Father, from whom all things came and through whom we live; and there is but one Lord, Jesus

Christ, through whom all things came and through whom we live. But not everyone knows this. (vss. 4–7, NIV)

Here Paul summarizes a Christian doctrinal novelty, a uniquely Christian claim about the divine. He centers this confession between Judaism on the monist side and Hellenistic polytheism on the pluralist side.

To take the latter first, Paul rejects the Greek pantheon not because Greek gods are "promiscuous, quarrelling, incestuous, and fratricidal," as James Burtchaell describes them – the sort of company one would not want to keep even for a weekend, let alone a lifetime.[4] Paul rejects them rather because they are unreal, mere nothings in the world. Accordingly he simplifies and substitutes: There are not many gods, but one God, the Father. There are not many lords, but one Lord, Jesus Christ.

On the other hand, where Judiasm is concerned, Paul echoes the great Old Testament monotheistic claim of Deuteronomy 6:4, the so-called *Shema:* "Hear, O Israel, the Lord our God, the Lord is one." While reaffirming the *Shema,* Paul explicitly identifies this one God with the person called "Father" and then adds a second focus of interest. "For us," he says, "there is but one God, the Father . . . *and* there is but one Lord, Jesus Christ" (italics added).

Paul's claim is scandalous. For "Lord" is a divinity title in Paul's usage. Thus, not surprisingly, the Lord Jesus Christ in this passage is a cosmic mediator in creation and providence. He is the one "through whom all things came and through whom we live." Elsewhere in Pauline literature, Jesus Christ is claimed to be equal with God, to be a cosmic ruler and savior, a person in whom the fullness of the Godhead lodges. He is a person, indeed, to whom Paul and other Christians *pray.*[5]

So beyond the Old Testament claim of one God – a claim Paul interprets as confession of one Father – there is also this second person, equal with God, fully divine, and a proper object of Christian prayer. Paul calls this person Lord, and identifies him as Jesus the Christ. This is the person the apostolic father Justin Martyr boldly called "a second God in number."[6]

Paul is more circumspect. But he does simultaneously distinguish God the Father from Jesus Christ and ascribe divinity to both. There is for us one God, the Father, and one Lord, Jesus Christ.

Ephesians 4:4 adds that there is also one Spirit. The Spirit in Pauline literature is probably a distinct personal being. The Spirit searches, for example, and intercedes. The Spirit apportions gifts and can be grieved.[7] These are personal acts and capacities. The biblical locutions "Spirit of God" and "Spirit of Christ" moreover suggest that the Spirit is a person distinct from God and Christ, even if closely associated with them. Further, the Spirit is almost surely a *divine* being. The Spirit performs such acts proper to God as pouring out the love of God and regenerating human beings.

Moreover the Spirit can be blasphemed – which, in the New Testament, is usually an act of verbally injuring someone divine.[8]

To summarize, in Pauline literature we clearly have two distinct divine persons and probably we have three. Moreover, in Paul and the New Testament generally, the appropriateness of recognizing full three-person trinitarianism is increased by the appearance of a dozen or so trinitarian formulas. One thinks, for example, of the formula at the end of 2 Corinthians, often still used as a worship benediction: "May the grace of the Lord Jesus Christ, and the love of God, and the fellowship of the Holy Spirit be with you all." In such formulas, the names of Father, Son, and Spirit appear in close contiguity. This is significant. For if in the case of two of the three designations we know the referent to be a divine person, then likely the same sort of entity is referred to in the third case.

So far, then, we have in Paul one God, one Lord, and one Spirit. I might add that Paul's habit of reserving the designator *God* for the Father, and indicating the divinity of the Son and Spirit in ways usually other than calling them *God* straight out, is typical of the New Testament generally. This habit, combined with biblical characterizations of the Father as generator and sender, lies behind a Christian trinitarian tradition, especially pronounced in the Greek East, of regarding the Father as God proper, as the source or font of the divinity of Son and Spirit. The latter two may be fully divine, but they are derivatively so.

So much for Paul. Through John's Gospel runs an even richer vein for the church's doctrine of the Trinity – a wide, deep, and subtle account of divine distinction within unity. In John, Father, Son, and usually the Spirit or Paraclete are clearly distinct divine persons who play differentiated roles within the general divine enterprise of life-giving and life-disclosing. Yet they are primordially united – a claim typically made in the Fourth Gospel by the use of two similar words, *en* and *hen*, i.e., "in" and "one."[9] Father and Son are said to be in each other. This is the base claim for the Greek Fathers' doctrine of *perichōrēsis*, a sort of intratrinitarian hospitality concept. According to this concept, each trinitarian person graciously makes room for the others in his own inner life and envelops or enfolds that person there. Each is *in* the other two.

In John, Father and Son are also said to be one with each other. Though the relation of in-ness and oneness is not clearly set forth, it is close in context and apparently in concept. Perhaps in-ness is the main exhibition of oneness.

In any case, the primal unity of Father, Son, and Paraclete is revealed, exemplified, and maybe partly constituted by common will, work, word, and knowledge among them, and by their reciprocal love and glorifying.[10] These same six phenomena both distinguish the three persons and also unite them, typically by a functional subordination relation that obtains among the three.'

Take will as an example. In John's Gospel, the Son of God is on a mission: He does not do his own will, but that of his Father, the one who sent him. Though the Son has a will of his own, he subordinates it to his Father's.[11] The Spirit in John is in turn subordinate to the Son. He operates as almost pure agent, bestowed on the community of believers by Jesus the Son,[12] and sent as Paraclete to combine the functions of advocate and comforter.

Yet this very superordination and subordination of wills that distinguish the three persons also unite them. For in fact only one divine will is expressed – that of the Father who sends the Son and who, with the Son, sends the Paraclete. The sending idea itself, given the šālî(a)ḥ tradition of the Old Testament and rabbinic Judaism, suggests both that "the one who sends is greater than the one sent" and also that the one sent is an almost perfect duplicate or representative of the sender.[13]

The presentation of both divine subordination and divine unity in the Fourth Gospel would complicate later trinitarian debate, not least the Arian debate of the fourth century. For, on the one hand, there is little doubt that John presents at least a functional hierarchy, with the Father ultimately in control. Son and Spirit seem comparatively unoriginal. On the other hand, the Son appears to be equally divine with the Father. For if the Father is the "only true God," the Son is also God (*theos*) and "the God" (*ho theos*).[14] He speaks throughout the Gospel with "the accent of deity."[15]

And if divine nature (perfect will, love, glory, etc.) is revealed by heavenly origin and divine work, then with due hesitation the Paraclete/ Spirit, "the other Counselor" besides the Son, may be added to the Johannine concept of God. Altogether, where trinitarian issues are concerned, John's Gospel is the acme of New Testament witness and reflection, a pretty well-developed base for the Christian doctrine of the Trinity. In fact, John's presentation of transcendent in-ness and oneness, exhibited by various divine excellences, lies behind the Christian trinitarian habit of sometimes using the locution "one God" as a designator for the whole Trinity,[16] and, alternatively, of sometimes using "God" or "one God" as a designation for the divine essence or nature or substance.[17]

This last possibility, incidentally, especially when combined with philosophical precommitments to particular understandings of the divine nature, can quickly generate remarkable difficulties and ambiguities that push us into an intellectual atmosphere quite remote from the deliverances of the Gospel of John. For instance, theologians with a strong commitment to simplicity theory[18] tend to see the divine essence as a concrete thing – "deity itself," or "the most divine thing" – with which each trinitarian person is identical.[19] Such theologians would naturally read the fifteenth verse of the Athanasian Creed ("The Father is God, the Son is God," etc.) as claiming that the Father is (identical with) the divine essence, the Son is (identical with) the divine essence, etc.

On the other hand, theologians with more modest theories of divine simplicity also use *God* with reference to the divine essence, but for them the designator functions only sortally and adjectivally. For them, the obvious way to read verse 15 of the Creed is as follows: "The Father is (wholly) divine, the Son is (wholly) divine," etc. Such a reading appears to maintain some continuity with the Fourth Gospel presentation.[20]

Statement of a social theory

A person who extrapolated theologically from Hebrews, Paul, and John would naturally develop a social theory of the Trinity. Accordingly, I want to propose such a theory. I want first to state the theory generally, and then to address such specific issues as the relation of persons and essence, the definition of modalism, and finally, the question how social trinity theory qualifies as monotheistic.

Let me propose generally, then, that the Holy Trinity is a divine, transcendent society or community of three fully personal and fully divine entities: the Father, the Son, and the Holy Spirit or Paraclete. These three are wonderfully unified by their common divinity, that is, by the possession by each of the whole generic divine essence – including, for instance, the properties of everlastingness and of sublimely great knowledge, love, and glory.[21] The persons are also unified by their joint redemptive purpose, revelation, and work. Their knowledge and love are directed not only to their creatures, but also primordially and archetypally to each other. The Father loves the Son and the Son the Father. Extrapolating beyond explicit New Testament teaching, let us say that the Father and Son love the Spirit and the Spirit the Father and Son. The Trinity is thus a zestful, wondrous community of divine light, love, joy, mutuality, and verve.

Each member is a person, a distinct person, but scarcely an *individual* or *separate* or *independent* person. For in the divine life there is no isolation, no insulation, no secretiveness, no fear of being transparent to another. Hence there may be penetrating, inside knowledge of the other as other, but as co-other, loved other, fellow. Father, Son, and Spirit are "members one of another" to a superlative and exemplary degree.

And this is no accident. We ought not to picture the Holy Trinity as a set of three miscellaneous divine persons each of whom discovers he has the generic divine essence and all of whom therefore form an alliance to get on together and combine their loyalties and work. We ought to resist every Congregational theory of trinity membership. The biblical materials rather suggest that besides the common or generic divinity each possesses, Father, Son, and Spirit bear a much closer relation to each other as well – a derivation or origin relation that amounts, let us say, to a personal essence. The Spirit, for instance, is *of* God or of the Father; he is moreover the Spirit of Christ, or of the Son. The Spirit is thus relatively unoriginal by comparison with Son and Father in turn.

The Son, meanwhile, is of the Father or from the Father. It is true that the classic doctrine of the eternal generation of the Son by the Father has been somewhat disenfranchised by modern translations of John 1:14 and 18, and of John 3:16 and 18. The "only begotten" Son is now the "only" Son (RSV) or the "one and only" Son (NIV). Such biblical language as Son "of the Father" still suggests, however, both kinship and derivation. One might suppose, therefore, that these two persons are essentially related to each other not only generically but also in some quasi-genetic way. For the Son is not only equally divine with the Father; he is also the *Father's* Son. He is, so to speak, his Father all over again. We could say, then, that Father and Son are not just members of the class of divine persons, but also members of the same family. This is doubtless part of what the author of the Fourth Gospel means when he presents the Son as being in the Father and the Father in the Son. The mysterious in-ness or oneness relation in the divine life is short of personal identity, but much closer than mere common membership in a class. For it includes a divine kinship relation as well.

As Christopher Stead suggests, the Nicene *homoousios* clause probably means something similar. The everlasting Son and Father are of one substance or being: generically, they are both wholly divine (and, of course, this claim all by itself would have been strong enough to rout Arius). But the Nicene Fathers probably meant something stronger. By their famous clause they likely meant to say that the two trinitarian persons, besides having generic equality, are moreover related by quasi-genetic derivation. As a stream from a source, or a twig from a branch, or a child from a parent (all common fourth-century illustrations), so the Son is of or from the Father.[22] Medievals sometimes said the Son is of the *womb* of the Father (*ab utero Patris*).[23]

Suppose, then, that each of Father, Son, and Spirit possesses the whole generic divine essence and also a personal essence that distinguishes that person from the other two. Both kinds of essences unify. The generic essence assures that each person is fully and equally divine. The personal essences, meanwhile, relate each person to the other two in unbreakable love and loyalty. For the Father has the essential personal property of being permanently related to the Son in an ineffable closeness akin to a parent-child relation. The Son has the essential personal property of being permanently related to the Father in an ineffable closeness akin to a child-parent relation. Let us say, extrapolating from Scripture, that the Spirit has the essential property of being the Father and Son's loyal agent.

They in turn have a complementary property: it is essential to them to *have* the Spirit as their loyal agent.

Now the section of the Toledo Creed with which I began yields a standard, summary claim that in the divine life there are three persons and one God, or three persons and one substance. Putting together the biblical materials with the statement of social trinity theory just offered, we can see how such a standard claim would be construed in strong trinitarian perspective.

So far as the three persons are concerned, I think I have given good reasons for supposing that at least Paul and John present Father, Son, and Spirit as distinct knowers, lovers, glorifiers. I now want to add two comments: first, these authors seem not to confine their view of the personhood of the Son of God to the time of the Incarnation. In their view the Son is also personal in a preexistent, or, better, preincarnational state, and also in an exalted state. John says Jesus Christ shared glory with the Father before the world began. He was with God in the beginning (17:5, 1:1). In the Philippians kenosis hymn, Paul says Jesus Christ was preincarnationally in the form of God, but emptied himself, taking on the form of a human servant, finally being exalted by God the Father (2:6–9). Jesus Christ appears to have been a divine person before he additionally became a human person in incarnation and exaltation. Indeed, this states-of-Christ Christology, shaped like a parabola, has been regnant for most of the history of doctrine, from at least the time of Hilary of Poitiers.

Second comment: it is usual for historians and theologians to claim that, whatever the biblical authors believed, the Church Fathers had a thinner and more modalist-tending concept of the personhood of the threeness in God than we might suspect if we attended simply to their selection of *persona* and *hypostasis* as threeness terms.[24] Where a trinitarian person is concerned, the Fathers are said to have had in mind less a distinct center of consciousness than a role or part, as, for instance, in the locution *dramatis personae*.

I believe that this judgment is historically false, or largely false. It may be that consciousness was not as prominent a component of the concept of personhood for the Fathers as it was after Descartes, but it should be noted that Tertullian, who fixed the Latin vocabulary, used *person* as a threeness term in ways that fit nicely with social trinitarianism. He argued against Praxeas, for instance, that one divine monarchy does not entail just one divine monarch. For, says Tertullian, even in earthly monarchies several "persons" or "officials" administer it – for example a father and a son. So also in God.[25]

Further, the Fathers routinely identified the error in modalism as belief in only one divine person. For example, Novatian complained that modalists overlook the fact that Father and Son are as plainly two persons as are Paul and Apollos.[26]

This is a doubly telling complaint. It tells us, first, that Novatian thought the distinction between Father and Son to be like that between Paul and Apollos – who are clearly two persons in a full sense of the term. Novatian's complaint also tells us that he thought modalists lacked a full enough sense of personhood. Their problem is clearly not that they believe in only one role: no modalist ever suggested that. Their problem is rather that they believe in only one person. They may believe in three roles or parts played by one person; what they lack is belief in three persons.

I conclude that biblically and historically one is justified in speaking of three persons in God in a rich sense of *person*.

But, now, what about the claim that there is only one God? How, exactly, may social trinitarians cling to respectability as monotheists?

In, appropriately enough, three ways. First, if *God* is used as the peculiar designator of the Father, as the New Testament typically uses it (see, e.g., 1 Cor. 8:6 above), then Father, Son, and Spirit are all divine persons, but there is only one font of divinity, only one Father, only one God in *that* sense of *God*.

Second, suppose *God* is used as the name of the divine essence, as it is in much of Latin Christianity. Then there are three divine persons, but only one generic divinity, one *divinitas* or *deitas* or *theotēs;* one Godhood or Godhead or Godness – that is, only one God in *that* sense of *God*. Of course, social trinitarians will regard the divine essence as abstract, not concrete, and, as suggested above, will use *God* with reference to it as a predicate adjective instead of a predicate nominative. On this view, the generic divine essence is a set of excellent properties severally necessary and jointly sufficient for their possessor to be divine: Father, Son, and Spirit each *has* this essence, though none *is* it. In any case, social trinitarians delightedly affirm that there is exactly one such divine essence, and, in so doing, affirm a typically Cappadocian view.[27]

Third, according to another standard habit,[28] *God* is properly used as designator of the whole Trinity – three persons in their peculiar relations to each other. This particular usage is a favorite among social trinitarians: there are three divine persons, but only one divine family or monarchy or community, namely, the Holy Trinity itself.

Each of these ways of using the designator *God* is perfectly standard and familiar in the Christian tradition. And in each case, social trinitarianism emerges as safely monotheistic. For it shares the general Christian conviction that there is only one Father, only one (general as opposed to personal) divine essence, and only one triune God.

On not three Gods

So why, then, is social trinitarianism from its embryonic formulations in Gregory of Nyssa to such twentieth-century versions as those of Hodgson, Moltmann, and Brown, often accused of tritheism?

Karl Barth, for example, says in the *Church Dogmatics* that "by Father, Son and Spirit we do not mean what is commonly suggested to us by the word 'persons'. . . [rather] the one 'personality' of God, the one active and speaking divine ego, is Father, Son, and Holy Spirit. Otherwise we should obviously have to speak of three Gods."[29]

I think it is quite clear that Barth's position here is biblically and historically eccentric. For if it is tritheist to believe that *Father, Son,* and *Spirit* designate distinct persons, then Paul and the author of the Fourth Gospel must be regarded as tritheists. And they are good company for tritheists to keep.

Indeed, Barth's claim seems eccentric even by comparison with such classic Western trinitarianisms as that of Augustine. Like Barth, Augustine does have a strong simplicity theory according to which, in God, persons and divine attributes are identical, as are persons and the sum of attributes, the divine essence. According to Augustine, this divine essence is "the thing itself that God is."[30] For Augustine, God the Trinity is the only instance of Godness, or *divinitas,* or the essence of God. God the Trinity is indeed identical with Godness-itself, the only divine thing. And each of Father, Son, and Spirit is identical with that thing.[31] So Godness itself, the only divine thing, the Trinity, and each of Father, Son, and Spirit – all these turn out to be really the same thing.

Accordingly, in book 5 of *De Trinitate* Augustine says with respect to each attribute that it has only one instance in the divine life. Thus with respect to greatness, for instance, the Father is great, the Son is great, and the Holy Spirit is great, and yet there are not three greatnesses (not *tres magnitudines*), nor even three who are great (not *tres magni*), but only one great thing (only *unum magnum*).[32]

And, of course, so far Augustine sounds like a Barthian. But in fact Augustine's theory is mixed. For besides the heavily Neoplatonic sections of simplicity theory in *De Trinitate* (especially books 5–7), Augustine also has places that are quite pluralist. Much of book 15, for instance, drives toward the conclusion that we will be seriously misled if we imagine Father, Son, and Spirit to be merely faculties of one divine person called *God.* For, says Augustine, each person is living; none lacks perception and understanding. Each is "most powerful" and "most just."[33] Augustine deliberately says that each of the persons (a term of which he is admittedly wary) is a rememberer, a thinker, a lover, a willer.[34] Indeed, Father and Son mutually know and love each other. Even the Spirit who *is* love, who is the *vinculum caritatis* between Father and Son – even the Spirit loves.[35] Elsewhere Augustine speaks of Father and Son sharing a "society of love" and a unity of will like that of cooperative human beings.[36]

In sum, Augustine has biblical materials that lead him to talk as if Father, Son, and Spirit are distinct persons. He also has Neoplatonic convictions that lead him to assert claims from which it seems to follow that *Father, Son,* and *Spirit* are, in effect, three names for the divine essence conceived of as self-related according to paternity, filiation, and procession. How these two tendencies in Augustine cohere is remarkably hard to see.

But unlike Barth, Augustine nowhere explicitly denies that Father, Son, and Spirit are distinct thinkers, lovers, and willers. In fact, he affirms that they are thinkers, lovers, and willers, and his language suggests that he thinks of them as distinct thinkers, lovers, and willers. When one recalls that contemporaneous Greek theories of the Trinity – that of Gregory of Nyssa, for instance – have three persons *without* severe and competing simplicity statements,[37] the historical judgment on Barth emerges. His claim that there is only one person in God fits with just half of Augustine's theory – the Neoplatonic half. And Augustine's type of trinitarianism is only half the Christian tradition – the Western half. Indeed, Barth's statement that there is only one person in God looks strikingly like what Tertullian, Novatian, Hilary, and Gregory of Nyssa identified as the heresy of modalism.[38] Barth smooths out the apparent incoherence in Augustine in a monist direction. Oddly, his consistency makes him vulnerable to the charge that he is a classic trinitarian heretic.[39]

So the first defense of social trinitarianism against the charge of tritheism is this: to say that Father, Son, and Spirit are the names of distinct persons in a full sense of *person* scarcely makes one a tritheist, Indeed such a claim makes oneself an ally with the best-developed biblical presentation on the issue and with three-quarters of the subsequent theological tradition. It is quite acceptable in both cases to believe in three full persons, and the believer who does this emerges untainted.

Second defense: In the fourth and fifth centuries, when the doctrine of the Trinity was being fully developed, there were particular limits on orthodoxy and, accordingly, particular positions outside orthodoxy. As already suggested, virtually everybody who writes on the Trinity during this period identifies the monist heresy as some form of modalism (Sabellianism, for instance), and then specifies that modalism is unacceptable because it allows belief in only one person. I now want to add that the heresy on orthodoxy's pluralist side is specifiable as well. And it is surely not the view that God includes three distinct persons: that view lies at the heart of orthodoxy, agreed to by Cappadocians and Augustinians alike. What is rather heretical is belief in three *ontologically graded* distinct persons. It is Arianism that Hilary, Augustine, and the Cappadocians identify as pluralist heresy. For if Sabellians confound the persons, Arians are said to be guilty of "dividing the substance."[40] That is, Arians have a Son and a Spirit who are less than *homoousios* with the Father. The Son, for example, lacks the whole divine essence because he lacks everlastingness: he is in fact a creature. Arianism, as Jaroslav Pelikan points out, thus became the standard tritheist heresy because, despite Arius's own insistence on the unity and simplicity of God, Arians worshipped Christ and the Spirit and baptized in their names *while refusing them full ontological deity.*[41] This, as Gregory of Nyssa says, makes the Son a "bastard" and the Trinity a pagan "plurality of gods."[42] For the whole Augustinian age, and for centuries afterward, modalism and Arianism are the opposite trinitarian heresies and, here again, social trinitarianism affirms the standard trinitarian tradition.

So a second proper defense of social trinitarianism is that it falls safely to the monist side of classically defined tritheism.

Third, several objections to strong trinitarianism cluster around the question of intratrinitarian relations, and whether we can really conceive of three distinct persons, each of whom is fully divine, that nonetheless together constitute only one complex, worshippable unit – that is, one triune God.

Deep in Western trinitarian reflection is the conviction that any multiplication of the divine essence, such that there really are three instances of it, three distinct bearers of it, would imply that the resultantly distinct persons would each be finite, limited by the other two. Thus, in a medium-famous passage Donald Baillie issues what might be called "Baillie's Challenge":

> If we regard the three *personae* of the Trinity as quite distinct persons or personalities in the full modern sense, we seem to imply that they are *parts* of God, and it is difficult to remedy this by going on to speak of their being united in the highest conceivable kind of unity. If they are three distinct Persons, are they limited by each other, so that they are *finite* Persons? Or if that is rejected as intolerable, and it is maintained that each has the divine attribute of infinity, is it not very difficult to think of *three infinite Beings,* of the same essence, coexisting with each other as distinct entities? Yet I do not see how the interpretation in question [the social analogy] can avoid that difficulty.[43]

What must be said to this?

First, on the question of limit and finitude, one is tempted to reply to Baillie by pointing out that on his notion of limit God would apparently be limited by the existence of any other persons at all, including human persons. These are, after all, entities distinct from God whose existence affects God and, so to speak, requires God's acknowledgment. In fact, God's existence is in general limited to being *God's* existence, in distinction from the existence of creation. That is the main burden of denying pantheism. Further, each person in God is limited by his own nature to doing what is right instead of wrong, wise instead of silly, and the like. So one cannot mean by the doctrine of God's infinitude that God has no "boundaries" or limits whatever.

Given this properly limited understanding of divine infinity, could there be three equally infinite divine beings? Baillie declares that it is very difficult to think of such a state of affairs. He does not exactly state the nature of his difficulty, but perhaps he has in mind a sort of bizarre scenario once sketched by C. Stephen Layman. In a striking paper, "An Ontology for Trinitarian Relations,"[44] Layman muses over the following questions: If three divine beings are equally infinite, would they not also be independent? Would it not be possible, then, that one or two might break away from the Trinity and establish a rival kingdom? Would the one or two who were left be able to take up the slack? Worse, if all three persons are fully omnipotent, could not one or two destroy the other(s)?

The answer to these questions is plainly negative. To see why this must be so, one has only to compare them with questions about any divine person's ability to harm, alienate, or destroy *himself.* No fully divine person could do that – surely not the God Donald Baillie acknowledges. No more could any of the social trinity persons leave the others derelict, or compete for intergalactic dominion, or commit intratrinitarian atrocities. For just as it is a part of the generic divine nature to be everlasting, omnipotent, faithful, loving, and the like, so it is also part of the personal nature of each trinitarian person to be bound to the other two in permanent love and loyalty. Loving respect for the others is a personal essential characteristic of each member of the Trinity. Each divine person has general, generic *aseitas* vis-à-vis creation, but within the Trinity each essentially has interdependence, agapic regard for the other, bonded fellowship. Such is the proper response to Baillie's challenge, so it seems to me, and to Layman's musings.

But if the persons are interdependent in this way, can one still say they are *free?* Joseph Bracken has suggested that freedom includes "the power of radical self-disposition."[45] Is this so? And would a free person thus be likely, or at least able, to issue a declaration of independence from time to time?

Not necessarily. It is no abridgment of divine freedom – in any significant sense of freedom – that a divine person cannot do what is contrary to his nature! It is no more embarrassing to the personal freedom of Father, Son, and Spirit that they cannot ruin each other or abandon each other than it is to generic divine freedom that no divine person can cause his own demise. Thus, for each person to exist in, and *only* in, society with the other two is no defect or weakness. On the contrary, it is the ultimate grounding and vindication of the fact that perfect love always respects the *other*. In social trinity perspective, Father, Son, and Spirit are not independent persons. Each is essentially the fellow of the other two. And such interdependency is a vice only to egoists and individualists. At the heart of the universe it is a splendid divine excellence.

The third defense of social trinitarianism comes, then, to this: If belief in three *autonomous* persons or three *independent* persons amounts to tritheism, the social analogy fails to qualify. For its trinitarian persons are essentially and reciprocally dependent.

Finally, I want to raise once more the question of Trinity and simplicity and observe a particular definition of tritheism that is generated by a simple Trinity position. In referring to Augustine earlier, I noted that Augustine holds out for three distinct persons, but also claims each is identical with the divine essence. The result is a position according to which even if Father, Son, and Spirit are distinct persons and each is great, still there are not in the divine life three who are great. When this Augustinianism gets lifted out of *De Trinitate* and reproduced in the Athanasian Creed of the late fifth or early sixth century, we seem to have an ancient ecumenical confession that ratifies as conventionally Christian a peculiar result of Augustinian simplicity doctrine, namely, the Creed's denial in vss. 7–14 that in God there are three "increates," three "infinites," three "eternals," three "almighties." Such denials the Creed apparently regards as entailing and entailed by the summary claim in vs. 16 that "there are not three Gods, but there is only one God."

So tritheism here seems to be any claim to the effect that there are three eternals or three who are eternal, three Gods or, apparently, three who are God. And this would be a hard doctrine for many Christians, including social trinitarians, to handle.

Still, matters are complicated by two facts: one is that in verse 6 the Creed says that it is the *Godhead* (*divinitas*) of Father, Son, and Spirit that is one. The Creed then adds, seemingly in apposition, that the glory and majesty of the three are equal. This has led such commentators as J. N. D. Kelly to suggest that what is really targeted in 7–14 is Arianism, that is, the denial of *co*-infinity, *co*-eternality, *co*-omnipotence, and so forth.[46] What there are not three of in each case is qualitatively different divine *properties* rather than qualitatively equal divine persons. Possibly Kelly is right about this.

The second complicating fact is that book 5 of Augustine's *De Trinitate,* from which the Creed is largely taken, interprets the "one God" claims as specifically affirming one essence, not only, but also one *Trinity:* "For as the Father is God, the Son is God, and the Holy Spirit is God," says Augustine, "which no one doubts to be said in respect to substance, yet we do not say that the very supreme Trinity itself is three Gods, but one God."[47] I do not myself believe that Augustine was content with affirming one generic divine essence and one Trinity; I believe what he says in effect also affirms that there is only one person. For Augustine wants to say that God the Trinity is identical with Godness itself, that is, with *divinitas,* with the only divine thing. And he also wants to say that Father, Son, and Spirit are each identical with that thing. But whether the Athanasian Creed goes quite so far I leave as an open question. Perhaps it does not, and can therefore, as suggested above, be read more than one way.

By the time of the Fourth Lateran Council in the thirteenth century, however, this matter gets confessionally tightened up. For in the interim the interesting trinitarianisms of Gilbert of Poitiers and Joachim of Fiore appear. Both seem to have denied simplicity in the Holy Trinity: both seem to have distinguished between Father, Son, and Spirit, on the one hand, and *divinitas,* on the other. Moreover, Gilbert seems also to have distinguished between the generic divine essence and the personal essences of each of the three. Bonaventure at any rate criticized what he took to be Gilbert's distinction between "that by which the Father is God" and "that by which the Father is Father."[48]

In condemning such views, the Fourth Lateran Council says the following:

> We ... believe and confess ... that there is one highest, incomprehensible and ineffable thing [or reality (*res*)] which is truly Father, Son and Holy Spirit, at the same time three Persons and each one singly a Person; and therefore in God there is only Trinity, not quaternity. For each of the three Persons is that thing, that is, that divine substance, essence or nature ... and that thing is not generating, nor generated, nor proceeding, but it is the Father who generates, the Son who is generated, and the Holy Spirit who proceeds; so that there may be distinction of persons but unity in nature.[49]

Here is confessional *simplicitas* in all its glory. One cannot hold that God the Trinity is a complex of persons, personal relational essences, and a generic essence, for in God there is exactly one thing, the divine essence, and each person *is* that thing. That is all there is. As Thomas Aquinas would put it later, "everything which is not the divine essence is a creature."[50]

Lateran IV apparently rules out the possibility that each person might be an *instance* of the essence, generically conceived, for then, apparently, God would be a quaternity of four things – an essence plus three exemplifications of it.

Accordingly, in the Western High Middle Ages tritheism might plausibly be said to be any trinitarian view that distinguishes the persons from each other while refusing to affirm their simultaneous identity with the one divine essence or thing. Beyond Arianism, medieval tritheism is any denial of such trinitarian simplicity.

And, of course, on this standard, social trinitarianism of the sort I have been proposing will have to plead guilty.

But is the standard itself plausible? And are we simply obliged to accept it, plausible or not? Do we take for granted an aggressive, Western version of trinitarian simplicity theory – as if the claim that each of the divine persons is identical with the divine essence is as much a trinitarian given as the claim that each person is distinct? Are we simply obliged to accept such a version of simplicity, and then struggle with the "mystery" or sheer incoherence it introduces into the doctrine?

Surely not. For one thing, as is sometimes admitted even by its supporters,[51] simplicity theory of the Augustinian, Lateran, and Thomistic sort cannot claim much by way of biblical support. Paul and John do not state, or even suggest, that Father, Son, and Spirit are finally just the same object. The whole drift of their thought appears to go just the other way. Simplicity doctrine finds its way into Christian theology via Neoplatonism, and ought therefore to be viewed with the same cool and dispassionate eye as any other potentially helpful or harmful philosophical contribution to theological elaborations of biblical truth. Simplicity theories are negotiable in ways that Pauline and Johannine statements are not.

Second, trinitarian simplicity theory of the Lateran sort is clearly much more Western than Eastern. As shown above with respect to Gregory of Nyssa, those who accept some version of simplicity as a helpful component of any formal statement of the doctrine of the Trinity are quite within their rights to choose a more modest and less mystifying version like Gregory's rather than one of the much more ambitious and troublesome Western versions.

Third, the Lateran standard for trinitarian orthodoxy is of very doubtful coherence. For it claims that Father, Son, and Spirit are distinct persons, but also each identical with the one divine thing or reality. And, of course, it would not take a student of logic very long to show from the latter statement that they are therefore identical with each other. If so, on the Lateran version of trinitarian simplicity the three trinitarian persons are not really and ontologically distinct, but only logically or notionally or nominally. The incoherence of a statement that has distinct persons each identical with the same thing comes out in the generation statements: the divine thing does not generate, get generated, or proceed, despite the fact that Father, Son, and Spirit, identical with it, do. How are we to imagine this?

In the *Summa theologiae,* Thomas Aquinas offers an exceedingly subtle and often exquisitely difficult exploration of these matters. He seeks to explain, for instance, how fatherhood and sonship are real relations in God that are really, and not just logically, distinct,[52] but also how

> a real relation in God is in reality identical with nature and differs only in our mind's understanding, inasmuch as relation implies a reference to the correlative term, which is not implied by the term 'nature'. Therefore it is clear that in God relation and nature are existentially not two things but one and the same ... Nothing in God can be attributed to him in any other way than as being identical with him, since he is absolutely simple.[53]

But how can three things (the divine relations) that are really distinct each bear an identity relation to the divine nature or essence, differing from it "only in our mind's understanding"? That is, how can three things identical with some fourth thing remain distinct? Thomas offers an example from Aristotle, namely, that of action, passion, and motion:

> Although action is the same as motion, and likewise passion, still it does not follow that action and passion are the same; because action implies reference as of something *from which* there is motion in the thing moved, whereas passion implies reference as of something *which is from* another. Likewise, although paternity, like filiation, is really the same as the divine essence, nevertheless, these two in their own proper notions and definitions import opposite relations. Hence they are distinguished from each other.[54]

What does all this come to? Surely action and passion are logically distinct as are paternity and filiation. Indeed, the logical distinctions here are in both cases complementary: they are what Thomas calls "relations of opposition." But how does that observation help Thomas? For his project in this article is to show that paternity and filiation (and, by extension, Father and Son)[55] are not only logically distinct but also really distinct. That is because "if the relations were not really distinguished from each other, there would be no real trinity in God, but only a logical trinity, which is the error of Sabellius."[56]

Thomas does show, I think, how one thing, such as a one-person God, might have logically distinct self-relations. For this one-person God, perhaps being Father and being Son would be like being a subject and being an object. Suppose, for instance, that the one-person God loves himself. He as loving subject is logically distinct from himself as loved object. Still, he and himself are nonetheless really (i.e., ontologically) only one person. And, I take it, transposed into trinitarian terms, the affirmation of only one person is the Sabellian error Thomas is trying to avoid – and this would be true even if, in some appropriate sense, "being a subject" and "being an object" are real relations, and really distinct ones.

If, on the other hand, Thomas meant by his analogy of action, passion, and motion to suggest only that Father, Son, and Holy Spirit are all personally distinct instances or instantiations of Godness, real personal exemplifications of *divinitas* – just as action and passion are kind instances of generic motion – then Thomas would have a much milder version of simplicity than Lateran IV and a much more understandable one. I think it wholly doubtful that he can be taken thus, but if he could, then the social trinitarian would happily agree, reserving only the right to add that each of these kind instances is a person possessing his own distinguishing personal essence as well as the kind essence he instantiates. This latter claim – that there are two sorts of essences in God, personal and generic – would then become the point of contention between the social trinitarian and Thomas, rather than the formal claim of trinitarian simplicity.

I conclude that, either way, medieval simplicity doctrine is not so very much for the social trinitarian to worry about. If it is interpreted as claiming that the only real distinctions between Father, Son, and Spirit are in our understanding, not in the absolute nature of God, and that the persons are therefore not really persons in a full sense of the term, the social trinitarian will resist in order to protect the biblical givens. If, on the other hand, Thomas's simplicity claim means no more than that each trinitarian person is an instance of exactly one essence (as the action-passion example suggests) then the social theorist will so far agree. But of course clarity on these matters depends to a large degree on an ability to understand typical medieval simplicity claims, which is exceedingly hard to come by.

Certain recent writers have stated the trinity-simplicity doctrine in more modern terms. Bernard Lonergan, for example, has an interesting variation on traditional formulations, wishing to speak not of three persons identical with some one essence, but rather of three centers of one consciousness. Lonergan seems to hold both that there is only one real consciousness in the divine life and also that the three persons are each self-conscious and other-conscious. This is, at least, the way Joseph Bracken represents Lonergan's view.[57]

Let us briefly consider this view, whether or not Lonergan holds it. Suppose there is only one consciousness in the divine life, only one flow of thought and perception. This generic flow could contain within it knowledge of the truth that the Father is distinct from the Son and that each is distinct from the Holy Spirit. And, accordingly, each person, tapping terminal-like into the general flow, could know this truth. The Father, for instance, could know specifically the truth of the proposition, *The Father is a center distinct from Son and Spirit*. And the Son could know that same proposition: But the trouble is that, on this scheme, what the Father could not know is the truth of the proposition, *I am the Father*. And what the Son could not know is the truth of the proposition, *I am the Son*. For, if the Father knew the truth of the proposition *I am the Father*, he would know something different from what is known by the Son and Spirit – who could not know the truth of that proposition. In other words, if the Father were truly self-conscious, he would have to have a partly different consciousness from that of Son and Spirit. It could not be the case that Father, Son, and Spirit each had precisely the same consciousness while each was moreover distinctly self-conscious.

But suppose Lonergan were to concede this point, dropping the claim that each person is self-conscious and holding out for the more modest claim that the three persons are distinct but non-self-conscious centers of exactly one consciousness.

I believe that although this revised position improves in coherence, it loses a lot in other ways. For one thing, it does not accord at all well with the Scriptures. The Fourth Gospel, for instance, presents Father and Son as each quite capable of distinguishing himself from the other. For another thing, it is hard to see why distinction among persons should be a perfectly Godly phenomenon, but self-referential knowledge of such distinction divinely unavailable. Indeed, it would seem peculiar that we humans should be able to distinguish ourselves from other humans, but divine persons be unable to do anything analogous.

Once more, simplicity theory ends up complicating trinity doctrine quite needlessly. Its lease ought not to be extended.

Altogether, I suggest that a social doctrine of the Trinity, untroubled by the severest forms of simplicity theory, enjoys a solid biblical base, a safe position within the boundaries of classical fourth-century orthodoxy, and, finally, the ability to turn back usual complaints that it succumbs to tritheism.

Notes

1. Denz. 528–529 in *The Teaching of the Catholic Church,* comp. Josef Neuner and Heinrich Roos, ed. Karl Rahner, trans. Geoffrey Stevens (New York: Alba House, 1967), pp. 94–95.

2. R. C. Moberly, *Atonement and Personality* (London: John Murray, 1913), pp. 86, 167; Taymans d'Eypernon, *Le Mystère primordial: La Trinité dans sa vivante image* (Brussels: Édition universelle, 1950), p. 52.

3. Joseph A. Bracken, "The Holy Trinity as a Community of Divine Persons," *Heythrop Journal* 15 (1974): 166–182; *What Are They Saying About the Trinity?* (New York: Paulist Press, 1979); *The Triune Symbol; Persons, Process, and Community* (Lanham, Md.: University Press of America, 1985); Jürgen Moltmann, *The Trinity and the Kingdom,* trans. Margaret Köhl (San Francisco: Harper and Row, 1981).

4. James T. Burtchaell, *Philemon's Problem: The Daily Dilemma of the Christian* (Chicago: ACTA Foundation, 1973), pp. 12, 18.

5. Phil. 2:5, 10; 2 Tim. 2:10; Col. 1:19; 1 Cor. 16:22.

6. *Dialogus contra Tryphonem* 128.4.

7. 1 Cor. 2:10; Rom. 8:26; 1 Cor. 12:11; Eph. 4:30.

8. Rom. 5:5; Jn. 3:5; Mk. 3:29.

9. E.g., 10:30, 38.

10. E.g., 4:34; 5:19–22, 15:26; 3:34; 16:14; 10:14f.; 10:17, 14:31; 8:50, 5:41, 16:14.

11. Jn. 17:24, 4:34.

12. Jn. 20:22.

13. *Theological Dictionary of the New Testament,* s.v. ἀποστελλω, ἀπόσταλος, by Karl H. Rengstorff, pp. 415, 421.

14. Jn. 1:1c, 20:28.

15. Archibald M. Hunter, *According to John: The New Look at the Fourth Gospel* (Philadelphia: Westminster Press, 1968), p. 23.

16. E.g., Augustine, *De Trinitate* 1.6.9.; 5.8.9.

17. E.g., the Belgic Confession 1: "We all believe ... that there is one only simple and spiritual Being, which we call God (Nous croyons tous ... qu'il y a une seule et simple essence spirituelle, laquelle nous appelons Dieu éternel ...)," and 8; "We believe in one only God, who is one single essence in which are three persons (Nous croyons en un seul Dieu qui est une seule essence, en laquelle il y a trois personnes)."

18. The doctrine of divine simplicity, in its most aggressive medieval versions, holds that in God there is really no distinction or "composition" at all – not between form and matter, or potentiality and actuality, or substance and accident, or essence and existence, or person and essence. The last of these is especially controversial where the doctrine of the Trinity is concerned. Thomas Aquinas, *Summa theologiae* 1a q. 3 is classic on the general doctrine. For trinity and simplicity, see 1a qq. 28–30 and 39–40.

19. See below on Augustine, the Fourth Lateran Council, and Thomas Aquinas.

20. For elaboration of ways to read the Creed (including vs. 16), given various uses of *God,* see my essay, "The Threeness/Oneness Problem of the Trinity," *Calvin Theological Journal* 23 (1988): 37–53.

21. There are special problems that are generated by the traditional incarnation doctrine for generic essence formulations within trinity doctrine. How, for instance, does one handle the fact that the fully divine incarnate Son of God was apparently non-omniscient?

22. G. Christopher Stead, *Divine Substance* (Oxford: Clarendon Press, 1977), pp. 247–250.

23. E.g., Creed of the (Eleventh) Council of Toledo (675), Denz. 526.

24. E.g., Claude Welch, *In This Name: The Doctrine of the Trinity in Contemporary Theology* (New York: Charles Scribner's Sons, 1952), p. 269.

25. Tertullian, *Adversus Praxean* 3.

26. *De Trin.* 27.

27. For elaboration, see my "Gregory of Nyssa and the Social Analogy of the Trinity," *The Thomist* 50 (1986): 325–352, esp. pp. 338–351.

28. That of Augustine, for instance. See n. 16.

29. Karl Barth, *Church Dogmatics,* ed. G. W. Bromiley and T. F. Torrance, various translators, 4 vols. (Edinburgh: T. & T. Clark, 1936–69), IV/1, pp. 204–205.

30. *De Trin.* 2.18.35.

31. Ibid. 5.10.11; 5.11.12. Augustine denies here that in the divine life greatness and that which is great because of greatness are two things. See also 7.6.11: There are not three species – Father, Son, and Spirit – of God conceived as genus; nor are there three individuals – Father, Son, and Spirit – of God conceived as species. For whether conceived of as genus or species, God, or the essence of God, has exactly one instance – God the Trinity itself. And here Augustine has in mind that the essence of God is *self*-exemplifying, for (5.11.12) God the Trinity is his own deity.

32. *De Trin.* 5.10.11.

33. Ibid., 15.23.43; 15.5.7.

34. Ibid., 15.7.12.

35. Ibid., 15.17.18; 15.19.36.

36. Ibid., 4.8.12.

37. Gregory's simplicity theory, unlike medieval Latin versions, nowhere includes the claim that Father, Son, and Spirit are identical with the divine essence; indeed, Gregory explicitly denies that they are. For him, it is not God who is simple, but rather the divine essence in which the persons share, i.e., not *ho theos,* but *to theion.* This means that the divine essence, like the generic essence of human beings, is available only whole, never in parts or shares. Whoever has any divine excellence has the whole essence. And Gregory is very clear that such simplicity of the divine essence is quite compatible with multiple exhibitions of it in personal hypostases. See Gregory, *Contra Eunomium* 1,22, 10.3, 11.1; see also Basil Krivocheine, "Simplicity of the Divine Nature and Distinctions in God, According to St. Gregory of Nyssa," *St. Vladimir's Quarterly* 21 (1977):104, and my "Gregory of Nyssa," pp. 341–343.

38. See above for Tertullian and Novatian. See also Hilary of Poitiers, *De Trinitate* 2.23; Gregory of Nyssa, *Contra Eun.* 1.19.

39. Someone might challenge the consistency thesis on the ground that Barth's language *re* Father, Son, and Spirit is often richly communal. Barth does indeed speak of intratrinitarian "connexion and fellowship" (*CD* III/2, p. 324) and of "interplay" and "relationship" among Father, Son, and Spirit (IV/1, p. 203). In fact, Barth famously takes the "Let us" of Gen. 1:26 as a trinitarian cohortative that attests the "plurality in the divine being . . . the differentiation and relationship, the loving co-existence and coopera- tion, the I and Thou, which first take place in God himself" (III/1, p. 196). However, in these same places Barth takes pains not to be misunderstood. The "I and Thou" in God, contrary to the case with humans, is within an "individual." This individual is "I only in relation to himself who is also Thou, and Thou only in relation to himself who is also I" (ibid.). Again, "the one 'personality' of God, the one active and speaking divine Ego, is Father, Son and Holy Spirit" (IV/1, p. 205). See also II/1, p. 284, where God is "*a* person," and p. 299, where God is "*an* acting subject" (my italics). Perhaps the best case for Barth's trinitarian orthodoxy could be put like this: in case Barth's communal and plural language is to be given the same weight, on the one hand, as his formal repudiation of what it suggests, on the other, then Barth is merely baffling like Augustine, and not modalist. Unhappily, neither of these is a particularly attractive option.

40. As in the Athanasian Creed, vs. 4. See also Hilary of Poitiers, *De Trin.* 1.11.17; Augustine, *De Trin.* 7.4.9; Gregory of Nyssa, *Contra Eun.* 2.6.7.

41. Jaroslav Pelikan, *The Christian Tradition: A History of the Development of Doctrine,* 5 vols. (Chicago: University of Chicago Press, 1971–1989), 1.200.

42. *Contra Eun.* 1.19.

43. Donald Baillie, *God Was In Christ: An Essay on Incarnation and Atonement* (New York: Charles Scribner's Sons, 1948), p. 141.

44. Los Angeles, 1978 (mimeographed). See also Layman's "Tritheism and the Trinity," *Faith and Philosophy* 5 (1988): 291–298.

45. "Trinity as Community," p. 180.

46. *The Athanasian Creed: The Paddock Lectures for 1962–3* (London: Adam & Charles Black, 1964), pp. 76–80.

47. *De Trin,* 5.8.9.

48. Pelikan, *The Christian Tradition,* 3.278.

49. Denz. 804, in Rahner, ed., *Teaching of the Catholic Church,* p. 98.

50. *Summa Theologiae (ST)* Ia q. 28, a. 2, s.c. in *Basic Writings of Thomas Aquinas,* ed. Anton C. Pegis, 2 vols. (New York: Random House, 1945), 1.284.

51. E.g. by Mark Pontifex, *Belief in the Trinity* (New York: Harper & Bros., 1954), p. 31.

52. *ST* Ia q. 28, a. 1, a. 3, s.c.

53. *ST* Ia q. 28, a. 2, and ad 1, in Blackfriars edition, 61 vols. (Cambridge: Blackfriars, 1964-), 6.31.

54. *ST* Ia q. 28, a. 3, ad 1, Pegis ed., p. 287.

55. Given q. 29, a. 4, where Thomas claims that the divine relations are the divine persons ("God's Fatherhood is God the Father, who is a divine person"), what is said in the present discussion on the distinction of real relations applies equally to the distinction of persons (Blackfriars ed., 6.61).
56. *ST* Ia q. 28, a. 3, s.c., Pegis ed., p. 286.
57. *What Are They Saying?* pp. 5–8.

CHAPTER 6

A LATIN TRINITY

Brian Leftow

Latin models of the Trinity begin from the existence of one God, and try to explain how one God can be three Persons. I offer an account of this based on an analogy with time-travel. A time-traveler returning to the same point in time repeatedly might have three successive events in his/her life occurring at that one location in public time. So too, God's life might be such that three distinct parts of His life are always occurring at once, though without any succession between them, and this might give God the triune structure Christian theology believes He has.

The Athanasian creed has it that Christians

> worship one God in Trinity ... the Father is God, the Son is God and the Holy Spirit is God. And yet they are not three Gods, but one God.[1]

Such odd arithmetic demands explaining. Some explanations begin from the oneness of God, and try to explain just how one God can be three divine Persons.[2] As Augustine, Boethius, Anselm and Aquinas pursued this project, let us call it Latin Trinitarianism (LT). I now sketch a Latin view of the Trinity and argue that it is coherent.

The Latin view

On LT, there is just one divine being (or substance), God. God constitutes three Persons. But all three are at bottom just God. They contain no constituent distinct from God.[3] The Persons are somehow God three times over, since as the Athanasian Creed puts it, "we are compelled by the Christian verity to acknowledge every Person by Himself to be both God and Lord."[4] Thus too the Creed of the Council of Toledo has it that

> although we profess three persons, we do not profess three substances, but one substance and three persons ... they are

not three gods, he is one God . . . Each single Person is wholly God in Himself and . . . all three persons together are one God.[5]

Again, Aquinas writes that

among creatures, the nature the one generated receives is not numerically identical with the nature the one generating has . . . But God begotten receives numerically the same nature God begetting has.[6]

To make Thomas' claim perfectly plain, let us talk of tropes. Abel and Cain were both human. So they had the same nature, humanity. Yet each also had his own nature, and Cain's humanity was not identical with Abel's: Abel's perished with Abel, while Cain's went marching on. On one parsing, this is because while the two had the same nature, they had distinct tropes of that nature. A trope is an individualized case of an attribute. Their bearers individuate tropes: Cain's humanity is distinct from Abel's just because it is Cain's, not Abel's.

With this term in hand, I now restate Thomas' claim: while both Father and Son instance the divine nature (deity), they have but one trope of deity between them, which is God's.[7] While Cain's humanity ≠ Abel's humanity, the Father's deity = the Son's deity = God's deity. But bearers individuate tropes. If the Father's deity is God's, this is because the Father *just is* God: which last is what Thomas wants to say.

On LT, then, there clearly is just one God, but one wonders just how the Persons manage to be three. If the Father "just is" God, it seems to follow that

1. the Father = God.

If "each single Person is wholly God in Himself," and both Son and Father have God's trope of deity, it seems also to follow that

2. the Son = God.

But then since

3. God = God,

it seems to follow that

4. the Father = the Son,

and that on LT, there is just one divine Person.

(1) and (2) raise another problem. Cornelius Plantinga writes that an

> incoherence . . . comes out in the generation statements:
> the divine thing does not generate, get generated or proceed,
> despite the fact that Father, Son and Spirit, identical with it, do.
> How are we to imagine this?[8]

Plantinga's point is this. According to the Nicene Creed,

5. the Father generates the Son.

But the claim that

6. God generates God

is either unorthodox or necessarily false. Nothing can "generate" itself,
i.e. bring itself into existence. So if (6) asserts that something "generates"
itself, it is necessarily false. But if (6) asserts that one God "generates" a
second God, it implies polytheism, and so is unorthodox. Now the
Nicene Creed commits Christians to (5). In conjunction with (1) and
(2), (5) yields (6). So if LT is committed to (1), (2) and (5), LT entails
either unorthodoxy or a necessary falsehood. Of course, avoiding this
problem by rejecting (5) is just unorthodoxy of a different stripe.

The other options for LT are to reject all or just some of (1), (2), and
the cognate claim that the Spirit is God. Rejecting all also seems to wind
up unorthodox. For then there seem to be four divine things – Father,
Son, Spirit and God. But if "each single Person is wholly God in Himself," each includes God somehow. So surely God is not a fourth divine
thing in addition to any Person.[9] And in any case, on the doctrine of the
Trinity, there are at most three divine things. That's why it's a doctrine
of Trinity, not Quaternity. Rejecting just some can trim the number of
divine beings to three – e.g. by accepting (1) but denying (2) and that
God = the Spirit. This would retreat to a form of Trinity rejected well
before Nicaea. It also raises the question of just what the relation between
God and the Son is.[10]

Everything is either God, an uncreated object distinct from God or
a creature. To call the Son a creature is to embrace Arianism. If the Son
is a creature, it's hard to see how He can be fully divine, or even divine
at all–divine/creaturely seems an exclusive disjunction. But Scripture
does not let Christians deny all deity to the Son.[11] Further, whether
or not the Son is *as* divine as God, if He is created, He is a divine being
who *is not God*. The positing of divine beings in addition to God is of

course polytheism. So it is easy to see why the early Church found Arianism unacceptable.

If the Son is an uncreated item discrete from God, it is false that God has made all that He does not include, which flies in the face of Scripture and Creed.[12] To call Him divine, uncreated and discrete from God is to opt for a polytheism even clearer than Arianism's. But if the Son is not a creature or an uncreated item discrete from God, He is in *some* way God.[13] How then, if not by simple identity? One option here would be to say that God is always Father, but only temporarily Son, or necessarily the Father but only contingently Son. This avoids polytheism: God *is* in some way Son. If there are no temporary or contingent identities, it is consistent with denying (2). But of course it leaves us the question of just what God's relation to the Son *is*. The clearest account of this seems to be Modalism: the being who is always, necessarily the Father, contingently and temporarily takes on a second role, as Son, in such a way that (so to speak) when the Son was on earth, nobody was home in heaven, and the Father counts as crucified. Modalism sits ill with Scriptural passages which seem to treat Father and Son as two separate persons, e.g. Christ's saying "I have come down from heaven not to do my will, but to do the will of him who sent me" (*John* 6:38) and praying "Father, glorify me in your presence with the glory I had with you before the creation of the world" (*John* 17:5). Such texts make it clear why the early church found Modalism unacceptable. It thus seems that LT cannot be coherent, monotheist and orthodox. I now suggest that LT can be all three, and speculate as to how it may be so.

Time-travel, tap-dancing, and the Trinity

You are at Radio City Music Hall, watching the Rockettes kick in unison. You notice that they look quite a bit alike. But (you think) they must just be made up to look that way. After all, they came on-stage at once, each from a different point backstage, they put their arms over each others' shoulders for support, smile and nod to each other, and when the number is over, they scatter offstage each in her own direction. So they certainly seem to be many different women. But appearances deceive. Here is the true story. All the Rockettes but one, Jane, called in sick that morning. So Jane came to work with a time machine her nephew had put together for the school science fair. Jane ran on-stage to her position at the left of the chorus line, linked up, kicked her way through the number, then ran off. She changed her makeup, donned a wig, then stepped into her nephew's Wells-o-matic, to emerge in the past, just before the Rockettes went on. She ran on-stage from a point just to the right of her first entry, stepped into line second from the chorus line's left, smiled and whispered a quip to the woman on her right, kicked her way through the number, then ran off. She then changed her makeup again . . . Can one person thus be wholly in many places at once? The short answer is: she is in many places at the same point in *our* lives, but not the same point in *hers*. If Jane travels in time, distinct segments of her life coincide with the same segment of ours. To put this another way, Jane's personal timeline intersects one point in ours repeatedly.

Now in this story, there is among all the Rockettes just one trope of human nature. All tropes of human nature in the Rockettes are identical. But consider this argument:

1a. the leftmost Rockette = Jane.
2a. the rightmost Rockette = Jane.
3a. Jane = Jane.

So

4a. the leftmost Rockette = the rightmost Rockette.

The argument appears sound, but doesn't shorten the chorus line. There is just one substance, Jane, in the chorus line. But there *is* also an extended chorus line, with many of *something* in it. Many what, one asks? Some philosophers think that Jane is a four-dimensional object, extended through time as well as space – that not Jane's life but Jane herself has earlier and later parts.[14] If this is true, each Rockette is a temporal part of Jane.

If (as I believe) Jane has no temporal parts, then not just a temporal part of Jane, but Jane as a whole, appears at each point in the chorus line, and what the line contains many of are segments or episodes of Jane's life-events. This may sound odd. After all, Rockettes dance. Events do not. But what you see are many dancings of one substance. What makes the line a line is the fact that these many events go on in it, in a particular set of relations. Each Rockette is Jane. But in these many events, Jane is there many times over. She plays different causal roles, once (as the leftmost Rockette) supporting the second-from-left Rockette, once (as the second-from-left) being supported by the leftmost, etc. And she has genuine interpersonal relations with herself in her other roles. She leans on herself for support, smiles to herself, talks (and talks back) to herself. The talk may even be dialogue in the fullest sense. In changing makeup, wig, etc., Jane might well forget what she said when she was leftmost in the line, and so a remark she hears when she is one in from the left might well surprise her, and prompt a response she did not anticipate.[15] The Wells-o-matic lets the one Jane be present at one time many times over, in many ways, as the leftmost Rockette, the rightmost, etc. It gives us one

Jane in many *personae*. If we give the name "Rockette" to what we see many of, it lets the one Jane be (or be present in) many Rockettes. The Wells-o-matic allows this by freeing the events composing Jane's life from the general order of time.

Is time travel genuinely possible? I travel in time into the future if, with no gaps in my existence, periods of suspended animation, time spent unconscious, or subjective slowing in my experience, I find myself at a point in world-history beyond where the biological aging of my body and (say) the time on my watch would date me: if, say, I step into a machine, step out 10 seconds later by watch- and body-time, and find that it is next year. If this is an acceptable description of futureward time-travel, then the Special Theory of Relativity entails that it occurs. For the theory entails that the time of an accelerated object dilates: if we mount a sufficiently precise clock on a body A, accelerate A a while, then compare the A-clock with one which has not been accelerated, the A-clock will be found to have run more slowly. If A-time thus dilates, the A-clock travels into the future *per* the description above. Experiments have confirmed that time-dilation occurs.[16]

In some models of the universe consistent with General Relativity's field equations and requirements on the universe's mass-energy distribution, physical objects can travel into the past. This is reason to call pastward time travel physically possible.[17] Paradoxes threaten stories of pastward time travel ("suppose I went back and killed my earlier self before he got into the time machine . . ."). Some think these reason to call it conceptually impossible.[18] But they may not be. According to Earman, these paradoxes

> bring out a clash between Gödelian time travel and what might be held to be conceptual truths about spatiotemporal/ causal order. But in the same way the twin paradox of special relativity theory reveals a clash between the structure of relativistic space-times and what were held to be conceptual truths about time lapse. The special and general theories of relativity have both produced conceptual revolutions. The twin paradox and the [time-travel paradoxes] emphasize how radical these revolutions are, but they do not show that these revolutions are not sustainable or contain inherent contradictions.[19]

In other words, if the physics clashes with our pre-theoretic intuitions, it may be the intuitions (and *a fortiori* philosophical theories built on them) which should give. And the paradoxes are not necessarily intractable. It would take a full paper of its own fully to motivate a solution to the time-travel paradoxes. But it would be good to say something to suggest that these can be solved, or at least come as close to solution as matters for my purposes. For I go on to model the Trinity on a time-travel case.

Time-travel paradoxes

The "killing my earlier self" paradox is the most disturbing intuitively. This paradox applies to Jane: can Jane as rightmost turn and kill Jane on her left, before next-left Jane made it to the time machine to re-emerge and take her rightmost place? A "no" answer seems untenable. Surely it's physically possible for Jane to pick up a knife on the way to her rightmost station, turn toward the next person in line, etc. But if yes, then there is a physically possible world in which Jane arrives at a point in her personal future after (it seems) having made it impossible for herself to get there. Moreover, Jane's killing her earlier self seems to generate a contradiction: Jane does travel back in time this last time, else she could not commit the murder, but if Jane does commit the murder, Jane dies before returning to the time-machine and so does not travel back in time. So if yes, it is apparently within Jane's power to make a contradiction true.

For my purposes, I need not suggest a full solution to this paradox. I want to suggest by analogy with a time-travel case that it is possible that God be a Latin Trinity. That is, I want to suggest that for all we know, this is how it is with God in some metaphysically possible world. To suggest this, I need only make out the analogy (which I have already begun to do) and make a case that there is a metaphysically possible world containing pastward time travel. To do this last, I need only point to the physics and suggest that in some world with such a physics, the paradoxes would not arise. A full solution to the time-travel paradoxes would show in effect that time-travel is compatible with all the facts about our own world. I need not argue this, for my claim is only that a Latin doctrine of the Trinity has likenesses to something found in *some* metaphysically possible world.

Now the paradox above is that seemingly we cannot grant either that Jane can or that she cannot kill her past self. To show that there is a possible world immune from this paradox, we need only show that there is a possible world conforming to an appropriate solution to the General Relativity equations in which an analogue of one or the other claim is true. I suggest that in some such GR-world, a creature just like Jane and in her situation simply cannot kill her past self. We think that Jane can kill her past self because we think she has libertarian freedom and the physical possibility of so using it. But it is within God's power to make creatures very like us save that they lack libertarian free will, and to site them in an appropriate GR-world physically deterministic at the macro-level. Suppose that God makes such a creature, Janet, and sets her in such a world which physically determines that she does not kill her past self when she emerges from a time-machine. Then there is no possible world indiscernible from Janet's up to the time at which she exits the machine in which she kills her past self. It is just not possible that she do so given these antecedents. Physical determinism and the lack of libertarian free-dom can occur in an appropriate GR-world. So the "retro-suicide" par-adox does not entail that pastward time travel does not occur in any possible world. And I do not need to claim that time travel can occur in *our* world to claim that a Latin Trinity exists in some world. For that mat-ter, I don't need to claim this to assert that a Latin Trinity exists in our world. For if physical indeterminism and created libertarian freedom did in fact rule time travel out of our world, they would not also rule out a Latin Trinity. These things have no bearing at all on God's nature, since I do not claim that God travels in time, and in any case they exist only logically after God has His nature.

A second sort of paradox can be built on the first, and to this I now suggest a full solution. Suppose that rightmost-Jane knifes the next per-son in line. Next-left Jane, stunned and confused by the attack, picks up a knife to defend herself on the way back to the time-machine, and in her confusion attacks in the wrong direction when she emerges: she attacks herself because she was attacked. A causal "loop" runs from next-left Jane's being attacked to the attack by rightmost Jane, and so the being-attacked is in its own causal ancestry. Every event in the causal loop is fully explained causally by immediately prior events. The puzzle is that *globally,* each event seems its own full explanation – since in tracing its ancestry, we find our way around the loop to the event itself – and that since nothing can explain its own occurring, it seems that globally, each event has no full explanation at all, despite having a *local* causal explana-tion. Putting it another way, there seems no real reason that Jane has a knife-wound. She has it at every point in the loop due to something earlier in the loop, but there seems no answer to the question of why there is ever any time at all at which Jane has a wound.

This is a paradox, but is it an impossibility? Quantum theory suggests that we must learn to live with events with no full physical causes. "No event causes itself" looks like a necessary truth, but it doesn't rule loops out. In the loop, no event *locally* causes itself. Nor does any event *globally* cause itself. Globally – that is, taking into account all events in the loop-events in the loop are uncaused, at least physically. The loop offends against intuitions that favor principles of sufficient reason, but it is impossible only if some fairly strong PSR is a necessary truth. If one is, of course, one can run powerful arguments for the existence of God. So atheists, at least, might not wish to push this sort of objection. Of course, an atheist might Chisholm away at PSRs to produce one gerrymandered to keep both loops and God out. But such a principle would quite likely forfeit its claim on our intuitions, and so provide no real *reason* to think loops impossible. And even theists needn't push PSR objections. For given a PSR strong enough to yield God, an explanation of the entire loop's existence is available from outside the loop. It is that God brought it into existence: the reason Jane has a wound is that God brought this about, by conserving the entire loop.[20] So I claim that an intuitively plausible PSR strong enough to rule loops out will rule God in. But with God ruled in, loops become compatible with the PSR after all. I conclude that the possibility of loops is an oddity, but does not rule time travel out.

Retro-suicide and causal loops yield the strongest objections I know to the possibility of time-travel. I suggest that the loop paradox dissolves on inspection, leaving us with an oddity that falls well short of contradiction, and that there is a possible world containing time-travel in which retro-suicide is not possible. But even if I turn out wrong about these things, Jane's story is consistent and broadly conceivable. Even if pastward time travel is in some way impossible, we have detailed physical models of the world in which it can occur. It is physically impossible that there be frictionless planes, but talk about them – detailed physical models in which they occur – can clarify the behavior of actual physical things. More to the point, time-travel stories may have at worst the status of intuitionist logic. I hold that classical logic is true, and necessarily true. If it is, there are no intuitionist possible worlds – it is not, for instance, possible for some p that $\neg\neg$ p be true and p not be true. The distinctive theses of intuitionism state metaphysical impossibilities. But they are internally consistent, comprehensible impossibilities. We know in great detail how logic would be were they true- so to speak, we have detailed logical models of the world in which they occur. We understand intuitionist theses full well, we can reason consistently within intuitionist strictures, and – here's the most important point – we can even appeal to intuitionist theses to clarify other things which may be metaphysically possible or even true ("if the future is indeterminate, then it is as if for some future-tensed propositions, negation behaves intuitionistically"). So even if pastward time travel is impossible, talk about it may help us clarify other, genuinely possible things.

Further, *if* pastward time-travel is impossible, this is due to the nature of space, time, and the causal order within them: in short, because of the relations which link events located in space and time. If pastward time-travel is impossible, what pastward time-travel stories show us are relations time-bound events cannot instance because they *are* time-bound. The classic Latin Trinitarians agree that God is not in time. If He is not, then if there *are* such things as events in His life, they are free from temporal constraints. They need not be related as events in time are. Again, if God *is* in time, it does not follow that events in His life are ordered as other temporal events are. Even if they have some temporal properties, they might not have the full complement of ordinary temporal properties.[21] If God's life is at least as free from ordinary temporal ordering as a pastward time traveler's would be, it is conceivable and so may be possible that in His life, one substance is three Persons in some form of social relation – as in Jane's case one substance is (or is present in) many Rockettes. So we need not suppose that God travels in time to draw this moral: God's life may be free from time's bonds. If it is, its events may be strangely structured, and this may be relevant to the doctrine of the Trinity.

Events and the Trinity

There is one Jane, but she was present many times over in the chorus line. At one point in our lives, many discrete maximal episodes in her life were co-present. These episodes were discrete in that along Jane's own personal timeline, they did not overlap (they were strictly successive). These episodes were maximal in that any point during each included one event in Jane's life of which every other event occurring at that point in Jane's life was part, and at any point we could say, for a shorthand, simply that *that* event was occurring. Suppose, then, that God's life has the following peculiar structure: at any point in our lives, three discrete parts of God's life are present. But this is not because one life's successive parts appear at once. Rather, it is because God always lives His life in three discrete strands at once, no event of His life occurring in more than one strand and no strand succeeding another.[22] In one strand God lives the Father's life, in one the Son's, and in one the Spirit's. The events of each strand add up to the life of a Person.[23] The lives of the Persons add up to the life God lives *as* the three Persons. There is one God, but He is many in the events of His life, as Jane was in the chorus line: being the Son is a bit like being the leftmost Rockette.

Of course, the cases also differ. Not all of Jane's life is on display in the chorus line. But every event in God's life is part of the Father-Son-Spirit chorus line; God does not live save as Father, Son and Spirit. Jane has just one life, with a peculiar episode partway through. It does not consist of anything else that counts as an entire life. God's life always consists of three other things which count as entire ongoing lives.[24] While the disruption between Jane's personal timeline and the sequence of events in ordinary public time had a special cause, God's life just naturally runs in three streams. Again, along Jane's personal timeline, first she only dances in one spot, then she runs to the machine, then she only dances in another spot. Jane dances in one spot only after she dances in another. Not so for God: God always lives in all three streams. God's life always consists of three non-overlapping lives going on at once, none after the other, as the series of positive numbers consists of two non-overlapping series, the positive rationals and irrationals, "going on at once" within the series, neither after the other.

Jane's story includes an account of how the many Rockettes are generated (the time-travel story) which involves succession. This account does not rule out Jane's existing at all times, and even having three streams of her life going at all times. For suppose that Jane exists at all public times. Then if public time has a first and last instant, the time-machine brings it about that after Jane's life at time's last instant comes a next instant of Jane's life located at time's first instant.[25] There is no public time after public time's last instant or before its first, but in Jane's life, her personal time, there is a period after the last instant of time (one which begins Jane's life's second stream, at time's first instant) and one before public time's first instant (namely, her entire first life-stream).[26] If time has a finite length but no last instant, there is a further puzzle. Suppose that the Wells-o-matic sends Jane pastward at some particular time. If time has no last instant, there is time *after* that time. So it seems that Jane misses some of time the first time around, in which case it's not true that her first life-stream exists at all times. But suppose e.g. that there is a last full second followed by an open period not more than a second long. Then we can simply say that Jane spends all of that open period in the machine, and that the machine brings it about that the first period of Jane's second life-stream succeeds the period she spent in the machine. If time has an infinite future, there is no particular problem in saying that infinite periods of Jane's life succeed one another. Such number-series as 1, 3, 5 . . . 2, 4, 6 . . . are mathematically unproblematic. Jane's life in this case would consist of minutes paired 1:1 with the members of some such series. What's puzzling is again just when the machine sends Jane back. One way to dissolve the puzzle is just to have Jane live in the machine for all time after a particular point, and say that the machine links her time in it to her life's second stream earlier in time. It should be clear from what I've said how the time-machine scenario can handle further permutations on the length and topology of time. So talk of time-travel can even provide some model of a life which always has three streams. Jane's generation-account, again, involves succession. Whatever account we give in God's case will not. But here my point is simply that we can make some sense of there being a life so structured as to have three discrete streams going on at once, even if that life includes all of time. I do not claim that the analogy is perfect.

Some might say that what makes the time-travel story comprehensible is precisely what's missing in the Trinitarian case.[27] Parts of Jane's life *succeed* parts of Jane's life, and so we can make sense of her winding up as three dancers at once as we watch her. But Persons' lives do not succeed Persons' lives. Instead, I've said, God just always lives in three streams. So how does one better understand the Trinity *via* the time-travel analogy? In Jane's story, again, three streams of events going on at once, which initially seem like three lives, turn out to be the life of one individual. On the surface, it might seem that what makes the story work is the succession between the life-segments. But it's more basically the causal relations between her life-segments. These are segments of one individual's life not because they succeed one another in a timeline but because the right causal relations link them. For one can imagine (borrowing an illustration from Lewis[28]) that when Jane enters the time-machine, she is annihilated and replaced by an atom-for-atom duplicate put together by the machine, with Jane existing at all times up to t in her personal timeline and the duplicate existing from Jane-time t onward. In this story, the duplicate is an "immaculate replacement" for Jane – its timeline succeeds and continues hers without a gap. But clearly the resulting life is not a further part of Jane's. Now some argue that the difference between duplicate-succession and continued existence is primitive and ultimate – that identity over time is a brute matter, not grounded in relations among the events of a life.[29] But if it is not, it rests largely on causality. The duplicate's life does not continue Jane's *inter alia* because the causal relations between the events aren't right – the positions, motion etc. of the atoms constituting Jane's body (and Jane herself, on materialism) don't directly cause those of the duplicate's atoms.[30] Conversely, on materialism, it's because (*inter alia*) these atoms' present motion is caused in the right way by the immediately prior motion of the atoms in Jane's body that this person's life continues Jane's, and so this person is Jane. If Jane has a soul and continues to exist only if it does, still causation is relevant, for the same soul continues to exist only if its earlier states contribute causally to appropriate sets of its later.[31] Succession by a duplicate isn't continued existence, and so doesn't give us a case of three streams of one life going on at once, because the causal relations between the relevant streams of events aren't right. Causal relations at least help determine the identity of the substance in the differing streams of Jane's life; it's (perhaps *inter alia*) because the right causal relations link them that they are successive stages of one life, as vs. successive smoothly continuous lives of duplicate Janes. And if this is correct, it lends itself to Trinitarian use.

As causal relations between the event-streams in the Jane case help make them streams within one life, we can suppose that causal relations do the like without succession in the Trinitarian case: that is, we can suppose that causal relations between the event-streams involved are what make them all streams within one individual's life. The causal relations involved are those of the Trinitarian processions: the Father "begetting" the Son, the Father and the Son "spirating" the Spirit. Nobody has ever claimed to explain how these work, so I'm at no disadvantage if I do not either. Every Trinitarian has claimed that whatever these relations amount to, they yield distinct Persons who are the same God. I say the same. The time-travel analogy makes this point: causal relations between streams of events going on at once and apparently involving wholly distinct individuals can make them streams of events within a single life. That point applies univocally to the Trinitarian case. Those who hold that the Son eternally proceeds from the Father hold that there eternally is a causal relation between them such that the events of the Son's life and the events of the Father's are events within the life of one single God. They leave the mechanism involved a mystery. The time-travel case shows that there is some intelligible story one can put where the mystery is in a structurally similar case. This does not remove the mystery, but it domesticates it a bit: thinking about time-travel shows us that causation can do the kind of thing Trinitarians claim it does. In Jane's case, ordinary identity-preserving causal relations link events in her life as each Rockette, and the causal relation which makes what look like three individuals' lives into the lives of one individual – the one the time-machine induces – directly links only the ends of various short event-streams, not the events in the middle. The Trinitarian relations of generation directly link entire streams: every maximal event in the Father's stream has or contains a begetting relation to an appropriate event or set of events in the Son's stream. But we know of nothing that would make this impossible – why *can't* causal relations which turn what are apparently three lives into one life link more than just the end-segments of streams?

If one asks what sort of persons the Persons are, on this account, the right answer is that they are whatever sort God is – the Persons just *are* God, as the Latin approach will have it. The Persons have the same trope of deity. Numerically the same substance generates their mental episodes. Just as Jane has her own thoughts while she is the left – and rightmost Rockettes, God has His own thoughts as Father and Son. But just as Jane does not think her leftmost thoughts at the point in her life at which she is rightmost, God does not think His Father-thoughts at the points in His life at which He is Son. Just as Jane can token with truth "I am the leftmost Rockette" and "I am the rightmost," God can token with truth "I am the Father" and "I am the Son." But just as Jane cannot token both claims with truth at the same points in her life, God cannot token with truth "I am the Son" at points in His life at which He is Father.[32] Just as Jane at the leftmost spot on the chorus line has no internal access to and is not thinking the thoughts she thinks at the rightmost spot, God as Father has no internal access to and is not thinking the thoughts of God as Son.[33] So the Son is distinct from the Father as leftmost Rockette is from rightmost, and the Son's mind is distinct from the Father's as leftmost's is from rightmost's.

On my account, the Persons' distinctness, like the Rockettes', depends on that of events involving a particular substance. Their identities are event-based; facts about events in God's life are what make Him triune. There is reason to say that at least one classic Latin account of the Trinity is in this way event-based. Aquinas begins his *Summa Theologiae* Ia account of the Trinity with questions on Persons' procession from Persons (q. 27), relations among Persons (q. 28) and finally the Persons themselves (q. 29). The first claim in his positive account of procession is that "all procession is according to some action"[34] that Persons proceed from Persons because of some divine act. The story Thomas tells of some of these acts is this.[35] God understands Himself. This is a divine act – God *does* something.[36] Because God does something, His understanding Himself is what we would call an event.[37] According to Thomas, because God understands Himself, His mind naturally generates an "understood intention," something expressing the content of His self-understanding. This is His "inner Word."[38] The coming to be of this "intention" is the Word's proceeding from the Father. Now "coming to be" suggests a process. This is misleading, as the Word is generated instantaneously and so exists co-eternal with God's self-understanding.[39] As Thomas points out, what's left when we remove this misleading implication is just an eternal relation of origin.[40] But this is a *causal* relation. And so its distal term is a caused state of affairs, the Word's existing. The obtaining of a caused state of affairs as and because it is caused is (I'd argue) an event.[41] One can call this event the Word's filiation. Because the Word proceeds, God's initial self-understanding has a relational property: it is the cause of an understood intention. Because it has this property, God's understanding Himself is also the Father's fathering the Son, His having the causal relation of paternity. For Thomas (following Augustine and Boethius), the Persons are distinguished solely by relational properties (being the Father of, being the Son of). That is, the only difference between God the Father and God the Son is that one is someone's Father (and no one's Son) and the other is someone's Son (and no-one's Father). These relational properties are exemplified entirely because certain acts – events – take place in God's inner life (self-understanding, inner expression; fathering, filiation): this is why Thomas orders *ST*'s Trinity treatise to move from acts to processions to relational properties, and only then to Persons. In fact, Thomas says, the relational properties' being exemplified just is the acts' taking place.[42] So what distinguishes God the Father from God the Son is simply which act God is performing. God the Father is God fathering. God the Son is God filiating, or being fathered. The Persons simply are God as in certain acts – certain events – in His inner life.[43] These events have no temporal sequence. None succeeds the other, for none are in time. As they are not in time, they have no temporal parts. God just eternally *does* the acts which constitute His life; these acts render Him triune.

Aquinas attempts to explain why God's self-understanding renders Him a Father and a Son, when our own acts of self-understanding do not do this to us.[44] But we needn't tackle this issue, at least for now.[45] One *could* suggest that it's just a primitive fact about the kind of thing God is that one stream of His life generates a second stream, and the two together generate a third stream, as it is about our kind that that this does not happen to us.[46] Explanation has to stop someplace, and the doctrine of the Trinity is supposed to be in the end mysterious.

Preserving the persons

To be minimally acceptable, an account of the Trinity must be coherent and orthodox. So an event-based account must at least show that it can deal with (1)-(4) and the "generation" argument. On an event-based account, on one reading, (1)-(4) is sound but irrelevant. If God as the Persons is relevantly like Jane as the Rockettes, then just as (1a)-(4a) did not shorten the chorus line, (1)-(4) do not collapse the Trinity. (1a)-(4a) did not shorten the chorus line because the real force of (4a) is

> 4a*. the substance who is the leftmost Rockette = the substance who is the rightmost Rockette.

(4a*) is compatible with the sort of distinction leftmost and rightmost have. To eliminate Rockettes, one would have to infer from (1a)-(3a) not (4a) or (4a*), but that the episode of Jane's life in which she is the leftmost Rockette and has not previously been any other Rockette is the last episode on her timeline in which she is any Rockette. It's obvious that (1a)-(3a) cannot by themselves yield this conclusion. The Trinitarian parallel is clear: (1)-(3) do not license the conclusion that the events (life) in which God is Father are the only events (life) in which He is any Person.

On the present view, the generation argument loses its sting. For it assigns (5) the sense

> 5a. God in the event(s) in which He is Father generates God in the event(s) in which He is Son.

(5a) asserts something relevantly like event causation within God's life: it causally links one segment of God's life to another. This does not entail that a second God exists *or* that one item causes itself to exist.[47] (5a) so taken still yields (6), but also so interprets (6) as to make it harmless. And in fact, the event-causal relations involved here provide a natural hook on which to hang an account of the Persons' generation-relations.

Thus one could simply concede (and ignore) these arguments. But in fact, there is more than one way to read them. On the second reading, thinking about time-travel suggests that they are in an unusual way unsound and invalid.

Timelines and soundness

For an argument to be sound, all its premises must be true at once. We see all the Rockettes at once. So of course it seems to us that (1a)–(3a) are all true at once. For that matter, we tend to think all identity-statements true omnitemporally if true at all (or at least true for all time after their subjects begin to exist[48]), and so again true at once (once their subjects exist). But when Jane has gone home, nothing satisfies the description "the leftmost Rockette" (though Jane of course satisfies "the person who *was* the leftmost Rockette"). If nothing satisfies "the leftmost Rockette," the description does not refer. And if the description does not refer, (1a) is not true. If we see (1a) as omnitemporally true (or as true for all time after Jane starts to exist), this is because we treat "the leftmost Rockette" as temporally rigid, picking out Jane at all times if it picks her out at any (or all future times once it picks her out at any). But we needn't. And read as involving a temporally non-rigid description, (1a) can cease to be true. This might suggest that (1a) is not "really" an identity-statement, that at some deep level it is "really" the predication that Jane is the leftmost Rockette. I take no stand on this. What's clear is that the predication can cease to be true, and on the non-rigid reading, the identity-statement is true only as long as the predication is.

With the descriptions rigid, (1a)–(4a) is sound but irrelevant: we took the descriptions as rigid in the last section. Now let us read (1a) and (2a) non-rigidly. If we do, an ambiguity emerges. (1a)–(3a) are all true at the same point in our lives. So for us, the argument is sound (though still irrelevant). But on Jane's timeline, things differ. When Jane is the leftmost Rockette, she has not yet lived through dancing in the rightmost Rockette's spot – even if she has a perfect memory, she has no memory of this. Jane then shares the stage with the rightmost. So Jane is then living through existing simultaneously in public time with her dancing in the rightmost Rockette's spot. But still, on Jane's timeline, (2a) is not yet true, because Jane has not yet done what she must to satisfy the description "the rightmost Rockette," even though (1a) and (2a) are true at once on *our* timeline. So too, when (2a) is true on Jane's personal timeline, (1a) has ceased to be true. Jane *recalls* dancing in the leftmost spot, and so qualifying for the title "the leftmost Rockette," and one can only remember what has happened in one's past. Dancing as leftmost is something she *once* did but is no longer doing – on her timeline. This is so even though Jane is then living through existing simultaneously in public time with her dancing in the leftmost spot. So on Jane's personal timeline, with its premises read non-rigidly, (1a)-(4a) *is never sound*.

This suggests that there is actually a tense involved in (1a) and (2a), at least when we treat the descriptions as non-rigid. The ordinary-language sentences (1a) renders are after all "Jane is the leftmost" or "Jane is identical with the leftmost" (and so for (2a)). In these, "is" is present-tensed. Whether non-rigid (1a) and (2a) are true at once depends on whether the present the tense brings in is Jane's own or that of the public timeline. So here is the ambiguity: the non-rigid-description reading of (1a)-(4a) is sound (though as irrelevant as the rigid reading) if the tenses invoke the public timeline, but never sound if they invoke Jane's. If pastward time-travel can occur, it's Jane's timeline that counts: that (1a)-(4a) is sound along the public timeline is irrelevant. To show why, I now sketch another problem about time-travel.

In the same period of public time, Jane does (as rightmost) and does not (as leftmost) remember exiting the stage after the leftmost Rockette danced her number. So it seems that time-travel entails a flat-out contradiction. To avoid this, the defender of time-travel must relativize Jane's remembering somehow. One option would be to relativize to different places: Jane recalls this in the rightmost but not the leftmost spot, and it is no contradiction to recall-this-in-the-rightmost-spot at t but not recall-this-in-the-left-most-spot at t, even though it is one to recall this and not recall this at t. But this is unintuitive, it's hard to avoid the feeling that if Jane remembers in one spot then Jane remembers *simpliciter* (which re-instates the contradiction), and it isn't sufficiently general, as it would not handle time-travelers not located in space (angels, perhaps). Another option would be to relativize to different temporal parts of Jane – the rightmost part does recall and the leftmost does not – and reject the move from Jane's part's remembering then to Jane's remembering then or else parse "Jane remembers then" strictly in terms of her temporal parts. But that Jane has temporal parts so ordered implies that Jane has a personal timeline distinct from the public timeline.[49] So if relativizing to Jane's timeline will solve the problem by itself, it's a cheaper solution: it doesn't commit one to temporal parts. It's better, then, to relativize to Jane's time-line, i.e. to say that there's no contradiction involved in Jane's time-travel because Jane recalls and does not recall at different points in her life. But this dissolves the problem only if Jane's personal timeline takes precedence over the public time-line: that is, only if that Jane recalls P at a point in her life coinciding with public time t does not imply that Jane recalls P at t *simpliciter*. For of course, if this did follow, the original contradiction would be re-instated. Pastward time-travel is possible only if it does not involve the contradiction above. The best way to block the contradiction is to relativize Jane's recalling to her timeline. But this works only if facts about the order of segments of Jane's own life supersede facts about the public timeline – only if, as it were, Jane while time-travelling is really in her own time even though every instant of her life coincides with some instant of public time. This last is exactly what one would expect if there can be pastward time-travel, in which individual timelines break free of the public timeline.

If time-travel can occur, then that P at a point in one's life which coincides with public time t does not entail that P at t. Nor does P's being so at public t entail that P is so at every point in one's life which coincides with public t. Jane exits the stage from her leftmost position at public time t+1. So at public time t, she has not yet made the exit, and does not remember it. As Jane exits the stage after her first dancing, her timeline has not yet diverged from public time. So if her not recalling this exit at public t, before she made it, entailed that she did not recall it at every point in her life which coincided with t, then she would both recall it and not recall it as rightmost. If time-travel can occur, then, that Jane does not at public time t recall her exit does not entail that Jane does not recall this at every point in her life which coincides with t. Not all facts about the public timeline impose themselves on the time-traveler's timeline.

There are stages of our lives at which Jane is presently both the leftmost and the rightmost Rockette. During any such stage, (la)-(4a) is sound. But Jane's life has no such stage. For again, as we watch the Rockettes, we see all at once events that for Jane are successive, i.e. not all co-present. On her timeline, when she is presently the rightmost Rockette, being the leftmost Rockette is in her past.[50] Now if time-travel can occur, facts about time-travelers' personal timelines supersede facts about public time. That (1a)-(3a) are all true at once in public time does not entail that they are all true at once during Jane's life, even though all segments of Jane's life coincide with public times. So if time-travel can occur, the fact that (la)-(4a) is sound in public time does not matter. Along Jane's timeline it is wrong to treat (1a)-(4a) as a proof, even though we would be right to do so. Even if the argument were able (as it were) to shorten the chorus line, it would do so only if it were sound along Jane's timeline.

It would strengthen my overall case if I could show that what must be so if time-travel is possible is so – i.e. that for quite general reasons, personal timelines supersede public time. For the nonce I can only suggest something weaker. There is not (say I) some single substantival entity, Time, which passes at Newton's "uniform and equable rate." What we call time's passage is just a function of what events occur, and how they occur. Events compose all timelines, public and personal. So at the very least, there is no *a priori* reason that we should treat public time as having priority over personal, and able (as it were) to impose itself upon it. For both are wholes composed equally of the same basic parts. They simply arrange those parts differently, if they differ. Now in some cases, parts compose wholes only by composing larger parts of those wholes: players compose baseball leagues only by composing those leagues' teams, atoms compose walls only by composing bricks which compose walls. It is at least arguable that public time is really just the fusion of personal times – that events compose public time only by composing personal times which compose public time. If this is not just arguable but true, of course, then traits of personal times take precedence.

Soundness and Trinitarian timelines

In any case, the Trinitarian parallel to my treatment of Jane is clear. On my account, God's life runs in three streams. In one stream, (1) is so. In another, (2) is so. In no stream are both so. So in no stream of God's life are (1)-(4) or the generation-argument sound. For this fact to matter, past-ward time-travel need not be possible – though if it is, that of course is helpful. It need only be the case that as in my treatment of the time-travel case, facts about God's personal timeline(s) supersede facts about the public timeline. I now argue that if God is atemporal, they do, while if God is temporal, it is at least coherent to maintain that they do.

If God is atemporal, as the classic Latin Trinitarians held, His life is wholly independent of time, and so the public timeline does not constrain it. Facts about the order of events in His life supersede facts about the public timeline in almost the sense facts about Jane's timeline do. If time-travel can occur, "P at a point in one's life which coincides with public time t" does not entail "P at t," nor *vice-versa*. It's hard even to come up with a sense in which a timeless God's life would coincide with times.[51] But just suppose that if God is timeless, then there is *some* sense in which (1) is so at a point in God's life coinciding with all times – after all, at every time, if one asserts (1), what one asserts is true. Even so, it does not follow from this that (1) is so *at* any t. For if God is timeless, no event in His life occurs at any time. But if (1) were the case at t, this would be because an event helping make it so occurred at t: what is true then is true then because part of what makes it so occurs then.[52] So if God is timeless, it's not true in his case that for all P, if P at a point in His life coinciding with t, then P at t. If God is timeless, then even if P is true of Him and it is now t, it is not the case that P *at* t. Instead, P is so without temporal location.

The reverse entailment, from "P at t" to "P at some point in God's life coinciding with t," seems to fail as well if God is timeless. For at t, all and only those events before t are such that their happening is in the past. But at no point in God's life is this so. If for God anything is in the past – over, done and gone – God has a past, and so is temporal. Even if we waive this and allow that somehow, things can have happened for a time-less God, still if only *some* of time has happened for Him, then for Him, time has reached only that point – and so the rest of it lies in His future, and so He has a future and is again temporal. Moreover, if God's life does not occur in time, no facts about public time are relevant to "when" in His life claims are true. Events occur at different points in public time, but on any account of divine timelessness, they are given "all at once" for God- that is, at the same point(s) in His life. So events' order for God differs from their order in public time – though of course God knows what their order in public time *is*.

One might think that the public timeline imposes itself on God's this way: if God is atemporal, at every moment of time t, it is timelessly so that (1) and (2). So (1) and (2) are the case at t timelessly, and so the case at one time timelessly. However, timeless facts obtain, but not *at* any time. So "at t, it's the case that timelessly P" does not entail "it's the case at t timelessly that P." Further, suppose that (1) and (2) are the case at one time timelessly (whatever this might mean). This would not make (1) and (2) true at the same point in God's life. A parallel case can show this. Suppose God were temporal, but His personal time were simply a series of periods wholly discrete from our time – none before, during or after any period in our time. Then God's time would be related to ours just as the life of a timeless God would be, and it would be true that

A. for each public time of ours t, at t, somewhere in God's own time, (1) and somewhere in God's own time, (2).

But (A) would not entail that (1) and (2) are true at once in God's own time. Times discrete on God's own timeline would not be collapsed into one because there is a second time to each period of which each has exactly the same temporal relation, namely none at all. If this isn't clear intuitively, consider a spatial parallel: suppose that there is a second space, consisting of points with no spatial relations at all to ours. Then (let's say)

B. for each place of ours p, it is the case at p that in the second space, both a dog and a cat are located somewhere.

But (B) does not entail that the dog and the cat occupy the same place. So if God is timeless, facts about the public timeline and about God's life's relations to it cannot supersede facts about when within God's life (1) and (2) are true. If (1) and (2) are true only in discrete parts of God's timeless life, facts about our time cannot make them true "at once."

Now if God is timeless, it is just timelessly the case that God's life has three "streams." That is, it consists of three aggregates of events each with the right internal relations to count as a single life and the right generation relations to set it off from events in the other sets.[53] If there is no temporal relation between these streams, and facts about our time cannot make them true at one time, then it is not the case that (1) and (2) are true at one time-period. But this is not enough to show that (1)-(4) and the generation argument are never sound for God. For suppose that there were neither time nor God – that there was only a three-dimensional space. If there is no time, no claims are true at one time. But surely the argument "this is a space; any space has dimensions; so this space has dimensions" would be sound. Again, plausibly mathematical truths are timeless. If so, none are true at one time. But even so, surely some mathematical arguments are sound. So the truth about soundness must be that an argument is sound only if none of its premises' being true is separate temporally or in some other relevant way from the rest's. In the case of mathematical truths, there is no relevant separation. In God's case, there is (1) and (2) are true only in non-overlapping parts of God's life which are relevantly like temporal maximal episodes. This makes (1)'s and (2)'s being true relevantly separate, as does the parallel gap in Jane's life between (1a)'s and (2a)'s being true. The separation in Jane's case is discreteness along a private timeline. If God is timeless, the discreteness of episodes in His life is not along a timeline. But (I now suggest) it is enough like discreteness along a timeline in its *causal* aspects for Jane's case to be relevant to God's.

In Jane's case, the separation of what occurs all at once in public time into different segments of one life is there due to causal relations among the segments. These events' causal relations make them parts of one and the same life. They also account for the events' discreteness, for they include relations events cannot bear to their own parts. Events are discrete if they have no parts in common. If event A causes all parts of event B, it follows that B and A share no parts, as no event causes the occurrence of its own proper parts, and so that A and B are discrete. By causing B, A accounts for B's existence and its having the parts it does. B's having just the parts it does establishes B's discreteness from A. So by causing B, A accounts for B's discreteness from A. Finally, these events' causal relations make them temporally ordered non-simultaneous parts of Jane's life (even though they are simultaneous parts of public time) if they include causation of a sort involving temporal precedence.

Now if a life is temporal, then if two of its segments are discrete, it follows that either one immediately succeeds the other or there is a temporal gap between them. Because of this, propositions can be true in one segment but not the other. So if a life is temporal and two of its segments are discrete, then due to this they stand in a relation which lets propositions be true in one but not the other. I now generalize from this, and say that if segments are discrete yet in one life, then due to this they stand in a relation which lets propositions be true in one but not the other, whether or not the life is temporal. I do so based on my brief rejection above of substantival time. For non-substantivalists about times, times just are sets or fusions of co-occurring events. If so, then if truths can differ at different times, they can equally differ at different sets or fusions of co-occurring events: to relativize truths to times is to relativize them to events. If relativizing to events is fine for temporal events, why would things differ for atemporal?

If this is true, then if causal relations account for the segments' discreteness and their being in one life, they also account for the fact that propositions can be true during one of these segments which are not true during the other. Nor does time play the essential role here. By starting something new of a temporal sort, A's causal powers make time pass. It's not that A places B at a later point in time and so lets B make true truths A did not. It's rather that A brings B about, and so makes things true which were not true before, and so makes B's time a later one. Facts about time are not basic but derivative. It's causation which makes the temporal facts about A and B what they are. The real story about the relations between segments of Jane's life, the one which lets them have different properties while we watch them all at once, is causal, not temporal.

In Jane's case, all the segments occurred in one public-temporal period, but causal relations between them made them discrete segments of one life, with truths unique to each. In a timeless God's case, all the segments occur at once in the eternal present, but causal relations between them make them discrete segments of one life. Here too, then, there are truths unique to each. There is no temporal separation along a private timeline in this case. But I've suggested that it is causal, not temporal features that matter here, and in any case there is a more profound temporal disconnect, in that there are no temporal relations *at all* between the segments – only causal ones. Causation, not time, accounts for the distinctive features of Jane's case. I've claimed that the causal relations involved in Trinitarian generation are enough like those involved in time-travel that the key features of Jane's case carry over. If this is correct, arguments sound in public time need not come out sound along the "time" line of the Trinitarian lives.

The remaining question, then, is whether there is some analogue to a public timeline within timeless eternity, which might make (1) and (2) true at once for God. The short answer is: there is, but it can't, any more than the fact that the many Janes all dance at once in public time can make the segments of Jane's life we see in the chorus line simultaneous in Jane's private time (which would be to collapse them all to a single segment). Causal relations between the lives of the Persons make them both discrete as lives and yet lives of one God. This is the mystery of the Trinitarian generations; I have not claimed to crack it. That there is one eternal present is the public timeline of eternity. That the events occur at one present does not eliminate the discreteness of the events whose one present this is any more than it did in Jane's case. Again: it is causal relations between events in Jane's life which both make them discrete – as effect from cause- and unite them into one individual's life, even if all these events are linked by time-travel and occurring at one present. So too, causal relations make the Persons' lives both discrete and the lives of one God, even if linked by Trinitarian generation and occurring at one eternal present. Causal relations so bind Jane-events that (1a)-(4a) fails, even if all the Rockettes kick at once in public time. So too, I suggest, causal relations among the atemporal events of an atemporal God's life block (1)-(4) even if the Persons share a single eternal present. If all of eternity is a single present and God's life has discrete parts, what follows is simply that God's life is relevantly like a time-traveler's, with discrete parts occurring at once in such a way as to respect the discreteness of the parts. I submit, then, that if God is timeless, (1)-(4) and the generation argument are not sound on His "time"-line. (1) and (2) are never true at the same points in God's life even if they share a single eternal present.

Each Rockette is Jane. But in terms of Jane's personal timeline, in the way just set out, each is not Jane *while* the others are Jane. Let "while*" be a connective relativized to a particular timeline, and making no reference to general, public time. Then Jane is not the leftmost Rockette while* she is the rightmost, though her being both coincides with the whole of the public time her number involves. In the same way, each Person is God, but God is not the Father while* He is the Son.

What if God is temporal?

If God is temporal, facts about His timeline might equally well supersede facts about the public timeline. A temporalist could assert that they do without argument, making it simply part of his/her particular conception of God's eternality. But some temporalists, at least, could offer an argument that this is so. For some temporalists maintain that God has made time, or that it is as it is because He is as He is: that God's being has some sort of causal priority to time's existing or having its character.[54] If either is true, then surely God gives time such a nature as permits Him to exist as His nature dictates. If God determines time's nature, then even if He is temporal, if God's nature is such that His life should consist of three streams related relevantly like streams of a time-traveler's life, nothing in the nature of time will preclude this.

Sortals and soundness

No infant is a man. But Lincoln was infant and man: "that infant" and "that man" picked Lincoln out at different points in his life. Now consider this argument:

7. that infant = Lincoln,
8. that man = Lincoln,
9. Lincoln = Lincoln,

and so

10. that infant = that man.

Taking the descriptions as temporally rigid, the argument is sound, but of course does not prove that someone is both infant and man at once. Taking the descriptions non-rigidly, (7) ceases to be true when Lincoln ceases to be an infant, well before Lincoln is an adult. So the argument is never sound. One might think (10) true even so. But more precisely, what's true is that the person who was that infant = the person who is that man. Strictly speaking, reading the descriptions non-rigidly, (10) is false. For an identity statement is true only if the terms flanking "=" refer to the same item at once, and if we take them non-rigidly, "that infant" and "that man" never refer to the same item at once[55]: nothing is a man while* it is an infant. Let me now introduce a technical term, "phased sortal."[56] "Infant" and "man" are phased sortals: they pick out a substance under a description which essentially involves a particular phase of its life. Identity-statements linking temporally non-rigid descriptions involving mutually exclusive phased sortals cannot be true. So with the descriptions non-rigid, (7)-(10) is not only never sound but has a false conclusion.

In the Rockette case, "the leftmost Rockette" and "the rightmost Rockette" act as mutually exclusive phased sortals picking out Jane, if we're dealing only with Jane's own timeline. So too, on the account of the Trinity I've been suggesting, "Father" and "Son" are mutually exclusive phased sortals picking out God. (1) and (2) are never true at once*: God is not Father while* He is Son. And (4), like (10), cannot be true – though it is of course true that while* God is the Son, God is the God who is also the Father.

Trinitarian lives and validity

Once temporary identities enter the picture, identity-statements are implicitly relativized to times (or something time-like). If so, then if we let "t"s refer to times on Jane's timeline, with the descriptions read non-rigidly, we really have

1b. $(t_1 \not\!\!\!= t_2)$(Jane = the leftmost Rockette),
2b. $(t_3 (>t_2) \not\!\!\!= t_4)$(Jane = the rightmost Rockette), and
3b. (t)(Jane = Jane).

(1b)–(3b) are all true. But what I now argue suggests that the move from them to (4a) is invalid.

Here is an argument philosophers have discussed at length[57]:

11. Necessarily, 9 is greater than 7.
12. 9 = the number of the planets. So
13. Necessarily, the number of the planets is greater than 7.

The premises are true, yet the conclusion is false, since there could have been just 6 planets. So obviously, something goes wrong here.

(11) asserts of 9 that it has a property, being greater than 7, in all possible worlds. (12) is true, but not in all possible worlds. "9" and "the number of the planets" actually refer to the same number. But they need not have. Neptune and Pluto might never have formed, or might have formed but never been caught by the Sun's gravity. So it could have been the case

that there were just seven planets. If it had, "9" and "the number of the planets" would not have had the same referent. So it is possible that "9" and "the number of the planets" do not refer to the same number. (13) asserts in effect that "the number of the planets" picks out a number larger than 7 in every possible world. But as we have seen, this is not true. So this inference from necessarily Fx and x=y to necessarily Fy is invalid. One moral one might draw from this is that in a modal context (i.e. within the scope of "necessarily"), the fact that two terms "a" and "b" actually refer to the same thing (i.e. that an identity-statement like (12) is true) does not suffice to warrant substituting "b" for "a." What is required instead to have a valid inference (one which cannot take us from true premises to a false conclusion) is that "a" and "b" refer to the same thing in every possible world. For consider by contrast

11. Necessarily, 9 is greater than 7.
12a. $9 = 3^2$. So
13a. Necessarily, 3^2 is greater than 7.

"9" and "3^2" refer to the same thing in every possible world. And thus both premises and conclusion are true.

Times are like possible worlds – both are items at which propositions can be true- and temporal contexts can be like modal contexts. Consider this argument:

11b. 9 is always greater than 7.
12. 9 = the number of the planets. So
13b. The number of the planets is always greater than 7.

Here we go astray as in (11)-(13). For not all the planets formed simultaneously, our sun existed before it had any planets, and the universe existed even before our sun did: (13b) is false. To see why we went astray, let us parse the argument a bit more perspicuously, as involving a temporal operator which quantifies over times as "□" does over possible worlds:

11c. At all times (9 is greater than 7).
12. 9 = the number of the planets. So
13c. At all times (the number of the planets is greater than 7).

The problem is that while (12) is true, it is not true at all times. As the problem parallels that above, one can draw a parallel moral. In a universal-temporal context, even if "a" and "b" now refer to the same thing, it is valid to substitute "a" for "b" only if "a" and "b" always (i.e. at all times) refer to the same thing. This explains the invalidity of the move from (1b)-(3b) to (4a).

I now suggest that the identities in (1) and (2) do not license the universal inter-substitution of terms denoting the one God – that is, that the move from (1), (2) and (5) to (6) is invalid. To move from Jane's case to the Trinity, we need just note that on non-substantival theories of time, times just *are* sets or mereological fusions of events.[58] So if it makes sense to index propositions to times (i.e. treat times as items at which propositions can be true), it can also make sense to index propositions to sets or fusions of events. This (I now submit) is what we must do on the present account of the Trinity. On this account, whether or not God is temporal, there are items *like* times in God's life – sets or fusions of events in God's life at which propositions are true. These are the sets or fusions of just the events of each Person's life.

The generation argument, again, moves from

1. the Father = God
2. the Son = God, and
5. the Father generates the Son,

to

6. God generates God

(5) is true at all Trinitarian lives: it is the Trinitarian equivalent of a necessary or omnitemporal truth. But (1) and (2) are like (12). As (12) is true only at some possible worlds and times, (1) and (2) are each true only at some Trinitarian lives. So though (1) and (2) are true, they do not make it valid to substitute "God" for "the Father" and "the Son" in (5), for reasons akin to those operative in the modal and temporal arguments above. The basic point of the Rockette analogy is that one should approach the Trinity by asking in what ways God's life is free from ordinary temporal relations. I suggest that it is free enough from ordinary temporal ordering that we can say that God lives His life in three streams at once, index Trinitarian truths to appropriate sets of events, then use this indexing to block the move to (6). Of course, one can also block the move to (4) this way.

The menace of Modalism

Accounts of the Trinity must skirt the Scylla of tri-theism and the Charybdis of modalism. Tri-theists so emphasize the separateness of the Persons as to wind up affirming three separate Gods, not three Persons in one God. Modalists so emphasize the unity of God as to wind up affirming one God who has three modes of appearing or of dealing with us, not one God in three Persons. Or so we think. It is no easy thing to say just what Modalism *was,* or exactly why it was rejected, as the Church Fathers who fought it seem to have suppressed all copies of the works they deemed heretical. Still, scholars have pieced together some sense of it from quotes, allusions and (perhaps biased) descriptions which survive in non-Modalist works, and at least on the depictions of Modalism one finds in standard theological dictionaries, my account seems comfortably far from it.[59] Such works describe Modalism as holding that all distinctions between Persons are impermanent and transitory[60], or "are a mere succession of modes or operations,"[61] that

> the one God becomes Trinitarian only in respect of the modes of His operation *ad extra*[62],

that

> God is three only with respect to the modes of His action in the world[63],

that

> the one God . . . has three manners (modes) of appearance, rather than being one God in three Persons.[64]

and that for Modalism,

> the three Persons are assigned the status of modes or manifestations of the one divine being: the one God is substantial, the three differentiations adjectival . . . the Modalist God metamorphosed Himself to meet the changing needs of the world[65],

and so there is

> a Trinity of manifestation, not even a Trinity of economy, still less a Trinity of being.[66]

Nothing in my account of the Trinity precludes saying that the Persons' distinction is an eternal, necessary, non-successive and intrinsic feature of God's life, one which would be there even if there were no creatures, If one asserts all this, one asserts a "Trinity of being," with no reference to actions *ad extra* or appearances to creatures. Further items on an anti-Modalist checklist: does the view set out here entail that the Father is crucified? No, though the God who is the Father is crucified — at the point in His life at which He is not the Father, but the Son. Can the view deal adequately with the anti-Modalist texts cited above? On the present view, the Son cannot token truly "I am the Father," though He can token truly "I am the God who is (at another point in His life) the Father." Nor can the Son say truly that

14. I am at one point in my life the Father and at another the Son,

since at no point in the Son's life is He the Father. The Son can say truly that

15. I am the God who is at one point in His life the Father and at another the Son,

i.e. that He is God, and God is both Father and Son. But this is so on any Latin view of the Trinity. A natural question here is, "if the Son just *is* God, can't the Son use 'I' to refer to God, not to the Son, and if He does, can't He assert (14) truly?" But if the Son so uses "I," what He asserts is in effect (15), not (14). On any Latin approach, for a tri-personal God, "I" cannot be purely referential, a term whose contribution to the content of a sentence is simply an individual to whom God refers. For if there is just one individual, God, in the three Persons, then a purely referential "I" would always contribute simply God to a sentence's content. No Person could speak as "I" and refer to Himself as a Person; the Son could not say with truth, "I am not the Father," for His "I" would refer to God, and God *is* the Father. So on any Latin approach, if Persons can speak as themselves, and the Son can know that He is not the Father, God's "I" always includes a mode of presentation, a sense under which the speaker conceives and refers to Himself. When the Son speaks as the Son, He presents Himself to Himself as the Son, and so the Father is never other than another "I," who as such has His own mind and will. This is enough to make adequate sense of the texts, given the way my view guarantees the real distinctness of Father and Son.[67] And this is why if the Son uses 'I' to refer to God, what He asserts comes out as (15): the "I"'s mode of presentation builds "the God" etc. into the content of His claim.

The question is sure to come, though: aren't your Persons still "modes," if not modes of appearance, "adjectival" rather than "substantial"? One reply is that on the present account, each Person is as substantial as the one God is, since each Person is God in a different "part" of His life. If an infant isn't a mode of a substance, neither is a Son. Again, arguably a person could be a substance despite having identity-conditions that depend on events: Locke, for instance, rested the identity-conditions for persons on certain relations among mental events, and while he has of late been charged with many things, turning persons into events, accidents or modes has not been among them. Most latter-day Lockeans see persons as substances which are also material objects, or at least supervenient on them.

God's life is not constrained by time. If it is at least as free from time's bonds as a pastward time-traveler's would be, this provides a way to make sense of the doctrine of the Trinity – orthodox sense, or so I've argued. Note that in this last statement, pastward time-travel serves only as a model for the Trinity. While I have used pastward time-travel as a model, my view is not hostage to whether such travel is possible. My account is metaphysically possible if pastward time travel is, and I have in fact suggested that time travel is possible. If time travel is not, my account is still at least as conceivable as time travel is, and the impossibility of time travel may not count against my account's possibility, even as the impossibility of intuitionist logic does not count against the possibility of an indeterminate future. There is more to say here – in particular, about *why* God is a Trinity, and what sort of persons Persons are. But this will have to do for now.[68, 69]

Notes

1. *The Book of Common Prayer* (N.Y.: Seabury Press, 1979), 864–5.
2. Others start from the threeness of the Persons, and try to say just how three Persons can be one God. I discuss these in "Anti Social Trinitarianism," in Steven Davis and Daniel Kendall, eds., *The Trinity* (New York: Oxford University Press, 1999), 203–48.
3. LT's partisans up to Scotus all accept a strong doctrine of divine simplicity. So while they acknowledge that Father and Son stand in the generative relations of paternity and filiation, they deny that these relations are *constituents* of the Persons. Aquinas, for instance, asserts that the Father is identical with the relation of paternity just as God is with the divine nature, deity (*ST* Ia 29, 4). While divine simplicity no longer commands the wide assent it did, we would still not incline to see relations as constituents of particulars standing in them – save on "bundle" theories of substance, which few now favor.
4. *Common Prayer,* 865. So also Barth: "in . . . the inner movement of the begetting of the Father, the being begotten of the Son and the procession of the Spirit from both . . . God is once and again and a third time" (Karl Barth, *Church Dogmatics* II: 1, tr. G. Bromiley and T. F. Torrance (Edinburgh: T & T Clark, 1957), 615. At the back of this is of course *John* 1:1, "the Word was with God, and the Word was God." If the Word is God and is with God, God is with God – and so (it seems) we have God twice over.

5. Quoted in Cornelius Plantinga, "Social Trinity and Tritheism," in Cornelius Plantinga and Ronald Feenstra, eds., *Trinity, Incarnation and Atonement* (Notre Dame, In.: University of Notre Dame Press, 1989), 21. [The previous chapter in this volume.]

6. S. Thomae de Aquino *Summa Theologiae* Ia (Ottawa: Studii Generalis, 1941) 39, 5 *ad* 2, 245a. My translation. See also Edmund Hill, *The Mystery of the Trinity* (London: Geoffrey Chapman, 1985), 103.

7. For Thomas, talk of tropes is not strictly appropriate here, since in fact God is identical with the divine nature (so e.g. Aquinas, *ST* Ia 3, 3). For the nonce this need not concern us.

8. Plantinga, "Social Trinity," 40.

9. A common constituent of three things which never existed save as included in one of them might to philosophers seem a fourth thing in addition to any of the three though included in all. But the language of the New Testament sits ill with this. References to "the God and Father of our Lord Jesus Christ" and "God the Father," or to God simply as Father, are too numerous to list. These would not be appropriate if God were something like a part of the Father. Again, according to *John* 1:1, the Word *was* God. This does not suggest that God was part of the Word.

10. Henceforth I will not discuss the Spirit where the points to be made exactly parallel those made about the Son.

11. So e.g. *John.* 1:1 and 20:28; *Romans.* 9:5; *I Corinthians* 16:22; *I John* 5:20.

12. So e.g. *Isaiah* 44:24 "I am the Lord, who has made all things," *Romans* 11:36: "from Him and through Him . . . are all things," and the Nicene Creed's statement that orthodox Christians believe in "one God . . . creator of heaven and earth, and of all things visible and invisible" (*Common Prayer*, 358) (putative uncreated items presumably are visible or invisible).

13. There is one other alternative, that the Son be divine, uncreated, and distinct but not discrete from God. If the Son is not discrete from God, the Son overlaps God. If he overlaps God but is distinct from God, either (a) God has a constituent the Son lacks, but every constituent of the Son is a constituent of God, or (b) the Son has a constituent God lacks, but every constituent of God is a constituent of the Son, or (c) God and the Son share a constituent but each also has a constituent the other lacks, or (d) they overlap despite sharing no constituents. Or (a) the Son is part of God: God is a whole composed of persons. As parts are basic and wholes derived on (a) the three are basic, the one derived: (a) is not a version of LT. (b) was rejected in n. 9. (c) is a form of polytheism. (d) would assert a primitive constitution relation between God and the Son. I am skeptical that there is such a relation.

14. So e.g. Mark Heller, *The Ontology of Physical Objects* (N.Y.: Cambridge University Press, 1990).

15. Even if Jane later in her life knows what Jane earlier in her life is going to say to her, this need not unfit the analogy for Trinitarian purposes. It is hard to see how one Person could surprise another.

16. See e.g. Edwin Taylor and John Wheeler, *Spacetime Physics* (San Francisco: W.H. Freeman and Co., 1963), 89, and J. Hafele and Richard Keating,

"Around-the-world Atomic Clocks: Predicted Relativistic Time Gains and Observed Relativistic Time Gains," *Science* 177 (1972), 166–70.

17. So John Earman, "Recent Work on Time Travel," in Steven Savitt, ed., *Time's Arrows Today* (N.Y.: Cambridge University Press, 1995), 268–310.

18. So e.g. Richard Swinburne, *Space and Time* (N.Y.: The MacMillan Co., 1968), 169.

19. Earman, "Recent Work," 281.

20. This doesn't take away Jane's agency or freedom. For both can figure in every *local* explanation along the loop. That divine conservation is compatible with creaturely agency and freedom is non-negotiable for Western theists. Arguably conservation differs from creation only in that we call the same divine action creation when what God causes begins to exist and conservation when it continues to exist (so e.g. Scotus, *Quodlibet* 12). If this is true, the compatibility of creation and libertarian freedom/agency is equally non-negotiable, and I could as easily have spoken of God as creating the loop.

21. Keith Ward speculates that a temporal God may be free from the usual temporal ordering (*Rational Theology and the Creativity of God* (N.Y.: The Pilgrim Press, 1982), 164-70); Philip Quinn advances the same notion in some detail in unpublished comments given at the 1993 APA Central Division meeting. Swinburne (*Christian God,* 137–44) and Alan Padgett (*God, Eternity and the Nature of Time* (London: The MacMillan Press, Ltd., 1992)) suggest His freedom from other aspects of time.

22. In saying this I use an ordinary, intuitive concept of an event. On some theories of events (e.g. Kim's), such things as God's being divine and God's being omniscient count as events. (For Kim's theory, see Jaegwon Kim, "Events as Property-Exemplifications," in Douglas Walton and Myles Brand, eds., *Action Theory* (Dordrecht: D. Reidel, 1980), 159–77.) If you hold such a view, modify this claim to: the strands have in common only those events involved in God's bare existence and having His nature, not any events composing His conscious life or involving His agency. Any other modifications to accommodate theories of events would not (I think) affect the basics of the view I am setting forth.

23. For now I do not take up just what makes this so.

24. If we are reincarnated, we have lives which consist of other items which count as complete lives. So the Trinitarian claim is at least as coherent as belief in this sort of reincarnation.

25. If so, Jane's life fails to be continuous. It is not even dense, as there is no time, public or Jane-private, between Jane's life at public time's last instant and her life's next instant. On the other hand, there is no temporal *gap* between Jane at the last instant and Jane's next either. If Jane's life always has three segments ongoing, then it consists of three discrete segments with zero duration between them. In that sense, the segments' endpoints are closer together than any two points in a continuous stretch of time. No qualms about Jane's identity between time's last instant and her next ought to arise, then. If we found that time was universally discrete in the small, consisting of chronons (as some have argued), we would not conclude that

no-one is identical over any long duration. We would adjust our account of identity over time to allow for this, speaking of not-quite-continuous duration where we used to speak of continuous. We can do the like for Jane.

26. In principle then, as a referee pointed out, Jane could live an infinite life by looping back endlessly through a finite period of public time. (She'd need infinite space to do this, as otherwise she would eventually run out of room – the whole universe would be filled nothing but time-travelling Janes. But there's no reason to think infinite space impossible.) But this does not entail that public time is infinite. Its properties arise out of the properties of all personal/private times. Even given Jane's peculiar life, all personal times might have the following trait: either they end no later than a particular instant – say, the Big Crunch – or they continue through that instant to some instant which as of the Big Crunch has already been occupied.

27. An anonymous referee raised this.

28. David Lewis, "The Paradoxes of Time Travel," in David Lewis, *Philosophical Papers,* v. 2 (N.Y.: Oxford University Press, 1986).

29. *Op. cit.,* 73.

30. So e.g. Trenton Merricks, "There Are No Criteria of Identity," *Nous* 32 (1998), 106–24.

31. It's not enough to have Jane that the atoms making her up at t be those which made her up just prior to t. There is also a causal condition, that her atoms be moving in ways their prior motion directly accounts for. A Star Trek transporter beam story can make this clear. One can suppose the beam to work by disassembling us into our constituent atoms, accelerating these to a destination, then rebuilding someone looking just like us from them there. Most people, given this description, will think of the transporter as a way to get killed, not a way to be transported: we do not survive being smashed into our constituent atoms, even if something is rebuilt from them later which looks like us. Now let's modify the case: suppose the disassembly is literally instantaneous, and the transporter sends one's atoms to their destination so fast that there is no time between our standing here whole and something looking just like us standing there whole at destination. I suggest that even so, our intuition that we don't survive the process doesn't change. For what matters here is our belief that we don't survive being disassembled into atoms, not any fact about how fast the bits are reassembled. Disassembly and smashing are precisely situations in which there is massive interference with the movements our atoms would otherwise be making, and given the intervention of the beam, the positions, motion etc. of Jane's atoms prior to teleportation don't directly cause those of the duplicate's atoms at the destination point. So (I claim) the transporter story supports the text's claim that it defeats a claim of continued existence that the positions, motion etc. of the atoms constituting Jane's body don't directly cause those of the duplicate's atoms,

32. The causation here is "immanent," not "transeunt." See Dean Zimmerman, "Immanent Causation," *Philosophical Perspectives* 11 (1997), 433–71.

33. When Jane is the rightmost Rockette, she *used to be* the leftmost, even though she is rightmost and leftmost during the same period of public

time. So strictly, she could say both that she is and that she used to be the leftmost, depending on whether she tensed the verbs to the public or to her personal timeline. But as we see in greater detail below, if time-travel is possible, the personal timeline takes precedence. I suggest below that something similar holds in the Trinitarian case.

34. Even if the Father reads the Son's mind, He reads it "from without."

35. Aquinas, *ST* Ia 27, 1, 182a2–3.

36. Thomas' story about the Spirit's proceeding is the same in all respects that matter to my point. So I needn't go into it here.

37. As Thomas sees it, this act is by nature rather than choice (*ST* Ia 41, 2). But that it is not in all respects free does not entail that it is not something God does. Even coerced acts are acts.

38. Though as Eleonore Stump pointed out to me, Thomas likely does not have a single concept that does the work of our event-concept.

39. *Summa Contra Gentiles* IV, 11.

40. *Ibid.*

41. *ST* Ia 41, 1 *ad* 2.

42. Some would rejoin: for Thomas, the Word's existing, caused or not, is atemporal (*ST* Ia 10, 1 *et* 4). So it can't count as an event. Well, if that's right, a timeless God can't act, either. For a case that a timeless God can, see my *Time and Eternity* (Ithaca, N.Y.: Cornell University Press, 1991), 291–7. For a more general case in favor of non-temporal events, see my "The Eternal Present," in Gregory Ganssle and David Woodruff, eds., *God and Time* (N.Y.: Oxford University Press, 2001), 21–48. In any case, that Thomas believes that some acts are atemporal is irrelevant to the fact that his Trinity-account is act-based, and so event-based.

43. *Ibid.*

44. Actually, things get a bit more complex than this. Due to the impact of his doctrine of divine simplicity, there are really two accounts of the Trinity in Thomas. I've given one; in the other, it might be better to say that the Persons *are* events in God's inner life.

45. See e.g. *Compendium of Theology* I, 41. The explanation has a surprising feature: while we might think the doctrine of divine simplicity a hindrance to the doctrine of the Trinity (how can a simple God contain Triune complexity?), Aquinas argues that the reason God is a Trinity and we are not is precisely that God is simple and we are not.

46. Here is at least a gesture at a different explanation. Suppose that as Aquinas thought, there are just three discrete maximal episodes in God's life: three events such that everything God does, thinks or experiences is part of just one of these. Then if God is timeless, these events are somehow all *there,* timelessly. They do not cease to occur. Neither does one take another's place. Yet as they are discrete, they do not overlap: one does not occur *within* another. What there timelessly is to the reality of God, then, is God in one episode, and in the second, and in the third. God might differ from episode to episode, as Father differs from Son. As events are natural causal relata, it would not be surprising if (say) God in one episode had causal relations He did not have in others, e.g. becoming incarnate in just one episode.

Perhaps, in short, God's timelessness plus an assumption about God's life can generate a Latin Trinity-*given* the tenability of the notion of an atemporal event.

47. This is of course the pattern of generation-relations Western Christians posit between the Persons.

48. Thus it is a case of immanent, not transeunt causality.

49. But even here, one has to wonder. Is it really still true that Lincoln = Lincoln? "Lincoln = Lincoln" is after all a more precise rendering of "Lincoln is Lincoln." The latter is present-tensed. Perhaps if Lincoln no longer exists, nobody has any longer the property of identity with Lincoln.

50. If Jane had just one temporal part at public time t, she would be like the rest of us. Her personal timeline would not diverge from public time at t. If Jane has distinct temporal parts at public t, then one of them is in the other's past along Jane's timeline. But along the public timeline, whatever is at t when t is present is present. So if Jane has distinct temporal parts at public t, her timeline diverges from that of public time.

51. Another angle on the same fact: on Jane's timeline, there are times between the leftmost and the rightmost Rockettes' arrivals onstage. There are none in our timeline – for us, all Rockettes step onstage from backstage at once.

52. If P is present-tense and true, an improper part of its truthmaker is at t. If P is past-tensed and true, a proper part is: that Casesar crossed the Rubicon is true due to an event now over (the crossing) and one now going on, which makes it later now than the crossing and so makes it correct to use the past tense. The life is so if P is future-tense and true. If God is timeless, "God knows that 2 + 2 = 4" has no temporal tense at all. Its truthmaker thus lies entirely outside time.

53. Stump and Kretzmann's ET-simultaneity is one attempt (Eleonore Stump and Norman Kretzmann, "Eternity," *Journal of Philosophy* 78 (1981), 429–458).

54. Talk of atemporal events may cause pain here; see *ops. cit.* n. 37.

55. See e.g. William Craig, "Timelessness and Omnitemporality," and Alan Padgett, "God the Lord of Time," in Gregory Ganssle, ed., *God and Time* (Wheaton, Ill.: Intervarsity Press, 2001).

56. How about "remember that infant I pointed out to you years ago? That man over there, the President, is that infant"? This is loose speech for "that man *was* that infant," i.e. "the person who is that man was that infant."

57. See e.g. David Wiggins, *Sameness and Substance* (Cambridge, Mass.: Harvard University Press, 1980), 24ff.

58. Its *locus classicus* is W.V. Quine, *From a Logical Point of View* (N.Y.: Harper and Row, 1961), 147–8.

59. Such theories face a variety of philosophical problems. Many can be treated along lines laid out in Graeme Forbes, "Time, Events and Modality," in Robin Le Poidevin and Murray MacBeath, eds., *The Philosophy of Time* (N.Y.: Oxford University Press, 1993), 80–95, and Jan Cover, "Reference, Modality and Relational Time," *Philosophical Studies* 70 (1993), 251–277.

60. The more extended account one finds in J.N.D. Kelly, *Early Christian Doctrines* (N.Y.: HarperCollins, 1978), rev. ed., 119–126, merely validates the briefer dictionary descriptions quoted below.

61. F.L. Cross, ed., *The Oxford Dictionary of the Christian Church* (N.Y.: Oxford University Press, 1997), 1097.

62. *Ibid.*, 1102, in an account of Patripassionism, which overlapped Modalism.

63. Karl Rahner and Herbert Vorgrimler, *Dictionary of Theology* (N.Y.: Crossroad, 1981), 312.

64. J. Komonchak, M. Collins, D. Lane, eds., *The New Dictionary of Theology* (Wilmington, Delaware: Michael Glazier, Inc., 1987), 668.

65. Donald McKim, *Westminster Dictionary of Theological Terms* (Louisville, Ky.: Westminster John Knox Pres, 1996), 176.

66. H.E.W. Turner,. "Modalism," in Alan Richardson and John Bowden, eds., *The Westminster Dictionary of Christian Theology* (Philadelphia, Pa.: Westminster, 1983), 375.

67. *Ibid.*

68. In the *John* 17 text cited, the Son prays to the Father. This is like one Rockette's talking to another.

69. My thanks to Jeff Brower, Paul Reasoner, Eleonore Stump, Dale Tuggy, Dean Zimmerman and an anonymous referee for comments.

CHAPTER 7

THREE PERSONS IN ONE BEING: ON ATTEMPTS TO SHOW THAT THE DOCTRINE OF THE TRINITY IS SELF-CONTRADICTORY

Peter van Inwagen

Enemies of the Church have frequently contended that the doctrine of the Holy Trinity is not only false, but violates various elementary logical principles. In this essay, I show that, on one understanding of the doctrine, this charge is unfounded.

Enemies of the Church have frequently contended that two of its central doctrines are not only false but violate various elementary logical principles. These two doctrines are, of course, the doctrine of the Incarnation of the Word and the doctrine of the Holy Trinity. I shall investigate the contention that the doctrine of the Trinity is logically self-contradictory.

I shall proceed as follows. I shall try to imagine a way of stating the doctrine of the Trinity that has the following feature: when the doctrine is stated in this way, it can be *shown* not to be self–contradictory. I shall leave the following question to theologians (for I am a philosopher, not a theologian): Is what I describe as 'a way of stating the doctrine of the Trinity' properly so described – or should it be called a way of *mis*stating the doctrine of the Trinity? I claim only this: a strong case can be made for the thesis that the formulation of the doctrine of the Trinity I shall propose does succeed in being a statement of what has historically been called 'the doctrine of the Trinity'; and an even stronger case can be made for the thesis that this formulation is *consistent* with historical orthodoxy. Even if these theses are false, they are, in my view, plausible enough to be worthy of a considered refutation.

My project, therefore, belongs to Christian apologetic. It is a Christian philosopher's attempt to meet a certain kind of philosophical attack on Christian belief. Whether my attempt at apologetic in fact *distorts* Christian belief is a point on which I humbly (and sensibly) defer to trained theologians. In matters of speculative theology – and particularly when the question at issue is whether certain theological speculations are in accord with historical orthodoxy – theologians must sit in judgement over mere philosophers. (Just as, in my view, bishops and councils must sit in judgement over theologians.) I claim only one kind of authority that is denied to theologians: I am the ultimate arbiter of what my own words mean. If a theologian tells me that my proposed way of stating the doctrine of the Trinity is wrong (that is, that what I have proposed as a way of stating 'the doctrine of the Trinity' has implications inconsistent what the Church has always understood by 'the doctrine of the Trinity'), I allow myself only one defense: 'If I had said what you think I've said, you'd be right; but I didn't say what you think I said.'

Now a qualification. When I said I should propose a way of stating the doctrine of the Trinity, I spoke loosely. What I am going to propose a statement or formulation of is a *part* of the doctrine of the Trinity, the part that is alleged to violate certain principles of logic. In one sense, there can be no more important questions of Trinitarian theology than those raised by the *filioque*. These questions are important because they have consequences for the immensely important task of restoring Christian unity. But these questions would not interest those enemies of the Church who attack the doctrine of the Trinity on logical grounds. They attack aspects of the doctrine that are common to the Eastern and the Western understandings of the Trinity (if indeed there is still any difference between Eastern and Western understandings of the Trinity). Their attacks are not directed at theses concerning the relations the persons of the Trinity bear to one another, but are directed, so to speak, at the persons themselves. But it is time to turn from the abstract to the concrete and to see how the attacks I am going to consider have been formulated. I am going to concentrate on attacks made by present-day unbelievers, but these attacks do not differ in their essential content from those made by Socinians in the seventeenth century, and I should be surprised if similar objections to Trinitarianism had not been raised by Jewish and Muslim philosophers and theologians – although I cannot speak to this question of my own knowledge. The essential points made in these arguments, moreover, were known to the great Trinitarian theologians of the first millennium, and to the philosophers and theologians of the Latin Middle ages.

I will consider two arguments. Here is the first.

> The term 'God' applies without qualification to the Father, to the Son, and to the Holy Spirit. The Father is not the Son; the Son is not the Holy Spirit; the Holy Spirit is not the Father. Hence, there are at least three Gods.

We may compare this argument with the following argument:

> The term 'king' applies without qualification to Gaspar, to Melchior, and to Balthasar. Gaspar is not Melchior; Melchior

is not Balthasar; Balthasar is not Gaspar. Hence, there are at least three kings,

and we may note that the former argument and the latter appear to be logically identical, and that the second is certainly logically valid. But monotheism is essential to Christian belief, and indeed, to the doctrine of the Trinity; therefore, the doctrine of the Trinity is logically self-contradictory. For this argument to be valid, the word 'God' must be understood as what linguists call a count-noun, that is a noun that, like 'king,' has a plural form (and in languages that have an indefinite article, can follow the indefinite article). But this seems to be so: We say, "There is one God, the Father Almighty, maker of heaven and earth" and "Our God is a God of love" and "The doctrine of the Trinity does not imply that there are three Gods"; and each of these sentences is grammatically correct.

Here is the second argument:

> The Father is God. The Son is God. Hence, the Father is the Son.

We may compare this argument with the following argument:

> The capital of Russia is Moscow. The largest city in Russia is Moscow. Hence, the capital of Russia is the largest city in Russia,

and we may note that the former argument and the latter appear to be logically identical, and that the second is certainly logically valid. But it is essential to the doctrine of the Trinity that the Father is not the Son; therefore, the doctrine of the Trinity is logically self-contradictory. For this argument to be valid, the word 'God' must be understood as a proper name – like 'Moscow' or 'Zeus' or 'Socrates.' But this seems to be so: We say, 'O God make speed to save us' and 'The peace of God, which passeth all understanding, keep your hearts and minds in the knowledge and love of God'; and each of these sentences is grammatically correct.

We have noted that these two arguments presuppose two different grammatical functions for the word 'God.' But this does not imply that at most one of the two arguments is logically valid, for the word 'God' does function both as a count-noun and as a proper name. In every language I know of, a proper name can function, or one might say, be forced to function as a count-noun. (Here is an example used by the German philosopher Frege: Trieste is no Vienna.) But the use of God as a count-noun in the first argument is not a case of a proper name being *forced* to function as a count-noun. No force is required when we choose to employ 'God' as a count-noun. It is part of the meaning of 'God' that it has a dual grammatical function, that it is syntactically ambiguous as it were: it can function both as a count-noun and as a proper name. And if we suppose that 'God' functions as a count-noun at each of its occurrences in the first argument, the premises of that argument seem to be true. If, moreover, we suppose that 'God' functions as a proper name at each of its occurrences in the second argument, the premises of *that* argument seem to be true. (The fact that God has a proper name in the more usual sense – as we learn from Exodus 3:14 – does not affect the point that the word 'God' often *functions* as a proper name. I may mention in this connection that Professor Peter Geach has argued that 'God' is never a proper name, owing to the fact that, in translations from one language to another, the word is itself translated – the word that means 'God' in the original language is replaced with a word of the other language that means 'God' – and is not merely phonetically adapted. A contrastive example will make Geach's point clear. The English word 'God' is a true translation of the Russian word 'Bog,' to which it bears no phonetic resemblance and to which it is etymologically unrelated. By way of contrast: the English proper name 'Moscow' is not in anything like the same sense a translation of 'Moskva'; it is merely an adaptation of the name Russians have given to their largest city, a phonetic adaptation that was made because it is easier for someone whose tongue is accustomed to the vowel-and-consonant patterns of English to say 'Moscow' than to say 'Moskva.' Whether or not this argument of Geach's is cogent, its target is not the thesis that I have endorsed. I have not said that 'God' is a proper name as 'Yahweh' is a proper name, but only that in some contexts it functions logically like a proper name. More exactly: I have not *said* this; I have said only the second of the above arguments depends on the word's so functioning, and that examination of the way the word is used seems to endorse the thesis that it can so function.)

Now what shall we say of these two arguments? I have heard of (but cannot cite) theologians who are, in effect, willing to concede that our two arguments are logically valid and that their premises are true. They concede, therefore, that the doctrine of the Holy Trinity is internally inconsistent; and they go on to say that it is nevertheless to be believed. Having made these concessions, they proceed to deprecate 'merely human logic.' Their point (so I have been told) is not that the doctrine is not inconsistent but seems to be inconsistent owing to the deficiencies of merely human logic; it is rather that it is only because of the deficiencies of merely human logic that inconsistency (at least in theology) seems objectionable. This position has (to be gentle) little to recommend it. If one maintains that something is to be believed, one thereby commits oneself to the thesis that that thing is true, for to believe something and to believe that it is true are one and the same thing. And nothing that is true can be internally inconsistent. If a theological doctrine or political ideology or scientific theory comprises three statements, and if that doctrine or ideology or theory is true, then its three constituent statements must be individually true. We might put the matter this way: every 'part' of anything that is true must also be true, and anything that is true is consistent with anything else that is true – and an inconsistent doctrine or ideology or theory is one such that some of its parts are inconsistent with others of its parts. Those who are willing to believe what is logically inconsistent have failed to take account of the logically elementary fact that a truth cannot be inconsistent with a truth.

I have said that I could find no theologian who has actually said that inconsistencies were to be believed. Professor Geach claims to be able to identify (although he does not provide explicit citations of) certain medieval Latin thinkers who held a closely related thesis: that there are bodies of truth – just those that comprise the doctrines of the Trinity and the Incarnation – that somehow constitute exceptions to logically valid principles or reasoning. These medievals, Geach says, appended the following warning to their statements of certain rules of logical inference: *Haec regula habet instantiam in mysterio Sanctae Trinitatis.* (Here is a gloss: WARNING: Do not use this rule when the subject-matter of your reasoning is the mystery of the Holy Trinity; applied to that subject-matter, the rule can license the inference of false conclusions from true premises.)

To say this, or anything like this, is to misunderstand the concept of logic. Nothing is, or could be, above, beyond, or outside the province of logic. The idea does not make sense. And, certainly, it is blasphemous to say that any part of Christian theology is above, beyond, or outside the province of logic. Jesus Christ, in addition to being the Way and the Life, is the Truth. In him there is no darkness at all. In him there is no falsehood. The faith we have from him, and from the Holy Spirit whom he has sent to us, is therefore entirely true, true in every part. And nothing that is entirely true can be above, beyond, or outside the province of logic, for (as I have said) a truth cannot be inconsistent with a truth. If, *per impossibile,* there were some doctrine, some ideology, some theory, that was above, beyond, or outside the province of logic, it would not be entirely true; for what is entirely true is logically internally consistent, and what is logically internally consistent conforms to the rules of logic and cannot therefore be said to be above, beyond, or outside the province of logic.

To say this, however, is not to say that Christian doctrine (or, for that matter, a scientific theory like quantum mechanics; the suggestion has been made that quantum mechanics has just this feature) cannot be in violation of principles of reasoning that are generally *believed* to be logically correct. It is to say that Christians are committed to the thesis that if an essential Christian doctrine violates some principle of reasoning, then that principle is not logically correct, however many reputable professional logicians believe it to be logically correct. Logic – and this statement pertains to the *essence* of logic – makes a universal claim. It claims to apply to the whole of the Real – and nothing has a securer place in the Real than God, who alone can say, 'I should be real if nothing else was.' (The Austrian philosopher Alexius Meinong believed there to be – in a sense of 'to be' he was never able adequately to explain – things that lay outside the Real, and he believed that some of these violated the principles of logic. He thereby denied the universal claim of logic, whose scope he confined to the Real. He in fact denied that, 'I pertain to the whole of the Real' *is* a claim to universality. His philosophy, however, seems to me to be nonsense, and – *I* say – unless one is prepared to follow Meinong into nonsense, one must accept the claim of logic to be of absolutely universal applicability.)

I said I should propose a way of stating the doctrine of the Trinity that was demonstrably consistent. I am not the first to have proposed to do this. Certainly various heretics have. Very roughly speaking, their heresies fall under two headings: modalism and tritheism. Modalism is the heresy that the Father, the Son, and the Holy Spirit are three modes in which the one God is known by us or presents himself to us – three faces that God shows us, so to speak, as God's Ape does in the *Inferno*. Tritheism is, of course, the heresy that there are three Gods: that God the Father is one God, God the Son another God, and God the Holy Spirit a third God. I shall take it for granted that everyone present will agree that modalism is a heresy. It might be thought equally clear that tritheism was a heresy. ('Hear, O Israel, Yahweh our God is one Yahweh.') But there is a modern attempt at a demonstrably consistent statement of the doctrine of the Trinity – at least I should be willing to say that its consistency was demonstrable – according to which there are three Gods, and its author's defense of its historical orthodoxy is well thought out and not simply to be dismissed. (I have in mind Professor Swinburne's important essay on the Trinity, 'Could There Be More Than One God?') But whether Professor Swinburne's account of the Trinity is, or is consistent with, historical orthodoxy is a subtle question, and one that is not, in the end, to be answered by a philosopher. What I can do, as a philosopher, is to exhibit the consequences of his theory – subject, of course, to correction by Professor Swinburne, whose authority to contend that I have got him wrong and whose authority to contend that I have made a mistake in reasoning are both unassailable. I shrink from the risks implicit in criticizing the work of a philosopher who is not only alive but is present as I speak, and will say nothing in detail about his views. I have mentioned these views only to make the point that the question whether tritheism is a heresy is a subtle question – and to make the related point that the question 'What, exactly, *is* tritheism?' is likewise a subtle question. I am happy to make these points because, if any charge of heresy were to be lodged against my own speculations concerning the Trinity, it would certainly be that I have fallen into some form of tritheism. No one – I certainly hope this is so – could reasonably accuse me of having embraced modalism in any form.

My attempt to state the doctrine of the Trinity (and I do intend presently to get round to doing it) rests on the contention that certain rules of logical inference that are commonly supposed to be valid are not in fact valid, that these rules must be replaced by other rules, rules that *are* valid, and that the doctrine of the Trinity does not violate any valid rule of logical inference.

That part of logic whose rules the doctrine of the Trinity is in violation of (or is in violation of if the two arguments I set out earlier are valid) is the logic of *identity*. According to standard textbook logic, the logic we have from Frege and Russell, there is a relation called identity. This relation is defined by two properties. First, everything whatever bears this relation to itself. Secondly, this relation forces indiscernability. That is to say, if a thing x bears identity to a thing y, then whatever is true of x is true of y and whatever is true of y is true of x. From these two defining properties of identity (it is easily shown) two other important properties of identity immediately follow: identity is *symmetrical* (that is, if a thing x bears the relation of identity to a thing y, then y bears the relation of identity to x), and identity is transitive (that is, if x bears identity to y and y bears identity to z, then x bears identity to z). These properties of identity entail the validity of four principles of reasoning or logical rules. In stating these rules, I will use the words 'is identical with' instead of 'bears the relation of identity to.'

The rule of *Reflexivity* tells us that if we are engaged in a piece of reasoning, and if a name like 'Ivan the Terrible' occurs in this reasoning, and if this name (unlike, say, 'Zeus') actually designates something, we may introduce the sentence formed by surrounding the phrase 'is identical with' with two occurrences of that name into our reasoning. For example, if the name 'Ivan' occurs in our reasoning, and if 'Ivan' designates something, we may introduce into our reasoning the sentence 'Ivan is identical with Ivan.' This rule, moreover, applies not only to names but also to any phrase that purports to designate a single thing; 'the first czar' for example: Reflexivity licenses us to include in any piece of reasoning the sentence 'the first czar is identical with the first czar.'

In stating the rule 'Reflexivity,' I had to strain to state it generally (and a logician will tell you that I did not really succeed, since I said nothing about what logicians call 'variables,' a point I will concede). In the sequel, I will not even attempt to give general statement of the rules whose validity follows from the properties of identity; I shall instead proceed by example and illustration.

The rule called *Leibniz's Law* or *The Indiscernibility of Identicals* (note that I did not say 'The Identity of Indiscernibles'!) allows us to introduce the following sentence into our reasoning:

> If Moscow is identical with the city in which the Kremlin stands, then Moscow is populous if and only if the city in which the Kremlin stands is populous.

In this example the first or 'if part of the statement is true, and the predicate 'is populous' in fact applies to the one thing that is both Moscow and the city in which the Kremlin stands. But I must point out that logic is in a certain sense blind to truth, and that Leibniz's Law would allow us to introduce the following sentence into our reasoning:

> If Helsinki is identical with the capital of Japan, then Helsinki is a moon of Jupiter if and only if the capital of Japan is a moon of Jupiter.

No doubt no sane person would *want* to introduce this sentence into any piece of reasoning; but a madman who did so would be reasoning logically – something madmen are often very good at. (And, anyway, when you think about it, isn't it *true* that *if* Helsinki is identical with the capital of Japan, then Helsinki is a moon of Jupiter if and only if the capital of Japan is a moon of Jupiter?)

The rule called *Symmetry* (its validity can be proved, given the validity of Reflexivity and Leibniz's Law) licenses inferences like these:

> Cicero is identical with Tully; *hence*, Tully is identical with Cicero
> Peter the Great is identical with Catherine the Great; *hence*, Catherine the Great is identical with Peter the Great.

The rule called *Transitivity* (its validity can be proved, given the validity of Reflexivity and Leibniz's Law) licenses inferences like these:

> Byzantium is identical with Constantinople; Constantinople is identical with Istanbul; *hence*, Byzantium is identical with Istanbul

> Turgenev is identical with Dostoevski; Dostoevski is identical
> with the author of *Anna Karenina; hence,* Turgenev is identical
> with the author of *Anna Karenina.*

Infinitely many other rules of inference involving the phrase 'is identical with' can be proved valid given the defining properties of identity.
Some of them are even interesting and important; Euclid's Law, or the
Substitution of Identicals, for example, which allows us to infer 'Tolstoy
was excommunicated' from the two premises 'The author of *Anna
Karenina* was excommunicated' and 'Tolstoy is identical with the author
of *Anna Karenina,*' but one must make an end somewhere, and perhaps
at least the most general features of the logic of identity are now reasonably clear. And this logic of identity is all but universally regarded as an
established part of logic. 'How, ask the proponents of the validity of these
rules, could they fail? Consider Transitivity. Suppose that the sentence
"Byzantium is identical with Constantinople" is true; if this sentence is
true, that must be because there is a single thing, a certain city, that bears
the two names "Byzantium" and "Constantinople."' And if 'Constantinople is identical with Istanbul' is true, that can only be because there is a
single thing, a certain city that bears the two names 'Constantinople'
and 'Istanbul.' It obviously follows that this 'certain city' bears the two
names 'Byzantium' and 'Istanbul' (we have said so), and that, therefore,
'Byzantium is identical with Istanbul' is true.

Now consider the first of the two anti-Trinitarian arguments I set out
a moment ago. This argument depends on the idea of number; the idea
expressed by the question 'How many?' Number is explained in terms of
identity. The proposition that there is exactly one phoenix can be
expressed this way:

> Something x is a phoenix and any phoenix is identical with x.

(For this sentence would be false if there were no phoenixes, and it
would be false if there were two or more phoenixes: it is true in just
exactly the remaining case, the case in which the number of phoenixes
is one.) The proposition that Mars has exactly two moons can be
expressed this way:

> Something x is a Martian moon and something y is a Martian
> moon and x is not identical with y and any Martian moon is
> identical with either x or y.

If we delete the last clause from this sentence (thus):

Something x is a Martian moon and something y is a Martian moon and x is not identical with y,

the result is a way of expressing the proposition that there are *at least* two Martian moons. (The truncated sentence is false if Mars has no moons or has only one; it is true otherwise.) Now consider the sentence

Something x is a God and something y is a God and something z is a God and x is not identical with y and x is not identical with z and y is not identical with z.

This sentence says that there are at least three Gods. Now suppose someone says these things:

The Father is a God
The Son is a God
The Holy Spirit is a God
The Father is not identical with the Son
The Father is not identical with the Holy Spirit
The Son is not identical with the Holy Spirit.

If these six things are true, then it would seem that we have our 'x,' our 'y,' and our 'z,' and it would seem, therefore to follow that there are at least three Gods. And are these six things true? Well, I concede that it might be hard to get a Christian to give his unqualified assent to any of them. Christians who speak a language that uses the indefinite article are likely, to say the least, to feel uncomfortable saying 'The Father is a God.' But consider: they will want to say the following two things: 'The Father is God' and 'God is a God'; does that not commit them to the truth of 'The Father is a God,' however reluctant they may be actually to utter these words? As to the final three sentences, perhaps these two will make the Christian uncomfortable. But they will certainly want to say these two things:

The following is true of the Son: that he is begotten of the Father

The following is not true of the Father: that he is begotten of the Father.

And it follows from these two sentences by Leibniz's Law that the Father is not identical with the Son: for if the Father were identical with the Son, then everything that was true of the Father would also be true of the Son. It would seem, therefore, to follow by the logic of identity from things all Christians assent to that there are at least three Gods. And, since it is an essential element in the doctrine of the Trinity that there is one God, and one only, a logical contradiction can be deduced by the logic of identity from the doctrine of the Trinity. What I have just done, of course, is to present our first argument in a form which makes its reliance on the standard logic of identity explicit. This was a rather complex undertaking. To present our second anti-Trinitarian argument in this form, however, is simplicity itself:

> The Father is identical with God
> The Son is identical with God
> *Hence,* by Symmetry, God is identical with the Son
> *Hence,* by Transitivity, the Father is identical with the Son.

And this conclusion certainly contradicts the doctrine of the Trinity. For one thing, as we have seen, it would imply – given that the Father begets the Son and given the standard logic of identity – that the Son begets the Father. For another, it would imply that there was a single thing for which 'the Father' and 'the Son' were alternative names – as there is a single thing for which 'Constantinople' and 'Istanbul' are alternative names – and this is modalism. Might the Christian respond by simply denying the premises, by simply denying that the Father is identical with God and that the Son is identical with God? (The Christian might appeal to Leibniz's Law to establish this: God comprises all three persons of the Holy Trinity; the Father does not comprise all three persons of the Holy Trinity; hence, the Father is not identical with God.) But this response leads to 'counting' problems, like those on which our first argument turns. The Father is, as we have seen, a God. And God is certainly a God. Therefore, if the Father is not identical with God, there is something x that is a God and there is something y that is a God and x is not identical with y. That is to say: there are at least two Gods.

It has long seemed to me that the problems our two anti-Trinitarian arguments raise are insoluble, if the standard logic of identity is correct.

That is, it has seemed to me that the doctrine of the Trinity is self-contradictory if the standard logic of identity is correct. I wish, therefore, to explore the possibility of rejecting the standard logic of identity. But it is not possible to reject the standard logic of identity root and branch. There is obviously much that is right about it. I wish therefore, to investigate the possibility of a logic that preserves what is obviously right about the standard logic of identity, but which differs from the standard logic in a way that does not allow the deduction of a contradiction from the doctrine of the Trinity.

The logic of identity I shall propose turns on the idea that there is not one relation of identity but many. Thus, I do not so much propose a logic of identity according to which the rules governing identity I have laid out above are invalid as a logic according to which they are vacuous: I deny that there is one all-encompassing relation of identity for them to govern. When I say that there is no one all-encompassing relation of identity, I mean that there is no relation that is both universally reflexive and forces indiscernibility. When I speak of 'many relations of identity,' I have in mind relations like these: 'being the same horse as,' 'being the same artifact as,' and 'being the same apple as.' I call these *relations of relative identity,* since the use of any of them in an assertion of sameness relativizes that sameness to a *kind;* it is for that reason that each of the phrases I have mentioned contains a count-noun like 'horse' or 'artifact' or 'apple.' Thus, one might call the relations expressed by the phrases 'horse-identity,' 'artifact-identity,' and 'apple-identity.' In pieces of reasoning whose validity turns on relations of relative identity, count-nouns will occur only in phrases like the ones I have used as examples – 'horse' will occur only in the phrase 'is the same horse as,' and so on. Having said this, I qualify it: I will allow predicates not of this form to occur if their form is that illustrated by 'is a horse.' I allow this because predicates of this sort can be regarded as mere abbreviations for phrases of the sort I allow 'officially.' For example, 'Bucephalus is a horse' can be understood as a mere abbreviation for 'Bucephalus is the same horse as Bucephalus.' Since 'Bucephalus is the same horse as Bucephalus' expresses (so I contend) the thought expressed by the ordinary sentence 'Bucephalus is a horse,' it is clear that the logic of relations of relative identity must have no rule corresponding to the rule Reflexivity. If we had such a rule, or, rather, if we had a separate rule of reflexivity for every relation of relative identity, this would have disastrous consequences. For example, the 'horse'–rule would allow us to introduce the sentence 'Tolstoy is the same horse as Tolstoy' into our reasoning. And we do not want that, for that sentence says that Tolstoy is a horse.

I also decline to allow anything corresponding to Leibniz's Law – that is to supply each relation of relative identity with its own little version of Leibniz's Law. The logic of relative identity thus does not give us its permission to introduce into our reasoning the sentence

> If Bucephalus is the same horse as Alexander's favorite horse, then Bucephalus was fond of apples if and only if Alexander's favorite horse was fond of apples.

If the logic of relative identity does not give us its permission to introduce this sentence into our reasoning, neither does it forbid us to do so. I myself think that this sentence expresses a truth, even a necessary truth, and I am therefore perfectly willing to introduce it into my reasoning (and would be equally willing to introduce any sentence built round 'is the same horse as' in the same way), but I would justify this willingness by an appeal to what I believe to be features of horse-identity, features that (in my view) may not be shared by all other relations of relative identity.

I in fact allow only two logical rules to govern reasoning about relations of relative identity. First, Symmetry, which is illustrated by this inference:

> Bucephalus is the same horse as Alexander's favorite horse;
>
> *hence,* Alexander's favorite horse is the same horse as Bucephalus.

Secondly, Transitivity:

> Byzantium is the same city as Constantinople; Constantino-ple is the same city as Istanbul; *hence,* Byzantium is the same city as Istanbul.

(In the standard logic of identity, Symmetry and Transitivity are derived rules; in the logic of relative identity, they must stand on their own.) Now let us apply these ideas to the doctrine of the Trinity. Suppose we have the two relations of relative identity:

> is the same being (substance, *ousia*) as
> is the same person as.

I shall not attempt to explain what either of these phrases means in any philosophically satisfactory way, but I shall make two remarks. First, I use 'being' for whatever it is that 'there is one of' in the Trinity, and I use 'person' for what it is that 'there are three of' in the Trinity. Secondly, there has been some debate about the relation between 'person,' the technical term of Trinitarian theology, and 'person,' the word of ordinary speech. Without attempting to resolve this debate, I will say that I regard 'x is the same person as y' as meaning more or less the same as 'x is someone and y is someone – but not someone else.' But nothing I shall say here depends on whether I am right about this. Now it might be thought that all this apparatus of relative identity does not enable us to escape the force of the skeptic's arguments. Consider the second argument. May the skeptic, even if he has only relations of relative identity at his disposal, not present the following argument?

> The Father is the same person as God
> The Son is the same person as God

>*Hence,* God is the same person as the Son
>*Hence,* The Father is the same person as the Son.

And is it not true that the Father and the Son are both the same person as God? One way to answer this argument might be to say that strictly 'person' applies only to the three 'persons' of the Trinity, but does not apply to the Godhead. I will not say anything of this sort. It seems to me that in Holy Scripture God frequently refers to himself as 'I' – depending on how you understand the Hebrew of Exodus 3:14, it may even be that his name is 'I Am' or 'I Am who Am' – and it would, I believe, be heretical to maintain that the God who speaks in the Hebrew Bible is simply God the Father, one of the persons of the Trinity. No, the theologians tell us, and I think that nothing else makes sense in the light of the doctrine of the Trinity, the God who spoke to Moses and Elijah and Ezekiel was the Triune God. And if this is so, God, the Triune God, must be a person. I would say, rather, that the defect in this argument comes from the way it uses the terms 'the Father,' 'the Son,' and 'God.' It uses these phrases as what logicians call 'singular terms' by which they mean terms that bear a relation called 'denoting' or 'reference' or 'designation' or 'naming' to a single object. But the very notion of a singular term is infected with the idea of the single all–encompassing relation of identity that we have rejected. If, for example, 'Catherine the Great' is a singular term, it follows that if 'Catherine the Great' denotes x and also denotes y, then x is identical with y. A logic that, like the logic of relative identity, rejects the very notion of a single, all-encompassing identity relation, must, therefore reject the notion of a singular term. But singular terms pervade, or seem to pervade, all our discourse, religious and non-religious. If we 'reject' singular terms we must find something to put in their place, something to do at least some of their work. I will show by example how to do this. Let us first consider the word 'God.' One thing we must be able to say that we ordinarily say using this singular term (at least it appears to be a singular term) is this: God spoke by the prophets. Suppose we introduce the predicate 'is divine' to express the divine nature or Godhead. Instead of saying 'God spoke by the prophets' we may say this:

>Something is divine and anything divine is the same being
>as it, and it spoke by the prophets.

(Here I use 'something,' 'anything,' and 'it' as logicians do: when one is speaking very generally, one many use these words to speak of, well, *anything,* including human beings, angels, and God himself.) Now what of singular terms that purport to denote the individual persons of the Trinity, terms like 'the Father,' 'the Son,' 'the second person of the Trinity,' and 'he who proceeds from the Father'? The Father, the Son, and the Holy Spirit are individuated; each is made *who he is* by, the relations that hold among them. The Father, for example, begets the Son, the Holy Spirit proceeds from the Father through the Son (or perhaps proceeds from the Father alone), and the Father proceeds from no one and is unbegotten. Suppose we so understand the predicates 'begets' and 'is begotten' that no one but the Father begets and no one but the Son is begotten. We could then understand theological sentences that contain 'the Father' and 'the Son' after the following models:

> The Father made all things
> Something begets and whatever, begets is the same person as it and it made all things
> All things were made through the Son
> Something is begotten and whatever is begotten is the same person as it and all things were made through it.

Now, what of our embarrassing argument? Is the Father the same person as God? Is the Son the same person as God? If these things are conceded, does it follow that the Son is the same person as the Father. The statement 'The Father is the same person as God' would be written like this:

> Something x begets and whatever begets is the same person as x and something y is divine and whatever is divine is the same being as y and x is the same person as y.

And similarly for 'The Son is the same person as God':

> Something x is begotten and whatever is begotten is the same person as x and something y is divine and whatever is divine is the same being as y and x is the same person as y.

But 'The Son is the same person as the Father' would be written thus:

> Something x begets and whatever begets is the same person as x and something y is begotten and whatever is begotten is the same person as y and x is the same person as y.

And this last statement does not follow from the first two, despite the fact that the rule Transitivity applies to the relation 'is the same person as.' I will in fact show you how to prove that the last statement does not follow from the first two – using devices from what logicians call the theory of models. Consider the following little story:

There are exactly two dogs in Ivan's shop. They are of the same breed and are for sale at different prices. One barks at the other, and the other never barks at all.

This little story is sufficient for the truth of the following two statements (if we consider 'Ivan's shop' to comprise the whole universe):

Something x barks and whatever barks is the same price as x and something y is a dog and whatever is a dog is the same breed as y and x is the same price as y.
   Something x is barked at and whatever is barked at is the same price as x and something y is a dog and whatever is a dog is the same breed as y and x is the same price as y.

Now consider the following statement:

Something x barks and whatever barks is the same price as x and something y is barked at and whatever is barked at is the same price as y and x is the same price as y.

This statement is *not* true in our story, for one thing in the story barks, another is barked at, and they are for sale at different prices. Now consider this question: does the third statement follow from the first two by the standard logic of the textbooks? Unless our story about Ivan's shop is self-contradictory, the answer to this question must be No, for the standard logic of the textbooks is known to have this property: if a story is not self-contradictory, then no statement that is false in the story can be deduced by the rules of the standard logic of the textbooks from any set of statements that are true in the story. But our little story of Ivan's shop and its canine inhabitants is obviously not self-contradictory, and, therefore, the third statement does not follow from the first two.

Now let us return to our three theological statements, our statements that represent 'The Father is the same person as God' and 'The Son is the same person as God' and 'The Father is the same person as the Son.' Does the third, which is certainly inconsistent with the doctrine of the Trinity, follow from the first two (which I, at least do not find objectionable) – I mean does it follow given the logic of relative identity that I have presented? The answer to this question is, No it does not follow, and this may be shown as follows. If it did follow, then it would be possible explicitly to write down the steps of the reasoning, each valid according to the logic of relative identity, by which the third statement was deduced from the first two. That reasoning could, by a purely mechanical set of transpositions of terms, be turned into a piece of reasoning, valid according to the standard logic of the textbooks, by which 'Something x is barked at and whatever is barked at is the same price as x and something y is a dog and whatever is a dog is the same breed as y and x is the same price as y' follows from the story of Ivan's shop. And we have seen that this statement does not follow from that story by the standard logic of the textbooks. If all this is too complicated to take in at one sitting, here is a statement of what I claim to have shown that is not too wide of the mark.

Suppose this set of statements was self-contradictory: 'The Father is the same person as God. The Son is the same person as God. The Father is not the same person as the Son.' It would follow that the simple story of Ivan's shop – There are exactly two dogs in Ivan's shop; they are of the same breed and are for sale at different prices; one barks at the other, and the other never barks at all – was self-contradictory; but this simple little story is obviously not self-contradictory.

In a talk of this length I cannot say enough to establish my general thesis, or even to discuss our first anti-Trinitarian argument. My general thesis is this: All the constituent propositions of the doctrine of the Trinity can be expressed in the language of relative identity, and they can be shown to be mutually consistent, given that the correct logic of identity is the logic of relative identity. That is to say, they can be shown to be mutually consistent if a certain simple story about everyday life – a story hardly more complicated than the story of Ivan's shop – is not self-contradictory. And it will be evident to anyone that this simple little story about everyday life is not self-contradictory.

PART III

THE INCARNATION

INTRODUCTION

The Incarnation is the first aspect of the work of Christ, whereby the Second Person of the Trinity assumed a human nature in order to bring about the reconciliation of some fallen human beings with God. This doctrine has been the subject of considerable interest in recent philosophical theology. Much, though not all, of this work has been an attempt to shore up traditional, Chalcedonian Christology (that is, Christology which takes its point of departure from the so-called 'definition' of the person of Christ given by the ecumenical Council of Chalcedon in AD 451).

Taking a rather different approach, Peter Forrest offers an updated version of kenotic Christology. This family of views can be traced back to post-Reformation Lutheran thought. However, kenotic Christology had been relegated to the dustbin of ideas until recent philosophical-theological work which salvaged this amendment of Chalcedonian thought by emphasizing how Christ 'emptied himself' in order to become human, in accordance with the great Christ-hymn of Philippians 2. Forrest argues that a kenotic account of the Incarnation avoids certain problems besetting more traditional, Chalcedonian alternatives, by providing a story that makes sense of how a divine person can 'empty himself' in order to become human.

Eleonore Stump is well known for her work in medieval philosophical theology, and has recently produced a critically acclaimed study of the philosophy of Thomas Aquinas. In her essay, she sets out Aquinas' compositional account of the Incarnation. This is the view, according to which the Incarnation involves the assumption by the Second Person of the Trinity of a human body and human soul, which, taken together, form one whole composed of three parts. Stump's essay is noteworthy for her clear articulation of Thomas' Aristotelian account of Christ's constitution, and her use of the idea of properties being 'borrowed' by wholes (like the God-Man) from their parts (e.g. natures) in order to rebut certain philosophical problems concerning the hypostatic union.

The third essay in this part is an interesting and constructive essay by Thomas Flint. He is a defender of Molinism, or the doctrine of God's middle knowledge.[1] Molinism is a doctrine that originated with Louis de Molina, a post-Reformation Jesuit thinker who sought to reconcile a robust account of human free will with the meticulous providence of God. His solution to what is usually called the 'freedom-foreknowledge dilemma' (roughly, the problem generated by conjoining a (libertarian) account of human freedom with the idea that God foreknows and fore-ordains all that comes to pass) was to conceive of God's knowledge in three 'phases' or 'moments' – a logical distinction, not a temporal, sequential one. God has 'natural' knowledge of all necessary truths. God also has 'middle knowledge', that is, knowledge of all contingent truths (including all truths about what free human creatures will do in all the possible circumstances they might be placed in). The divine nature has no control over this 'middle knowledge', so-called because it sits midway in the logical moments of divine knowledge between the 'natural' knowledge of God and his 'free' knowledge. But, taken together with his 'natural' knowledge, God knows all that will result from his actualizing any given possible world, including the states of affairs that will obtain in such worlds given the myriad free choices of his human creatures. Upon this basis, God chooses to create one particular world from all those that are possible, and that he can actualize (there are, possible but non-actualizable worlds on this way of thinking, as Alvin Plantinga has pointed out[2]). Divine 'free' knowledge is consequent upon 'middle' knowledge, and God's act of creation. It consists of all the contingent truths God knows that are under his control, having created the world he does create, rather than some other, possible world. In this essay, Flint applies the doctrine of middle knowledge to the Incarnation with some surprising, and theologically creative, results.

Finally, in this part, and despite its title Thomas Morris's essay is a summary statement of his influential 'two-minds' Christology, set forth in what is widely regarded as the most important recent monograph on Christology by a philosophical theologian, *The Logic of God Incarnate*.[3] Morris's account could be thought of as an attempt at updating a broadly Chalcedonian orthodoxy. In his book and in this essay, he argues that deploying a number of simple metaphysical distinctions enables us to see that the classical account of the person of Christ is not incoherent. Hence, his task is an apologetic one, showing that certain intellectual objections to the Incarnation, and specifically, certain putative epistemological objections to the doctrine, can be removed or set aside.

Notes

1. The standard contemporary account of Molinism is Thomas P. Flint, *Divine Providence* (Ithaca: Cornell University Press, 1998). Alfred Freddoso has translated the relevant part of Louis de Molina's massive *De Concordia* in *On Divine Foreknowledge: Part IV of the Concordia*, trans. Alfred J. Freddoso (Ithaca: Cornell University Press, 1988), which also has a useful introduction to Molinism.

2. See Alvin Plantinga, *The Nature of Necessity* (Oxford: Oxford University Press, 1974).
3. (Ithaca: Cornell University Press, 1986).

Suggested further reading

- Adams, Marilyn McCord, *Christ and Horrors: The Coherence of Christology* (Cambridge: Cambridge University Press, 2006).
- Crisp, Oliver D. *Divinity and Humanity: The Incarnation Reconsidered* (Cambridge: Cambridge University Press, 2007).
- Evans, C. Stephen (ed.), *Exploring Kenotic Christology: The Self-Emptying God* (New York: Oxford University Press, 2006).
- Hick, John, *The Metaphor of God Incarnate* (Louisville, KY.: Westminster John Knox, 1996).
- Leftow, Brian, 'A Timeless God Incarnate' in Stephen T. Davis, Daniel Kendall and Gerald O'Collins (eds), *The Incarnation* (Oxford: Oxford University Press, 2002), pp. 273–299.
- Morris, Thomas V., *The Logic of God Incarnate* (Ithaca: Cornell University Press, 1986).
- Swinburne, Richard, *The Christian God* (Oxford: Oxford University Press, 2004), chs. 9–10.

CHAPTER 8

THE INCARNATION: A PHILOSOPHICAL CASE FOR KENOSIS

Peter Forrest

Abstract: As a preliminary, I shall clarify the kenotic position by arguing that a position which is often called kenotic is actually a quasi-kenotic version of the classical account, according to which Jesus had normal divine powers but chose not to exercise them. After this preliminary, I discuss three problems with the strict kenotic account. The first is that kenosis conflicts with the standard list of attributes considered essential to God. The second problem is posed by the Exaltation, namely the resumption by Jesus of normal divine powers after his life on Earth. Finally there is the problem of how it was possible for Jesus to be the same person as the pre-incarnate Word. My solutions to these problems constitute my defence of a strict kenotic account of the Incarnation.

Introduction

The purpose of this paper is to compare two rival accounts of the Christian doctrine of the Incarnation, the classical and the kenotic, defending the latter. These accounts agree that the second divine person, the Word, remained divine at the Incarnation. They disagree, however, in that the kenotic account denies that Jesus had the powers *normal* for a divine person. Here the plural 'powers' is a reminder that I am including both the power to act and the power to know. So the normal divine powers would include a capacity to act and know far exceeding the human, without the implication that these capacities are exercised.

As a preliminary, I shall clarify the kenotic position by arguing that a position which is often called kenotic is actually a quasi-kenotic version of the classical account, according to which Jesus had normal divine powers but chose not to exercise them. I suggest that Thomasius, the source of nineteenth- and early twentieth-century kenotic theories, and Stephen T. Davis, often cited as a philosopher defending kenosis, held the quasi-kenotic theory. This might suggest that my terminology is eccentric, so if readers prefer, they could re-label quasi-kenosis as moderate kenosis, and kenosis in my sense as extreme kenosis. In that case this paper is a defence of extreme kenosis as a serious alternative to both the classical account and moderate kenosis. This dispute over terminology is not entirely trivial, however. For mine is the natural one if we are primarily interested in the relevant philosophical issues, whereas the alternative might be more appropriate if we were considering Scripture or the beliefs of the early Church. For I doubt if such considerations would distinguish between quasi-kenotic and kenotic accounts except via philosophical argument such as I provide in this paper.

After this preliminary, I reply to three objections to the kenotic account. Of these the most widespread is that it conflicts with the standard list of attributes considered essential to God, including immutability. I consider but reject as ad hoc the strategy of merely qualifying the standard list of divine attributes. Instead I offer the more robust reply that the objection is based upon a misguided conception of the divine. After that I turn to the problem posed by the Exaltation, namely the resumption by Jesus of normal divine powers after his life on Earth. Finally I tackle a question which defenders of kenosis must answer: how is it possible for Jesus to be the same person as the pre-incarnate Word? I offer a suggestion as to how the conditions for personal identity can be met in the case of the Incarnation.

Quasi-kenosis and qualified kenosis

A kenotic account of Incarnation is contrasted with the classical account according to which the Word never ceased to have normal divine powers. Now those who hold the classical account may well do so because they consider that divinity entails omnipotence and omniscience. But I want to leave open the possibility that, even prior to the Incarnation, God had freely given up some power for the sake of creatures, perhaps in order to ensure their freedom. So normal divine powers may or may not be taken to imply omnipotence and omniscience. I am, of course, assuming that, but for the Incarnation, the Word would have had vastly greater powers than any human being. In particular these powers would not have been spatially limited.

With that qualification, then, I mean by a quasi-kenotic account one according to which Jesus possessed but chose never to exercise these normal divine powers. This comes in a number of versions which may be illustrated by supposing that we grant that water was turned into wine at Cana.[1] On the kenotic account Jesus did not and could not work this miracle. Instead he exercised a perfectly normal human power of praying for a miracle. On an unqualified classical account Jesus, having normal divine powers, exercised the power directly to turn water into wine. According to the least kenotic version of the quasi-kenotic account Jesus could have directly turned water into wine but chose not to, praying instead for a miracle. On another version he had no power directly to turn water into wine but could have decided to reacquire that power. And, if we insist, we can iterate the distinction between having a direct power and having the power to acquire a direct power, but there would be little point in such iteration. Now I shall assume that having the power to acquire the power to do X is already having the power to do X, but is not having the power directly to do X. Hence even if Jesus had no power directly to turn water into wine he had the power indirectly to do so if he had the power to acquire the power directly to do so, or, implausibly, the power to acquire the power to acquire the power directly to do so.

Thomasius argued that the 'omni' properties of omnipotence, omniscience, and, he added, omnipresence, were not essential divine attributes because they were relative, presupposing there exists a universe to have power over, to know, and to be present in.[2] These 'omni' attributes are, however, said to be manifestations of the essential divine attributes. This suggests that the essential divine attributes include the power to be omnipotent, omniscient, and omnipresent, which would make Thomasius a proponent of the quasi-kenotic version of the classical account.

Davis distinguishes omnipotence and omniscience *simpliciter,* which he denies are essential for divinity, from qualified senses which are essential.[3] He distinguishes between having a power and choosing to exercise it and he identifies omnipotence and omniscience *simpliciter* with the nonessential total exercise of the essential divine power. So his is, in my terminology, also a quasi-kenotic classical account.

Some attempts to qualify kenosis result, then, in versions not of the kenotic account but of the classical one. To further clarify the position which I am defending, I note that a kenotic account is, however, quite compatible with some other qualifications. The first of these is that, as Davis and others have pointed out, being truly human does not entail being a normal human being.[4] So, for instance, I hypothesize that Jesus had some memories of his pre-incarnate state. The next is that I hold that Jesus resumed normal divine powers, hence the kenosis of the Incarnation is qualified by its temporary character. One reason for holding this doctrine of the Exaltation, as it is called, is that it makes sense of the Ascension without requiring an otherwise unnecessary hypothesis about space.[5] Jesus did not go anywhere – by becoming omnipresent he went everywhere. A more important reason is that the love which is an excellence does not involve reckless sacrifice, such as taking a serious risk of drowning in order merely to retrieve an object of sentimental value to your beloved. Kenosis is easily accused of recklessness and permanent kenosis really would be. And if that is not persuasive I suggest that the divine joy experienced by the persons of the Trinity requires normal divine powers. So, out of love for each other, none of them would permanently abdicate their powers.

Although I am not committed to this, we might also suppose that the temporary character of kenosis is not merely true but is essential for being a divine person. So no divine person could abdicate power permanently. I mention this largely because Morris, who eventually rejects the kenotic account, provides a sympathetic interpretation of it in which the 'omni' properties are not essential. Rather the essential properties have the qualification 'unless freely and temporarily choosing to be otherwise'.[6]

Kenosis and the essential divine attributes

The most widespread objection to kenotic accounts is that the 'omni' properties are essential divine attributes, so divine persons cannot lose them, whether they want to or not. A similar objection is that to be unchanging is essential to being divine, so divine persons could not lose any attributes, even if not considered essential on other grounds.

Here we could distinguish between: (a) an attribute being necessary *de dicto,* that is, necessary if something is to belong to the kind, divine person; and (b) an attribute being necessary *de re,* that is, necessary for the existence of the person in question, whether or not that person ceases to be divine. As Morris points out, if the 'omni' attributes were necessary *de dicto* but not *de re* then kenosis would be possible but would imply that the Word ceased to be divine.[7] If, however, the 'omni' attributes were necessary *de re,* then the Word could not lose them, except perhaps by ceasing to exist. In whichever sense we take it, if the 'omni' attributes are necessary then the kenotic account as I have stated it is false. For I am proposing that Jesus was truly divine but lacked normal divine powers.

At this point defenders of the kenotic theory are tempted to qualify the standard list of attributes. Morris suggests the qualification 'unless freely and temporarily choosing to be otherwise'.[8] I think he is right, but by itself this provides no defence against the objection that a divine person is immutable. For an immutable divine person cannot choose to be otherwise. In any case, unless some further rationale is provided, the method of qualifying traditional attributes is ad hoc and so a weakness in an account.

The problem, as I understand it, is not with the kenotic account of the Incarnation itself so much as the attempt to combine that account with a classical conception of the divine. The problem is solved by adopting a more thoroughly kenotic theology. To argue for this I first note that there can be various different *conceptions* of God without any ambiguity in the *concept* of God.[9] This may be illustrated by means of a once common abuse of students by philosophy lecturers. A purportedly unbiased discussion of the Argument from Evil would begin with something not discussed at all – a definition of God as omnipotent, omniscient, and morally good. Any students who suggested qualifying these attributes would be told they had changed the topic. But that is not a definition, at least not in the sense of an accurate analysis of our concept of God. Far better is St Anselm's 'that than which no greater can be conceived of', although, for various reasons I would then gloss 'greater' as 'properly more awe-inspiring'. For present purposes these details may not matter much, so let us just talk of a perfect being. Our conceptions of God are based upon (implicit) inferences about what sort of entity a perfect being would have to be. For a start I share with most Christians a personal conception of God, namely that a perfect being would be either a person or a community of persons. But it does not follow that a pantheist who rejects the personal conception of the divine is using the words 'divine' and 'God' differently from me.[10] Rather there is a different conception because an inference I find obvious has been rejected by the pantheist. Likewise the philosophy lecturer who defined God as omnipotent, omniscient, and morally good was mistaking the 'omni' God conception for a definition. This 'omni' God conception is based upon an (implicit) inference that a perfect being would' obviously' have to have the maximum amount of power, knowledge, and goodness.

Now the Anselmian definition coheres well with a process of subration or *aufhebung* whereby we progress from more to less inadequate conceptions of God as we conceive of something greater than anything we had previously conceived of. The central thesis of kenotic theism is that we should progress beyond the 'omni-God' conception to that of the kenotic God who out of love abandons absolute power, while retaining sufficient power to warrant total trust. It follows that there is nothing ad hoc about Morris's 'unless freely and temporarily choosing to be otherwise' qualification to the 'omni' attributes. Likewise, there is nothing ad hoc in first replacing the divine attribute of immutability by the power to remain unchanged and then qualifying that power with the 'unless freely and temporarily choosing to be otherwise' qualification.

The resulting conception is of a God who had the power to remain forever unchanging, as an omnipotent and omniscient being. Such a being, even if a single person, would have been great, but there is something greater yet, namely a community of divine persons who are able and willing to abandon their initial omnipotence and omniscience.[11]

I now turn to three objections to the account I have just given of the divine attributes. First, there is Feenstra's objection that Morris's qualification is too permissive. I am committed to that qualification, so I need to consider Feenstra's objection. It is that, given Morris's qualification, all three divine persons could simultaneously abdicate the powers normal for a divine being.[12] I shall restate this problem as an inconsistent tetrad:

(1) Each divine person has the unqualified power to abdicate normal divine powers.
(2) If a number of persons have the unqualified power to do something then it is possible that they all exercise that power.
(3) If all divine persons exercise the divine power to abdicate normal divine powers then God as a whole would cease to have normal divine powers.
(4) But necessarily God retains normal divine powers.

Feenstra rejects (1), and after some discussion, suggests instead that a divine person has the essential attribute of only being able to abdicate divine power by becoming kenotically incarnate which can only happen for the purposes of redemption.[13] Not only does Feenstra's qualification seem rather ad hoc, it does not prevent the possibility of all three persons simultaneously abdicating normal divine powers by becoming incarnate. For that might happen if there were three planets whose inhabitants simultaneously required redemption. So I shall not reject (1).[14] Now (3) could only be rejected if we thought of God as something additional to the community of divine persons, which is not merely an unnecessary complication, but would seem to suggest that creation is the work of some impersonal force which operates through the divine persons who are not therefore free. This would conflict with my personal conception of a perfect being. Therefore to defend my position I should abandon either (2) or (4). First consider (4). I ask why we would object to the idea that God as a whole, and not just one (or two) divine persons, might abandon normal divine powers? The only reason I can think of is that it would be foolish or wrong to do so. Perhaps this is because it would interfere with the life of the Trinity, or because God needs to exercise providential care over the universe or perhaps because God's continual activity is required to keep the universe in existence, and it would be wrong having created the universe just to let it cease to exist. Now it has been pointed out that none of these reasons require the retention of *full* divine powers.[15] While I grant this I note that the problem being discussed can be restated with the phrase 'normal divine power' interpreted as 'sufficient divine power to sustain a universe in existence'. And rejecting (4) will not solve the restated problem. So there is a case for retaining (4) but I note that it depends on the thesis that God is necessarily good.[16] Otherwise we could say that we have every reason to hope the divine persons would not do anything as rash as simultaneously abandoning normal divine powers, but that this is nonetheless possible.

I now argue that if we accept the thesis of necessary divine goodness, as I think we should, then (2) should be abandoned. (And if we do not accept that thesis we can reject (4).) Now (2) seemed plausible only because we took it for granted that if a person has a power it is possible for that person to exercise it, and then we asked ourselves what could possibly prevent several persons simultaneously exercising their powers. But I reject what was taken for granted. Having the freedom to exercise a power is compatible with necessarily never exercising it. For, a necessarily good person will necessarily never exercise the power to act wrongly, a necessarily wise person will necessarily never exercise the power to act foolishly, and so on. The necessity governs the intentions, and so does not interfere with the freedom to act in accordance with other, impossible, intentions.

I grant that this is a compatibilist position, reconciling necessity and freedom, but it is not an attempt to reconcile causal determinism and freedom. If someone is caused by earlier events to act in one way rather than another that, I grant, is not freedom. The sort of moderate compatibilism I am here considering occurs when no earlier event causes the divine person to act one way or the other. It is just that the divine character is necessarily such that wrong or foolish acts are never performed. To those who reject even this moderate compatibilism I have a doubly *ad hominem* argument. Can God create something God has no power over – a stone too 'heavy' for God to 'lift'? It would seem that an essentially omnipotent God has less power than one who is not essentially omnipotent, because an essentially omnipotent God lacks powers of self-limitation.[17] Now the classical conception of God as omnipotent is based on the assumption that power contributes to greatness. So as an *ad hominem* we can argue in favour of the kenotic conception of God as having once been omnipotent but as having exercised a kenotic power of self-limitation. Against this, defenders of the classical conception could provide the compatibilist reply, namely that God has the power of self-limitation but necessarily does not exercise it. This is fair enough except that I am engaged in an *ad hominem* against those who deny such compatibilism.

The above reply to Feenstra's objection might make us reconsider the question of divine immutability. The kenotic account was that divine persons are under no compulsion to change but may freely do so. Now it could be objected that while this is adequate as part of an account of divine greatness, there is another reason for holding that God is immutable. For, as Davis observes in his discussion notes, Geach argues that a mutable God would have to have a cause, but God has no cause.[18] But, as Davis points out, Geach's argument seems to depend on a strong version of the Principle of Sufficient Reason, namely that anything changeable has a cause, not the less controversial version that anything that comes into existence has a cause.[19] Or we might replace the strong version with the appealing principle that every change has an intuitively adequate explanation, where in the case of divine changes the divine motives of goodness and love would be adequate as explanations of the change.

The Exaltation

Does a kenotic account of the Incarnation require the Exaltation? Or might, instead, the kenosis be permanent? One reason for rejecting permanent kenosis is the thought that the Word might have extra-terrestrial incarnations and that the saving power of these would require resumption of normal divine attributes before the further incarnation. But that is too speculative to be of much weight. Instead, as I have already mentioned, permanent kenosis would be reckless. Moreover it would conflict with the love for the other divine persons. For surely giving is part of loving and giving is frustrated by lack of means.

Feenstra in his discussion notes the problem posed by the Exaltation. If, as Baillie argues, the 'distinctive' divine and human attributes are incompatible then the Exaltation requires that Jesus lose his humanity on resuming normal divine powers.[20] The simplest response to this is that of Brown and others cited by Feenstra: deny the humanity of the exalted Christ. I would be reluctant to adopt this response because of its incompatibility with traditional devotion to Jesus as mediator between the purely divine and the purely human. Moreover, it is excluded by the considerations of personal identity to be discussed at the end of the paper. Feenstra considers two other solutions: arguing that kenosis is required for becoming human but not for remaining human; and arguing that the Incarnation does not imply kenosis even though the Incarnation was accompanied by kenosis.[21] These two solutions agree that the kenosis could come to an end even though Jesus continued to be human, or, in a minor variant, resumes humanity in the future after a non-human interlude. And that is the position which I shall defend.

This leaves me with the following problem: why should we abandon the classical account of the earthly life of Jesus if we are to assume just that account of his exalted life?[22] The answer to this question depends on the reasons we have for preferring a kenotic to a classical account. Since the purpose of this paper is merely to defend the kenotic account I will not discuss those reasons in detail. I shall merely claim, without further argument, that while being human is compatible with having normal divine powers there are some limitations which a person of normal divine powers could not have, but which in the Incarnation reveal the nature of divine love. I shall call these limitations the *paradoxical* attributes because there is an air of Kierkegaardian paradox in Jesus' possession of a limitation necessary for revealing that which is unlimited. I believe, but shall not here argue, that Jesus had two such paradoxical attributes: his capacity to share human suffering at its worst, namely suffering unrelieved by any accompanying joy; and his capacity to be genuinely tempted. These paradoxical attributes were required in order for Jesus to reveal divine love but not in order for him to be human. Having revealed divine love there is no need for him to go on revealing it. Hence the exalted Christ can be human while having the normal divine powers even though the purpose of the Incarnation required that Jesus, while on earth, did not have these powers.

How is kenotic incarnation possible?

The defence of a kenotic account of the Incarnation is incomplete until we answer some awkward questions concerning personal identity, questions which have been unduly neglected. For unless it is possible, and not merely conceivable, that the human being Jesus is the very same person as the pre-Incarnation Word, not even divine power can bring it about.

There are two main contenders for theories of personal identity: versions of the Simple View and versions of the Psychological Continuity Theory. The former asserts that either personal identity cannot be further explained or is explained by positing some enduring component or constituent of a person, such as a Cartesian ego or, on Swinburne's current version of the Simple View, a thisness.[23]

The Psychological Continuity Theory comes in many versions but the following is representative. It asserts that: (i) persons are essentially historical beings, so that to be a given person is to be as that person now is and to have had that person's history; (ii) a person's history is a sequence of stages which are (a) explanatorily connected in the appropriate way, that is, later stages are as they are largely because earlier stages were as they were, and (b) there are no abrupt changes or discontinuities in the sequence of stages; (iii) a person at one time is said to be the same person as a person at another time only if one of the histories is part of the other.

I am not asserting that there is nothing more to personal identity than the conditions given in this account. For a start even though persons are essentially historical every person has to be a person of some kind, and, I assume, no one can remain the same person if they lose one of the attributes characteristic of that person-kind. Hence I assume that a divine person cannot cease to be divine. Furthermore, just as according to moderate dualists the mental depends upon but is not fully explained by the physical, likewise it can be said that being the same person is a mysterious matter which is not fully explained in terms of such necessary and sufficient conditions which we are able to formulate for personal identity. The Psychological Continuity Theory, then, might not be the whole truth concerning personal identity. But I am not concerned with the whole truth, merely that part of the truth which makes it problematic to say of a certain human being, Jesus, that he is the very same person as the Word.

The Psychological Continuity Theory has the consequence that a person could undergo fission, which, in the human case Swinburne takes as a reason for holding the Simple View, positing thisnesses. But, for good reasons, he rejects this in the divine case, where it would have the further disadvantage of making the Trinity problematic.[24] I am inclined to reject the Simple View in all cases, but, fortunately, this issue need not be decided here. For I note that if we hold the Simple View, the possibility of a kenotic incarnation would be trivial in two ways. First it would be trivial in the sense that the required identity of thisness or ego may simply be asserted. But second, it would be trivial in the sense that nothing much has been accomplished. For the point of the doctrine is not to assert the unity of the human and the divine in some ontological sense with no consequence, which is what identity of thisness would amount to. Even were the Simple View correct Christians would need to assert in addition the psychological continuity of the humanity and divinity of Jesus, resulting in discussions just like those which arise for the Incarnation if we assume the Psychological Continuity Theory.

As far as the dispute between the Simple View and Psychological Continuity is concerned, then, we should concentrate on the latter. Before doing so, however, we should briefly consider two other, less popular, theories of personal identity. There is the possibility of requiring both a strictly identical component, say a thisness, and psychological continuity. But given the triviality of the implications of the Simple View for the Incarnation that would leave us with the same problem as with

Psychological Continuity. There is also, of course, the theory that to be the same person there must be the same living organism. Although this would be inconsistent with the Incarnation as usually stated, it would not be a genuine threat to Christianity. For were we to accept that theory, then psychological continuity would be more significant for us than personal identity. So rather than reject the doctrine of the Incarnation, we should reformulate it as asserting the psychological continuity of the humanity and divinity of Jesus.

Regardless of just which is the best theory of personal identity we should, therefore, assume the Psychological Continuity Theory when discussing the Incarnation.

Prior to the Incarnation, the Word enjoys normal divine powers. Perhaps these are limited by previous kenotic acts such as granting free will to some creatures. Nonetheless, on the kenotic account there is an infinite difference between the power and knowledge of the pre-incarnate Word and the powerlessness and ignorance of Jesus at birth. So how could there be continuity? But even supposing continuity, we might wonder whether the enormous difference between the two states is compatible with personal identity. And there is a third problem, to do with the explanatory connection. To be sure there is no problem with the pre-incarnate Word causing Jesus to be born with certain characteristics. This requires only that either at creation or subsequently the Word guide humanity's and Israel's history providentially. But there is still a problem for psychological continuity. For how can it be that the details of Jesus' life on Earth are explained by the details of earlier stages of the Word?

First let us consider the continuity problem. There is no difficulty with a continuity between the finite and the infinite provided it is possible for a process to be made up of an actual infinity of stages. We may suppose that to have divine power is to have knowledge of an infinity of possible worlds, knowing which parts of them are actual and which merely possible, and to be able to actualize any part that is not actual but still possible.[25] We may think of this infinite domain of possibilities as divided into infinitely many portions, each comparable to that which a human being can know and have power over. Whatever infinity we are considering, removing the knowledge and power piece by piece must, in an infinity of stages – the same infinity – reduce the divine consciousness to a human one. Instead of one big act of kenosis there could be a kenotic process made up of an infinity of small kenotic acts whereby the Word gradually comes to have purely human powers.

There are three possible objections to this account of continuity. First there are those who deny the actual infinity. Clearly they would reject the account I gave of the divine knowledge and power, but they would also reject the idea that there could be an actual infinity of real stages in any process. They may well be right, but if they are then the same objection holds to any continuous process, such as that occurring in Zeno's paradox of Achilles and the tortoise. Hence whatever we say of the latter we can say of the process of kenosis.[26]

The second objection is that, given the usual ideas we have about time, we cannot have a process made up of more than countably many stages yet there must surely be uncountably many possible worlds. Suppose I grant the impossibility of a process with uncountably many stages. I could still insist that continuity requires only that at each stage an infinitesimal proportion of the divine power and knowledge be removed from the Word, even if each infinitesimal proportion is itself infinite. Since anything, however large, can be thought of as made up of countably many parts which are infinitesimal as proportions of the original, it would follow that only countably many stages are required.

The final objection is, I think, the most important. It is that as kenosis occurs there should be physical correlates to the process – something should happen in the universe. But, the objection goes, this would be contrary to the laws of nature and, more serious, noticeable. My reply is that either, as I hold, free acts are quite compatible with the laws of nature or these laws have exceptions which accommodate free acts. I see no reason why the act of kenosis should raise problems not already there in the case of free human acts. To reply to the more serious part of the objection, we need to speculate about the physical correlates of a gradual restriction of the Word's powers. To illustrate the sort of speculation we might come up with, let us concentrate on the moral order and let us suppose that it has been decided that providential guidance for human beings is divided up as follows: that which provides the basic understanding of morality and a command-like motivation to act rightly comes from the first person, that which provides the practical wisdom to act rightly rather than merely with good intentions comes from the third, and that which provides the opportunity for repentance or change of heart comes from the second, the Word. We may also suppose that to rebel freely against the divine will expressed by the guidance of the first two persons nullifies the guidance of the third until there is repentance, and, as a result, general moral principles are respected but misapplied. That in turn results in appropriate guilt but no effective means for improvement. If that were so, then as the Word underwent kenosis, humans were increasingly left without any providential guidance towards repentance, which therefore becomes haphazard. This would result in a gradual deterioration of the moral order, accompanied by an increase in guilt and a corresponding increase in misguided ways of trying to eliminate guilt, such as human sacrifice. Such a deterioration would have been of immense importance but not perhaps that noticeable to historians.

Gradual kenosis does not by itself establish the psychological continuity between the pre-Incarnation and post-Incarnation stages. For the psychological states of Jesus must be explained by and continuous with earlier stages. Here, I suggest, we need to consider character, projects and memories. As regards character, continuity could be ensured by Jesus having perfect love. And Jesus' project seems to have been to call as many as he could to repentance, leading to friendship with himself and reconciliation with the first person. And we may assume that this is a continuation of the distinctive role of the Word in human affairs. We still need to give an account of Jesus' memories. Now full recall is not required for psychological continuity, but I do not think the continuity of character and projects is sufficiently great to establish psychological continuity if Jesus had no memories of the pre-Incarnation state. So I am committed to something that might seem all too classical to those attracted by kenosis, namely that Jesus had some sort of memories of his former state. My commitment might surprise those who would insist that in the ordinary human case persons could survive total amnesia. But the case of the Incarnation lacks those factors which replace memory in the case of total amnesia: the continuity of body image; and the continuity of routine behaviour patterns, such as the way of eating, the way of dressing, the way of walking, and so on.

We should suppose, then, that Jesus had a memory of the life of the Trinity, and in particular of what the first person was like, which he could not communicate to his disciples. Perhaps this memory would, in neurophysiological terms, be somewhat like the recollection of a mystical experience. But in any case we may suppose it to be connected with his incapacity to sin and his having perfect divine love.

For personal identity the successive stages should not merely be continuous but earlier stages should explain later ones, and explain them in the appropriate way. If we ignore the proviso that the explanation be appropriate then we have no problem. The Word providentially arranges for the occurrence of the requisite kind of human being to occur just as the last of the normal divine powers is abdicated. The proviso cannot, however, be ignored. For an appropriateness condition is standard in accounts of memory and psychological continuity more generally. For example, you do not remember your first birthday if you have an apparent memory caused by seeing a video recording of the event, even though that apparent memory depends, in detail, on the events of your first birthday. Likewise, it is doubtful if psychological continuity is ensured if a human being dies and eventually leaves no trace but God then decides to recreate a qualitatively identical person at the Resurrection of the Dead. Hence it is not sufficient for an incarnation that the Word providentially arranges for a perfect human being to have the appropriate character, projects and apparent memories, while simultaneously abdicating all power.

The appropriateness requirement is, I submit, satisfied if and only if the divine kenosis itself may be said to cause the existence of the human being who was Jesus, with that character and projects, and with those memories, which, as a consequence are genuine, not merely apparent, memories. This might prompt a re-description question directed at the kenotic account. What, it could be asked, is the difference between the divine kenosis causing Jesus' existence and the hypothetical situation in which the Word ensures the occurrence of a human being with appropriate character projects and 'memory' at just the moment that all power and knowledge are abdicated? In either case the Word gradually restricts power and knowledge and ceases to have anything like normal divine powers just prior to the coming into existence of the human being, Jesus, who has the appropriate character, projects, and memories. In either case we have for each stage S of the kenosis a set of possibilities $P(S)$ which the Word has power to actualize at stage S, where if S^* is later than S then $P(S^*)$ is contained in $P(S)$. Fortunately this redescription question can be given a precise answer. The product of the process of kenosis is specified by the intersection of the $P(S)$, that is the by the set of possibilities which the Word has the power to actualize at every stage in the process. In the case of total abdication this intersection would be empty. In the case of the Incarnation this intersection is just the set of possibilities which Jesus has the power to actualize by making such free choices in his life as he can make.[27]

A corollary of this is that Jesus must have been excepted from any divine kenosis by which the Word ceased to have power over human affairs, for the sake of our freedom. For were Jesus not such an exception then the Incarnation would have resulted in a total abdication of the Word's power rather than the required continuity between the Word's power and that of Jesus.

Finally, I need to consider whether the exalted Christ could be identical to the human being Jesus if, as Brown suggests, he is no longer human. The problem here is that a purely divine Christ would have the same sort of knowledge of what it was like to have been Mary, or John, as of what it was like to have been Jesus. It is only if the exalted Christ knows some things in the divine way and others in a human way that he can have the memories which seem to be required for him to be identical with Jesus, rather than anyone else who came to share in the Word's project of reconciling humanity to the God. I conclude that the identity of Jesus with a purely divine person prior to the Incarnation is less problematic than any supposed identity with a purely divine person after the Exaltation.[28]

Notes

1. Or that the water was annihilated and wine created *ex nihilo*. For present purposes this will not be distinguished from the turning of water into wine.
2. See Ronald J. Feenstra 'Reconsidering kenotic Christology', in Ronald J. Feenstra and Cornelius Plantinga Jr (eds) *Trinity, Incarnation and Atonement: Philosophical and Theological Essays* (Notre Dame IN: University of Notre Dame Press, 1989), 130.
3. Stephen T. Davis *Logic and the Nature of God* (London: Macmillan, 1983), 125–126.
4. *Ibid.,* 125.
5. As C. S. Lewis noted, twentieth-century ideas about space and time make a fairly literal interpretation of the Ascension more believable than they have been at any time since the medieval world view was abandoned. For there is nothing in contemporary physics that excludes treating heaven as a parallel universe literally less than a mile from ours – or an inch. So Jesus might have moved continuously from our universe to heaven. But why hypothesize this without good reason?
6. Thomas V. Morris *The Logic of God Incarnate* (Ithaca NY: Cornell University Press, 1986), 99.
7. *Ibid.,* 93.
8. *Ibid.,* 99.
9. I am indebted to Fred d'Agostino for helping me see just how important the Rawlsian concept/conception distinction is in so many contexts.
10. I am indebted to Michael Levine for drawing this to my attention.
11. See my 'Divine fission: a new way of moderating social trinitarianism', *Religious Studies,* 34 (1998), 281–298.
12. Feenstra 'Reconsidering kenotic Christology', 140.
13. *Ibid.,* 142.
14. Feenstra also considers the suggestion that only one of the three persons has the capacity to become incarnate. He rejects this because it contradicts the orthodoxy that the three persons are coequal (142).
15. By one of the anonymous referees for *Religious Studies* [the journal in which this paper first appeared].
16. For a discussion of this see Morris *The Logic of God Incarnate,* ch. 5.
17. The classical reply here is that 'a stone too heavy for God to lift' is incoherent because, God being omnipotent, there cannot be such a stone. So, it is said, the supposed power is not a genuine one. But incoherence requires more than necessary falsehood. It requires, at least, inconsistency with the definition of God. So this classical reply is itself based upon the incorrect premise that our *concept* of God is of an omnipotent being.
18. Davis *Logic and the Nature of God,* ch. 3.
19. *Ibid.,* 50–51.
20. Feenstra 'Reconsidering kenotic Christology', 144.
21. *Ibid.,* 147–148.

22. I take it that this is Baillie's objection when, in a passage quoted by Feenstra, he says 'The presupposition of the [kenotic] theory is that the distinctive divine attributes ... and the distinctive human attributes ... cannot be united simultaneously ...'; (Feenstra 'Reconsidering kenotic Christology', 144).

23. Richard Swinburne *The Christian God* (Oxford: Clarendon Press, 1994). ch. 2.

24. *Ibid.*, 163–169.

25. God's actualizing preexisting *possibilia* is Plantinga's way of describing the divine creative power. I prefer to describe it in terms of God increasing the determinacy of an indeterminate actual world. Some might object to the (moderate) modal realism implicit in either of these descriptions. Presumably they can be paraphrased so as to avoid ontological commitment to *possibilia*.

26. Either a small finite number of comparatively small discontinuities occur and this is compatible with the persistence of the same objects or there is a continuous process but its infinitely many stages are not real stages of which the process is the sum but rather Whiteheadian extensive abstractions from the process.

27. Here I agree with both Morris and Swinburne in assuming that it is metaphysically impossible for Jesus, being divine, to choose the bad. Nonetheless, I hold that he had the ordinary human power to do so. But even if he did not he would still have had the power to choose the lesser good.

28. I would like to express my gratitude to the anonymous referees for *Religious Studies* for their most helpful comments.

CHAPTER 9

AQUINAS' METAPHYSICS OF THE INCARNATION

Eleonore Stump

Introduction

Aquinas' interpretation of the metaphysics of the incarnation is an attempt to make sense out of a theological doctrine bequeathed to him as a traditional and central part of Christian belief. In this chapter, I want to explicate his interpretation of the doctrine and go some way towards defending it. It is *not* my intent to argue that the formulation of the doctrine he accepts as traditional is the only orthodox one, or that his interpretation of that formulation is the only appropriate interpretation of the doctrine, or that his interpretation is the best way to understand biblical statements about the nature of Christ. It is also *not* part of my purpose to show that Aquinas' interpretation is completely intelligible and coherent or philosophically defensible in every respect. Rather, my aim in this chapter is a limited one: to explicate Aquinas' interpretation of the doctrine of the incarnation in terms of his metaphysics in such a way as to clarify and support both his understanding of the doctrine and his metaphysics.

The formulation of the doctrine of the incarnation which Aquinas accepts and takes as binding on Christians is the one put forward at Chalcedon in AD 451: Christ is one hypostasis, one person, with two natures, one fully human and the other fully divine. Stating the Chalcedonian formulation is one thing; explaining what it means is another. Aquinas relies heavily on his general metaphysical theory to provide one interpretation of the Chalcedonian formulation. His interpretation is so thoroughly rooted in his general metaphysics that it is not possible to grasp this part of his philosophical theology without some understanding of his metaphysics.[1] On the other hand, the doctrine of the incarnation stretches that metaphysics almost to breaking-point. Consequently, in the course of considering the incarnation, Aquinas is compelled to explain his metaphysics with some care, in order to argue that, contrary to appearances, the doctrine of the incarnation does not serve as a counter-example to any of his general metaphysical claims. Some of his most helpful explanations of various parts of his metaphysics can thus be found in his discussions of the incarnation.

I shall begin by laying out just the parts of Aquinas' metaphysics which in my view are particularly important with regard to the doctrine of the incarnation. After that, I shall turn to Aquinas' interpretation of the doctrine of the incarnation itself. I shall be concerned primarily with the way in which Aquinas understands the Chalcedonian formula, the resources his interpretation of the formula has for handling familiar objections to the doctrine of the incarnation, and the view of the mind of Christ to which his interpretation is committed.

Matter and form

Aquinas thinks that a macro-level material thing is matter organized or configured in some way, where the organization or configuration is dynamic rather than static. That is, the organization of the matter comprises causal relations among the material components of the thing as well as such static features as shape and spatial location.[2] This dynamic configuration or organization is what Aquinas calls 'form'.[3] Furthermore, a thing has the properties it has, including its causal powers, in virtue of having the configuration it does; the proper operations and functions of a thing derive from its form.[4]

Prime matter is matter without any form at all, 'materiality' (as it were) apart from configuration. When it is a component in a matter-form composite, prime matter is the component of the configured composite which makes it the case that the configured thing can be extended in three dimensions and can occupy a particular place at a particular time. Prime matter does not by itself occupy a place or extend through dimensions; it needs to be configured by forms in order to do so. But prime matter is the component of the configured whole which allows the configured whole to be spatially extended; form alone cannot be spatially extended.[5]

Aquinas takes it that the forms of material objects can be divided into two sorts, substantial forms (that is, the substantial forms of things that are primary substances) and accidental forms. For present purposes we can understand his distinction between substantial and accidental forms in this way. A substantial form of a material thing configures prime matter.[6] For this reason, configuration by a substantial form brings it about that a thing which was not already in existence comes into existence. Since any thing that comes into existence exists as a member of a kind, the substantial form of a thing is thus also responsible for a thing's belonging to a particular primary kind or lowest species.[7] The change produced by the advent of a substantial form is consequently a generation of a thing.[8]

From Aquinas' claim that a substantial form configures prime matter, it follows that no part of a substance counts as a substance in its own right as long as it is a component of a larger whole that is a substance.[9] Otherwise, the substantial form of the whole would configure parts which have their own substantial form, and so the form of the whole would configure matter-form composites, rather than prime matter. Consequently, the substantial form, which a part of a whole would have if it existed on its own, is absent when it becomes part of a composite substance and is replaced instead by the one substantial form of the composite.[10] Or, to put the same point the other way around, if we divide a composite substance into its parts, we may turn what was one substance into several substances.[11]

So a substance comes into existence when prime matter is configured by a substantial form. If its constituents existed as things before being woven together by that configuration, they cease to exist as things in their own right when they are conjoined into the whole, and a new thing is generated.

Individuation and identity for material substances

Aquinas thinks that a substance is always individuated by its substantial form, which is unique to it.[12] A thing is *this* thing just in virtue of the fact that the form which conjoins the parts of it into one whole is *this* form. So, for example, a substance such as Socrates is this human being in virtue of having *this* substantial form of a human being; what is necessary and sufficient for something to be identical to Socrates is that its substantial form be identical to the substantial form of Socrates.[13]

But what makes something *this* substantial form rather than some other? For any species of material thing, there are many individuals within a species, and the species-conferring configuration, the substantial form, of each member of the species will therefore be the same. Aquinas designates the collection of the species-conferring properties a thing has in virtue of having a substantial form of a certain sort with the Latin term translated 'nature'. The nature of a thing is what is signified by the species name of the thing, and a thing's nature is given by its substantial form.[14] The human nature of Socrates is the same as the human nature of Plato insofar as they are both human beings, and so the species-conferring configuration of Plato is the same as the species-conferring configuration of Socrates. How, then, are the substantial forms of material objects such as human beings individuated?

Aquinas' response to this worry is expressed succinctly in his well-known line that matter individuates.[15] When Aquinas attempts to explain the concept of matter relevant to individuation, he tends to speak of it as signate matter[16] or as matter under indeterminate dimensions,[17] that is, matter which is extended in three dimensions but where the degree of extension in any dimension is left open or vague rather than being specified. Now any actually existing matter has determinate dimensions. But the particular degree of extension in a dimension is one thing; the materiality, as it were, of matter is another thing. The determinate dimensions of a material thing have to do with exactly what space that thing occupies at a given time; the materiality of the matter is responsible for the space-occupying feature itself. That is, matter is the sort of thing which is *here* now,[18] in a way that numbers, for example, are not. This feature of matter, however, can be considered without specifying the precise spatial locations that the matter occupies. When Aquinas talks of matter under indeterminate dimensions, it seems to me that he is attempting to call attention to this feature of matter.

No doubt, one could wish for a great deal more clarity and precision with regard to the notion of matter Aquinas has in mind when he claims that matter individuates. But perhaps this is enough to point us in the right direction for making sense of his concept of substantial forms that are individual rather than universal. For Aquinas, what individuates Socrates is *this* substantial form of a human being; and a substantial form of a material substance such as a human being is *this* substantial form in virtue of the fact that it configures *this* matter.

Constitution and identity

It is important to see that on Aquinas' views of matter and form constitution is not identity,[19] and a whole is something more than the sum of its parts. One might wonder whether Aquinas is entitled to this claim if, as I claimed above, he takes the form of the whole to include the properties of the parts, as well as the causal relations among those parts. What else could there be to the configuration of the whole? Some confusion arises in considering this question because we can understand the properties of the parts in more than one way. In particular, when we include under the properties of the parts the relations and causal interactions among those parts, we can be thinking of these properties either as (i) the properties the parts have when they are taken *singillatim* (as e.g. the properties including causal powers which the constituent atoms of a molecule have considered on their own, when they are not configured together into the molecule), or as (ii) the properties the parts in fact have when they are in the whole (as e.g. the properties the atoms of a molecule have when they are configured into the molecule). If we understand the properties of the parts in sense (i), it is true to say, as biochemists do, that the features of a whole protein (such as its folded shape) cannot always be derived from even perfect knowledge of the properties (including the causal powers) of the atoms which are constituents of the protein. This is so because a large protein achieves its biologically active form, including its folded shape, only with the help of certain enzymes acting on it; and so the properties of the whole are a function of something more than the properties of the parts taken *singillatim*. But if we understand the properties of the parts in sense (ii), then in effect we are smuggling the configuration, or the form of the whole, into the properties of the parts of the whole. In sense (ii), it would be very surprising if there were properties of the whole that were not a function of the properties of the parts of the whole. Nonetheless, in sense (ii), the properties of the whole are a function of the properties of the parts *in the configuration of the whole*. Consequently, in either sense (i) or sense (ii), the parts alone are not all there is to the whole; the configuration of the whole is also required. A whole is thus not identical to its constituents alone.

The general designation Aquinas uses for a thing which has a particular substantial form is the Latin 'supposit'[20] or the Greek term transliterated into Latin as '*hypostasis*'.[21] A supposit is a particular or individual just in the category of substance.[22] The Latin term translated 'person' is Aquinas' technical term for an individual substance of a rational nature.[23] For Aquinas, although the existence of *this* substantial form is necessary and sufficient for the existence of a supposit, a supposit is not identical with its substantial form alone. The substantial form is only a constituent of the supposit.[24]

To begin with, any thing which has a substantial form necessarily also has accidents, even though it is not necessary that it have one accident rather than another. So a substantial form is not the only metaphysical constituent of a thing; any thing will also have accidents as metaphysical constituents. In addition, for material things, the matter which the substantial form configures is also a constituent of a supposit.[25] So a supposit has more metaphysical constituents than just the substantial form. If, however, a supposit were identical to its substantial form alone, then these other metaphysical constitutents would not be constitutents of the supposit itself.

If constitution is not identity, then we need to consider the relation of the composite whole to its parts. The constitution relation lets us make a distinction among the properties appropriately predicated of the composite whole. The whole can have a property either in its own right or else in virtue of the fact that one of its constituents has that property in its own right.[26] Consider, for example, the molecule CAT/Enhancer-Binding Protein (C/EBP), which is important in regulating DNA transcription, is a dimer, each of whose subunits is a protein which is coiled with an alpha helix coil.[27] The molecule thus has the property of being coiled in the alpha helix manner, but it has that property in virtue of the fact that it has two parts which are coiled in that way. Each of these parts of the molecule, however, is coiled in the alpha helix manner in its own right. On the other hand, the whole molecule has the property of regulating DNA transcription, and this property it has in its own right, in consequence of the shape of the molecule as a whole, which allows it to fit into one of the grooves of DNA.

Adopting a term from Lynne Rudder Baker,[28] we can say that the whole molecule 'borrows' some of its properties from its constituents, and it has these properties only in virtue of the fact that the constituents have them in their own right. Baker emphasizes the fact that a property borrowed from a part is nonetheless genuinely to be attributed to the whole. She says,

> Borrowing walks a fine line. On the one hand, if x borrows H from y, then x really has H – piggyback, so to speak. . . . if I cut my hand, then I really bleed . . . I borrow the property of bleeding from my body, but I really bleed. But the fact that I am bleeding is none other than the fact that I am constituted by a body that is bleeding. So, not only does x really have H by borrowing it, but also – and this is the other hand – if x borrows H from y, there are not two independent instances of H: if x borrows H, then x's having H is entirely a matter of x's having constitution relations to something that has H non-derivatively.[29]

Although Aquinas does not draw this distinction among properties explicitly, his metaphysical views about constitution provide for it, and he relies on it in one place after another. So, for example, he argues that whatever follows naturally on the accidents or the parts of a supposit is predicated of the whole supposit on account of the accident or part in question. A man is thus said to be curly on account of his hair or seeing on account of the function of the eye, on Aquinas' view.[30] Similarly, in discussing the powers of the soul, the substantial form of a human being, Aquinas says: 'We *can* say that the soul understands in the same way that we can say that the eye sees; but it would be more appropriate to say that *a human being* understands *by means of* the soul'[31] (emphasis added). Here a property (understanding) of a metaphysical part, the soul, and a property (seeing) of an integral part, the eye, are transferred to the whole, the person, which in effect borrows these properties from its parts.

Incarnation: the doctrinal claims

With this much work on Aquinas' metaphysics, we are now in a position to turn to his interpretation of the Chalcedonian formulation of the doctrine of the incarnation. The Chalcedonian formula says that Christ is one person with two natures. On Aquinas' understanding of the doctrine, the one person of Christ[32] is the second person of the triune God.

There is some ambiguity in the notion of person in the case of Christ, as Aquinas himself recognizes.[33] Because Christ is one and just one person, and a person is a substance of a particular sort, there is just substance in Christ. That substance is composite. It includes a human soul and body and the divine nature. So Christ is one composite person. On the other hand, the second person of the Trinity, who is identical with his divine nature, is a constituent of the composite Christ. So in the case of Christ 'person' can refer either to the substance which Christ is, or to the second person of the Trinity in his incarnate state. I shall use the expression 'the person of Christ' to refer to the incarnate second person of the Trinity; to refer to the composite person which the incarnate Christ is, I shall use the expression 'the person Christ'. Nonetheless, it does not follow that there are two persons or two substances in Christ. The human nature, body and soul, are assumed by the second person of the Trinity and united to him in a union of person. Consequently, the new composite is the same person as before the incarnation. For some discussion of the metaphysical difficulties of this claim, see the discussion below regarding the notion of a union in person in the incarnation. Finally, it is worth noticing here that this ambiguity does not mean that the term 'person' is equivocal. In either of its ambiguous uses as regards Christ, it means *an individual substance of a rational nature*. The divine nature includes the cognition of reasons, and the deity is one thing; so the Boethian definition of person fits the persons of the Trinity, too, as long as we are careful not to define the terms in that definition in such a way as to make them incapable of applying to what is simple. When the second person of the Trinity assumes a human nature, it does so in a union of person, so that the resulting composite is still only one supposit. Since this supposit is an individual substance and one which is rational, the composite incarnate Christ is still an individual substance of a rational nature.

All that is true of deity is true of the person of Christ. He is outside time; his knowledge, power, and goodness are not limited, and so on. In short, because the person of Christ is the second person of the Trinity, divine nature is the nature of that person.[34]

At a certain moment in time, the second person of the Trinity assumed a human nature. That is to say, the second person added to himself another nature, in addition to the divine nature already his own.[35] As I said above, for Aquinas, the nature of a material substance is conferred by a substantial form which is an individual; and a substantial form is an individual in virtue of configuring matter. So when the second person of the Trinity assumes human nature, he assumes a particular substantial form and the matter it configures.[36]

Like every other human substantial form, the substantial form assumed by Christ configures matter into a human body and confers those properties essential to human beings, including rationality. In virtue of having two natures, Christ therefore has two operations.[37] In his divine nature, he has the operation proper to the deity. In his human nature, Christ has a complete and fully human mind, and he also has a rational appetite, that is to say, a complete and fully human will. Since intellect and will also characterize the divine nature, in virtue of having two natures Christ also has two intellects[38] and two wills,[39] one human and one divine.[40]

Furthermore, different things can be true of these intellects and these wills. The human intellect can fail to know something that the divine intellect knows.[41] It is impossible that Christ sin, in either his divine or his human will.[42] But it is possible for the human will to be out of accord with the divine will, at least as regards desire, without sin. Consequently, Christ's human will can desire what the divine will rules out.[43] When the human will of Christ desires not to die, there is a non-sinful discord of this sort between the divine and the human wills.[44]

For these reasons, the multiplicity of the natures is preserved on Aquinas' interpretation. However the unity of Christ is to be explained, it is not a unity of nature.

Now for a subsisting thing to have a complete human nature is just for it to have a human soul and body and thus to be a human substance. But to be an individual human substance is to be a human person. Consequently, it seems as if there must be a human person as well as a divine person in Christ. Aquinas' response to this sort of worry is to grant that in general a human soul configuring a human body composes a human body but that in the special case of Christ there is a human soul and body but not a human person. Because the substantial form and the matter it configures are part of a larger composite, which includes the second person of the Trinity and the divine nature, in this one case, the substantial form of a human being and the matter it configures do not constitute a human person. If they existed on their own, outside the composite which is the incarnate Christ, the human soul and body of Christ would certainly constitute a human person. But conjoined in Christ, they do not, in virtue of being subsumed into the larger whole.[45] There is therefore just one person in Christ, and that person is divine.

The two natures of Christ are united into one thing in this one person, so that the unity of the incarnate Christ is a unity in person. (Since the person is a supposit or a hypostasis, this unity is sometimes also referred to as 'a hypostatic union'.)

There are perhaps three main questions to ask of this, as of any other, interpretation of the Chalcedonian formula of the doctrine of the incarnation.

First, does the interpretation succeed in preserving the Chalcedonian formula, or does it instead alter the doctrine, overtly or by implication, in the process of interpreting it? An interpretation of the doctrine which explicitly or covertly multiplied the persons or conflated the natures of Christ into one, for example, would be an interpretation which was not successful in preserving the Chalcedonian formula.

Second, does the interpretation give us a logically coherent position? An interpretation which in effect predicates contradictory attributes of one and the same thing would not be a logically coherent position. Does the interpretation have the resources to show that in predicating the attributes of divinity and humanity of one and the same thing, it is not simply making inconsistent claims?

Finally, we ordinarily think of a person as an entity with a mind and a will. Even in the bizarre human cases we know of in which there seem to be multiple personalities in one organism; one personality at a time is present in a body, so that there is one will and one mind operative at a time. There are those rare cases of dicephalic twins where one physically indissoluble biological organism is governed by two minds and two wills, but just for that reason most of us suppose that such an organism is governed by *two* persons, not one. Apart from worries about the logical coherence of the doctrine of the incarnation, is there any way to explain the claim that there is one person with two minds and two wills which makes psychological sense? What would it be for one person to be split in this way and yet constitute one person? Or, to put the same point another way, how could two minds constitute one person without thereby collapsing into one mind? If one mind knows the date of the Last Judgement and the other mind does not, what are we to say about the mental or cognitive state of the one person?

If Aquinas' interpretation does not have the resources to answer this third question, it will in effect have multiplied the persons in Christ. If, as things are in this world, two minds cannot comprise one person even if both minds are in one organism, then however much Aquinas may insist on the Chalcedonian orthodoxy of his interpretation, his interpretation will deviate from the Chalcedonian formula in virtue of holding that there are two minds in the incarnate Christ. On the other hand, unless there is some way of making sense of the claim that one thing can have contradictory human and divine attributes, Aquinas' interpretation will not be successful in modelling the Chalcedonian distinction of the natures of Christ. If his attempt to keep the doctrine of the incarnation from logical incoherence by segregating the apparently incompatible attributes into distinct natures is nothing but a complicated way of predicating incompatible properties of the same thing, then on his interpretation there will in effect be just one complicated nature of Christ, a conjunctive nature having incompatible divine and human properties.[46] In effect, then, Aquinas' interpretation will have conflated the natures.[47]

For these reasons, the question whether Aquinas' interpretation of the doctrine is faithful to the Chalcedonian formulation is best answered by considering whether or not Aquinas' interpretation has the resources to deal successfully with the second and third questions.

Logical incoherence

There is certainly a *prima facie* case to be made for the objection that the doctrine of the incarnation attributes contradictory properties to one and the same thing. On the doctrine of the incarnation, one and the same thing is said to be limited in power and not limited in power, for example. Being limited in power and not being limited in power are contradictory properties, and both properties are attributed to Christ. So, on the face of it, it seems as if the objection is right.

One traditional way, employed also by Aquinas, of defending the Chalcedonian formula against this objection is by means of reduplicative propositions.[48] According to the reduplicative strategy, the fact that both limited and unlimited power are attributed to Christ does not show the Chalcedonian formula of the incarnation to be incoherent, because omnipotence is predicated of Christ in his divine nature and lack of omnipotence is predicated of him in his human nature.[49] Christ *qua* God is omnipotent; *qua* human, he is not. Consequently, on the reduplicative strategy, the attributes that are incompatible with each other are also segregated from each other in the incarnate Christ in virtue of inhering in different natures of his.

The reduplicative strategy is not much in favour in contemporary philosophical theology. One apparently plausible criticism of it runs along these lines. For any reduplicative proposition of the form 'x as A is N and x as B is not N', if 'the reduplication predicates being A of x and predicates being B of x' and if 'being N is entailed by being A, and not being N is entailed by being B',[50] then the reduplicative proposition is nothing more than a complicated way of predicating contradictory attributes of its subject, X.[51]

Aquinas' metaphysics, and especially his attitude towards constitution, give a response to this sort of objection to the reduplication strategy, however.[52] On Aquinas' view, there is a distinction between a property a whole has in its own right and a property it has in virtue of having a constituent that has that property in its own right; as I explained above, a whole can borrow a property from one of its constituents.

This distinction gives us one helpful way to analyse *qua* locutions of the form *x qua A is N*. In such a locution, the property of being N is predicated of *x,* but it is predicated of *x* just in virtue of the fact that *x* has a constituent *C* which has the property of being *N* in its own right. So, for example, '*C*/EBP *qua* dimer with coiled subunits has the property of being coiled in the alpha helix manner' predicates a property of the whole molecule which it borrows from a part. *C*/EBP has a constituent *C* – in this case, a coiled subunit of the dimer – which has in its own right the property *being coiled in the alpha helix manner. Being coiled in the alpha helix manner* is thus predicated of *C*/EBP in virtue of the fact that the molecule's dimer subunit is coiled in that way. On the other hand, *C*/EBP is a conglomerate of two such dimer subunits which bend away from each other in a limp Y-shape at one end of the molecule. So this is also true: '*C*/EBP *qua* Y-shaped is not coiled in the alpha helix manner.' Here again a borrowed property is being attributed to the whole. *C*/EBP has a constituent *C* – in this case, the Y-shaped end of the molecule – which has in its own right the property *not being coiled in the alpha helix manner.*

Someone might suppose that when in a *qua* locution we attribute to the molecule *C*/EBP the property *being coiled,* we are in effect just attributing to it the property *having a coiled part,* and when we attribute to it the property *not being coiled,* we are just attributing to it the property *having a part that is not coiled.* Clearly, there is no incoherence here, but that is because these are not incompatible properties. But, then, on this way of analysing the relations of part to whole, the properties which really are incompatible – *being coiled* and *not being coiled* – are not attributes of the molecule; they are attributes only of its parts.

But this line of argument cannot be right. A thing which has a coiled part really is itself coiled in some respect or to some degree. Similarly, in virtue of having a part that is Y-shaped, the whole itself is really not coiled in that respect or to that degree. If a student, seeing a diagram of the molecule for the first time, were to try to describe it to someone unfamiliar with its shape, she might well say, 'Well, it's a sort of complicated coiled, Y-shaped molecule.' So the incompatible properties *being coiled* and *not being coiled* are attributes of the whole molecule, not just of different parts of the molecule. But because these are borrowed properties, since the molecule does not have these properties in its own right, there is no incoherence in the claims that the molecule is both coiled and not coiled.

As long as *qua* locutions are understood in this way, it is clear that both *qua* locutions – '*x* as A is N' and '*x* as B is not N' – can be true without any violation of the laws of logic. The two *qua* claims taken together do not have the result that we are making inconsistent claims or that we are giving a logically incoherent account of x. Although contradictory attributes are being predicated of the same subject, they are not being predicated in the same respect. C/EBP is coiled in virtue of having a constituent which is coiled in the alpha helix manner, and it is not coiled in virtue of having a constituent which is Y-shaped.

Someone might suppose that we should simply reidentify the characteristics which are being attributed to the whole. Someone might hold, that is, that C/EBP has the properties *being coiled with respect to its alpha helix constituents* and not *being coiled with respect to its Y-shaped constituent*. On this way of understanding the characteristics in question, it is easier to see that the simultaneous predication of these attributes does not violate any laws of logic, and this feature of this way of specifying C/EBP's characteristics is no doubt an advantage. On the other hand, this formulation may make it seem as if the characteristics in question are in fact just characteristics of the constituents of the molecule and not characteristics of the whole molecule; and that is a significant disadvantage of this formulation. Some theological claims central to Christianity require attributing to the whole composite that is Christ properties had in their own right only by a constituent of the composite. So, for example, a central Christian claim is that Christ died on the cross. Here the property of dying on the cross is attributed to the whole. It is, however, not possible that immutable, eternal deity die. Human beings can die; God cannot. Therefore, it is true that Christ dies only in the case that a property had in its own right by a constituent of Christ, the human body and soul, is also properly attributed to the whole. For this reason, as well as for the metaphysical reasons given earlier, it seems to me better to say that a whole borrows properties of its parts, so that the whole can be said to be coiled, for example, in virtue of having a part that is coiled.[53]

Analogously, some of the properties attributed to Christ are properties borrowed from his constituent natures. So, for example, Christ is limited in power and not limited in power, but he borrows the first attribute from his human nature and the second from his divine nature. So he has the property of being limited in power just by virtue of having a constituent, namely, human nature, which has the property of being limited in power in its own right; he has the property of not being limited in power just in virtue of having a different constituent, divine nature, which has the property in its own right. Because the incompatible properties are borrowed properties, Christ does not have them in the same respect. And so it is no more incoherent to attribute both properties to Christ than it is to attribute being coiled and not being coiled to C/EBP.

In correspondence, Brian Leftow has suggested that some of Christ's divine properties, such as the property of being omnipotent, should be considered properties had in their own right by the whole Christ; on this view, a property such as being omnipotent is not a borrowed property for Christ. Leftow argues that a being having both a fast and a slow body would have the property *being fast* in its own right, because 'one is fast if one can run fast on some occasions (e.g. when using the right body)'. Analogous reasoning suggests that *being omnipotent* is a property the whole has in its own right also. My purpose in this chapter is only to show the way in which Aquinas' metaphysics supports the reduplicative strategy, and so it does not matter for my purposes exactly which properties of Christ's are borrowed and which are had by the whole Christ in their own right. But I am inclined to think that whether or not a property such as *being fast* is equivalent to a property had by a whole in its own right or to a borrowed property depends on the reasons for the ability in question. C/EBP has the property *able to reconfigure DNA on some occasions* in virtue of the shape of the molecule as a whole, and so the property in question is appropriately considered a property the whole has in its own right. But it has the property *being able to uncoil* only in virtue of the fact that it has a coiled part, and so this property is borrowed from a part. Because running fast for normal human beings requires a co-ordination of the whole body, from brain to toes, the property *being* fast does seem to be a property had in their own right by whole human beings. But in the case of Christ, who is a composite of one person and two natures, the property of being unlimited in power is a property had by the whole only in virtue of the fact that one constituent of the whole has this property. Furthermore, if all the constituents of Christ other than the divine nature were removed, what remained would still be omnipotent. By contrast, it is not the case that we could remove all but one constituent of a human body and still have a fast human being. For these reasons, it seems to me that *being fast* is disanalogous to *being omnipotent*, so that *being omnipotent* is a borrowed property of Christ's.

Someone who rejects the reduplicative strategy might repudiate this attempt to resuscitate it in connection with the Chalcedonian formula, on the grounds that the case of the C/EBP molecule and the case of the incarnate Christ are not suitably analogous. The molecule has integral or physical parts – the dimer subunit, the Y-shaped end of the molecule – which have certain properties, and we attribute those properties to the whole molecule only because the molecule has these integral parts. But in the case of Christ, the natures are not integral parts: insofar as they are any sort of part at all, they are metaphysical parts. Metaphysical parts aren't physically segregated bits of the whole, and so it seems that a whole cannot borrow properties from them. Consequently, it appears that the original objection to the reduplicative strategy still stands. The reduplicative strategy can be defended against that objection by the notion of borrowed properties only in the case the properties are borrowed from physical constituents of the whole.

This conclusion, however, and the line of thought that supports it seem to me mistaken. It is true that the case of Christ differs from the case of the molecule insofar as the parts in question in the case of Christ are not integral or physical parts. But it is false that a whole borrows properties from its parts only in the case the parts are physical parts. Consider, for example, Mark Twain's *Letters to the Earth*. This work is a passionate indictment of Christianity based largely on a dark and hard-hitting review of the suffering in the world and what Twain takes to be the insipid nature of Christian attempts to explain it away. As such, *Letters to the Earth* is a serious complaint against Christianity, and Twain meant it to be. On the other hand, the attack is carried out by means of Twain's characteristic biting humour. As such, *Letters to the Earth* is comic. So the work *qua* attack on Christianity is serious (and therefore not funny): *qua* work of satire, on the other hand, it is very funny. In fact, one might argue that a satire is a work which uses various forms of humour as a means to a sober end. Jokes and sarcasm are parts of the whole which are woven together by the configuring serious purpose. The comic bits and the overriding purpose are therefore some sort of constituents of the whole, but certainly not integral or physical constituents. Nonetheless, it is clear that the whole can borrow properties from these constituents, just as the molecule can borrow properties from its integral constituents. That is why Twain's work taken as a whole is correctly characterized both as a hilarious piece of satire and as a deadly earnest attack on religion. Because the properties of the whole are borrowed from the constituents in this way, there is no more incoherence in saying of the work that it is funny and not funny than there is in saying that C/EBP is coiled and not coiled. The work is funny in one respect and not funny in another, just as C/EBP is coiled in one part and not coiled in another.

So a whole can borrow properties from its constituents even if those constituents are not integral or physical parts of the whole. Consequently, there is no reason for denying that Christ can have properties borrowed from either his human nature or his divine nature, even if the natures are not integral parts of Christ and the properties are contradictories. Because each of the incompatible properties is had in its own right by a different constituent of the whole and because they attach to the whole only derivatively, in consequence of the fact that the whole has these constituents, there is no incoherence in attributing both otherwise incompatible properties to the whole.

Therefore, the objection to the reduplicative strategy fails. The objection would succeed if the attributes in question were attributes of the whole not borrowed from the parts. In that case, incompatible properties would be predicated of the same thing in the same respect, and that would be incoherent. But the point of the reduplicative strategy is to segregate the incompatible properties into different constituents of the whole and to attribute them to the whole derivatively, and Aquinas' metaphysics of composite things supports this use of the reduplicative strategy. Aquinas' metaphysics therefore provides a way to support his interpretation of the Chalcedonian formula against the charge of incoherence.

Conclusion: one person and two natures

The preceding considerations make clear, I think, that Aquinas' interpretation of the doctrine of the incarnation succeeds in remaining faithful to the Chalcedonian formula it wants to explain. Aquinas' metaphysics includes an understanding of constitution which supports the reduplicative strategy. It thus has the resources to ward off the charge that the doctrine of the incarnation is logically incoherent. Furthermore, it does so in virtue of keeping the natures separate, so that the distinct properties of the two natures are separated from each other and not joined together into one super-nature. In addition, the reduplicative strategy can be shown to work even for properties involving intellect and will, such as the properties of knowing and not knowing something. So Aquinas' interpretation stays true to the Chalcedonian formula at least in this respect: Christ is *one* person, and there are *two* natures in Christ.

I conclude therefore that Aquinas' interpretation of the doctrine of the incarnation, as it is explained and supported by his metaphysics, is a philosophically sophisticated, rich and powerful account which is faithful to the Chalcedonian formula and successful in defending it against some of the formidable objections commonly levelled against it.[54]

Notes

1. So e.g. I disagree with much of Richard Cross's otherwise excellent analysis of Aquinas' account of the incarnation because I understand the underlying metaphysics differently from the way in which he does; see R. Cross, 'Aquinas on Nature, Hypostasis, and the Metaphysics of the Incarnation', *Thomist,* 60 (1996), 171–202.
2. That is why Aquinas thinks that at the instant of death the form of a human being is replaced by a different form, even if the general shape and appearance of the body remain the same. Once a human being dies and the soul is

gone, he says, we use such words as 'flesh' or 'eye' equivocally if we apply them to the corpse (*Quaestiones disputatae de anima*, 9 corpus). At death, the matter of the body is configured in a substantially different way and so has a form different from the one it had before death. See e.g. *In De anima.* 2. 1. 1. 226; see also *Sententia super Metaphysicam*, 7. 1. 11 (1519). For a helpful discussion of the relation of a thing's form to its nature, see also *ST* 3a. 2. 1 and *SCG* 4. 35 (3728–29).

3. For a very helpful attempt to explicate a notion at least closely related to the Aristotelian concept of form which is at issue in this part of Aquinas' metaphysics, see K. Fine, 'Things and their Parts', *Midwest Studies in Philosophy*, 23 (1999), 61–74. Fine does an admirable job of discussing this notion in the context of contemporary mereology and showing that the Aristotelian notion can do what cannot be done equally well with mereological schemes. He also makes a very helpful distinction between what he calls 'temporary' and 'timeless' parts. This distinction has some resemblance to the distinction I make later in the chapter between integral and metaphysical parts (though perhaps Fine himself might think the resemblance attenuated).

4. See e.g. *SCG* 4. 36 (3740).

5. Cf. *De principiis naturae*, 1–2.

6. For the claims about what substantial and accidental forms configure, see e.g. *De principiis naturae*, 1.

7. For the claims about what the forms bring into existence, see e.g. *De principiis naturae*, 1; see also *ST* 3a. 2. 6 objs. 2–3, the replies to the objections, and *ST* 3a 3. 7 ad 1.

8. See e.g. *SCG* 4. 48 (3834).

9. Cf. *ST* 3a. 2. 1, *Compendium theologiae*, 210 (406) and 212 (418), and *SCG* 4. 35 (3733).

10. See e.g. *Compendium theologiae*, 210 (406), where Aquinas explains this general point in connection with the composition of the incarnate Christ, and *SCG* 4. 49.

11. See e.g, *Compendium theologiae*, 212 (418).

12. I discuss below Aquinas' claim that in the special case of material objects substantial forms are individuated by matter, so that matter is the ultimate individuator for material objects.

13. *Expositio super librum Boethii De trinitate*, 4. 2; see also *ST* 1a. 119. 1 and *Quaestiones disputatae de potentia*, 9, 1.

14. See e.g. *De unions verbi incarnati*, 1; see also ibid. 2 ad 6 where Aquinas explains that the name of a species signifies a nature.

15. See *De ente et essentia*, 2. Perhaps the most detailed exposition of this view of his is in his *Expositio super librum Boethii De trinitate*, 4. 2; see also *ST* 3a. 3. 7 ad 1 and *SCG* 4. 30 (3780–1).

16. *De ente et essentia*, 2.

17. *Expositio super librum Boethii De trinitate*, 4. 2. Aquinas does not always describe his position on this score in the same way; e.g. in *De ente et essentia*, 2 he explains signate matter as matter under determinate dimensions. The variation in terminology suggests to some scholars either a development in

his thought or a series of changes of mind. The issue is complicated, and so I am leaving it to one side here. Cf. *Sententia super Metaphysicam,* 7. 1. 2 (1283) for a helpful discussion of matter and its dimensions.

18. Cf. *Expositio super librum Boethii De trinitate,* 4. 2.

19. See, e.g. *Sententia super Metaphysicam,* 7. 1. 17 (1672–74). There Aquinas says that in cases in which the composite is one thing, the composite is not identical with its components; rather the composite is something over and above its components. See also *De unione verbi incarnati,* 1. For interesting contemporary arguments against the reduction of wholes to their parts, see M. Johnston, 'Constitution is not Identity', *Mind,* 101 (1992). 89–105, and L. Rudder Baker, 'Why Constitution is not Identity', *Journal of Philosophy,* 94 (1997). 599–621. For an excellent discussion of the constitution relation, see L: Rudder Baker, 'Unity Without Identity: A New Look at Material Constitution'. *Midwest Studies in Philosophy,* 23 (1999), 144–165.

20. In the case of the incarnate Christ, the thing which has a human substantial form is the whole composite, and not just the human nature. Or, to put the same point another way, the substantial form of a human being which is part of the human nature of Christ is *had* not by the nature of which it is one constituent but by the whole composed of all the constituents of Christ.

21. See e.g. *Compendium theologiae* 1. 210 (405–6) and *SCG* 4. 49, (3846). The terms 'supposit' and 'hypostasis' are not synonymous for Aquinas, strictly speaking, because although they pick out the same thing in reality (for this point see e.g. *SCG* 4. 38 (3766)), they pick out under slightly different designations, because 'suppositum' is a term of second intention and 'hypostasis' is a term of first intention. For the distinction, see. *De unione verbi incarnati.* 2. This complexity of medieval logic is one I will ignore here for the sake of brevity.

22. Aquinas gives a helpful explanation of his use of these terms in *De unione verbi incarnati,* 2: see also *Quaestiones quodlibetales,* 5. 2. 1. Strictly speaking, because God is simple, God does not belong in any of the Aristotelian categories. Consequently, strictly speaking, God is not a substance, and the person of Christ is not a supposit in virtue of being the second person of the Trinity. On the doctrine of divine simplicity, however, it is not possible to give an appropriate formulation which is in accordance with the doctrine, and Aquinas himself is willing to use the relevant terms broadly, rather than strictly, in the case of Christ. I follow his lead here.

23. *ST* 3a. 2. 2.

24. Eric Olson argues that a human person is identical to a living organism but that the persistence of only a small, living biological part of the organism (a part of the brain, namely, the brainstem) is necessary and sufficient for the existence of that organism: see E. Olson, *The Human Animal* (Oxford: Oxford University Press, 1997). That is, although a human being is not identical to a living brainstem, what a human being is identical to – a living biological organism – is such that it can exist when it is composed only of a brainstem. Aquinas' views are similar. A human being is not identical to a soul. But what a human being is identical to – a particular in the species

mortal rational animal – is something that in certain circumstances can exist when it is composed of nothing more than a soul. And so Aquinas' position can be thought of as the metaphysical analogue of Olson's: the persistence of a small, living metaphysical part of the whole human supposit is necessary and sufficient for the existence of that human being. It doesn't follow that a human being is identical to his soul any more than it follows from Olson's view that a human being is identical with a part of his brain. For Aquinas, a soul is not identical to a human being; but a human being – a mortal rational animal – is such that, although it is naturally embodied, it is also capable of persisting for a time in an unnatural disembodied condition. In the same way, a living biological organism which is a human being is naturally and ordinarily composed of more than just a part of the brain; but, if Olson is right, it is also capable of persisting for a time in an unnatural, severely reduced condition. I am grateful to Scott MacDonald, whose persistent questions on this score helped me to see this point.

25. See e.g. *SCG* 4. 40 and *De unions verbi incarnati*, I where Aquinas says that a suppositum will not be the same as a nature in anything in which there is either accident or individual matter, because in that case the suppositum is related to the nature by means of an addition. See also *SCG* 4. 40 (3781) where Aquinas explains the distinction between a singular and its quiddity or nature, and goes on to explain that a supposit such as Socrates is not identical to his substantial form because he is also constituted of designated matter.

26. Baker speaks in this connection of something's having a property independently, rather than in its own right, and she gives a helpful analysis of what it is for anything to have a property independently. See Baker, 'Unity Without Identity', 151–60.

27. A helpful discussion of this molecule and its properties can be found in S. L. McKnight, 'Molecular Zippers in Gene Regulation', *Scientific American*, 264 (1991), 54–64.

28. See Baker, 'Unity Without Identity', 151–60.

29. Ibid.

30. *SCG* 4. 48 (3835).

31. *ST* Ia. 75. 2 ad 2.

32. See e.g. *ST* 3a. 2. 3–4 and 17. I; *De unione verbi incarnati*. 4.

33. Cf. *ST* 3a. 2. 4.

34. See e.g. *ST* 3a. 2. 4.

35. See e.g. *ST* 3a. 2. 8.

36. *ST* 3a. 2. 5 and *Compendium theologiae*. 209 (402–4).

37. *De unione verbi incarnati,* 5.

38. *ST* 3a. 9. 1.

39. *ST* 3a. 18. 1.

40. Strictly speaking, this locution is inaccurate. The divine nature is simple, and so it is not accurate to speak of the divine person as having an intellect and a will. But the locutions needed to try to speak accurately in accordance with the doctrine of divine simplicity are so clumsy that Aquinas himself does not always avoid the simpler but inaccurate locutions. Having noted

the constraints of divine simplicity, in the rest of the chapter I shall avail myself of the simpler locutions such as that used here, which describes the person of Christ's having an intellect and will.

41. See e.g. *QDV* 20. 1 and 4.
42. *ST* 3a. 18. 4.
43. *ST* 3a. 16. 5, but see the qualification in 6.
44. See ST 3a. 15. 4–6.
45. *ST* 3a. 2. 3 ad 2.
46. In correspondence, Brian Leftow has asked whether it is so much as possible to avoid attributing a conjunctive nature to Christ. If Christ is human and divine, then it seems as if he has one nature, namely, the nature of being human-and-divine. I think, however, that Aquinas' metaphysics rule out such a conjunctive nature, and I also think that Aquinas is concerned to make sure that his views do not conflate natures in Christ. On Aquinas' view, a nature is something conferred by a substantial form (or a form which is a substance in the case of immaterial things). If there were only one nature in Christ, then there would be only one substantial form, or one form which is a substance. But the substantial form of a human being does not configure all the components of the incarnate Christ, because it does not configure the second person of the deity; the substantial form of a human being configures matter. The form which is the second person of the Trinity does not configure all of the components of the incarnate Christ either, however, because the second person is not a form configuring matter. So there is not one substantial form (or one form which is a substance) which configures all the components in the incarnate Christ: rather there are two such forms. Consequently, there are two natures, not one. It is for this very reason that Aquinas has so much difficulty in explaining what kind of union of the components there is in the incarnate Christ, as I explain below.
47. For an example of a contemporary interpretation of the Chalcedonian formula which suffers this sort of defect, see T.V. Morris, *The Logic of God Incarnate,* (Ithaca, NY: Cornell University Press, 1986). Morris attempts to keep the two natures of Christ distinct, but the nature of his attempt makes it seem as if he has in fact conflated the natures. So, Peter van Inwagen, commenting on Morris's interpretation, says, 'One might wonder whether it is not a form of monophysitism' ('Incarnation and Christology', in *The Routledge Encyclopedia of Philosophy* (New York: Routledge: 1999, 725–32, at 730)). See also my review of Morris's book in *Faith and Philosophy,* 6 (1989), 218–23.
48. Aquinas uses or discusses the reduplicative strategy in many places. See e.g. *ST* 3a 16. 10–12 and *Compendium theologiae,* 210 (407), 229, and 232.
49. Cf. *ST* 3a 13. 1.
50. Morris, *Logic of God Incarnate,* 48.
51. See van Inwagen, 'Incarnation and Christology', 730–1, for a helpful and succinct expression of the challenge to the reduplicative strategy, which he calls 'a predicative solution'. Van Inwagen says: A satisfactory predicative solution must supplement the abstract theses . . . [which give a reduplicative

form to statements predicating attributes of Christ] with some sort of reply to the following challenge: Where F and G are incompatible properties, and $K1$ and $K2$ are "kinds", what does it mean to say of something that it is F *qua* $K1$ but G *qua* $K2$? – or that it is F *qua* $K1$ but is not F *qua* $K2$? And can any more or less uncontroversial examples of such pairs of statements be found?' This section of my chapter is an attempt to show that Aquinas' metaphysics has the resources to respond to this challenge, and the example of the borrowed properties of C/EBP is an attempt to provide a more ordinary and less controversial case of such pairs of statements.

52. A different and elegant solution to the problem of the apparent logical incoherence of the doctrine of the incarnation can be found in P. van Inwagen, 'Not by Confusion of Substance, but by Unity of Person', in A. G. Padgett (ed.), *Reason and the Christian Religion: Essays in Honour of Richard Swinburne* (Oxford: Clarendon Press, 1994). Van Inwagen provides an analysis of reduplicative propositions in terms of relative identity. On this interpretation, God is the same person as the human being Jesus of Nazareth, but not the same substance or being. Aquinas considers a solution of this sort himself (see ST 3a. 2. 3 and *De unione verbi incarnati*, 2), but he rejects it, as he has to do. On his metaphysics, a person is an individual substance of a rational nature, and so for any individuals x and y, x is the same person as y only if x is the same substance as y.

53. I am grateful to Scott MacDonald and Brian Leftow for making clear to me that this paragraph needed to be added.

54. I am grateful to William Alston, Lawrence Dewan, Brian Leftow, Scott MacDonald, and Gerald O'Collins for comments on an earlier draft of this chapter on the metaphysics.

CHAPTER 10

THE POSSIBILITIES OF INCARNATION: SOME RADICAL MOLINIST SUGGESTIONS

Thomas P. Flint

Abstract: The traditional doctrine of the Incarnation maintains that God became man. But was it necessary that God become the particular man He in fact became? Could some man or woman other than the man born in Bethlehem roughly two thousand years ago have been assumed by the Son to effect our salvation? This essay addresses such questions from the perspective of one embracing Molina's picture of divine providence. After showing how Molina thought his theory of middle knowledge helps alleviate a traditional Christological puzzle, the essay turns to the aforementioned questions concerning God's incarnational alternatives and suggests some fairly radical answers. Finally, the essay presents two substantial objections to these radical answers and argues that these objections fail.

According to traditional Christian belief, the salvation of mankind was achieved through the death and resurrection of Jesus Christ. Atonement, Christians believe, crucially involved Incarnation; for us humans to be saved, it was necessary (or at least eminently fitting) that God become man. But was it also necessary that God become the particular man He in fact became? Was the specific human being who was born in Bethlehem roughly two thousand years ago the *only* man through whom God could have reconciled the world to Himself? Or could that same salvific end perhaps have been attained had God the Son united Himself with some other man or woman? Were St Peter or St Paul candidates? How about St Augustine, or Mother Teresa, or Billy Graham? Moving a tad further afield, how about another Bill – Bill Clinton? Could he have been the instrument of divine salvation rather than – well, rather than what he is? Finally, were any of us candidates? Could the Word of God have become incarnate in you, or in me?

This is the family of questions I intend to address in this essay. They are not, I think, questions Christians are accustomed to asking themselves. But they arise quite naturally when we begin to think seriously about divine providence. After all, a central part of God's providential plan for His world involved Incarnation and Atonement. In thinking about how providence operates and how to reconcile that providence with both divine and human freedom, it is natural to wonder what options, if any, were available to God with respect to the Incarnation.

Before examining these questions, though, I need to do three things. First, I will very briefly outline the account of divine providence that I will be assuming to be correct. Second, I will quickly recount what I see as some of the essentials of the standard Christian picture of the Incarnation. And third, I will offer a cursory explanation of how the account of providence I defend offers us an intriguing perspective on that traditional Incarnational picture.[1] With these three preliminaries in place, the stage will be set to usher in our questions concerning God's incarnational alternatives, and to suggest some fairly radical answers. Finally, I will present two substantial objections to these radical answers and argue that these objections fail.

The Molinist account of providence

The account of divine providence I defend stems from the writings of the sixteenth-century Iberian philosopher Luis de Molina. According to the Molinist picture, God's exercise of providence is dependent upon His middle knowledge – His knowledge of contingent truths over which He has no control. The truths in this category that are of greatest interest to us are what I have elsewhere called *counterfactuals of creaturely freedom*.[2] These counterfactuals are conditionals that, speaking loosely, tell God how any creature who does or might exist would freely act in any set of circumstances in which that creature could be created and left free.[3] Given His knowledge of such counterfactuals, God can, by carefully selecting both the beings He creates and the situations in which He places them, arrange things in such a way that His goals for the world are attained with certainty, but attained largely through the free acts of His creatures rather than through His causally determinative initiatives.[4]

As I see it, Molinism is the natural product of two more basic views: a strong traditional notion of providence (including universal divine foreknowledge and specific sovereignty) and a libertarian picture of freedom. Since Christians have good reason to be attracted to each of these two positions, and since the only way consistently to hold both is to adopt the Molinist account of providence, Molinism is, I contend, the position most worthy of Christians' support.[5]

This account of the dialectical situation is, of course, extremely controversial. But that controversy is not my focus in this paper. Rather, my goal is to examine some of the implications of this picture of providence on our understanding of the Incarnation. Before we can do that, though, a few remarks on the doctrine of the Incarnation are in order.

Incarnation and the human nature of the Son

Christians contend that Jesus Christ is both truly and fully divine and truly and fully human. The second person of the Trinity, who possessed his divine nature from eternity, took on (or, as it is often put, *assumed*) a human nature at a precise point in time. In becoming incarnate, the Son took on whatever exactly we humans are. And what are we? Are we simply bodies of a particular type? Immaterial souls? Body–soul composites? Something else? Whatever it is that a human being is, that is what the Son assumed in becoming a man. Following much of the traditional discussion of these matters, I will speak of the Son as assuming an *individual human nature*.[6] In further deference to tradition – and because I find the position plausible – I will also assume in what follows that individual human natures are divinely created body–soul composites, though I don't think much of what I say hinges on this assumption.

As I understand it, the traditional doctrine of the Incarnation implies that the individual human nature assumed by the Son – a nature that I will call CHN – has a unique metaphysical status.[7] Most of us human persons are nothing other than individual human natures – that is, wholes made up of body and soul. Hence, whatever can be said of my individual human nature – of the body–soul composite that I am – can equally be said of me, of this specific person. As the medievals would put it, most individual human natures just are *supposita,* or ultimate subjects of predication. If we wish to avoid the Nestorian heresy, though, we cannot say this about CHN, for if CHN were a *suppositum* distinct from the Son, then the Incarnation would yield two persons rather than one. What we need to say in this special case, then, is that CHN is not a *suppositum*; rather, the ultimate subject of whatever properties CHN has is not that body–soul composite itself, but rather the Son, the eternal and divine person who is united to and sustains in being this individual human nature.[8]

CHN, then, was born in Bethlehem, spoke with Mary Magdalene, cured the blind and the lame, was kissed by Judas, accepted death on a cross, and so on. In making such statements, of course, we are not saying that CHN was the *person* who did or suffered all these things. For the only person involved in the Incarnation is the Son, the selfsame person who existed eternally before CHN came to be. Still, because the Son did these things through the created body and soul that make up CHN, it is entirely appropriate to see CHN as the immediate, and the Son as the ultimate, possessor of the characteristics involved.

Molinism and the freedom of the Son's human nature

Molina clearly believed that his theory of middle knowledge had significant ramifications for our understanding not only of the general notion of divine providence, but also of the specific doctrine of the Incarnation. In particular, he seems to have felt that it was only by adopting a Molinist stance that we can resolve a particularly thorny Christological puzzle.[9]

The puzzle he had in mind concerns the freedom of the human nature assumed by the Son. On the one hand, we seem committed to saying that CHN cannot sin. For, since the Son is the only person involved in the Incarnation, it follows that what CHN does, the Son does. But the Son, as an essentially divine and hence essentially morally perfect being, cannot sin. On the other hand, to say that CHN was not free to sin seems to lessen (perhaps even to eliminate) the meritorious nature of CHN's accepting death on a cross.[10] Furthermore, denying CHN true moral freedom makes it difficult to see how we can take Christ's life as a model for our own. The book of Hebrews (4.15) tells us that we have in Jesus a Saviour 'who in every respect has been tested as we are, yet without sin'. How can we take this claim seriously if we insist, not simply that CHN passed all such tests, but that CHN couldn't possibly have failed them?

Our quandary, then, is how to ascribe to the Son the impeccability his divine nature entails while also ascribing to him the kind of freedom his human nature and salvific mission seem to involve. Molina's solution to this puzzle, translated into contemporary language, seems to have been this. There is no possible world in which an assumed human nature sins. So, if CHN is assumed, it follows that CHN remains sinless. But being sinless does not entail being unable to sin, and as we have seen, CHN needed such freedom. It follows, then, that God must have arranged things in such a way that (i) CHN was placed in *freedom-retaining circumstances* (i.e. circumstances that left open to CHN the genuine option to sin), and yet (ii) CHN did not in fact sin in those circumstances. And how did God manage to arrange things in this way? By employing His middle knowledge as to how CHN would freely react if placed in various different circumstances. Given this middle knowledge, God decided both to assume CHN and to place it only in those circumstances in which He saw that CHN would freely avoid sin.

A bit of formalization might prove helpful here. Suppose that, prior to making any creative decision, God saw that each of the following contingent counterfactuals was true:

(1) If CHN were placed in lifelong freedom-retaining circumstances
    C, CHN would freely sin.[11]
(2) If CHN were placed in lifelong freedom-retaining circumstances
    D, CHN would freely refrain from sinning.[12]

In knowing (1), God would know that He could not create CHN, assume CHN, and place CHN in C. In knowing (2), though, God would know that He could create and assume CHN and place CHN in D. Since the circumstances D are freedom-retaining, CHN's freedom to sin would be assured. But God would know with certainty that CHN would not in fact employ its freedom wickedly. Therefore, both the freedom of the assumed human nature and the impeccability of the divine person assuming that nature would be safeguarded.

Suppose we call an individual human nature *assumable* if and only if there are lifelong freedom-retaining circumstances such that the nature would remain sinless if placed in those circumstances.[13] Let us also agree to call a conditional that specifies circumstances in which a nature would freely refrain from sinning a *counterfactual of assumability.* Our conditional (2), then, is a counterfactual of assumability, one that tells God that CHN is assumable.

So Molinism seems to have an unexpected payoff when we turn our attention to the Incarnation: it does indeed offer us the resources to propose an intriguing solution to our Christological puzzle, a solution that applies a full-blooded libertarian sense of freedom to CHN without involving the Father in any risk that His anointed one might turn against Him.

Incarnational alternatives: six radical Molinist theses

We are now, at long last, prepared to consider the questions with which we began. What options, if any, did God have with respect to the Incarnation? Was the particular human nature He in fact assumed – the one we have been calling CHN – the only one He could have assumed? Or is it at least possible that He could have achieved the salvation of the human race by taking on some other human nature – even yours or mine?

As I see it, Molinism forces upon its adherents no particular answers to these questions. But it docs, I think, open the door to certain responses that might initially seem rather radical. Indeed, 'open the door' seems to me too feeble a metaphor. More apt would be a picture of one swimming in a river where the current will naturally take one downstream unless considerable effort is expended to go in some other direction. If the river is Molinism, the flow, it seems to me, is decidedly toward those radical downstream waters.

I propose to present the drift toward this radical Molinist stance via a series of six loosely related theses, each arguably a tad more radical than its predecessor. My contention is not that the propositions in question are connected in a tight logical sense; just about anywhere in the series, one can declare 'So far, but no farther!' without fear of logical infelicities.[14] Still, I think there is a natural momentum at work here, such that, at any point in the series, acceptance of the earlier members makes acceptance of their successor seem eminently plausible. What might have looked like a radical modification of the doctrine of the Incarnation thus begins, little by little, to appear but a natural development of the doctrine.

Thesis 1: Necessarily, being assumable is a contingent feature of any assumable individual human nature

As we have seen, a human nature is assumable just in case there is a true counterfactual of assumability about that nature. For example, (2)'s being true entails that CHN is assumable. Now, counterfactuals of assumability are one and all contingent propositions. Since their antecedents make no claims concerning the actual assumptions of the natures involved, it is possible that any such counterfactual be false. Furthermore, it seems evident that counterfactuals of assumability are logically independent of one another; the truth or falsity of one such conditional entails nothing whatsoever about the truth or falsity of any other. So it's necessarily the case that, for any individual human nature, it's possible that every counterfactual of assumability about that nature be false. From this, of course, it follows that, necessarily, every human nature is such that, in some possible world, that nature is not assumable. So if a nature is assumable, that is only a contingent fact about the nature in question.

Thesis 2: It's possible that CHN was neither assumed nor assumable

This claim is virtually impossible to deny if thesis 1 is accepted. If every individual human nature is, at best, only contingently assumable, then CHN was only contingently assumable. From this it follows that there are possible worlds in which CHN was not assumable, And it seems obvious that, if there are worlds in which CHN was not assumable, there are worlds in which CHN was not assumed.[15]

Thesis 3: It's possible that there be an individual human nature distinct from CHN that was both assumable and assumed

If God knows by middle knowledge truths about how CHN would freely act if placed in the kinds of lifelong freedom-retaining circumstances which assumption might prescribe, there seems no reason to doubt that He knows such counterfactuals about other individual human natures as well. If He does, He surely might know that one of these other human natures was assumable. But suppose He saw that one such nature (call it X) was assumable, but that CHN was not assumable. It seems natural to conclude that, under such conditions, God might choose to create and assume X rather than CHN. So there are indeed possible worlds in which God assumes an individual human nature distinct from CHN.

Thesis 4: It's possible that CHN exist as an independent, unassumed suppositum

Suppose that, as thesis 2 tells us is possible, CHN were neither assumable nor assumed. Suppose also that, as thesis 3 maintains could be the case, some nature other than CHN were assumed. Would it follow that CHN does not exist at all – that God decided not to create CHN? On the surface, there seems no good reason to think so. Knowing that the counterfactuals of creaturely freedom are not propitious in the way assumability requires would, of course, preclude God's becoming incarnate via CHN. But why think it would preclude God's creating CHN and interacting with it as He interacts with his other human creatures? Given God's omnipotence, we ought not postulate limitations upon God's creative freedom unless we have a solid reason so to limit His options. Thus, it seems prima facie reasonable to assert that God could have created but not assumed CHN. And from this it follows that CHN was not (in the contemporary sense) *essentially* united to and sustained by a divine person.

Thesis 5: There are in the actual world individual human natures distinct from CHN that were assumable

Even if, as thesis 3 asserts, there are possible worlds in which a human nature other than CHN is assumable, it could be that no such nature actually exists. The fact that, in some possible world, God creates and assumes X gives us no right to conclude that God even creates X in the actual world, let alone that He assumes it here. Still, it seems hard to believe that, aside from CHN, *none* of the individual human natures God in fact created were, like CHN and X, assumable. We know that God has brought into existence billions and billions of such natures. While it is undeniably possible that not a single one of these natures (other than CHN) was assumable, such a claim hardly seems plausible. To be sure, we have no way of knowing *which* individual human natures were assumable – no way of knowing for sure, say, that Billy Graham *was* assumable, but Bill Clinton *wasn't*. Still, it would be highly presumptuous of us to suppose that *none* of the body–soul composites we bump into on a daily basis was such that the Son might have assumed it as easily as he in fact assumed CHN. Though not demonstrably true, then, thesis 5 still seems eminently reasonable.

Thesis 6: Necessarily, every human nature is possibly assumed

This claim follows from two other necessary propositions which, once one has moved through thesis 5, must surely seem credible. The first of these propositions is the claim that:

> (a) Necessarily, for any individual human nature N, it's possible that N is assumable.

That is, for any human nature, there is a counterfactual of assumability about that nature such that, in some possible world, that counterfactual is true.

Now, to reject (a) would be to say that, in some possible world, there is an individual human nature which is not even possibly assumable. To say that a nature is not possibly assumable, though, is to say that, in every possible world, every counterfactual of assumability about that nature is false. But this would in turn be to say that every counterfactual of assumability about that nature is necessarily false. Since counterfactuals of assumability are only contingently true or false, though, the denial of (a) hardly seems reasonable. And the same, one might argue, goes for:

> (b) Necessarily, if an individual human nature N is assumable, then it's possible that N is assumed.

To say that a certain nature is assumable, of course, is just to say that there are lifelong freedom-retaining circumstances in which that nature could be placed and in which it would remain sinless. Obviously, the fact that a nature is assumable hardly entails that the nature *is* assumed. But it seems far more reasonable to say that assumability entails at least the *possibility* of assumption. If God is omnipotent, and if He knew by middle knowledge that a certain human nature was assumable, then He would know that there is a feasible world in which that nature is assumed, for He would know that assuming the nature was one of the options open to Him.[16] To deny such an option to God would be once again to restrict divine freedom without reason.[17]

So there seems to be a strong case for saying that both (a) and (b) are true. And if they are, then thesis 6 can hardly be denied. We thus seem justified in concluding that, in every possible world, every individual human nature is such that it is assumed in some possible world. And this means, among other things, that each and every one of us is much more similar to CHN than we might have thought. For each of us is such that we are possibly united to a divine person in precisely the way that we believe CHN is in fact united. And that, it seems to me, is a claim that should, for most of us, alter our perception of the doctrine of the Incarnation – not in the sense of being at odds (so far as I know) with any official Church teaching concerning the Incarnation, but in the sense of construing that doctrine in a far more inclusive manner than most of us would reasonably have anticipated. To return to one of our earlier examples, we can hardly look at Bill Clinton in quite the same way if we believe that this very man is in some other possible world assumed by the Son of God.

Two objections to radical Molinism

There are many objections that might be raised to these six theses, or to the manner in which I have ordered them, or to the grounds offered in support of them. I propose here to address only two such objections. As we shall see, the first of these criticisms can be met much more readily than can the second. My intention, though, is to show that neither is fatal to the radical Molinist claims I have just outlined.

The first objector suggests that the radical position we have proposed is indicative of the arrogance endemic to academics engaged in philosophical theology. For what have we defended if not the idolatrous claim that each of us might have been God? Every individual human nature, according to thesis 6, is possibly assumed. But I, of course, just am an individual human nature. So *I* am possibly assumed. That is, in some possible world, I am united to the Son of God. But this means that, in some possible world, I am divine. But surely, the objector concludes, no true Christian can possibly agree to so patent a clouding of the distinction between the divine and the human. As our colleagues and spouses will quickly attest, we philosophers may often *act* as if we think we're God, but not even the most conceited among us *really* believes that such an identification is a genuine possibility. Since thesis 6 requires that this ludicrous position be embraced, none of us can reasonably view it as a live option – however much we might *wish* it were true.

Perhaps the first thing to say in response is that, if one is overly 'concerned about clouding the distinction between the divine and the human', one's problem is apt to be more with the doctrine of the Incarnation itself than with our Molinist extension of the doctrine. More seriously, though, I think the charge that thesis 6 clouds this distinction more than a Christian can tolerate is without foundation. For that thesis simply does not entail that there is a possible world in which I am God. What it entails is that there is a possible world in which I am assumed by a divine person. But to be assumed by a divine person is not to be a divine person; nor is it to be divine.

Take the case of CHN, which we Christians believe was in fact assumed by a divine person. Is CHN *itself* a divine person? No, for CHN is not a person at all; *pace* Nestorianism, the *only* person involved in the Incarnation is the second person of the Trinity. Is CHN *itself* divine? Again, I think we must answer, no. CHN is united to the Son in an unfathomably intimate way, but not in such a fashion that CHN is no longer distinguishable from the Son. And one of the principal ways in which the two are to be distinguished is that only the latter is strictly and unqualifiedly divine.

What is in fact true of CHN, according to thesis 6, is possibly true of each of us. But then, in affirming that each of us is possibly assumed, one is not saying that each of us is possibly divine, or possibly a divine person. And so our first objection has been met. Molinists, like other philosophers, may still need to plead guilty to the charge of arrogance, but it is at least not arrogance on quite so gargantuan a scale.

The second objection contends that the radical position outlined above is committed to a noteworthy ontological claim: that *being a person* is a quality which an individual human nature either has or lacks contingently. As we have seen, orthodoxy entails that CHN is not itself a person, for there is only one person involved in the Incarnation, and that person is the Son. Even so, if thesis 4 is true, CHN could have been a person, for it could have been created without being assumed by God, in which case it would have been a *suppositum* in its own right. So, according to thesis 4, an individual human nature which is *not* a person contingently *lacks* the property of being a person. Thesis 6, on the other hand, entails that human natures which *are* persons *possess* this property only contingently. If every human nature is possibly assumed, then each human nature is such that it could have existed without itself being a human person. For if a nature is assumed, that nature is not itself a person, but is instead sustained by the Son. If thesis 6 is accepted, then, human natures which are persons are only contingently so. Therefore, theses 4 and 6 taken together entail that individual human natures cannot be either essentially persons or essentially not persons.

Why think this commitment puts the radical Molinist in jeopardy? Because, some would argue, being a person cannot have so tenuous a tie to a nature. Alfred Freddoso, for example, asks us to consider the following valid argument which Socrates might offer:

(3) I am identical with Socrates.
(4) I cannot exist without being a person.

So,

(5) Socrates cannot exist without being a person.

The radical Molinist view we have examined would accept (3) but reject (5); hence, it must be denying (4) as well.[18] 'But this', says Freddoso, 'is a manifest repugnancy which flouts our deepest convictions about ourselves and which the doctrine of the Incarnation can in no way be thought to sanction'. Such a view, he concludes, is 'utterly bereft of merit'; it is, as he puts it elsewhere, 'extraordinarily implausible' and 'wholly unacceptable'.[19]

Freddoso's attack is clearly rich in rhetorical flourishes. Unfortunately, it seems relatively poor in logical force. Freddoso is surely right in suggesting that (4) seems to have the ring of truth to it, for denying it might be thought equivalent to asserting that I could exist in an utterly non-personal manner. But reflection on the Incarnation should teach us, if nothing else, that we need to lend an especially close ear to propositions involving natures and persons. In fact, those who reject (4) needn't claim that a human nature could exist where no person exists. They might instead be maintaining only that the human nature need not be identical to that person. That is, they might be replacing (4) with:

(4*) I cannot exist without either being a person or being sustained by a person.

Human natures which are not assumed satisfy (4*) by themselves being persons. Natures (such as CHN) which are assumed satisfy (4*) by being sustained by a divine person. So far as I can see, (4*) adequately supports the intuition Freddoso sought to encapsulate via (4), and manages thereby to defend the radical Molinist stance in a manner which is neither unacceptable, nor implausible, nor repugnant, nor bereft of merit.

Of course, one might seek to push the radical Molinist in an even more radical direction, and seek thereby to discredit the position itself. For example, one might argue that, if we grant that an individual human nature might be only *contingently* a person, we have no reason to doubt that such a nature might be only *temporarily* a person. That is, the radical Molinist should concur with Scotus and Ockham in contending that assumption could be a temporary episode in a nature's life – that the nature might be, say, unassumed (and hence a person) on Monday, assumed (and hence not a person) on Tuesday, and then unassumed (and hence once again a person) on Wednesday.[20]

While I concede that the radical Molinist *could* adopt this position, it seems to me that she *needn't* do so, and hence needn't be marred by the blemishes which allegedly disfigure it. Indeed, she might think there is good reason *not* to adopt the Ockhamist view that personhood could be temporary, for she might think there are sound moral or metaphysical reasons for God not to treat a human nature in this way. On the one hand, to 'cut loose' an assumed nature would surely be a most ungracious act on God's part. For to dissolve so intimate a union with a human nature would be to deprive it of an infinite good, and to do so without sufficient moral cause, for, as we have seen, an assumed nature commits no sin. On the other hand, to assume a nature which at first existed on its own would be to eliminate that nature's personhood. What was a human person would, via assumption, cease to be one. Where we once had two persons – the Son and the nature in question – we would now have only one. To be sure, if union with the Son really is the infinite good we asserted it to be, then God could hardly be thought to have harmed a nature by assuming it, for the nature would have lost a finite good (being a person), but gained an infinite one (being sustained by a divine person). Still, I think one can justifiably doubt that a good God would play this game of metaphysical tag with His universe. Far better and wiser, one might think, would be a God who creates certain types of things – iguanas, rabbits, human persons – and endeavours to perfect them as they are, without robbing them of the goods they naturally possess.

Indeed, it seems to me that the position I have suggested here – that being a person is always a contingent but never a temporary feature of an individual human nature – has a notable proponent in Thomas Aquinas. As Freddoso has shown, there is strong textual support for the claim that Aquinas would have rejected the Ockhamist contention that a human nature could be temporarily assumed.[21] But does it follow that Aquinas would also have denied the radical Molinist claim that personhood could be a contingent feature of a human nature? 'Here', Freddoso concedes, 'things get a bit murkier'.[22] Indeed they do. Freddoso attempts to extend St Thomas's arguments against the Ockhamist position into arguments against the radical Molinist one, but it is far from clear that such extensions are justified. Furthermore, Freddoso offers not a single passage from Aquinas which seems at odds with the radical Molinist claim. This is especially interesting since there *are* Thomistic passages that prima facie seem to be assuming that what I have called CHN *could* have been a human person. For example, in his reply to the third objection to the Second Article ('Whether the Son of God Assumed a Person') of Question 4 in Part III of the *Summa Theologica,* Aquinas says:

> Absorption does not here imply the destruction of anything pre-existing, but the hindering what might otherwise have been. For if the human nature [i.e., CHN] had not been assumed by a Divine Person, the human nature would have had its own personality; and in this way is it said, although improperly, that the Person *absorbed the person,* inasmuch as the Divine Person by His union hindered the human nature from having its personality.[23]

As Freddoso notes, the Latin term *personalitas,* unfortunately translated here as 'personality', has nothing to do with 'character traits and temperament', but instead stands simply for *personhood*–i.e. for the property of being a person.[24] On the surface, then, it surely looks as though Aquinas is, in effect, saying here that CHN might have existed as an unassumed human person. Freddoso would no doubt respond that St Thomas may have been thinking of the conditionals involved here ('if the human nature had not been assumed') as having impossible antecedents.[25] While I grant that this is possible, Aquinas gives us absolutely no hint in such passages that he thinks of the antecedents as impossible. Hence, it seems to me that a philosopher with no axe to grind would be unlikely to see him as making such a tacit assumption. And thus my inclination (for what it is worth – this is really a matter for Thomistic scholars to decide) is to see St Thomas as an advocate of the radical Molinist claim that a nature could contingently lack personhood.

I see no reason to assume, then, that one who thinks of personhood as a contingent feature of a human nature is thereby committed to thinking of it as possibly only a temporary feature.[26] The radical Molinist view seems to be genuinely independent of the Ockhamist stance, and thus not automatically discredited by the supposed implausibility of the latter. And so our second objection to our six theses seems inconclusive at best.

Conclusion

I have argued in this paper that Molinism seems naturally to engender an understanding of the possibilities of Incarnation that, I suspect, few Christians consciously embrace. We have examined two objections to this radical Molinist view, and seen that neither offers a convincing refutation of it. Of course, it hardly follows that the Molinist would be fully justified in wedding herself to such a view. Perhaps one of the objections we have explored can be easily recast in a more potent fashion; perhaps other difficulties with one or more of our six theses can be readily detected. Still, until such objections can actually be mustered, I think the radical view is well worth the Molinist's serious attention. And, of course, since I also think Molinism is well worth the attention of every serious Christian, it follows that, on my view, the radical position is one that all Christians would do well to consider carefully.[27]

Notes

1. For much richer presentations of the issues addressed in these three sections of the paper, see my '"A death he freely accepted": Molinist reflections on the Incarnation', *Faith and Philosophy*, 18 (2001), 3–20.
2. See Thomas P. Flint. *Divine Providence: The Molinist Account* (Ithaca NY: Cornell University Press, 1998), 40.
3. Why do I say 'speaking loosely' here? Because the counterfactuals cannot refer to the creatures themselves. Why not? Because they need to guide God in His creative decisions; hence, they need to be available to Him logically prior to His determining which beings to create. Some of the counterfactuals, then, will turn out to be about 'possible but non-actual beings'. If we feel (as we should) that, strictly speaking, there *are* no possible-but-not-actual beings, then we can stipulate that the relevant counterfactuals refer to creaturely essences rather than to creatures themselves. For more on this issue, see Flint *Divine Providence: The Molinist Account*, 46–50.
4. For more on Molina's view as set forth in his *Concordia*, see Alfred J. Freddoso (ed. and transl.) *On Divine Foreknowledge: Part IV of the Concordia* (Ithaca NY: Cornell University Press, 1988). Further references to this work will refer to it simply as *Concordia*.
5. The position sketched here is defended in much greater detail in my *Divine Providence: The Molinist Account*, Pts 1 and 2.
6. Contemporary readers inclined to read the term *nature* as referring to a type of property should make special note of the fact that the kind of natures I am thinking of here are concrete particulars, not abstract objects.
7. Many contemporary theorists would deny this traditional understanding of the Incarnation. For example, some would say that the Son did not assume a distinct created human soul, but simply acquired particular properties

(e.g., being related to a specific human body in a certain way); taking on such properties, they suggest, is sufficient to make the Son human. (See, for example, Richard Swinburne *The Christian God* (Oxford: Clarendon Press, 1994), ch. 9, especially 212–215.) Though entering this controversy is beyond the scope of this paper, it seems clear to me that the alternatives are markedly inferior with respect to avoiding Christological heresies.

8. I have chosen to avoid masculine pronouns for CHN in order to preclude Nestorian readings of sentences involving such pronouns. Hence, I shall consistently refer to CHN as *it* rather than as *he*.

9. For Molina's discussion of this issue, see *Concordia,* 265–273.

10. I am assuming here that Jesus had a moral obligation to abide by the Father's will that he accept death on a cross. In other words, the refusal of the human will to align itself with the divine will would have been sinful. Like Molina (and, I might add, his opponents such as Zumel), I find this assumption eminently reasonable. Those who doubt it, though, should note that the puzzle we are discussing remains so long as we grant that, at *some* point in his life, Jesus was free with regard to *some* morally significant activity.

11. By *lifelong* circumstances, I mean circumstances that specify a complete set of situations in which CHN might be placed over the course of its life.

12. Note an important fact about the antecedents in (1) and (2). Middle knowledge, as we saw, is knowledge of contingent truths. So (1) and (2) are part of middle knowledge only if they are contingently true or false. But neither of these conditionals could be contingent if the circumstances mentioned in their antecedents included CHN's being assumed, for as we have seen, it is impossible for an assumed human nature to sin. Neither *C* nor *D,* then, can include CHN's being assumed. And from a Molinist perspective, this restriction makes perfect sense. For the circumstances in which a creature acts includes only those states of affairs over which the creature has absolutely no control *B,* that is, only those states of affairs that still would have obtained no matter what action within its power the creature had performed. But *CHN's being assumed* is not a state of affairs that was in this sense beyond CHN's power during CHN's earthly existence. For if CHN was significantly free, then it had the power to do something (namely, sin) such that, were it to have done it, it never would have been assumed. *CHN's being assumed,* then, was not a hard, fixed, settled state of affairs so long as CHN was significantly free, and hence cannot plausibly be included in the circumstances in which CHN acted. For a related discussion, see my 'A new anti-anti-Molinist argument', *Religious Studies,* 35 (1999), 299–305.

13. I presuppose here that if a nature freely refrains from sin, then the circumstances in which it acts leave it genuinely free to sin. A nature can be in lifelong freedom-retaining circumstances, then, only if it faces morally significant choices.

14. I say 'just about anywhere' rather than simply 'anywhere' because it is very hard to see how a Molinist could deny thesis 1, or (having accepted thesis 1) deny thesis 2.

15. It should be obvious in any event that there are worlds in which CHN isn't assumed. For surely there are worlds in which there *are* no individual

human natures. In such worlds, of course, CHN doesn't even exist, and so a fortiori isn't assumed.

16. To say that a world is feasible is to say that the world is one which God in fact has the option to actualize, given the truths He knows via middle knowledge. Given Molinism, the set of feasible worlds is necessarily a proper subset of the set of possible worlds. (For more on feasibility and possibility, see my *Divine Providence: The Molinist Account,* 51–54.) As the discerning reader will note, the argument in the text would support a claim somewhat stronger than (b), namely, (b*) 'Necessarily, if an individual human nature N is assumable, then there is a feasible world in which N is assumed'. Since (b*) is not needed to support thesis 6, though, I have focused on the weaker (b) instead.

17. Could it be that assumability is but *one* of *several* necessary conditions for being assumed? Perhaps. But, defenders of thesis 6 might ask, what would the *other* necessary conditions be? More precisely, what other conditions might there be which a human nature that was assumable might fail to satisfy? If we cannot come up with some plausible candidates, then why think there *are* other interesting necessary conditions?

18. In saying that the radical Molinist accepts (3), I mean, of course, that she would think that (3) is true when said by Socrates. And in saying that she rejects (5), we are assuming that 'Socrates' is being used as a name for the relevant body-soul composite.

19. Alfred J. Freddoso 'Human nature, potency and the Incarnation', *Faith and Philosophy,* 3 (1986), 37.

20. *Ibid.,* 30–38.

21. *Ibid.,* 45–48.

22. *Ibid.,* 48.

23. Translation by the Fathers of the English Dominican Province, in *Summa Theologica,* vol. 4 (Westminster MD: Christian Classics, 1981), 20–47.

24. Freddoso 'Human nature', 50, n. 7.

25. For Freddoso's discussion of such conditionals, see *ibid.,* 43–45.

26. Not surprisingly, there *are* some interesting properties in the neighborhood that *do* seem to be temporary properties. For example, it *does* seem plausible to say that *being human* (i.e., *being a man*) was an on-again, off-again property of the Son. The Son was not human (prior to the Incarnation), then human (from the birth to the death of CHN), then not human (from the death of CHN to the Resurrection), then human (after the Resurrection). Or so at least Aquinas (quite reasonably, I think) believed; see *Summa Theologica,* Part 3, Q. 50, Art. 4. It's also intriguing to note that, even if *being a person* is a property that *cannot* be a temporary feature of an individual human nature, *being part of a person* is a property that *can* be a temporary feature of a *part* of an individual human nature. The human soul, as part of an individual human nature, is part of a person before death, and part of the same person once reunited with its body after the general resurrection. But between death and resurrection, there is no body-soul composite, and hence no individual human nature, and hence no person. The sole exception here would be the soul of CHN, which remained united to the Son

during the three days between the Crucifixion and the Resurrection. The typical human soul that survives death, though, is (prior to the resurrection) neither a person not a part of a person. (See again Aquinas, *Summa Theologica,* Pt 1, Q. 29, Art. 1.) Thus, the soul is first part of a person, then not part of a person, then once again part of a person.

27. A version of this paper was given at the Wheaton College Philosophy Conference in October 2000. In addition, earlier versions of a much longer essay that included an ancestor of this paper were presented to the Notre Dame Center for Philosophy of Religion Discussion Group and at the Society of Christian Philosophers session at the American Philosophical Association Eastern Division Meetings in December 1998. I am grateful to those who attended these various sessions (especially the members of the Center for Philosophy of Religion) for their help with the paper. Special thanks also go to David Hunt, William Craig, William Hasker, Hugh McCann, Scott Davison, Stewart Goetz, and Paul Griffiths for stimulating and challenging comments and questions.

CHAPTER 11

RATIONALITY AND THE CHRISTIAN REVELATION

Thomas V. Morris

Now there was a man of the Pharisees, named Nicodemus, a ruler of the Jews. This man came to Jesus by night and said to him "Rabbi, we know that you are a teacher come from God; for no man can do these signs that you do unless God is with him." (John 3:1–2)

Since at least the time of Nicodemus, people have reasoned about the identity of Jesus. It has been the most widespread view of Christians throughout the centuries that it is eminently reasonable to believe Jesus to be, not just a teacher come from God, but God himself, incarnate in human nature. In the letter to the Hebrews, it is said that:

> In many and various ways, God spoke to our fathers by the prophets; but in these last days he has spoken to us by a Son, whom he appointed heir of all things, through whom also he created the world. He reflects the glory of God and bears the very stamp of his nature, upholding the universe by his word of power (Heb. 1:1–3a)

Christians have always believed that the supreme self-disclosure of God has occurred in the life and death of Jesus. He who has seen him has seen the Father. It is the insistence of traditional orthodox Christians that this is true precisely because Jesus was himself literally divine. More precisely, it is the claim of traditional Christology, and the central commitment of distinctively Christian belief, that Jesus was, and eternally is, God the Son, the Second Person of the divine Trinity in human nature. To reveal himself to us, God became one of us. To save humanity, he took on humanity.

In recent years, however, the fundamental Christian claim about Jesus has undergone a barrage of criticism. Numerous critics, including many prominent theologians who continue to align themselves with the Christian church, have alleged that it is no longer possible that it be rational for well informed intelligent people to accept the doctrine of the Incarnation. This allegation has been made in a number of ways and stands nowadays as a foregone conclusion in many centers of higher education, including numerous seminaries and schools of divinity. I believe it is a view which richly deserves to be challenged.

In this essay, I want to examine some important facets of this question as to whether it is possible that it be reasonable or rational to believe Jesus to be God Incarnate. In particular, I want to take a look at some considerations which have been thought by many recent critics to constitute obstacles for a positive answer to this question and see how a perspective on the Incarnation can be developed which will allow these potential obstacles to be overcome. Thus, we shall be dealing here with some basic epistemic matters concerning the doctrine of the Incarnation. My aim here, however, is not to marshal evidence or other sorts of epistemic support in favour of the doctrine. I shall not try to prove, argue, or in any other way show that Jesus was God Incarnate. Not even the more modest task will be attempted of showing that all Christians ought to adopt this traditional understanding of Jesus over any of the alternative conceptions of him developed by a number of contemporary theologians, although I believe this is the case. On this occasion, I shall focus on what are, in principle, only some of the epistemic dynamics of the incarnational claim – some of its logical relations to the sorts of epistemic considerations in the light of which its rational affirmation would be possible or impossible. What I do hope to indicate, in a positive vein, is that contrary to what many critics have argued in the recent past, it is possible that it be rational to believe Jesus to be God Incarnate. To put it a bit more strongly, I hope to go some way toward showing that none of the major criticisms of a philosophical nature directed against the doctrine of the Incarnation in the last few years provides any good reason at all to think that it cannot be rational to believe that the pinnacle of divine revelation has consisted in God's coming among us as one of us. The belief that Jesus was God Incarnate can be an eminently rational belief to hold.

The present essay will be an exercise in Christian philosophical theology, an intellectual enterprise which I take to be a necessary component in any comprehensive, broadly orthodox theology. Of course, Christian theology is not just apologetics. It is not even primarily apologetics. Yet, especially in our time, it must prominently involve apologetics. And this is something we need not regret. For in attempting to answer our critics, we very often come to see features of our beliefs we otherwise might have overlooked. It is my hope that in taking even a brief look at each of the challenges I want to address, we shall begin to attain a richer perspective on one of the most central and important Christian beliefs about the self-disclosure of God.

God in Christ: the possibility of rational belief

In the past, many people, including some friends of the Christian message as well as numerous foes, have believed the doctrine of the Incarnation to be ultimately beyond the scope of reason. Some have believed this because they have taken the doctrine to be inexpungibly obscure to the point of being without clear sense or determinate, cognitive meaning. If it were beyond the scope of reason on this ground, or on any other ground, it would not be such that belief in it could be rational, or in accord with reason.

What are we to make of this sort of view? I think it will be interesting here to quote at length a line of reasoning presented some time ago by John Wisdom:

> It has been said that once at least a higher gift than grace did flesh and blood refine, God's essence and his very self – in the body of Jesus. Whether this statement in true or false is not now the point, but whether it's so obscure as to be senseless. Obscure undoubtedly it is but senseless it is not. For to say that in Nero God was incarnate is not to utter a senseless string of words nor merely to express a surprising sentiment; it is to make a statement which is absurd because it is against all reason. If I say of a cat, 'This cat is abracadabra' I utter a senseless string of words, I don't make a statement at all and therefore don't make an absurd statement. But if I say of a cat which is plainly dead 'In this cat there is life' I make a statement which is absurd because it is against all reason. The cat is not hunting, eating, sleeping, breathing; it is stiff and cold. In the same way the words, 'In Nero God was incarnate' are not without any meaning; one who utters them makes a statement, he makes a statement which is absurd and *against* all reason and therefore *not* beyond the scope of reason. Now if a statement is not beyond the scope of reason then any logically parallel statement is also not beyond the scope of reason. ….The statement 'In Jesus God was incarnate' is logically parallel to 'In Nero God was incarnate.' The latter we noticed is not beyond the scope of reason. Therefore the statement 'In Jesus God was incarnate' is not beyond the scope of reason.[1]

It is not merely the case that we have no reason to believe that Nero was God Incarnate; that would be compatible with our also having no reason to believe he was not God Incarnate. And in that case, the claim, and claims of its type, could be beyond the scope of reason. Wisdom's point is that we have very good reason, as decisive a grounding as we could want, for believing that the wicked man Nero was *not* God Incarnate. And surely to this, everyone in possession of the Judeo-Christian conception of God would agree. Any claim that Nero was God Incarnate we would label as nonsense or absurd. Now it happens to be the case that many critics of orthodox Christian doctrine within the contemporary academic theological community have called the traditional claim that Jesus was literally God Incarnate nonsense or absurd. But even these critics, or at least the vast majority of them, surely would recognize something clearly wrong with the Nero claim which is not wrong with the parallel claim about Jesus. The Nero claim is nonsensical or absurd on properly epistemic grounds, and thus in an epistemic sense – It stands in flagrant contradiction to all we know about the character of the man Nero, in light of the concept we have of God. It is something about Nero himself, his particular personality and character, which would make a claim to his deity particularly absurd, and markedly inferior in an epistemic sense to the parallel claim about Jesus. It is this that Wisdom would have us attend to.

The Christian claim has been said by some critics to be nonsensical or absurd in a logical, or semantic, or conceptual sense. That this is not the case can be held to be evinced by the comparative difference in *prima facie* epistemic status we sense between the claim about Nero and the claim about Jesus, given what we know about the two of them on the human level. Thus, as Wisdom indicates, neither of these statements is unintelligible. And neither is beyond the scope of reason. The difference we feel between them witnesses to that.

If Wisdom has indeed successfully indicated to us that the doctrine of Incarnation is not beyond the scope of reason, has he shown that the possibility is open that it may be rational or reasonable to endorse this doctrine? The answer to this question is clearly 'No,' for the claim that Jesus was God Incarnate could fall within the scope of reason in much the same way as would a claim that, for example, Jesus was a married bachelor, for all that Wisdom shows. Wisdom does draw our attention helpfully to a difference between the Nero claim and the Jesus claim. But the claim of deity for Nero could be absurd in a way in which the claim of deity for Jesus is not absurd without its following from this that the claim about Jesus is not absurd in any sense at all, and such that it is even possible that it be rational to endorse it.

As a matter of fact, various contemporary theologians have thought the incarnational claim about Jesus to be patently incoherent and thus absurd in a logical or conceptual sense. From this point of view, it would be possible to believe Jesus to be God Incarnate and to be rational in so believing only if one rationally could fail to see the patent incoherence of the claim. A certain significant degree of ignorance or obtuseness would be required, if this were to be possible at all. A number of philosophers have offered persuasive arguments in recent years to the effect that it is possible rationally to believe the impossible, or necessarily false. However, if 'incoherent' means more than merely 'necessarily false', if 'patently incoherent' means something more like 'analytically false' or *'a priori* impossible', then it is less likely, to say the least, that anyone would be able rationally to believe a patently incoherent doctrine, for it is highly unlikely that belief in the truth of an analytically false, or *a priori* impossible, proposition can reasonably be ascribed to a person at all. If a patently incoherent proposition is such that one cannot understand it without seeing it to be false, and it is impossible to believe a proposition to be true without understanding it, and, moreover, it is impossible to believe a proposition to be true while seeing it to be false, then should the doctrine of the Incarnation be patently incoherent, it would not be possible rationally to believe it, because it would not be possible to believe it at all. Furthermore, understood in this way, it is clear that nothing could count as a positive epistemic consideration in favour of the truth of a patently incoherent claim. If the incarnational claim endorsed by traditional Christians had this status, there could be no positive epistemic ground for believing it true. As, for example, Grace Jantzen has said:

> If the claim that Jesus is God incarnate is on an epistemological level with 'Jesus was a married bachelor' then no matter how much evidence we could discover for his having said so, his disciples and others having believed it, and the early church having affirmed it, the claim must still be rejected: such 'evidence' would be strictly irrelevant.[2]

And this is certainly correct. Nothing can count as evidence or any other form of epistemic grounding for belief in a proposition the very understanding of which suffices for seeing its falsehood.

The charge of patent incoherence has been repeated in various forms quite often in recent years by critics of the doctrine of the Incarnation. Basically, the sort of argument most of them seem to have in mind is roughly something like the following: On a standard and traditional conception of deity, God is omnipotent, omniscient, incorporeal, impeccable, and necessarily existent, among other things. Moreover, by our definition of 'God', such properties as these are, so to speak, constitutive of deity – it is impossible that any individual be divine, or exemplify divinity, without having these properties. To claim some individual to be divine without being omnipotent, say, or necessarily existent, would be on this view just as incoherent as supposing some individual to be both a bachelor and a married man at one and the same time. By contrast, we human beings seem clearly to exemplify the logical complement (or 'opposite') of each of these constitutive divine attributes. We are limited in power, restricted in knowledge, embodied in flesh, liable to sin, and are contingent creations. Jesus is claimed in the doctrine of the Incarnation to have been both fully human and fully divine. But it is logically impossible for any being to exemplify at one and the same time both a property and its logical complement. Thus, recent critics have concluded, it is logically impossible for any one person to be both human and divine, to have all the attributes proper to deity and all those ingredient in human nature as well. The doctrine of the Incarnation on this view is an incoherent theological development of the early church which must be discarded by us in favor of some other way of conceptualizing the importance of Jesus for Christian faith. He could not possibly have been God Incarnate, a literally divine person in human nature.

As I have addressed this challenge to the doctrine of the Incarnation in great detail elsewhere, I shall give only a relatively brief indication here of how it can be answered.[3] A lengthy response is not required in order for us to be able to see how this currently popular sort of objection can be turned back. A couple of very simple metaphysical distinctions will provide us with the basic apparatus for defending orthodoxy against this charge, which otherwise can seem to be a very formidable challenge indeed.

As it is usually presented, the sort of argument I have just outlined treats humanity and divinity, or human nature and divine nature, as each, constituted by a set of properties individually necessary and jointly sufficient for exemplifying that nature, for being human, or for being divine. Such an argument depends implicitly on a sort of essentialist metaphysic which has been around for quite a while, and which recently has experienced a resurgence of popularity among philosophers. On such a view, objects have two sorts of properties, essential and accidental. A property can be essential to an object in either of two ways. It is part of an individual's essence if the individual which has it could not have existed without having it. It is a kind-essential property if its exemplification is necessary for an individual's belonging to a particular kind, for example, human-kind. Human nature, then, consists in a set of properties severally necessary and jointly sufficient for being human. And the same is true of divine nature. The critic of the Incarnation begins with the simple truth that there are properties humans have which God could not possibly have, assumes that these properties, or at least some of them, are essential properties of being human, properties without which one could not be fully human, and then concludes that God could not possibly become a human being. The conclusion would be well drawn if the assumption were correct. But it is this assumption that we must question.

Once a distinction betweeen essential and accidental properties is accepted, a distinction employed in this sort of argument against incarnation, another simple distinction follows in its wake. Among properties characterizing human beings, some are essential elements of human nature, but many just happen to be common human properties without also being essential. Consider for example the property of having ten fingers. It is a common human property, one had by a great number of people, but it clearly is not a property essential to being human. People lose fingers without thereby ceasing to be human. Further, consider a common property which safely can be said to be a universal human property, one had by every human being who ever has lived – the property of standing under fifteen feet tall. Obviously this is not an essential human property either. At some time in the future, an individual might grow beyond this height, certainly not thereby forfeiting his humanity. So it is not a safe inference to reason simply from a property's being common or even universal among human beings that it is an essential human property, strictly necessary for exemplifying human nature.

The relevance of this distinction to the doctrine of the Incarnation should be obvious. It is common for human beings to be less than omnipotent, less than omniscient, contingently existent, and so on. And any orthodox Christian will quickly agree that apart from Jesus, these are even universal human properties. Further, in the case of any of us who do exemplify these less than divine attributes, it is most reasonable to hold that they are in our case essential attributes. I, for example, could not possibly become omnipotent. I am essentially limited in power. But why think this is true on account of human nature? Why think that any attributes incompatible with deity are elements of human nature, properties without which one could not be truly human?

An individual is *fully human* just in case that individual has all essential human properties, all the properties composing basic human nature. An individual is *merely human* if he has all those properties *plus* some additional limitation properties as well, properties such as being less than omnipotent, less than omniscient, and so on. Some examples of this *merely x/fully x* distinction may help. Consider a diamond. It has all the properties essential to being a physical object (mass, spatiotemporal location, etc.). So it is fully physical. Consider now a turtle. It has all the properties essential to being a physical object. It is fully physical. But it is not merely physical. It has properties of animation as well. It is an organic being. In contrast, the gem is merely physical as well as being fully physical. Now take the case of a man. An embodied human being, any one you choose, has mass, spatio-temporal location, and so forth. He is thus fully physical. But he is not merely a physical object, having organic and animate properties as well. So let us say he is fully animate. But unlike the turtle he is not merely animate, having rational, moral, aesthetic, and spiritual qualities which mere organic entities lack. Let us say that he belongs to a higher ontological level by virtue of being fully human. And if, like you and I, he belongs to no higher ontological level than that of humanity, he is merely human as well as being fully human.

According to orthodox Christology, Jesus was fully human without being merely human. He had all properties constitutive of human nature, but had higher properties as well, properties constitutive of deity, properties which from an Anselmian perspective form the upper bound of our scale. What is crucial to realize here is that an orthodox perspective on human nature will categorize all human properties logically incompatible with a divine incarnation as, at most, essential to being *merely human*. No orthodox theologian has ever held that Jesus was merely human, only that he was fully human. It is held that the person who was God Incarnate had the full array of attributes essential to humanity, and all those essential to divinity.

I am suggesting that armed with a few simple distinctions the Christian can clarify his conception of human nature in such a way as to provide for the coherence and metaphysical possibility of the traditional doctrine of the Incarnation. But I am sure it will be objected by many that to use these distinctions to explicate what Chalcedon and the rest of the church has had in mind about Jesus is to land oneself in some well known absurdities. On the Chalcedonian picture, Jesus was omniscient, omnipotent, necessarily existent, and all the rest, as well as being an itinerant Jewish preacher. But this has appeared outlandish to most contemporary theologians. Did the bouncing baby boy of Mary and Joseph direct the workings of the cosmos, from his crib? Was this admittedly remarkable man, as he sat by a well or under a fig tree actually omnipresent in all of creation? Did this carpenter's son exist *necessarily?* These implications of orthodoxy can sound just too bizarre for even a moment's consideration.

A couple of ancient claims are sufficient to rid orthodoxy from any such appearance of absurdity. First of all, a person is not identical with his body. Even a modern materialist who holds that all personality necessarily is embodied need not deny this. So the necessary existence of God the Son, with its implications that he cannot have begun to exist and cannot cease to exist, does not entail that the earthly body in which he incarnated himself had these properties. Secondly, a person is not identical with any particular range of conscious experience he might have. With this in mind, we can appreciate the early view that in the case of God Incarnate, we must recognize something like two distinct ranges of consciousness.[4] There is first what we can call the eternal mind of God the Son with its distinctively divine consciousness, whatever that might be like, with its full scope of omniscience. And there is a distinctly earthly consciousness which grew and developed as the boy Jesus grew and developed. It drew its visual imagery from what the eyes of Jesus saw, and its concepts from the languages he spoke. The earthly range of consciousness, and self-consciousness, was thoroughly human, Jewish, and first century Palestinian in scope.

To be as brief as possible here, we can view the two ranges of consciousness as follows: The divine consciousness of God the Son contained, but was not contained by, the earthly range of consciousness. Further, there was what can be called an asymmetric accessing relation between the two (think of two computer programs or informational systems, one containing but not contained by the other). The divine mind had full access to the earthly experience being had through the incarnation, but the earthly consciousness did not have such access to the content of the over-arching omniscience of the Logos. This allows for the intellectual and spiritual growth of Jesus to be a real development. It also can help account for the cry of dereliction. We have in the person of Jesus no God merely dressed up as a man. No docetic absurdities are implied by this position. Nor is it Nestorian. Nor Apollinarian. There is one person with two natures, and two ranges of consciousness. He is not the theological equivalent of a centaur, half God and half man. He is fully human, but not merely human. He is also fully divine. There is, in this doctrine, no apparent incoherence whatsoever. Thus, there seem to be no good logical or conceptual grounds for thinking that there can be no rational belief that Jesus was God Incarnate.

But before concluding too hastily that it is at least possible for belief in the Incarnation to be rationally grounded, we would do well to consider briefly a problem which has been raised by Francis Young. Young has said:

> ... it is now accepted by the majority of Christian theologians that Jesus must have been an entirely normal human being, that any qualification of this implies some element of docetic thinking, and that docetism, however slight, undermines the reality of the incarnation.
>
> I therefore pose the following conundrum:
> *If Jesus was an entirely normal human being, no evidence can be produced for the incarnation.*
> *If no evidence can be produced, there can be no basis on which to claim that an incarnation took place.*[5]

If it is assumed, as I would suspect it is by Young, that the belief that Jesus was God Incarnate cannot be a reasonable or rational belief to hold unless there can be evidence on which to base it, this argument, or conundrum, immediately becomes an argument to the effect that, on a certain assumption concerning what the doctrine of the Incarnation itself requires with respect to the humanity of Jesus, we find that it cannot be reasonable or rational to believe that Jesus was God Incarnate.

It is true that in order to avoid the docetic tendency which some critics have claimed plagues traditional theology, we must maintain the full, complete humanity of Jesus. But Young has a genuine problem here for incarnational belief only if in order to avoid docetism we also would have to hold that Jesus was *merely* human, and thus different from ordinary human beings such as you or me in no metaphysical way which could possibly be empirically manifested. But as we have seen, there is an important distinction to be drawn between being fully human and being merely human. Jesus can be fully human without being merely human. At least, that is the orthodox claim as I have articulated it. His complete humanity is thus compatible with his belonging to the higher ontological level of deity as well, and being such that his deity as well as his humanity is manifest in his life. We need not hold that Jesus was merely human in order to avoid docetism and uphold the doctrine of the Incarnation. If we did hold this, it is clear that we would be fleeing docetism only to fall into the grasp of psilanthropism, and thereby relinquish the doctrine just as certainly, only in a more currently fashionable way. On a careful understanding of the logic and metaphysics of the Incarnation, we can thus see that Young's 'conundrum' cannot even arise. So, once again, we find that what has been taken to be a problem for the traditional position that it is possible for belief in the Incarnation to be rational is in actuality no problem at all. None of the considerations we have examined so far has had the slightest tendency to block in principle the possibility of rationally discerning God in Christ.

But there is one more major sort of objection many recent critics have lodged against the doctrine of the Incarnation, along with the beliefs about divine-human relations it presupposes. The doctrine of the Incarnation is one component in a much larger doctrinal scheme encompassing the themes of creation, fall, and redemption. Contemporary critics of the traditional renderings of these themes often have pointed out that they originally where enunciated and developed in pre-scientific conditions and thus within the context of a very different sort of world-view from the one which modern scientifically minded people have today. They have then usually gone on to suggest that religious claims which may have made a great deal of sense in their original context have lost much, if not all, of their plausibility in the modern age. It is interesting to note that this is a general point made repeatedly in recent years by many prominent professors of Christian theology as well as by critics avowedly outside the communion of the church.

Now, I think we must recognize that many professedly Christian theologians during the past century or so have appeared a bit overly ready to beat a hasty retreat in the face of almost any specious argument or other consideration against the traditional affirmations of the faith they are supposed to be representing. Often they seem inclined to relinquish or 'reinterpret' important doctrines on no better grounds than that those beliefs can appear to some secular critics to be somehow out of step with the march of science. There have been those such as Rudolf Bultmann, for example, who claim to be unable to believe in the literally miraculous while at the same time availing themselves of the comforts of modern technology. But of course such cases as these may be of more interest to psychologists than to anyone seeking to determine the objective status, truth value, or rationality of orthodox Christian beliefs. Occasionally, however, an interesting and even challenging philosophical or theological problem can be extracted from the often vague misgivings of such critics of orthodoxy. Let us consider various ways in which such a challenge might be thought to arise here against the doctrine of the Incarnation.

It has been suggested many times during the past two hundred years that this doctrine, which made a great deal of sense to many people living within the geocentric world-picture of Ptolemaic cosmology, is rendered in some sense absurd by modern accounts of the immensity and nature of our universe. The problem seems to be something like this: During the times when the Chalcedonian understanding of Christ was developed and reigned supreme, it was believed by great numbers of people, including the best educated, that we human beings live in a relatively circumscribed universe, the entirety of which has been created for the benefit of human life, which represents the special crowning act of divine creation, situated, appropriately at the hub of the cosmos, around which all else literally as well as figuratively revolves. Within such an overall perspective, it would have seemed in no way incongruous, but rather could have appeared supremely fitting, that the Creator of all take such interest in his human creatures as to step into his world himself and take a part in the human drama, being enacted, as it was, on the center stage of the universe. An anthropocentric world-view provided the cosmological backdrop and framework for a literally anthropomorphic theology – God become a man. The importance of the earth and the importance of humanity rendered this incarnation of deity intelligible and appropriate.

However, during the past few centuries this world-view, and the framework it provided, has been destroyed, chipped away bit by bit by the onslaught of scientific discovery until nothing of it remains. Actually, it is quite a variety of scientific discoveries, assumptions, hypotheses, speculations, and methodological implications which have seemed to many people to have had the net result of demoting human-kind from its traditionally exalted place in the universe to what can appear to be a relatively unexceptional and terribly insignificant role in the cosmic process. I shall not attempt to delineate here the variety of negative effects modern science has been perceived to have on religious doctrine. Numerous books exist which thoroughly document the so-called 'history of the warfare between science and theology.' But it will be of some interest to at least indicate a couple of points at which scientific developments have been thought to have this de-valuing impact on our view of humanity, and thus on the system of Christian doctrines, including centrally that of the Incarnation, in which the value of human beings seems clearly to be assumed to be great.

Some critics appear to think that the sheer size of the universe renders humanity unimportant in the cosmos, and Christian doctrine thus implausible. Of course, it is no modern novelty to juxtapose the immensity of the universe to the religious emphasis on man. The psalmist, for example, wrote long ago:

> When I consider Thy heavens, the work of Thy fingers, the moon and the stars, which Thou hast ordained: What is man that Thou dost take thought of him? And the son of man that Thou dost care for him? (Psalm 8:3, 4)

This is an expression of an attitude of wonderment, and perhaps astonishment, that amidst the grandeur of the heavens, human beings should be especially valued by God. The attitude of modern critics, however, is that of simple disbelief. Of course, the psalmist was not aware as some of us are today *how* immense the heavens might be. But it is a bit difficult to see exactly what it is about distinctively modern knowledge of the scale of the universe which is thought to show the absurdity of any religious beliefs based on the assumption that the earth and human beings are important to the Creator of all.

Now, it is clear that in many contexts size and value are in direct correlation, the latter depending on the former. For example, all other things being equal, a large army is of greater value than a small one, if one seeks protection of one's country from an enemy. But this dependence of value on size is only relative to some contexts having to do with instrumental value, and clearly does not hold true in either all or even most such contexts. And when it comes to considerations of intrinsic value, the sort of value ascribed to human beings by Christian theology, questions of size or physical magnitude are simply irrelevant. It is just absurd to argue: Small therefore unimportant. Critics often accuse Christian theologians of being anthropomorphic in their thought. But here it seems to be the critics who are anthropomorphizing, or better, anthropopathizing, with the assumption that if there were a God, he would not deign to notice or value anything as small and insignificant on the cosmic scale as the earth and its inhabitants. On the Christian picture, God is sufficiently unlike a man that his attention and care can extend fully to every part of a universe, however large, to the point of being infinite in space and time.

So I think we are safe in concluding that if any discovery of modern science undercuts the Christian belief that God so valued us that he became a man, it will not be any discovery concerning the sheer size of the universe. But as with the link between relative size and value, there have been traditionally believed to be a number of other signs, or even requisites, of human importance which have been undercut by the advance of the sciences. For example, in many primal religions an equation is held between spatial centrality and importance. Anthropologists have found many tribes who hold as a sacred belief the claim that their village, or a fire in the center of the village, is located at the center of the world, or at the center of the entire cosmos. Their importance to the gods is held to be tied to their central location. Such a view also can be seen in the Ptolemaic cosmology and in the many theological and philosophical speculations arising out of that cosmology. In light of this apparently natural equation of importance and spatial centrality, reflected also in non-spatial uses of the notion of centrality, it is easy to understand the resistance many Christian theologians and clerics once felt toward any transition away from a geocentric cosmology. But again, outside a very few contexts of instrumental value considerations, it is simply wrong to think there to be a necessary link between spatial centrality and value. Modern critics who cite the transition from a Ptolemaic to a Copernican to a contemporary cosmology as counting against or as undercutting traditional Christian claims that the earth and humanity are sufficiently important as to render appropriate a divine incarnation on earth are making the same mistake with respect to value theory as the ancients whose views they deride.

There are other lines of reasoning which have been used to support the conclusion that the doctrine of the Incarnation is a cosmologically incongruous claim, but all of them suffer from the same, or similar, sorts of glaring debilities as those two arguments we have just examined.

It is a bit surprising to find that a challenge to Christian belief which seems to have such widespread emotional appeal for critics has so little substance when examined closely.

Experience and affirmation

If it is possible that it be rational to believe Jesus to be God Incarnate, how is it possible? On what grounds, or in what circumstances, could a person be rational in believing Jesus to be literally God in human nature? What is required for rationality here? What will suffice? Can it be that any Christians who hold to an incarnational Christology, or more simply ascribe deity to Jesus, are rationally justified in so doing? And if so, how so?

If we survey a good, deal of relatively conservative theological litera-ture relevant to the topic, we often find writers of an orthodox bent producing arguments of one kind or another for the deity of Jesus, argu-ments which they apparently attempt to use to ground the propriety or reasonableness of affirming the doctrine of the Incarnation. A number of these arguments can be put quite concisely as producing their common desired conclusion from a simple two premise structure. Among the arguments frequently to be found are, for example, the following:

(1) *The Soteriological Argument*
    (a) Jesus can forgive us our sins and offer us salvation.
    (b) Only God can forgive us our sins and offer us salvation; thus
    (c) Jesus is God.
(2) *The Liturgical Argument*
    (a) Jesus is properly worshipped.
    (b) Only God is properly worshipped; thus
    (c) Jesus is God.
(3) *The Revelatory Argument*
    (a) Jesus reveals God perfectly.
    (b) Only God can reveal God perfectly; thus
    (c) Jesus is God.

Such arguments, of course, hardly ever appear in such pared-down form. Usually, the (a)-premise is defended as part of the distinctively Christian proclamation throughout the centuries and as either given in Christian experience or assumed in Christian practice. The (b)-premise is seen as a product of conceptual truths concerning the concepts involved: in each case the concept of God and, respectively, the concepts of sin, forgiveness, and salvation in the first argument, that of worship in the second, and revelation in the third.

These are clearly instances of deductively valid argument forms. And if the (b)-premise in each case is a conceptual truth, it follows that it will be reasonable to accept the conclusion of each argument if it is reasonable to accept its (a)-premise. But of course, it is also true that it is reasonable to accept the (a)-premise in each case only if it is reasonable to accept the claim of deity for Jesus. And that is precisely the question at issue. Such arguments as these clearly can serve a function within the context of an incarnational Christian faith – the function of explicitly displaying important logical relations between and among various central commitments of such a faith. A function they cannot perform is that of endowing incarnational belief with a rationality or reasonableness it otherwise would lack apart from their construction.

Can there be a deductively valid argument for the truth of the doctrine of the Incarnation which can function in such a way as to provide a person with a rational belief in it which, without the argument, he would not have, all other things being equal? In order to enhance our perspective on this question, let us look at one more relevant form of deductive argument.

In one of his contributions to the Incarnation debate, Brian Hebblethwaite sketched a number of arguments for the preferability of the Chalcedonian characterization of Jesus over the reduced claims for his status propounded in more recent times.[6] In a response to Hebblethwaite, Keith Ward wrote:

> Hebblethwaite introduces the remarkable argument that 'if God might have become a man, but did not, then the reduced claims for what God has done in Christ fail to satisfy'. It is difficult to formalize the argument; but it seems to go like this: 'if x is logically possible; and if we think it better that x, then x.' It is the sort of argument sometimes produced for the doctrine of the Assumption of Mary: 'God could have done it; he should have; so he did.'[7]

Consider for a moment Ward's attempt to formalize the argument he finds in Hebblethwaite. He first offers us the schema

(A) 1. x is logically possible
     2. We think it better that x; thus,
     3. x

and then apparently means to paraphrase it, or at least apply it in such a way that a parallel schema, each of whose premiseforms he apparently takes to be entailed by the corresponding premise-forms of (A), will result which relates directly to theological argument:

(B) 1. God could have done *x*.
     2. God should have done *x*; thus,
     3. God did *x*.

It is Ward's contention that using arguments of the form of (A) in theological matters will yield arguments of the form of (B), and will have, to say
the least, untrustworthy results. Ward seems to view the sort of theological
argument represented in (B) as having all the benefit of theft over honest
toil – that of providing an easy route to results we have no right to.

   Of course, the first thing that should be pointed out about what Ward
says and seems to assume here is that (A) clearly neither is equivalent
to (B) and thus properly paraphrased by it, nor does it even entail (B).
The many qualifications we must introduce into a careful definition
of omnipotence have taught us that (A)–1 does not entail (B)–1. And
certainly (A)–2 does not entail (B)–2. We can be wrong about what
states of affairs would be or would have been, better than others; moreover, even when we are right in such judgments, we are not always discovering divine obligations to bring about such states of affairs.

   Since (A) does not entail (B), (A) can be a fallacious form of argument
without its following that (B) is as well. And this, as a matter of fact, is
the case. Arguments of the form of (A) are obviously fallacious. The
world does not necessarily conform itself to our preferences. But, interestingly, arguments of the form of (B) are not fallacious. The (B) schema
is a deductively valid one, given the concept of God as a necessarily good
being. If we could know, concerning some possible action, both that
God could have done it and that he should have done it, then we also
could know that he did it. Applying this to the doctrine of the Incarnation, if we knew or had reason to believe the two premises in the following argument, our knowledge or reasonable belief would be transmitted
to its conclusion:

(C) 1. God could have become incarnate in human nature as Jesus of
         Nazareth,
     2. God should have become incarnate in human nature as Jesus of
         Nazareth; thus,
     3. God did become incarnate in human nature as Jesus of Nazareth.

As I have indicated already, a couple of simple metaphysical distinctions
will suffice to defend the truth of (C)–1. But, in light of the epistemic
realities for religious belief with which we live, it is difficult to see how
anyone might be in better epistemic position with respect to (C)–2 than
with respect to (C)–3. It is thus hard to see how the reasonableness of a
belief that (C)–3 could be thought to be based on or grounded in an
argument such as (C) operating on an independently reasonable belief

that (C)–2 and (C)–1, given the epistemic conditions we are all in with respect to God's actions, and the principles of his actions.

It seems to me that vast numbers of Christians are reasonable in believing Jesus to be God Incarnate, and it is my guess that many of them have never reflected on or in any other way entertained proposition (C)–2, the claim that God should have become incarnate, and have no reasonable belief that it is true. Moreover, many who have considered it would, *I suspect,* maintain a properly pious agnosticism about it, while whole-heartedly and reasonably endorsing the doctrine of the Incarnation. And further, I would expect that any Christians who would affirm (C)–2 would do so on the basis of, among other things, their prior belief that Jesus was God Incarnate. So even in their case, the reasonableness of the latter belief would in no way depend on the reasonableness of the former – quite the opposite.

I have introduced this excursus into Ward's remarks along the way to making a very simple point. If it is reasonable to believe Jesus to be God Incarnate, that reasonableness is not likely produced by means of, or grounded in, any such deductive argument. It seems to be the case that deductive arguments for the Incarnation will always have at least one premise whose positive epistemic status is no greater or more obvious than that of the doctrine itself. In the Soteriological, Liturgical, and Revelatory arguments, it will be reasonable to believe the premise in question, at best, *if and only if* it is reasonable to believe Jesus to be God Incarnate. In the argument (C), gleaned from Ward's remarks on Hebblethwaite, it will be reasonable to believe the more controversial premise at best *only if* it is reasonable to believe in the Incarnation. In none of these cases do we find a prior, independent reasonableness transmitted to and conferred upon the incarnational belief from more evident beliefs. So if it can be, or is, reasonable to believe Jesus to be God Incarnate, then most likely that reasonableness will neither consist in nor be provided by the having of such a simple deductive argument.

It is natural to ask next whether some form of inductive, or non-deductive, argument could render belief in Jesus' deity reasonable. Consider for a moment that form of reasoning in which Nicodemus engaged concerning Jesus, and from which this chapter began. We can represent the structure of his argument as

(N) 1. Jesus performed a certain class of acts *M* (acts such as tradition-ally have been classed as miracles)
    2. No one can perform acts of class *M* unless he is a teacher come from God; thus,
    3. Jesus was a teacher come from God.

And again, this is a deductively valid argument concerning the status of Jesus. As Nicodemus appears to have reasoned to the conclusion that Jesus was a teacher come from God, many Christians of conservative theological orientation talk as if they themselves have reasoned, or as if they are convinced that a rational non-believer could reason, from empirically ascertainable facts about the circumstances, character, and deeds of Jesus to the much stronger conclusion that he was and is God Incarnate. They could have in mind an argument such as (N), where M now presumably would include, say postresurrection activities of the risen Christ, and which would employ a substituted second premise such as

2′. No one can perform acts of class M unless he is God,

from which it would follow validly that Jesus was God. Or they could have in mind a probabilistic transform of the revised (N), in which case the simple, categorical claim of deity for Jesus would not validly follow, but the weaker claim that it is probable that Jesus was divine would. Or it could be the case that many Christians who reason about Jesus in the tradition of Nicodemus have something in mind which cannot be captured by any such simple, two-step deductive argument. Perhaps there is a complex non-deductive form of argument to the best explanation which they have in mind, and which cannot be so simply represented. Thus, they would argue that the best explanation for a certain range of facts about Jesus is that he was God Incarnate.

On the one hand, it is clear that most mature Christians who affirm the divinity of Jesus see their belief as anchored in the empirical realm. They see their incarnational belief as in accord with their own personal experience, with the experience of other Christians throughout the centuries, and with the apparent though sometimes elusive manifestations of deity in the empirical realm which the New Testament documents appear to record surrounding the person of Jesus. But on the other hand, it seems not to be the case that there is any single, isolable form of non-deductive argument typically relied upon by such Christians to get from distinct facts about the portrayal of Jesus in the New Testament, from facts about the experience of Jesus on the part of fellow believers through the ages, or from features of their own experience to a conclusion that Jesus is God the Son, the Second Person of the Divine Trinity. Nor is it obvious that any account of their reasonableness in so believing must involve the production of such an argument.

It does not seem that the reasonableness of incarnational belief is provided by deductive arguments from premises it is independently reasonable to believe, nor does it seem to be provided by any single sort of non-deductive argument consciously entertained or used by believers. Could it then be a simple function of direct experience? Could it be the case that traditional Christians have just *seen* Jesus to be God Incarnate, and that their belief in his deity, thus generated, is reasonable precisely in light of that experience?

Grace Jantzen once wrote:

> Clearly, any doctrine which wishes to affirm that Jesus of Nazareth is God the Son, the Second Person of the Holy Trinity, is going well beyond the boundary of empirical observability. Indeed, what would it be *like* to make that sort of observation? Even the question seems misphrased. No list of empirical data, whether these are taken strictly as sense data or more broadly as observation of speech and behaviour patterns could ever entail the conclusion reached by the centurion in the Gospel: "Truly this man was the Son of God."[8]

Sense data reports underdetermine statements about physical objects. Reports about the disposition and behavior of physical objects (such as arms, legs, mouths, and even brains) arguably underdetermine claims about the distinctively mental properties of persons. And claims about the divine can seem to be even more remote from any reports about what is experienced in the empirical realm. For example, a few years ago an article appeared in which it was argued that not even God could know from observation, or even from observation enhanced by inductive reasoning, that he is God, i.e. that he exemplifies the distinctively divine attributes.[9] Consider omnipotence alone. No matter how many extraordinary tasks a being has attempted to perform and has carried out successfully with no difficulty or strain whatsoever, it will not follow from his record of accomplishments, however astounding, that he is literally omnipotent. Thus, no matter what we observe a being do in the empirical arena, a full report of our observations will not entail the proposition that the being in question is omnipotent. If seeing that an individual is God requires seeing that he is omnipotent, necessarily good, omnipresent, omniscient, ontologically independent, and the like, then the prospects for just directly seeing that Jesus is God look pretty dim, to say the least.

But does experiencing Jesus as divine require this sort of 'seeing-that' relation? Clearly, in undergoing the processes which sense data theorists have characterized as the having of percepts or sense data, we most often reasonably take ourselves to be experiencing physical objects. Likewise, in experiencing the dispositions and behaviors of certain sorts of physical objects in certain sorts of circumstances, we reasonably take ourselves to be experiencing or observing the mental qualities of other persons, e.g. their anger, happiness, irritation, tranquility. It is true that if the observational experience of a table were to be reported in purely sense data language (supposing that to be possible), the report would not entail any appropriately related proposition about a physical object. But this does not prevent our sense experience being experience of physical objects. Likewise, the lack of entailments between reports about Jesus cast in this-worldly terms and the appropriate propositions concerning his deity need not preclude the possibility of an experience of Jesus as the infinite God Incarnate through the sort of finite range of experience of him available to an ordinary human believer.

Suppose that, as many theologians have suggested through the centuries, there is an innate human capacity which, when properly functioning, allows us to see God, or, to put it another way, to recognize God when we see him, in the starry heavens above or in the moral law within. If there is such a capacity to recognize God both in his products, and where he is distinctively present and active, and if he is personally present and active in the life of Jesus of Nazareth as the ultimate subject of that life, then we would expect him to be recognized in his incarnate form by those whose relevant capacity for seeing is sufficiently unimpeded.

Many children believe that Jesus is divine upon being told so by their elders. They believe it on testimony. They do not believe it on the basis of any argument or inference from the general reliability of testimony, from the particular reliability of the elders in question, or from any fact or belief about testimony at all. They just believe it on the occasion of being told it, like so much else they believe. And surely they are not irrational in so believing. But perhaps small children are not yet at any age of epistemic accountability. Perhaps as children mature, we expect them to start hooking up their beliefs into coherent pictures of the world. What was once a properly basic belief for the young child, a belief not based on any epistemically more secure beliefs by standard basing relations, and not requiring such basing, may later come to stand in such relations in the young person's noetic structure that it is no longer among his basic beliefs, but that it is nonetheless still among his beliefs that it is reasonable for him to have.

Likewise, many people who become Christians, or who come to see Jesus as divine, come to believe in his divinity upon seeing the portrait of him in the Gospels, or upon experiencing what they take to be his presence in prayer or his power transforming their lives. They do not base their belief on any argument or inference from the details of the scriptural account or from the features of their own personal experience. They merely find themselves believing on having some such appropriate

originating experience or experiences, experiences which they take to
be experiences of God Incarnate. But as the Christian who holds such a
belief matures in his faith, he comes to know much better the testimony
of scripture and of other believers to the reality of what he has taken
himself to have experienced. I want to suggest that the Christian who
originally attains a belief that Jesus is God Incarnate either from testimony or from his own experiences, of the sorts indicated, can reasonably
take up such a belief, and as he matures, reasonably take much of what
he subsequently learns of the Christian story, and from his own experience, to be corroboration of that belief. Instances in the life of Jesus, for
example, as recounted in the Gospels, can reasonably be thought by a
responsible reader to attest to his divinity. As we have seen in discussing
the conundrum for incarnational belief which Francis Young attempted
to formulate, the metaphysics of the Incarnation allow Jesus' divinity to
be manifested through displays of knowledge and power often catego-
rized as miraculous, as well as in other ways. And, despite what some
critics seem to imply, one need not be exceedingly naive concerning the
vicissitudes of New Testament criticism in order to be reasonable in so
reading the Gospels as to find corroboration in them for a belief in the
Incarnation.

The dynamics of reasonable belief are extremely complex and are far
beyond the scope of the present essay to lay out in any general way, even
for the restricted, though highly controversial, class of religious beliefs
such as the one which is our proper focus. One feature of reasonable
belief maintenance, however, which should be mentioned here is the
following: Whenever one holds a belief which is challenged by apparently powerful considerations which one understands, one's maintaining
of the belief will continue to be reasonable to the same degree only
if one is able to locate a sufficient response to the newly introduced
challenge. For many sophisticated Christians of an orthodox persuasion
in recent years, the challenges to the doctrine of the Incarnation which
we have been reviewing in this study have constituted potentially the
most difficult obstacles to the continued reasonableness of their belief
that Jesus was God Incarnate. The availability of such perspectives as
I have been attempting to sketch out constitutes, I think, a response to
those challenges sufficient to block any negative net impact on the reasonableness of endorsing the incarnational claim. A traditional believer
who has grown in the maturation of his faith and who has faced and met
such challenges as those we have considered can be held to have attained
the sort of corroboration and defense of his incarnational belief which
can secure the reasonableness of his maintaining that conception of the
status of Jesus which most often arises from the simple founts of testimony and experience.

If there is an innate human capacity which, when properly functioning, allows us to recognize God when we see him, then if Jesus is God
Incarnate, it is clear that there are widespread and deeply rooted impedi-
ments to this capacity's functioning. It seems likely, in light of what has
just been adumbrated, that a reasonable belief that Jesus is God Incarnate
will arise and flourish only with the removal of some of these impedi-
ments from the life of a person. And this is just the insight we can derive
from the original Nicodemus story when we see that Jesus' response to
Nicodemus' simple *modus tollens* argument, whose conclusion fell well
short of the mark, is not the glaring *non sequitur* it can initially appear, but
rather is a profound indication of the truth, or rather of the only way to
come to the truth about who he is. The story, in John 3:1–3, from which
we began this essay, will bear repeating:

> Now there was a man of the Pharisees, named Nicodemus,
> a ruler of the Jews. This man came to Jesus by night and said
> to him, "Rabbi, we know that you are a teacher come from
> God; for no one can do these signs that you do, unless God is
> with him."

And then the key:

> Jesus answered him, "Truly, truly I say to you, unless one is
> born anew he cannot see the kingdom of God."

In Matthew 17:15–17 we find this exchange between Jesus and his
disciples:

> He said to them: "But who do you say that I am?" Simon
> Peter replied, "You are the living Christ, the Son of the living
> God." And Jesus answered him, "Blessed are you, Simon
> Bar-Jona! For flesh and blood has not revealed this to you, but
> my Father who is in heaven.

And in the Apostle Paul's first letter to the church at Corinth (I Corinthians 12:3), we find the succinct claim that

> . . . no one can say "Jesus is Lord" except by the Holy Spirit.

A full account of the epistemic status of Christian doctrine would be
quite complex and would require, at its core, what we might call a Spirit
Epistemology. The remarks of the present essay have been laid out in
broad strokes and have hinted at no more than a very few elements of

such an account in even the case of the one tenet of orthodox Christian belief which is our present concern. Yet, despite the severe limitations of what I have undertaken to say here, it seems to me that on the basis of the few considerations we have been able to reflect on, however briefly, we can conclude that from these quarters, there seems to be no obstacle in principle to the acceptability of the widespread Christian assumption that it is possible that it be rational to believe Jesus to be God Incarnate.

Notes

1. John Wisdom, *Paradox and Discovery*, (Oxford: Basil Blackwell, 1965), 19-20.
2. Grace Jantzen, 'Incarnation and Epistemology,' *Theology* 83 (May 1983), 171.
3. The challenge is addressed in chapter nine of *Understanding Identity Statements* (Aberdeen: Aberdeen University Press and Humanities Press, 1984), in 'Divinity, Humanity, and Death,' *Religious Studies* 19 (December 1983), 451–458, and in 'Incarnational Anthropology,' *Theology* 87 (September 1984), 344–350. It is explored in much greater detail in chapters one through six of *The Logic of God Incarnate* (Ithaca: Cornell University Press, 1986).
4. One contemporary theologian who has hinted repeatedly at the importance of this view is Brian Hebblethwaite. See for example his article 'The Propriety of the Doctrine of the Incarnation as a Way of Interpreting Christ,' *Scottish Journal of Theology* 33 (1980), 201–222.
5. Frances Young, 'Can There Be Any Evidence,' *Incarnation and Myth: The Debate Continued,* ed. Michael Goulder (Grand Rapids: Eerdmans, 1979), 62.
6. Brian Hebblethwaite, 'Incarnation – The Essence of Christianity?' *Theology* 80 (1977).
7. Keith Ward, 'Incarnation or Inspiration – A False Dichotomy?' *Theology* 80 (1977).
8. Grace Jantzen, 'Incarnation and Epistemology,' 173, 174.
9. See Richard Creel, 'Can God Know That He is God?' *Religious Studies* 16 (June 1980), 195–201.

PART IV

SIN AND ORIGINAL SIN

INTRODUCTION

The doctrine of original sin presents some of the most difficult problems for the contemporary theologian. There are various accounts of the doctrine in the tradition with no single agreed definition of the doctrine, unlike the Chalcedonian 'definition' of the person of Christ. However, many theologians distinguish between Adam's primal sin, which began the corruption of human nature; original sin, which is the morally vitiated condition passed down from Adam to his progeny; and original guilt, which is the guilt associated with this condition. Quite how original sin and guilt are transmitted from Adam to his posterity is a hoary old theological conundrum. But quite apart from problems arising from particular aspects of the doctrine, there are well-known difficulties for defenders of this doctrine concerning how the Primeval Prologue of Gen. 1–3 relates to contemporary scientific theories about human development. This difficulty is undoubtedly one of the most profound contemporary theological problems, with insufficient work having been done on it by contemporary systematic – or philosophical theologians. The essays in this part reflect this general trend. Rather than focusing on whether the traditional theological account of this doctrine can be retained in light of contemporary scientific thinking, the essays reprinted here focus on issues having to do with the coherence or internal logic of the concept of sin as well as the doctrine of original sin, and on the relationship between theological accounts of original sin and more philosophical theories of sin.

In his essay, moral philosopher Robert Adams attends to issues at the interface between the doctrine of original sin and more philosophical accounts of sin, particularly that given by Immanuel Kant. Adams concludes that the traditional doctrine may need some revision, but a robust account of sin can be had in which some of the insights provided by Kant might figure.

The work of Oxford philosophical theologian Marilyn Adams engages with both medieval philosophy and theology. These twin concerns are reflected in her essay, where she considers the concept of sin as 'uncleanness', with particular reference to the medieval mystical theologian, Julian of Norwich.

The third essay, by Keith Wyma, engages with the traditional doctrine of original sin. He attempts to show that being created by God in a state of original sin may be compatible with divine justice, and that actual sins performed by those in a state of original sin are the responsibility of those sinful individuals, for which they are justly blameworthy.

Suggested further reading

- Crisp, Oliver D., *Jonathan Edwards and the Metaphysics of Sin* (Aldershot: Ashgate, 2005).
- Quinn, Philip L., 'In Adam's Fall, We Sinned All' *Philosophical Topics* (1988) reprinted in Christian Miller, (ed.) *Essays in the Philosophy of Religion* (Oxford: Oxford University Press, 2006), pp. 209–233.
- Quinn, Philip L., 'Disputing the Augustinian Legacy: John Locke and Jonathan Edwards on Romans 5: 12-19,' in Gareth Matthews, (ed.) *The Augustinian Tradition* (Berkeley: University of California Press, 1999), pp. 233–250.
- Rea, Michael C., 'The Metaphysics of Original Sin' in Peter van Inwagen and Dean Zimmerman, (eds), *Persons, Human and Divine* (Oxford: Oxford University Press, 2007), pp. 319–356.
- Swinburne, Richard, *Responsibility and Atonement* (Oxford: Clarendon Press, 1989), ch. 9.
- Wainwright, William J., 'Original Sin' in Thomas V. Morris (ed.), *Philosophy and the Christian Faith* (Notre Dame: University of Notre Dame Press, 1988), pp. 31–60.

CHAPTER 12

ORIGINAL SIN: A STUDY IN THE INTERACTION OF PHILOSOPHY AND THEOLOGY★

Robert Merrihew Adams

MUCH THAT HAS BEEN SAID about the relation of Christian theology to other disciplines in a modern (or "postmodern") intellectual environment assumes a deep opposition between Christian traditions and the secular liberalism of the modern West. I have never been able to see an irreconcilable opposition here. For it seems to me that I have lived my whole life as a member of a tradition that fuses versions of Protestantism and modern liberalism – a tradition whose most typical American exemplar, perhaps, is Reinhold Niebuhr. Niebuhr blended those sources with an illuminative power that may have been as effective for his generation as St. Thomas Aquinas's fusion of Aristotelianism and Augustinianism was for his generation.[1] Many American Catholics have a similar experience of a tradition combining liberal and Christian strands, in a Catholic version, with John Courtney Murray, perhaps playing something like Niebuhr's role; but I will leave it to them to speak for themselves.

Niebuhr's work was at once social criticism, political ethics, and Christian apologetics. Its apologetic force lay in its showing that Christian thought could illuminate contemporary moral situations and depended, therefore, on its having an appeal to experience and to contemporary moral sensibilities that was independent of any appeal to religious authority. This is exemplified in Niebuhr's most famous intellectual project, his exposition and rehabilitation of the doctrine of original sin. While the exposition is rich with biblical and theological allusions, and is clearly inspired by religious sources, Niebuhr's version of the doctrine can easily be read as a mainly empirical thesis.

Behind Niebuhr's treatment of the subject lies Kant's – not in Niebuhr's consciousness,[2] but in the line of historical development. Kant is one of relatively few modern philosophers to pay much attention to questions of sin and forgiveness. What is striking, for our present concern with the relation of Christianity to philosophy, is that Kant sees these topics both as historically Christian and as belonging to the realm of *Religion Within the Limits of Reason Alone* – as topics to be treated by *mere* reason, *bloße Vernunft*. In the present essay I will try to illuminate the relation of Christian theology to philosophy by recounting and reflecting on some of the history of the doctrine of original sin, beginning and ending with Kant.

What led Kant to a theory of original sin?

It may seem strange that Kant should be interested in such a doctrine at all, since it is commonly understood to involve the ascription to us of guilt for the sin of Adam, whereas Kant is committed to ascribing moral merit and demerit only on the basis of the free acts of one's own will. Kant is well aware of this problem, and tries to work out a form of the doctrine that is compatible with his voluntarism. But why should he take an interest in this subject at all?

It is foreign to much of the current lively interest in Kant's ethics, which has only recently begun to take seriously the difficulty of isolating his permanently interesting ethical theses from his religious views and his metaphysical hypotheses about noumena, or timeless things in themselves. Perhaps, indeed, a fragment of Kant's ethics, consisting chiefly in the Categorical Imperative, can be isolated in this way from his metaphysics and philosophical theology. But there is much more to Kant's moral thought than the Categorical Imperative, and his interest in the problem of original sin[3] arises naturally from something that has a pretty good claim to be regarded as the first principle of his moral philosophy, as it is enunciated in the very first sentence of the body of the *Groundwork of the Metaphysics of Morals:* "Nothing can possibly be conceived in the world, or even out of it, which can be called good without qualification, except a good will."[4]

Of course, in order to understand this principle or interpret it, we have to have some sense of what Kant means by "a good will." What is it to have a good will? What is a good will? A preoccupation with the Categorical Imperative, as a source of ideas for developing criteria for the evaluation of actions, may mislead us here, tempting us to think that for Kant having a good will must be a matter of acting voluntarily in accordance with the moral law, which he calls *pflichtmäßig handeln* (acting in accordance with duty). But that is quite explicitly not what Kant means by "having a good will." Having a good will for Kant is not *pflichtmäßig handeln* but *aus Pflicht handeln*, not acting in accordance with duty, but acting out of duty – in other words, acting from a certain motive.

In support of this view Kant appeals, very plausibly, to ordinary moral judgment. If we think people are acting in accordance with duty only because they fear punishment, or because they hope for some reward from other people, or merely because what they are doing happens to be expedient for purposes that have nothing to do with morality, we do not give them much credit for it. But if they do it because they believe it is right, that seems morally worthy.

Kant makes no appeal to religious authority, and none seems needed to sustain this point. At the same time, it is obvious that his conception of a good will resonates with the emphasis on good motivation in the Bible and in Christian traditions. How much is Kant influenced, and how much is our "ordinary" moral judgment influenced, by that background? It might be hard to say.

Furthermore, Kant understands the good will, not as a particular act, but as something more global. The good will, for Kant, is the moral agent him- or herself being rightly motivated, or something approaching that. This comes out in several ways. For one thing, it is quite clear that the question about the good that grips Kant's interest is not "Was that a good act?" or "Was that an act deserving of reward?" The question that grips his interest is, rather, "Is my will good?" or "Am I a person well pleasing to God?" or "Do I deserve to be happy?" – questions, in other words, about himself as a whole, not about particular acts. He insists also that a good will (or, for that matter, a bad will) is not to be inferred, even with probability, from a single action; rather, such an inference should take into account a course of life continued over some time.[5]

A good will, therefore, is a motivational state, and a very comprehensive one. In saying that nothing is unqualifiedly good except a good will, Kant is proclaiming, first of all, that the value of morality is intrinsic, not merely instrumental; and, second, that moral worth depends on one's motivational state. The first of these convictions grounds Kant's interest in problems of guilt and forgiveness. His theory of original sin is strongly rooted in the second conviction, about the moral value of motivation.

We can trace, in Kant's *Religion Within the Limits of Reason Alone,* a rationale for belief in original sin that begins with his conviction that moral worth depends not merely on our action, but chiefly on a disposition (*Gesinnung*) which is, as he puts it in the *Religion,* an "ultimate subjective ground" of choice (p. 20). This disposition consists, I take it, of the most basic maxims or principles of action we adhere to, together with such facts as how strongly or weakly we adhere to them and any motives we may have for our adherence.

The second point in the rationale is that if we consider any act that we perform at any time, we see that this act proceeded from an ethical disposition that we already had. This seems to follow from the very structure of human action. As Kant says, "The ultimate ground of the adoption of our maxims . . . is posited as the ground antecedent to every use of freedom in experience (in earliest youth as far back as birth)" (p. 17). Our actions must, therefore, be traced ultimately to a disposition that we did not adopt by any action that we have performed in time. Kant is prepared to call this original disposition an "inborn natural constitution" (*Beschaffenheit*) (p. 20) precisely and only in the sense that it has not been acquired in time. It would seem to follow also that having it is not voluntary, since we have never adopted it.

In the third place, while our original constitution could have been wholly good, Kant believes that experience constrains us to judge that that is not the case, and that in each of us, before we performed any evil act in time, there was a propensity (*Hang*) to evil included in our ethical disposition. For immoral action proceeds from a disposition that is morally flawed. If one did not already have such a corrupt propensity, Kant thinks, one would not do wrong.

It would be consistent with these first three points to maintain that while our original bad disposition preceded any act in time and thus could not have been adopted by such an act, the good or bad disposition that we now have as adults was determined, not by the original disposition, but by our voluntary acts in the past, and can, thus, be regarded as voluntarily adopted. But, in the fourth place, Kant denies that we have that kind of control over our ethical disposition. He says that while "it must be possible to overcome [*überwiegen*] [the propensity to evil] because it is found in man as a being that acts freely," it "cannot be eradicated [*vertilgt,* or (p. 27) *ausgerottet*] because this could happen only through good maxims, which cannot take place when the ultimate subjective ground of maxims is presupposed as corrupt" (p. 32). Thus, our predicament in original sin is serious indeed.

In spite of having said all this, Kant quite explicitly holds that we are to blame for this condition. "We are accountable," he says, "for the propensity to evil . . . despite the fact that this propensity is so deeply rooted in the will that we are forced to say that it is found in man by nature" (p. 30). And he ascribes to us guilt (*Schuld, reatus*) for the propensity to evil (p. 33).[6]

I want next to examine more closely the epistemological status of Kant's theory of original sin, in comparison with traditional Catholic and Protestant views. This will help, to prepare us for an historical and comparative consideration of the issue that most interests me in all this, which is the relation between voluntariness and our accountability for motivational states. Finally, I will discuss the treatment of it in Scholastic philosophy, the Protestant Reformers, and Kant.

The epistemological status of original sin

In the rationale that I traced in the previous section, the first point, that moral worth depends on disposition, is integral to Kant's ethical theory;

I have already discussed its grounds. The second point, that every act in time proceeds from a disposition that we already have, and the fourth, that a propensity to evil cannot be eradicated by human powers, belong to a clearly philosophical analysis of human action. The crucial third step, that our original disposition includes a propensity to evil, is justified by appeal to experience. Kant says that we are "evil by nature" in the sense that "evil can be predicated of man as a species; not that such a quality can be inferred from the concept of his species (that is, of man in general) – for then it would be necessary; but rather that from what we know of man through experience we cannot judge otherwise of him, or, that we may presuppose evil to be subjectively necessary to every man, even to the best" (p. 27). Thus, Kant presents the claim that we are evil by nature as an empirical thesis about human beings as we now actually find them. The empirical character of his theory of original sin is closely connected with his relation to theological tradition on three different issues.

(1) Kant's theory of original sin is not grounded in any appeal to the authority of the Bible. It does not essentially depend on the story of the Fall of our first ancestors from innocence, narrated in the second and third chapters of Genesis. For Kant denies that the evil in us was caused by their sin. "Of all the explanations of the spread and propagation of this evil through all the members and generations of our race," he says, "surely the most inept is that which describes it as descending to us as an inheritance from our first parents; for one can say of moral evil precisely what the poet said of good: 'race and forebears, and what we have not done ourselves, I hardly count as ours'" (p. 35).[7]

This rejection of the hereditary character of original sin is the chief departure from theological tradition in Kant's views on the subject. He does find a use for the Genesis story of the Fall, but it is merely illustrative. According to him, we have sinned in Adam only in the sense that we have sinned as he did. A line Kant quotes from Horace aptly expresses the religious significance Kant finds in the story of Adam and Eve: "*Mutate nomine de te fabula narratur*" (Change but the name, of thee the tale is told) (p. 37). In other words, the point of Genesis 2 and 3, for Kant, is to provide a parable or model for the understanding of our own sin.

It is of interest to note that Kant has largely been followed in this by the most influential Protestant writers on original sin in the nineteenth and twentieth centuries, such as Schleiermacher, Kierkegaard, and Reinhold Niebuhr. Despite various differences among them, it is true of all these theologians that Adam and Eve play no crucial role in their conception of original sin. The only importance that the Genesis story of the Fall has for any of them is "Of thee the tale is told." Niebuhr is quite explicit about this, declaring: "When the Fall is made an event in history rather than a symbol of an aspect of every historical moment in the life of man, the relation of evil to goodness in that moment is obscured."[8]

(2) It follows that there is room in Kant's theory for only one of the two leading ways of thinking of original sin that are found, often in combination, in the history of the doctrine. The first of these ideas is that guilt is imputed to all of us for Adam's sin, because we all, in some sense, sinned in him, or were in him when he sinned. Here the sin in question, of which Adam and we are guilty, is the sin that he sinned in eating the forbidden fruit. For this idea Kant has no use, because Adam's sin plays no essential part in his theory, and, more fundamentally, because he rejects any ascription to us of guilt or responsibility for another agent's act.

The other way of thinking of original sin is as a morally corrupt condition, a state or disposition, that we all were in at birth. This is not a sin that Adam committed, but a sin that is in us, at birth. To be sure, it was Adam's sin that led to our being in this condition, on the traditional account; but the condition was in us, and we are individually guilty for it, with a guilt that is not merely imputed to us. The corrupt condition is conceived as at least largely a motivational state; in this conception of original sin, therefore, we are held accountable for motivational states.

The first idea, of imputed guilt for Adam's sin, is probably what many people think of first in connection with the doctrine of original sin. But I think, in fact, it is the second idea, of the morally corrupt condition in which we all were born, that has been the more important in the history of the doctrine.[9] To conceive of original sin, as Kant does, exclusively in terms of a corrupt condition is, therefore, a less radical departure from theological tradition than his denial that either corruption or guilt is inherited from our first parents.

(3) The treatment of the doctrine of original sin as an empirical thesis about a corrupt condition found in human beings as we observe them is facilitated by another position characteristic of Protestant theology. One of the original topics of controversy between Protestants and Catholics in the sixteenth century was whether original sin remains in those who have been baptized. The Reformers held that it does, whereas the Council of Trent maintained that both the guilt of original sin and any sinful corruption are cleansed away by baptism and that although some consequences of the Fall remain in the baptized, the consequences are not sin. An exploration of some of the ramifications of this dispute will shed light on the epistemological status of claims about original sin and will also provide important background for our subsequent discussion of approaches to the relation between voluntariness and accountability for motivational states.

Underlying the debate about the consequences of baptism is a dis-agreement about what happened in the Fall. According to the Scholastic theology that is reflected in the thinking of the Council of Trent, the Fall did not corrupt human nature. What happened was, rather, that Adam and Eve lost, and lost not only for themselves but also for their descend-ants, a gift that they had been given in addition to their nature. This preternatural gift, which was called "original righteousness," or "original justice" (*justitia originalis*), consisted, first of all, in an orientation of the soul toward God, which made the soul able to know and love God more fully than it naturally could. It carried in its train an ordering of the powers of the human soul and body, such that all of them, including all the emotions and desires and all the functions of the body, obeyed the highest part of the soul, the reason, more fully and perfectly than would have been naturally possible.

Original righteousness was lost in the Fall and is not restored com-pletely by baptism. Baptism provides something that is in some respects as good and in some respects even better – a sanctifying grace, which makes it possible again for the soul to know and love God properly if it makes proper use of its freedom. But sanctifying grace does not com-pletely restore the ordering of all the powers of the soul and body. It does not remove the natural independence of the desires and emotions from the reason, which constitutes, so to speak, a natural disorder within us.

This disorder is called "concupiscence." Concupiscence is not nice but, being natural, is not itself sin. It can be called "tinder for sin" in the baptized, the idea being that this lack of natural agreement between the desires and the reason is there waiting to burst into flame if sin comes along to set it off. But it is not ignited unless the soul, by its own free will, sins. Consequently, any sin occurring in someone who has been baptized is not "original" sin, but "actual" sin.

The Reformers held a different view of the matter. According to them, a corruption that is itself sin remains after baptism and even after the fullest regeneration that is possible for us in this world. Regeneration does remove any guilt that may be imputed from Adam's sin. And as long as the Christian is in a state of grace, justified by faith, the corruption that remains is not imputed as liability to punishment. The corruption is in itself sin, however, and the regenerate person is "at once righteous and a sinner" (*simul justus et peccator*), in Luther's famous phrase.

This is connected with the Reformers' view that what was lost in the Fall was not a preternatural gift, but something that belonged to human nature. Our nature itself having been corrupted, the ensuing disorder in us, which the Reformers also called "concupiscence," cannot be excused as natural. Protestants were accordingly prepared to say that concupiscence is in itself sin.

I think it follows from this disagreement that the Catholic and the Protestant doctrines of original sin have rather different subject matters and different epistemological bases. The Protestant doctrine is not primarily about infants. Claims about infants get involved in it, but it starts with a morally corrupt condition discoverable in all of us as adults. Then the observation that this corrupt condition can be traced back before any sinful act of ours yields the conclusion that it was already in us as infants.

The Protestant doctrine of original sin, thus, has a largely empirical basis in our experience of the thinking and behavior of human adults and children. The Genesis narrative of the Fall has undoubtedly played an important part in Protestant theology. But the identification of original sin as a persisting evil, observably at work in baptized adults, has enabled Kant, and leading post-Kantian Protestant theologians, to retain the main substance of the Protestant doctrine without any essential dependence on the story of Adam and Eve.

The Catholic doctrine of original sin, on the other hand, at least in its sixteenth-century context – a society where almost everyone was baptized soon after birth – is mainly about infants and secondarily about members (mostly remote in space or time) of non-Christian societies. It is obviously, I think, much less empirical than the Protestant doctrine. For original sin itself, as opposed to the tinder left behind after it, is something that no one, on the Catholic view, would have experienced in a society where everyone had been baptized as an infant.

Motives and the will: scholasticism

Let us return now to the crucial difficulty about the relation between voluntariness and our responsibility for motivational states. This problem has a long history in the Christian ethical tradition. For it is characteristic of that tradition to see ethical goodness and badness as depending heavily on motivational states and especially on our deepest motivation, on what Kant would call our "ultimate subjective ground" of choice. Among the chief sins are hate and indifference toward God and our neighbors and misdirected or disordered love. I will discuss three different ways in which the idea of voluntariness has historically been related to this conviction of our accountability for motivational states.

The first approach I want to discuss is that which prevailed among Scholastic philosophers and theologians such as St. Thomas Aquinas. They held both that we are directly accountable for love and hate and certain other motives and that we are directly accountable only for what is directly voluntary. What enabled them consistently to hold both these positions is that, on the Scholastic view, love and hate are acts of the will and, thus, directly voluntary. They are acts of the will in the sense that they are the will doing what it is a faculty for doing: namely, being for and against things.

This is not to say that we are directly accountable for all our motivational states. Scholastic philosophy does not hold us directly accountable for hunger and thirst, for example. That is because they are not acts of the will but, rather, acts of another faculty, the sensory appetite (*appetitus sensitivus*). Thus, the distinction between what is and is not directly voluntary, on the Scholastic view, is drawn on the basis of a faculty psychology. I will elaborate on certain important points in this. I want to say, first, something about the will and about love and hate as acts of the will; second, something about the sensory appetite; and, finally, something about concupiscence.

First, the will Aquinas calls the will "the intellectual appetite" (*appetitus intellectivus*). We are accustomed to use the word "appetite" mainly for desires for physical satisfactions. Obviously, it has a broader meaning in St. Thomas's term. Any faculty of going for something or against something is an "appetite," in his sense. It is interesting, and I suspect significant of the Scholastic background of eighteenth-century German philosophy, that *appetitus* has a closer translation in Kant's German than in our English; it is precisely a *Begehrungsvermögen*.

More important for our present purpose, the notion of an intellectual appetite, or a will in Aquinas's sense, is broader, in another direction, than the notion that I think most of us usually have of the will. This appetite or appetitive power is a faculty not only of controlling actual behavior, but also of intending, desiring, enjoying, and their opposites. This is also quite clearly the case with the Kantian *Begehrungsvermögen*. It is explicit in Aquinas. He says of the will,[10] for instance, "The appetitive part has not only this act, that it seeks [*appetat*] what it does not have, but also that it loves what it has and delights in it."[11] It is a standard Scholastic view that enjoyment (*fruitio*) is an act of the will.

The will, of course, is not just any appetite. It is specifically an intellectual appetite, because it is situated in the reason — that is, because it always involves an understanding of its object. As Suárez puts it, "*Actus voluntatis non potest ferri in incognitum*" (an act of the will cannot be directed to something unknown).[12]

In speaking of the acts of this intellectual or rational appetitive faculty, later Scholastics distinguished two kinds of acts of the will. They distinguished "elicited" from "commanded" acts of the will. The commanded acts of the will are those that consist partly in events other than the operation of the will itself — for example, acts that consist partly in motions of the limbs. The idea that inspires this way of speaking is that,

in order to move the limbs, the will has to command another and inferior faculty to move the limbs. The will cannot move them all by itself,
and if it were disconnected from the inferior faculty by some paralysis,
the will could not move them at all.

The elicited acts of the will, by contrast, are those that consist entirely
in the operation of the will itself. In these the will does not depend on
any inferior faculty to accomplish the act; and for that reason the elicted
acts of the will were regarded as more fully within the will's control than
its commanded acts. Motivational states belonging to the will, such as
love and hate, being seen as internal to the will, were classified as elicited
acts of the will.

The word *act,* of course, is being used here in a broad sense in which
being in a motivational state over an indefinitely protracted period of
time can count as an act. Any actualization of a power or faculty is an act
in this sense; it does not have to happen at an instant or in a minute. The
Scholastic notion of "act" is not essentially episodic.

Hunger and thirst, as I have noted, were not viewed in Scholastic
philosophy as acts of the will. They were assigned to a different faculty,
called the "sensory appetite" (*appetitus sensitivus* – or, in Kantian German,
the *sinnliches Begehrungsvermögen*). Aquinas says that "the sensory appetite
is an inclination following a sensory apprehension" (ST, I, q. 81, a. 2). The
sensory appetite presupposes a sensory apprehension of its object, as the
will (the intellectual appetite) presupposes an intellectual understanding
of its object. The desires or cravings that belong to the sensory appetite
are not voluntary, because they are responses, not to intellectual apprehension of an object, but only to sensory stimulation. Aquinas holds that
the will, and, indeed, the soul, cannot completely control the sensory
appetite, because the sensory appetite, unlike the will, "is a power [*virtus*]
of a bodily organ" (ST, I–II, q. 17, a. 7).

The notion of concupiscence is closely connected with that of a
sensory appetite. The word *concupiscence* (*concupiscentia*) has at least three
senses in Saint Thomas. (1) In the first sense, the Latin word *concupiscentia*
originally meant desire rather generally. In New Testament contexts,
for example, it is a translation of the Greek *epithymia,* which, while it
sometimes has a sensual flavor to it, really is a general word for desire.
Sometimes Aquinas uses *concupiscence* in this general sense, speaking for
example, of a "*concupiscentia sapientiae*" (a concupiscence for wisdom,
a desire for wisdom), which is an act of the will, according to Aquinas,
because it has a nonsensible object and occurs without passion or excite-
ment of the mind (*animus*) (ST, I, q. 82, a. 5). However, this is not the
typical use of *concupiscence* in Aquinas or in other Scholastic sources.

(2) Most commonly, and in the second sense, concupiscence is one of
the two main functions of the sensory appetite. The other function is

anger, very broadly construed. "The object of the power of concupis-cence," Aquinas says, "is sensible good or evil, simply understood, which is the delightful or the painful"; whereas "the object of the power of anger is the same good or evil according as it has the nature of the ardu-ous or difficult" (ST, I–II, q. 23, a. l).[13] In this sense concupiscence is sim-ply a natural function of our sensory appetite.

(3) But there is still a third sense. *Concupiscence* can also mean, in Aquinas, the disorder (*inordinatio*) by which other powers of the soul besides the will "are inordinately turned toward a changeable good" (ST, I–II, q. 82, a. 3). On Scholastic and Tridentine views, this disorder is a deplorable but natural result of the natural operation of sensory powers, once original sin removes the restraint of the preternatural gift of origi-nal righteousness, which in Adam restrained this disorderly operation.

It is with regard to this third sense, from the Scholastic point of view, that controversy arose with Protestants as to whether concupiscence is sin. Catholic theologians held that concupiscence in this sense, not being a function of the will, and hence not voluntary, cannot be imputed as sin in its own right. They accommodated biblical texts that could be alleged as evidence for an opposing view by saying that concupiscence, as a dis-order in the functioning of the nonvoluntary powers of the soul, can be called "matter of original sin" in the unregenerate.[14]

There is, I think, at least one feature of these Scholastic views about sensory concupiscence that will be retained in a plausible account of our responsibility for motivational states. There are desires that seem to be merely natural responses to sensory stimulation, or to something as primitive, cognitively, as sensory stimulation. An example would be the desire for food when one's blood sugar level is low. It would be bizarre to hold us directly accountable for these desires, even if they happen to be desires that, in a particular situation, it would be wrong to act on. Scholasticism seems to be right about that. I will argue that the Reform-ers, or some of them, also agree with it.

Motives and the will: the reformers

The simplest thing to say about how the Reformers deal with the prob-lem of relating our accountability for fundamental motivational states to considerations of voluntariness is that they deny that we are accountable only for what we freely and voluntarily do. They take the view, in effect, that freedom is not necessary for accountability. This is obviously con-nected with their doctrines of grace and predestination, and perhaps, indeed, largely motivated by those doctrines. However, it seems to me that we can find, in the Reformers, particularly in Philip Melanchthon, indications of other, more narrowly philosophical objections to the Scholastic solution of the problem; and that is what particularly interests me here.

Melanchthon focuses on an issue about control, which I think will seem obvious to us, once we think about it, but which, rather strikingly, is hardly mentioned in Scholastic discussions of the problem that I have read. Melanchthon acknowledges that our will has a control–a "liberty," as he puts it–over the motions of our limbs; but he denies that the will has that sort of control over our own emotions (*affectus*), such as love and hate. He writes:

> If you estimate the power of the human will as touches its natural capacities according to human reason, it cannot be denied but that there is in it a certain kind of liberty in things external. These are matters which you yourself experience to be within your power, such as to greet or not to greet a man, to put on a certain attire or not to put it on, to eat meat or not to eat it as you will. . . . In truth, however, because God does not look upon external works but upon the inner motions of the heart, Scripture has recorded nothing about such freedom. . . . On the other hand, internal emotions are not within our power. For by experience and practice we have found out that the will of its own accord cannot assume love, hate, or the like emotions, but that one emotion is conquered by another. So much so that, for instance, because you were offended by someone you at one time loved, you now cease to love him; for you love yourself more ardently than you love anyone else.[15]

In Scholastic terms, Melanchthon is claiming here that certain commanded acts of the will are more within the control of the will than such elicited acts as love and hate – which is just the reverse of the Scholastic view that the elicited acts are more within the control of the will than the commanded acts. Why would he think that? Melanchthon argues as follows:

> We learn from experience and practice that we cannot take on or put off the love or hate of any thing. Suppose you love a girl; that you think six hundred times to yourself that from now on you will neglect her – that is a frigid and fictitious thought of the understanding, not a decision of the will. For the heart cannot decide against itself. Suppose you hate an enemy, or that you envy an enemy something; that you think

six hundred times that you are going to return to friendship
with him is a frigid and fictitious thought, until a stronger
emotion conquers this emotion.[16]

Concluding, or deciding, by a conscious decision of the intellect and will
that one ought to change one's love or hate, and consciously resolving to
do so, will not produce the desired change. Melanchthon claims that that
is a fact of experience; and it seems to me that that is true. There is a kind
of direct voluntary control that we have over the motions of our limbs
in certain circumstances – when we are not paralyzed, for example – and
that we do not have over our loves, hates, desires, and many other elicited
acts of the will, in the Scholastic sense, though we often wish we did
have this power over them.

I believe that, in modern thought, faculty psychology has been discarded in favor of this sort of control as a criterion of the voluntary.
Modern thought has predominantly adopted a conception of the voluntary according to which the directly voluntary is only that which is
within our control in approximately the way and the degree in which
the motions of our limbs normally are. I think we see this change, this
shift of focus, taking place in Melanchthon.

It is true that in the 1521 edition of the *Loci Communes* he has not
completely made the shift, at least as regards his use of the term *will*. For
he ascribes emotions to the will, saying, "Nor will I hear the sophists
if they deny that the human emotions, such as love, hate, joy, sorrow,
envy, ambition, and the like, pertain to the will. For now, nothing is said
about hunger or thirst. But what is the will, if not the fountain of the
emotions?"[17]

Here we still see something of the Scholastic conception of the will,
as a faculty of, among other things, loving and hating. But the question
as to what faculty these things are operations of is clearly much less
important to Melanchthon than the question of control.

Taking love and hate and the like to be involuntary because they are
not controllable in the relevant way is, of course, not to deny that love
and hate are operations of the will in the Scholastic sense of "the will."
This point has often been acknowledged by Protestant writers – as, for
example, in the following statement by the seventeenth-century
Reformed theologian François Turretin:

> In the first place, "voluntary" is said either strictly or broadly.
> In the former sense, it is said for that which happens through
> the actual motion of the will. In the latter sense, it is said for
> that which in any way either affects the will or inheres in it or
> depends on the will. Here, indeed, we are not concerned with

the voluntary broadly speaking. For we do not deny that sin is in the will, and can to that extent be called "voluntary," at least with regard to the subject in which it inheres. But we are concerned with the voluntary strictly speaking, which involves an act of choice [*prohaeresis*] and of the will. And in this sense we deny that all sin is *hekousion* [voluntary].[18]

In other words, Turretin would not deny that all sin is voluntary in relation to a criterion of the voluntary drawn in the Scholastic manner from faculty psychology, but he does deny it in relation to a criterion based on control.

It is doubtful whether Protestants should grant, as Turretin seems to do here, that all states that are directly and inherently sinful are in the will, even in the Scholastic sense. For some states regarded by Protestants as inherently sinful, such as unbelief, are cognitive states, and it is not clear that they should be regarded as inhering in the will rather than solely in the intellect. But we need not pursue this issue here.[19]

It will be more important to say something about the Protestant treatment of concupiscence as sin. Luther was vehemently attacked for holding that concupiscence is sin. Catholic writers have sometimes accused Protestants of meaning that there is fullfledged sin in the sensory appetite as such. But this seems at least not to have been Melanchthon's meaning, so far as I have read him. It is noteworthy that, in one of the passages I have quoted, Melanchthon says, "Nothing is being said here about hunger or thirst." In excluding hunger and thirst from consideration when he talks about the emotions of the heart that God is concerned with and that we are accountable for, Melanchthon is ruling out precisely the cases where it is most plausible to say, "This is not imputable because it is a natural response to a sensory stimulus."

There was a great deal of talking past one another going on in the dispute about concupiscence. I think that the Protestants, for the most part, were abandoning the Scholastic use of *concupiscence* in favor of a different use based on their exegesis of the Bible. Their use of the word was influenced, for example, by the fact that "Thou shalt not covet," in the Tenth Commandment, was rendered in Latin as *Ne concupisces,* with the verb related to *concupiscentia* (concupiscence) used for "covet." This was important because this is the one of the Ten Commandments in which a motivational state seems to be explicitly forbidden in its own right. Expounding this commandment, Melanchthon says,

For it does not only condemn here those vicious emotions to which "consent" is given, as they say;[20] it also condemns the wicked inclination itself, which is a certain perpetual aversion from God and a stubborn opposition fighting against the law of God, and which begets an infinite confusion of appetitions, even if consent is not always given. . . . And enmity against God is not to be understood as a light evil, for it includes many plagues: doubts about God, aversion from God, grumbling against God when we are punished; also infinite wandering and errant motions against the law of God – namely, confidence of one's own wisdom and powers, contempt of others, envy, ambition, avarice, flames of libido, desire for vengeance.[21]

We see here something interesting about the use of the word *concupiscence* and the conception attached to it. On one hand Melanchthon wants to seize on the commandment "Thou shalt not covet," understood with the use of the word *concupiscence,* to oppose the idea that nothing is inherently sinful except what involves a full, conscious, voluntary consent. On the other hand, if you look at the sorts of things that he brings under this heading of concupiscence (or *Ne concupisces*), it is quite clear that very few of them are matters of natural response to sensory stimulus. Melanchthon just is not interested in connecting concupiscence with sensation. Because it has nothing to do with the use of these terms in Scripture, which is his primary concern, the fact that that connection was crucial in the Scholastic tradition seems to be of no importance to him.

This disregard for Scholastic tradition may be due in part to influences of Renaissance humanism, but Melanchthon is doubtless driven here primarily by his interpretation of the Bible and by Martin Luther's religious experience and religious vision. Behind what Melanchthon says, however, there is also a more narrowly philosophical point of some interest – a point distinct from the one about control that I mentioned before. If we ask ourselves how we should classify such a state as antagonism toward God, or sexual lust for another person, the Scholastic theory offers essentially two alternatives: either a natural response to a sensory stimulus or a conscious consent of the will. To be sure, this dichotomy is modified by a gradation of degrees of consciousness, but that seems to be the only sort of modification that fits into the theory. Even with this modification, the dichotomy seems to me – and I think it seemed to Melanchthon – a Procrustean bed; it simply is not all that plausible to try to fit such states as antagonism toward God or sexual lust for another person into that dichotomy, and Melanchthon does not want to do it.

The Protestant reaction to this situation, I take it, was largely to give up faculty psychology as a criterion of ethical accountability. I have a lot of sympathy for that response. Another alternative, however, would be to try to develop a more adequate faculty psychology that could be used to provide a criterion for ethical accountability and to relate accountability for motivational states to considerations of voluntariness; and in a way, that was Kant's approach.

Motives and the will: Kant

Protestant though his theory of original sin is in other respects, Kant's treatment of moral responsibility has more in common with the Catholic and Aristotelian Scholasticism that was so deeply entrenched in the German universities. In the first place, he was not willing to give up the thesis that we are accountable only for our free and voluntary actions. And, in the second place, like the Scholastics, he finds the criterion of accountability in a distinction between active and passive faculties, and sometimes calls the passive one "sense," and the active one "reason" or "intellect."

We must not suppose, however, that Kant conceives the distinction of faculties just as the Scholastics did. For Kant, a desire or inclination of the sensory faculty need not be in any simple way a response to sensory stimulation. Reason may be very much involved in its formation.[22] What is crucial, for Kant, in the distinction of faculties is that the self is passive in its sensory functioning – that it has no power to determine that functioning by a choice moved only by pure practical reason – whereas it is active in the functioning of its rational power of choice. Accordingly, Kant says that sensory pleasure (*Lust*) and displeasure (*Unlust*), or desire and inclination, are given causally prior to any decision of the will, whereas pleasure and displeasure that follow the decision of the will are intellectual.[23]

There is another and even more important difference between the Kantian and the Scholastic distinction of faculties. The Scholastic faculties are part of an essentially empirical psychology. The Kantian faculties are not. For the crucial move in Kant's reconciliation of the doctrine of original sin with his insistence that "nothing is ethically, that is, imputably evil but that which is our own act"[24] is to deny that the relevant act of will is accessible to empirical observation.

Kant holds, as we have seen, that our fundamental ethical disposition and our propensity to evil were not adopted by any act in time. How, then, can they be imputably evil? Kant's answer is that they were adopted by a free and voluntary act, but it was not an act in time. Being outside of time, which is the necessary form of all our experience, this act is also outside our experience. It is neither an empirical nor a temporal event.

It might be thought that, by its very meaning, the word *act* can only signify an event in time. But Kant holds that there are two senses in which the word *act* can be used: in the first, it refers to acts occurring in time, empirical acts; in the second, it applies to something that is not an event in time: namely, to an act of the self as a being that transcends time. The latter, according to Kant, is the sort of act by which we freely and voluntarily adopt our most fundamental maxims, our ethical dispositions. "The propensity to evil, then, is an act in [this] sense, and at the same time the formal ground of every unlawful act in the [other] sense."[25]

This explanation, which Kant gives quite explicitly, is in full agreement with his metaphysics. His talk of timeless acts, with its implication that the choosing self has an existence outside of time, is unpalatable to most of us. But Kant is already committed to a distinction between things as they appear to us ("phenomena") and things as they are in themselves ("noumena"), and to the thesis that it is only the phenomena that are in time, and the noumena have no temporal properties or relations. Time and again, beginning with the Antinomy of the first *Critique*, Kant appeals to this distinction to resolve a paradox. Here he uses it to enable us to see the holding of an attitude, the having of a motive – indeed, the having of a propensity to evil – as a free act, and thus to see ourselves as free, not only in what we would ordinarily think of as actions, but also in the having of motivational states. The faculty psychology, therefore, which grounds Kant's criterion of ethical accountability is a psychology of noumenal faculties, a distinction between those things in which we are active and those in which we are passive, as we are in ourselves, outside of time.

Within the framework of Kant's metaphysics this is not merely an ingenious but also a reasonable solution of the problem. It is perfectly intelligible and coherent if Kant's conception of the phenomenal/noumenal distinction is intelligible and coherent.[26] This does not necessarily commend his solution to those of us who are not prepared to accept his phenomena/noumena distinction as it applies to the self. Still, there is something I like about it. It exemplifies a more general idea, that our ethical motives and dispositions may be something that we are doing, something that we ourselves spontaneously produce, even if we do not acquire them by anything that we experience as an act of choosing them.

This idea is not necessarily tied to the notion of timeless noumenal action. The view is gaining currency again that not only events, but also substances, or, at any rate, persons, can be causes and that free actions are not caused by preceding events but by their agents. And if persons can in this way be spontaneous causes of their actions, why can't they also in the same way be spontaneous causes of their motivational states? Why not, indeed?[27]

Conclusion

Even if we believe in original sin, few of us would adopt without qualification Aquinas's or Melanchthon's or Kant's theory of the matter. Certainly, I would not. But we can learn from all of them. One thing we can learn is that a theory of original sin will draw on a variety of sources. We should not have expected it to be otherwise. Any such theory will obviously draw inspiration from the Bible and Christian tradition. The thinkers I have discussed differ in the extent to which exegesis of Scripture or other authoritative texts governs their thought on the subject, but they all draw on ideas of the Christian tradition, and they all are giving form to a conviction of the central ethical importance of good motives. This conviction is very deeply rooted in the Christian faith and its primary texts, though (at least in our culture) it can also appeal to moral common sense.

At the same time, it is clear that, on pain of schizophrenia, a theory of original sin will be part of a more comprehensive psychological theory and will draw on materials of psychological theorizing that are not specially Christian. Many of the differences among the historic figures I have examined arise from differences in their nontheological views.

It is hardly imaginable that Kant would have written as he did on this topic if he had not thought a lot about Christianity. His treatment of it demonstrates the depth of his engagement with Christian theology and provides grounds for classifying him as a Christian philosopher, if not an orthodox one. Nonetheless, Kant proposes the possibility of a theory of original sin that makes no essential appeal to religious authority. This possibility is important to the apologetic role of the concept of original sin exemplified in the thought of Reinhold Niebuhr.

More surprisingly, perhaps, the history we have surveyed suggests ways in which philosophical understanding may depend on an understanding, if not an acceptance, of theology. We have seen that important parts of the development of conceptions of the voluntary and of moral responsibility from the Middle Ages into the early modern period took place in the context of discussions of original sin. It would be fatuous to expect to comprehend the former without some understanding of the latter.

Questions and answers

Q: I very much admired your carefully reasoned exposé of Kant's theory and of what preceded it. I think you indicated quite well how this is a beautiful instance of how theology can directly influence philosophy without killing its autonomy. I have two historical points and one point of exegesis. It is interesting historically that the interpretation of Adam as merely a model is very much present in the earliest Fathers. For example, we find that Irenaeus and also the entire Antiochian school of exegesis had basically that idea, contrary to the Alexandrian school. The other point, where I'm not sure I completely share your interpretation, if I understand it, is on Kierkegaard. It is not the case that Kierkegaard says simply, "Each one is responsible for his own sins and for nothing more." He does say that, but that is not the whole story. There is also this element in Kierkegaard, that the situation, as he says in *The Concept of Dread,* fundamentally changes with the entrance of sinfulness in the human race, and he explicitly appeals to Romans 5:10. He does not want a purely liberal interpretation of that text as a model. He says, "We are a species, and when sinfulness once enters that species, the whole situation of the species changes." And, consequently, there is an accumulation of what he would call then a concupiscence that grows ever more intense as human beings become more sinful.

Finally, the one small question of exegesis. There is one thing I have never understood in Kant's interpretation of original sin, and I am wondering whether you can perhaps enlighten us a bit further than you have done so far on that point. When Kant speaks of "the evil disposition" or the "disposition toward evil" which affects all human beings, he speaks of a free and voluntary act, but not in time. I do not understand how such a thing could be compatible with any kind of responsibility for it, because it seems to me that the notion of voluntariness he invokes here explicitly would require at least consciousness of it, and that for consciousness of that original act in time, it is not sufficient in this case to say, "Well, I'm discussing the matter on a nonempirical level." When it comes to voluntary acts, there is no other level but the empirical, one would think.

A: Those are very good questions. Let me say, first, that I certainly do not disagree with what you have said about the early Fathers. I have not studied the Antiochians on this, but I certainly agree about Irenaeus. In general, I guess, I have found plausible those interpretations which suggest that what we think of as a traditional codifying of the doctrine of original sin is enormously influenced by Augustine, and that things that happened before or independently of Augustine in the Christian tradition show a much greater variety of uses of the Genesis narratives.

With regard to Kierkegaard, it has occurred to me that I might be incautious in what I said about him here, and I want to think more about that, and I thank you for raising the issue.

On the interpretation of Kant, I think I want to stick by what I said. It seems to me that it is clear that he says that the most fundamental

maxims are adopted by an act that is not an act in time. It cannot, therefore, be an act of which we have experience in his system. What is our
cognitive relation to it? At a minimum, it is an act in which he thinks we
have moral grounds for believing. Is it an act of which we have some sort
of consciousness, perhaps by reflection? Well, I haven't worked that out.
I think that this is a very interesting issue and would relate, specifically,
to what view one would take in the rather controversial interpretation
of things he says about the fact of reason and, in general, the view one
takes of his theory of freedom. So, while I'm not sure that I have an
answer to that question you raise, I think it's a very goôd question.

Q: I was both instructed and persuaded by your reading of the complex passages in Kant.[28] I would like to hear more, however, on your
references to Reinhold Niebuhr and to Thomas Aquinas on at least a
general way of formulating one of the issues they have both shared in,
the move from original sin to personal sin, and the understanding of the
responsibility and the freedom that is present in the human situation.
Surely, one of the most puzzling concepts in Niebuhr, and one of the
controversial and influential, was precisely his insistence that sin is inevitable but not necessary.

There have been, as I'm sure you know, analyses of Thomas Aquinas
in a more contemporary setting on this issue. Most famously, Bernard
Lonergan's *Grace and Freedom* suggests that Thomas's view is really not
confined only to the passage you cite or to the understanding you cite
of original sin, but pertains to the movement from original to personal
sin. I have always been persuaded by Lonergan's reading, though, as he
admitted himself, it's a contemporary reading, as is Niebuhr's of the Protestant tradition. In Lonergan's reading, as I remember it, the question in
Thomas Aquinas is how much deliberation do you need for a free act?
To use, not Thomas's example but Lonergan's: we eat breakfast everyday,
but we very rarely explicitly deliberate about that act of eating breakfast.
Nevertheless, if pressed, one would say one freely eats breakfast.
Thomas's psychological theory is very much like that, especially in the
Summa. I think Lonergan is right to read Thomas as positing a difference.
It is like Niebuhr's problem with "inevitable" and "necessary." Thomas's
problem, as Lonergan reads him – correctly, I think – is distinguishing
the difference between classical and statistical necessity. How much deliberation do we need for a particular free act? The movement from original to personal sin is on that model. The movement from "eventually
we're going to be tired and exhausted and not able to deliberate; that is
the effect of original sin" gives us to an inevitability, but not a necessity,
to sin. That can be retranslated into contemporary terms from the philosophy of science of a statistical but not classical necessity. So, I suppose

all I am saying is that it would be helpful to hear further your own reflections on Niebuhr and a comparison with Thomas, which has been made by John Courtney Murray, as a matter of fact.

A: Thank you. I have to say I'm not familiar with Lonergan's interpretation of Aquinas and am therefore reluctant to comment on it. The other point you raised, about Niebuhr, is a very good one, and it's well worth comparing Kant with Niebuhr on this. This is a point on which Kant differs, I think, from Niebuhr and, indeed, from most of the other people I was talking about. You are absolutely right about what Niebuhr says, and Kant says nothing of the sort. In fact, one of the most disturbing points in Kant's analysis, from a theoretical point of view, is that he doesn't really say much to account for the universality of original sin; he attests that it's an empirical fact. There's a reason why he doesn't: Kant, in a certain sense, is not about to explain the radical evil in human nature. He is trying to explain *how* it happens, but he is not about to explain *why* it happens.

Now, Niebuhr – and in this I take it he's following Kierkegaard – tries to give an explanation of why it's there. Kant does not want to do that, because to give an explanation of why it's there would be to offer a rationale for it, and, of course, Kant's ethical theory is so profoundly and fundamentally a theory of practical rationality that Kant is totally committed to the view that, at bottom, radical evil is thoroughly irrational. So, we have in Kant no analogue; there is no analogue, I think, to Niebuhr's claim that it's inevitable but not necessary. No, it's not inevitable; it's just a fact, a fact that it's too late for us to change in some way – although there is also the theory of the overcoming of evil by good.

That is a difference between Kant and Niebuhr, and I think a difference profoundly rooted in Kant's ethics.

Q: Like the other speakers, I'd like to thank you for a very informative and illuminating discussion. I'd like to suggest and question a couple of things. One is the idea in itself of calling this "original sin." After all, everyone knows that there is weakness, vice, turmoil, and disorder in the human condition. For people like Aristotle or Plato, it's easier to handle it. It's simply the way things are, then we try to become better through virtue and good actions. Once you put that into a context of creation, you've got to say, "Well, where could this have come from?" And it couldn't have come from God. Therefore, there must have been something that brought it about. I think that kind of negative theology – not about the best but about the worst, in this case – is part of the sense of original sin, and perhaps it has something to do with Kant's appeal to the ultra-noumenal here, some kind of action that we never really experienced as a root, that is the theological source for this. That's one point I'd like to make.

The other is that I really enjoyed your analysis of faculties, issues of guilt, and the shifts that occurred within them. That was extremely illuminating. I wonder if you think the Scholastic and the Reformist traditions had enough of a role for character of the dispositions that are shaped through earlier actions. It seems to me that we're left with a radical difference between a choice and something that's there by nature. In between, there's something that would be *ethos,* the way we are because of the way we've acted or because of a certain endowment at birth. Within that area could there be an element of freedom, but freedom that is not as punctual as a single choice?

A: That was a very interesting question about the role of character – two very interesting questions. Let me start with the second one about the role of character. I'm not sure why it is, but it's clear that the notions of character and of virtue and vice have, in fact, tended to play a smaller role in Protestant ethics than in Catholic ethics. The emphasis in Protestant ethics has fallen more punctually on particular actions and their particular motives. That probably has something to do with the notion of obedience being very central to the Protestant interpretation of biblical ethics. The Protestant emphasis on grace and forgiveness also supports this thinking. Forget about the past; this is what God says to you now – obey now. There's that sort of mood in Protestant ethical thinking which probably has been less conducive to emphasis on the virtues and vices and the ethics of character.

There is perhaps a deeper reason. I'm not very confident about this, but it may be that, even in Scholastic ethics, for all the talk about character, it may not be so natural to plug that right into the issues of accountability, sin, and so forth because of what is clearly recognized in Aristotelian traditions as the social nature of the formation of character. I think there is something in all Western Christian traditions that tends to zero in on the individual when we start thinking about sin, and that may be a mistake in Western Christian traditions.

Q: I agree, and it seems to me it's because you have this eternal destiny there as a kind of ultimate horizon, so that the actual life and the human situation pales in comparison with whether or not you're guilty for eternity.

A: Yes.

Q: I think that is true, that it's downplayed even in the Catholic tradition.

A: Right. I suppose that's also connected with the fact that in the Christian tradition, individuals have an eternal destiny. Communities, except for the Church Universal, don't. And the Church Universal is, I think even in Catholicism, a little bit too ethereal to grip our emotions in the way that the Jewish sense of the Jewish people grips Jewish emotions.

Remind me again of the other point; I thought it was a very interesting one.

Q: The contrast between treating human vice and wickedness and so forth as original sin, as coming from original sin, is related to creation, because where else would it come from, but from within ourselves? Do you agree?

A: Yes. Certainly. To finish with a little note of possible disagreement with the other speaker this morning,[29] there's a point here at which I suppose I feel a strong resistance to disconnecting the Christian tradition from certain metaphysical drives, although I can also see interesting possibilities in trying to disconnect it. That is, the Christian tradition, at least in the West, has had a strong drive to develop an integrated picture of the world, its history, and its relation to God with God at the absolute origin, and that, of course, creates problems about how evil gets there. And there is, I think, a clear contrast with Judaism on that. The Jewish tradition has been much more relaxed about that. The rabbis talked about the "evil impulse" without worrying how it got there, and as people like John Levinson have been reminding us, the Jewish tradition has been much more relaxed in general about playing around with nonmonistic treatments of the problems of evil. That's true.

And while I see some attractions in those Jewish alternatives, I must say I find myself very reluctant to give up the traditional Western Christian impulse to try to get the picture whole, which I think does, indeed, account for a lot of what goes on in discussions of original sin, both in the most consciously theological and most consciously orthodox thinkers and also in the most liberal such as Kant, who still, as I argue, is very much a Christian philosopher.

Notes

★ A version of this essay was presented as a lecture at a National Endowment for the Humanities Institute on Kant's moral philosophy at The Johns Hopkins University in the summer of 1983, and later at Reed College. I am indebted to many, and especially to Marilyn McCord Adams, for helpful comments. It is a pleasure to thank the Center of Theological Inquiry in Princeton for fellowship support during part of the writing, and Princeton Theological Seminary for hospitality and use of its library.
1. See Alasdair MacIntyre, *Whose Justice? Which Rationality?* (Notre Dame, Ind.: University of Notre Dame Press, 1988), chap. 17 (for a verdict on liberalism quite different from mine); and *Three Rival Versions of Moral Enquiry: Encyclopedia, Genealogy,* and *Tradition* (Notre Dame, Ind.: University of Notre Dame Press, 1990), chap. 7 (on the limited influence of Aquinas in his own time).

2. Niebuhr's acknowledgment of Kant's theory, in a footnote, seems to me to reflect only a superficial engagement with Kant on this point. See Reinhold Niebuhr, *The Nature and Destiny of Man: A Christian Interpretation*. I. *Human Nature* (New York: Scribner's, 1941), p. 120.

3. The same is true of his interest in the problem of the justification of the sinner, which is also treated in *Religion Within the Limits of Reason Alone*.

4. Immanuel Kant, *Fundamental Principles of the Metaphysics of Morals,* trans. Thomas K. Abbott (New York: Liberal Arts Press, 1949), p. 11.

5. Immanuel Kant, *Religion Within the Limits of Reason Alone,* trans. Theodore M. Greene and Hoyt H. Hudson (New York: Harper Torchbooks, 1960), pp. 16, 62ff. Henceforth, I will cite this text by parenthetical page references. I have also used the German text, in the Philosophische Bibliothek series, *Die Religion innerhalb der Grenzen der bloßen Vernunft,* ed. Karl Vorländer, 8th ed. (Hamburg: Felix Meiner, 1978).

6. He says here that this guilt is "intentional" (*vorsätzlich*) with respect to wickedness, but "unintentional" with respect to frailty and impurity. I take it that the point is that wickedness involves a full, though conditional and not necessarily conscious, acceptance of violation of the moral law, whereas frailty and impurity do not.

7. I have slightly modified the translation of the German, and translated the quotation from Ovid.

8. Niebuhr, *Nature and Destiny of Man,* p. 269.

9. Calvin, for instance, who can hardly be accused of not believing in original sin, characterizes it as "a hereditary depravity and corruption of our nature," and declares that "not only has punishment fallen upon us from Adam, but a contagion imparted by him resides in us, which justly deserves punishment. . . . For that reason, even infants themselves, while they carry their condemnation along with them from the mother's womb, are guilty not of another's fault but of their own" (*Institutes of the Christian Religion,* trans. Ford Lewis Battles, ed. John T. McNeill, 2 vols. Library of Christian Classics 20–21 [Philadelphia: Westminster Press, 1960], II.i.8, p. 251).

10. In this passage he speaks specifically of God's will, but I think it clearly applies to the will generally.

11. St. Thomas Aquinas, *Summa Theologiae* (hereafter, ST), I, q. 19, a.1, *ad primum*. Henceforth I will cite this text by parenthetical references.

12. Francisco Suárez, *De voluntario et involuntario,* VI.iv.2 (*Opera omnia* IV. [Paris: Vivès, 1865], p. 245). I am ignoring a distinction between a "higher" and a "lower" reason that figures in some Scholastic discussions of the will.

13. Somewhat freely translated, for the sake of clarity.

14. Catholic theology gives a complicated account here because it is recognized that both St. Augustine and St. Paul refer to concupiscence as sin in certain contexts. In order to accommodate Scholastic doctrine to this way of speaking, it is said that concupiscence can be called "sin" because it proceeds from sin and incites to sin. In the unregenerate, moreover, who still have original sin, concupiscence can be regarded in some sense as the matter of original sin – the form being the lack of original righteousness. In the baptized, as I have noted above, Catholic theology would speak of

concupiscence as "tinder for sin." Strictly speaking, however, concupiscence, not being voluntary, cannot be imputed as sin in its own right, according to Catholic theology.

15. *The Loci Communes of Philip Melanchthon* [1521], trans. Charles Leander Hill (Boston: Meador Publishing Co., 1944), pp. 75f. I have slightly modified the translation.

16. Philip Melanchthon, *Loci Communes in ihrer Urgestalt,* ed. G. L. Plitt and Th. Kolde (Leipzig, 1900), p. 79. This passage is from the second edition of the *Loci,* published in 1522.

17. *Loci Communes,* trans. Hill, p. 76; translation modified.

18. Franciscus Turretinus, *Institutio Theologiae Elencticae,* Part I (New York: Robert Carter, 1847), p. 537 (Locus IX, q. ii). A similar distinction, explicitly aimed, like Turretin's, against the "Papists and Socinians," can be found in Turretin's younger Lutheran contemporary David Hollaz. The explicit Protestant rejection of the doctrine that all sin is voluntary can be found quite clearly as early as Melanchton's 1531 *Apology for the Augsburg Confession.* For references to Melanchthon and Hollaz, see Karl Hase, *Hutterus Redivivus,* 7th ed. (Leipzig: Breitkopf und Hartel, 1848), p. 194n.

19. I have discussed it elsewhere: see my "The Virtue of Faith," *Faith and Philosophy,* 1 (1984): 3–15, esp. 4–6, and "Involuntary Sins," *The Philosophical Review,* 94 (1985): 3–31, esp. 17–21.

20. The reference is to a Scholastic notion of "consent."

21. From the 1543 edition of the *Loci Communes* (*Corpus Reformatorum* XXI, col. 710).

22. See Kant's account of the "predisposition to humanity" in *Religion Within the Limits of Reason Alone,* p. 22.

23. Immanuel Kant, introduction to *The Metaphysics of Morals* (pp. 211f. in the Prussian Academy edition of the original German); pp. 8f. in Kant, *The Doctrine of Virtue,* trans. Mary J. Gregor (New York: Harper Torchbooks, 1964).

24. *Reason Within the Limits of Reason Alone,* p. 26.

25. Ibid., p. 26.

26. Whether it is consistent with Kant's theology of regeneration is another question. Philip Quinn argues for a negative answer in his excellent paper "Original Sin, Radical Evil and Moral Identity," *Faith and Philosophy,* 1 (1984): 188–202; but I am not completely convinced. See also Quinn's later paper, "Christian Atonement and Kantian Justification," ibid., 3 (1986): 440–62, esp. 448.

27. I have developed this suggestion, without reference to Kant, in "Involuntary Sins," 24–31.

28. Editor's note: The questioner is David Tracy, one of the symposium speakers.

29. Editor's note: John Caputo is being referred to here.

CHAPTER 13

SIN AS UNCLEANNESS

Marilyn McCord Adams

What is sin?

Sin was a rare topic during the first twenty of the last thirty years of analytic philosophy of religion. That it came up at all was due to the popularity of Free Will approaches to the problem of evil, which fix on traditional doctrines of the Fall and assert their logical possibility or truth as the explanation of evil's origin and/or Divine permission of it. Such Free Will approaches envision an "original position" in which incompatibilist free creatures are competent choosers placed in a utopian environment: that is, they have enough cognitive and emotional maturity to grasp and accurately apply relevant normative principles, while (on the occasion of choice) their exercise of these abilities is unfettered by unruly passions or external determinants of any kind. The possibility envisioned is that such creatures should choose contrary to their normative judgments, thereby introducing evil into the world. Even so, Free-Will-Defending philosophers such as Alvin Plantinga[1] have chosen not to speak of *sin*, but of *moral* agency and responsibility, of **moral** goodness or turpitude. And this preference is of a piece with the widespread but unspoken agreement to discuss both the concept of God and the problem of evil within the parameters of religion neutral value-theory.[2] Little wonder if the relation between the concepts of sin and immorality should seem puzzling now![3]

One obvious way to connect them starts with a religion-neutral view of human beings and the norms pertaining to them, and then identifies sin with violations of some or any of these norms, with or without the stipulation that to call them "sin" adds a reference to God.[4] With Basil Mitchell's "Plain Moralist,"[5] many Free-Will-Defenders readily identify the normative principles relevant to sin with moral principles (and so conceive of sin *moralistically*). Agreeing that "moral-ought" implies "can", they readily conclude that sin is, in the first instance and the primary sense, a matter of wrongful choices by fully competent, incompatibilist free creatures (and so to think of sin *voluntaristically*).

This straightforward strategy for dealing with the concept of sin has the vices of its virtues. For if it renders the concept of sin palatable to secular thinkers, it runs the risk of being religiously inadequate. First of all, the Biblical catalog of sins includes, not only (i) conscious voluntary actions, but also (ii) emotions (e.g., anger) and cognitive states (e.g., belief) not within our (direct) voluntary control, (iii) dispositions, habits, inclinations that resist the normative ordering of the self,[6] and (iv) states or conditions of uncleanness (e.g., the abominations of Leviticus). Plain Moralists with the courage of their convictions dismiss (iv) uncleanness as a primitive category deservedly supplanted by the ethical,[7] while refusing to count us responsible for any of (ii) or (iii) that are not within our power.[8] And in general, among those who equate sin with the immoral, disagreements about which (if any) of (ii) or (iii) count as sin would parallel disputes about which are genuinely morally wrong, morally vicious or bad. Second and more importantly, this strategy makes the notion of sin *anthropocentric*, by conceding that the norms relevant to sin lie within the province of religion-neutral value theory. One impli- cation is that a human being who conformed to all such norms would be sinless; where the standards are moral principles for (i) voluntary action, Pelagianism is ready in the wings.[9]

My own contention is that "sin" is a fundamentally theological notion, signifying some sort of impropriety in the relation between created per- sons and God. The difficulty cannot be moral *at bottom*, because (as I have maintained in other papers[10]) the network of moral considerations, rights and obligations is *not* one that connects God with His free creatures. Rather morality is a human institution, roughly the best framework humans generally can master and/or apply on a large scale to promote friendly and curtail anti-social behavior and attitudes.[11] Moreover, the network of *moral* considerations, rights, and obligations presupposes a commensuration among the agents connected thereby. But God and creatures are ontologically incommensurate. This is why God has no *obligations* to creatures, and why creatures' obligation to obey God can- not be *moral* strictly speaking.[12] To identify sin with moral wrong-doing thus threatens either to trivialize sin or to make an idol of morality.

My purpose here is to commend the alternative view, that *the funda- mental obstacle to Divine-human relations lies in the very incommensuration of Divine and created natures*. To lend vivacity and plausibility to this idea, I will begin with category (iv), by exploring three accounts of sin as uncleanness. With the first two – drawn from Rudolf Otto's justly famous book *The Idea of the Holy* and from Mary Douglas' work in the social anthropology of religion – I follow out the methodological axiom of John Locke and David Hume: that considerable insight into a concept is gained by reflecting on its genetic origins. The third reflects on religious experience a different way, and is found in Julian of Norwich's *Revelation of Divine Love*. I will consider this breaking of disciplinary ranks justified if it manages to dislodge philosophical myopia regarding the nature of sin.

Sin as uncleanness and the idea of the holy

In *The Idea of the Holy*, Rudolf Otto offers a rational reconstruction of our supposed derivation of the idea of God ("the Holy" or "the numen") from religious experience.[13] Otto's approach is particularly apt for our purposes, because it results describe the Holy, and human relationship to the Holy at one and the same time. Since sin is a sometime feature of the latter, Otto's search for the genetic roots of the idea of the Holy promise to identify those of our notion of sin as well.[14]

(2.1) Otto's Procedure: (i) Recall how Otto identifies as paradigm religious experience which content-wise is *of* God (the Holy, the numen), in which God is presented as something other than the self, and which is attended by a full range of feeling accompaniments.[15] By analogy, one might identify a paradigm experience of a tiger as a visual experience in which the tiger is presented to me as something other than myself, and which is accompanied by a wide range of feelings, such as terror, awe, and admiration. (ii) My experience provides with two sources of tiger-descriptions. Most obviously, I can read off a characterization of the tiger from its visual appearance (e.g., as being huge in size, and as having orange and black stripes, long claws, and sharp teeth). In addition, I can infer features of the tiger from the feeling accompaniments, according to the following pattern: "Feeling Φ accompanies my experience of *x*; therefore I experience *x* as the logically appropriate object of feeling Φ". For example, terror accompanies my vision of the tiger chasing me; therefore I experience the tiger as a logically appropriate object of terror – i.e., as terrifying and terrible! Where ordinary objects are concerned, information from the one source can be checked against and/or corrected by that from the other. For example, I may be terrified of lady bugs, but they (as harmless to human well-being) are not logically appropriate objects of terror. Or a detective may have a funny feeling that something is wrong, although everything looks fine. Otto insists, however, that because God (the Holy, the numen) is so different from and so much bigger than we are, we cannot read off a characterization of God from the "visual" content of religious experience; instead, we can characterize God *only* as the logically appropriate object of the feelings that normally accompany paradigm religious experiences that are content-wise of Him. For present purposes, we need not accept this strong thesis, that religious feelings are our only root to God-characterizations. We can profit from his remarks so long as we concede the weaker claim that religious feelings *contribute* to the content of our idea in the way he describes.

(iii) According to Otto, our efforts thus to articulate our idea of the Holy are further complicated by the fact that such religious feelings are *sui generis* and only analogically related to those that accompany our experience of ordinary objects (e.g., our fear of loose tigers versus our dread of grave yard ghosts on Halloween). This means we will have to proceed by comparison and contrast, and must be alert to the fact that feeling-vocabulary will often be used analogically.

(iv) Finally, Otto hypothesizes that, in addition to reason and the five senses, humans are endowed with a special faculty for religious experience, a faculty for having experiences in which God is presented as something other than the self, and for having a wide range of feeling-accompaniments.[16] Moreover, such religious feelings can be triggered in different degrees by situations other than paradigm religious experience (e.g., by telling ghost stories or watching horror movies). Thus, Otto expects most (if not all) of his readers to have had the feelings to which he refers in his reconstruction.

(2.2) Otto's Results: Drawing on various religious texts including the Bible, Otto identifies and classifies religious feelings and infers the consequent God-characterizations as follows:

Feeling Experience of Myself	*Characterization of God/Holy/Numen*
A. *Tremendum*	
1. Fear, dread	1. Aweful, eerie, weird, dreadful
2. Creature-feeling	2. Powerful, plenitude of being
3. Radically threatened	3. Living, urgent, active
B. *Mysterium*	
1. Angst, stupor	1. Wholly other
2. Attracted	2. *Fascinans*
C. *Augustus*	
1. Profane, unclean	1. August, holy

(A) First, God is experienced as a worthy object of trembling and terror. For, Otto claims, *(A1)* paradigm religious experiences would be accompanied with something like my fear of a loose tiger, but different from it in the direction of my reactions to graveyard ghosts on Halloween. Stories of ghosts and active corpses make flesh creep and blood run cold; they seem eerie, uncanny, and weird.[17] Biblical examples include God's smoking pot covenant with Abraham in Genesis 15:7-12. Abraham splits and arranges the animals for the ratification ceremony, and shoos the birds away all day long. Then, "as the sun was going down, a deep sleep fell on Abram; and lo, a dread and great darkness fell upon him" (Gen. 15:12) and "behold, a smoking fire pot and flaming torch passed between these pieces. On that day the Lord made a covenant with Abraham, saying, 'To your descendants I give this land . . .'" (Gen. 15:17-18).

Again, *(A2)* paradigm religious experiences would be accompanied by creature-feeling, the sense of being radically weak and impotent in relation to something overwhelmingly efficacious; of being (in Anselm's words) "almost nothing" in relation to an infinite ocean of being (Damascene's words). In Biblical language, it is the experience of hearts melting, of strength draining out, of being utterly undone at the very sight of the other.[18] Moreover, *(A3)* in paradigm religious experience, I would not only experience myself as utterly unable to affect what has an overwhelming capacity to affect me; I would experience myself as *on the verge* of being ruined, done in, or annihilated, and accordingly experience the Holy as living, urgent, active.[19] Thus, the voice of the Lord is said to shake the wilderness (Ps.29:8), to make the oak trees writhe, and to strip the forests bare (Ps.29:9); His presence, to make mountains skip like rams and little hills like young sheep (Ps.114:4,6) and to cause seas and rivers to flee (Ps.114:3,5). Again, in preparation for the Sinai summit, God warns Moses that the people must consecrate themselves and not touch the mountain, lest the Lord "break out against them" (Exodus 19:12-15, 21-24) as He later did against Uzzah who reached forth his hand to steady the ark (II Samuel 6:1-11). When the time came for the Sinai meeting, the people were so terrified at the thunder and lighting, the trumpet blasts, and smoking mountain that they insisted on dealing with God only through mediators like Moses (Exodus 20:18-20).

(B) Otto's second category, the *Mysterium*, breaks down into two parts. On the one hand, in paradigm religious experience, I would experience *(B1)* great anxiety, I would feel stupefied, at a loss for words. Thus, when God finally grants Job a hearing, Job stammers, "Behold, I am of small account; what shall I answer thee? I lay my hand on my mouth. I have spoken once, and I will not answer; twice, but I will proceed no further" (Job 40:3-5). And, seeing Jesus transfigured, Peter suggests three tents "not knowing what he said" (Luke 9:33). Otto infers, one experiences God as wholly other, utterly unique and unlike the ordinary objects of our experience.[20] On the other hand, *(B2)* I would feel powerfully attracted to the Holy.[21] For instance, the psalmist writes, "As a deer longs for the water-brooks, so longs my soul for you, O God. My soul is athirst for God, athirst for the living God; when shall I come to appear before the presence of God?" (Ps.42:1-2) Or again, "O God, you are my God; eagerly I seek you; my soul thirsts for you, my flesh faints for you, as in a barren and dry land where there is no water" (Ps. 63:1). And, "How dear to me is your dwelling, O Lord of hosts! My soul has a desire and longing for the courts of the Lord; my heart and my flesh rejoice in the living God" (Ps.84:1). Accordingly, the Holy is experienced as fascinating and enticing.

(C) Finally, Otto claims, in paradigm religious experience, I would experience myself as profane, unclean, sinful. Thus, when Isaiah sees the Lord in the temple, he cries, "Woe is me! For I am lost; for I am a man of unclean lips, and I dwell in the midst of a people of unclean lips; for my eyes have seen the King, the Lord of hosts!" (Isaiah 6:5) Likewise, faced with God, Job gasps, "I had heard of thee by the hearing of the ear, but now my eye sees thee; therefore I despise myself and repent in dust and ashes" (Job 42:5-6). And Peter, seeing the miraculous draught of fishes, falls down before Jesus, saying, "Depart from me, for I am a sinful man, O Lord" (Luke 5:8). Conversely, God is experienced as pure and holy.[22]

Drawing Otto's conclusions together, we see that feelings in category *(B1)* reveal God to us as "separate" in the sense of being radically unlike anything else in our experience. Those in category *(A)* tell us that this Wholly Other is radically dangerous to the health of beings of our kind, while category *(C)* shows normative priority to lie on the side of God. As Otto himself insists, all of these characterizations are pre-moral,[23] because what, in the first instance, evokes the feelings from which the descriptions are derived, is the sheer presence of Divine *nature* to human *nature*, quite apart from any exercise of agency on either side. For Otto, it is a further step – what he styles a "*moralizing*" of the concepts – when the feelings arising from the interaction of the natures are projected onto the personal characters, policies, and choices of God and creatures (so that, e.g., so that "powerful" in *(A2)* and 'threatening' in *(A3)* are transmuted into "wrathful"; "fascinating" and "attractive" in *(B2)* into "gracious" and "benevolent"). Thus, the devaluations of creatures in *(A2)* and *(C1)* have nothing to do with the unique conditions or behavior of individuals; but pertain to individuals *qua* members of a certain kind. *(A2)* simply expresses the ontological incommensuration between God and creatures, while *(C1)* is a relative devaluation consequent upon it. It follows that on Otto's analysis, the notion of sin is, in its genetic origin, pre-moral. Creatures are to be characterized as sinful or unclean, because the radical incommensuration of Divine and created natures obstructs relations between God and creatures, and the problem lies, not in any flaw in the Divine nature, but in the radical limitation and finitude of created natures in comparison to God.[24]

Sin and the sociology of uncleanness

Even if we agree that Otto's focus on religious feeling catches something fundamental and *Uralt* that should not be lost sight of in our attempts to understand God and Divine-human relationships; and that part of the soul of religion is lost, when theological concepts are entirely cut off from these feeling roots, we might consider Otto's reflections on genetic origins inconclusive. After all, so much Biblical attention to Divine-human relationships revolves around themes of covenant, commandments, obedience and disobedience — notions which seem prima facie congruent with the voluntaristic/moralistic common-places about sin mentioned in section I. To undermine this objection, I turn now to the work of Mary Douglas, which provides a framework of ideas relative to which the Biblical structure of covenants and commandments emerge as a solution to the more fundamental problem of the incommensuration between Divine and created natures. Theoretically, her conceptual apparatus has the advantage over the Plain Moralists'. For Douglas can provide a *unified* sociological explanation of why Biblical legislation ranges over, not only morally wrong acts, but also conditions of ritual uncleanness. Not only does her account make the notion of uncleanness foundational; it sheds light on the legal/anti-nomian controversy in the New Testament as well.

In her fascinating book *Purity and Danger*, Douglas offers a sociological explanation of the function of cleanliness metaphors and institutions in terms of twin ideas: *that dirt is stuff out of order,*[25] and *that stuff out of order is both powerful and dangerous.*[26] (i) Order and boundaries come in many varieties. Within society, social classes or castes, governmental, social, and familial roles give definition and create order. In the world at large, national boundaries, treaties, and international agreements give structure and definition to relations among nation states. Likewise, in nature, genus and species boundaries give structure and definition to plant and animal worlds. (ii) Disorder is experienced as doubly dangerous: fundamentally, because order confers identity on individuals and groups by giving them definition — what compromises identity threatens existence[27]; pragmatically, because order makes reality predictable and so enables individuals and groups to plot survival — and prosperity-strategies. At the same time, disorderly elements seem powerful, not only because they threaten to disrupt the old, but also because they symbolize creative potential for the new. Again, powers outside the order may bring super-structural blessing as well as curse, and so may be objects of admiration as well as terror.[28]

(3.1) Sample Applications: Thus, Douglas remarks, the numen or numenal individuals (such as, witches, medicine men, pregnant women, ghosts, madmen, saints) are felt to be *powerful, dangerous, and/or attractive,* because they fall between the cracks of social, political, and/or natural categories.[29]

Again, Douglas explains, where group boundaries (whether social, political, or natural) are under assimilative pressure, communities tend to meet the threats to group identity by evolving codes and regulations that clarify and strengthen group definition. And such institutions often metaphorically express the resolution of the problem, by positing sharp distinctions between the clean and the polluted. Douglas sees "the abominations of Leviticus" in this light.[30] *Etymologically, "holy" means separate,*[31] so that, on the one hand, holiness involves the clear and distinct separation of one thing from another. Thus, animals are clean or unclean, insofar as they perfectly conform to or compromise the species boundaries of rudimentary zoology. Those which fall between the taxonomical cracks or blur them by participating partly in one category and partly in another are unclean (Lev.11:3-7, 26-28). Similarly, swarming things are unclean, because their motion is indeterminate, no more of one sort than another (Lev.11:10-11, 29-38, 41-43).[32] Likewise, *because "holy" symbolizes the whole, complete, or perfect,*[33] things which are defective members of their kind (such as the lame, the blind, those with crushed limbs or sex organs; Lev.21:17-21; 22:20-25; cf. Lev.1:3,10) are unclean.[34] And *because holiness implies purity, being of the same kind all over and through and through,* it follows that hybrids (such as mules; Lev.19:19), mixtures (such as linsey-woolsey), and those with blotchy or blemished surfaces (people who are partially leprous, partially mildewed walls or cloth, etc.; Lev.13; Lev.22:4) are unclean. Again, *because the human body is itself an image of society*, bodily emissions symbolize ruptured group definition. Hence, bodily discharges of whatever sort (including menstrual blood, Lev. 12:1, Lev.15; and semen; Lev. 22:4) render one unclean.[35]

(3.2) Douglas Adapted: It is not clear to me whether Douglas intends a sociological *reduction* of religion generally, or of such institutions of purity and danger in particular. Happily, we need not embrace any reductive program to accept her generic thesis – that human perceptions and responses to others are profoundly shaped, both individually and collectively, by social context and institutions – or to profit from her more precise observations about how a thing's relation to social structure, or a group's position in its wider context, affect ascriptions of purity and pollution, danger and power. Adapting Douglas' ideas, I want now to propose an account of the function of covenants and commandments in ancient Israel, which harmonizes with my contention that, at the most basic level, sin is a disorder arising in Divine-human relationships because of the incommensuration of natures.

The application is straightforward. Because Divine and created natures are incommensurate, God will be unclassifiable relative to any merely human order (social, political, international) or to any human perception of natural order. Since we are unable to fit Him into any of our categories, we experience God as *(B1)* wholly other, and therefore as utterly unpredictable, as arbitrary power *(A2)*, at once dangerous *(A3)* and attractive *(B2)*. Given that roles not only confer identity, but define relationships, the possibility of Divine-human interactions seems like-wise jeopardized.

However intimidating the Divine *nature* ("no one can see God and live"), Biblical religion insists on a relentless Divine will to intimate, beneficial relations with His human creatures, a goal which requires Him to overcome human terror at His presence. One Biblical solution has *God* create an order, which assigns God and creatures roles, and issue a set of laws and commandments that define and structure Divine-human relations, thereby making them possible, tolerably safe, and potentially wholesome. In doing so, God accommodates Himself to the human condition by using analogues of human institutions: the Genesis 15:7-16 covenant with Abraham is modelled on ancient business deals; the Sinai covenant on international treaties (Exodus 20; Deuteronomy 5-8); and various liturgical rules on courtroom etiquette. On the other hand, the incommensuration between God and creatures accounts for a certain arbitrariness (e.g., which clan is eligible for priesthood, Temple decora-tions, etc.) and historical relativity in the content of the rules (e.g., pork and honeyed sacrifices are forbidden (Lev.2:11-13) because they were typical of Canaanite religion, which was exerting assimilative pressure on Israelite culture).

Since only God can assign God a role, the *norm* for God-creature interactions is God's social order, the Divinely imposed suzerainty cove-nant. Cast in the language of purity and pollution, since God is Holy, His people must be metaphorically holy; and God takes the initiative to make this possible by providing covenant obligations in terms of which to "separate" Israel from other nations (cf. Lev.19:2; 20:7, 26; 22:31-33). Thus, creatures are out of order and so unclean, when they fail to con-form to God's laws. The notion that disobedience to Divine laws has bad consequences for the human violator and/or his community, remains legal on the surface – the Sinai covenant is sealed with conditional curses (Deuteronomy 28:1-14), and specific penalties for law-breakers are pre-scribed in the code itself. Nevertheless, the laws themselves are not invariably voluntaristic/moralistic (cf. Levitical laws regarding *uninten-tional* sins which must nevertheless be expiated by sacrifice, and pollution legislation which concerns states and conditions outside the agent's voluntary control).[36] And underneath lies the fact that the Law was God's gift, a protective shield and framework; to break it, exposes the creature to the terrors of unstructured contact with the Divine.

3.3. A Christian Alternative: The Christian answer to the incommensu-ration problem is different: in a word, it is Christ Jesus Himself! *The per-son of Christ* declares that, despite Douglas-Ottonian appearances, created proximity to the Divine is *not metaphysically ruinous*. Christ is the eternal Word made flesh (John 1:14), the One who "bears the very stamp" of

God's nature (Hebrews 1:3) and at the same time is "like us in every respect" (Hebrews 2:17), partaking of the same flesh and blood nature (Hebrews 2:14). In Chalcedonian language, Divine nature and human nature are united in one person or *suppositum*, without confusion, change, division, or separation. According to medieval theology, the *suppositum* that is the Divine Word (God the Son) assumes and "supposits" an individual human nature. And although the Divine Word assumed the human nature contingently and could shed it at will, the Divine Word will remain united to that human nature forever.[37]

The work of Christ proclaims that God is an extra-structural figure relationship with whom will involve trials and suffering but be dominated by blessing. Because of the incommensuration problem, God will be experienced by any human consciousness as powerful and dangerous if also attractive (see sections 2 and 3.1 above). Because God's ways are higher than our ways, both beyond and contrary to our comprehension, "yes" to Divine vocation means exchanging citizenship in the earthly homeland for that in a heavenly country (Hebrews 11:8-16) and accepting to become "strangers and exiles upon the earth" (Hebrews 11:13). Although God is the ideal city-planner, the Christian should not expect to grasp the structure of the Kingdom of God in a more than fragmentary way – enough to know that it so fails to be congruent with human social divisions – e.g., between Jew and Greek, male and female, slave and free, rich and poor – as to explode them. On Douglas' model, the disciple risks becoming a displaced person who falls between the cracks of human social organization, oneself a liminal figure liable to evoke fear and hostility from others who remain imbedded in the merely human social institutions.

The letter to the Hebrews implies that Christ, in His human nature, reacted to His vocation with all the normal human fears and anxieties: He learned obedience through suffering (Hebrews 5:8; cf. 2:10), was tempted in all respects as we are (Hebrews 4:15), even prayed with loud cries and tears in Death's dark hour (Hebrews 5:7). Nevertheless, He chose to tolerate these psychic storms of Ottonian feelings and to trust God for goods as yet unseen. The incongruity between earthly and heavenly cities brought Him trials, and eventually failure and ruin by human standards, but God exalted Him to a position of intimacy and honor at God's right hand (Hebrews 8:1-2). Similarly, the letter-writer explains, such trials are the discipline by which God the Father teaches human beings how to be citizens of the city which He has prepared (Hebrews 12:7, 10, 13). The resurrection and exaltation of Christ are offered as assurance that blessing has the last word!

Finally, the letter-writer concludes, human approach to God is not, as for the Israelites at Mt. Sinai, towards "naked" Divinity, but through Jesus

(Hebrews 12:18-24), a person of our own nature, our pioneer (Hebrews 2:10) and companion, a priest who knows how to sympathize with us (Hebrews 4:15), who intercedes for us at God's right hand (Hebrews 7:24-25). Jesus Himself furnishes human beings safe passage into the holy of holies through the curtain of His flesh (Hebrews 10:19-20).

Sin as uncleanness and the tender loving care of Mother Jesus

If the Bible represents God as overcoming the barrier of ontological incommensuration by taking the initiative to establish a covenant relationship with human beings, the problem of sin re-arises with human non-compliance to its terms (from a Christian point of view, summarized in the First and Second Great "Love" commandments). Julian of Norwich analyzes this failure, not as rebellion that results in guilt, but as incompetence issuing in uncleanness, requiring a Divine Mother's loving care.

(4.1) *Psychological Prototypes*: Since Julian's account of Divine-human relationships emphasizes family as well as courtly models, we can best harvest her insights by taking a brief detour through developmental psychology. Beginning with Freud, psychologists have argued that (T1) religious belief reflects a projection of childhood models of parent-child relationships. Freud himself took the psycho-dynamics of the little boy's Oedipal struggle as the psychological prototype of human religion. God is a projection of the primal horde father within every human male, and the God thus projected is omnipotent, harsh, and demanding, threatening violent punishment of the slightest infractions of his arbitrary commands. As an atheist, Freud wanted to work (T2) a psychological reduction of religious belief, and so maintained that as therapy undid unconscious ego strategies, unconscious projections would be withdrawn, resulting in the end of religious delusion.

Others, influenced by Freud but uninterested in (T2) a psychological reduction of religion, have thought that Freudian dynamics nevertheless help to explain why people conceive of God as they do. Anna Maria Rizutto has documented striking parallels between people's pictures of God and their view of parent and family figures, and sees this psychic interference as explaining why some people believe in God and others don't. For her, therapy can help transform one's picture of God. But (not-T2) the psychodynamic explanation of people's conceptions of God is logically compatible with the reality of God as a spiritual being who is more or less different from these conceptions.

If humans inevitably conceive of the God-creature relationship on analogy with some developmental model or other of human relationships, the *theologian's* question becomes which developmental prototype would be the least inaccurate. This choice is crucial for soteriology, because the meaning of sin and suffering varies so considerably from model to model.

To appreciate this point, we must review briefly what these earlier phases are. (i) According to developmental psychologists, to begin with, a child's psyche is bombarded with stimuli from within and from without, and is a booming, buzzing confusion with no center or organizational principle. The child does not at first distinguish self from world (or not-self), but actively gropes for some way to center or organize this psychic material. (ii) At the age of three months, the child is able to focus on a human face (or just a drawing of one) and use that to center himself and his world. The presence of the face is a major organizer of the personality. We may call this the stage of **semi-differentiation**. In a way, the child differentiates the face as an object within the matrix of his psyche. But insofar as the face is the center of *the child's* personality and world, the child does not fully distinguish the face from the matrix which is itself. Usually, the face is that of the mother or adult care-taker, and so is experienced as an identity-conferring, loving other who orders the cosmos. To be sure, the child experiences heat and cold, wet and dry, hunger and digestive pains, and – to put it mildly – it does not understand why the psyche "has" to include these things. But insofar as the mother is indeed nurturing, the child will experience the face-centered world as a place made hospitable through the agency of the face.

(iii) At the age of six months, the child learns to recognize the absence of the face, and so experiences the face as something not entirely reliable. This makes the child realize it has to fend for itself, and here begins a long process of ego-development.

(iv) In the course of this ego-development, the child learns to move and walk, etc. And if the mother continues to be nurturing, she will respect and support the child in its moves towards independence. When the child takes the first step and then falls at the second, the mother will admire and be delighted in the first, and will in no way blame the child for the fall but will encourage it to get up and try again. The nurturing mother will thus exercise a kind of delicate courtesy and respect for the child's developing ego, and will not blame or shame it but will seek to provide a context of unconditional love and support within which these competencies can grow.

(v) Not until a year and a half or so later does the child reach the stage on which Freudian history of religions fixated, the stage at which the child is mature enough to construct the world as a place containing the big powerful authority figure who holds it accountable for obedience and disobedience with rewards and punishments.

Julian's dominant conception of God as a loving and nurturing heavenly Mother draws on psychological prototype from phases of child-development earlier than Freud's.

(4.2) Metaphysical Mothering: Julian agrees with Otto about the ontological incommensuration between God and creatures, and acknowledges a deep human propensity to fear the Divine presence. Nevertheless, she insists, the enormous metaphysical difference does not show itself in the need for separation or distance between God and creatures, but rather the radical metaphysical dependence of creatures on Him. For Julian, the developmental prototype of this dependence relation is the relation of semi-differentiation between a three to six-month old infant and its mother/adult care taker. Thus, she describes the relationship between God and the human soul in terms of *mutual indwelling.*[38] The human soul is a "glorious city," "a resting place"[39] where Christ makes Himself completely at home[40] and where the Blessed Trinity lives eternally.[41] Again, God is "the foundation of our nature"[42] and "the ground of our life and existence,"[43] in such a way that "all souls to be saved in heaven forever are joined and united in this union and made holy in this holiness."[44] Bringing her metaphysical remarks into explicit juxtaposition with the mother-image, Julian declares, "the Trinity is our Mother, in whom we are enfolded"[45]; Christ's "the tender love" that "enfolds," "embraces," and "completely surrounds us, never to leave us."[46] From a metaphysical point of view, human beings never get beyond the stage of semi-differentiation: for "our Saviour himself is our Mother"; "we are forever being born of him, and we shall never be delivered."[47]

Of course, human adults do not invariably *experience* themselves in relation to God the way a six month old does in relation to its mother. But Julian insists that those who pursue the path of self-knowledge will find it so. For it is

> easier for us to get to know God than to know our own soul. For our soul is so deeply set in God, and so deeply valued, that we cannot come to know it until we first know God, its Creator, to whom it is joined.[48]

Inevitably, "we come to know both together," because

> God is nearer to us than our own soul, for he is the ground in which it stands, and he is the means by which substance and sensuality are held together so that they can never separate.[49]

If the child finds a center for its personality in the mother's face and so does not know itself apart from knowing the mother, so also it cannot know the mother in the stage of semi-differentiation apart from knowing itself.

(4.3) Sin as Incompetence and Uncleanness: According to Julian, the evaluative truth about the human condition finds its developmental prototype in the pre-Oedipal stages, where the emotional developmental agenda is to establish a favorable balance of trust over mistrust, of autonomy over shame and doubt.

Following tradition, Julian analyzes sin as a disordering of two parts of human nature: an essential/inward/higher/godly nature which is superior to and ought to govern the sensual/outward/lower/animal nature.[50] Implicitly drawing on Romans 7, she insists that sin does not occur in the higher nature, but rather is a defect of the lower nature in not conforming to the higher.[51] Unruly desires and sinful inclinations are rooted in our sensuality.[52] Nevertheless, God regards both parts of human nature as good, and willed from eternity that they should be created and joined to one another. The soul's higher essential nature, both Christ's and ours, were created simultaneously and immediately united to God and hence to God the Son. But sensuality was joined to God the Son at His Incarnation,[53] so that God Himself is the means whereby our two natures are inseparably united.[54] The Divinely purposed conformity of the lower to the higher nature occurs first in the person of Christ; their realignment in us, perfected in heaven, is His saving work.[55]

Julian's picture is distinctive because of her contention that psychological bad government results, not from rebellion, which would make the sinner guilty, but from incompetence, which threatens autonomy and produces shame. This diagnosis is already implicit in the Parable of the Lord and the Servant, which Julian received after persistent inquiries into the origin and purpose of pain and sin:

> . . . I saw physically before me two people, a lord and his servant. And God showed me its spiritual meaning. The lord is sitting down quietly, relaxed and peaceful: the servant is standing by his lord, humble and ready to do his bidding. And then I saw the lord look at his servant with rare love and tenderness, and quietly send him to a certain place to fulfil his purpose. Not only does that servant go, but he starts off at once, running with all speed, in his love to do what his master wanted. And without warning he falls head-long into a deep ditch, and injures himself very badly. And though he groans and cries and struggles, he is quite unable to get up or to help himself in any way. To crown all, he could get no relief of any

sort: he could not even turn his head to look at the lord who loved him, and who was so close to him. The sight of him would have been of real comfort, but he was temporarily so weak and bemused that he gave vent to his feelings as he suffered his pains.[56]

The fall is sin and is incurred in the course of trying to obey God's will. It is a result of our "blindness,"[57] "weakness,"[58] and "ineffectiveness."[59] When we sin, we are like two-year olds who fail the competence-test in toilet training. Sins are "foul, black, shameful,"[60] "vile"[61] deeds, which leave us "befouled"[62] and "really unclean."[63] "Our heavenly Mother Jesus" wants us to run to Him and cry

> with the humility of a child, 'Kind, thoughtful, dearest Mother, do be sorry for me. I have got myself into a filthy mess, and am not a bit like you. I cannot begin to put it right without your special and willing help."[64]

We need to be "purged"[65] or "cleansed"[66] to arrive at a sinless state, "clean,"[67] "pure,"[68] and "holy."[69] In other words, "Mommy, please change my diaper!"

(4.4.) Love in Place of Blame: Human beings respond to sin three ways. We feel *grief*[70] at the pain it causes[71]; *shame* because it prevents us from doing what we, in our essential nature, want[72]; and *fear* that God will be angry with us, blame us, punish if He does not forgive us.[73] Holy Mother Church encourages the last, and it would be appropriate if sin were a matter of the creature's autonomous (and hence guilty) rebellion.

Yet, Julian reports, she *saw* something different. God's love for us is eternal and entirely undisturbed by our sin.[74] God judges us according to our essential nature, and His first verdict was to join human nature to Himself.[75] Further, as much as she looked, Julian found no anger in God[76]: for anger is inconsistent with peace and contrary to "the integrity of His love," "to the nature of his power, wisdom, and goodness."[77] As angerless, God cannot strictly speaking forgive us, if "forgiveness" signifies the removal of anger[78]; if it means that sin is not held against us, our forgiveness is guaranteed.[79] Instead of blaming us,[80] God "overlooks"[81] and "excuses"[82] our sin and "never faults those who are going to praise Him forever."[83] He regards our incompetence with sympathy and pity.[84] Julian is convinced that the worst punishment the elect will ever have to suffer is enduring our weakened condition and the struggles between our higher and lower natures, during our lives in this world.[85]

(4.5) Sanctification as Development: God gauges His expectations to our condition, as children[86] whom it will take the whole of this passing life

to rear up.[87] Our developmental goal is to become persons who can enjoy God's astonishing love for us; our developmental agenda in this world is to learn to love God and trust Him humbly and wholeheartedly.[88] The first step is to appreciate the ontological incommensuration between God and creatures: "...to realize the littleness of creation and to see it for the nothing that it is."[89] If theophany convinced Mary,[90] our humility grows when we meet awareness of our incompetence with hatred of whatever makes us sin, and the choice to trust God's love instead of accusing Him for our pains.[91] For Julian, the contrast between Divine and human reactions to sin estimate the wideness of God's love: awareness of sin moves us to fear of God's anger and repentance in hope of forgiveness, all which yields to surprise at His "friendly welcome"[92] and the recognition that our sin "has made no difference at all to his love."[93] Moreover, this lesson repeats; it spirals and deepens, so that the more the soul sees of Divine courtesy and love, the more it hates sin and the greater its sense of shame; the humbler it becomes, the broader its appreciation of Divine love.[94]

(4.6) The Motherhood of Jesus: Childhood growth and development needs a mother's tender loving care. According to Julian, Jesus Christ is the paradigm-case Mother:

> A mother's is the most intimate, willing, and dependable of all services, because it is the truest of all. None has been able properly to fulfil it but Christ.[95]

In His divine nature, Mother Jesus *creates* us and joins us inseparably to the Godhead forever; God the Son is Mother of our sensual nature, by taking it on Himself in the Incarnation.[96] Mother Jesus "*carries* us within himself in love."[97] Julian was allowed mystically to enter the wound in His side into a place "large enough for all saved mankind to rest in peace and love,"[98] like baby kangaroos in their mother's pouch. Mother Jesus *bears* us with the labor pangs of His suffering and death on the cross.[99] Yet, we are never more than semi-differentiated from Mother Jesus: "our Saviour himself is our Mother for we are ever *being born* of him, and shall never be delivered!"[100] If only we could see this truth, we should be as satisfied and content as the three to six month old infant, enfolded in its mother's arms and gazing into her face.[101] Where earthly mothers feed with their own milk, Mother Jesus *feeds* us with Himself, and leads us to His breast through His open side.[102] Mother Jesus "functions as a kindly nurse who has no other business than to care for the well-being of her charge,"[103] to rear us up in those virtues which will enable us to enjoy Him forever.[104] Mother Jesus *guides* us by His laws,[105] and sometimes *punishes to correct* faults.[106] Like any mother, Jesus sometimes allows His children to learn the hard way, but never allows the situation to become dangerous or life-threatening for them.[107] When we fall, it is the gracious touch of Mother Jesus that enables us to get up and try again.[108] Whenever we are frightened, whether by suffering or our own disobedience and failures, Mother Jesus wants us to run to Him at once and cling to Him forever.[109] Thus, Julian declares,

> ...Jesus Christ who sets good against evil is our real Mother. We owe our being to Him – and this is the essence of motherhood! – and all the delightful, loving protection which ever follows.[110]

"Jesus is the true Mother of our nature, for he made us. He is our Mother, too, by grace, because he took our created nature upon himself."[111]

> And she invites us to find blessed assurance in those bonds of motherly love which sin and death cannot break.[112]

(4.7) Honor Cancels Shame: According to Julian, God will finally solve the problem of sin, not by a debt-moratorium lifting the burden of guilt, but by Divine courtesy canceling shame. Strictly, "courtesy" signifies an elaborate etiquette governing royal courts and conventionally defining behaviors as symbolic of worth and valor. Julian retains the heraldic imagery of the Parable of the Lord and the Servant, but interprets it kenotically, reversing lordly and servant roles. She envisions God as a great king who pays His creatures the unsurpassable honor of genuine and spontaneous, intimate and loving friendship.[113] Not at all condescending,[114] Our Lord is so "utterly kind and unassuming"[115] that He does not hesitate to become human in order to serve us.[116] The passion of Christ is a deed of knightly valor, which Lord Jesus gladly undertook to honor and please His Lady, the soul. Julian reports on her vision of the crucifixion that

> . . . our good Lord Jesus Christ said, 'Are you well satisfied with my suffering for you?' 'Yes, thank you, good Lord,' I replied. 'Yes, good Lord, bless you.' And the kind Lord Jesus said, 'If you are satisfied, I am satisfied too. It gives me great happiness and joy and, indeed, eternal delight ever to have suffered for you. If I could possibly have suffered more, I would have done so.[117]

Calculating the magnitude of the deed, Julian reckons that the hypostatic union between Divine and human natures strengthened the manhood of Christ to suffer more than the whole human race could suffer.[118] In comparison with other feats possible for Him (such as the creation of countless worlds), Julian estimates His "willingness to die times without number" and yet "count it as nothing for the love of us"[119] "the greatest gesture our Lord God could make to the soul of man."[120] Lord Jesus Christ, our knight in shining armor, will present elect souls to the Father in worship, whereupon the Father will gratefully receive them and grant them to the Son[121] as His happy reward.[122]

During this passing life, God shows His royal friendship for us, by the great courtesy with which He corrects us: "he holds on to us so tenderly when we are in sin" and exposes our "foul" condition "by the gentle light of mercy and grace," to protect us from despair.[123] He greets our repentance with "friendly welcome" as to loved ones released from prison.[124] Our entrance into heaven will not begin with court flattery and thanksgiving from servants to the Lord; rather God will honor His servants by showing His gratitude to them: "Thank you for all your suffering, the suffering of your youth!"[125] Julian observes, not even the whole history of human suffering could have merited such heavenly gratitude; moreover, it will be public, and the pleasure of it will last eternally. Further, not only will the wounds of sin finally heal into honorable battle scars, but also God will compensate us for suffering through them with a "great, glorious, and honorable reward."[126] "So shall shame be turned to greater honour and joy."[127]

Conclusion

I want now to draw the threads of the above discussion together, to sketch a Christian account of sin, which I find preferable to its moralistic competitors and worthy of further development.

Theologically, sin is an impropriety in the relation between God and created persons. My three exhibits – from Rudolf Otto, Mary Douglas, and Julian of Norwich – suggest a two-tiered understanding, where sin is to be identified, at both levels, with uncleanness rooted in incompetence, and seen as a problem for Divine-human relations to which Divine love is an indispensable solution.

Fundamentally, sin is uncleanness arising from the incommensuration of Divine and created natures, in the incapacity of any finite being to do or to be anything, naturally or intrinsically, worthy of God. The latter claim divides into two: that finite creatures are not naturally or intrinsically valuable enough either to command God's love or to be or do anything that could render Him fitting honor. Developing the first point, the great Franciscan theologians, Scotus and Ockham, measure the gap between finite and infinite by their intuition that if it is rational to love valuable things in proportion to their intrinsic worth, yet it is not necessarily irrational not to love finite goods even a little bit, not always foolish to love the lesser more than the greater.[128] As for the second claim, to be natural signs of value, by nature the currency of honor, things have to be sufficiently valuable in themselves. Cardboard crowns and plastic rings are not naturally suited to honor kings, but rather gold and diamonds.

This ontological incommensuration of natures is a metaphysically necessary consequence of what God and creatures are, not the outcome of the free and contingent exercise of anyone's agency, created or Divine. It follows that the disproportion between finite and infinite can never change: there neither is, was, nor could be a time, whether in the mythological past or the eschatological future, in which God and creatures existed and were of metaphysically comparable size. Likewise, if sin is fundamentally a consequence of what God and creatures *are*, and the normative priority lies with God, then the logically appropriate feeling response for creatures is not guilt (which befits a rebellious use of free agency) but a sense of taint and shame.

Immutable as the ontological incommensuration itself is, the resultant *formal* obstacles to relationship can be easily overcome by Divine fiat: just as governments confer value on relatively worthless paper through legislation stipulating a value-equivalence to silver and gold; so God, the creator and governor of the universe, can simply count finite creatures as valuable by loving them, declare *ex officio* certain conditions and deeds of creatures to be honorific of Him. The result is to create *at the second level a "stipulative" or "statutory" contrast* among created beings and doings between what is sinful and what is worthy and acceptable and righteous in God's sight.

Specific items – the sorts and conditions of ritual uncleanness, morally wrong actions and moral vices, thoughts, emotions, and unconsciously acquired habits – enter the Biblical catalog of sins at the second, stipulative or statutory level. If some second-level sins are within our power to do or withhold in the sense normally required for moral responsibility, others just happen to us (e.g., states of ritual uncleanness) and still others, while caused by our substance, lie outside the conscious control of mature agency (e.g., neurotic childhood adaptations). Since, from a Biblical point of view, the *content* of Divine stipulations is summarized in the First and Second Great Commandments (to love God with one's whole self, and to love one's neighbor as oneself), human agency is once again reduced to a posture before God of incompetence and shame! Some (e.g., Aquinas and Julian of Norwich) diagnose our difficulty as the incapacity of the higher, intellectual or spiritual nature to subordinate the lower, sensual nature. Others (e.g., Reinhold Niebuhr and Basil Mitchell; cf. St. Anselm on post-lapsarian condition of rational creatures) locate it in a dominant psycho-biological drive toward self-centeredness.

At the secondary content level, as much as the foundational formal level, gratuitous Divine Love is the solution to created incompetence, uncleanness, and shame. For Divine Love guarantees the being and well-being of each created person. And Divine pedagogy trains the soul, guiding its unlearning of ego-centricity, teaching it new skills, making trust and self-giving love possible. The soteriological syllabus spirals through stages in which God creates structures to house the relationship until the creature believes enough in Divine Love to do without such definitive structures. The ultimate cure for shame is not the achievement of natural competence (although we grow towards it in this passing life, and its fulfillment is promised in the eschatological future), because even at our created best, our finitude would leave us, naturally and intrinsically, unworthy to appear in the presence of God. Rather the Love of the Infinite Creator, identifying with His creature in the Incarnation, serving His creature in His passion, showing eternal gratitude to His creature for the earthly service of a created life – God Himself many ways honoring His creature, finally overcomes our shame!

Notes

1. *The Nature of Necessity*, Oxford at the Clarendon Press, 1974, ch. IX, pp. 164-93. John Hick, writing as a theologian and proceeding historically from Augustine, does talk about **sin**. Cf. *Evil and the God of Love*, Harper and Row, 1966, 1978, pp. 64–69, 87–89.
2. Cf. my "Problems of Evil: More Advice to Christian Philosophers," *Faith and Philosophy* 5 (1988), pp. 121-43; esp. pp. 127–135.
3. In the lead paper of a recent symposium, Basil Mitchell remarks: "The word 'sin' is unlikely to be found in the index of a book on moral philosophy. It belongs to the vocabulary of theology. But the serious student of both subjects is bound to wonder how the concept of sin is to be related to the topics that interest moral philosophers. The problem is complicated by the evident fact that 'sin' is what W. B. Gallie has called an 'essentially contested concept' and that unanimity is as rare among moral philosophers as it is among theologians. It is not a matter, therefore, of applying an agreed philosophical method to a clearly defined theological concept, but of looking for a way of thinking about sin which is theologically defensible and which can approve itself to a reasonably sympathetic moral philosopher." ("How is the Concept of Sin related to the Concept of Moral Wrongdoing?" *Religious Studies* 20, pp. 165–73; quoted passage on p. 165.)
4. Thus, Mitchell (*op.cit.*, p. 165) and co-symposiast David G. Attfield ("The Morality of Sins," *Religious Studies* 20, p. 228) agree that "sin" connotes a reference to Divine disapproval. By contrast, Robert Merrihew Adams, who does not in general follow the strategy I am sketching, offers the term "sin" to secular as well as religious moralists ("Involuntary Sins," *Philosophical Review* XCIV (1985), 3–31).

5. Cf. Mitchell, "How is the Concept of Sin related to the Concept of Moral Wrongdoing?" *Religious Studies* 20, pp. 165–68.

6. The rabbis spoke of the evil *yezer* or evil heart (cf. 2 Esdras 3:20–26). Reinhold Niebuhr speaks more concretely of an innate anxiety over finitude which leads to individual and collective self-deception and prideful self-assertion at the expense of others (*The Nature and Destiny of Man*, Charles Scribners' Sons, 1941, chapter vi, pp. 164–69; chapter vii, pp. 179–88; chapter viii, pp. 209–210; chapter ix, pp. 247, 249. Basil Mitchell remarks on an insidious self-centeredness that leads to self-deception ("How is the Concept of Sin related to the Concept of Moral Wrongdoing?" *Religious Studies* 20, pp. 168–67).

7. As Mitchell notes ("How is the Concept of Sin related to the Concept of Moral Wrongdoing?" *loc.cit.*, p. 165: "It is...the definitive stage in the development of ethical monotheism when men came to see that it was *unrighteousness* rather than *ritual uncleanness* that incurred the wrath of God."

8. David G. Attfield measures the category of "inward thoughts and emotions," failures to exemplify ideals, collective or public sins, and cultic acts, against Tennant's criterion that "sin must be a violation of a moral law" and excludes those that are not within our direct voluntary control ("The Morality of Sins," *Religious Studies* 20, pp. 227–32).

9. Note that those who, like Reinhold Niebuhr, locate the root of sin in a built-in self-centeredness arising from anxiety over finitude, still take an anthropocentric approach to sin. For this diagnosis of the human condition is one shared by atheistic and theistic existentialists alike. Likewise, those who would characterize sin as sickness or defection from a norm naturalistically conceived. For the diagnosis is arrived at on religion-neutral territory; the reference to God is still secondary in the order of explanation.

10. Viz., "Problems of Evil: More Advice to Christian Philosophers," *Faith and Philosophy* Vol. 5, No. 2 (1988), pp. 121–43; and "Theodicy without Blame," *Philosophical Topics* Vol. XVI (1988), pp. 215–245.

11. Cf. my "Theodicy without Blame," *Philosophical Topics* (Fall 1988), sec. 5.3, pp. 230–33. Mitchell seems to agree, when he distinguishes "what other people have a right to blame us for" from "what we should be ready to confess as a sin to God" as follows: "I am answerable to other men, that is to say morally responsible for, my failure to fulfil my duties and obligations towards them, but I am answerable to God for my failure to love my neighbor as myself." ("How is the Concept of Sin related to the Concept of Moral Wrongdoing?" loc.cit., pp. 169.)

12. "Theodicy without Blame," sec. 5, passim.

13. *Idea of the Holy,* Oxford University Press: New York, 1958, ch. III, pp. 8–11. I am particularly indebted in this section to Nelson Pike, who used regularly to begin his courses on the nature and attributes of God with a unit on Otto. For years, I have followed Pike's practice (as well as many interpretive details) in my own teaching.

14. *The Idea of the Holy,* ch. VII, pp. 41–49.

15. *The Idea of the Holy,* ch. III, pp. 8–11.

16. *The Idea of the Holy,* ch. XIV, pp. 112–116; ch. XVII, pp. 136–42.

17. *The Idea of the Holy*, ch. IV, pp. 13–17.
18. *The Idea of the Holy*, ch. III, pp. 8–11, 20–21.
19. *The Idea of the Holy*, ch. IV, pp. 23-24.
20. *The Idea of the Holy*, ch.V, pp. 25–26, 29; Appendix I, pp. 179–86.
21. *The Idea of the Holy*, ch.VI, pp. 31–32.
22. *The Idea of the Holy*, ch.VIII, pp. 50–57.
23. *The Idea of the Holy*, ch.VIII, pp. 50–59.
24. Commenting on the difference between moral devaluation and that involved in (A2) and (C1), Otto writes, "Mere morality is not the soil from which grows either the need of 'redemption' and deliverance or the need for that other unique good which is likewise altogether and specifically numinous in character, 'covering', and 'atonement'. There would perhaps be less disputing as to the warrant and value of these later in Christian doctrine *if dogmatic theology itself had not transferred them from their mystical sphere into that of rational ethics and attenuated them into moral concepts.*" (*The Idea of the Holy*, ch.VIII, p. 53) Again, "'Atonement'...is a 'sheltering' or 'covering', but a profound form of it...Mere awe, mere need for shelter from the *tremendum,* has been elevated to the feeling that man in his 'profaneness' is not *worthy* to stand in the presence of the holy one, and that his own entire personal unworthiness might defile even the holy itself . . ." Cf. *ibid.,* pp. 55–56.
25. Mary Douglas, *Purity and Danger: An analysis of concepts of pollution and taboo.* Routledge & Kegan Paul: London, 1966, Introduction, p. 2; ch. 2, pp. 35–36; ch. 10, pp. 160–61.
26. *Purity and Danger*, ch. 3, pp. 49–50; ch. 6, pp. 94–113.
27. *Purity and Danger*, ch. 1, pp. 2–3; ch. 2, p. 36.
28. *Purity and Danger*, ch. 6, pp. 109–13; ch. 10, pp. 160–79.
29. *Purity and Danger*, ch. 6, pp. 95–98.
30. *Purity and Danger*, ch. 3, pp. 49–57.
31. *Purity and Danger*, ch. 3, pp. 49–51.
32. Likewise for rules about sexuality (Lev. 18:6–20): "...Holiness means keeping distinct the categories of creation. It therefore involves correct definition, discrimination, and order. Under this head all the rules of sexual morality exemplify the holy. Incest and adultery (Lev. xviii, 6–20) are against holiness, in the simple sense of right order. Morality does not conflict with holiness, but holiness is more a matter of separating that which should be separated than of protecting the rights of husbands and brothers." (Cf. *Purity and Danger*, ch. 3, p. 53.)
33. *Purity and Danger*, ch. 3, pp. 51–2.
34. *Purity and Danger*, ch. 3, p. 53.
35. *Purity and Danger*, ch. 7, pp. 114–28.
36. For a discussion of this legislation, see Jacob Milgrom, *Cult and Conscience: The Asham and the Priestly Doctrine of Repentance*, E.J.Brill: Leiden, 1976.
37. Cf. my paper "The Metaphysics of the Incarnation in Some Fourteenth Century Franciscans," in *Essays Honoring Allan B. Wolter.* Edited by William A. Frank and Girard J. Etzkorn. The Franciscan Institute, St. Bonaventure University: St. Bonaventure, N.Y. 1985, pp. 21–57.

38. *Revelations of Divine Love*, translated by Clifton Wolters, Penguin Books, 1966, ch. 54, p. 157. (Hereafter *RDL* followed by chapter number, period, then page number: e.g., *RDL* 54.157.) Cf. *RDL* 9.75.
39. *RDL* 81.206.
40. *RDL* 67.183.
41. *RDL* 1.63.
42. *RDL* 56.162.
43. *RDL* 78.201.
44. *RDL* 53.157.
45. *RDL* 54.158.
46. *RDL* 5.67–68; cf. *RDL* 5.69.
47. *RDL* 57.164.
48. *RDL* 56.160.
49. *RDL* 56.161.
50. *RDL* 19.93; cf. *RDL* 37.118, 57.163.
51. *RDL* 51.144; 57.163.
52. *RDL* 37.118.
53. *RDL* 57.163; 158.166.
54. *RDL* 56.161.
55. *RDL* 56.161.
56. *RDL* 51.141.
57. *RDL* 11.80–81; 64.178, 66.181–82; 72.190.
58. *RDL* 51.144, 64.178, 66.181–82, 74.194.
59. *RDL* 51.144, 62.174.
60. *RDL* 10.78, 40.121.
61. *RDL* 40.122, 78.201.
62. *RDL* 39.120.
63. *RDL* 63.175.
64. *RDL* 61.172-73.
65. *RDL* 27.104.
66. *RDL* 27.104, 39.120.
67. *RDL* 12.82-83, 27.103, 28.105, 40.123.
68. *RDL* 20.94.
69. *RDL* 28.105.
70. *RDL* 13.83.
71. *RDL* 27.104.
72. *RDL* 13.83, 29.120, 40.122, 66.181.
73. *RDL* 45.131, 46.133–34.
74. *RDL* 53.155, 82.207.
75. *RDL* 45.131.
76. *RDL* 13.84, 45.131, 46.133, 49.137–38.
77. *RDL* 48.136, 46.133.
78. *RDL* 49.137.
79. *RDL* 41.121.
80. *RDL* 27.104, 39.120, 45.131.
81. *RDL* 28.105.
82. *RDL* 52.154.

83. *RDL* 53.155.
84. *RDL* 28.105, 51.144–45, 82.207.
85. *RDL* 39.120, 40.122, 63.175, 77.199.
86. *RDL* 28.105, 63.176.
87. *RDL* 52.153, 56.161, 58.165, 82.207.
88. *RDL* 61.173; cf. 7.72–73, 10.79, 52.151-52.
89. *RDL* 5.68.
90. *RDL* 7.71; cf. Otto's account in section (2.2) above.
91. *RDL* 36.117, 52.153, 79.202, 81.206.
92. *RDL* 40.121–22; cf. 38.118–19, 39.120.
93. *RDL* 61.172.
94. *RDL* 40.122.
95. *RDL* 60.169, 170.
96. *RDL* 58.165.
97. *RDL* 60.169; cf. 57.163.
98. *RDL* 25.100
99. *RDL* 60.169–70.
100. *RDL* 57.164.
101. *RDL* 47.134–35; 54.158; 72.191.
102. *RDL* 60.170.
103. *RDL* 61.173.
104. *RDL* 58.166–67.
105. *RDL* 55.158.
106. *RDL* 61.171–72.
107. *RDL* 61.172.
108. *RDL* 52.153.
109. *RDL* 61.172.
110. *RDL* 59.168.
111. *RDL* 59.168.
112. *RDL* 78.201.
113. *RDL* 5.67, 7.72.
114. *RDL* 7.72.
115. *RDL* 10.79.
116. *RDL* 6.70; 7.72–73.
117. *RDL* 22.96.
118. *RDL* 20.94.
119. *RDL* 22.96–97.
120. *RDL* 22.97.
121. *RDL* 23.98–99.
122. *RDL* 23.98–99.
123. *RDL* 40.121.
124. *RDL* 40.121.
125. *RDL* 14.86.
126. *RDL* 14.85, 39.120–21.
127. *RDL* 39.121.
128. Cf. my "The Structure of Ockham's Moral Theory," *Franciscan Studies* 46 (1986), pp. 1–35; esp. pp. 5–6, 18–23.

CHAPTER 14

INNOCENT SINFULNESS, GUILTY SIN: ORIGINAL SIN AND DIVINE JUSTICE

Keith D. Wyma

As a college sophomore taking a course in Reformed theology, I was troubled by the doctrines having to do with original sin. Eventually I raised my questions in class. "How can it be just," I asked, "for God to create me in an already-sinful state? And if I *start* life with original sin, and so am sinful such that I *cannot help* but do evil, how can it be just on God's part to condemn and punish me for it?" In response, the professor stared at me, drew a long nasal breath, and in stern tones of righteous indignation proclaimed, "Well, I think that's the kind of question a good Christian just wouldn't ask!" After enduring the resultant witch-burning glares of my classmates, I shut my mouth and kept mum for the rest of the course.

But my questions remained, and they nag at me to this day. Apparently, I still just am not a good Christian (although good enough to have restrained my spiteful urge to identify the school and professor . . .). I see these questions as necessary for Christians to address, since they pose a serious challenge to Christian attempts to reconcile a just God with the evil humans do. For the doctrine of original sin seems to cripple the human freedom that crucially supports Christian theodicy. If we are born guilty of sin, then apparently at least some of our sin cannot be directly traced to any identifiable free choice on our own parts. Also, if original sin makes further sinful action inevitable, it's hard to see how those resultant sins can be attributed to our free and responsible action. In that case, though, it's not clear how God can escape responsibility for those sins; and it certainly seems that he cannot justly blame and punish us for sins we did not choose or could not help but commit.

In this paper, then, I shall examine original sin with two purposes: first, to show that creating us in the state of original sin can be compatible with God's justice; and second, to show how the sins we perform from that state can still be our responsibility and thus justly be blameworthy.

Before analyzing aspects of the doctrine of original sin, however, we had better look at the doctrine itself. Christian thinking on this topic mostly reflects the view of Augustine of Hippo. Augustine set the tone for later Catholic theologians, including Thomas Aquinas. Moreover, the primary Reformers Luther and Calvin were both deeply influenced by Augustine. According to Augustine, then, since Adam's fall, every human being has been born already carrying the guilt and punishment of that first sin (not including those with miraculous births like Christ's, of course). Somehow Adam's sin has been transmitted and attributed to us (Augustine, *Confessions* VIII.*x*(22), X.*xx*(29)). Biblical texts appealed to in support of this view include Psalm 51:5, "Behold, I was brought forth in iniquity, and in sin my mother conceived me," and Romans 5:12, 18-19, "... through one man sin entered into the world, and death through sin, and so death spread to all men, because all sinned.... So then... through one transgression there resulted condemnation to all men ... through the one man's disobedience the many were made sinners ..." (NASB). Each of us thus begins life a guilty sinner condemned by God's righteous judgment (Augustine, *Confessions* I.viii(11-12)). Worse, the depravity of our faculties, which is part of the death-sentence punishment of that original sin, ensures that we cannot help but sin in our later actions (*On Free Choice of the Will* III, xix.180, 184, 185). Therefore, on our own we cannot please God by our actions (*Retractations* II, 4). This picture, or slight variations on it, has since dominated Christian doctrine on original sin.

In investigating this doctrine, the first difficult issue that I shall focus on concerns how we should understand God's justification in creating Adam's progeny in an already-sinful state. For it seems that God does us wrong by creating us in the punitive, morally-unable condition of original sin. Among its physical and mental effects, original sin damages our faculties for deciding upon and executing action, particularly as they relate to our abilities to know and to do the good. Does God not owe us a "clean slate" starting point? How can God justly extend the disordered faculties imposed on Adam as punishment for his transgression to us, who did not actually commit that sin?[1] In response to these questions, I shall propose two possible justifications. While they have distinct bases, they lend each other support, so that their combined justification will be stronger than either alone.

The first justification points to our complete inability to assert any moral obligation upon God with regard to the status of our creation. That is, in creating us, God graciously grants existence to us; it is as if God were giving us a gift. Since this existence is neither earned by us nor otherwise owed to us – after all, *before* we exist we cannot be the objects of any moral duty – it follows that we cannot make any claims on God as to *how* we shall exist. For example, that I exist at all is essentially a gift to me; with regard to moral obligation, God's act in creating me was *supererogatory* (at least in respect to any moral claims on *my* part). Given that, how could I possibly make any moral complaints about the qualities of that gift? May I accuse God of injustice because I'm not as insightful, not as good a writer, as I might have been? No. If God had chosen to create me in an earlier time period or in a nation racked by war, famine, or disease, could I claim that I was being wrongly treated, since I was being denied the easy, comfortable life I might have had? No. If God had chosen to create me with less ability or opportunity – or even let me be born with serious mental or physical disabilities or both – would that impugn God's justice? No. Why not? Because in a situation of non-obligatory giving, the amount of the gift is also a non-obligatory matter. God may give more or less ability or opportunity, as he pleases. In short, the initial circumstances of our lives and the innate extents of our capabilities – moral and otherwise – lie beyond the reach of moral obligations we can claim upon God.[2]

Moreover, this point is strengthened by the fact that the very nature of creaturely existence involves finitude. Any creature must fall short of the omnipotence of God; possession of that trait would imply divinity. However, to be less than omnipotent implies *some* limit to one's power to act. And if there must be limits to any creature's innate capacities to act, then where those limits fall is a matter for God's free discretion. For there is no point at which a capability-limit might be set such that no creaturely complaints might result.[3] Consider, for example, my ability to learn: it's good, but not great. I learn well enough to understand what I'm taught in most, but not all, areas. I never did gain a truly solid grasp of differential calculus. That failure bothers me; perhaps it even hindered my career choice – avoid engineering and physics, young man! Because of those sorts of hindrances, I have complained to God that I should have had more capability in these areas. But suppose God suddenly infused me with greater ability in all those areas. Differential calculus comes easily; I can jump higher, palm the ball, and dunk; and so on. But now I complain about difficulties with time-space theory, or my inability to "sky" and throw down jams off alley-oop passes. Shall God relent and increase my abilities again? And again when I complain that I can't leap tall buildings in a single bound? In truth, there is no discernible optimal ability-limit. Whatever the capacity and wherever the limit, ability-failures would remain possible, and creaturely complaints might be made. Thus God's creative choice is unconstrained by any set of capacities and limits that *should* or *ought* to be utilized; he may simply choose as he pleases.

To apply the general point to our question about original sin, our moral capacities to identify and to perform the good, or to identify and to avoid evil, must have some boundaries. As finite beings, we creatures necessarily have some circumstances possible in our lives such that under those conditions we could not know or could not do the good.

Again, though, given that there must be some limit set, it is entirely up to God's free choice where to place that boundary. Therefore, even if we recognize our moral capacities, in the state of original sin, to be severely diminished in comparison to what they could be (or to what Adam's were before the Fall), that does not mean God has done us wrong. Were our moral capacities even lesser or greater, God would not thereby have done morally worse or better by us. For this reason, that we are created in a state of original sin, possessing moral capacities on a par with Adam's punitively weakened ones, does not impugn God's justice. Indeed, if Adam had never existed, God would still not wrong us by creating us with the moral capacities that we in fact have.[4] We simply receive what abilities God chooses to give us, with no question of justice involved at all.

But I think this justification faces some immediate objections. First, it has not explained how Adam's sin can be attributed to us; rather it treats our originally-sinful state as if God might have created us with it whether Adam fell or not. But a key aspect of original sin is that we receive it *from Adam* somehow, because of what he did. We're born in a punitive state through, and because of, him and our relation to him. Yet this justification conveys no sense of that, and so is incomplete.

Second, and more damagingly, this justification seems outright mistaken in that it ignores a crucial difference between our moral capacities and any other abilities we might possess: God does not demand a specified level of achievement in our use of those other abilities. Perhaps God may create me fast, slow, or even without legs; but he doesn't require me to run quickly. Perhaps he may create me with a low or high IQ; but he does not demand that I solve multivariable equations. Yet God does command me to do right. How then can he justifiably create me with an inability to do so? If God lays a demand, an 'ought', upon us, he must supply the 'can', the ability to carry out what's required. Yet in our condition of original sin, it appears impossible for us to meet the moral demands of God. Therefore, it seems that in the case of our moral capacities, God's choice of where to set our ability-limits is constrained by considerations of what he requires from us. But our originally-sinful condition seems to violate those constraints; God still appears unjust for creating us in such a state, while commanding us to do what that state renders impossible.

The former objection can be met, I believe, by appealing to the second potential justification, to which I shall turn next. Some help also will be offered for the latter, and more troubling, objection; but that will not have a complete defense until we see the second main argument of the paper. I think the interpretation of our moral obligations and moral inabilities included there will provide a plausible response. However, for complete consistency even that rebuttal will need to be accompanied by a minor revision to our understanding of original sin itself.

For now, though, let me lay out the second piece of the first main argument justifying God's creation of us in an already-sinful state. This justification utilizes counterfactuals of freedom and God's so-called middle knowledge. Counterfactuals of freedom are conditional (or "if-then") statements about free-willed agents, telling what they would have freely done, if circumstances had been different from what they were or are. For example, "If Bill Clinton were propositioned by one of his current interns, he would freely refuse," and, "If Judas had repented and asked for for giveness instead of committing suicide, God would freely have forgiven him," are both counterfactuals of freedom. Moreover, many theologians and philosophers have thought that God's omniscience implies knowledge of which counterfactuals of freedom are true, including those concerning possible-but-uncreated free agent creatures. That is, in deciding whom to create, and in what conditions and circumstances to place them, God would have reference to truths about what any possible creature would freely do, in any circumstances possible for it. Those truths constitute what has been labeled God's "middle" knowledge (because it falls between God's knowledge of necessary truths prior to creation, and his knowledge of contingent truths about the world posterior to creation).

Unfortunately, the very possibility of true counterfactuals of freedom and very existence of God's middle knowledge are highly controversial. I cannot here present the argument in their favor; yet I do think they can be rationally defended.[5] For the purposes of this paper, then, I will operate under the assumption that such a defense is available, and that it is plausible that there are true counterfactuals of creaturely freedom, which God knows through his middle knowledge.

Now, all possible humans (presuming humans to be free agents) would then be the subjects of counterfactuals truly describing what they would freely do, in whatever states of affairs they might be found. God, in considering whom to create and where and when to place them, could make use of those truths. In creating Adam's progeny, God could restrict himself to the set of possible humans who would freely have done as Adam did in the circumstances of his temptation and fall. That is, I propose that the humans who exist, and who have existed and who will exist, constitute some subset of those possible humans who would freely have fallen, just as Adam did.[6] Thus, Adam's rebellion becomes a kind of paradigm for all of us, since his action represents what each of us would have done in his place. In him, we all sinned, *figuratively* speaking.

Because of that, God can justifiably create us in the same state to which Adam was punitively condemned. There's no point in replaying the Fall over and over to the same result. It's as if God said to himself, "The first scene will always be the same, so let us join the action *in media res;* begin with the second scene, where the lives follow their own unique paths." This justification then helps to make sense of why our state of original sin traces back to Adam. Because we are the ones-who-would-freely-have-acted-as-he-did, our relation to Adam allows the punishment his rebellion received to be applied to us as well. His action stands in for ours; on account of what he did, we too suffer the consequences and share in his condemned state.

Moreover, this justification also offers some vindication for God's creating us in a state from which we cannot fulfill his moral demands. God knows that even if we were created with more perfect moral capacities, like Adam's initially, so that we would be fully capable of carrying out his moral commands, we still would *not* do so, as Adam did not. Therefore, if we would not obey even if we could, God need not ensure that we could. It would be useless overdevelopment to give us increased moral capacities. For that reason, setting the limits to our moral capacities truly does resemble setting the boundaries of any of our other abilities; all such limiting falls to God's unconstrained, free choice, since it is not a question of moral obligation for God.

With both justifications in place, we can see each strengthening the case for original sin's being compatible with God's justice. In the first proposal, we saw how God's choices regarding the initial conditions and capacities of a creature's existence are completely free and unconstrained by moral obligations to the created being. That establishes the general point that even if our native abilities and capacities are not sufficient to succeed at all we might attempt with them, we do not thereby possess grounds to complain against God's justice to us. So although our moral abilities are recognizably impoverished, that does not necessarily imply God has wronged us. In spite of the fact that we ourselves committed no actual sin to bring on the punitive reduction of our moral abilities, God can still justifiably create us in such a reduced condition.

The second proposal showed how our originally-sinful state traces back to Adam's rebellion through our counterfactual concurrence with his action. If God creates only from among those possible humans who would freely have done as Adam did, then he can justifiably skip the replays of the Fall and simply start us out in post-Fall condition. Moreover, this justification provides a plausible interpretation for the biblical passages on original sin. Sin and death (i.e., the punishment for sin) "entered into the world" and "spread to all" because Adam's action was just what we would freely have done in his place; thus "through one transgression there resulted condemnation to all." Further, this proposal aids the first by supplying reason to think that God justifiably could create us with moral abilities insufficient to the moral directives he issues. If it is true that we would have rejected those commands anyway, even if we could have kept them perfectly, then it seems pointless for God to have to give us those higher abilities.

However, a significant obstacle remains in that even though we can now see how God might be justified in creating us in the disordered and limited condition of original sin, we still have not seen how God can justly *blame* us for being in that state. That is, one piece of the standard view on original sin is that it is a state not simply of disorder but of *guilt* (it's a *sin,* after all). We inherit more than Adam's post-Fall faculties; we also receive his guilt. Yet the proposed justifications don't seem to imply that. If it's true that we would have rebelled as Adam did, it's one thing to skip giving us his test; but it seems a much farther step to blame us for failing it. As an analogy, take one of the unfortunate subjects of Stanley Milgram's famous experiments involving authority and electric shock. Suppose a test subject has displayed willingness to inflict extreme pain on the word of an authority. Further suppose this confirms that the subject would also have been willing to follow orders in carrying out Hitler's genocidal plan in Nazi Germany. Let's say, then, that it's true of this subject that she would freely have helped to commit genocide if her governmental authorities had told her to. Do we then blame her for the Nazi atrocities? Does this counterfactual concurrence make her guilty of those crimes? No; because although she would have committed the acts, she in fact did not. Similarly, it seems unjust for us to share Adam's guilt, as only he actually committed the transgression in question.

On that account, even with the justifications in place, the predominant view on original sin needs alteration. I propose this: the state itself of original sin should be understood more as a *shortfall* than as a *transgression.* That is, rather than being a kind of wrongdoing, original sin resembles the Old Testament states of *uncleanness.* Having leprosy might have indicated imperfection that made an Israelite unfit to enter the wholly perfect presence of God, but it didn't count as a crime against the Almighty. Similarly, the disorder of original sin might in itself prevent one from being fit to see God; so original sin still needs fixing and baptism is not in vain (one of Aquinas' concerns should original sin not be a source of guilt [*On Evil,* q.4, a.1, resp.]). However, seen this way, original sin does not constitute a damning offense. Original sin is a sinful state in that its disorder disposes us to become actual sinners (and even inevitably so, as we shall see), but is not in itself grounds for guilt.[7] It is a state of *innocent sinfulness.*

I conclude this portion of the argument by appealing to authority for legitimization. In formulating my view, I was troubled by its implications in altering the traditional Christian doctrine; my position seemed on the fringes of orthodoxy and perhaps even slightly heretical. However, I have lately discovered that my explication closely matches statements by Zwingli and Wesley on original sin.[8] So it turns out Christian thinking on this point is not monolithic. And if my position prevents me from being a "good Christian," at least I'm in good company.

However, in beginning the second main argument, I seem to have undercut myself. If the first argument establishes the innocence of the initial sinful state of original sin, and if the disordered disposition of that state makes committing sins inevitable, then apparently these further sins will not be reason for guilt, either. As an analogy, consider a drunk person, who may be held responsible for things she did while inebriated and unable to control her actions *if* she freely and knowingly drank herself to that condition. Yet suppose she was the thirsty but unwitting victim of spiked punch at a Sunday school party – if she had no control over getting drunk, can she be blamed for her subsequent blacked-out drunken brawl with a deacon? Seemingly not. Similarly with the innocent sinfulness of original sin: we don't enter that state by any actual action or choice on our parts. This starting point is beyond our control. However, that initial disposition ensures that we will actually commit sins; such necessity seems to take those actions out of our control, too. Therefore, it appears that we cannot be considered guilty of those, either. If God holds us responsible for them, he seems to accuse us unjustly. Yet vindicating God's accusation is the second goal of this paper's argument. Has my earlier position made that impossible?

I think not, based on an important distinction between the inevitability of *sinning* and the inevitability of *committing a particular sin*. I believe a correct view of original sin includes the former but not the latter. The disordered faculties of post-Fall humanity make sinning unavoidable, but that doesn't mean they necessitate committing any particular sin. Because of the inescapability of sinning, it may not make sense to hold us accountable for entering the general state of being sinners. Yet we may still bear responsibility for the specific sins we commit. I thus propose that not only should the initial disposition of original sin be considered guiltless, but so also should the necessarily-subsequent *state* of being a sinner. However, that excuse does not extend to committed sinful *acts;* for those, responsibility, blame, and punishment can justly be assigned.

It works like this – suppose that my original sinfulness necessitates the following (vastly simplified) disjunction:

> (S1) Four-year-old Wyma covets his older brother's Christmas present, *or* (S2) seven-year-old Wyma falsely accuses his younger brother of breaking a lamp, *or* (S3) ten-year-old Wyma mocks a classmate's disability, . . . *or* (S*n*) twenty-year-old

Wyma presents a false I.D. to buy beer,... *or* (Sz) on his death-bed Wyma curses God.

I cannot, then, complete my life without making at least one disjunct true. However, that does *not* mean I must make true any *particular* disjunct. Suppose further that at ten, I mock my classmate and that, astonishingly, it is my first sin. The disjunction is now true; I'm a sinner. More precisely, though, (S3) is now true; I'm an uncharitable mocker. Given original sin, I could not help but become a sinner, but I needn't have been uncharitable to my classmate. Thus, I can bear no guilt for being a sinner, but I can be held responsible for my uncharitable act. In judgment God might ask, "Could you have avoided mocking that classmate?" My honest reply would have to be affirmative. "Then," God might justly respond, "We condemn you for your mockery; proceed to your punishment."

Or again, consider this analogy: a man is kidnapped by terrorists who rig him with a bomb controlled by a "deadman" switch in the form of a spring-compress-grip. If the man relaxes his grip, the spring decompresses and the bomb detonates. The terrorists then bind, gag and conceal the man on the side of a continuously busy roadway. Eventually he must tire and release his grip, and the bomb will destroy whatever vehicles are passing. He lets go at time $t(n)$. The resultant explosion takes eleven lives (including his). In judgment God asks if the man could not have released the grip earlier at $t(n-1)$ or even held it a bit longer to $t(n+1)$. The man responds affirmatively. Obviously, the man can't be held responsible for detonating the bomb; in no way could he have avoided that (or his own death). But can he be held responsible for the *particular other deaths* he caused? I think so – although admittedly to a diminished degree in these circumstances; for *those* deaths weren't necessary, but occurred through the man's chosen and avoidable release at $t(n)$. It can legitimately be asked: why did the man trigger the bomb when he did? Suppose he answers this question with, "I saw my hated business rival's car passing, and thought, 'that cheat really deserves to be blown up.'" Wouldn't the man then at least be responsible for the act of killing his rival (and perhaps so to a lesser degree, regarding killing the others caught in the blast)? Cases like this show that we are willing to assign responsibility and blame, even in circumstances similar to our condition due to original sin.

My thesis would have a problem accounting for guilt assigned to persons who refrained from sinning until their last possible action. If I were to live sinlessly my whole life, but then, because of original sin, were to curse God on my deathbed (Sz), it isn't clear that I could be held responsible for that act. That *specific* action would become unavoidable, and guilt for it appears to be excluded. Similarly, the kidnap victim might well remain entirely blameless, if he only released the trigger in dying of exhaustion. However, with regard to sinning, the simple truth is that no one who survives past (early) childhood waits till the end of his or her life to sin.[9] Indeed, God might – through his middle knowledge – choose to create only those possible humans who freely would sin in some action prior to their last opportunity. In that way, God could preserve the justice of his condemnation for our sins, by eliminating any instances in which someone's committed sin would be unavoidable due to original sin.

However, my view still faces the objection that our responsibility for our sins may be significantly diminished; therefore, punishment might be inappropriate. As admitted above, the kidnap-victim certainly bears less responsibility for the death of his business rival than if he had set up the bomb himself. But the key is, he is responsible to *some* extent and does incur *some* blame. Similarly, lessened responsibility for sin may still allow God justly to blame and punish us. Even hell might yet be justifiable punishment. Aquinas points out that any unrepented sin against the infinite majesty of God constitutes an infinitely grave and eternal offense (*On Evil,* q.1, a.5, rep.15; q.2, a.10, resp; q.7, a.10, rep.1). And infinity reduced by any portion or percentage leaves infinity, so an eternity in hell might be appropriate punishment even for diminished-responsibility sins. Thus, while our responsibility for our committed sins might be lessened by the necessitating impact of original sin, that guilt is not removed. On that account, God justly can punish us for those sinful acts.

Further, by placing the focus of responsibility and blame on specific committed sins, this argument can offer additional support for the paper's first main point. One problem for the first argument – that God could be justified in creating us in the state of original sin – was that God's moral demands seemed illegitimate, given his creating us in a condition from which we are unable to fulfill those demands. However, we now see that God's moral requirements can be understood from two perspectives. First, we might think that God commands us not to be sinners. Second, we might view God's laws as forbidding us to commit any particular sins. From the prior perspective, God requires more than we are capable of doing, given original sin – but not so, from the latter. Even while acting from original sin's disordered disposition, we still possess the freedom to perform or to avoid individual sins as their opportunities arise. Therefore, if God's moral law forbids specific commissions of sins, then it does *not* demand more than we're capable of doing.

Now perhaps this seems like a distinction without a real difference. After all, if I'm able to refrain from performing (S1), and from (S2), and from (S3), and so on through (Sz), doesn't that mean that I'm able to refrain from becoming an actual sinner? Shouldn't the conjunction of the possible refrainings imply that the disjunction of possible sins may be false? No. Even if it's possible for me to refrain at every opportunity to sin that I face, that does not mean it's possible for me to refrain from becoming a sinner. I think we frequently see analogous examples of this point. As I write this, my beloved Indiana Pacers have just lost to the boorish Miami Heat. The loss snapped a twenty-five home-game winning streak. Could the Pacers have won the game? Yes. For each of the particular home games remaining this season, can the Pacers win it? Yes. Could the team then have won a home-streak stretching from November of '99 (when the actual streak started) through the end of the '00 season? Regretfully, I think not. In general, it is within the team's power to win *in each* game they play, but it's beyond their ability to win *all* their games. Or again, consider an alcoholic who cannot make and successfully execute a decision to stay sober "for the rest of her life," but who can refrain from taking *this* drink and thereby can stay sober "one day at a time." I believe we occupy a similar position with respect to our original-sin-diminished ability to keep the moral law.

Moreover, I think this paper's interpretation of the moral law is plausible beyond the considerations of the immediate issue. After all, the divine commandments direct *specific* actions – to refrain from stealing, to honor one's parents, to love one's neighbor, etc. – so this perspective seems biblically grounded. Further, with this support added to the earlier argument, we can conclude that God's justice is not violated by creating us in an already-sinful state; for in spite of first appearances, our *original* moral abilities are not insufficient to meet his moral demands.[10] So this interpretation solves the problem that dogged the first argument.

In summary, then, I propose that original sin necessitates our becoming sinners; it makes it unavoidable that we shall actually commit sins. Given its unavoidability, I do not think the *state* of being a sinner can count as blameworthy or as a source of guilt. However, original sin does not necessitate the commission of any *particular* sinful action. Hence God may justly blame and punish us for our committed sins, which confer guilt because of their avoidability.

Joining this argument to the first, I submit that God's moral uprightness and justice are compatible with creating us in the severely limited and disordered condition of original sin, but that we are guilty and blameworthy only for the individual sins we actually commit. We cannot claim any moral obligation on God with respect to the status of our creation – i.e., to the capacities and powers we possess by nature – no matter the limits imposed. Moreover, God might justifiably create us in the punitive state earned by our first parent, if God knows through his middle knowledge that we would freely have rebelled just as Adam did. However, while our creation in original sin is thus morally justified, that does not make original sin a morally guilty state. Further, if original sin necessitates that we actually sin, the state of being an actual sinner remains guiltless too. But by distinguishing the necessity of sinning from the necessity of committing a particular sin, we can see how our individual sins may not be necessary, but rather may be freely committed. Thus God can justly blame and punish us, because those sins can still be matters of responsibility and guilt.

I think this view of "innocent sinfulness and guilty sin" upholds the righteousness of God; preserves the essential inheritance and corruptive power of original sin; and leaves human freedom intact enough to provide grounds for moral responsibility, so that our committed sins may be our own and no fault of God's. On that account, in contrast to my professor's warnings, I think my questioning has brought me to a more convinced reverence for God's holiness, and to a more convicted realization of my own guilt.

Notes

1. Of course, original sin was passed to us through both Adam and Eve, but because the Bible translation I use speaks of "through one man," I shall utilize that phraseology and refer to the Fall as *Adam's* sin.

2. Please note that I am not claiming that God has, or can have, *no* moral obligations to us *at all*. Some thinkers have made this much stronger claim – cf. Marilyn Adams, "Duns Scotus on the Goodness of God," *Faith and Philosophy* 4:4 (October 1987): 486–505; and William Alston, "Some Suggestions for Divine Command Theorists," in *Divine Nature and Human Language:. Essays in Philosophical Theology* (Ithaca, N.Y.: Cornell University Press, 1999); and a rebuttal of that position in Eleonore Stump's "God's Obligations," in *Philosophical Perspectives 6: Ethics,* ed. James E. Tomberlin (Atascadero, Ca.: Ridgeview Publishing Company, 1992) – but I do not. Moreover, my argument parses God's goodness and distinguishes between God's justice and his love and benevolence. So this point may commit me to maintaining that God could create us in *any* circumstances and with *any* capabilities (even, for instance, giving us lives of unending, unrelieved, unredeemed, mind-numbing suffering) and not violate justice; but it does *not* imply that God could do so and remain loving and benevolent. So while it might not be unjust for God to create in that way, God's character is necessarily such that he would/could never do so. It may seem that original sin makes for human lives that show that God has, in fact, acted in an unloving or malevolent manner, but that is another argument.

3. Several philosophers have made similar points, going back at least to Descartes in his *Meditation IV*, which deals with the explanation for the possibility of erroneous belief.

4. Augustine makes almost this same point: "If, therefore, a soul should start out – before it has sinned or even been alive – in the state that another soul was in after a blameworthy life, it still possesses no small amount of good. Therefore, it owes thanks to its Creator . . . ." (*On Free Choice of the Will*, trans. Anna S. Benjamin' and L. H. Hackstaff [New York: Macmillan, 1964], III, xx.190). Here, I agree with Augustine, and the Medievals generally, that existence is itself a good thing – even when that existence is drastically limited or damaged.

5. For a thorough and well-argued defense of the possibility of true counterfactuals of freedom, see Thomas P. Flint's *Divine Providence: The Molinist Account* (Ithaca, N.Y.: Cornell University Press, 1998).

6. It might be asked, at this point, why God would choose to create from this set. That is, if God has middle knowledge, why wouldn't he simply create only those humans whom he knew would *not* fall? One answer might rely on Alvin Plantinga's notion of 'transworld depravity'. If every possible human is essentially such that in any world in which she exists, she freely does *some* evil, then God's choice would be constrained to the set of would-be-Adams ("God, Evil, and the Metaphysics of Freedom," in *The Problem of Evil*, ed. Marilyn McCord Adams and Robert Merrihew Adams [New York: Oxford University Press, 1990], pp. 83–109, esp. 101–5). Alternatively, one might appeal to supralapsarian notions that fallen-then-redeemed humanity makes for a better world than unfallen humanity (cf. Plantinga's "Supralapsarianism, or 'O Felix Culpa'" in Peter van Inwagen ed., *Christian Faith and the Problem of Evil* (Grand Rapids: Eerdmans, 2004)). In either case, it would involve argument beyond the scope of this paper.

7. Surprisingly, even Augustine shows some support for this point. He writes, ". . . if ignorance of the truth and difficulty in behaving rightly are the natural points from which man begins . . . no one properly condemns the soul because of its natural origin" (*On Free Choice*, III, xxii, 220).

8. Zwingli, from his *Fidei Ratio,* and Wesley from *On Original Sin* and the *Confession of American Methodists,* quoted in William T. Bruner, *Children of the Devil* (New York: Philosophical Library, 1966), pp. 186–87, 193, 200.

9. Here it might be objected: But what about infants who die unbaptized? They clearly don't commit any actual sins. Are they condemned merely because of original sin? In fact, I think my view can answer this query better than the traditional, main stream view of original sin. It seems quite possible that such infants would be *saved,* for if Christ's death-to-sin can be shared by the living through baptism, couldn't it also be shared by the dead through death itself? So perhaps infants lose their original sinfulness in death, and thus approach judgment as true innocents. Note, too, that even if older, guilty sinners also share in Christ's death when they die – and so lose the defect of original sin – they would still be subject to judgment for their committed sins (unless they had accepted Christ, of course). Thus, while

universal infant salvation is compatible with my view, universal salvation is certainly not entailed by it.

10. Note that I do not claim that no one ever finds herself in the position of necessarily committing a particular sin, only that that never happens based *solely* on original sin. Such necessary sinning may still occur in other ways – perhaps through sinfully-entered dilemmas, or through the force of sinfully-gained habits – but that need not impugn the moral abilities we are originally given.

PART V

THE ATONEMENT

INTRODUCTION

Traditionally, the work of Christ has been divided into two parts: his active work in becoming human at the Incarnation; and his passive work in atoning for sin on the cross, including the resurrection from the dead. There is no ecumenical agreement on the nature or scope of the atonement. This has led to the proliferation of a number of different models of the atonement in the history of Christian thought.[1] Recently, systematic theologians have begun once again to consider the doctrine of the atonement in detail, with a number of writers questioning received models of the atonement, particularly the penal substitution theory. The interest in the atonement from philosophical theologians includes a number of the traditional atonement theories, as reflected in the essays selected here. Oliver Crisp explores the governmental theory of the atonement, often – perhaps mistakenly – associated with the Dutch Arminian lawyer-theologian Hugo Grotius (1583–1645). He argues that there are two strands to this atonement-theory. The first is broadly Arminian, associated in particular with American Methodism of the nineteenth century. The second is more 'Calvinistic', drawing on the New England theology stemming from the work of Jonathan Edwards (1703–1758). He defends the New England theologians and disciples of Edwards who offer a robust theory of the atonement that deserves more serious consideration than it is often accorded in the literature.

Although not a *Christian* philosopher, David Lewis is widely regarded as one of the most important metaphysicians of the later twentieth century. In his essay, he sets out an argument in partial defence of one of the core claims of penal substitution. Advocates of this theory of atonement claim that Christ acts on behalf of fallen human beings by taking upon himself the penal consequences of human sin, and being 'punished' in place of (some number of) fallen humanity. Most of those who take this view think God the Father imputes our sin to Christ, and imputes Christ's righteousness to those who trust in Christ. Hence, though Christ is innocent, he is treated as if he was guilty of sin and 'punished' in our place, while those who trust in Christ are treated as if they were righteous on account of the merits of Christ. One problem with this is that there does not seem to be an analogue in human justice for this sort of penal arrangement, which raises a question about the justness of this account of the atonement. Lewis argues that this reasoning is in fact mistaken. There are analogues for penal substitution in natural justice, and these analogues should give those who think penal substitution a hopeless account of the atonement pause for thought. For if such analogues exist, then it seems that penal substitution looks a lot less implausible as a means of punishing sin, than some have thought.

In a similar vein, the late Philip Quinn's essay is a rehabilitation of the Abelardian account of the atonement. Abelard's account is often characterized as a reaction to the satisfaction or commercial theory of atonement advocated by Anselm of Canterbury (1033–1109) in his magisterial *Cur Deus Homo*.[2] Whereas Anselm conceived of the work of Christ as satisfying divine wrath for sin, Abelard, so this story goes, thought of Christ's work as a demonstration of divine love that calls forth a corresponding act of love from fallen humans, who are enjoined to imitate Christ as a moral exemplar. Quinn argues that this way of thinking about Abelard's doctrine of the atonement is a caricature. In fact, examination of key aspects of Abelard's account shows that his doctrine of Christ's work is hardly the meagre account it is often portrayed as in textbooks of Christian theology.

Richard Swinburne is perhaps the most important and widely read philosophical theologian at work today. In his book *Responsibility and Atonement*, he sets out an account of the atonement that draws upon the satisfaction tradition of Anselm, with certain important qualifications. Atonement, Swinburne tells us, has to do with four elements: repentance, apology, reparation and penance, and all of these aspects are present in the work of Christ. Although God could have forgiven human sin without an act of atonement, he chooses to bring about the reconciliation of (some number of) fallen human beings by the work of Christ because this is a most fitting and good act of God. Like Anselm, he conceives of the work of Christ as an act of supererogation, which generates a merit sufficient for the salvation of (some) fallen human beings. In the essay reproduced here, Swinburne gives his rendition of the 'Christian scheme of salvation'. The scope of the paper is broader than the atonement, but the atonement plays a central role, as he sets forth his distinctive understanding of what the work of Christ is about.

Notes

1. R. S. Franks's *The Work of Christ* (London: Thomas Nelson, 1962 [1918]) is still a standard work of reference on the history of the doctrine of the atonement.
2. See *Anselm of Canterbury, The Major Works*, Brian Davies and G. R. Evans (eds) (Oxford: Oxford University Press, 1998).

Suggested further reading

- Brümmer, Vincent, *Atonement, Christology and The Trinity: Making Sense of Christian Doctrine* (Aldershot: Ashgate, 2005), ch. 4.
- Crisp, Oliver, 'Original Sin and Atonement' in Thomas P. Flint and Michael C. Rea (eds), *The Oxford Handbook to Philosophical Theology* (Oxford: Oxford University Press, 2009), pp. 430–451.
- Cross, Richard, 'Atonement without Satisfaction' in *Religious Studies* 37 (2001), pp. 397–416.
- Porter, Steven, 'Swinburnian Atonement and the Doctrine of Penal Substitution' in *Faith and Philosophy* 21 (2004), pp. 228–241.
- Swinburne, Richard, *Responsibility and Atonement* (Oxford: Oxford University Press, 1989).

CHAPTER 15

PENAL NON-SUBSTITUTION

Oliver D. Crisp

The governmental, or Grotian, theory the atonement is often given short shrift in histories of Christian doctrine. And in recent theology it is hardly mentioned at all, even where the atonement is discussed. Yet this theory of the atonement offers a robust understanding of the nature of Christ's work that is a theologically interesting alternative to its near-relatives, the satisfaction theory of the atonement and the penal substitution theory of the atonement. In this essay, I shall outline and discuss one version of this doctrine. We shall see that, although there are problems attending this theory of the atonement, it is a way of thinking about the work of Christ that should be taken more seriously than it often is by contemporary theologians.

Terminological distinctions

Let us begin with a few words of terminological clarification, before setting out one version of the doctrine, and analyzing it. Although this theory of the atonement is often spoken of as the Grotian theory, or the governmental view, I shall avoid speaking of it as such. There are several reasons for this. The first is that there is some dispute about the geneal-ogy of the doctrine. The Dutch Arminian lawyer-theologian, Hugo Grotius (1583–1645), is often credited with first articulating it,[1] but his view is not as clearly 'governmental' as some commentators seem to believe it to be.[2] It may be that Grotius' doctrine of the atonement was more like a species of penal substitution with elements that sound like the developed governmental view of the atonement I wish to focus on.[3] In which case, Grotius' doctrine is a sort of theological hybrid, or at least, an intermediate species of atonement theory, and one that I do not intend to discuss here.

Secondly, there are distinct strands of this doctrine. Although they share a common core of ideas about the nature of the atonement, they also differ in important respects, as we shall see. One strand of the doctrine that has been held by a number of classical Arminian divines claims Grotius as its founder. Whether this is historically accurate or not, I shall refer to this Arminian version of the theory as the 'Grotian' version.

In this respect, in what follows, the 'Grotian' version of penal non-substitution bears the same relationship to Grotius as Nestorianism does to Nestorius in discussion of Christology. Whilst there may be some dispute about whether the historical Grotius was a Grotian about the atonement or not, it is certainly true to say that a particular brand of theology associated with American Methodism in the nineteenth century tended to think of its version of penal non-substitution as a 'Grotian' doctrine.[4]

But there is a second strand to this doctrine of the atonement often called the Edwardsian, or Edwardean view, which was a product of the New England theology of the nineteenth century. Whilst here is not the place to trace the development of this American understanding of the atonement in detail, it is worth pointing out that what I shall say here is certainly in keeping with much of what we might call the full-blown version of the doctrine espoused by nineteenth century 'Edwardeans', that is, theologians who aligned themselves with the theological teaching of the philosophical theologian, Jonathan Edwards. In particular, the version of the doctrine I shall lay out has important affinities with the definitive Edwardean account of the doctrine, given by the son of Jonathan Edwards; Jonathan Edwards Jr.[5] I shall refer to this way of thinking about penal non-substitution as the 'Edwardean' or the 'New England' version of the doctrine. (The choice of the term 'Edwardean', rather than 'Edwardsian' is significant. It distinguishes this historical school of theology from the contemporary study of the theology of Jonathan Edwards Sr. This is because the Edwardean doctrine of the atonement, like several other aspects of the New England theology, represents a doctrine that is significantly different from the stated views of Jonathan Edwards Sr.[6]) There may be other versions of the doctrine I am not aware of.[7] Be that as it may, these two strands will be sufficient for what follows.

In order to prevent misunderstanding, when the theory as a whole is referred to, irrespective of regional differences, I shall avoid speaking of it as either Grotian or Edwardean. Instead, I shall refer to it by what I take to be the central and defining notion that shapes the entire doctrine, namely, that Christ's work is a species of *penal non-substitution*. This has two components. These are, roughly, that the atonement has some important relation to the divine law that can be construed as penal; and that Christ's death is not a matter of his being a substitute with some forensic relationship to us, upon whom the wrath of God is visited.

It is also worth making clear that this essay is not principally concerned with the intricacies of historical exegesis (important though that enterprise undoubtedly is[8]), but with setting forth one, broadly Edwardean, version of this doctrine. To put the same point rather differently, if my argument diverges in points of detail from those of other theologians who have taken this view in the past, it may still offer an interesting way of thinking about a version of this particular theory of atonement. It is rather like one conductor's interpretation of a great piece of orchestral music. It might be that the conductor in question interprets the piece of music in a way that departs from conventions, perhaps even from the manner in which the piece has recently been played. Some reviewers might be shocked by this; even offended at the temerity of the conductor. But, provided the conductor has followed the musical score for the particular piece of music, it is difficult to argue that his interpretation of the music is wrong, or inaccurate, or mistaken. (Of course, if he had interpolated his own musical flourishes, or ignored important aspects of the scoring, such as time, musical punctuation and so on, then the dissenters would have good reason to grumble. But musical scores admit of a variety of quite diverse interpretations without departure from the letter of the score.)

What I am attempting to do is something like this. I want to give a contemporary re-telling of an old theological argument. Whilst I shall be sensitive to the logical form this argument takes, I shall feel free to present the argument in my own language, using a contemporary idiom and literature, where appropriate. We shall proceed by teasing out the internal logic of the argument. Then, we will turn to objections to the argument. What we shall see is that the doctrine is problematic, but not always for the reasons offered in the secondary literature on the subject.

Laying out the argument

(a) The necessity of the atonement

To begin with, let us set out the argument. There are five major components to the version of the doctrine we shall consider. The first of these concerns the necessity of the atonement. On reading some modern critics of the penal non-substitution theory one could be forgiven for thinking that all defenders of penal non-substitution deny that the atonement was necessary. For instance, Robert Letham in his brief discussion of the subject asserts that this theory introduces an element of arbitrariness into the doctrine of God, because it states that God could have chosen some other means of salvation than the one he did chose.[9] There are several aspects to this criticism that we need to distinguish. These have to do with the nature of the necessity of the atonement, and whether penal non-substitution introduces an element of arbitrariness into the doctrine of God. Let us consider each of these issues in turn.

First, we turn to the question of the necessity of the atonement. Letham appears to have in mind the Grotian version of penal non-substitution, which does claim that the atonement is not *absolutely* necessary. The nineteenth century American Methodist and advocate of the Grotian version of penal non-substitution, John Miley, states '[w]hile thus asserting the intrinsic evil of sin, Grotius denies an *absolute necessity* arising therefrom for its punishment. The punishment of sin is just, but not in itself an obligation.'[10]

The real problem with Letham's charge is that it is not sufficiently discriminating. Unlike what I am calling the 'Grotian' version of penal non-substitution, the Edwardean version of the doctrine affirms the absolute necessity of the atonement. So Letham misrepresents penal non-substitution if he means to imply that all those who have espoused the doctrine deny the absolute necessity of the atonement.[11] On the contrary, at least one of the New England divines who takes this view was at pains to argue that the atonement is, in fact, 'absolutely' necessary. Jonathan Edwards Jr. in his *Three Sermons on the necessity of the Atonement and the consistency between that and free grace in forgiveness* says, '[t]hat we are forgiven through the atonement of Christ, and can be forgiven in no other way, the Scriptures very clearly teach.' Moreover, 'The Scriptures also teach the absolute necessity of the atonement of Christ, and that we can obtain forgiveness and salvation through that only.'[12]

The younger Edwards does not offer a precise explanation of what he means by the 'absolute necessity' of the atonement as a term of art, although he does have more to say concerning this absolute necessity later in the same sermon. For instance, at one point he remarks that 'it is necessary on the same ground, and for the same reasons, as punishment would have been necessary, if there had been no atonement made. The ground of both is the same.'[13]

Nevertheless, the term was a common one in post-Reformation Reformed dogmatics.[14] Francis Turretin makes this point in his discussion of the necessity of the atonement in his *Institutes of Elenctic Theology*, where he states that, aside from the Socinian denial of the necessity of the atonement, there are two principle views taken by classical divines. These are the *hypothetical necessity* and the *absolute necessity* of the atonement. According to some theologians the atonement is hypothetically necessary because God could have ordained some other mode of atonement. Augustine seems to have held this view, and there was a vigorous discussion around these issues in post-Reformation Reformed theology.[15] However, those who take the hypothetical necessity view usually claim that, although there were other avenues by which God could have liberated fallen humanity apart from the death of Christ, nevertheless the atoning act of Christ on the cross was the most fitting means of satisfaction.

The element of necessity involved in this view seems to depend upon its being decreed by God on this basis, that is, on the basis of being the most suitable means of salvation, although other means were possible. Hence there is an important connection between this and the medieval distinction between the absolute and ordained power of God (*potentia absoluta et ordinata*).[16] We might put it like this: according to his absolute power, God could have ordained one of several means of salvation, including the cross of Christ. But, given considerations about the fittingness of the cross as the most suitable means of satisfaction, God decreed this means, rather than any other means, according to his ordained power. By contrast, says Turretin, defenders of the absolute necessity of the atonement claim that 'not only has [God] not willed to remit our sins without satisfaction, but [he] could not do so on account of his justice. This' observes Turretin, 'is the common opinion of the orthodox (which we follow).'[17] It should be clear from this that the younger Edwards' doctrine of the absolute necessity of the atonement is part of a larger tradition of Reformed thinking on this matter. It is certainly not the case that a defender of penal non-substitution is committed to the denial of the necessity of the atonement.[18]

But it is also true that there is nothing about the structure of penal non-substitution that requires adherence to a doctrine of the absolute necessity of the atonement. Defenders of penal non-substitution regard the atonement as a means of vindicating the moral law and government of God, rather than as a means to satisfying divine retributive justice.[19] This means that the connection between the absolute necessity of the atonement and divine retribution that Turretin envisages is not a factor that bears upon the thinking of the advocate of penal non-substitution. So one key element that motivates a number of the Reformed Orthodox to opt for the absolute necessity of the atonement, namely, the idea that the nature of divine retributive justice is such that it must be satisfied either in the punishment of sinners, or in the atoning work of some suitable vicar, is not an issue facing those who defend penal non-substitution.

For this reason it should not be surprising that there is a difference of opinion between the Grotians and Edwardeans, on this particular matter. As we have already noted, John Miley, as an important representative of the 'Grotian' stream, claimed that 'Grotius denies an absolute necessity arising therefrom for its punishment.' He goes on to add, 'the punishment of sin is just, but not in itself an obligation. The intrinsic evil of sin renders its penal retribution just, but not a requirement of judicial rectitude.'[20] This is important. It means that, according to this Grotian way of thinking, divine rectoral justice can be decoupled from divine retributive justice for the purposes of satisfaction. In this context, *rectoral justice* is that aspect of divine justice whereby God rightly governs the cosmos in accordance with his moral law. *Retributive justice* is that aspect of divine justice whereby God's wrath is meted out to those creatures who transgress the divine law, who remain the objects of divine wrath and are not the objects of divine mercy.[21] Whereas the former must be satisfied in some sense, there may be a relaxation of the requirements of divine retributive justice so that Christ may act in a manner consistent with rectoral justice (hence the 'penal' element to this theory) but without acting so as to satisfy divine retribution as a penal substitute (which has direct bearing upon the non-substitutionary element to the doctrine). In short, for advocates of the Grotian version of penal non-substitution, rectoral justice *must* be satisfied, whereas retributive justice *may* be satisfied. God may waive the satisfaction of divine retributive justice and remain perfectly just in so acting because this aspect of God's distributive justice may be relaxed. The same cannot be said of rectoral justice, which is dependent on the divine moral law, and therefore may not be relaxed without vitiating God's just and moral rule of the created order.

A similar story concerning what we might call the internal structure or logic of divine justice can be found in the Edwardean version of the doctrine, but with several important qualifications. The younger Edwards claims that the atonement is absolutely necessary because God must either punish sin or offer some act of atonement. So, unlike the Grotian view, the Edwardean view states that the punishment of sin is an obligation, at least in the sense that, once God has created the sort of world he has, it is incumbent upon God to ensure that either sin is punished in the person of the sinner, or some suitable act of atonement is made in the person of a vicar. Where the Edwardean and Grotian views agree, it is concerning the notion that rectoral justice *must* be satisfied whereas retributive justice *may* be relaxed, so that Christ's atonement satisfies the former, not the latter, such that this constitutes an act rectorally sufficient for the vindication of divine justice and the upholding of divine moral government, consistent with the moral law.[22] This is a very important component of penal non-substitution. It means that rectoral justice is somehow more fundamental to the nature of God than retributive justice is.

The defender of penal non-substitution is committed to the view that Christ's atonement does not satisfy divine retribution. Christ is, after all, not a penal substitute whose atoning act is a work of supererogation that can be imputed to fallen human beings. What the advocate of penal non-substitution can say is that the atonement satisfies the rectoral justice of God, because it enables God to continue to govern the world justly and morally. The implication is that God sets to one side the demands of retributive justice on account of the suitably equivalent act of atonement offered by Christ for fallen humanity. This in turn means that fallen humans have their sins remitted, provided they choose to avail themselves of the benefits of Christ.

However, it seems to me there may be good reason for the defender of penal non-substitution to opt for the hypothetical, rather than the absolute, necessity of the atonement. This was the position taken by Grotians like Miley, who says at one point:

> Only a divine person could redeem the world; and the redemption could be effected only by a great personal sacrifice. The necessity is from the office which the atonement must fulfil. But, with the profoundest conviction of truth in these facts, we should greatly hesitate to say – indeed, we do not believe – that in the resources of infinite wisdom the precise manner of the mediation of Christ was the only possible manner of human redemption.[23]

I take Miley to be saying that Christ, the only possible holder of this office of Redeemer, could carry out the duties of that office in some other way than the way he did carry them out.[24] On this reading, Miley's reservations have to do with the apparently counterintuitive consequences of adhering to the absolute necessity of the atonement. For commitment to the absolute necessity of the atonement has the implication that there was no possible world or state of affairs in which God could bring about this salvation by some other means. And this looks odd. To make this clear, let us distinguish several theological claims about the necessity of atonement. The first is this:

1. Atonement was necessary for the salvation of some number of fallen human beings.

This presumes that God could not bring about human redemption without atonement, contrary to Socinianism. But – crucially – it does not entail that God was bound to provide some means of atonement. He could have punished sinners instead. To this extent, advocates of the hypothetical- or absolute necessity of the atonement are in agreement. The problem with (1) as it stands is its ambiguity. It could mean one of two things:

2. Some act of atonement was necessary for the salvation of some number of fallen human beings.

Which is the central claim made by defenders of the hypothetical necessity doctrine, including Miley amongst the Grotians. Alternatively, it could also mean:

3. A particular act of atonement was necessary for the salvation of some number of fallen human beings.

This is the claim being made by the younger Edwards and Turretin,
corresponding to the absolute necessity of the atonement. Clearly, the
hypothetical necessity claim is weaker than the absolute necessity claim
in the sense that the hypothetical claim says only that some act of atonement was necessary not the particular act Christ did in fact perform.

What we have seen is that defenders of penal non-substitution, in
common with the Reformed Orthodox, deny God was bound to save
some number of fallen human beings. God had the option to punish all
human beings instead. On the related question of whether God was
bound to deploy the particular means of atonement he did deploy, the
logic of the Grotian version of penal non-substitution is consistent with
the claims made by some of the Reformed Orthodox like William Twisse
or the early John Owen, that God was so bound once he opted to save,
rather than to punish, some number of fallen human beings. However,
the qualification 'once he had opted to save . . . some number of fallen
human beings' is vital. It would not be true to say the Grotian view
entails that God was bound to bring about atonement by the means he
did, and that no other means of atonement was open to God, *all things
considered*. It would only be true to say that, on the Grotian conception
of things, God was bound to ordain the means of atonement he did once
he had opted to provide one particular means of salvation to fallen
human beings in Christ's atoning work on the cross. And this is in keeping with those members of the Reformed Orthodox who opted for the
hypothetical necessity of the atonement. It seems a lot less counterintuitive than the doctrine of absolute atonement opted for by the younger
Edwards in common with Reformed Orthodox divines like Turretin.

In a similar way, it could be that, once Vincent van Gogh had committed himself to painting sunflowers using the materials he had to hand,
the only alternative was to not paint the picture. He could not use
some other medium for painting the picture than he had before him at
that time. However, at some earlier point in time Van Gogh could have
bought some other paints – perhaps some water-based paints rather than
oil-based ones. Then he would have been in a position to make a very
different choice when it came to painting the picture. But if Van Gogh
did not opt to buy the water-based paints at an earlier moment in time,
it is not an option for him to use water-based paints to paint his picture,
when he has committed himself to spending time painting with what he
has to hand, and all he has to hand are the oil-based paints.

Secondly, and much more briefly, we come to the charge of arbitrariness.
If, like Miley, we opt for the hypothetical necessity of the atonement,

does this make the atonement an arbitrary matter, as Letham suggests it does? Not necessarily. Miley is careful to argue that there are parameters within which there were options for the mode of satisfaction (once again, in keeping with those of the Reformed Orthodox who held to the hypothetical necessity of the atonement). Recall his comments, cited earlier, to the effect that atonement could only come about by great personal sacrifice to the one atoning, and where the agent of atonement was a divine person. Moreover, the atonement must be able to satisfy the rectoral justice of God. The contours of this particular aspect of the Grotian version of penal non-substitution might be objectionable for other reasons. But there is nothing *arbitrary* about such an arrangement, neither in the sense of being some chance event, nor in the sense of being solely dependent upon the divine will. And it should be quite clear from the foregoing that Edwardeans like the younger Edwards, committed as they were to the absolute necessity of the atonement, can hardly be said to make the atonement into an arbitrary matter. Indeed, the facts support precisely the opposite conclusion.[25]

(b) Divine will, moral law and atonement

However, although the Grotian version of the doctrine is consistent with the hypothetical necessity of the atonement, there is a deeper problem that needs addressing. It may be that critics of the doctrine like Letham are attempting to get at this deeper issue, but have conflated it with the question of the necessity of the atonement, a particular understanding of which the Grotians did affirm.

The deeper issue to which I am alluding has to do with the relation between the divine will, moral law and atonement. In his account of Grotius' position, L. W. Grensted says,

> Grotius follows Socinus in asserting God's supreme freedom. As Ruler of the universe He may secure the ends of His government in whatever way He will. It is true that there is a law imposing death as the punishment of sin, yet the incidence of this law is entirely subject to the freedom of God.[26]

He goes on to cite Grotius to this effect:

> All positive laws may be relaxed, in the absolute sense . . .. For a law is nothing internal to God, nor is it God's very will, but a certain effect of that will. But that the effects of the Divine will are mutable is most certain.[27]

This is clearly an instance of the doctrine of legal voluntarism, according to which the moral law is established solely by an act of divine will.[28] Suppose Nimrod decides to found a new state, and has himself crowned as its prince. And suppose he has the power to inaugurate a new legal system for this new realm because he is its absolute monarch. What will he decree? We might think that a just prince would make certain things illegal and others permissible *because they are somehow inherently moral or immoral acts*. For instance, murder, rapine and theft appear to be obvious candidates for juridical censure. But, Nimrod might see things differently. Perhaps his conception of law is merely *the legislative encoding of his particular will,* whatever that may be. Then, that which is moral or immoral depends upon what the Prince says will be moral or immoral, at least, for the purposes of the state over which Nimrod presides. In which case, he might decide to make murder, rapine and theft permissible, rather than proscribed activities. And once he has decreed the body of laws that make up the legislation of his new kingdom, they are binding upon all its citizens. This story of Nimrod is an example of legal voluntarism at work. What Nimrod ordains becomes law; and Nimrod ordains what he wants, what he wills. There is, according to Nimrod's way of thinking, no set of necessary moral truths that constrain him as he issues his legislative decrees. It is a matter of sheer will.

At first glance, Grotius, as reported by Grensted, appears to hold something like this view with respect to the ordination of the divine moral law – after all, Grensted tells us that, for Grotius, 'God may secure the ends of his government in whatever way he will.' Moreover, even the incidence of retributive punishment for sin is 'entirely subject to the free will of God'. This seems to suggest that the law of God is nothing more than what God wills is the case. To put it in the language of Plato's Euthyphro Dilemma, what God wills is holy; it is not the case that what is holy is what God wills. According to Grensted, Grotius seems to think this is important because it enables him to account for the relaxation of divine retribution in the atonement, whilst retaining the notion that the atonement is just because it satisfies rectoral justice (which involves the notion of decoupling retribution from rectoral justice, mentioned earlier). In other words, God may will that one part of the law is relaxed because the whole law is his creature: he has ordained the existence of retributive justice, and he can suspend its requirements, opting for the satisfaction of a broader, less onerous aspect of justice instead – which is none other than rectoral justice.

Assume, for the moment, that some Grotian does hold to this doctrine of legal voluntarism. It is certainly consistent with the hypothetical necessity of the atonement, provided that the moral law is binding once God has ordained it. Even if one does not believe that God is obliged to act in certain ways (as some theologians have argued),[29] it may be that God 'binds' himself to the law he ordains once he has ordained it. For, plausibly, even God cannot go back on a promise once he has uttered it. He could be 'bound' to act in a way consistent with his own words without being bound by any *prima facie* obligation towards his creatures as well. One might think that the divine law is 'binding' on God because he cannot go back on the laws he has ordained once he has ordained them, on pain of contradicting himself, or being inconsistent with what he has previously said concerning the moral law. In which case, if this sort of scenario does obtain in the case of God's relation to the moral law, it would be true to say that, having ordained the moral law, God must act in a way consistent with that law, even though it is his creature, an abstract entity brought into being by a sheer act of will. We might then be able to speak of the hypothetical necessity of the atonement on this basis. The atonement is necessary once God has ordained it rather than some other means of salvation, and this atonement is requisite to salvation because God has ordained the laws he has, although he could have ordained some other set of law had he chosen to do so.

But, without important amendments being made to it, this version of voluntarism faces very serious objections. For one thing, if God could have ordained some other set of laws than he did ordain, what is the relation between the moral law and God's character? If some other set of laws than the one God did decree is consistent with divine justice, are there sets of laws that are inconsistent with it? Surely there are. A set containing the law 'it is obligatory to hate God and despise all his statutes' would not appear to be consistent with divine justice. But then, even if some version of legal voluntarism makes sense, how the doctrine is framed and in what way it circumscribes what laws God could have ordained consistent with his justice, are important considerations that any defender of this doctrine will want to be cognisant of.[30]

I suggest that some moderate form of voluntarism consistent with this reasoning, is behind the Grotian doctrine. But even if this is not the case, a Grotian mindful of these problems could modify her voluntarism accordingly: God ordains the laws he does, and could not have ordained any laws inconsistent with his divine character. Yet, given this restriction upon what God could have willed, it would still appear to the case that God could have ordained other laws than he did. For it seems consistent with God's holy character to say (a) there are certain moral laws that are necessary, (b) there are certain moral laws that are contingent and (c) at least some of those moral laws that are contingent might have been different. Quite which laws fall into this category of contingent laws that might have been different is another matter, and venturing a guess as to which sorts of laws this might include is a hazardous philosophical endeavour.

Nevertheless, so the moderate Grotian might claim, for all we know, this might be true, even if we cannot isolate every moral tenet that might have been different. For it is conceivable that a general principle could apply across a certain set of circumstances although we cannot work out when or where it applies in every instance. Then, the precise set of laws God ordains is an act of will in an important sense, albeit in a way that takes account of the fact that the moral law of God is circumscribed by his divine character in significant respects.

But the defender of penal non-substitution need not subscribe to a version of the legal voluntarist doctrine. If the hypothetical necessity of the atonement is consistent with divine voluntarism, it is certainly consistent with a non-voluntarist understanding of the generation of divine law. For suppose the divine law is fundamentally an expression of the divine character. It truly reflects who God is, and God could not have brought about some other set of laws without acting in a way that conflicted with his divine justice. It might still be the case, given this non-voluntaristic account of the generation of the moral law, that more than one means of salvation is available to God, consistent with his moral law.

And as with voluntarism, a non-voluntaristic doctrine of the generation of the moral law could be modified to make it less stringent. Suppose, as before, that the divine law is fundamentally an expression of the divine character. God could not have brought about a set of laws inconsistent with his character in general, and his divine justice in particular. Yet it is still possible for God to have brought about some other set of laws than the ones he did, if it is granted that (a) some moral laws are contingent, and (b) in at least one instance, God could have brought about a different contingent moral law, consistent with his divine character. It may also be that (c) there was a set of laws, or certain cluster of possible sets of moral laws, that better suited the divine purposes and divine character, all things considered, than other, possible sets of laws consistent with the divine character. In which case, God's choice of laws, or choice of the particular set from the set of laws consistent with the divine character (if he had a choice about the matter) may have been circumscribed by a criterion of 'fittingness' or 'suitability'.

(c) Sin and its penal consequences

We come to the third component of penal non-substitution, which has to do with the doctrine of sin. Defenders of this theory, in both Grotian and Edwardean guises, affirm robust doctrines of sin, where sin is taken to be some transgression of the divine law. But according to penal non-substitution, sin and guilt, and the penal consequences thereof, are non-transferable. My sin and guilt cannot be imputed or transferred to another, who may suffer in my place. Nor may the penal consequences of my sin be transferred to another. This notion is contrary to the logic of penal substitution, which requires, in its traditional form, that Christ in acting as a penal substitute, takes upon himself the penal consequences of my sin and guilt (not, it should be pointed out, my sin and guilt *simpliciter*, although popular versions of the doctrine often mistakenly assert this).

That said, on penal non-substitution Christ's atoning work does have this relationship to the law: he suffers instead of fallen human beings, so that the rectoral justice of God may be satisfied and the divine moral government upheld. Hence, there is an important 'penal' element to the doctrine, although not in relation to the retributive justice of God, as is the case with satisfaction or penal substitutionary theories of atonement. A similar point is made by Edwards Amasa Park in discussing the main issues in the Edwardean version of penal non-substitution. He says,

> Our Lord suffered pains which were substituted for the penalty of the law, and may be called punishment in the more general sense of that word, but were not, strictly and literally, the penalty which the law had threatened.[31]

There are, I presume, crimes the punishment of which is like this. For suppose a man is apprehended speeding in his automobile. It is not inconceivable that he be offered either a short custodial sentence or a fixed penalty fine as a means of atoning for his sin. We might think he deserves the custodial sentence, strictly speaking, although the fine is a fitting substitute of comparable worth (where the fine is suitably onerous). This is just what the defender of penal non-substitution maintains happens in the case of Christ's atonement. Christ offers, as Hugo Grotius maintained, a suitable equivalent (*solutio tantidem*) to the punishment due for sin, which God the Father may accept in place of punishing the sinner.[32] God may only accept such an equivalent to the punishment due for sin, provided it satisfies the requirements of divine rectoral justice. Assuming the suitable equivalent does satisfy rectoral justice, God may relax the demands made upon the sinner by divine retribution (as we noted earlier in distinguishing between the fact that according to penal non-substitution rectoral justice *must* be satisfied, whilst retributive justice *may* be satisfied – to which we should add the qualification 'in circumstances where atonement by a suitable equivalent consistent with the satisfaction of rectoral justice is not forthcoming'.) So Christ's atonement has an important relation to the divine law, and one which we might term 'penal', if our understanding of what constitutes a penal act is broad enough to admit not just of punishments due for sin, according to divine retributive justice, but also equivalent substitutes, sufficient to satisfy divine rectoral justice (along with the relaxation of retributive justice).

(d) The solutio tantidem

However, this raises an important question that goes to the heart of penal non-substititution, which is, in what sense is the atonement a suitable equivalent to punishment for sin? Horace Bushnell, in characterising the New England (i.e. Edwardean) version of penal non-substitution says,

> Our New England teachers …. began to conceive that Christ in his cross, maintained the righteousness of God without punishment, by what was expressed, to the same effect as in punishment, of God's abhorrence to sin. Christ, they conceived, has simply shown, by his death, the same abhorrence to sin that would have been shown by the punishment of the guilty. The righteousness of God therefore stands even and fair, even though punishment is released.[33]

Similarly, Park observes,

> The humiliation, pains, and death of our Redeemer were equivalent in meaning to the punishment threatened in the moral law, and thus they satisfied Him who is determined to maintain the honor of this law, but they did not satisfy the demands of the law itself for our punishment.

To which he adds,

> The active obedience [of Christ], viewed as the holiness of Christ was honorable to the law, but was not a work of supererogation, performed by our Substitute, and then transferred and imputed to us, so as to satisfy the requisitions of the law for our own active obedience.[34]

The central notion standing behind these citations is that Christ's suffering on the cross was not a species of penal substitution. His death was a means of satisfying the demands of the moral law so that God could forgive sin without punishing the sinner. Yet Christ's work on the cross is not a substitutionary work, strictly speaking. Although he suffers rather than the sinner, *he does not stand in the place of the sinner with respect to the penal consequences due for sin.* Christ's death is not a punishment at all;

it stands in the place of the rightful punishment due to sin. Yet it is perfectly just because it satisfies rectoral justice.

Understanding the concept of 'suitable equivalence' is crucial to grasping this central claim of penal non-substitution. But it is sometimes overlooked or misunderstood. For instance, Robert Letham claims that on the 'Grotian' theory of the atonement (as he characterises it) the connection between sin and punishment is severed. God punishes, not because his righteous character requires it, but because he freely chooses to punish 'in order to govern the human race more effectively.'[35] But, as with his previous comments, Letham is only partially right. Let us take the two aspects of Letham's attack in reverse order. It should be clear from what has already been said about the necessity of the atonement that the second aspect of Letham's objection – to do with God being able to freely choose to punish or refrain from punishing sinful human beings - is not representative of either strand of penal non-substitution, although, for different reasons. Nevertheless, neither the Grotians nor the Edwardeans would concede that God could freely refrain from punishing sinful human beings *absent atonement*. Nor would they recognise Letham's charge that God's character may not require the satisfaction of justice. This bespeaks a failure to understand the careful distinction defenders of penal non-substitution make between the requirement to satisfy rectoral justice and the fact that retributive justice may be relaxed. In other words, there is nothing in the logic of penal non-substitution that denies that God's righteous character requires the satisfaction of divine justice. The real issue here, which Letham overlooks, is whether rectoral justice can be decoupled from retributive justice, so that the latter may be relaxed, whilst the former is enforced, as penal non-substitution maintains.[36]

The first part of Letham's criticism fairs little better. It is true that the logic of penal non-substitution makes a sharp distinction between punishments as satisfaction of the divine law on the one hand, and the free offer of divine grace on the other. This, in the original 'Grotian' form of the doctrine, was a concession to Socinian attacks upon penal substitution. The problem, as the Socinians saw it, was that punishment of sin seems inconsistent with the free offer of grace and forgiveness.[37] If Trevor forgives Wayne, remitting the debt he owes Trevor, no further satisfaction is required: Wayne is forgiven; any penal consequences attending his crime are remitted. However, if Trevor requires satisfaction from Wayne, then Wayne must pay whatever the penal consequences of his crime are. But once Wayne has paid these penal consequences, atonement has taken place. No debt remains. But note that, on the Socinian view, remission of sin and satisfaction for sin are mutually exclusive notions. Either one's sin is remitted, or it is satisfied, but not both.[38]

Against this Socinian objection to the atonement as satisfaction of debt, defenders of penal non-substitution claim that atonement involves the provision of a suitable equivalent to such payment, which is consistent with the divine law. So, the satisfaction of retributive justice due for sin is not met, according to penal non-substitution. Instead, Christ's death is treated as *equivalent in value* to the punishment that would have been due for sin. (Equating 'sufficient equivalence' with 'equivalent in value' is an important consideration for penal non-substitution, as we shall see in a moment.) In this way, advocates of penal non-substitution sought to outmanoeuvre the Socinians by showing that atonement is not about satisfaction of retributive justice, but of providing some means, consistent with divine moral government, of forgiving sinners. Sin and punishment are held apart in the sense that the punishment due for sin is not visited upon fallen human beings and no penal substitute is offered in place of the sinner. But it is not true to say that penal non-substitution *severs the connection* between sin and punishment. For defenders of penal non-substitution maintain that Christ's death on the cross is a suitable equivalent to the punishment due for human sin. As the younger Edwards maintained:

> The followers of Mr. Edwards [i.e. Jonathan Edwards Sr.] have proved [sic] that the atonement does not consist in the payment of a debt, properly so called. It consists rather in doing that, which, for the purposes of establishing the authority of divine law, and of supporting in due tone the divine government, is equivalent to the punishment of the sinner according to the letter of the law. Now, therefore, God, without prostration of his authority and government, can pardon and save those who believe. As what was done to support the divine government was not done *by the sinner*, so it does not at all diminish the free grace of his pardon and salvation.[39]

Interestingly, both traditional arguments for penal substitution and penal non-substitution rely upon the notion of a forensic fiction at critical junctures. In the case of penal substitution, the fiction is that God treats Christ as if he were the guilty party, visiting upon him the penal consequences of human sin. In the case of penal non-substitution, God treats Christ's death as if it were a moral equivalent to the sin of humanity, so that it balances out the scales of divine justice. God may remain a moral governor of the universe because Christ's work stands in for the punishment that is due for sin. But it is not that punishment.[40]

There are other contemporary theologians besides Letham, whose discussion of penal non-substitution is sometimes wide of the mark

because it assumes that penal non-substitution is identical with the
Grotian version of the doctrine. Take, for instance, Wayne Grudem's
comment that penal non-substitution 'takes away the objective character
of the atonement by making its purpose not the satisfaction of God's
justice but simply that of influencing us to realise that God has laws that
must be kept.'[41] It is simply not the case that the doctrine of suitable
equivalence that lies at the heart of the case for penal non-substitution
entails a denial of the objective character of the work of Christ. Christ's
work is 'objective' if we understand by this that Christ's work is the
means by which we are saved. Nor does it reduce the efficacy of Christ's
work to influencing fallen humanity into realising that God's laws must
be kept. No advocate of penal non-substitution would claim that the
work of Christ has this merely 'subjective' component. Furthermore,
Grudem, like Letham, fails to see the connection between the concept
of a suitable equivalent and the requirement that divine rectoral justice
be satisfied. In so doing both these recent expositors of the work of
Christ misrepresent key aspects of penal non-substitution. What they
criticise is not penal non-substitution but a straw man.

(e) Suitable equivalence and acceptance

A fifth component of this view is related to the previous point about a
suitable equivalent to punishment for sin. It is not the case that Christ's
suffering and death is accepted by God the Father instead of full punishment due to human sin, despite the fact that it has an inferior value
to the punishment due to human sin. This is the medieval doctrine of
acceptation and it is excluded if the suffering and death of Christ are
taken to be both suitable and of (at least) equivalent value to the punishment due for human sin.[42] In fact, at one point in the first of his *Three
Sermons*, the younger Edwards argues that a lesser degree of suffering
than that which Christ in fact endured may be equivalent to the curse
of the law borne by the sinner 'on account of the infinite dignity and
glory of his person'.[43] But this is not the same as acceptation. For Edwards
Jr. is not claiming that the sufferings of Christ are of *less value* than the
sufferings that would be endured by the sinner absent atonement. Rather,
he is claiming that Christ might have endured less suffering than he did
endure, and *this still be equivalent* to the suffering that would have been
endured by sinners absent atonement.

   There are at least two ways that this insight might be cashed out.
First, it could be argued that there is some threshold of suffering equal
to the punishment that would be suffered by fallen human beings absent
atonement, and that the suffering of God Incarnate is at least equivalent

to, or perhaps greater than, that threshold of suffering. This brackets out the question of whether Christ's sufferings have an infinite value. Such a manoeuvre might be thought advantageous because it avoids the need for long explanations of how it is that the sufferings of God Incarnate have an infinite value, rather than some colossal, but finite value.[44] In light of this, we might call it the 'thin' doctrine of the equivalence of Christ's suffering. However, not everyone will think the concession involved in the thin doctrine is an advantage. Hence, it could also be argued that the suffering endured by God Incarnate has an equivalence equal to the total suffering that would befall sinners absent atonement because of what the younger Edwards calls 'the infinite dignity and glory of his person'. Let us call this the 'thick' version of the doctrine. Both of these views seem consistent with the letter of Edwards Jr.'s sermon, but the latter appears to be more in keeping with what he says about the 'infinite dignity and glory' of Christ's person. If a person has an infinite dignity and glory, it might be thought that an act of atonement endured by such a person has an infinite value because any atoning act performed by such an individual has an infinite worth on account of the glory and dignity of his or her person.[45]

However, it might also be thought that this 'thick' way of construing the younger Edwards' assertion seems to contradict his claim about the absolute necessity of the atonement, mentioned earlier. But this would be a mistake. The point being made here concerns the *value* of the sufferings of Christ, not the *mode* of suffering Christ endured. If Christ is God Incarnate, and if, with the vast majority of the Christian tradition we affirm that his sufferings have the value they do in virtue of 'the infinite dignity and glory of his person', it makes sense to think that the suffering endured by God Incarnate on the cross has a value equivalent to the suffering of all merely human beings (perhaps an infinite value) because it is a person of 'infinite dignity and glory' who is suffering.

But, in fact, there are two strengths to the thick view too. Let us call these the 'thicker' and 'plain thick' versions of the 'thick' position just outlined. As the titles of these two versions of the 'thick' doctrine suggest, the 'thicker' version is stronger than the 'plain thick' version. On the 'thicker' reading of his words, Edwards Jr.'s point has to do with the fact that any amount of suffering endured by Christ is of a qualitatively different nature to any suffering that might be endured by someone who is merely human. This is a somewhat counterintuitive claim, to be sure. Normally we would think that being pricked by a pin involves less suffering than, say, having a limb removed in a farming accident, or having third degree burns over most of one's body. There is, we might think, a different quantity of pain endured in each of these instances. And we might also think that there are different qualities of pain too. Plausibly, psychological abuse is qualitatively different from physical abuse. These things are difficult to quantify not least because there is no reliable means of measuring one sort of pain against another, even where the two instances seem to be similar sorts of pain – a mild and a severe back pain, for example. Yet there does seem to be a deep intuition that different levels of pain involve different levels of suffering and that there are different sorts of pain human beings can endure.

But this 'thicker' reading of the younger Edwards means that any instance of suffering Christ endured, however trivial, has an infinite worth because it is a being of infinite worth that is suffering, and, somehow, the worth of his person translates to the value of the suffering he endures, however slight. This seems peculiar. But perhaps the reason why Christ's suffering has a different value than mine is that he suffers as the God-Man, whereas I do not (leaving to one side the thorny question of what it means for *God* Incarnate to suffer). Even if this assertion is on the right lines theologically speaking,[46] there is still the matter of apparently different orders of magnitude of pain (the pinprick, the crucifixion) generating the same value in the case of Christ's suffering, for the purposes of salvation. But maybe this can be overcome as well (if Christ is a person of infinite worth and this somehow translates to an infinite value placed upon any instance of suffering he endures, then it looks like any instance of suffering he endures has this value because he has this worth).

Nevertheless, even if we grant that *any* instance of suffering Christ may have endured had an infinite quality because of the 'infinite dignity and glory' of the person suffering, this does not necessarily mean that any act of suffering endured by Christ was an atoning act. I presume that Christ suffered all sorts of pain in his life prior to the cross. But those pains do not have the same salvific value as the work on the cross. And this is true even if we admit a robust doctrine of the active and passive obedience of Christ. One reason for introducing such a theological distinction is to demarcate those aspects of Christ's suffering that are part of his larger work of humiliation consonant with scriptures like Phillipians 2, in contrast to that aspect of his suffering that had a specific soteriological orientation of the sort we find spoken of in other Scriptures, like Isaiah 53. Had Christ lived a blameless life but not died on the cross we may surmise that he would have endured much suffering and privation, maybe even suffering that has an infinite value, but not the suffering requisite to salvation, in fulfilment of Scripture.

Now, consider the 'plain thick' version of our original 'thick' doctrine. On this view, it is not necessarily the case that every instance of suffering endured by Christ had an infinite value, although his work in his capacity as the mediator the New Covenant (that is, his priestly work) does have this value. This has the advantage (if it is an advantage) of remaining

agnostic about whether every instance of suffering endured by Christ
had an infinite value, as per the 'thicker' version of the doctrine.

Whether one opts for the 'thicker' or just 'plain thick' versions of
the 'thick' doctrine, it should be clear that the point being made by the
younger Edwards concerning the nature of the sufferings endured by
Christ is not necessarily in conflict with a doctrine of the absolute necessity of the atonement. Provided some account can be given of the way
in which Christ's suffering on the cross is distinct from other aspects of
suffering associated with his state of humiliation, and that this is consonant with his work on the cross being absolutely necessary, in fulfilment
of Scripture and in accordance with divine moral government, then the
younger Edwards's position seems consistent.[47]

Objections to penal non-substitution

We are now in a position to assess penal non-substitution. There are several serious problems facing the doctrine. The first objection concerns
whether penal non-substitution makes the atonement superfluous to
salvation. Thus, Wayne Grudem asserts of penal non-substitution, that

> it makes the actual earning of forgiveness for us something
> that happened in God's own mind apart from the death of
> Christ on the cross – he had already decided to forgive us
> without requiring any penalty from us and then punished
> Christ only to demonstrate that he was still the moral gover-
> nor of the universe. But this means that Christ (on this view)
> did not actually earn forgiveness or salvation for us, and thus
> the value of his redemptive work is greatly minimized.[48]

But as we have already noted, this does not apply to the Edwardean strand
of the doctrine. So this criticism can be dismissed without further ado.

Secondly, from the foregoing it is clear that penal non-substitution
denies punishment is a requirement for atonement to take place. Strictly
speaking, Christ is not punished. God the Father, instead of punishing
sinners for their sin, afflicts Christ in their stead. But afflicting someone
who is innocent of any crime instead of punishing someone who is guilty
of that crime is surely unjust. Charles Hodge says something similar to
this:

> Suffering inflicted for the good of others is not punishment
> any more than suffering inflicted for the good of the sufferer.
> The amputation of a crushed limb is not of the nature of
> punishment . . .. And the sufferings of Christ, if incurred in

the discharge of his mission of mercy, and not judicially inflicted in the execution of the penalty of the law, had no more tendency to show God's abhorrence of sin than the sufferings of the martyrs.[49]

And, of course, Hodge is right. Christ is not punished according to penal non-substitution. But, as has already been mentioned, the same is true of penal substitution. According to the logic of traditional versions of penal substitution, Christ is not punished, in a strict and philosophical sense of 'punishment'. He cannot be punished because punishment presumes guilt on the part of the one being punished, and Christ is not guilty of sin. It would make little sense to claim, 'I am punishing this innocent'. Surely, in the case of such utterances, 'language has gone on holiday', as the later Wittgenstein put it. It makes no more sense to say 'I am punishing this innocent' than it does to say 'I am setting light to this non-flammable substance'.

If penal substitution does not allow that Christ is punished for sin, strictly speaking, it does allow that Christ is treated as if he was the sinner, taking upon himself the penal consequences of sin in his capacity as penal substitute. In other words, penal substitution also means Christ is afflicted for a sin that is not his own. If the issue here is to do with punishing an innocent in place of the guilty, then, once again, there is parity between penal substitution and penal non-substitution (and, indeed, other theories of the atonement, such as non-penal substitution – sometimes called vicarious penitence – and satisfaction). This does nothing to alleviate the problem posed by this criticism. It merely points out (*tu quoque*) that these are not problems peculiar to penal non-substitution, but are issues shared by other, similar views of the nature of the atonement. And since Hodge adheres to the penal substitution view of the atonement, it is a problem he has in common with defenders of penal non-substitution.

A third line of attack has to do with whether penal non-substitution is really a theory of atonement at all. Christ does not stand in the place of sinful humanity to offer himself up instead of them, thereby providing atonement for their sin. Instead, his death has a suitably equivalent value to the punishment that would be visited upon sinful humanity without this act. But Christ's work on the cross – or the whole of his work from the incarnation onwards – does not actually effectually atone for any fallen human beings. His work is necessary for atonement, but it is not sufficient. Instead, it is one condition for the sufficiency of the atonement. Without the faith of the individual sinner, it atones for nothing.

We might put it like this. According to penal non-substitution the atonement is not *sufficient* for salvation, strictly speaking, although it is *sufficient to removing any obstacle to salvation*. It is rather like presenting a starving man with a feast. In sitting the man down before this culinary cornucopia, one is removing any obstacle to his remaining hungry. But this is not sufficient, in and of itself, to prevent the man from starving to death, if he chooses not to eat.[50] Although different strands of penal non-substitution supply alternative explanations, or reasons for why this is the case (which is one sort of difference between the two versions of penal non-substitution) it is true to say that both Grotian and Edwardean advocates of the doctrine take the potentially universal scope of the atonement, and its insufficiency for salvation without the exercise of human volition and the interposition of the Holy Spirit, very seriously indeed.

This criticism is really a version of the stock-in-trade objection mounted by Calvinists against the Arminian doctrine of the efficacy of the atonement. The idea is that if the atonement is not effectual, that is, does not actually redeem any particular individuals, then Christ has died in vain. For, possibly, no fallen human being will avail themselves of the benefits of Christ's work. In which case, none of fallen humanity would be saved, which appears to be a rather unpleasant prospect. (Nor need this be thought of as some merely possible, but not actual, world: for all we know every human being is without saving faith at the moment of death, either through failing to believe in Christ, having false or pseudo-faith, or through rejecting that faith at some moment prior to death – in which case no one is saved.)

However, on the Edwardean version of the argument this is not the case. The Edwardeans claimed that God truly offers the benefits of Christ to all humanity irrespective of whether or not they are among the elect. In this way, justice can be done to those passages of Scripture that suggest the scope of salvation is universal in extent, if not in efficacy (e.g. John 3: 16). Although fallen human beings are naturally capable of turning to Christ (there is no natural impediment to them doing so, no malfunctioning faculty or organ that prevents this outcome), neverthe-less, on this Edwardean view, no human being will come to Christ with-out the prevenient grace of God expressed through the work of the Holy Spirit. This is because human beings suffer from a moral inability to turn to Christ. This moral inability, according to some of the earlier Edwardeans at any rate, is a serious and crippling condition. Sin so affects fallen humanity that no individual will ever freely choose Christ because they are in a fallen state. So, without the internal working of the Holy Spirit, no human being will be saved. Thus, atonement is not the reason why some are elect and others are not; this is down to the sovereign electing will of God, expressed through the secret work of the Holy Spirit in the hearts of men and women.

The implication of this view is that God is not bound to save any fallen human being. After all, fallen human beings are culpable for their sin and salvation is an act of sheer grace. But, because of Christ's work, any fallen human being who does turn to Christ for salvation in virtue of the internal and efficacious work of the Holy Spirit, will be saved. This does have the unfortunate consequence that Christ's work does not bring about reconciliation for sin, strictly speaking, but merely makes the benefits of atonement available to all. But it does attempt to marry the biblical affirmation of the universal scope of atonement with the particularism of other passages of Scripture, beloved of certain Calvinists. Whether it is successful or not, and whether this really constitutes an act of atonement, or not, is another matter.

But even here, an advocate of penal non-substitution could dissent from the prevailing opinions of his peers and embrace the Reformed doctrine of particular redemption. Then, Christ's work is hypothetically or, alternatively, absolutely necessary; it has a suitably equivalent value to the punishment of sin; and it brings about the reconciliation of a particular number of fallen human beings (usually thought of in terms of some number less than the total number of humanity). There is nothing about the logic of penal non-substitution to prevent it being taken in a more traditionally Calvinist direction than is found in the Edwardean version of the doctrine.

Conclusions

I have argued that there are five major issues in the penal non-substitution doctrine of atonement. Through failure to understand all of these components of the doctrine, or through failure to see that there is more than one version of the doctrine, several of its recent and older critics have ended up mounting arguments that have no purchase in penal non-substitution. When the doctrine is considered sympathetically, it becomes clear that what it promises is a way of circumventing serious difficulties to do with penal substitution raised by the Socinians. It also retains a robust doctrine of the necessity of the atonement and the satisfaction of divine justice in the person of the God-Man – despite the fact that several prominent critics of the doctrine claim that it does away with a strong doctrine of divine justice. Its central claim is that Christ is capable of offering up an atoning act suitably equivalent in value (i.e. (at least) inversely proportional) to the punishment that would have been meted out for sin. This too is often overlooked or underplayed in accounts of penal non-substitution.

We have also seen that there are several criticisms of the doctrine that do have purchase. The first is that it shares a problem in common with penal substitution concerning the fiction at the centre of both doctrines. Christ is not punished for sin, according to penal non-substitution.

But then, he is not punished for sin according to traditional penal substitution theories of atonement either (although, for different reasons). The second is that it may be faced with difficulties over the question of the sufficiency of Christ's atoning act if read along Grotian or Edwardean lines, although there is nothing preventing a defender of penal non-substitution from advocating a doctrine of particular redemption. I suggest that these two issues present real and pressing theological difficulties for penal non-substitution, and that these problems, not those found in a number of traditional accounts of this doctrine, are the concerns that need to be addressed by its advocates.

Notes

1. This was Grotius' response to Faustus Socinus, entitled *Defensio Fidei Catholicae de Satisfactione Christi* (A defence of the Catholic faith concerning the Satisfaction of Christ), published in 1617.
2. For useful summaries of Grotius' doctrine of the atonement, see Robert S. Franks, *The Work of Christ, A Historical Study of Christian Doctrine* (London: Thomas Nelson, 1962 [1918]), pp. 389–409 and L. W. Grensted, *A Short History of The Doctrine of The Atonement* (Manchester: Manchester University Press, 1920), ch. XII.
3. This is the view of Garry Williams in 'A Critical Exposition of Hugo Grotius' Doctrine of the Atonement in *De Satisfactione Christi*', unpublished D. Phil Thesis, Oxford University, 1999. Compare the comments of the nineteenth century American Methodist theologian, and defender of a governmental theory of atonement, John Miley: 'It is rarely the case that the originator of a new theory, especially in a sphere of profound and broadly related doctrinal truth, clears it of all alien elements or achieves completeness in scientific construction. Such, on this subject [viz. the atonement] is the fact with Anselm. It is also true of Grotius.' *Systematic Theology, Vol. II* (Peabody, Mass.: Hendrickson, 1989 [1893]), p. 161.
4. Hereinafter, where reference is made to the Grotian version of penal non-substitution, it will be assumed that the reader understands that this should not be taken to mean the Grotian view is necessarily exactly the same as the view of Hugo Grotius. Whether there is a legitimate development from Grotius to the Grotians rather like there is a legitimate tradition of doctrinal development from Calvin through the Calvinists, is a matter beyond the scope of this essay.
5. Jonathan Edwards Jr., was the son of the better-known Jonathan Edwards (1703–1758) that most readers will be aware of. An able theologian in his own right, Edwards Jr., along with other 'Edwardeans' like Joseph Bellamy and Samuel Hopkins (both students of Edwards Sr.) were torch-bearers for what became known as 'the Edwardean theology', and, latterly, 'New England' and 'New Haven' theology in the nineteenth century. Edwards Jr. wrote three very influential sermons on the nature of the atonement, which constitute one of the clearest expressions of the Edwardian version of the doctrine. They can be found in *The Atonement, Discourses and Treatises by Edwards, Smalley, Maxcy, Emmons, Griffin, Burge and Weeks,* ed. Edwards Amasa Park (Boston: Congregational Board of Publication, 1859), pp. 1–42.

6. There has been some discussion about the relationship between the Edwardean doctrine of the atonement and the teaching of Jonathan Edwards Sr., but more work is required. Edwards Sr. appears to have held a version of satisfaction theory, although at times he writes as if he were a defender of penal substitution. But, curiously, he also wrote a laudatory preface to Joseph Bellamy's treatise *True Religion Delineated*, which sets out an early version of Edwardean penal non-substitution. (Bellamy had been a student of Edwards Sr.) This is a puzzle that cannot be unravelled here, which is reason enough to distinguish the views of Edwards Sr. and the study of his thought (Edwardsianism) from the doctrine espoused by the New England divines (Edwardean).

7. Charles Hodge mentions the German 'Supernaturalists' of the nineteenth century as holding a doctrine of atonement *similar* to, but not exactly the same as, the 'governmental view'. See *Systematic Theology Vol. II* (London: James Clarke, 1960), pp. 576–578.

8. The two standard treatments of the historical background to the rise of the New England theology and its doctrine of the atonement are Frank Hugh Foster's *A Genetic History of The New England Theology* (Chicago: University of Chicago Press, 1907) and George Nye Boardman, *A History of New England Theology* (New York: A. D. F. Randolph, 1899). Also worth noting is Edwards Amasa Parks' essay, 'The Rise of The Edwardean Theory of The Atonement' in Parks, ed., *The Atonement*. There have been several recent essays that bear upon this subject. See, for example, Joseph A Conforti, 'The New England Theology from Edwards to Bushnell' in *Encyclopedia of American Cultural and Intellectual History, Vol. I,* eds. Mary Kupiec Cayton and Peter W. Williams (New York: Charles Schribner's Sons, 2001): 205–214; Mark Noll, 'The Contested Legacy of Jonathan Edwards in Antebellum Calvinism: Theological Conflict and The Evolution of Thought in America' in *The Canadian Review of American Studies* 19 (1988): 149–164; and Douglas A. Sweeney, *Nathaniel Taylor, New Haven Theology, and The Legacy of Jonathan Edwards* (New York: Oxford University Press, 2003), pp. 104–108. See also *The New England Theology*, eds. Douglas Sweeney and Alan Guelzo (Grand Rapids, MI.: Baker Academic, 2006), which offers a useful overview of the whole literature and is the only modern reference work on this subject.

9. Robert Letham, *The Work of Christ* (Leicester: IVP, 1993), p. 169. Similar sentiments can be found in the older dogmatic literature. See, for instance, William G. T. Shedd's comments that Grotius' notion of law 'reduces everything back to the arbitrary and optional will of God', in *A History of Christian Doctrine Vol. 2* (Eugene, OR.: Wipf & Stock, 1999 [1864]), p. 355.

10. Thus John Miley, *Systematic Theology, Vol. II* (Peabody, MA.: Hendrickson, 1989 [1893]), p. 162. Emphasis added.

11. Of course, he might mean that the logic of this view *entails* the denial of the absolute necessity of the atonement. Making good on this claim would depend on showing that the Edwardean version of the doctrine is somehow internally disordered, affirming something that is inconsistent with the logic of penal non-substitution. But, as will become clear, I think this is not the case.

12. Jonathan Edwards Jr. 'Three Sermons on the Necessity of the Atonement and its consistency between that and free grace in forgiveness' (1785), in Park, *The*

Atonement, p. 4. Hereinafter cited as *Three Sermons*. All references to the *Three Sermons* are to this edition.

13. Edwards Jr., *Three Sermons*, p. 6.

14. Compare Heinrich Heppe: 'From the beginning of the seventeenth century recognition of "the absolute necessity of the vicarious sacrifice" became predominant in Reformed theology.' *Reformed Dogmatics*, trans. G. T. Thomson (London: Harpercollins, 1950), p. 469.

15. For useful discussion of this matter as it bears upon the change of mind John Owen had on the necessity of the atonement, see Carl Trueman, 'John Owen's Dissertation on Divine Justice: An Exercise in Christocentric Scholasticism' in *Calvin Theological Journal* 33 (1998): 87–103. For Augustine on this matter, see *De Trinitate* 13. 10. Other Reformed theologians who took the hypothetical necessity view include William Twisse (c.1578–1646), one time prolocutor of the Westminster Assembly and Samuel Rutherford (c.1600–1661), Professor of Divinity in St. Mary's College, University of St. Andrews.

16. The absolute power of God has to do with divine power absent his decrees, roughly, what God is able to do as an absolute sovereign. His ordained power has to do with divine power circumscribed by the divine decrees, that is, what God has ordained he will do. Thomist theologians were principally responsible for the development of this distinction.

17. Francis Turretin, *Institutes of Elenctic Theology, Vol. II*, trans. George Musgrave Giger, ed. James T. Dennison, Jr. (Phillipsburg, NJ.: Presbyterian & Reformed, 1994), XIV. X. IV, p. 418.

18. It might be thought that the views of the younger Edwards are anomalous, or even that this claim about the necessity of the atonement is inconsistent with the rest of his views. But neither of these things is true, as a careful reading of the literature on this theory of the atonement would show.

19. Although, in Garry Williams' estimation, this is not the view Grotius himself held. See 'A Critical Exposition', pp. 105–150.

20. Miley, *Systematic Theology, Vol. II*, p. 162.

21. Some theologians place divine retributive justice within a broader notion of divine distributive justice, which has two aspects. According to the first, God distributes his justice positively in *renumerative justice*, giving some creatures rewards according to his grace, and visits his wrath upon sinners in *retributive justice*. But, for present purposes, what is important is the distinction between the satisfaction of rectoral justice and the relaxation of retributive justice. For more on this, see Louis Berkhof, *Systematic Theology* (Edinburgh: Banner of Truth, 1988 [1939]), p. 75. Compare William Shedd, *Dogmatic Theology, Third Edition,* ed. Alan Gomes (Phillipsburg, NJ.: Presbyterian and Reformed, 2003), p. 292.

22. Park says, 'the sufferings of our Lord satisfied the general justice of God, but did not satisfy his distributive justice.' *The Atonement,* p. x.

23. Miley, *Systematic Theology, Vol. II*, p. 165.

24. As it stands, it could also be read to mean some other divine person could carry out this office of Redeemer. But I presume that Miley does not mean this. Most theologians in the western tradition have maintained that it was most

suitable that the Son of God become Man. Some have maintained that the Triune relations in the ontological Trinity preclude the incarnation of divine persons other than the Son. I presume Miley falls into one of these two groups, although I have not found an explicit avowal of this in his *Systematic Theology*.

25. Of course defenders of penal substitution are not subject to this sort of criticism, because conventionally, advocates of that theory claim the atonement is not just dependent on the divine will, but reflects the character of God in the expression of his divine justice. And, as I have already pointed out, this is consistent with opting for the hypothetical necessity of the atonement, as some Reformed Orthodox did.

26. Grensted, *A Short History of The Doctrine of The Atonement*, p. 293. Similar sentiments can be found in the Lutheran dogmatician Francis Pieper in *Christian Dogmatics, Vol. II,* (Saint Louis, Mo.: Concordia Publishing House), p. 359.

27. From Grotius, *Defensio Fidei Catholicae de Satisfactione Christi*, p. 3, cited in Grensted, ibid.

28. Could Grotius' view be consistent with some weaker notion of legal voluntarism with respect to the punishment of infringements of the divine law? Perhaps. For example, it could be that it is not necessarily the moral law that is, as it were, immediately and wholly dependent on the divine will, but the punishments the moral law requires that may, in some instances – like divine retribution – be relaxed according to the divine will. This is an attractive prospect, but does not appear to be what Grotius says – at least, not according to Grensted, and other interpreters, like Shedd in *A History of Christian Doctrine, Vol. 2*, p. 356 ff.

29. For a recent discussion of this issue, see Thomas Morris, *Anselmian Explorations* (Notre Dame: University of Notre Dame Press, 1989).

30. Alternatively, one could deny that divine justice is essential to God. No defender of penal non-substitution I know of would welcome that, for reasons that are too obvious to need rehearsing here.

31. Parks, 'Introductory Essay' in *The Atonement*, p. x.

32. Carl Trueman discusses this point in the context of John Owen's engagement with Grotius in *The Claims of Truth, John Owen's Trinitarian Theology* (Carlisle: Paternoster, 1998), pp. 210 ff.

33. Horace Bushnell, *The Vicarious Sacrifice* (London: Alexander Strahan, 1866), p. 306.

34. Park, 'Introductory Essay' in *The Atonement,* p. x.

35. Letham, *The Work of Christ*, p. 168. Garry Williams points out that this sort of criticism goes back to F. C. Baur in the nineteenth century, whose misreading of Grotius became influential because it was adopted by Frank Foster in his 1909 English translation of *De Satisfactione*. See Williams, 'A Critical Exposition', p. 125.

36. The reader's attention is drawn once again to the work of John Miley *Systematic Theology, Vol. II,* p. 162, in this regard.

37. This problem is also central to Jonathan Edwards Jr.'s discussion of the atonement. See his 'Remarks on The Improvements Made in Theology by His Father, President Edwards', in *The Works of Jonathan Edwards, D. D., Late President of*

Union College, Vol. 1, ed. Tryon Edwards (Andover, MA.: Allen, Morrill & Wardwell, 1842), p. 485, cited in *The New England Theology*, eds. Sweeney and Guelzo, p. 128.

38. Compare Faustus Socinus in *De Jesu Christo Servatore*, 3. 2. 240: 'There is no need for remission – indeed, remission is an impossibility – where the debt no longer exists.' Cited by Alan Gomes in '*De Jesu Christo Servatore*: Faustus Socinus on the Satisfaction of Christ', *Westminster Theological Journal* 55 (1993): 226.

39. Jonathan Edwards, Jr., 'Remarks on The Improvements Made in Theology by His Father, President Edwards', cited in *The New England Theology*, eds. Sweeney and Guelzo, p. 128. Cf. Edwards Jr.'s opening comments in the first of his *Three Sermons*, concerning the debt-forgiveness problem in the atonement: 'Having from my youth devoted myself to the study of theoretic and practical theology, this has to be been one of the *gordian knots* it that science', p. 3.

40. John Miley also notes the parity between penal substitution and what he calls the governmental view of the atonement. He observes that according to both theories, sin is not punished in Christ, strictly speaking, because Christ is not guilty of sin. Penal substitution claims the penal consequences of my sin are imputed to Christ. But this means treating Christ as if he were a sinner, which is what defender of penal non–substitution requires too. See Miley, *Systematic Theology Vol. II*, p. 156 ff.

41. Wayne Grudem, *Systematic Theology* (Leicester: IVP, 1994), p. 582.

42. The qualification inserted here 'of (at least) equivalent value' is given because a number of classical theologians argued that Christ's suffering and death have an infinite value in virtue of the fact that they are offered up by God Incarnate. But the argument actually only requires that Christ's suffering and death has a value at least equal to that of sin.

43. Edwards, *Three Sermons*, p. 10.

44. Although, note that even the claim that Christ's suffering and death is at least equivalent to the threshold of suffering that fallen humans would endure is consistent with the notion that the nature of Christ's sufferings have an infinite value.

45. This notion has been disputed in the recent literature by Marilyn Adams in 'Hell and the God of Justice' in *Religious Studies* 11 (1975): 433–447. I have attempted to rebut this criticism in 'Divine Retribution: A Defence', *Sophia* 42 (2003): 35-52.

46. And much more would need to be said about this by way of supplying an argument for this claim, for it to begin to look plausible. But we cannot pursue that in this context.

47. But what does it mean to say that Christ's work is of infinite value because it is the work of the theanthropic person of Christ, if, with classical theologians, we affirm that Christ's divine nature is incapable of suffering? This is a hoary old theological conundrum. One ready solution offered to it involves the use of reduplication: Christ suffered *qua* man, not *qua* God, and it is this suffering that has infinite value. But, far from solving the problem, this only throws it into stark relief: if only Christ's *human* nature can suffer, then how is Christ's death of any greater value than the death of any other human being? Perhaps a better solution lies in claiming that it was *God Incarnate* who suffered, not Christ

qua man. The idea here is that the subject of Christ's suffering is the Incarnate Second Person of the Trinity, not merely his human nature, just as it was the Incarnate Second Person of the Trinity who ate broiled fish with his disciples in John 21, or was hungry, or thirsty in Luke 4: 2 and John 19: 28 respectively. This distinction is a subtle but important one that promises a way of holding on to divine impassibility and the possibility of God Incarnate. A recent treatment of this question that takes this sort of line is Thomas Weinandy's *Does God Suffer?* (Notre Dame: University of Notre Dame Press, 2000), ch. 8.

48. Grudem, *Systematic Theology*, p. 582.
49. Hodge, *Systematic Theology, Vol. II*, p. 579.
50. This view, commensurate with traditional Arminianism, was also part of the New England version of penal non-substitution. The New England theologians, following, but adapting, and eventually subverting a distinction introduced by Jonathan Edwards Sr., claimed that there is no *natural* impediment to any human being turning to Christ for salvation. What prevents this outcome is a *moral* inability to do so. Thus, they sought to overcome the injustice they perceived in the Calvinistic doctrine of limited atonement (how can those who are never given the chance to repent be justly cast off by God?), whilst retaining an explanation of why some human beings refuse salvation, in keeping with the secret election of God. This is an important matter, but there is not space to develop it here. Edwards Sr. discusses this natural and moral (in)ability in *Freedom of the Will, The Works of Jonathan Edwards, Vol. 1,* ed. Paul Ramsey (Hew Haven: Yale University Press, 1957), p. 362 ff. This distinction is discussed in Oliver D. Crisp, *Jonathan Edwards and the Metaphysics of Sin* (Aldershot: Ashgate, 2005), ch. 4.

CHAPTER 16

DO WE BELIEVE IN PENAL SUBSTITUTION?

David Lewis

Imagine that an offender has a devoted and innocent friend. The offender has been justly sentenced to be punished for his offence. But the friend volunteers to be punished in his place.[1] If the friend undergoes the punishment that the offender deserved, does that render it permissible (or even obligatory) to leave the offender unpunished? Is that any reason at all in favour of sparing the offender?

Mostly we think not. It is unheard of that a burglar's devoted friend serves the burglar's prison sentence while the burglar himself goes free; or that a murderer's still-more-devoted friend serves the murderer's death sentence. Yet if ever such a thing happened, we surely would hear of it – for what a newsworthy story it would be! Such things do not happen. And not, I think, because a burglar or a murderer never has a sufficiently devoted friend. Rather, because the friend will know full well that, whatever he might wish, it would be futile to offer himself as a substitute for punishment. The offer would strike the authorities as senseless, and they would decline it out of hand.

Even if the friend managed to substitute himself by stealth, and arranged for it to be found out afterward that he had been punished in place of the offender, the scheme would fail. Once the authorities learned that the offender had gone unpunished, they would get on with the job. However much they might regret their mistake in punishing the innocent friend, they could not undo that mistake by failing to punish the guilty offender. That would merely add a second mistake to the first.

We can say, if we like, that the offender 'owes a debt of punishment'. But the metaphor is misleading. As we mostly conceive of them, the condition of owing a debt and the condition of deserving to be punished are not alike. In the case of debt, what is required is that the creditor *shall not* suffer a loss of the money he lent; what happens to the debtor is beside the point. Whereas in the case of a 'debt of punishment', what is required is that the debtor *shall* suffer a loss; there is no creditor. (Society? – Not really. The creditor is supposed to be the one who suffers a loss if the debt is not paid. But sometimes, what with the cost of prisons, society will suffer more of a loss if the debt is paid.) This is common ground between alternative conceptions of the function of punishment. Perhaps the guilty ought to suffer a loss simply because it is better that the wicked not prosper; or as an expression of our abhorrence of their offences; or as a means to the end of reforming their characters; or as a means to the end of depriving them of the resources – life and liberty – to repeat their offences; or as a means of deterring others from similar offences. Punishment of innocent substitutes would serve none of these functions. (Not even deterrence, since the deception that would be required to make deterrence effective could not be relied upon.)

What function would we have to ascribe to punishment in order to make it make sense to punish an innocent substitute? – A compensatory function. Suppose that the offender's punishment were seen mainly as a benefit to the victim, a benefit sufficient to undo whatever loss the offender had inflicted upon him. Then the source of the benefit wouldn't matter. If the offender's innocent friend provided the benefit, the compensatory function would be served, no less than if the offender himself provided it.

But our actual institutions of punishment are not designed to serve a compensatory function. A murderer's victim cannot be compensated at all, yet we punish murderers just the same. A burglar's victim can be compensated (so long as the victim is still alive), and may indeed be compensated, but not by the punishment of the burglar. How does it benefit the victim if the burglar serves a prison sentence? The victim, like anyone else, may be pleased to know that wrong-doing has met with its just reward; but this 'compensation', if such it be, could not (without deception) be provided by the punishment of the burglar's innocent friend.

We can imagine a world in which the punishment of burglars really is designed to serve a compensatory function, and in such a way as to make sense of substitution. But when we do, the differences from actuality are immense. Suppose, for instance, that the burglar was required to serve a sentence of penal servitude as the victim's personal slave. Then a compensatory function, would indeed be served; and punishing an innocent substitute could serve that function equally well. Or suppose the burglar was to be hanged before the victim's eyes. If the victim took sufficient pleasure in watching a hanging, that might compensate him for the loss of his gold; and if he enjoyed hangings of the innocent no less than hangings of the guilty, then again punishment of a substitute could serve a compensatory function.

A one-sided diet of mundane examples might convince us that we do not believe in penal substitution; we agree, in other words, that the substitutionary punishment of the innocent friend is never any reason to leave the offender unpunished. But of course we do not all agree to this. For many among us are Christians; and many among the Christians explain the Atonement as a case of penal substitution. They say that when Christ died for our sins. He paid the debt of punishment that the sinners owed; and thereby He rendered it permissible, and thereby He brought it about, that the sinners (those of them that accepted His gift) were spared the punishment of damnation that they deserved.

Although these Christians do believe in penal substitution in the context of theology, they do not seem to believe anything out of the ordinary in the context of mundane criminal justice. We do not hear of them arguing that just as Christ paid the debt of punishment owed by all the sinners, so likewise other innocent volunteers can pay the lesser debts of punishment owed by burglars and murderers. ('Innocent' not in the sense that they are without sin, but only in the sense that they are not guilty of burglary or murder.) Why not? I think we must conclude that these Christians are of two minds about penal substitution. Their principles alter from one case to another, for no apparent reason.

My point is not new (though neither is it heard as much as we might expect). Here is a recent statement of the point by Philip Quinn:

> In [medieval legal] codes, the debt of punishment for even such serious crimes as killing was literally pecuniary; one paid the debt by paying monetary compensation. What was important for such purposes as avoiding blood feud was that the debt be paid; who paid it was not crucial. . . . But our intuitions about the proper relations of crime and punishment are tutored by a very different legal picture. Though a parent can pay her child's pecuniary debts, a murderer's mother cannot pay his debt of punishment by serving his prison term. . . . So to the extent that we think of serious sins as analogous to crimes and respect the practices embedded in our system of criminal law, we should expect the very idea of vicarious satisfaction for sin to seem alien and morally problematic.[2]

However, the heart of the rebuke against those Christians who explain the Atonement as a case of penal substitution is not that they are out of date and disagree with our 'intuitions'. Rather, it is that they disagree with what they themselves think the rest of the time.

An impatient doubter might say that it is pointless to rebuke these Christians for their on-again-off-again belief in penal substitution. The prior problem lies elsewhere. Even if their (sometime) principle of penal substitution were right, and even if they themselves accepted *it single-mindedly*, still they would be misapplying it. For in the case of the Atonement, the supposed substitution is far from equal. Evil though it is to be put to death by crucifixion, even if the death is temporary and foreseen to be temporary, still the eternal damnation of even one sinner, let alone all of them, is a far worse evil. How can the former be a fair exchange for the latter, even if we grant in general that such exchanges make sense?

But to this question the Christians have an answer. They may say, with scriptural support, that what happened to Christ on the cross was something very much worse than crucifixion. He 'bore our sins', whatever that means, and He found Himself forsaken by God.[3] Perhaps these evils, if not the crucifixion itself, were an equal substitute for the deserved damnation that the sinners escaped in return.

An alternative answer is on offer. Perhaps Christ paid only some small part of the debt of punishment that the sinners owed; only just enough so that, if they had paid it for themselves, it would have been the penance required as a constitutive element of sincere repentance. Thereby He made it possible for them to repent, and when they repented the rest of their debt was forgiven outright.[4]

So we can see, at least dimly, how our doubter's inequality objection might be fended off. And if it is, we are back where we were before: the real problem is with the very idea that someone else can pay the sinners' debt of punishment.

Those Christians who explain the Atonement as a case of penal substitution, yet do not in general believe in the principle they invoke, really are in a bad way. Yet the rest of us should not be overbold in rebuking them. For we live in the proverbial glass house. *All* of us – atheists and agnostics, believers of other persuasions, the lot – are likewise of two minds about penal substitution.

We do not believe that the offender's friend can serve the offender's prison sentence, or his death sentence. Neither can the friend serve the offender's sentence of flogging, transportation, or hard labour. But we do believe – do we not? – that the friend can pay the offender's fine. (At least, if the offender consents.) Yet this is just as much a case of penal substitution as the others.

Or is it? You might think that the proper lesson is just that the classification of fines as punishments is not to be taken seriously. Consider a parking space with a one-hour limit. If you want to park there for an hour, you pay a fee by putting a coin in the meter. If you want to park there for two hours, you pay a fee at a higher hourly rate; the fee is collected by a more cumbersome method; and the fee is called a 'fine'. But what's in a name? The function served is the same in either case. The fee helps pay the cost of providing the parking place; and, in a rough and ready way, it allocates the space to those who want it more in preference to those who want it less. Since those who want it more include some who want to make a gift of it instead of using it themselves, and since some of these may want to make a gift of two-hour rather than one-hour use, the payment of others' 'fines' fits right in. Paying someone else's 'fine' for two–hour parking is no more problematic than buying someone else a pot of beer. It has little in common with the penal substitution we mostly do not believe in.

Agreed, But set aside these little 'fines' that are really fees. Some fines are altogether more serious. They are as much of a burden as some prison sentences. (If given the choice 'pay the fine or serve the time', some would choose to serve the time.) They convey opprobrium. They serve the same functions that other punishments serve. They do not serve a compensatory function, since the fine is not handed over to the victim. Yet if the offender is sentenced to pay a fine of this serious sort, and his friend pays it for him, we who do not otherwise believe in penal substitution will find that not amiss – or anyway, not very much amiss.

You might think that in the case of fines, but not in other cases, we accept penal substitution because we have no practical way to prevent it. Suppose we had a law saying that a cheque drawn on someone else's bank account would not be accepted in payment of a fine. Anyone sentenced to pay a fine would either have to write a cheque on his own bank account or else hand over the cash in person. What difference would that make? – None.

If the friend gives the offender a gift sufficient to pay the fine, we have a *de facto* case of penal substitution. Whoever may sign the cheque, it is the friend who mainly suffers the loss that was meant to be the offender's punishment. What happens to the offender? – His debt of punishment is replaced by a debt of gratitude, which may or may not be any burden to him; he gets the opprobrium; if the friend has taken the precaution of withholding his gift until the fine has actually been paid, he may need a short-term loan; and there his burden is at an end. Whereas what happens to the friend, according to our stipulation of the case, is that he suffers a monetary loss which is as much of a burden as some prison sentences. The transfer of burden from the offender to the friend may not be quite complete, but plainly the friend is getting much the worst of it.

How to prevent *de facto* penal substitution by means of gifts? Shall we have a law that those who are sentenced to pay fines may not receive gifts? (Forever? For a year and a day? Even if the gift was given before the case came to trial? Before the offence was committed? If the recipient of a generous gift afterward commits an offence and uses the gift to pay his fine, could that make the giver an accomplice before the fact?) Such a law would be well-nigh impossible to get right; to enforce; or to square with our customary encouragement of generosity even toward the undeserving. We well might judge that what it would take to prevent *de facto* penal substitution in the payment of fines would be a cure worse than the disease.

Here we have the makings of an explanation of why we sometimes waver in our rejection of penal substitution. It would go like this. In the first place, we tolerate penal substitution in the case of fines because it is obviously impractical to prevent it. Since, in the case of punishment by fines, the condition of being sentenced to punishment is the condition of owing a debt – literally – the metaphor of a 'debt of punishment' gets a grip on us. Then some of us persist in applying this metaphor, even when it is out of place because the 'debt of punishment' is nothing like a debt in the literal sense. That is how we fall for such nonsense as a penal substitution theory of the Atonement.

Well – that might be right. But I doubt it; the hypothesis posits too much sloppy thinking to be credible. The worst problem comes right at the start. If we were single-mindedly against penal substitution, and yet we saw that preventing it in the case of fines was impractical, we should not on that account abandon our objections to penal substitution. Rather we ought to conclude that fines are an unsatisfactory form of punishment. (Serious fines, not the little 'fines' that are really fees.) We might not abandon fines, because the alternatives might have their own drawbacks.[5] But our dissatisfaction ought to show. Yet it does not show. The risk of *de facto,* penal substitution ought to be a frequently mentioned drawback of punishment by fines. It is not. And that is why I maintain that all of us, not just some Christians, are of two minds about penal substitution.

If the rest of us were to make so bold as to rebuke the Christians for their two-mindedness, they would have a good *tu quoque* against us. A *tu quoque* is not a rejoinder on behalf of penal substitution. Yet neither is it intellectually weightless. It indicates that both sides agree that penal substitution sometimes makes sense after all, even if none can say how it makes sense. And if both sides agree to that, that is some evidence that somehow they might both be right.

Notes

1. A. M. Quinton once argued, in 'On Punishment', *Analysis* 14 (1954), pp. 133–142, that punishment of the innocent is logically impossible, simply a contradiction in terms. Maybe so. Nevertheless, since abuse of language makes for easier communication than circumlocution or neologism, I shall speak of the innocent volunteer being punished. I trust that the reader will understand: I mean that the volunteer undergoes something that would have constituted punishment if it had happened instead to the guilty offender.
2. Philip Quinn, 'Aquinas on Atonement', *Trinity, Incarnation and Atonement,* ed. R. Feenstra and C. Plantinga (University of Notre Dame Press, 1989), pp. 171–72. See also Eleonore Stump, 'Atonement According to Aquinas',

Philosophy and the Christian Faith, ed. T. Morris (University of Notre Dame Press, 1988), pp. 61–63.

3. How could Christ have been forsaken by God when He *was* God? – perhaps God the Son found Himself forsaken by the other persons of the Trinity.

4. See Richard Swinburne, 'The Christian Scheme of Salvation', *Philosophy and the Christian Faith,* ed. T. Morris (University of Notre Dame Press, 1988), pp. 15–30 [reprinted as Chapter 18 in this volume]. Although Swinburne's theory of the Atonement is not the standard penal substitution theory – it is rather a theory of *penitential* substitution – Swinburne by no means abandons the idea of substitution. 'God . . . can help us atone for our sins by making available to us an offering which *we* may offer as *our* reparation and penance . . .' (p. 27, my emphasis).

5. Might we console ourselves with the thought that, although penal substitution has not been prevented, cases of it are at least not frequent? – That might not be much of a consolation. For if cases are rare, those few cases that do occur will seem all the more outrageous.

CHAPTER 17

ABELARD ON ATONEMENT: "NOTHING UNINTELLIGIBLE, ARBITRARY, ILLOGICAL, OR IMMORAL ABOUT IT"

Philip L. Quinn

It was, according to a prominent English philosopher and theologian, a moment of theological recovery. "For the first time – or rather for the first time since the days of the earliest and most philosophical Greek fathers – the doctrine of the atonement was stated," Hastings Rashdall says, "in a way which had nothing unintelligible, arbitrary, illogical, or immoral about it."[1] Rashdall, who coined the term 'ideal utilitarianism' and ably advocated the position since then so called, made this remark in his Bampton Lectures of 1915, published in 1919 under the title *The Idea of Atonement in Christian Theology.*[2] He was referring to the account of atonement set forth by Peter Abelard in his *Commentary on Paul's Epistle to the Romans.* In this essay I argue that there is a lot to be said for Rashdall's strongly positive evaluation of Abelard's account of the Atonement.

As two good recent books on atonement make clear, Rashdall's view is not the conventional wisdom of our own times. In *The Actuality of Atonement,* Colin Gunton, who is Professor of Christian Doctrine at King's College, London, does not so much as mention Abelard; Abelard is not listed in the book's index of names or in its bibliography.[3] And in his *Responsibility and Atonement,* Richard Swinburne, who is Nolloth Professor of Philosophy of the Christian Religion at Oxford, dismisses Abelard in a single sentence; he claims that "Abelard's exemplary theory of the atonement, that Christ's life and death work to remove our sins by inspiring us to do penance and good acts, contains no objective transaction."[4] Implicit in this remark is a criticism of Abelard's account of atonement that is often thought to be devastating. The charge is that Abelard's views on atonement are exemplarist in character. But what exactly does the charge come to: What is exemplarism? Why is it a bad thing to be an exemplarist? And is Abelard guilty as charged? These are questions to which I shall offer answers in the course of the present discussion.

The difficulty is not, I think, that it is false or unorthodox to claim that Christ's life and death are an inspiring example. Thomas Aquinas, who is surely a sound guide on this point, explicitly endorses this claim.

When enumerating some of the benefits that accrue to us as a result of the Incarnation, he includes on a list of five that contribute to our furtherance in good both having our charity kindled because God's love for us stimulates us to love in return and being inspired to do good because God himself sets an example for us.[5] And Gunton remarks that if "we are to establish a case for an objective, past atonement, it cannot be at the cost of denying the subjective and exemplary implications."[6] So the difficulty must rather be that exemplarists are explicitly or implicitly committed to the view that Christ's life and death are no more than an inspiring example, a paradigm of Christian existence. Such an exclusive view would, it is alleged, leave out something important about Christ's atoning work. Exemplarists are thus to be faulted because they have an incomplete doctrine of the Atonement. What they say is sound as far as it goes, but it is not the whole truth.

What objective transaction or past fact do the exemplarists neglect? For historical reasons, it would be virtually impossible to get agreement on an answer to this question among Christian theologians or philosophers. In this respect, there is a sharp contrast between the doctrine of the Atonement and other central Christian doctrines such as the Incarnation and the Trinity. Under pressure from theological controversy, the early church felt itself obliged to formulate the fairly precise definitions of such doctrines that we find expressed by the familiar Nicene and Chalcedonian formulas. Such definitions have operated as a traditional constraint on theological theorizing. Nothing similar happened in the case of the doctrine of the Atonement, and so the history of theological reflection on it is richly pluralistic. It is a colorful tapestry of scriptural motifs and theological elaborations.

In the present context, it turns out to be useful to impose some taxonomic order on the otherwise bewildering variety of accounts of the Atonement by thinking of them as falling at various places in a spectrum. At one end of this spectrum would be accounts that emphasize one motif to the exclusion of all others if there were any such purely monistic accounts. The theory Anselm proposes in *Cur Deus homo* falls close to this end of the spectrum. According to Anselm, God became human in order to pay a debt that human sinners owe but cannot pay and thereby to spare sinful humans the punishment that would otherwise be consequent upon their inability to pay this debt.[7] So Anselm understands the Atonement almost exclusively in terms of the legalistic category of making satisfaction for a debt of sin. At the other end of the spectrum would be accounts that incorporate several motifs and treat them all as being of more or less equal importance. The account Gunton sets forth in *The Actuality of Atonement* is an example of such egalitarian pluralism. It focuses on three ideas: Christ's work as a victory over demonic forces, Christ's work as a contribution to cosmic justice, and Christ's work as a priestly sacrifice.[8] All three motifs are taken to be metaphoric in nature; they are not to be confused with theories and must be understood in suitably nuanced and qualified ways. But when properly understood, each of these metaphors has something vital to contribute to our admittedly imperfect grasp of the complex mystery of the Atonement. In the middle of the spectrum are accounts that draw on a plurality of motifs but assign pride of place to some and relegate others to subordinate roles. The story Aquinas tells in the *Summa Theologiae* furnishes an instance of this kind of hierarchical pluralism. Like Anselm, Aquinas thinks that the principal function of Christ's atoning work is to make satisfaction for human sin by paying a debt of punishment human sinners cannot pay.[9] Aquinas holds that the power to do this comes from Christ's Passion, but he insists that the Passion also has other functions. It contributes to the salvation of sinners by meriting grace for them on account of its voluntary character, by redeeming them from bondage to the devil through a ransom paid to God, and by reconciling them to God because it is an acceptable sacrifice. So although satisfaction is the dominant theme in Aquinas's account of the Atonement, he eclectically mobilizes other motifs to play subsidiary parts.

We can, I believe, clarify the question that needs to be put to Abelard's account of the Atonement if we ask where on this spectrum it is to be located. As we shall see once we begin to examine the texts, there is no room for doubt that Abelard makes much of the inspiring love displayed in God becoming incarnate and suffering unto death for his human creatures. But even if the exemplary motif is the dominant theme in Abelard's account, it does not follow without further argument that it is the only theme. Absent such argument, the possibility remains open that Abelard, like Aquinas, is a hierarchical pluralist and so is not an exemplarist in the sense of excluding part of the truth about the Atonement. Indeed, it could turn out that Abelard and Aquinas differ not so much over which motifs should be included in a fairly comprehensive account of the Atonement as over the more delicate matter of which themes are most important and deserve to be highlighted. And if this were so, Abelard too would be located somewhere in the middle of the spectrum in terms of which we are for present purposes ordering accounts of the Atonement. In that case, an evaluation of Abelard's account would involve the subtle task of determining whether it does a better job than its rivals in answering questions about which motifs ought to be regarded as central to a well-rounded doctrine of the Atonement and thus deserve emphasis in its presentation.

Should we embrace Abelard with the enthusiasm Rashdall displayed near the beginning of this century? Or should we write Abelard off as an exemplarist in the way Swinburne has done near the century's end? Let us look at what Abelard says with the possibility in mind that neither response rests on an adequate appreciation of the merits of his views.

The central motif of Abelard's account

Abelard interrupts his commentary on Romans 3 to raise the question of what Christ's death does to atone for our sins. It is the solution he proposes to the problems that come up in the course of this discussion that has given rise to the charge of exemplarism. So we need to look with particular care at what he actually says in this celebrated passage.

The passage begins with arguments against the view that sinners are rightfully held in bondage by the devil until Christ ransoms them by his death. On this view, the devil holds all mere humans in bondage by right because the first man, Adam, yielded himself to the devil's authority by an act of voluntary obedience. Being perfectly just, God respects the devil's rights and so will not free sinners from their bondage by force. Instead he ransoms them from captivity at the price of Christ's blood. Abelard has three objections to this view. Two hang on rather esoteric theological points. The first is that Christ redeemed only the elect, who were never in the devil's power. Alluding to Luke 16:26, Abelard contends that Abraham there declares that a great gulf has been fixed between the elect and the wicked so that the latter can never cross over to the former. From this Abelard concludes that "still less may the devil, who is more evil than all, acquire any power in that place where no wicked person has a place or even entry."[10] The second point is that the devil never acquired rights over the first humans because he seduced them by means of a lying promise. Alluding to Genesis 3:4, Abelard maintains that "the devil could not grant that immortality which he promised man as a reward of transgression in the hope that in this way he might hold him fast by some sort of right."[11] Presumably the thought here is that the first humans were willing to grant rights over them to the devil in return for immortality, but he did not actually acquire rights over them because he could not and so did not live up to his part of the bargain.

Abelard's third objection echoes a point that Anselm had made earlier.[12] He concedes that God may have given express permission to the devil to torture humans by way of punishment for their sins, but he denies that the devil on that account holds sinful humans in bondage as a matter of right. If one servant of a master seduces another to depart from obedience to the master, the master properly regards the seducer as much more guilty than the seduced servant. "And how unjust it would be," Abelard exclaims, "that he who seduced the other should deserve, as a result, to have any special right or authority over him!"[13] Even the express permission to punish sinners will, according to Abelard, be withdrawn if God chooses to forgive their sins and to remit the punishment for them, as Matthew 9:2 reports Christ did in the case of a paralytic. If God were mercifully to choose to forgive other sinners, Abelard argues, then "assuredly, once the sins for which they were undergoing punishment have been forgiven, there appears to remain no reason why they should be any longer punished for them."[14] So there really is no need for God to ransom human sinners from the devil. The devil has no rights over them which God must in justice respect, and God can retract the devil's permission to punish simply by forgiving them and remitting the punishment.

But this makes the following question all the more urgent for Abelard: "What need was there, I say, that the Son of God, for our redemption, should take upon him our flesh and endure such numerous fastings, insults, scourgings and spittings, and finally that most bitter and disgraceful death upon the cross, enduring even the cross of punishment with the wicked?"[15] Would it not be reasonable to suppose, Abelard asks, that the suffering and death of his Son should increase God's anger at sinful humanity because humans acted more criminally by crucifying his Son than they did by disobeying his first command in paradise in eating a single apple? Nor does it seem promising to think of Christ's atonement as a blood price paid to God rather than to the devil for the redemption of sinful humanity, for it appears to be inconsistent with God's perfect goodness that he should demand such a price. As Abelard puts the point, "How cruel and wicked it seems that anyone should demand the blood of an innocent person as the price for anything, or that it should in any way please him that an innocent man should be slain – still less that God should consider the death of his Son so agreeable that by it he should be reconciled to the whole world!"[16] And thus passionately put, the point has considerable force.

Having done his best to impress upon his readers the difficulty of the question, Abelard audaciously propounds an answer to it. The passage deserves to be quoted at length both on account of its intrinsic interest and because of the controversy to which it has given rise among scholars:

> Now it seems to us that we have been justified by the blood of Christ and reconciled to God in this way: through this unique act of grace manifested to us – in that his Son has taken upon himself our nature and persevered therein in teaching us by word and example even unto death – he has more fully bound us to himself by love; with the result that

our hearts should be enkindled by such a gift of divine grace, and true charity should not now shrink from enduring anything for him. And we do not doubt that the ancient Fathers, waiting in faith for this same gift, were aroused to very great love of God in the same way as men of this dispensation of grace, since it is written: "And they that went before and they that followed cried, saying: 'Hosanna to the Son of David,'" etc. Yet everyone becomes more righteous – by which we mean a greater lover of the Lord – after the Passion of Christ than before, since a realized gift inspires greater love than one which is only hoped for. Wherefore, our redemption through Christ's suffering is that deeper affection [*dilectio*] in us which not only frees us from slavery to sin, but also wins for us the true liberty of sons of God, so that we do all things out of love rather than fear – love to him who has shown us such grace that no greater can be found, as he himself asserts, saying, "Greater love than this no man hath, that a man lay down his life for his friends."[17]

The case for taking Abelard to be an exemplarist rests almost entirely on interpretation of this text.

Thus, for example, after setting forth his own translation of its first and last sentences, Robert S. Franks concludes that it is evident that Abelard "has reduced the whole process of redemption to one single clear principle, viz. the manifestation of God's love to us in Christ, which awakens an answering love in us."[18] Rashdall proceeds in a similar fashion. First he sets forth his own translation of the last two sentences of the quoted passage, and then he adds his translation of the somewhat different version of its first two sentences to be found in the charges against Abelard drawn up and transmitted to the pope by Bernard of Clairvaux. These texts constitute the bulk of Rashdall's evidence for the following strong claims about Abelard's views on the nature of Christ's atoning work:

> In Abelard not only the ransom theory but any kind of substitutionary or expiatory atonement is explicitly denied. We get rid altogether of the notion of a mysterious guilt which, by an abstract necessity of things, required to be extinguished by death or suffering, no matter whose, and of all pseudo-Platonic hypostatizing of the universal "Humanity." The efficacy of Christ's death is now quite definitely and explicitly explained by its subjective influence upon the mind of the sinner. The voluntary death of the innocent Son of God on man's behalf moves the sinner to gratitude and

answering love – and so to consciousness of sin, repentance, amendment.[19]

And, needless to say, Rashdall wholeheartedly approves of all these things he attributes to Abelard.

Is this an adequate summary of Abelard's account of the Atonement? We should, I think, approach this summary with some suspicion precisely because almost all the evidence for it comes from a single passage, albeit an eloquent one, that covers slightly less than one page out of a total of three hundred pages of text in the Corpus Christianorum edition of Abelard's *Commentary on Paul's Epistle to the Romans*. And even in and around this famous passage there are small clues indicating that Abelard's view is more complicated than Franks or Rashdall takes it to be. First of all, in the final sentence of the famous passage Abelard does say that our redemption through Christ's suffering frees us from slavery to sin, though, to be sure, he does not at this point offer an explanation of how it does so. Second, a few lines after the close of the famous passage Abelard indicates that the explanation of the manner of our redemption it proposes is incomplete but reserves further elaboration, for another treatise.[20]

Moreover, the translations of the famous passage provided by Franks and Rashdall give it an exemplarist flavor that is absent from the Latin original. In his "Was Abelard an Exemplarist?" which challenges Rashdall's interpretation of Abelard, Robert O. P. Taylor points to several instances of this in Rashdall. To my mind, the most striking among them is this one. The Latin that begins the final sentence of the famous passage goes as follows: "Redemptio itaque nostra est illa summa in nobis per passionem Christi dilectio." "But this," Taylor insists, "surely, means, 'Our redemption, therefore, is that supreme love which is *in us* through the Passion of Christ'."[21] The translation I quoted does convey the idea that the *dilectio* which is our redemption is something in us. But, as Taylor observes, this is not the idea conveyed by Rashdall's translation. Rashdall renders the Latin thus: "Our redemption, therefore, is that supreme love of Christ *shown to us* by His passion" (my emphasis).[22] Franks performs a similar transformation. His rendition of the Latin is this: "And so our redemption is that supreme love *manifested in our case* by the passion of Christ" (my emphasis).[23] In short, both Rashdall and Franks take Abelard to be saying that our redemption is the love Christ shows or manifests by suffering for our sakes. From this thought it is only a small step to the conclusion that Christ's love is no more than an example displayed for our inspection. But this is not the only possible, or even the most natural, reading of the text. And if we take seriously the idea that our redemption is a love in us through Christ's Passion, then it remains to be seen how the Passion of Christ actually works to implant or produce this love in us.

So it is not clear that the famous passage actually teaches that Christ's love is merely an example, "something displayed in the hope that we may see that it is so admirable that we ought to emulate or adopt it."[24] And even if by itself it will bear an exemplarist interpretation, it does not follow that exemplarism is the only motif at work in Abelard's thinking about the Atonement. As we shall next see, it is not.

Penal substitution in Abelard

A survey of medieval accounts of the Atonement, called "The Concept of Satisfaction in Medieval Redemption Theory", argues that the key elements of Scholastic thought on this topic are satisfaction for the dishonor of sin, substitution for the punishment imposed, and the restoration of humankind. Its author, J. Patout Burns, holds that "the first is a contribution of Anselm; the second derives from Abelard; the third becomes central only in the thirteenth century."[25] It would be easy to quarrel with the last of these conclusions on the basis of the famous passage previously discussed. After all, Abelard there tells us that our redemption not only frees us from slavery to sin but also wins for us the true liberty of sons of God, so that we do all things out of love rather than fear, and the latter effect of our redemption certainly seems to involve the restoration of fallen humans to a state of liberty God meant them to occupy. But more interesting in the present context is the claim that Abelard is the source of the idea that Christ substitutes for the rest of us in bearing the punishment due to us for our sins and thereby makes it possible for us to avoid undergoing such punishment. There is no hint of this in the famous passage on which those who take Abelard to be nothing but an exemplarist build their case.

Nevertheless, Abelard clearly does endorse the notion of penal substitution in the *Commentary on Paul's Epistle to the Romans*. In discussing Romans 4:25, where it is said that Christ was handed over to death for our sins, Abelard says this:

> In two ways he is said to have died for our faults: first, because the faults for which he died were ours, and we committed the sins for which he bore the punishment; secondly, that by dying he might remove our sins, that is, the punishment of our sins, introducing us into paradise at the price of his own death, and might, by the display of grace such that he himself said

"Greater love no man hath," draw our minds away from the
will to sin and enkindle in them the highest love of himself.[26]

So Abelard is committed to holding that Christ removes our sins in the
sense that he, who is innocent and so deserves no punishment, takes our
place and endures the punishment we deserve. It may be that this view
is illogical because it is logically impossible for one person to pay a debt
of punishment for sin another person owes. And it may be that it is
immoral in the sense that it is morally repugnant to imagine that the
suffering of an innocent person could remove the debt of punishment of
a guilty person.[27] But, if so, Rashdall is mistaken in claiming that there is
nothing illogical or immoral about Abelard's account of the Atonement,
for this view is part of that account.

Of course, as L. W. Grensted remarks in commenting on this passage,
Abelard's heart is really in the thought with which it concludes, the idea
that the grace displayed in Christ's dying may work an interior transformation in us by which our minds are drawn away from sin and toward
Christ in love.[28] So there is some grist for the exemplarist's mill even
here but not for the strong thesis that the only benefit conferred on sinful humans by Christ's Passion is an inspiring example of love. Scholars
such as Rashdall and Franks are, of course, aware that Abelard says
things which do not comport well with taking him to be a pure exemplarist, but they typically dismiss such embarrassing remarks. Thus, in
a note, Rashdall concedes that "it must be admitted that Abelard sometimes shows a tendency to relapse into views hardly consistent with this
position."[29] And when Franks encounters evidence that undermines his
contention that Abelard reduces the whole process of redemption to a
single principle, his reply is that "if Abelard does in other places present
views along different lines, and so himself controvert his own tendency
to a simplification of doctrine, this need not prevent our recognizing that
this tendency exists."[30] Grensted provides a more balanced assessment.
After citing the last sentence of the famous passage quoted and another
passage which expresses a similar thought, he concludes that they represent "an attempt to set the ethical, manward, aspect of Atonement in a
primary and not in a secondary place."[31] It does seem fair to say that the
dominant motif in Abelard's account is the power of love in us through
Christ's Passion to transform us both by freeing us from slavery to sin
and, more important, by winning for us the positive Christian liberty to
do all things out of love for God. Godward aspects of Atonement, such
as paying a debt of punishment owed to divine retributive justice, are
relegated to distinctly subordinate roles in Abelard's account. But they
are not altogether absent, and Rashdall is simply mistaken in claiming

that any kind of substitutionary or expiatory atonement is explicitly denied. On the contrary, as we have seen, substitutionary atonement is explicitly affirmed.

In terms of the taxonomy I have proposed, it thus seems best to classify Abelard as a hierarchical pluralist. Like Aquinas, he offers an account of the Atonement that has a dominant motif to which others are subordinated. But unlike Aquinas, for whom satisfaction for sin is the principal theme, Abelard proposes to make a love that transforms motive and character in redeemed humans the heart of the matter. Abelard's views were fiercely denounced by Bernard of Clairvaux and condemned by the church of his day. So it will be worth our while to look into the question of whether they, or modifications of them that are recognizably Abelardian in spirit, are theologically and philosophically defensible. It is to this question that I now turn my attention.

Is it ill-disguised pelagianism?

Rashdall is far from being the first to take Abelard's views on the Atonement to be exemplarist. Although he did not put it in these terms, Bernard clearly interpreted Abelard in this way. But while exemplarism pleases Rashdall, it horrified Bernard. In a passage of considerable rhetorical power in his letter to Innocent II, Bernard thunders against Abelard's account of the Atonement:. "He holds and argues that it must be reduced just to this, that by His life and teaching He handed down to men a pattern of life, that by His suffering and death He set up a standard of love. Did He then teach righteousness and not bestow it; reveal love and not infuse it; and so return to his own place?"[32] And later on in the letter he remarks with what strikes me as a touch of sarcasm: "If Christ's benefit consisted only in the display of good works, it remains but to say that Adam only harmed us by the display of sin."[33] But, though Bernard was an ecclesiastical administrator and politician of genius, and a formidable mystical theologian, he was far from being a fair-minded philosophical critic. As Grensted acknowledges, Abelard's "extremest statements were taken as representative of his whole position and were even exaggerated by Bernard's rhetoric."[34] Grensted maintains, however, that Bernard had put his finger on a real weakness in Abelard's position: a Pelagian tendency, which, if pressed to its logical conclusion, must belittle both the sin of humans and the grace of God and fail to appreciate both the solidarity of humankind in sin and the solidarity of the redeemed in Christ. If it were true that the sin of our first parents is no more than a bad example their descendants can freely imitate or shun, then it would seem that we no more need redemption from a fallen state of bondage to sin than they did in their prelapsarian state. By the same token, if it were true that Christ confers on us no more than the benefit of a good example we can freely follow or reject, then it would seem that whether we are justified in the sight of God is something wholly within our power to determine. So the Pelagian danger Bernard fears is that Abelard has rendered Christ's atoning work unnecessary for our salvation. On such a view, we are in principle capable of earning worthiness of salvation on our own.

Yet according to Richard Weingart, whose book on Abelard's soteriology is the most detailed recent treatment of the topic in English, it cannot be repeated too often that Abelard is no Pelagian. "Although he denies that Christ's work is one of appeasement or substitution," Weingart contends, "he never moves to the other extreme of presenting the atonement as nothing more than an inducement for man to effect his own salvation."[35] And there are texts in the *Commentary on Paul's Epistle to the Romans* in which Abelard explicitly denies that it is within the unaided power of mere humans in the postlapsarian state to make themselves worthy of salvation. In commenting on Romans 7:25, Abelard affirms that our redemption is "thanks to God, that is, not the law, not our own powers, not any merits, but a divine benefit of grace conferred on us through Jesus, that is, the savior of the world."[36] Nor does the famous passage I have quoted at length provide unequivocal evidential support for Bernard's charge that Abelard is committed to Pelagianism. Consider, for example, its third sentence. The Latin goes as follows: "Iustior quoque; id est amplius Deum diligens, quisque fit post passionem Christi quam ante, quia amplius in amorem accendit completum beneficium quam speratum." Those words can, I suppose, be read in a way that speaks, as the translation I quoted does, of everyone becoming more righteous after the Passion than before because a realized gift inspires greater love than one merely hoped for. But Rashdall himself offers a different translation. It goes as follows: "Every man is also *made* juster, that is to say, *becomes* more loving to the Lord after the passion of Christ than he was before, because a benefit actually received kindles the soul into love more than one merely hoped for" (my emphasis).[37] Noticing that there is some oddity in the fact that Rashdall uses both "made" and "becomes" to translate the word *fit,* once used and not repeated, Taylor asks "Why not translate *fit* as 'is made' in both cases?"[38] If we adopt the suggestion implicit in this rhetorical question, the result is this: 'Every man *is* also *made* juster, that is to say, *is made* more loving to the Lord after the passion of Christ than he was before, because a benefit actually received kindles the soul into love more than one merely hoped for.' And this translation, which speaks of everyone being made more loving because a received benefit kindles love more than one merely hoped for, resists being interpreted in a way that supports attributing Pelagian tendencies to Abelard. Hence, even if it is granted that the famous passage considered in isolation permits a reading that supports the charge of Pelagian tendencies, it does not follow and it is far from clear that it is best read in this way once contextual factors are brought to bear on interpreting it. And surely a factor that should be given appreciable weight is Abelard's explicit claim that we are saved, not by our own powers, but through a benefit of grace conferred on us through Christ.

As I see it, then, the import of the famous passage is to some extent indeterminate. By itself it does not answer such questions as these: By what mechanism does the love that is in us through Christ's Passion get implanted in us? How precisely are we made or do we become more just or righteous after Christ's Passion? And what exactly is the process by which the benefit of Christ's Passion operates to inspire or kindle love in us? Because Abelard's thought does not return clear answers to these questions, interpreters can reasonably disagree about whether it commits Abelard to Pelagian views or tends to do so. I doubt that further exegetical work on this passage would yield a conclusive resolution of those disagreements. But because the principle of charity requires us not to attribute inconsistency to a thinker of Abelard's stature if we can help doing so, I think it is best to read it in a way that harmonizes with Abelard's explicit denials of Pelagian views in other passages and so to interpret it in a manner that does not clinch the case for Bernard's charge that Abelard is a Pelagian. If, as Grensted says, Bernard has identified a real weakness in Abelard's position, it is the relatively harmless flaw of having an incomplete account of how the love manifested in Christ's Passion works upon the human heart and hence of not having said enough to preclude purely exemplarist or Pelagian readings. But it may well be, as Taylor claims, that Abelard considers love to be "a spiritual force exerted by the lover on the beloved, and, in a responsive heart, setting up a reflex, which tends to become permanent."[39] Such a conception of the transformative power of love could, perhaps, partly explain the efficacy of Christ's Passion. If it is Abelard's, however, he has not succeeded in making it clear either to friends such as Rashdall or to foes such as Bernard.

We may conclude that Abelard's account of the Atonement is neither as attractive as admirers such as Rashdall contend nor as unattractive as critics such as Bernard maintain. When the famous passage is interpreted in the light of its context, it offers no firm support for the conclusion that Abelard is either an exemplarist or a Pelagian, though it does suggest tendencies in these directions. Yet it did introduce a fresh motif into medieval discussion of the effects of Christ's life, suffering, and death, and it continues to speak with considerable power to some Christians in our own times. So it seems to me worthwhile to develop that motif with an eye to seeing whether it could play an important role in an account of the Atonement that would appeal to contemporary Christians. I devote the final section of this essay to a somewhat speculative sketch of one way in which such development might proceed.

Toward a constructive Abelardian contribution

My suggestion is that what Abelard has to contribute to our thinking about the Atonement is the idea that divine love, made manifest throughout the life of Christ but especially in his suffering and dying, has the power to transform human sinners, if they cooperate, in ways that fit them for everlasting life in intimate union with God. But before I begin to elaborate on this suggestion, I need to issue two disclaimers in order to head off potential misunderstandings. First, I am not henceforth claiming that Abelard actually held the views I am going to recommend. Although they are inspired by the famous passage and, I hope, faithful to its spirit, my aim in setting them forth is to make a contribution to philosophical theology rather than to textual exegesis. Second, I do not claim that the motif of transformative divine love is the only idea that can help us appreciate the Atonement. I am attracted to the view that the Atonement is a mystery not to be fully fathomed by human understanding but best grasped in terms of a plurality of metaphors and models: So I am willing to entertain the hypothesis, shared by Anselm and Aquinas, that it functions in some manner to persuade God to remit a debt of punishment human sinners owe but cannot by themselves pay.[40] But I do not think that such legalistic considerations are the heart of the matter or should be allowed to dominate our understanding of the Atonement. Abelard strikes me as being on target in emphasizing the interior transformations wrought in sinners by God's love for them, for I am of the opinion that Christian reflection on Christ's atoning work should be rooted in a lively sense of what God has graciously done in us. And this leads me to favor a conception of the Atonement like Abelard's in which other motifs are subordinated to the theme of the transformative power of divine love.

In order to make it quite clear, as Abelard in the famous passage does not succeed in doing, that this power exceeds any merely human example's power to inspire, it is important to insist that the relation between the operations of divine love and those of merely human love is not identity but analogy of some sort. To be sure, ordinary human love has some transformative power, and that is why the analogy shows promise of being useful in soteriology. Contemplation of the lives and deeds of saintly people such as Francis of Assisi and Mother Teresa can contribute causally to making us better persons. But if we assume that examples of this kind operate in influencing beliefs and desires wholly within a natural order of causes, we should then deny that this is the only way in which divine love can operate in influencing us in order to avoid the reductionistic implications of exemplarism. We should instead affirm that divine love also operates outside the natural order, within what theologians call the order of grace, to produce changes in us. On such a view, the love of God for us exhibited in the life of Christ is a good example to imitate, but it is not merely an example. Above and beyond its exemplary value, there is in it a surplus of mysterious causal efficacy that no merely human love possesses. And the operation of divine love in that supernatural mode is a causally necessary condition of there being implanted or kindled in us the kind of responsive love of God that, as Abelard supposes, enables us to do all things out of love and so to conquer the motives that would otherwise keep us enslaved to sin.

By insisting that this supernatural operation of divine love in us is causally necessary for fallen humans to act out of love in a way that grounds God's gracious bestowal of righteousness on them, an Abelardian account of the Atonement can avoid the danger of falling into Pelagianism. What is to be shunned is a view according to which fallen humans have it within their power to perform works that will justify them in the eyes of God apart from a divine assistance that goes beyond God's ordinary conserving activity. So if being a person for whom it is in character to act out of love is a large part of what freedom from bondage to sin involves, we should not suppose that becoming such a person is an accomplishment within the reach of the unaided powers of postlapsarian humans. A vexed theological question is whether this operation of divine love is a causally sufficient condition for transforming the personalities of fallen humans in such a way that they habitually act from responsive love. No doubt divine love could, if God so chose, work such a transformation because it is powerful enough to overwhelm the resistance of a stubbornly recalcitrant human will. But I am inclined to think that God does not in fact act in this way; instead he refrains from making the pressure of his love irresistible in order to leave room for a free human response to it. So I would say that the causal efficacy of supernatural divine love, though not by itself sufficient to work such transformations in the fallen human character, is a non-redundant part of any condition that is sufficient for this purpose. Thus we may come close to agreeing with Bernard by saying that God makes an essential causal contribution to the presence of love in us, and we may say that God infuses love into us and bestows righteousness upon us, provided it is understood that this is not a deterministic mechanical process and that we are free to reject these gracious divine gifts.

Finally, lest the merely exemplary power of love exhibited throughout the life of Christ and particularly in his suffering unto death be decoupled from the supernatural divine love that is necessary to transform the fallen human personality, an Abelardian account of the Atonement must insist that this supernatural transformative love somehow operates through Christ's life and especially through the Passion. I take it that this is a contingent fact; God could have used some other channel to make his transforming love available to a humanity ravaged by sin. But perhaps, as Aquinas claims, it was peculiarly fitting, for reasons we humans are unlikely to be able to comprehend fully in this life at least, that such love come to us through Christ's suffering rather than in some other way.[41] If so, there is an answer to Abelard's question about why Christ endured insults, scourgings and spittings, and finally a bitter and disgraceful death in terms of the appropriateness of this mode of access to divine love for members of our species, even if we do not know precisely what that answer is. Is Christ the exclusive channel through which transformative divine love comes to fallen humanity? If so, this is another contingent fact about how divine providence works. However, there is no good reason to deny that providence has arranged things in this fashion provided no human who could benefit from such love is excluded from access to it. It would, I think, be unfair and so unworthy of a perfectly good being to limit access to the benefits of transforming love to the members of a particular empirical church in a world like ours in which some who might respond positively to that love have, through no fault of their own, no chance to be members of the church in question. For all I know, however, God has made his transformative love available to all fallen humans, Christian and non-Christian alike, through Christ, though of course non-Christians who benefit from it will not, at least in this life, have true beliefs about the channel through which this gift comes to them if this is the case.

It might be objected that it is empirically implausible to suppose that the life and death of Jesus of Nazareth have had such an influence on subsequent history. If he had never lived, the human condition would now not be much different from what it actually is because other inspiring examples of love would have had approximately the same good effects. My response to this objection is skeptical. According to another scenario, the human condition would now be very much worse than it actually is if Jesus had never lived because fallen human nature would have been progressively enfeebled by an increasing burden of sin. I doubt that empirical information about the actual course of history by itself supports the counterfactual that underlies the objection rather than the rival counterfactual that I have set forth. Such empirical information together with certain background assumptions does lend differential support to the objection's counterfactual, but that information together with traditional Christian beliefs about original sin lends differential support to my rival counterfactual. In short, empirical information about the actual course of history alone does not settle the controversy about how much of a difference the life and death of Jesus have made to human history because such information by itself is insufficient to render plausible any particular view of what the subsequent course of history would have been like in the absence of those events.

It is no accident that the Abelardian account of transformative divine love I have been sketching bears some resemblance to accounts of the operation of grace formulated by other medieval theologians.

But many contemporary Christians do not find these highly metaphysical theories of grace credible. Speaking of Aquinas, Eleonore Stump admits that, because his account of grace is complex and problematic, the part of his theory of the Atonement that depends on it "may leave us cold and uncomprehending."[42] Part of the difficulty, as she diagnoses it, is that "he explains in medieval metaphysical terms what we would be more inclined to explain in psychological terms."[43] It seems to me that one of the advantages of the Abelardian emphasis on love in giving an account of the Atonement is precisely that it provides a model of psychological transformation rooted in ordinary human experience that can be analogically extended to divine action. Many of us have actually experienced the power of human love to influence our characters for the better by provoking a responsive love, and some of us have experienced the power of meditation on the example of love displayed in the life and death of Christ to contribute to bringing about such psychological improvements in us. So it is a genuine aid to understanding to think of the way in which God acts on us to help make us better in terms of a divine love that has among its effects making a contribution to implanting a loving disposition in us. Indeed, it does not appear to me farfetched to claim that we can in certain circumstances experience the pressure of this divine love on us in a manner analogous to the way in which we experience the force of human love. And this analogy may help us grasp the point Karl Rahner is getting at in maintaining that God's grace is experiential.[44]

We would do well not to underestimate the depth of the human longing to be able to love God. As a televangelist character puts it in a novel by Sarah Shankman, "*Of course* you think I'm a shuck. But that's because you don't come from what I come from. Don't know what I know. Don't know the mingy tight pinched little lives people like me grow up with. Don't know how much we'd love to *love* the Lord."[45] An Abelardian account of the Atonement is directly responsive to this longing because it focuses our attention on the way in which divine love contributes to kindling in us love to him who has shown us such grace that no greater can be found and thereby to making us better persons. And even traditional Christians who cannot accept Rashdall's attempt to reduce the role of God in soteriology to providing in Christ an example of love can endorse his claim that Abelard "sees that God can only be supposed to forgive by making the sinner better."[46] Or, if that rather casual remark seems not to leave enough room for free human response to the gracious initiative of divine love, the insight he attributes to Abelard might be more precisely formulated by saying that God can only be supposed to reconcile sinners to himself by contributing in an important way to making them better persons. Whatever we may think about other motifs such as penal substitution that show up in Abelard's comments on Paul's Epistle to the Romans and arguably have some role to play in a complete account of the Atonement, it is, I believe, safe to agree with Rashdall that there is nothing unintelligible, arbitrary, illogical, or immoral about the thought that the main thing the Atonement does to benefit us is to give us access to a divine love on whose power we must rely in order to become better persons.

My conclusion is that an account along the Abelardian lines I have been laying out shows a lot of promise of enriching our understanding of the mystery of the Atonement. Part of that promise stems from the fact that such an account's emphasis on the inward transformation of sinners would be in tune with the modern inclination to explain the Atonement largely in terms of its psychological, effects. Another part derives from the fact that such an account would, by virtue of highlighting the efficacy of the Atonement in improving the characters of sinners, be better balanced than satisfaction-theoretic rivals, such as those proposed by Anselm and Aquinas, which are dominated by legalistic concerns with paying debts of honor or punishment. It is not merely that, as Gunton suggests, we should not deny the subjective implications or psychological consequences of the Atonement. I would urge that we must in an Abelardian spirit acknowledge that the transformation of the sinful human subject wrought in large part by divine love channeled to us through Christ is the most important purpose the Atonement serves. Abelard's legacy is that this motif should dominate our thinking when we reflect on the benefits graciously made available to us through Christ's life, suffering, and death.[47]

Notes

1. Hastings Rashdall, *The Idea of Atonement in Christian Theology* (London: Macmillan, 1919), p. 360.

2. For a brief discussion of Rashdall's life and works, see A. K. Stout, "Hastings Rashdall," in *The Encyclopedia of Philosophy,* ed. Paul Edwards (New York: Macmillan, 1967), 7:68.

3. Colin E. Gunton, *The Actuality of Atonement* (Grand Rapids, Mich.: William B. Eerdmans, 1989).

4. Richard Swinburne, *Responsibility and Atonement* (Oxford: Clarendon Press, 1989), p. 162. A detailed discussion of Swinburne's impressive positive account of atonement is outside the scope of this essay.

5. Thomas Aquinas, *Summa theologiae* III, Q. 1, A. 2; hereafter *ST.*

6. Gunton, *The Actuality of Atonement,* p. 157.

7. Anselm of Canterbury, *Cur Deus homo* II, 6.

8. Gunton, *The Actuality of Atonement.* These motifs are elaborated in chaps. 3, 4 and 5.

9. Aquinas, *ST* III, QQ. 46–49. I argue for this interpretation of Aquinas in Philip L. Quinn, "Aquinas on Atonement", in *Trinity, Incarnation, and Atonement,* ed. Ronald J. Feenstra and Cornelius Plantinga, Jr. (Notre Dame, Ind: University of Notre Dame Press, 1989), pp. 153–77. Further support for this view is to be found in Romanus Cesario, *Christian Satisfaction in Aquinas* (Washington, D.C.: University Press of America, 1982). A rather different interpretation is set forth in Eleonore Stump, "Atonement according to Aquinas", in *Philosophy and the Christian Faith,* ed. Thomas V. Morris (Notre Dame, Ind.: University of Notre Dame Press, 1988), pp. 61–91.

10. Peter Abelard, *Commentaria in epistolam Pauli ad Romanos.* The Latin text is to be found in *Petri Abaelardi opera theologica,* Corpus Christianorum, Continuatio Mediaevalis 11, ed. E. M. Buytaert (Turnhout: Brepols, 1969). An English translation of selected passages is to be found in *A Scholastic Miscellany: Anselm to Ockham,* The Library of Christian Classics 10, ed. Eugene R. Fairweather (Philadelphia: Westminster, 1956). For the sake of convenience, I quote this translation whenever possible, but I also refer to the Latin text by page and lines. Thus the quoted material to which this note is appended is at Buytaert, p. 114, lines 149–51, and Fairweather, p. 281.

11. Buytaert, p. 115, lines 171–73; Fairweather, p. 281.

12. Anselm, *Cur Deus homo* I, 7.

13. Buytaert, p. 115, lines 161–63; Fairweather, p. 281.

14. Buytaert, p. 116, lines 198–200; Fairweather, p. 282.

15. Buytaert, p. 116, lines 205–9; Fairweather, p. 282.

16. Buytaert, p. 117, lines 234–38; Fairweather, p. 283.

17. Buytaert, pp. 117–18, lines 242–62; Fairweather, pp. 283–84.

18. Robert S. Franks, *The Work of Christ* (London: Thomas Nelson, 1962), p. 146.

19. Rashdall, *The Idea of Atonement,* p. 358.

20. Buytaert, p. 118, lines 271–74; Fairweather, p. 284.

21. Robert O. P. Taylor, "Was Abelard an Exemplarist?" *Theology* 31 (1935): 212.

22. Rashdall, *The Actuality of Atonement,* p. 358.

23. Franks, *The Work of Christ,* p. 145.

24. Taylor, "Was Abelard an Exemplarist?" p. 213.

25. J. Patout Burns, S.J., "The Concept of Satisfaction in Medieval Redemption Theory", *Theological Studies* 36 (1975): 304.
26. Buytaert, p. 153, lines 992–1000. (my translation).
27. I have pressed this objection against Anselm's account of the Atonement in Philip L. Quinn, "Christian Atonement and Kantian Justification," *Faith and Philosophy*, 3 (1986): 440–62 and against Aquinas's account in Quinn, "Aquinas on Atonement".
28. L. W. Grensted, *A Short History of the Doctrine of the Atonement* (Manchester: Manchester University Press, 1962), p. 109.
29. Rashdall, *The Idea of Atonement*, p. 363.
30. Franks, *The Work of Christ*, p. 148.
31. Grensted, *A Short History*, p. 105.
32. Bernard of Clairvaux, *Tractatus ad Innocentium II Pontificem contra quaedam capitula errorum Abaelardi*, quoted in Grensted, *A Short History*, p. 106.
33. Ibid.
34. Grensted, *A Short History*, p. 107.
35. Richard E. Weingart, *The Logic of Divine Love: A Critical Analysis of the Soteriology of Peter Abailard* (Oxford: Clarendon Press, 1970), p. 150.
36. Buytaert, p. 210, lines 779–81 (my translation).
37. Rashdall, *The Idea of Atonement*, p. 358.
38. Taylor, "Was Abelard an Exemplarist?" p. 211.
39. Ibid., p. 212.
40. In Quinn, "Aquinas on Atonement", I try to illustrate by means of a fable how such persuasion might work (pp. 174–75).
41. Aquinas, *ST* III, Q. 1, A. 2.
42. Stump, "Atonement according to Aquinas", p. 77.
43. Ibid.
44. Karl Rahner, *Fundamentals of Christian Faith*, trans. W. V. Dych (New York: Crossroads, 1982), p. 55.
45. Sarah Shankman, *Now Let's Talk of Graves* (New York: Pocket Books, 1990), p. 139.
46. Rashdall, *The Idea of Atonement*, p. 359.
47. An earlier version of this essay was presented at the Claremont Graduate School's Twelfth Annual Philosophy of Religion Conference. I am grateful to Richard Rice, my commentator on that occasion, and to Marcia Colish, Alfred J. Freddoso, John Hick, James Wm. McClendon, and Eleonore Stump for helpful advice and criticism.

CHAPTER 18

THE CHRISTIAN SCHEME OF SALVATION[1]

Richard Swinburne

Christianity offers to us salvation, salvation from the guilt of our past sin, salvation from our proneness to present sin, salvation for the enjoyment of the Beatific Vision of God in the company of the blessed in Heaven. This salvation was made available to humans by the life, death, and resurrection of Jesus Christ. This paper is concerned to analyze how this life, death, and resurrection made available salvation from the guilt of past sin. In so doing I shall be spelling out a theory of Atonement which I believe to be in essence very similar to the theory expounded by St. Thomas Aquinas and also to the view of Christ's death as a sacrifice developed in the Epistle to the Hebrews. I shall, however, start from scratch and try to avoid using their technical terms without definition and to avoid using their implicit assumptions without bringing them out into the open.

I

Before anyone can understand how Christianity provides salvation from the past, he needs to understand three crucial concepts – guilt, atonement, and forgiveness. These concepts are crucial for understanding relations between one person and another, as well as relations between humans and God; and it is tragic that so much modern moral philosophy has neglected their study. I shall need to devote the larger part of this paper to analyzing these concepts before applying my analysis to the Christian message.

Among good acts, some are obligatory – duties owed to particular individuals, such as keeping promises or educating one's children. Good acts which go beyond obligation are supererogatory good acts. Giving one's life to save the life of a comrade is a plausible example of such an act. The scope for goodness is unending; however many good acts one has done, there is always another one waiting to be done. But it is a matter of dispute how wide is the range of obligation. Whether our obligations are a narrow set which can easily be fulfilled or a large set (including duties to help the poor in distant lands), which leaves little room for supererogatory goodness, is disputed.[2] Wherever the line is drawn, guilt belongs to a person only in respect of his failure to perform his obligations, or his doing what it is obligatory not to do, i.e., something wrong. (I shall often omit this second negative clause in future discussions of guilt, for the sake of simplicity of exposition. It will be obvious how it is to be inserted.)

The guilt is objective guilt if the agent has failed to fulfill a moral obligation (or done an act obligatory not to do) whether or not he realized that this was his moral obligation or that he was failing in respect of it. I am objectively guilty for failing to educate my children properly even if I believe that I have no duty to educate my children or if I believe that sending them to a certain school, which unknown to me is totally incompetent, is educating my children properly. The guilt is subjective if the agent has failed to fulfill what he believes to be his moral obligation (or done what he believed to be obligatory not to do), whether or not there was such an obligation–so long as the agent was free to do or refrain from doing the action, in whatever sense of "free" makes him morally responsible for that action.

But the assertion that someone is guilty is not just an assertion about the past; it makes two further claims about the present. The first is that the guilty one owes something to the one whom he has wronged, his victim. If I fail in an obligation, I do not just do a wrong, I do a wrong to someone. If I promise you that I will give a lecture and then do not turn up, or if I kick you in a fit of anger, I have done a wrong to you. By hurting you, I put myself in a moral situation somewhat like the legal situation of a debtor who has failed to repay money borrowed from a bank. But the kind of debt owed by failure to perform one's moral obligations is often no mere financial one. Insofar as the victim is a person, that person is known personally to the wrongdoer, the failure is a failure of personal trust, and above all if there is ill-will (deliberate malice or negligence) on the part of the wrong-doer, then there is a totally new kind of harm involved–the harm done to personal relations by a wrong attitude by the wrongdoer. Yet there is still more to moral guilt than past failure and present debt. Through his past failure the guilty one has acquired a negative status, somewhat like being unclean,[3] which needs to be removed. By making a promise a person puts himself under certain obligations, but his status is in no way bad or unclean in consequence. There is more in the present to being guilty than incurring new obligations.

There is something wrong with a person even if his guilt is purely objective. If I unintentionally break your best vase or light the fire with the manuscript of your book, I acquire the status of a wrongdoer even if my actions were done in total ignorance of their nature or consequence (and even if I had taken all reasonable precautions to ensure that they had no such nature or consequence). It is, I suggest, a virtually unanimous moral intuition that this is so, that in such circumstances I acquire a status which needs purging by reparation if possible, and certainly by apology. This is because in interacting with my fellows, I undertake responsibility for seeing that certain things are done and certain things are not done (e.g., in holding your vase, I take responsibility for its not getting broken); and bad luck (my actions having bad consequences, despite my taking reasonable precautions) no more removes the responsibility, than it excuses you from repaying a man a sum of money which you have borrowed from him, even if you have that same amount stolen.

But of course the guilt is of a different kind if I knowingly fail in my obligations toward you – if my guilt is subjective as well as objective. Here again I suggest that a virtually unanimous moral intuition suggests that far more is wrong, and far more needs doing to put it right. If I deliberately break your best vase, it is no good my saying "I really am very sorry." I have got to make several speeches distancing myself from the act and I have got to make reparation very quickly. I have wronged you so much the worse that my guilt is of a qualitatively different kind. The Book of Numbers differentiated between "sins committed unknowingly" and "sins committed with a high hand" (i.e., knowingly), declaring various kinds of ritual reparation suitable for the former and some very serious punishment for the latter.[4] The reason for the vast difference is that when I deliberately break your best vase, I have failed not merely in my outward obligations toward you, but also in that attitude of purpose toward you which I owe you, the attitude of seeking no harm for you.

What if there is no objective guilt, but I fail in what I believe to be my obligations toward you? I try to break your best vase, but by accident break my own instead. Have I wronged you? My argument suggests that the answer is yes; and we can see that the answer is correct from considering more serious cases. I try to kill you but the shot misfires. From the obvious need for reparation of rather more than a short apology, we can see that wrong has been done and guilt acquired. Both subjective and objective guilt are stains on a soul requiring expunging; but subjective guilt is embedded in the soul while objective guilt lies on the surface.

Such, I have suggested by example, is the common understanding of moral guilt, the status acquired by one who fails in his obligations. When modern moral philosophers neglect this concept, they ignore the fact that letting someone down hurts, and matters. We cannot undo the past, but we can remove its consequences—How is the taint of guilt to be removed? For perfect removal, the guilty one must make atonement for his wrong act, and the wronged person must forgive him.

Atonement involves four components: reparation, repentance, apology, and what, for want of a better word, I shall call penance (though not all of these are always required). They are all contributions to removing as much of the consequences of the past act as logically can be removed. The consequences are, first, the harm caused by and distinguishable from the act of causing it and second, the purposive attitude of the guilty one toward the wronged one manifested in the causing of harm. By removing the former harm the guilty one makes reparation. Sometimes he can literally restore the status quo. If I steal your watch and have not sold it, I can return it to you. Sometimes I can only make things rather similar to the way they were, so that the victim is almost equally happy with the new state. I can compensate him adequately, that is. If I steal and sell your watch, I can buy you another one. If I smash up your car, I can pay for the repairs. Sometimes, alas, full compensation is not possible. If I run you over with my car, and paralyze you for life, nothing I can do can compensate you fully for that. Full reparation is not possible. But some things which I can do can compensate you in part. I can pay for wheelchairs and machines to lift you out of bed in the morning.

But the consequences of the act are not merely such harm, but the fact that by doing the act the guilty one has made himself the one who has harmed the wronged one. He cannot change that past fact, but he can distance himself from it by privately and publicly disowning the act. The wronged one has been hurt, and so it is to the wronged one that the disowning is owed and must be shown. But the disowning which is owed must be sincere and so must reflect the attitude that the guilty one now has and naturally expresses to himself. The natural expression to oneself is repentance, the public expression to the wronged one is apology. Repentance involves, first, acknowledgment by the guilty one that he did the act and that it was a wrong act to do. Thereby the guilty one distances the act from his present ideals. Repentance also involves a resolve to amend–you cannot repent of a past act if you intend to do a similar act at the next available opportunity. Preachers often draw our attention to the etymology of the Greek word translated "repent," $M\varepsilon\tau\alpha\nu o\varepsilon\hat{\iota}\nu$, which means literally to "change one's mind." By resolving to amend, the guilty one distances the past act from his present purposes. In acknowledging his initiation of the past act, but distancing it both from his present ideals and from his present purposes, the guilty one makes the sharp contrast between the attitude behind the past act and his present attitude. He disowns the past act publicly by expressing to the wronged one the repentance, which he expresses to himself privately, assuring the wronged one that he recognizes its wrongness and that he purposes to amend. There are conventional ways of doing this; one may say "I'm very sorry" or "I really do apologize." An agent cannot alter the fact that he did the past act, but what he can do is make the present "he" in his attitude as different as possible from the past "he" who did the act; that is the most he can do toward undoing the act.

The above account of repentance and apology applies insofar as there is an element of subjectivity in the guilt, insofar as deliberately or through negligence the guilty one has some moral responsibility for doing the harm. If the guilt is purely objective, arising from the performance of an unintentional act in which there was not even the slightest negligence involved (e.g., dropping your best vase when startled by a loud noise), an apology of a sort is still owed, for the reason that in interacting with others we accept responsibility in advance for not causing them certain kinds of harm. If unintentionally we are the agents of harm, we must distance ourselves from that agency. But insofar as we never intended it in the first place (and had every intention of preventing it), what we must do is to emphasize that our present benevolent ideals and purposes were our past ones also. An apology (but one which brings out the unintentional character of the action) is needed; but it needs behind it no repentance in the form of change of mind, only sincerity in the reemphasis of ideals and purposes.

Apology can often be very difficult. It costs many of us a lot to say "I'm sorry." But sometimes, for some people, apology can be very easy. We all know the smooth, amiable people who say "I'm frightfully sorry" with such a charming smile that our reaction is "Yes, but do you really mean it?" And what else can show "meaning it," what else can show the sincerity of the apology? You lend your friend a considerably large sum of money. He forgets to return it until you remind him five times; in consequence of which you have to borrow money yourself and disappoint your own creditors. He then acknowledges his wrongdoing and resolves not to do it again (publicly, and, let us suppose, also privately). He pays you the money back and compensates you financially for extra financial costs, and says he is sorry. And yet that is not quite good enough, is it? We feel something else is required. The "something else" would be some token of his sorrow – a favor which we did not expect, interest on the money which was not part of the original bargain, perhaps a bunch of flowers – something more than mere compensation.[5] The giving of the extra gift does not have the function of making clear something which was true whether or not the agent made it clear; that he meant the apology. Rather it is a performative[6] act whereby he disowns the wrong act (in a way which mere words do not do when the wrong is a serious one). By doing his act of disowning, by doing something which costs him time, effort, and money, he constitutes that act as a meant and serious act. To give what we cannot too easily afford is always a serious act. The penitent constitutes his apology as serious by making it costly.

With reparation, repentance, apology, and penance, the guilty person has done what he can toward removing his guilt, toward atonement for the past, toward making him and the wronged one at one again. Not all such are needed in every case. For some wrongs reparation is inappropriate—there is no reparation for an insult; for the less serious wrongs, penance is not needed. But sincere apology is always needed. In the case of subjective guilt, apology involves repentance of the kind described.

The final act belongs to the wronged party—to forgive. In making apology, reparation, and penance, I am giving you something. All gifts have to be accepted (explicitly or implicitly) or else they remain with the giver. Gifts are accepted by the recipient completing the process which the giver is trying to effect by presenting them to the recipient. You accept my box of chocolates by taking it from me, the elephant I give you by accepting responsibility for its upkeep. What I give you in making reparation, penance, and apology is my contribution toward destroying the consequences (physical and not so physical) of my act of hurting you. You accept my reparation and penance by taking over the money, flowers, or whatever. My apology is my disowning of the past act. You accept my disowning by forwarding the purpose I had in showing you this disowning—to make it the case, as far as logically can be done, that I was not the originator of an act by which I wronged you. You do that by undertaking to treat me and think of me in future not as one who has hurt you, by agreeing not to hold my act against me. Your acceptance of my reparation, penance, and, above all, apology, is forgiving. Forgiving is a performative act—achieved perhaps by saying solemnly "I forgive you" or perhaps by saying "that's all right" or maybe just by a smile.

A person's guilt is removed when his repentance, reparation, apology, and penance find their response in the victim's forgiveness. Can the victim forgive him without any act of atonement on his part? The victim can indeed disown the act, in the sense that he explicitly says something like "let us regard this as not having happened" and then acts as though it had not happened. Such disowning could be done at any time, even if the guilty one makes no atonement; but unless it was done in response to atonement it would not be acceptance of that. And it will not then suffice to remove guilt, for the guilty one has not distanced himself from that act. We can see this by example. I borrow your car and damage the bodywork. I do not even apologize, but all the same you say "That's quite all right." But I remain one who has wronged you and I need to purge myself of my guilt, as I may well realize in later life. A mere financial debt can easily be removed by the creditor, but the unclean status of guilt requires some work by the debtor.

Indeed, not merely is it ineffective but it is wrong, in the case of serious acts, for the wronged person to treat the acts as not having been done, in the absence of some atonement at least in the form of apology from the guilty person. In the case of acts done to hurt us which are not done with much deliberation and where the hurt is not great, this may indeed be the right course of action. (It would be wrong to treat very seriously acts which were not in their intentions or consequences very serious.) But this would be the wrong course in the case of a serious hurt, and, above all, one done deliberately. Suppose that I have murdered your dearly loved wife; you know this, but for some reason I am beyond the power of the law. Being a modern and charitable man, you decide to overlook my offence (insofar as it hurt you). "The past is the past," you say, "What is the point of nursing a grievance?" The party we are both going to attend will go with more of a swing if we forget about this little incident. But, of course, that attitude of yours trivializes human life, your love for your wife, and the importance of right action. And it involves your failing to treat me seriously, to take seriously my attitude toward you expressed in my action. Thereby it trivializes human relationships, for it supposes that good human relations can exist when we do not take each other seriously.[7]

It is both wrong and ineffective for a victim of a serious hurt to disown the hurt when no atonement at all has been made.[8] What, however, is within the victim's power is to determine, within limits, just how much atonement is necessary before he is prepared to give the forgiveness which will eliminate guilt. The guilty one must offer some atonement – certainly repentance and apology and some attempt at reparation insofar as it lies within his power. But the victim may, if he chooses, let the guilty one off from doing any more; his forgiveness, without insisting on more, would be efficacious. But if he chooses, the victim can insist on substantial reparation, and sometimes it is good that he should do so, that he should insist on the guilty one, for his own sake, making a serious atonement; for that allows him to take seriously the harm that he has done.

What now if the guilty one makes due amends, gives a serious apology with due reparation and penance, but the victim fails to forgive? Does the guilt remain? My answer is that it does remain initially; the victim has the power to sustain it for a while. But if the apology is pressed, the penance increased, and still the victim refuses to forgive, the guilt disappears. Ideally both those involved – the guilty one and victim – need to disown the act, but if the guilty one does all that he can both to disown the act and to get the victim to disown the act, he will have done all he can to remove his involvement in the act. All that is logically possible for the guilty one to do to remove his status has been done.

If by my past act I have wronged you, that gives you a certain right against me – a right to accept or ignore my plea for pardon. If we were to say that the guilty party had, as it were, a fixed fine to pay in the way of atonement, that guilt did not disappear before the fine was paid but that it disappeared automatically when the fine was paid, that would have the consequence that I can wrong you and then remove my guilt at will. That would not take seriously the fact that the act is an act by which you are wronged, and in the wiping out of which you ought therefore to have a say. One consequence of my harming you is that it is in part up to you whether my guilt is remitted. But although my act gives you a right against me, it does not give you an infinite right. The harm which I have done you and the guilt which in consequence I acquire is limited. Hence your power to keep me guilty is limited. The victim has the right, within limits, to judge when the guilty one's atonement suffices. He can take an apology which sounds sincere and so indicates repentance as sufficient, or refuse forgiveness until the apology is renewed with reparation and penance. He cannot forgive when the apology is totally casual and so shows no repentance, and if he refuses forgiveness after a serious, repeated genuine apology with reparation and penance, the guilt vanishes despite the lack of forgiveness. But, within those limits, the final remission of guilt depends on the victim.

There is, in general, no obligation on the victim to forgive. How can my hurting you and then trying to undo the harm, actions all of my choice and not yours, put you under an obligation to do something, which did not exist before? Barring an exception to be explained below, your positive obligations arise from your choices, including your acceptance of my favors, not from my choices. However, forgiving the serious penitent is clearly good – a work of supererogation. (There is, however, an obligation to forgive others, on anyone who has solemnly undertaken to do so. For this reason Christians, unlike others, have an obligation to forgive all who seek their forgiveness. For it is a central theme of the gospel, embedded in the Lord's Prayer, that God's forgiveness can only be had by those prepared to forgive others; Christians who accept God's forgiveness thereby undertake the obligation to forgive others.)

In this paper so far I have in general been assuming that a person acquires guilt and so the need for atonement and forgiveness only in respect of actions which he has done himself, that atonement is owed only to those hurt (in an obvious and direct sense) by his actions, and that he alone can make atonement for the actions which he has done. It is time to bring in third parties.

We live in a network of obligations, some of them undertaken voluntarily – as are our obligations to care for our spouses and children – and some of them incurred involuntarily, as are our obligations to care for our parents and other benefactors of our youth. Normally it is only the accepting of a benefit which creates any positive obligation, and that together with the accepting of the obligation is something which we do voluntarily. But the greatest benefits – of life, nurture, and initial education – are ones which a benefactor must convey without the recipient being able to choose whether to accept or refuse them – because only when he has them does he have the ability to accept or refuse benefits. A benefactor reasonably assumes that a recipient would, if he had the choice, accept such benefits; and the conferring of the benefit, given that reasonable assumption, creates, I suggest, an obligation on the recipient to do something in return–to care for parents, teachers, and other members of his nurturing community in their need.

The web of obligations to care stretches, further than to parents and teachers, spouses and children. Voluntarily we have accepted friendship and cooperation with many, and that acceptance brings obligations to help our friends in their need. Involuntarily we have received benefits from a very wide community in space and time, stretching back to the first human who was sensitive to moral distinctions, and first chose intentionally to confer what was good on his children including some knowledge of what was good and bad. Many of our benefactors are dead. But the dead can still be benefited by bringing about what they would wish to have brought about, e.g., by conferring benefits on their descendents, our siblings and cousins and ultimately all members of the human race.

Among our obligations to our benefactors is the obligation to make some good use of benefits received. Of course if some one gives us a gift, we are not obliged to use it exactly as they wish. For it is the essence of a gift that, within limits, the recipient can do as he wishes with it. If I "give" you some money and tell you exactly what to buy for me with it, I have not given you a gift. But there are limits as to what a recipient can do with the gift. To accept an expensive present and then to throw it away is to wrong our benefactor. A recipient has *some* obligation to try to put what he has been given to some good use.

Given this web of obligations, what guilt have we for the actions of others? Those who are responsible for the moral education of children often have some guilt for the wrong acts of the children. Of course, a parent cannot make his children be good; there are other influences on the child, and also in the view of many, the child has some indeterministic freedom of choice. But the parent has a responsibility to influence, and if bad behavior results when he has failed to do so, the parent has some responsibility for this. Also, there is the responsibility of a member of a community to deter a fellow member from doing some particular grossly immoral act, on which he is intent. A husband has a duty to try to deter his wife from shop-lifting; a German a duty to protest against his country's extermination of Jews. Failure to protest involves a share in the resulting guilt.

Yet with these exceptions a person is surely not responsible for, not guilty in respect of, the acts of others; above all, he is not guilty for the acts of others which he could not have prevented. And yet, there is a sense in which a person is "involved" in the objective or subjective guilt of others of his community–although he bears no guilt for it himself. Our duty to help others of our community in their need includes a duty to help them with perhaps their greatest need, to get rid of their burden of past guilt. I cannot share my friend's guilt, but I can treat it as my burden and help him to cope with it in the ways in which he needs to cope with it–to acknowledge that it is his, and to help him by atonement to get rid of it.

Just as others are involved in our moral failures, so they can indeed help us get rid of our guilt. But the word is "help"; unless the guilty party participates in the process of "atonement," his guilt is not removed. If my child damages your property, and I tell you that he apologizes profusely, I pay the damage and give you a bottle of whisky at Christmas, my child's guilt remains. But I can help my child carry out the process of atonement–first, by encouraging him to set about it and second, by paying such of the reparation and proper penance as lies beyond his resources.[9] I can even help him say the words of apology–go along with him to knock at your door and provide him with cues. But beyond that I cannot go, if the atonement is to be his. Some offerings which others may give us to use as our reparation and penance are ones useful for other purposes. When my child damages your window and I give him money in the hope that he will pay for the repair, he could use the money for another purpose. But if I tell him that if he orders the glazier to mend the window, I will settle the bill, he does not give in reparation something which he could have used for another purpose. Nevertheless, in allowing me to do this for him, especially if it was something which I could ill afford and which required trouble to arrange, he is doing the only thing he can do and thereby he is showing humility (in recognizing the wrong he has done and his inability to right it by himself) when he transfers my generosity to you. And that is sometimes all that a wrong doer without resources can do.

II

Such is the structure of guilt, atonement, and forgiveness. I now introduce a theological assumption–that there is a God, that is, a perfectly good, omnipotent, omniscient creator, who made the world and the natural laws which govern its operation and so (indirectly) made us and the framework within which we operate, that he became incarnate in Christ who was both God and man, lived a perfect human life, foreseeing correctly that such perfection would have the consequence that he would be crucified, intended that that life and death should be available to us to offer to God in full atonement for our sins, rose from the dead, founded a church to carry on his work and seeks our eternal well-being in friendship with himself. This very detailed assumption is of course provided by parts of the Christian credal package other than the doctrine of the Atonement. In calling it an assumption I do not, of course, in the least imply that it cannot be the subject of rational argument, only that I need to take it for granted in a short paper on another subject. My aim is to show that, given what I have shown about the nature of guilt, atonement, and forgiveness, my assumption has the consequence that Christ's life and death is indeed, as he intended, efficacious for anyone who pleads it as a perfect atonement for his actual sins and the sins of others with whom he is involved.

If there is a God, the moral worth of humans is far lower than it would otherwise be. As I have argued, we owe it to our parents and educators to obey them and to do what they wish to some limited extent, in view of all that they have done for us. A fortiori, if there is a God, we have a greater duty by far to obey his commands and fulfill his wishes. For our existence at each moment and all that we have depends on him; our dependence on our parents and educators is very limited in time and degree, and their ability to benefit us arises from God's gift to them. Our dependence on God is so total that we owe it to God not merely to obey any explicit commands—to worship and evangelize, say—but also generally to fulfill God's wish by making something good out of our lives, something better than what we owe to our parents and educators. When we fail in any objective or subjective duty to our fellows, we fail also in our duty to God our creator.

If, further, as I have assumed, God seeks our eternal well-being in friendship with himself, then there is a pattern of life and a goal of fulfillment open to us, which would not otherwise be available. The greatest human well-being is to be found in friendship with good and interesting people in the pursuit of worthy aims. God is a better friend with more interesting aspects of himself to reveal than human friends (given his necessity and perfect goodness an infinitely better friend with infinitely more aspects) and he has worthwhile tasks which humans can share with him in bringing themselves and others to reconciliation with each other and God, to growth in the contemplation of God and the universe which he made, and to beautifying that universe. If there is a God, such tasks will necessarily be vastly more worthwhile than secular tasks—for there will be a depth of contemplation of the richness of life of a person, God, open to us which would not be open if there is no omnipotent and omniscient being; and there will be the infinite time of an after-life which God, seeking our well-being, is able to make available to us to help in the beautifying of the world and the spiritual healing of our fellows. And God, unlike humans, is a necessary being, who is the ultimate source of being and therefore of a kind quite other than finite things; the entering into contact with him has a richness and mystery and meaning which Rudolf Otto so vividly described as the "numinous." The existence of God, which makes human moral worth far lower than it would otherwise be, makes our prospects for the future infinitely brighter.

If there is no God, humans have no obligations to give their lives to prayer or philosophical reflection or artistic creativity or helping to enrich the spiritual, intellectual, and physical lives of others, good though it is that these things be done. But if all talents depend totally on God, and if doing these things is the way to form our characters and those of others over a few years of earthly life to fit us for the life of heaven, then to use our lives in some such way passes into the realm of the obligatory.

Because of our total dependence on God, and because the possibilities for us are of a vastly different kind in quality and quantity, it follows that, if there is a God, acts which otherwise would be supererogatorily good or not good at all become obligations; and failure to perform them is a breach of obligation to God. Failure in a duty to God is called sin. If a person does what is wrong (whether or not he realizes it), he sins objectively. If he does what he believes to be wrong, he sins subjectively.

Yet we have sinned, all humans have sinned, all humans have sinned considerably. So much is obvious, given the understanding which I have spelled out of what sin is. Hence all of us are guilty for our own sins, and also in part for the sins of those whom we ought to have influenced for good but failed to influence, and are involved in the way, which I have analyzed, in the sins of so many others of the human race. This responsibility for and involvement in the sins of others is a natural understanding of one part of original sin. (Original sin involves both some element of guilt for the sins of others, which I have analyzed, and also a proneness or tendency to sin.)[10] Each of us suffers from the burden of actual and original sin.

And so, each human owes atonement to God for the sins which he has committed and he owes it to God to help others make atonement for their sins, atonement in the form of repentance, reparation, apology, and penance. If you take seriously the theological background to human wrongdoing, you realize both the extent of atonement needed and the difficulty of making it—especially in respect of reparation and penance. For if God has given us so much, we have a duty to live a worthwhile life; and, if we have failed to do so, it's going to be very difficult to find a bit extra to offer to God in compensation for past misuse. We are too close to the situation of the criminal who has spent his ill-gotten gains and is unable to make reparation. We need help from outside.

But why in that situation would a good God not simply ignore our sins? I argued earlier that it is wrong for any victim to ignore serious harm done to him by another—for it involves not taking the other seriously in the attitudes expressed in his actions. But why would not God forgive us in return for repentance and apology without demanding reparation and penance? Aquinas claimed that he could have done so if he had so chosen.[11] But since our actions and their consequences matter, it matters that if we do wrong, *we* should take *proper* steps to cancel our actions, to pay our debts, as far as logically can be done. Just as a good parent may put in the way of a child an opportunity for making amends (an opportunity which he would not otherwise have had) rather than just accept an apology, so a good God also may do just that. God cannot literally atone for our sins, but he can help us to atone for our sins by making available to us an offering which we may offer as our reparation and penance, and by encouraging us to repent and apologize. He could give to us the opportunity to be serious enough about our sins to use his life and death as man to be our atoning offering.

And what is a suitable offering to God for our sins? Many offerings might suit, but a perfect human life would suit very well. For our sins make our human lives less worthwhile than the lives we owe to God; the best way of making it up to him would be for us to offer him a life which is perfect and so better than the life which is owed to God. The best reparation is that in which the reparation restores the damage done rather than gives something else in compensation; and the best penance is that which more than makes it up to the victim in the respect in which he was harmed rather than in some irrelevant respect. Having damaged the rusty bumper of your car, I can do penance better by giving you a new bumper, rather than restoring the old one and giving you a box of chocolates at the same time. This is because penance, to be good, must evince a concern that the particular harm which was done was done. The living of perfect human life by God himself forms a far more perfect offering for us to offer to God than a perfect life lived by an ordinary human. For the ordinary human has an obligation to God to live a worthwhile life, and so some of the perfection of his life would be owed anyway. An incarnate God does not owe it to any benefactor to live any particular kind of life, and so the whole of the perfection of that life would be available to others to use as their offering.

So if, as our theological assumption claims, God did indeed become incarnate in Christ and lived a human life so perfect that it ended in a foreseen death, and if he intended that that life should be available to be used by us to make our atonement, it is indeed the sort of thing which we could offer to God as our reparation and penance. Whether or not it would be a full reparation for the sins of all humans, it is good reparation such that a good God could indeed forgive us without demanding more. Given that Christ the man who made the offering intending it to avail fully for our atonement, is also the God to whom it was offered, he will forgive us without demanding more.

Christ offered the sacrifice on behalf of all. But it can only atone for me, if I use it–if I join my feeble repentance and halting words of apology to it, if I use it to pay my fine, to make my peace. There has to be a formal association with it in the process of my disassociating myself from my own sins and from involvement in those of others. A further part of my theological assumption was that Christ founded a body to carry on his work. The Christian Church provides a formal ceremony of association in the pledges made by the candidate for admission in its initiation ceremonies of baptism and confirmation, and before participation in the Eucharist in which, as Paul put it, we "proclaim the Lord's death until he comes."[12]

I plead the sacrifice of Christ in joining and rejoining myself to the new humanity, the new and voluntary association of those who accept Christ's offering on their behalf, the Church. And as it is difficult to repent and utter the words of apology, that too, the Church in its evangelistic and pastoral capacity helps me to do.[13]

Notes

1. This paper has been read on many occasions. I am grateful to all who have provided those critical comments which helped me to give it its final form, and among them I am especially grateful to George Mavrodes and others who commented on the paper at the Notre Dame conference.
2. The importance of the notion of supererogation was first brought to the attention of modern moral philosophers by J. O. Urmson in his article, "Saints and Heroes," in *Essays in Moral Philosophy,* ed. A. T. Melden (Seattle: University of Washington Press, 1958), and reprinted in *Moral Concepts,* ed. J. Feinberg (London: Oxford University Press, 1969). For the history of this concept, and its elaboration and defence, see David Heyd, *Supererogation* (Cambridge: Cambridge University Press, 1982).
3. For this analogy, see St. Anselm, *Cur Deus Homo* 1.19.
4. Numbers 15:28–31.
5. "When anyone pays what he has unjustly taken away, he ought to give something which could not have been demanded of him, had he not stolen what belonged to another" (Anselm, *Cur Deus Homo* 1.11).
6. J. L. Austin introduced the terminology of "performative utterances" to describe such utterances as "I promise," "I solemnly swear," "I name this ship,"

which do not report already existing states of affairs but themselves bring about states of affairs. (See, e.g., his "Performative Utterances" in his *Philosophical Papers,* Oxford: Oxford University, 1961.) The man who promises does not report an interior mental act but creates an obligation upon himself to do something, an obligation which did not previously exist. Actions other than utterances may create or abolish states of people or relations between them, describable in such moral terms as responsibility and obligation. I convey money to you and thereby abolish my debt, and in the context of an auction a nod is enough to constitute a bid (i.e., a promise to pay).

7. To say that it would be wrong for me to treat an act done deliberately to hurt me as not having been done in the absence of some apology from the guilty person is not to say that one ought to seek revenge or continually harbor malevolent thoughts. It is only to say that I should not treat the wrongdoer with such disdain as to ignore his seriously intended actions.

8. Whether we call the disowning of a hurtful act by the victim "forgiveness," when no atonement at all has been made, seems to be a matter which requires a linguistic decision. In view of the fact that forgiving is normally thought of as a good thing, I suggest that a victim's disowning of an act hurting him is to be called "forgiveness" only when it is in response to some minimal attempt at atonement, such as an apology. One of the very few recent philosophical discussions of the issues of this paper is William Neblett's "The Ethics of Guilt," *Journal of Philosophy* 71 (1974): 652–663. As I do, he claims that men become guilty through performing wrong actions, and that this guilt needs atonement; but he claims that a man can be forgiven, even when he has not made atonement.

   One recent article, which in my view fails to see what forgiveness is about, is Anne C. Minas, "God and Forgiveness," *Philosophical Quarterly* 25 (1975):138–150. She claims that God cannot forgive because forgiveness is either changing one's moral judgment, or remitting deserved punishment, or abandoning a feeling of resentment; and she has arguments to show that a good God will not do any of these. However, forgiveness does not involve changing any moral judgment, and feelings need not be involved (I can easily forgive that which I do not resent). It is true that if I forgive you for some act, I ought not subsequently punish you for that act. Yet forgiveness still has application in contexts where there is no question of punishment.

9. Aquinas urges that although confession has to be made and contrition shown by the sinner himself, "satisfaction has to do with the exterior act, and here one can make use of instruments" (*Summa Theologiae* III q. 48, a.2, ad 1), i.e., one can use reparation provided by others.

10. For the history of Christian views of original sin, see N. P. Williams, *The Ideas of the Fall and Original Sin* (London: Longmans, 1927). For analysis and assessment of the doctrine of the proneness or tendency to sin, see my "Original Sinfulness," *Neue Zeitschrift für Systematische Theologie,* 27 (1985): 235–250.

11. St. Thomas Aquinas, *ST* III q. 46, a. 1–4.

12. 1 Corinthians 11:26.

13. The account of atonement which I have given in this paper is that provided in the New Testament by the metaphor of sacrifice. We make a sacrifice to God by giving him something valuable, often as a gift to effect reconciliation. This is, of course, the way in which the doctrine of Atonement is worked out in the Epistle to the Hebrews, and is, I think, despite the emphasis on the Law Court metaphor in the Epistle to the Romans, the way of expressing the doctrine which has the widest base in the New Testament.

INDEX

EXPOSURE

By the same author

Expensive Habits: The Dark Side of the Music Industry

The End of Innocence: Britain in the Time of Aids

The Wrestling

The Nation's Favourite: The True Adventures of Radio 1

Mauve

The Last Journey of William Huskisson

Our Hidden Lives

We Are At War

Private Battles

The Error World

EXPOSURE

THE UNUSUAL LIFE AND
VIOLENT DEATH OF
BOB CARLOS CLARKE

SIMON GARFIELD

EBURY
PRESS

1 3 5 7 9 10 8 6 4 2

Published in 2009 by Ebury Press, an imprint of Ebury Publishing
A Random House Group company

The Random House Group Limited Reg. No. 954009

Addresses for companies within the Random House Group can be found at
www.randomhouse.co.uk

A CIP catalogue record for this book is available from the British Library

The Random House Group Limited supports The Forest Stewardship Council (FSC),
the leading international forest certification organisation. All our titles that are
printed on Greenpeace approved FSC certified paper carry the FSC logo. Our paper
procurement policy can be found at www.rbooks.co.uk/environment

Mixed Sources
Product group from well-managed
forests and other controlled sources
www.fsc.org Cert no. TT-COC-2139
© 1996 Forest Stewardship Council

FSC

Designed and set by seagulls.net

Printed and bound in Great Britain by Clays Ltd, St Ives PLC

ISBN 9780091922580

For Lindsey and Scarlett

contents

dramatis personae

Barbara Altounyan, a television executive

Emma B, a model

Nicky Barthorp, a neighbour

Tamara Beckwith, a personality

James Betts, a photographer

Andrew Carlos Clarke, a brother

Bob Carlos Clarke, a photographer

Lindsey Carlos Clarke, a wife

Scarlett Carlos Clarke, a daughter

Jane Chesterton, a childhood friend

Sam Chesterton, a childhood friend

Emma Ford, a muse

Sue Frame, an ex-wife

Simon Garfield, a narrator

Philippe Garner, an expert

Allen Jones, an artist

Geraldine Leale, a friend

Simon Le Bon, a pop star

Jake Lingwood, an editor

Rupert Morris, a humanist

Ghislain Pascal, an agent

Marco Pierre White, a restaurateur

Paul Plews, a photographer

John Stoddart, a photographer

John Taylor, a pop star

Crena Watson, a photographer

This is a story about love, suicide, genius, photography, beautiful women and corrosive artistic despair, but it didn't start out that way. The original plan was to tell a story about a showbusiness agent, and the intention was to make it commercial and glossy and provide a backstage glimpse at celebrity, but then something happened to make it darker, or at least weirder. The biggest thing that happened was that people started to talk about things they had seldom talked about before.

Everyone interviewed for this book told their version of events to the best of their recollection, but inevitably there were some discrepancies, as well as jealousies and uncertain interpretations of incidents.

PART ONE

1. it was never my intention to do a hatchet job, said simon garfield

Simon Garfield

When you come out with a new book, the thing most people want to know is how you got the idea. With previous books, my answer has often been vague: the idea came together over several months; it probably grew out of a newspaper or magazine article; it may have been an extension of something I heard on the radio, or something someone told me over a drink. But the source of this book I can pinpoint precisely.

Of course, I wouldn't be telling you this if it were all straightforward. If it were all simple, you'd just be reading the book, with none of this preamble. The original plan was for a book called *The Agent*, and was to be about a man called Ghislain Pascal and his celebrity showbusiness clients. Ghislain, who was in his mid-thirties when I approached him about this project, was understandably open to the idea of having a book published about him. Who wouldn't be? How many other agents had received that level of attention? The only other one I can think of would be Max Clifford.

Ghislain Pascal

It was very rapid at the end. I didn't even think he'd last through Christmas, he was so bad. But obviously he did get through Christmas, and we went to Spain and he was on top form, and then we came back and he just deteriorated. He started losing weight. He was a thin guy anyway, but he lost any weight he had. He was gaunt. I remember taking him to lunch just to keep him occupied.

Simon Garfield

I had known Ghislain for a number of years (you pronounce it gee-la; he grew up in Tooting, south London), and I had always found him interesting and forthcoming. I had first met him in the mid-1990s, when *Esquire* magazine had asked me to write a profile of the model Caprice. Caprice was the latest hot blonde, and had a little more to offer than most (she was also appealingly weird, like when she told me that she once wanted to be President of the United States, but had since narrowed her ambitions and would settle for modelling for Debenhams). Her latest ultimate goal was to act opposite Tom Cruise in a movie. She said that Ghislain was 'very like me – ambitious and aggressive', but this was 'all a question of semantics', a phrase she used an unexpected amount. I asked her the difference between a model and a supermodel, and she said, 'It's a matter of semantics. A model becomes a supermodel when she starts making $10,000 a day.'

I went along to an advert she was filming at Shepperton Studios with Jonathan Ross for Pizza Hut. In the script, the two of them were having a blind date. In the breaks between filming, a stylist clipped a hair from Ross's nose and a food technician used tweezers to rearrange mushrooms on a cold pizza base. After the shoot it was time for what Pizza Hut's PR man called 'a bit of buxom and cleavage' – photos for the papers. I asked Caprice how she was feeling, and she said, 'I'm really full. In fact, I could puke!'

Ghislain Pascal had been Caprice's agent for about a year. On the way back from the film studios he told me that the aim was to make Caprice an international superstar. 'In England it's more or less sorted. She's always going to be a star here. But we're looking abroad. We're getting reports she's been voted number-one pin-up in Malaysia.'

I enjoyed Ghislain's sense of the absurd ('we're getting reports…'), and I decided to put him in the *Esquire* story, describing him as a man who 'looks like a French mime artist but operates like a street hawker'. The magazine ran the piece on its cover, not because the profile was particularly memorable, but because the photo was. This featured Caprice in black vinyl trousers and gloves up to her armpits. Apart from that, nothing. Her trousers (or perhaps tights/leggings/latex bottoms would be better, as there was certainly no possibility of a crease – put them in a trouser press and they would have melted) were tugged above her belly button, a rare instance of fetish-wear worn in the style of an old man, only this time there was no gusset, and were in fact so close to her skin that you could begin to discern her inner folds. She looked like she had been dipped in sump oil; in fact, the outfit had been squeezed into with the help of several assistants and a jelly lubricant, and she squeaked when she moved around the studio. When it was over, she would have to lie down as helpers tugged off her gear like a parent might remove a child's wet play clothes. The upper part of Caprice's body was naked, but less visible than her fans would have liked, as the elbows of her rubber gloves were folded into her stomach, pushing together her large breasts into perfect circles. They looked like small stone boulders. She was also wearing a black vinyl eye-mask, an alluring symbol of mystery and death, through which she looked at the photographer with professional indifference. Her blonde hair was centre-parted into loose plaits, and they looked charged with current, springing out from her shoulders in the shape of a bell. She stood at a gentle angle, leaning towards the right edge of the frame, and she looked both tough and ridiculous.

Not long after it appeared in *Esquire*, the image was reprinted on calendars and books, and in one book it was accompanied by a quote from another model named Gina: 'Sometimes, when I'm half naked and the photographer gets close, I think it would be okay if he just got into me. But most times if he tried anything, I'd bust his nose. I guess it's mostly a matter of timing.'

A while later, the photographer gave a signed print of it to Ghislain, and by then it had a new name: Masked Blonde. It was one of the finest contemporary examples of erotic photography, and even

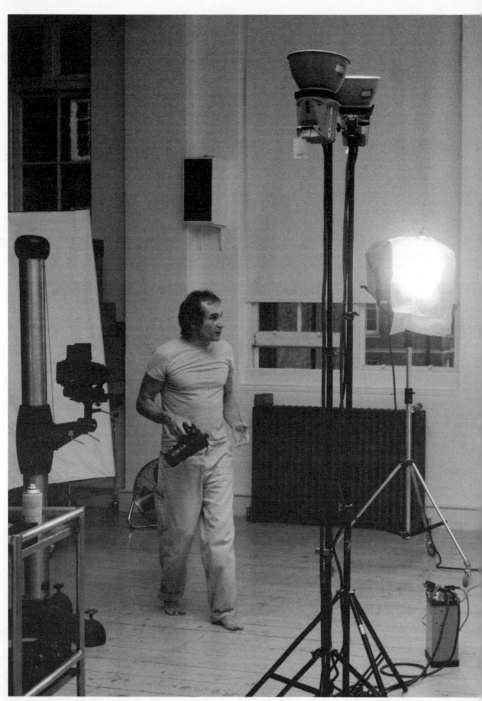

Bob Carlos Clarke in his studio.

if it didn't turn you on, you could appreciate the craft, the effort in its construction. It was almost pornography, and almost art. On the news-stands at the time, and even now on my desk in my study, it is a striking photo. It was taken by a man I had barely heard of called Bob Carlos Clarke.

Ghislain Pascal

At the end it was lots of things. He sold the Battersea studio. Lindsey and him decided they couldn't run that big studio – it was just too much money. He didn't like renting it out, because as soon as he rented it out he wanted it himself to shoot something. So listen, let's get rid of it. They sold it before Christmas for £2 million. They thought, with that money we can get a new studio. Then he rented a little place in the same Battersea complex. But it was dingy and cold. He wasn't happy with it, and he felt he couldn't photograph in it.

They did buy a new studio in Putney, and Lindsey was getting the builders in to work on it, so that was the light at the end of tunnel. And then Bob just started to lose it. He really lost his mind.

Simon Garfield

The plan was to focus on Ghislain. He would provide the narrative core of the book, and he would guide me (and I hoped the reader), through his slightly shrouded world of celebrity culture. I hoped he would do this by giving me unfettered access to his clients, and at the time of this idea these included Tamara Beckwith, Jacqueline Gold, Emma B, Nell McAndrew and Nancy Sorrell. This was not exactly an A-list line-up, but I would never have got close to an A-list without paying for it, and I was trying to earn money, not spend it. I had hoped that this 'fly-on-the-wall' approach, a well-trodden path but still entertaining, would be illuminating, funny and perhaps shocking. It would be enjoyable to do, as I'd attend premieres and product launches and go to people's clean homes, and ever since I began in journalism I had always liked looking around places I wouldn't otherwise enter. I knew this world was mostly nonsense, a sham for the media, which would then amplify or expose this sham to the public, but, even with this knowledge, I still got a vague thrill from spotting famous people and eating free things. Also, in the early 1980s one used to get great take-home bags stuffed full of perfumes or very useful merchandise, although these days it's mostly rubbish. Once I was given a Walkman, and once I got an early mobile phone, though obviously you had to sign up for an exorbitant contract.

Ghislain Pascal

I just knew that two or three weeks over Christmas was a long time for him not to be working. So having to spend Christmas with the family at the house in Chelsea, with Lindsey's mother – it would just do his head in. But it didn't – Christmas was fine. He didn't call me particularly. But then after Christmas and after Madrid he started to lose the way. He started talking gibberish. I've never seen it before. He would become paranoid about things, he'd be on the phone to me going, 'Why is that person using that picture – they shouldn't be using that picture.' Or, 'We shouldn't be using that picture, take it off the website – that model, she's now married to someone really rich and they're going to sue us!' I was like, 'Bob, please!'

Simon Garfield

It was never my intention to do a hatchet job. The targets were too easy for this, and I was too mature. I had learned my lessons. Once, when I was at *Time Out*, I had written that I hoped Annie Lennox would die in a plane crash, and although I didn't regret this instantly, I found it a tricky position to defend when the letters came flying in. Her publicist was shocked, as was Ruby Wax, who wrote in to the magazine to stick up for Annie and castigate me. At the time I was frightened of the admonishing power of Ruby Wax – can you imagine that?

I'm trying to think of some more usable stories about me and famous people. I once spent almost a week with U2 when they were at the height of their stadium fame in the late 1980s (i.e. before they turned ironic and Bono went nuts about good deeds), and I stayed in the same hotel as the band. My room was next door to The Edge ('Don't push me, I'm close to The Edge!' I remember telling my wife on the phone), and I accompanied the whole band and their

9

manager back to their hotel after a gig in New Jersey (champagne corks popping out of the limo's moonroof), and when I got back to London I wrote what I thought was a fairly positive piece, although amongst other criticisms I did mention that Bono looked a bit rough backstage and had spots, and after the story appeared Bono complained and didn't want to deal with me again.

A similar thing happened with Cher. I had flown out to Los Angeles to interview Cher on the set of her latest film. This was during that fortnight when Cher was the biggest star in the world, top of the album and film charts. I had agreed to promote her new album, and I had to completely ignore the film she was currently making: I had to sign a form saying that whatever happened, I couldn't say one word about this new film, not even the title. If I mentioned it even in passing I could be sued, or worse: the worse was that Cher would never speak to me again. With this agreed, I hung around the film set for what seemed like hours waiting for Cher to appear. I wasn't even allowed on the soundstage, but had to sit outside in the high heat, and after about two hours I began making polite noises about deadlines and how I was here all the way from London, and we had agreed 2pm, and how much longer would she be? No one knew or cared. Her publicist was apologetic, and said that everything was beyond her control. When Cher finally arrived there was another wait for an hour before she agreed to answer some obvious questions in a boring way. I then wrote the piece, and because I began it by saying that I had been kept waiting, Cher's agent called up to say I could never speak to her again. The agent also said she wouldn't let me speak to any of her other clients either, but when I asked who these other clients were, I was grateful.

Ghislain Pascal

I'm like, 'Put it into perspective, Bob. Let's worry about it when it happens.' He just became really paranoid. That's the only word, paranoid. The last time I saw him, I took him out to lunch in Battersea just to preoccupy him, and I was just like, 'Bob, you've really got to sort yourself out, you've got to move on. If your marriage is at its end, fine, move on, you can't dwell on it, if it's over it's over.' And then Lindsey turned up. She turned up because she was around the corner or something, and I didn't know she was coming. It was really weird. He just turned into this child. He was all doe-eyed and trying to put his arm round her and she was just…she was trying to be nice in front of me, but you could tell…a really awkward situation. And that was the last time I saw him. Shortly after that he told me he was going into the Priory.

Simon Garfield

The most uncomfortable interview I had conducted was with Joni Mitchell. It was about 1985, she had a new album out called *Dog Eat Dog*, and she had come to London to sit in a West End hotel for a couple of days to meet the press. This was something she didn't do often, and so it was a thrill to be given the chance to meet her. I had always loved *Blue* (who didn't?), and I had liked her freewheeling Californian symbolism with her long hair and thin face and apple-crunching toothiness, but any semblance of desire I had for her art or her person disappeared almost as soon as I walked into the hotel suite. I remember a black grand piano and several other people in the room, almost certainly including her publicist, her agent and her current love interest. I sat down and got out my tape recorder, but before I could turn it on she said there were one or two things she wished to get straight. This was unusual. As with George Michael and Cher, there were already agreements in place about when the piece would run and how prominently, and whether there were any subjects that were off-limits. But Joni Mitchell had other things on her mind.

She had in front of her a copy of last week's *Time Out*, in which I had reviewed her new CD in what I thought was a balanced way. It was a fairly poppy album with lots of synthesisers and sampling techniques (it was produced by Thomas Dolby), and some tracks I liked and some tracks I was iffy about. Unfortunately, Joni Mitchell was iffy about everything I'd written, and she started to go through each line of the review, asking me what I had meant by particular adjectives and descriptive phrases. Did I know, for example, the real meaning of the word 'crossover'? Could I explain how the song 'Shiny Toys' was in any way reminiscent of 'Big Yellow Taxi'? I had written the review in about an hour, and it was meant to be read in about one minute, as opposed to the academic scrutiny that it was now receiving. It was particularly gruelling because with every attempt I made to explain something there were further supplementary questions, and the glares from everyone else in the room made me stumble and sweat. It was four minds versus one, and they were prepared for the cross-examination and I wasn't. 'And finally,' Joni announced as I was getting ready to leave after twenty minutes' onslaught (the thoughts of actually conducting an interview with her had long evaporated), 'I am not American, I am Canadian.' I'm sure I knew this, but somehow I had got it wrong in the review, and it was a bad mistake to make, under the circumstances. As I left the hotel in the rain I resolved to cut down on my reviewing, and step up my profiling.

One of my profiles was of one of Ghislain's clients, Tamara Beckwith. Tamara was a 'socialite' with a wealthy father, and she had sprung to wider fame on a television programme about 'It Girls' – that is, girls who met up around Chelsea or Holland Park to talk about the best new shops and last night's parties. Ghislain had told me that Tamara was much more intelligent than the programme had made out, and was fun to be around, and I hoped I could write one of those pieces that attempt not to be patronising but usually are – one of those 'how the other half live' jobs, both respectful and open-mouthed, someone telling you about their fabulousness and nights on summer yachts without any comprehension of how they sounded to people in the real world. But what really got me interested in Tamara was her very flat chest. She had very tiny breasts, and she had made no attempt to enhance or hide them. On almost every picture of her they were poking out of a vest or cashmere sweater like doorbells, and I thought she was very self-confident to carry that off in a time of enlargements and Caprice and tanned cleavage.

Unfortunately, I didn't have the courage to ask her about her breasts when I met her, so we talked about her plans to establish a credible television career.

Ghislain Pascal

In Barnes. I chatted to him and it was fine. He called me from the Priory, because you're allowed your telephone in there. I spoke to

Lindsey and said I'm not sure if I should visit him or speak to him while he's in the Priory, because he was still ringing me up with this paranoia. 'My God, the *News of the World* is going to come round and they're gonna…' I was like, 'Bob, what the fuck are you talking about?'

Simon Garfield

But not in those words, surely. You'd be more placatory. You wouldn't say, 'Bob, what the fuck are you talking about?'

Ghislain Pascal

No, I'd say, 'Come on, Bob, get real.' But it was like talking to somebody who was in a totally different mental state. There was no sense to it. So I said to Lindsey, 'Do you think I should visit him?' She said, 'Maybe it's a bit early on.'

I said, 'Well, to be honest I don't think I should because every time he talks to me it's fuelling his paranoia.' Of course Lindsey was visiting him every day, so I was getting updates.

Simon Garfield

Tamara Beckwith told me about her desire to change her reputation. She wanted to lose her image as an 'It Girl' and 'Daddy's Girl' (her father was Peter Beckwith, the 'property magnate'). That was where Ghislain came in.

Ghislain Pascal

My first job was to keep her out of trouble. I didn't really know that much about her when we first met, just that she was this Society girl. She lived in Albert Hall Mansions by the Albert Hall, she shared with her sister, and her daughter was living in the family home in Wimbledon. She was still dating Michael Stone, Sharon Stone's brother. I got someone to pull up all the cuts from the newspapers, and they were all about her getting engaged to Michael Stone, her father saying they couldn't get married, then being arrested for drugs, being associated with Sylvester Stallone. She was a naughty Chelsea girl – you know, Amanda de Cadenet, that kind of set. She was at her worst ever behaviour. I would book her for jobs, and I had to turn up at her place and it took two hours to get her out of bed.

The gameplan was very simple. Basically she was in a mess. You'd turn on the television and they'd be debating her on *Kilroy* or *Vanessa* – this posh spoilt rich kid. So I said, 'You can't talk to the press, zip. You're not allowed to talk to anybody.' The plan was to shut all that down, and the aim was to get her work. All Tamara ever needs in her life is somebody to guide her. Money isn't the goal for her – if she wanted to make money she could have done the Paris Hilton thing ten years ago. All she wants is to have fun, but without upsetting her family. Her father has to be happy. At the beginning I never met Tamara's dad – just his people. And they obviously felt that she did need someone to help her, and the money was coming out of her trust fund. Obviously everything she earns by herself is nice – because it means it's her money, not her father's.

Simon Garfield

Ghislain is 'very hungry still', Tamara Beckwith told me once. 'Not a lot of fat on him. He's not into long waffly lunches like a lot of people. He can be incredibly blunt and he can lack charm. But he's a real softy underneath, though he likes to portray himself as quite hard.'

Bob Carlos Clarke told me, 'He's very straight. Any boy or girl who's good-looking in this town is like a carcass to predators. There are a lot of people who will just pick your bones and use you up, but Ghislain will always see your career as long-term.'

Ghislain Pascal

The thing that Tamara really liked in the early days was that I was at her beck and call 24 hours a day. If she wanted a cup of tea I would get up and make it. Her friends all said, 'I wish I had a Ghislain.' At that age I was fine doing it. She was 25/26 and I was 24. I wouldn't dream of doing that now. I used to go to everything with her, every single party she went to, just to stop the diarists talking to her. We wanted to build the image of her as a nice respectable party girl rather than just a wild party girl. So she became an It Girl, and her and Tara Palmer-Tomkinson were everywhere. It just became bonkers. They were never bosom buddies or called each other for conversation, they were just social friends. I remember we went to Brown's one night in its heyday. We went up to the VIP room – Cristal was coming out at £500 a bottle. When the bill came, everyone else disappeared, but Tamara paid it. It was £3,000. To me that was amazing, another world. I was earning £16,000 a year.

Tamara Beckwith

I got into a period where nobody could tell me anything.

I was hanging out with people who had no education and seemed to have fun all the time, and didn't have any family to keep them grounded. You start thinking: 'Oh, isn't that wonderful?'

The newspapers said that I was going out with Sylvester Stallone, Charlie Sheen and Robert Downey Jr. I did have dinner with them all, but does that mean I went out with them? These are just the sort of people I meet. I went to my friend's birthday dinner the other night and sat next to Gabriel Byrne, but it doesn't mean we then become a couple. Fascinating as he may be, it's not even the highlight of my week. On Saturday, I went out with Caprice and Rod Stewart to Mick Jagger's birthday party. What am I supposed to do? Not sit and talk to those people?

They're invariably smaller than you imagine. And the camera always puts on 10 pounds, so when you see them they're always much more dainty and more petite. A girlfriend of mine was engaged to Tom Sizemore, and they were filming *Heat* at the time, so she just called me out for supper. But then I turn up and it's supper with Tom Sizemore, Val Kilmer and Robert De Niro. De Niro was not the most fascinating dinner guest I've ever come across. I haven't yet met Al Pacino.

Ghislain Pascal

Tamara has always earned money for me. It's all in cycles – privileged posh girls, then Jade Goody, then posh girls again. In the mid/late 1990s she was earning really well. *OK!* magazine paid £30,000 to cover her birthday party. It was silly money. It's all changed now. I used to tell my clients, 'You should move house every year to get a *Hello!* deal, and you should get engaged and married few every years and you could fund your entire lifestyle.' She would get £6,000 for a personal appearance. She did photocalls for the lottery – there was one where she was pushing Tara Palmer-Tomkinson in a shopping trolley through Trafalgar Square, that was £6,000 for that. She did the Kentucky Fried Chicken with T P-T. They were behind a KFC restaurant serving. Crap, but they got paid loads of money.

Every time Tamara went to a premiere she would be in the papers. And obviously we are coming up with ideas all the time – turning up at *Unzipped*, the Isaac Mizrahi fashion film, with a see-through white dress and her white poodle; she was on the front page of two papers. It would never happen today.

The relationship with Michael Stone ended when he moved to London, because she couldn't deal with having somebody in the house all the time.

Simon Garfield

She told me that she was keen to do more television: she had already done a pilot for Channel 5 called *Tamara's World*. She was also keen to write a book, perhaps a *roman à clef*. 'So many funny stories,' she said. 'There was the Jack Nicholson one. Do you know that one?'

Tamara Beckwith

One night we went back to Jack Nicholson's house. I was with these two friends of mine. So I'm really over-excited being there, but at one point all the other people disappeared, paired off, and I was in his little sitting room. Not his *smart* sitting room, because there's more than one, but I'm in the little one, there all by myself, loads of champagne and everything. There's an occasional table with all his family photos on it, he'd just split up with that Rebecca Broussard at the time. And I suddenly realise that he's got these beautiful artworks. I'm not a big art buff, but I can recognise a couple. There's this Matisse, and I realise that one of them was a bit wonky, and I've got this disease where I can't stand anything not to be neat. So I go over, and I'm just about to straighten it, and he comes in behind me and shouts, 'DON'T TOUCH!!' And I was like, 'Oh no, I was just going to...' And he goes, 'Oh my God, we're hooked up to the Beverly Hills Police Station...' I was mortified, it looked as though I was going to steal it.

Then they all come back, and he does this thing where he chats to you, this thing which only a few men I've ever met do – he plays the goof. So he'll be talking, and on purpose he would flick his tie up so that it hit his hair; another person, if they did something like that, you would correct yourself, wouldn't you. But he pretends he hasn't noticed. So then the hair is off on a wonk. You can see the other girls totally fall for it: 'Oh, isn't he cute, what a little guy, you've got to take care of him...' But I'm thinking, 'No, no, no...'

Simon Garfield

Just before I met her she had done her own 'how the other half lives' story for *Marie Claire* magazine, about a single mother living on the breadline in Bristol.

Tamara Beckwith

The magazine thought I'd go up there, spend a bit of time, and then go to a hotel for the night. But you can't write about someone's life and then make it look like their house isn't good enough to sleep in. I couldn't just sneak back for breakfast and pretend to the reader I'd been there all night. I think people were gobsmacked that I wanted to stay. But, of course, when I got there I thought: 'Oh my God, what have I done?'

I didn't see a fresh piece of food the entire time I was there. They just ate fish and chips and pies and stodge. When I suggested changing things, they looked at me as if I was having the best laugh they'd ever heard.

They asked me, 'Do you really go to Gucci? Do you really have a different dress for each event?' We were flicking through their catalogues and I saw a couple of my girlfriends modelling things, and they were amazed that I knew them. I told them a whole bunch of inconsequential gossip. They wanted to know if Caprice was nice, and were those her real boobs? And when I walked in there was a picture of a model I used to know very well, a poster of a guy semi-naked holding a baby, and they said: 'You actually know him?' That was gold to them.

Simon Garfield

Towards the end of our first interview she mentioned her friend Bob Carlos Clarke, and what a 'complete madman' he was, 'but also shy'. She lived just behind King's Road in Chelsea, in the same street as Carlos Clarke.

Tamara Beckwith

A few months before the end we were doing the launch of something, and I was really brown and fit, and Ghislain arranged it for *Hello!* or *OK!*, and those were the best pictures Bob ever took of me. He did the pictures for my thirtieth birthday party at Home House and I've got all of those. Then there was another party from 1993 which he gave, that's in my downstairs office, it says Happy Bitchmas. He always used to love finding me – I'd be wandering around in my own world, the girl with too many bubbles. I was a bit too wild for him in one way, or the wrong way – I wasn't the girl who wanted to have sex with all the boys. Then he photographed my Christmas party, so he could come along and talk to everyone on the pretence of being the photographer, and all those pictures are in the down-stairs loo, and those were perhaps the last pictures he took.

Simon Garfield

Then in 2002, the *Observer* decided it wanted to do a special one-off magazine about celebrity, and the editor asked the paper's regular writers if they had any ideas. I thought of Ghislain immediately, and he said okay, so I arranged to catch up on his life. The piece began in the same place as my first story about him had ended – on the phone to Caprice. He was talking to her about the cover of *FHM* magazine, which had just come out.

Ghislain Pascal

It looks amazing, some of your best pictures. Not the cover so much, but the inside pictures are nice. The cover's not as nice – they've put in a fake background, put in a fake beach and all that kind of stuff. The inside pictures are full length, head to knee, a blue-and-white bikini with your hair hanging over your boobs. It looks great, but they've put in a fake beach!

Simon Garfield

FHM had put Caprice and five other models on the front of its November issue, accompanied by the cover line: 'Six ladies, one island, and five square inches of cloth'. Except there was no island.

The *Observer* story went on: 'Pascal is 29 and he takes 20 per cent. He says he would like to take 50 per cent. In return for his cut he provides a uniquely modern service – career guidance, public relations, brand development, product placement – operating a tiny but effective management and publicity company called Panic that exists to put his clients into magazines and catalogues and cable shows, and make them feel like permanent fixtures in a shifting world. He used to work in the charity sector, but now that he works in the amiable fluffhead sector he likes it much more.

'Refreshingly for a man who works in an industry infested with charlatans and sleazeballs, Pascal is a thoroughly likeable individual, and as soon as you learn to pronounce his first name, this slight figure will guide you through his unnatural but alluring world with generosity and skill. He may go further: in his everyday combination of combat trousers, Duffer T-shirt and pierced eyebrow, he may make you believe that the creation and maintenance of celebrity is an easy thing to do.'

Ghislain Pascal

I was just carrying on as normal. I thought, okay, he's in the Priory, he will get better, and he'll just come out and life will carry on. And then, it must have been about two weeks after he went in, on a Saturday morning, at about 11 o'clock, 11.30 I think it was, he called me, I was on my exercise bike, missed the call. I listened to the message, and it was another rambling message going, 'I've just been in Barnes, I've just seen one of the GDH pictures in a window of a hairdresser, have they got permission to use it, come on, Squirrel,' because he called me Squirrel, 'get on your bike, sort it out, I hope everything's going to be all right but I've just seen it so I'm letting you know.' And I'm like, oh, another message, didn't think anything of it, delete. I sent him a text saying, 'Of course it's all fine, it's part of the contract, they can use the image for in-store promotion.'

Went off to lunch, came back from Soho, literally got in the door, phone rang. It must have been 2.30 or 3, and it's Lindsey.

Simon Garfield

So when I had the idea of writing a book about this showbusiness world, I thought of Ghislain.

23/8/06
To Ghislain Pascal
Subject: Hi/Idea
Hi Ghislain,
 I hope all's well.
 Not sure if you're about at the moment, but I had an idea for something you might like and thought it would be good to meet up.
 Bests,
 Simon

[I wince when I see 'Bests' now. The cartoonist Glen Baxter had sent me some emails with it, and I thought he was up on things.]

A reply came back that afternoon:

Hi Simon,
 Great to hear from you. Yes very much around. Let me know when you want to meet up.
 Ghislain

I met him in September 2006 at a club near Trafalgar Square, and I tried to sound him out. I wasn't sure quite how interesting or entertaining his work would be (or whether this interest and entertainment would sustain a book), but if his clients were all up for it I thought it might be a worthwhile enterprise. Besides, I wanted to try something new, and I'd never started a book before without having a fairly clear picture of how things would turn out. Ghislain was quite keen, and said he would ask Tamara, Jacqueline, Nell and the rest, but feared that the book might be a bit boring. No, I insisted, I thought it would be fascinating.

Later that day he sent me an email:

Hi Simon,

Great seeing you for lunch today.

Liking your idea the more I think about it...obviously need to discuss much more so let me know when you want to come south of the river to get the ball rolling.

Ghislain

At the time it was impossible to know that he was right, that the book would turn out to be boring. It would be especially boring because Bob Carlos Clarke, who was Ghislain's most exciting client, and would have provided me with some nice anecdotes, had recently killed himself in a dramatic way.

2. can i start again? asked emma b

Simon Garfield

In early November 2006 I sent Jake Lingwood, my editor at Ebury Press, a proposal for the book. I had known Jake as a friend for a few years, ever since he got in touch with my agent and asked whether I had anything I was keen to write for him. Ebury was part of Random House, so clearly it had a lot of clout in the marketplace. Jake said he had liked a couple of books I had written, and after a few years he came up with an idea that he thought might suit me. This involved the Mass Observation archive at Sussex University, a huge collection of diaries and other writings collected from ordinary people from 1937. I edited three books of these diaries, covering the war years and the aftermath, and they were quite successful.

I had the idea for *The Agent* not long before the third diary book appeared in paperback. I went in to the Ebury office and mentioned it to Jake, and he was pleased with the idea, or at least the idea that I wanted to do something else for him, although I think he wondered whether the book was fully focused yet. Shortly afterwards I sent him an email:

Hi Jake,

Had a great lunch with Ghislain Pascal re the possibility of doing the book, and he's up for it. Nice coincidence: after our lunch he came into Ebury to talk about Jacqueline Gold. I'm going to his house/office in a couple of weeks to discuss things further. This is his client list – I'm obviously particularly taken with Emma B...

Best,

Simon

I attached a copy of my *Observer* article about Ghislain, and a link to the Panic website. The site contained potted histories of all those he represented, and the one for Emma B read:

After winning the 'Elite Model Look' in 1995 at the age of 15, Emma B starred in campaigns for Katherine Hamnett, Replay Jeans, Triumph, Joop, Top Shop, Lynx and Giant; appeared on the catwalk for Gucci, Christian Dior, Valentino and Hermès; and featured in the pages of Italian *Vogue*, *Allure*, *Elle*, *Marie Claire* and *The Face*.

She then moved from modelling to television, acting and singing, and began a relationship with the singer Brian Harvey. She co-presented the 26-part travel-based gameshow *Flying Start* for Carlton TV, and music show *The Mix* for ITV2; starred in the Channel 4 drama *It's A Girl Thing*; and released a single 'What You Need' through Warner Music.

Emma has appeared on numerous reality shows including *The Farm* (Five), and is currently appearing on Sky One's show *Cirque de Celebrité*. She has appeared on the cover of numerous men's magazines including *Maxim*, *Loaded* and *Front*.

As for Jacqueline Gold, she was writing a book for Ebury – an autobiography called *A Woman's Courage: The Inspirational Story of the Woman Behind Ann Summers* – in which she would reveal that she was abused by her stepfather. Ebury Press already published a successful series of Ann Summers erotic novels, with titles such as *True Passion: A Tale of Desire as Told by Madame B* and *Lost in Lust: More Tales from Madame B*. There was also *The Ann Summers Book of Red Hot and Rude Positions*. Jake feared that there might be some element of conflict or compromise, not least because if I upset

Jacqueline Gold in my book it might affect the possibility of Ebury publishing future titles on the Ann Summers list, including yet more tales from Madame B.

From Jake Lingwood

Hi Simon

Really pleased you had a good lunch.

I read your *Observer* piece and was surprised at how affectionate it was – good news, really, as Ghislain clearly has plenty of coals in the Ebury fire.

If you wouldn't mind writing an outline I think you should, as it's important we get the project as commercial-looking as possible. Because the content is quite close to home, we need to get folk to see beyond the subject and instead see a commercial, accessible book. Your *Observer* piece does that to some extent but what it doesn't really do is hint at narrative which, ultimately, will be what we need. If your outline can make encouraging narrative noises, even better. Is that OK?

A couple of weeks later, I completed the outline.

Hi Jake,

Here's the outline, at last. Inevitably it's one of those things that will only really take shape when it's under way, but Ghislain's up for it, and I think we'll get a really funny, insightful and original book. I'm very keen to start it.

Attachment:

The Agent

Or: How one man and four semi-famous quite rich women tried to get more famous and wealthier while still hanging on to what remained of their dignity.

What does it take to be successful in the modern world? How does one achieve fame and maintain it? What compromises must one make to attain one's goals? And how exciting and glamorous, in truth, is the exciting and glamorous life of the modern celebrity?

The Agent is a book about one man, four women, and their quest for fame and success. The man is Ghislain Pascal, a manager, agent and public relations practitioner – handsome, gay, early thirties – and the women are voluptuous and varied. There is Emma B, a slender *Vogue* and catwalk model at 15, a buxom star of reality television a decade later. There is Jacqueline Gold, chief executive of the Ann Summers and Knickerbox empires, purveyor of erotic lingerie and vibrating amusements to a grateful nation, one of the UK's most admired businesswomen. There is Nancy Sorrell, chief model for Ann Summers, an actor and singer and parent of twins with husband Vic Reeves. And there is Tamara Beckwith, model, journalist, actor, TV presenter, socialite and promoter of her own jewellery range on the QVC satellite shopping channel.

To a great extent, these women are trying to attain the same as all of us: happiness, individuality, a degree of financial comfort, flawless grooming, a sense of satisfaction and usefulness. But a life in the public eye is different and unpredictable, and is beset by insecurities and unusual values. *The Agent* is a book that examines the everyday details that determine success or failure. It will follow five lives into the worlds of glamour modelling, lacy underwear, television, men's magazines, newspapers and books, and will describe the process – the planning, meetings, modelling shoots, advertising and publicity campaigns, parties and launches – that propels or stalls a career.

In addition to these clients, Pascal also guides the careers of Nell McAndrew (fitness model, charity fundraiser, modern-day 'forces sweetheart'), Amanda Stretton (racing driver and television presenter), Gabrielle Richens (model and television presenter) and the estate of Bob Carlos Clarke, photographer of erotica, who once said to Pascal his work would be more valued after he died, and so it has proved. Pascal is also an astute observer of the profile of other celebrities, keen to point out misguided career moves and offer correctional advice. 'I look after the beautiful people,' he once proclaimed. He used to look after the model and presenter Caprice, who thought her career would flourish without him.

The Agent will incorporate insider knowledge and vivid anecdotes within a strong narrative drive, and the reader will gain unprecedented access behind doors normally closed. Combining the best elements of candid celebrity biography with strong journalistic insight, *The Agent* will provide a gripping and revelatory read.

80,000 words approx. Delivery August 2007.

I must have talked to Jake a few days after this, because the next email concerned the degree of control that Ghislain had over the final manuscript. The answer was: none, but he did have approval over other things.

Hi Jake,

Getting some great material with Ghislain: Wednesday was a meeting with three guys from a calendar company deciding whom to include in this year's UK's Hottest Babes, most of whom Ghislain represents. Lots of discussion about what the modern desperate man is looking for these days, and how much the company would have to pay to publish a Daniel Radcliffe calendar for this Christmas.

Ghislain would like a letter/email from you stating the following.

GP gets to approve:

1) Jacket image of him and any of his clients.

2) Text on back of jacket with sole aim of ensuring we are not being derogatory to him or his clients.

In addition:

3) GP will see the text of the book in advance of publication, at which point he will be able to correct any factual inaccuracies only. He does not have text approval. We also agree not to disclose any confidential business information. The text will be for GP's eyes only; his clients and/or any other third party will not see the text in advance of publication.

Things then went back and forth a bit between all parties, and there was much talk about images for the jacket. Ghislain wondered whether we could use an existing picture of him in a jacuzzi with a white shirt on, surrounded by some of his good-looking female clients in bikinis. The photo was by Bob Carlos Clarke.

From Jake Lingwood

Hi Simon

Ghislain says he's not sure he would want to do new photography. Unfortunately (for you!) when we talked about this in the last meeting, this was the key way for me to crystallise the book and the way it could be packaged in my mind. Of course, it's too early to commit to an idea, but I'd like to have the option. I have also written on the contract that it's your responsibility to deliver these guys in terms of a photo shoot.

J

Simon Garfield

Like you, I imagine, this correspondence was now sending me to sleep. I considered it one of those things that seemed important at the time, but would soon be consumed by other issues, such as content. Or so I hoped. In fact, to both Jake and Ghislain the jacket was the most important key to success – for Jake so that he could sell the book and create a marketing position that would enable his team to start showing it to booksellers, and for Ghislain partly for reasons of vanity, and to ensure that his clients would not be shafted.

We let it hang in the air for a bit. Jake was also keen to get more of a feel for the book itself, and he was wondering about a sample chunk he could show around. By this time I had actually begun to spend more time with Ghislain and his clients, and there had been one day in particular that I thought would give a good flavour of the book. My notes:

February 2007. We are travelling to a meeting at a television company – myself, Ghislain and Emma B, the tall blonde model in her early twenties. At the moment it is still just myself and Ghislain, as we are waiting in Ghislain's convertible Audi at Charing Cross, waiting for Emma B's train to arrive from Hastings. Emma B's full name is Emma Blocksage. The independent television production company is in Islington, and the woman we will be meeting is called Barbara Altounyan, the Director of Programmes at Flame TV, a company she manages with Roger Bolton, who also presents *Feedback* and a boring religious programme on Radio 4.

But we are early, so we stop at a café around the corner.

Emma B *(to me)*

I think I wanted to be famous ever since I was a very young girl. My whole world seemed to be looking up to pop stars and then film stars and wishing I was like them. I had no idea what being famous would involve, but now I know it hasn't put me off. I like hard work, and I will do almost anything. But I'm interested in lasting fame, not one of those examples from television where someone is absolutely everywhere for four weeks and then forgotten about. I want to be known for my skills as a model and hopefully an actress. Some people can do it and some people can't, and I think I'm one of the lucky ones. I don't wish to boast, but I do have very nice legs and boobs. I had the boobs done for myself, not Brian [Harvey, once in the band East 17] as some people think. Just as well, because now that I'm not with him any more I'm still with my boobs.

Simon Garfield

Ghislain had told me previously that Emma B was his 'reality star', his 'tabloid reality heaven'. She was not to be confused with the Radio 1 DJ of the same name.

Ghislain Pascal

She's my bimbo. I always need one of them, because that's how you make regular income. It's just a case of getting her into the big league. Sky One really loved her on *Cirque de Celebrité*, where she was runner-up, so I'm hoping they may come up with a show for her.

I had another television meeting with some friends of mine who have a production company, and we brainstormed Emma. The show we've come up with to pitch is called *I'm not a Bimbo, I've Got Brains*, or something. The thinking is, she goes off and learns about art, she learns about opera, she learns about ballet. Each week. There's loads of television shows a bit like that. It's a vehicle for her, but also the viewer learns a bit on each show, but then you have a bimbo fronting it. She'll be herself. She's not the brightest cookie in the box, but she's certainly not a Jade Goody. Or a Jordan. Okay, I don't think Jordan's thick. But she's not a Jade Goody. She's not going to come out and go, 'Ooh, is ice made out of water?' But she's not going to know anything about ballet. She has a council house background, so she has no cultural experience. I think it's quite a good formula. We thought BBC 3, but my friends said ITV.

And then there will be more of what we do already. *OK!* want to do another story with her this year about when her and Brian Harvey split. And we're doing some videos with her in January for Ann Summers online – quite funny. Like 'Emma B puts up a shelf'.

Simon Garfield

And then she bends over in a short skirt because she drops a nail?

Ghislain Pascal

Yes, tongue in cheek. You must come on that. They're just finishing the scripts.

Simon Garfield

Scripts?

Ghislain Pascal

They have to be funny, so that people will send them to each other. Two minutes each. Then she's in the windows of Ann Summers with Nancy Sorrell and Kate Lawler from January fifteenth, so that's always good, for Valentine's Day. In terms of all those girls you see in the papers every day, I think Emma is by far the sexiest. The *Sun's* current Page 3 Stunna is this girl called Keeley, and you look at it, and you think, why is everyone getting excited about that? But with Emma, you've never seen such good legs. Obviously her boobs are now ridiculous. She's now 34 double-D or something. She used to be 34 B, which is perfect lingerie-size tits, the face of Triumph, and she had a huge contract with Debenhams when I first met her. She couldn't possibly do any of those now.

Simon Garfield

Why did she have them done?

Ghislain Pascal

Because that's what she likes. A psychological thing. It's for herself.

Simon Garfield

What happens to them when she gets to 45?

Ghislain Pascal

They stay there. They're not going anywhere. They're in bags.

Emma B

And rich. I also want to be rich. When I was younger that didn't matter to me, but now that I've seen how much money you need to maintain a famous lifestyle then I really need to have that money. I don't think the money will make me happier, but it will make things easier. It would be very difficult to be famous without the money – imagine the Beckhams being poor. They just wouldn't be the Beckhams.

Ghislain Pascal (to Emma B)

The important thing is to be eager but not too eager. Don't just say yes to anything Barbara [Altounyan] suggests. Like any television company these days she has a lot of outlets, and she will make some serious programmes and some programmes that may seem crazy but pay the bills. Barbara is a wonderful person, but she can be very in your face. Once I was having dinner with her and Jacqueline, and her hair caught fire. Jacqueline noticed it first, and pointed it out – 'Er, Barbara, I think your hair is on fire…' and Barbara put it out quite nonchalantly, as if it was a weekly occurrence.

• • •

Barbara Altounyan

Well, Emma, it's lovely to see you. Do you have anything you'd particularly like to do?

Simon Garfield

We are in a small office in Islington. Barbara is mid-forties, frizzy mass of brown hair, small and stocky. She is sitting behind a desk, but occasionally stands up to place her legs astride an electric heater, the warm air circulating up her skirt. On the wall behind her is a

whiteboard with a list of possible ideas for television shows: Old
Dogs – Angry Yobs, Top Shop, Noel Gallagher at 40, Text a Celeb,
Gay Sex – Complicated Love, Castration – Have You Got the Balls?
Brown Like Me, Heart Transplants, Squaddies on Scrapheap, Rude
Magic, Holiday Hospital, Love Me Like I Wasn't Famous, Don't Ask
the Therapist, Cherie Blair's Family Law, Fat + Famous, Wicked
Stepmother, The Real Trisha/Jeremy Kyle, Band Therapy, Sell Your
House Live. Another list shows programmes currently in produc-
tion: Don't Get Done – Get Dom, and Crisis Hair.

Emma B
I'd be happy doing most things.

Barbara Altounyan
What sort of things are you passionate about?

Emma B
Apart from men?

Barbara Altounyan
Including men, if you like. You've had your boobs done, haven't you?

Emma B
And this afternoon I'm having botox.

Barbara Altounyan
Why on earth would you want to do that?

Emma B
My mother is having it done at the same time.

Barbara Altounyan
Are you close to your mother? Would she agree to be filmed?

Emma B
She's quite adventurous.

Barbara Altounyan

What I'd like you to do, Ghislain and Simon, is leave the room now. When you come back, Emma will have something to explain to you.

[Five minutes later]

Emma is a new presenter of a popular science show and will now explain something to you.

Emma B

Okay, Chaos Theory! Chaos Theory is when something happens that can't be explained but there is…an explanation for it. It is also when…can I start again?

Chaos Theorising is when a man, or woman, explains that although the things that happen are meant to…I'll try it once more…

Okay, Chaos Theory. It's when…

Barbara Altounyan

Shall I help you with it?

Emma B

I understood it when you told me about it, but now it's totally gone.

Simon Garfield

After this meeting, which didn't immediately result in an offer of work, I also composed a new outline of the book for Jake Lingwood.

The Agent is a book about one man, four women and their quest for celebrity and riches.

Ghislain Pascal is a handsome and fit man, and he used to be concerned about human rights, running the publicity unit of Survival International. But then he discovered the attractions of fame and glamour, and he transformed his life to look after the careers of those who wanted to become famous and wealthy.

His new clients were not endangered tribes in Borneo, but attractive women from Chelsea and the Home Counties, and they paid him thousands of pounds each month to boost their public profile in the media and improve their careers. This is the story of how he got on.

The women are voluptuous and varied. There is Emma B, a slender *Vogue* and catwalk model at 15, a buxom star of reality television a decade later. Emma B will do practically anything to become as famous as Jordan. There is Jacqueline Gold, chief executive of the Ann Summers and Knickerbox empires, purveyor of erotic lingerie and vibrating amusements to a grateful nation, one of the UK's most admired businesswomen. Although hugely successful, Jacqueline is keen to explore new career paths. There is Nancy Sorrell, chief model for Ann Summers, an actor and singer and parent of twins with husband Vic Reeves. Nancy wants to become the face of Mothercare. And there is Tamara Beckwith, model, journalist, actor, TV presenter, socialite and promoter of her own jewellery range on the QVC satellite shopping channel. Tamara, who is married to an Italian with fierce passions and jealousies, wants to appear in the pages of *Hello!* or *OK!* every week.

The Agent is also about the aftershock of fame, and what happens when the myth takes over. Pascal also represents the estate of his friend Bob Carlos Clarke, the glamour photographer who found fame with his subjects Rachel Weisz, Caprice and Marco Pierre White. But when his own looks started to fade...

As Pascal observes, he operates in a world where the work of his friend is worth more dead than alive, and his prints are now more in demand than ever.

The Agent will incorporate insider knowledge and vivid anecdotes within a strong narrative drive, and the reader will gain unprecedented access behind doors normally closed. Combining the best elements of candid celebrity biography with strong journalistic insight, the book will provide a gripping and revelatory read.

So much for that. Almost as soon as this new outline was sent, I began to wonder whether I had missed the real story. During the time I spent with Ghislain, much of his work was occupied with Bob Carlos Clarke – selling his photographs to collectors, protecting his copyright, caring for his archive with his widow Lindsey. Increasingly, Carlos Clarke seemed to be the key to understanding much of what Ghislain did. He had photographed most of Ghislain's clients and had entered their world, and they all had stories about him. But beyond this it seemed as though the issues I was originally keen to explore at the start of my book were also the ones that concerned the photographer throughout his life: the desire for fame and wealth, and how to square these ambitions with the need for acclaim and respect. What would one do and not do to achieve one's goals? Would a famous person ever be satisfied with their life? What about a creative person – was it possible to ever achieve artistic perfection?

It seemed to me that if I could get to the heart of Bob (as everyone called him, even those who hardly knew him, and especially those who weren't sure if Carlos was his middle name or part of his surname), then I could tell a darker story of brilliance gone awry, and of a tortured soul. My book would also then have a 'narrative arc', or at least a strict and dramatic ending. The real key to the story appeared to be his wife Lindsey, who began as his muse and then became his manager. If she was cooperative, then all the doors would suddenly be flung open, and soon I would be reading his school reports.

3. lindsey believes that few ever comprehended his inner torment, reported the *daily telegraph*

Simon Garfield

I don't know why it had taken me so long to grasp the significance of Bob. In February 2007, Ghislain had told me that Lindsey Carlos Clarke had agreed to do one interview about her husband and her life now, and he wondered whether I would be interested. The story would coincide with the first anniversary of his death. I said no, partly because I had other commitments at that time, but predominantly because I didn't realise what a good story this was. So Ghislain placed the piece with the *Daily Telegraph* and a journalist called Janie Lawrence turned up to see Lindsey at her home in Chelsea, and when I read the piece in the paper, accompanied by a good photo of Lindsey and some of Bob's pictures from the archive, I felt envious that I hadn't done it myself.

Daily Telegraph, 21 March 2007

Her husband may have been perceived as a charming and witty raconteur, but Lindsey believes that few ever comprehended his inner torment...

...she was pottering in the house with their 14-year-old daughter,

35

Scarlett, when there was a knock at the door. 'I thought it was the fish man but when I opened the door there were two policemen and a WPC. As soon as the woman said, 'What relation are you to Robert Carlos Clarke?', I knew…

Simon Garfield

Good as this article was, there were a lot of questions that arose from it. Such as, what were his inner torments? Why was she not shocked when the police called? Why did she spend the evening of his death at a cocktail party?

I sought out other newspaper cuttings to get a clearer picture, and inevitably these fell into two categories, those about or by him before he died, and the obituaries. The ones after he died tended to be more fawning, but even before he died the photographic journals gave him substantial analysis and reverence. 'Inspirational, passionate, and usually more than a little bit controversial, Bob Carlos Clarke has been one of the hottest names in UK photography across three decades,' wrote the *British Journal of Photography* in 2002. It noted that he had turned 50, and had begun to think about what makes a great photographer. 'It struck me that UK photographers reach an age when they become invisible,' he told the magazine. 'It doesn't matter how great they've been, they just fade into obscurity. Norman Parkinson once said to me that the secret is never to stay long enough in one place to become a target. A lot of young photographers have never heard of Don McCullin or Terence Donovan or Terry O'Neill, and yet they are among our greatest talents.' The wistful implication was: young photographers had never heard of Carlos Clarke either.

The newspaper stories contained information about his slightly troubled soul, particularly his desire not to be known as that man who does women in rubber. The *Independent* noted that he 'captured some of the most remarkable images of our celebrity-obsessed era', without actually being very interested in celebrity himself. *The Times* found that he was 'equally accomplished at creating still lifes and immaculately erotic commercial work', and noted that he regarded the still lifes – his stones near his Sussex beach house and salvaged objects from the Thames – as some of his best work, 'a judgement with which many concurred in the years before his tragic death in an accident, when just approaching the height of his powers'.

I also found some clippings that featured Bob's work as a starting point for a discussion about erotic art, or at least about sex. There was a piece on teenagers and sex in the *Sunday Times*, and there were many straight reports of his death, some of them inaccurate.

BBC News Online *(27 March 2006)*

Photographer Dies in Accident

Photographer Bob Carlos Clarke has died in an accident. He was in his 50s. Irish-born Clarke, who moved to Britain in 1964, was renowned for fashion, portrait and commercial photography, and creating a series of books.

In 1975 he graduated from the Royal College of Art with an MA in photography, and directed a series of high-profile advertising campaigns.

He was well known for capturing the female nude and a series of images showing a spoon and fork intertwined.

The Illustrated Delta of Venus, Obsession, The Dark Summer and *Shooting Sex* from 2003 are among his collections of photographs.

Simon Garfield

One of the best pieces about Bob was written by Tamara Beckwith for *Tatler*. Tamara knew people on the magazine, and they knew that she might produce a piece that was personal and affectionate.

Tamara Beckwith *(in* Tatler, *July 2006)*

In my late teens I, like every hardcore Chelsea girl and would-be model, was beyond desperate to shoot with the infamous, risqué Bob Carlos Clarke. He was fast and furious and seemed so cool (he even had a parrot – very Keith Richards). Born in 1950, he had grown up in County Cork, Ireland, the son of a retired major, and as a teenager in the 1960s had all the textbook wildness and sexual frustration that went with the territory. After Wellington College he'd become a photographer by chance, when he convinced a part-time model at his Sussex art school to pose naked for him. At the Royal College he completed an MA in photography and became interested in fetishistic images of rubber-clad women in high heels. Allen Jones, the British pop artist known for his erotically charged paintings and sculptures of women in similar outfits and positions, thought Bob should avoid being labelled an erotic photographer, but he had begun a life-long mission to capture these women on film.

Tamara Beckwith

The *Tatler* piece was my idea. I said to Ghislain that I thought it should be written, so I talked to him and Lindsey and my editor at *Tatler* and just got on with it.

Simon Garfield

I liked the way you began the piece by reporting from the funeral, and then opened it out.

Tamara Beckwith

I was away for the funeral.

Simon Garfield

So you did the classic journalistic thing and recreated it?

Tamara Beckwith

It wasn't in the original article, but *Tatler* added it.

It read: Brompton Cemetery: A jet-black coffin with a decadent plumage of blood-red roses and a former assistant snatching every moment on film. The funeral of Bob Carlos Clarke was a suitably theatrical farewell to a brilliant photographer and lover of the erotic, the dark and the dangerous – a man who thought in black and white, in life and art.

Simon Garfield

Her piece included memories of Bob from the television executive Claudia Rosencrantz, the photographer John Stoddart and Mandy Smith, who was photographed by Carlos Clarke at about the time she was going out with Bill Wyman, who was about twice her age.

John Stoddart

Bob was a real enigma. In his work he was utterly authentic and never dumbed-down – a genuine artisan. The work might sometimes have been classed as pornography but Bob always retained a high aesthetic. But there was increasing anger at the recent lack of recognition.

Simon Garfield

There was another account of Bob's life, and this one was even more authoritative. It had been composed in the days immediately following his death, and was delivered at the chapel at Brompton Cemetery by Rupert Morris 12 days after he died. Morris was trained as a minister by the British Humanist Association.

Rupert Morris *(6 April 2006)*

Our task today is to try to come to terms with the terrible shock of his death, to put his life in some kind of context, make sense of what we can, recall something of his unique, provocative charisma and lay him to rest.

I shall not detain you long before we move outside, but I'm going to begin with the most difficult bit, Bob's death: because it was so recent, so unexpected, and so hard to accept… In retrospect, the signs were there that he might choose one day to end his life in some sudden and violent way. His own work is full of allusions to such things, and many of you here may well have your own insights. For Lindsey certainly, the manner of his death, although deeply shocking and wounding, was not entirely a surprise.

Simon Garfield

Morris gave what I now consider to be a brilliant speech – obviously compassionate, but also brutally honest. Anyone who knew Bob was aware of the value he placed on bluntness and truth, and it was clear to me that Morris had obviously obtained some sort of instruction from Lindsey to reflect this in the directness and alacrity of his tone. One line in particular keeps returning: 'The horror of Bob's death still sends a shiver down our spines.' What did he mean? Why was it so awful?

Rupert Morris

We feel an extraordinary mixture of emotions today. There is anger, understandable anger, towards Bob for doing such a terrible thing; guilt – could we not have helped him, turned him away from self-destruction? Resignation – well if that's what he wanted, no one could have stopped him; regret – what a terrible, avoidable waste; then appreciation – for he was such an extraordinary, life-enhancing character that it is hard to envisage him just fading quietly away; and gratitude, for all that he gave you, and left behind with you.

4. i got really involved with him, said lindsey carlos clarke

Lindsey Carlos Clarke

I had a girlfriend, very pretty, who men were crazy for. She rang me up one day and said I've met this amazing photographer, you'd really get on well with him, he does such clever stuff. I didn't think much about it and then a few weeks later I got a phone call and he said, 'Hello, this is Bob Carlos Clarke, a friend of Geraldine's. I'd like to come and see you about maybe doing some pictures and I'd like to come and show you my portfolio.' Which was very odd for me, because as a model, I always went out to see them.

Rupert Morris

Bob certainly had a rich and colourful ancestry. The name Carlos has nothing to do with Spain. It was derived from a seventeenth-century forebear called Colonel Careless, a cavalier who helped Charles II hide in an oak tree to escape from his roundhead pursuers, and was rewarded when Charles became King by being allowed to assume the name of Carlos – and being given the land in London known as Carlos Place. In a later century the families of Carlos and Clarke came together. They were Protestant Irish aristocracy, and Bob's father was a chip off the old block, brave, self-willed, often outrageous.

Lindsey Carlos Clarke

I said, 'Well, you're very welcome to come and see me but I've actually got flu and I'm in bed because I've been working so much.' I remember him coming to the front door with this portfolio of pictures under his arm and he sat on the end of my bed and both of us were laughing because Bob was fantastically witty and funny and I looked at these photographs, which were amazing.

Rupert Morris

Major Charles Carlos Clarke had fought in two world wars, directed and managed Bostock's Three-Ring Circus ('Britain's Biggest!') and been married to two titled women before he met Bob's mother Myra. She came from an entirely different background, one marked by hardship and tragedy...Bob was clearly haunted by the old photographs he found among his mother's possessions after her death.

Lindsey Carlos Clarke

I was 23, just. And 1976 was that incredibly, incredibly hot summer and he asked me if I'd do some pictures for him, and I said yes, and we sort of became friends and we used to go out to dinner and I remember, I was earning very good money at that stage, and I remember going to Trader Vic's and we used to drink cocktails. Everyone was so obsessed by cocktails in the 1970s and I got on really well with him, and there was always a sexual innuendo there but I wasn't really...he was all right, I was busy in my life, and I sort of allowed things to happen, but what happened was I got really involved with him, in his whole psyche. He was such a magnetically creative man. Do remember I'd been brought up with someone like that so that was such a pull for me. We used to talk long into the night, ideas, you know, everything.

Ghislain Pascal

The first time I met Bob must have been 1995 or 1996. It was not long after I first started working with Tamara.

So she was booked to do a shoot for a trendy magazine, and Bob was booked to shoot it, and it was on the roof of the Whiteleys shopping centre. Tamara hadn't gone to bed the night before, she'd been to a nightclub, and the shoot was a complete disaster. She had to climb up these industrial ladders, and that's how I met Bob. He was on fiery form.

The piece never got published, but we started to get chummy. I started to learn who he was, and the studio was very impressive in Battersea. He shot Caprice, and it was that famous shoot of her in rubber, which was then used on the cover for *Esquire* for the piece you did, and then got used everywhere. That's the picture that's on my stairs.

Every year he did the Powergen calendar, and he got me involved in booking the celebrities. I did that for three years, and got all these different people, and it was working on those that we really got to know each other. What struck me about him most was his will, knowing what he wanted to do, and also how exciting he was to be with, always trying to provoke you and get into slightly risky situations.

Lindsey Carlos Clarke

When I met Bob I was already married to a guy in the music business. I got married very, very young, 19, which is pretty stupid. My mother said I only did it to shock her, because my parents were so laid-back and didn't get married for years, so I got married here at Chelsea Register Office.

He was a nice public school boy with long hair who played guitar, tall and blond, just what I wanted. My father said to me – my father was very small – he said to me I must marry a tall man to change the genetics. So I married him, and thought that was going to be lovely.

• • •

Simon Garfield

I love the way there's all this overlap between Bob and all your clients.

Ghislain Pascal

Yes, that's why it works. All our lives are intricately linked through Bob.

Simon Garfield

Will Scarlett talk? [Scarlett is Bob's daughter, 14 when he died.]

Ghislain Pascal

Probably not.

Simon Garfield

What about Marco Pierre White?

Ghislain Pascal

I can't get hold of him at the moment. He hasn't talked about Bob to anyone.

Simon Garfield

I know he's about to open a restaurant at Chelsea Football Club, so perhaps I could join that charabanc.

Ghislain Pascal

Tamara would be good. They live in the same road. He was at 41, and she's at 14, and Bob was always getting Tamara's mail.

• • •

Lindsey Carlos Clarke

I was a model. I came from quite a bohemian upbringing, so the nude thing or the shock thing was never a big thing for me. I never had a very pornographic body, so I could never do anything very exciting. But it was weird for me when those girls would come to Bob and say, 'I'd love to do a nude but I don't know if I can take my clothes off,' and you feel like saying, 'Well, don't bother then.' If you can't go for it, then don't, it's not going to mean anything. In the 1970s, working for things like the *Sun* newspaper, where there were four or five of us walking around naked, nobody really bothered or cared, and we were all, oh, I like your shoes, you know, not really interested at all. I did a commercial for something like Three Wishes and there must have been 50 crew there and I was a week naked being hoicked in and out of a bath, in there for hours covered in soap, and you never think about it unless someone's particularly disgusting. So when you've done that, I find people are uptight about talking about sex or nudity, I find them…get a life, did we live through the 1960s for this?

My name was Lindsey Rudland. At the time there was also Jilly Johnson, Nina Carter, blondes, and they had a group at one stage called Blonde on Blonde and they were a big hit in Japan. I was out of it when Samantha Fox came along. Bob photographed her. Things were really changing then.

Simon Garfield

Lindsey hadn't used her maiden name for years, but I'd had a look online and found that you could still buy merchandise with Lindsey Rudland's name and body on it. The *Sun* online store had ten photos of her from her Page 3 days, all with her boobs out with a lively big smile, and you could choose how you wanted to live with them in 2008: on a poster (four sizes), a mug, a mousemat, a coaster, a placemat or a T-shirt.

Lindsey Carlos Clarke

I did everything that blondes did in the 1970s. I did a lot of beauty for *Vogue*, with Barry Lategan I did hair products, I was never designed for catwalk because I'm not really tall enough, and in those days I had to say catwalk wasn't quite what happened. When the supermodel thing came along then it all became a different thing. But I worked for *Vogue* on a Monday, and the *Sun* newspaper on a Tuesday and it was perfectly normal.

In fact, everything was wonderful, everything was marvellous. As a designer I was earning 50 or 60 quid a week, considered good money, and then suddenly I was earning a thousand quid a week – a fortune. Nothing these days for a model, of course, but then it changed how I could run my life.

It wasn't what I thought I'd be doing when I was at school…

I went to a very smart school in Hampstead, lovely, I went to South Hampstead High School. I wasn't very good, but all the other girls were like Einstein.

And then I went to art school. My father was originally a free-lance artist, but then he ran a company called Four Square Publishing. He was a specialist hand-lettering artist, he did book jackets. When I was a little girl, he would do three layouts for each and then we'd sit in bed and the game was: which is the one they'll pick and which is the one you like? And they were obviously always different. At Four Square he was poached by a computer company who wanted someone to design all their stuff, because, as he told me, everybody will have a computer in their house at some point in the future. He took me to this room where there were these enormous big metal things, and I thought I don't want one of them anywhere near me. We lived in Richmond but then the department moved to Reading and I ended up at the Berkshire College of Art.

Simon Garfield
I wonder if you could tell me a bit more about your Page 3 work.

Lindsey Carlos Clarke
Page 3 was great in those days because most of the girls that did Page 3, it wasn't about having enormous bosoms. Girls that did it were always successful models and I loved working with them. I used to work with a photographer called Beverley Goodway – he was just a sweetheart. We could do all the poses. They often used to ring me on a Friday and say, 'Look, we're going to St Tropez, would you like to come?' and they always looked after you really well.

Simon Garfield
And did you become a *Sun* reader favourite?

Lindsey Carlos Clarke
Oh yes, there were men that sent me letters and things. You know they have to vet everything because sometimes you get killer letters, letters that say 'I'm going to cut you up with a knife', not that I ever

saw any of those, but I had hundreds of fan letters from army boys. I know it sounds naïve, but you just go to the studio and they come out on a Thursday or whatever and occasionally you saw them and you'd think, oh, there I am, funny picture they've chosen. And what have they written?, because they used to invent rubbish.

I've got one letter from a man who said he was so in love with me because I look just like a girl he saw at the bus stop except she was plumper and had dark hair. There was another man who wrote to me and asked if I'd like to go on a cycling holiday with him, and then there was another man who offered me £10 million to do some photographs. This was tempting until we realised he came from Rampton mental hospital. He gave me a date on which I could meet him and he would hand over the money. One year I was the *Sun*'s Christmas girl.

It's not like I was that good-looking, but you're not stupid about yourself, you know. Once I was picked up by a photographer when I was about 15, and he said, 'God, you look like Twiggy.' And Barry Lategan, who photographed Twiggy a lot, said I reminded him of Twig – it's something to do with the proportions of the face.

So this photographer picks me up at a school dance and gave me his number and said could he come to see me. He came and saw my parents and I was deeply suspicious and they said I could do some photographs with him but it was all very...I thought it was a bit odd. I just decided no. Later I met a friend of mine when I was a designer at Kids In Gear and she said you should be a model. My mother was extremely worried about the whole thing because she really wanted me to be a doctor or something, Einstein, you know – what she would have liked to have been.

There was lots of work for *Vogue*. I was never on the cover but I used to do a lot of close-ups, beauty work. I was Max Factor's face of '75, so I was all on all their hoardings and posters and things. No, I did love it, I did have a great time.

By the time I got together with Bob I had already started to know too much. I was seeing things in a different way. I was going to see photographers and they'd say, 'This is the layout,' and I'd say, 'That's awful, you can't make her arm do that,' and, 'You've got the wrong lighting – you need a reflector here.' I'd met Bob and I'd realised he really was, creatively, a force to be reckoned with but the problem was, he was absolutely no good at dealing with the nitty-gritty side of it at all, he was chaotic, and I just thought we should put this all together, because we could make this work.

I think this was 1980. I'd been modelling for six or seven years, I'd made good money, I bought a house, and by then I really had a different sort of dream. Bob was worried about the psychology of me giving up. He would work with the models and I would be an ex-model, which is really rather depressing, so I went out of my way on shoots not to look in any way a threat because it's very important that the models who came to us felt like queen bee, so you get the best out of her. So I was definitely in my overalls, and it never worried me, and I wasn't insecure about that at all. Models used to say, 'I think I'm going to be an actress,' and the only person that ever managed it was Joanna Lumley. So I found a different skill, which was making things work for Bob, clearing the way for him to do his best work.

Ghislain Pascal

If you did a Bob shoot, you knew you'd done one. You wouldn't go home thinking, 'Right, what's next?' You might need a day or two to recover. And some girls wouldn't come back. Some girls didn't get it and didn't like him – he could be explicit. But he wasn't coming on to them, he was just being Bob, he was just flirting. Most of the girls loved him. Bob was the real thing. He was the last of the maverick kind of proper full-on production photographers. With Bob you had the personality – it was always fun, he was such a big personality, he was always the star of the shoot – the celebrities just happened to be the people being photographed.

He always had lots of assistants – it was a big production number. He didn't like being out of his own environment. But in his studio you sat down for lunch at this big table, and he held court. It was a fun day out – it's not like photographers now, miserable as sin, you might get a hello or a sandwich if you're lucky and then they want you to fuck off.

He used to sit in meetings with people from Powergen and tell them they were a bunch of cunts. He had no concept of dealing with people – he would tell them exactly what he thought, and if they didn't like it he would tell them to fuck off, I don't want to do the fucking job then. But some clients want that: 'Oh my God, it's Bob Carlos Clarke! The legend!' They love all the girls and all the rubber that comes out.

Lindsey Carlos Clarke
So me and Bob had a two-year affair. Instead of starting off amazing and going the other way, which is what normally happens, it just became more and more special.

I'd spend the day with Bob and people got used to seeing us around, and then sometimes we'd have our partners with us, so we must be just good friends, but we weren't. My husband used to call us the master race, because I used to come home and say, 'We've had this amazing idea,' and he'd say, 'What have the fucking master race decided today?'

We got together finally in 1978, but after we'd been together for two years. It caused the most terrible two divorces.

Simon Garfield
Your own divorce was really acrimonious?

Lindsey Carlos Clarke
Horrible, horrible. We had a hideous divorce, just total hell.

Bob and I bought the first studio he had in Earls Court Square, it was on the first floor, and I remember we were traumatised by how much it cost and it was probably something like £15,000, and we stripped it all out and we had this huge room with a balcony. If you go back and look at his books like *Obsession*, all those pictures were done around that era. Then we sold my house in Fulham, I had a little tiny cottage, sweet, very St Ives, and we bought quite a big house in Fulham where we built a studio, and a drawing room on the top and we started to properly put ourselves together financially.

We made this pact that we were going to be like *The Hunger*, we were going to be absolutely out there, we were going to do what we wanted to do, you know, and have what we wanted to have, no marriage, yuk, no children. Then, when we decided we were too old, you know, it was going to be up and over the top together. Thelma and Louise before it happened, you know, it definitely was what our plan was. We were very young. I've heard people say, 'I don't think I'll make it past 30', and they're 17, and I think, I remember saying that.

The other thing I remember was that we all said to each other, 'Look at us, we're all beautiful and young, we're all models or photographers or actors and it's all going to last for ever.' It was just impossible to see how we could possibly fuck it up.

5. from one obsessive to another there's a kind of sympathy, said philippe garner

Philippe Garner

I find in life that one is always endeavouring to make some sort of connection with people, find shared territory, and when it's around something which is striking some deep and quite complex chords, it then becomes a more precious connection and I suppose that the chords that were being struck between me and Bob were all the darker resonances of his work.

Simon Garfield

I met Philippe Garner in a café near his office at Christie's in St James's, where he was in charge of photography and other artistic developments of the twentieth century, like modern design. But before then he was with the competition.

Philippe Garner

I was at Sotheby's for 31 years. In December 1971 I was asked to coordinate the first sale of photographs, which was the beginning of the modern photography auction market. I was 22, almost a child, but it meant I was able to grow up with the subject. Now I am 58, and have built up tremendous experience and expertise, and the flame of my passions remains completely undimmed. I regard it as one of the most precious forces in my life, because it keeps me curious. I think, what am I when I cease to be curious?

Simon Garfield

He'd been a fan of Bob's from the very early days. He seemed to understand not only the artistic process behind the photographs, but also the emotional forces that shaped them. I detected that he shared with Bob a deeply embedded yearning for beautiful objects. They were both dark aesthetes, although Philippe had the ability to stand back and articulate his passions.

Philippe Garner

For me there was always so much more than the obvious sexiness of the pictures. It was the shadows. It was the fact that these images really did come from a dark place, and the sexuality combined with all sorts of layers of fear and anxiety and guilt. I suspect that far more of us than would admit to it would in fact agree that the nature of sexual desire and sexual energy is very troubling and complicated and confusing and challenging. And it's not all sweetness and light, far from being just the search for some joy and fulfilment, you know, flowers bursting in spring. Very few people have a sexuality which isn't marked or traumatised in some way with elements of their upbringing, influences, things they've seen, tried to make sense of, and just by the very process of trying to manage those forces within you in a civilised social context, because there's always the polite exterior and the animal within, and it's not always a comfortable marriage and an easy thing to deal with.

Simon Garfield

One of my favourite books is that oral biography of Edie Sedgwick by Jean Stein and George Plimpton – just fantastic. I love talking to people and then cutting up their stuff.

Philippe Garner

That book is great! All of us become informed about things in a thousand and one different ways but the history of painting, photography, illustration, the history of picture-making is filled with explorations of the psyche which will very often include aspects of the sexual psyche as one section of the personality, and perhaps as the cement which binds so many other aspects of the personality. And with Bob...

Simon Garfield

Bob keeps changing, the project keeps changing. What I'm doing now is, well, it's changing shape every two weeks. By the time we leave this café it might be different again. There's a guy who you've met called Ghislain Pascal, who I've known for years, and we've done pieces together. He has always struck me as a very open and interesting young man who has some interesting clients.

I'd say he was mid-thirties. He used to do charity work, but then he decided he wanted to earn some money. I thought it might be rewarding to follow his life for a period of time.

Philippe Garner

Well, all of us are fascinated by the cult of celebrity. Even if we know it's a nonsense, we're fascinated by it. If you want to go back to the beginning of it you keep bumping up against Andy Warhol and everything he touched in his artistic-naïve way. He's like Voltaire's Candide, wandering in this world of wonder – film stars and beautiful people.

So here is Ghislain Pascal, who is making his living out of being the guide/mentor/conduit/go-between for these people with a quite varied range of talents for whom publicity and being in the public eye is their lifeblood, their essential requirement. For some of them it's all they do, for others it's a forum in which they ply their trade, whatever that may be. But in the end for a lot of them their look and their image is the product.

Simon Garfield

Yes, it's all thin air, and if you blow too hard it will just go. And that's Ghislain's job, making sure it all blows in the right direction. And he's very good at that. I began the book just a few months after Bob died, but I wasn't aware at the time just how he was linked in with so many of his clients.

I know you've written about Bob and are a great supporter, but I don't know very much about your background.

Philippe Garner

What we should actually do is meet up one Sunday afternoon and make you some coffee and I'll happily talk and talk. The best way we should do it is fresh, without thinking so much about it in advance. Let's be spontaneous and unscripted. I'm very interested in how people create their own personality and then sell it to others. It's about defining your identity, real or invented, and then seeing how comfortable you are with what you've created, and trying to survive within it. It's about balancing you the product and you the human inside you.

Simon Garfield

In Bob's case it all got tangled.

Philippe Garner

How do you reconcile your own sexuality, your own sex life? You're creating these shared fictional territories, and the whole thing is totally riveting to me.

Simon Garfield

Good – so you're interested not only in being in the book, but in the book itself. How did you begin your interest in photography?

Philippe Garner

I started collecting photos in 1962, when I was 13. I was cutting images out of magazines. From living in a child's world I started becoming much more interested in the bigger world. My conduit to so many things that intrigued me were the colour supplements that were first published in 1962. I used to spend long holidays in France, and had access to a family friend who was a very stylish woman with tons of fashion magazines, and I was free to go through them and cut things out.

I was building this world of style and fantasy – theatre, film, fashion, it was like a *musée imaginaire*, a world I wished to live in. The images, which I've still got in folders, became the reference points for what I now do professionally. So I am selling original prints of things I cut out as a teenager. My interest in photography has always been centred around images of style and seduction. I fell in love with certain actresses, and I don't feel I've ever grown up, because I have never denied that love, and I carry it with me, and I still idolise those figures and still enjoy that part of the imagination which one can people with one's goddesses. It doesn't impinge on my living a perfectly regular family life.

The photography of beautiful women has always held a kind of compulsive fascination for me. So over the years I have befriended a number of photographers for whom that is their professional pursuit, and one of them was Helmut Newton, who I enjoyed a very good relationship with – I was the first person ever to buy a photograph by Helmut Newton, and I'm still friends with his widow – and another was Bob.

Lindsey Carlos Clarke

Bob always hated the norm, the ordinary, the happy clappy family. I didn't like it either. When I was little I thought it was nice but as I got older I thought they had so many problems, families, there seemed to be so much intrigue. I liked the cleanliness of not having a big family. I used to watch people with their screaming children and go home and think, oh my God, what an awful thing to do. How could anybody do that?

So yeah, it was passionate with Bob; it was definitely an obsessive relationship without any question. The obsession, we were together all the time, 24/7, you know, we worked together, the books we did, the pictures we did, we used to find these girls in a club, do the hair, do the make-up, everything.

We only really became more detached when he became more

The young artist photographed by his mother.

successful. We were still of the same vision. Practically until he died we could go somewhere and both of us could go into a room and both notice the same thing, pick up on the same thing. Bob had an ability…He had a very dark, dangerous side to him, which obviously deeply appealed to me.

Philippe Garner

I think I first met him in the mid-1970s. I remember having seen some things published and wanting to buy the prints from him and seeking him out when they lived in Fulham, with a railway line at the end of the garden.

He was friendly, he was with Lindsey already by then, very welcoming. Because of my professional background, I often find that photographers are flattered and intrigued that a person who they perceive as a specialist with a wide understanding of the medium and its history might be interested in them. The door is always open, and 'welcome into my world and tell me, tell me, nourish me, tell me why you're drawn to my work'. They try to drain as much from you, to nourish their often slightly uncertain egos. I had that feeling with Bob. He was flattered that somebody with a real context of history and understanding of the medium was interested. And I think he recognised in me the fact that in my own way I am a very obsessive person. He could understand that if I wanted one or two of his pictures it was actually because I *needed* them.

It was that kind of level of fixation: here was something that triggered some responses in me that I had to get close to and really immerse myself in and assimilate. I wasn't a casual shopper, and I think from one obsessive to another there's a kind of sympathy. Without necessarily baring one's respective souls to the precise whys and wherefores of why you are the way you are, you kind of have an instinctive sympathy to somebody who can care so ridiculously much about things that would barely make a mark on other people's radars.

Lindsey Carlos Clarke

Having spoken one night in depth with Helmut Newton it was about always the edge, finding the edge, all artists or creative people

57

search for it but photographically what Bob wanted to get to was the edge of where you pushed art and pornography, and you came right in the middle. So difficult to get. Either it would be sentimental or it's just pornography and it was so exciting when you knew you'd got the shot. You could just feel it.

Philippe Garner

To her credit, Lindsey managed Bob's talent very well. She managed his psychology over so many years, navigating the very difficult periods, representing him to the world. And she would also be a great sounding board and support to him for the aesthetics of what he was doing. I suspect she would be the first to admit that she doesn't bring and hasn't brought to it the full panoply of historical critical analysis – if she had, it might have stopped him in his tracks. In the yin-yang of their relationship, my God, he needed her far more. There was a real dependency. Spending time alone with her after his death, and understanding all the signs and signals that one saw over the years, I think one realises the extent to which she was an absolute pillar for him. You know, just socially, just having a meal together, she'd be the one who, where necessary, would just lighten it up now and then, keep things moving.

Lindsey Carlos Clarke

When I first met him – when he sat on the edge of my bed – Bob had been having an affair with somebody else. I didn't know this at the time, of course. One day he arrived on her doorstep to find that she had been two-timing him. He was cheating, and being cheated at the same time. He was so angry, he said to this mate of his, 'I'm so pissed off about this, what am I going to do, how am I going to get back at her?' And they said, 'Fuck her best friend.' And that was me.

6. with her skirt tucked high into her knickers, said bob carlos clarke

Lindsey Carlos Clarke

I always imagined there was a big, dark mess in his head to do with his childhood that he never came to terms with, but it was probably even worse than I expected.

I mean, lots of people get sent away to school. Bob has some memory of it, but it's almost blanked out. He felt that he was taken out of his very cosy comfortable home and sent to the most awful prison-like situation which he hated every moment of, and everything about it. He wrote endlessly tear-stained letters home: get me out of here, this is so awful.

Bob Carlos Clarke *(from the first draft of his book* Shooting Sex*)*

Maybe I could blame my well-meaning parents for exiling me aged eight to a distant and dreadful preparatory school? Or perhaps my childhood in a southern Irish society where females were mainly wire-haired dowagers wreathed in the not-so-heady aroma of moth-balls, and leathery spinsters who ran riding schools.

1950s Ireland was no place for a libidinous adolescent, particularly a withdrawn Protestant boy in a land where all the hot talent was Roman Catholic and strictly off-limits. At parties Protestant girls looked plain and pasty, in pie-crust collars and pastel cashmere cardigans, compared with their RC counterparts, who seemed so alluringly bovine and brazen, and ate with their mouths open. I was once strapped to a particularly powerful one for a three-legged race. With her skirt tucked high into her knickers, she thundered off at breakneck speed whooping like a savage. She must have been about eleven years old, dress size fourteen, and I was eight, my skinny little leg welded to the muscle of her monumental calf. It was the closest I had ever been to the forbidden fruit, jolting along like a rag doll clamped with both arms to her Corinthian inner thigh, a kiss away from Heaven.

Simon Garfield

The problem, inevitably, is one of exploitation. To what extent is it acceptable to mine someone's past in search of clues to their work? And how does the biographer excuse the posthumous exploitation of someone so troubled? I'd like to excuse it on the grounds that he was also superbly talented, and passionate, and frail. But what do we gain from such a study? There is dark entertainment, and possibly an insight into our own behaviour. In Bob's case, I felt a growing sense of empathy. The more I talked to people, the more I heard aspects of a story that I thought were familiar, representing a common malaise. This began with the usual – the struggle to shake off, or at least deal with, a restrictive and stifling childhood. There were other shared problems that I hoped others would recognise in this driven man: a struggle between expectations and personal desire; a creative urge subdued; huge lust; a vague but constant belief that one could never express artistically what one felt inside. Later, there would also be the battles between art and commerce, about one's reputation and dignity, the balance between popular success and being true to oneself.

Bob Carlos Clarke

With an obsessive compulsion I've taken more or less the same photographs over and over again during the past three decades. It's not a job; it's an addiction. I could have entertained a fashionable

A-class drug habit, but chose instead to indulge what was, at a time when most of my world had gone stark raving gay, a highly unfashionable addiction to A-class females, and some others.

Who or what is responsible for this obsessive compulsion to shoot women? A little intensive psychoanalysis might get to the root of the problem, but it's something I've learned to live with. It's not about getting laid, although that's a tolerable side effect. Perhaps it's my way of compensating for the lost decade of female company from eight to eighteen. Photography isn't a cure, but it relieves the symptoms.

Lindsey Carlos Clarke

So Bob had been sent to Wellington, and been made to march around, and his brother Andrew was being given very much a different sort of laid-back lifestyle, and Bob really resented it. Bob held it against his mum, but it wasn't really her fault at all. I never met Bob's father because he died before I came on the scene. I met Myra, and she was quite a nervous, gentle sort of person, and she never put her hand up and said to her husband, 'You know what, I don't think this is a great idea.' So I think that was very big damage for him. When I spoke to the psychiatrist at the Priory, he said, 'You do know he was emotionally only eight years old?'

And I said, 'Christ, I thought he was at least 15.'

Bob Carlos Clarke

Situated in a Dublin suburb, my preparatory school was a grim prison to several hundred pallid boys in various stages of misery. Escapees were hunted down, dragged back for public humiliation and forced to wear striped pyjamas over their daytime uniforms. More inmates tunnelled out of Colditz than got away from this hellhole.

We were unequally divided into two factions, circumcised and uncircumcised, namely Roundheads and Cavaliers. In those days Cavaliers were an endangered species. A glimpse of one in the changing room was a red rag to a bully, attracting much cruelty, with lashings of Vicks VapoRub and elastic bands as the principal instruments of torture.

Lindsey Carlos Clarke

So, the school. Parts of it he just wouldn't talk about, and it took years and years and years and years to persuade him that he had to see somebody. He used to say, I'm perfectly fine.

I did persuade him to go and see somebody once, and he said, I'm not going again.

Why not?

I like being a shit. It's an addictive thing. I'm happy being the way I am. I like to hide behind this other persona.

But I think you have to get to a certain age in your life and look back and say, this was crap, this was awful, this was terribly difficult. You have to look back and go, God, it was amazing how I coped with that, and then move ahead. Give yourself a bit of praise, you know. But Bob carried it all with him.

Bob Carlos Clarke

I began to truly grasp the power of womankind when, aged eight, I was ripped from the bosom of my family for the first of a long and bitter taste of all-male educational institutions.

Of course I missed my mother and father desperately, but more significantly, I was to encounter so few females for the next ten years that I actually began to look out for them, like a train-spotter. In fact, sightings of attractive females were more like spotting UFOs, rare, remote and very brief.

From that interminable decade I can recall in detail every Close Encounter of the Woman Kind, for it was such encounters that sustained me, and reminded me that there was life beyond boredom and brutality.

Lindsey Carlos Clarke

You look at his work and you see lots of repression in there. Do remember also that he was brought up in Ireland. His parents weren't Catholic but they weren't allowed to have contraception, and Bob and his friends used to fly home from school with suitcases full of Durex thinking it was really funny. He was always told not to go with Catholic girls, all sorts of rules and regulations. His father was very proper: you couldn't say, 'Why don't you look in

Bob with his father and cereal bowl on the water in Ireland.

the mirror?' You had to say 'the looking glass'. In a way his mother became worse than his father because obviously it didn't come naturally to her. So she had to try to keep up with this figure of a father who was convinced you must behave in a certain way.

• • •

Sam Chesterton

Bob's thing was always to do with sex. He was rather precocious, he knew much more about it than I did, even though he was much younger. Or at least he thought he knew more, but he was easily embarrassed. When he was about 12 and I was 16 we were sent to the local shops to buy a rubber ball for our dog. We went to the shop, but it had turned from a toy shop to a chemist, and we didn't realise when we went in. So Bob asked for a rubber ball, and the shop assistant misheard and thought he said rubber gloves or something. She asked him if they were for men or women, and Bob came running out of the shop bright puce, his face almost on fire. He thought she was offering him something to do with sex. He had a very vivid imagination.

I'll tell you how I met Bob. I was born in 1946, so that makes me about four years older than him, but we were thrown together over the holidays, through our Anglo-Irish world. My mother was a Jameson, the Irish whiskey people. I was born in Dublin, and we moved to England when I was just a few weeks old. I was brought up in Kensington. My father's family had been there since the eighteenth century, when it was a village. The Chesterton estate agents business was established then – we managed the big local estates in Mayfair, and a lot of church property, a Dickensian business.

But we spent a lot of our summer holidays going back to Ireland. We used to go to County Waterford, because there was a wonderful cousin there called Tommy Jameson. He had been a famous cricketer, but he was rather scary because he smoked like a chimney and had had a tracheotomy. There was always this problem of were you going to understand what he was telling you?

And that's how we met Bob. As a family we went for the summer to Ardmore, and Bob's father Charlie had a little shack on the nearby beach in Ballyquin. We used to drive down there most days, or the Chestertons and the Clarkes would go on a day trip somewhere together.

Ballyquin was the best beach for kids, a huge expanse of sand. It was right over a sea-break, and if there was a storm the waves would crash right into it. They had no electricity in the shack, and there was always a smell of paraffin from their fridge and oil lamps. I think Bob's father had links with a tractor company because we always had these huge inner tubes to play with. And they had a canoe.

My mother and Myra were both great cooks, and they'd make fantastic picnics, and we'd go to the edge of the cliffs where there was a lime kiln and we'd light a fire and have barbecues. We'd go for the whole of August for about six years in our teens. Great days on the beach.

Jane Chesterton

It wasn't a very busy beach. We used to go shrimping and invent all these games. I was a year younger than Bob. I was completely besotted by him, thought he was wonderful, but to him I was probably the most irritating little bug.

This is his place here. Many of these photos were taken by our nanny I think. There's Bob, and his brother Andrew. That's Charlie, his dad. [The caption reads Charlie Clarke's Beach.] This is Molly Keane's house, the writer.

His mum Myra was so much younger than his father. His father was very charming, but he could be quite cranky. She was always cooking up great big teas, very motherly, a bit of a worrier, especially about Bob.

Lindsey Carlos Clarke

His father was about 30 years older than his mother, a military man. Eton, the whole works, and rather smart, rather upper crust, hung out with the Prince of Wales and Mrs Simpson. He was right in that world and could hunt and fight and do all those things that men are supposed to do, in uniform. And he was also quite wicked – used to write very funny poems.

His mother came from a working-class background, the daughter of a stonemason. Her mother died when she was very young and her brother killed himself when he was 12. He climbed up an electricity pylon and electrocuted himself. Yes, on purpose. We're not sure why, I have a theory that both her and her brother were interfered with by a relative – I'm not sure, it's only a theory I put together much later. She married an RAF pilot when she was 18 who went missing, probably killed, certainly never seen again. She then went with Bob's father, a much older man, whom she adored. She was his third wife.

She was quite creative. Myra could paint and I've recently found some photographs of hers, and you can definitely see the talent in there, the way she's lined them up. There's these pictures of Bob and Andrew, Bob's brother, playing on the beach together, and you can see she obviously had a visual skill.

She didn't want Bob to be sent away to school. In fact, she thought it was the most terrible thing. And then she had Andrew, who was eight years younger than Bob. So Bob went away to school, gets home, and finds somebody in his nest. He never got over it, never. He used to do terrible things to Andrew, terrible, terrible, terrible torturous things. You know, nail him into a box and roll him down a cliff. Wished he was dead.

7. it was always 'ha ha said the clown', said sam chesterton

Sam Chesterton

Bob's father Charlie was interesting – really an Edwardian character. He'd been a naughty boy by running off with his wife's secretary – Bob's mum Myra. He was incredibly stylish, a bit doddery. He wore this marvellous one-piece bathing suit with stripes. He was quite scrawny, wore a straw hat, had a moustache, smoked a lot. Myra fussed about him desperately and wanted to protect him. Once he was in a yacht that capsized in a local regatta, and she was in the most frightful state about it. He was brought back shivering.

He'd always have lobster and mayonnaise, and give these dinner parties and big Sunday lunches. The guests would include this wonderful pair of lesbians who would arrive driving their Bristol with their dogs. One of them was Master of the Waterford Hounds. We were always told to keep away – they were seen as a bad influence.

A lot of the houses at Ardmore were occupied by nuns, and you'd often see them paddling in the sea. Have you seen the photographs that Bob took of them later?

All the Anglo-Irish seemed to know each other. There was

another family in Ardmore called the Roach-Perks, half Anglo-Irish, half gypsy. One day Stella Roach-Perks opened up a hair salon in Ardmore, a bit unheard of. She had a huge beehive hairdo. There was a fairground at the back of the salon, and you could always hear the music coming through – it was always 'Ha Ha Said The Clown'. She lived in a caravan. Bob and I were allowed to collect the fares on the roundabout and dodgems.

Jane Chesterton

Sam has a much better memory than I do. Bob had a second life out there, and he was always running off. In the later years he had a motorbike that had no brakes, and he always pushed the edges, which was quite exciting. Sam will tell you about all the affairs he had with people – the girls saying, 'You have to wear three condoms because then I can still be a virgin.'

Sam Chesterton

When he was a bit older he became involved with one of the Sylvester-Carr sisters. There were six of them, from Dublin. The younger one, Barbara, took a great fancy to Bob. He was probably about 16, and she dragged him off one weekend and he came back so exhausted. He said, 'She made me wear two condoms.'

• • •

Bob was quite cheeky, so there was quite a lot of 'Do what your father says'. Andrew was the little protected one, and Bob was the one who had to show a good example and try a bit harder. After his father died he always romanticised things. His aunt, whom he never met, his dad's sister – he loved the idea of her driving racing cars and parachuting and becoming virtually a heroin addict.

And there was another thing that lurked in the background that you might not have heard about. Myra's brother committed suicide. He climbed on to an electric pylon and held on to the wires. Bob always talked about that with a kind of admiration and awe.

Simon Garfield

In the sense that he saw it as courageous to do something so dramatic?

Sam Chesterton

Yes, he revelled in the lunacy of it.

Bob Carlos Clarke

In the late 1920s, Dad was a director of Bostock's Three-Ring Circus, billed as 'Britain's Biggest'. Those that remembered him said he had a good eye for the public performance, and also enjoyed an intense private relationship with his troupe of agile trapeze artists.

Looking through the papers and photographs in his old tin trunk took me back to an era when he was my age and younger. Glimpses of gone for ever good times, horseplay on a tennis court with some fun-loving flapper, and later, on a warship off Murmansk, melting chunks of ice to make tea. So much life trapped in these fading little pictures, and through a magnifier so much detail: the tennis girl's fluttering hands, the glint in my father's eye, the photographer's silhouette reflected in the little tin of melting ice-water.

In contrast to my father's charmed life, my mother's had been tough, going downhill when she was eight with her mother's death from cancer, and at twelve the suicide of her teenage brother whom she adored. Effectively abandoned by her philandering father, a weasel-faced monumental mason specialising in tombstones, she soon married Rob Watson, a handsome young farmer and RAF bomber pilot.

Within a year he was shot down and lost somewhere in Egypt. She was still only 18, and for many years afterwards she clung to the idea that he would return.

Once again, it was the discovery of old photographs that seemed significant. I'd never really noticed my mother using a camera, but the few 35mm films shot by her were composed and timed intuitively. It seemed sad that she'd never had a chance to develop her ability.

Sam Chesterton

I don't remember much interest in photography on the beach. But in the years following he went back there, probably when he was at Worthing. He took a picture of his mother after she was widowed. He always perceived her loneliness, and the photo showed her out in the sea on her own, in a rubber bathing hat seen from behind. All you can see is a little black blob with the sun on the water.

I remember going out to Cork to visit Myra with Bob and Sue. That was so sad. Myra was falling apart a bit.

Simon Garfield

Rubber ball, rubber bathing hat, rubber johnnies – surely this couldn't all be just an easy coincidence.

Jane Chesterton

He loved the beach and it represented freedom. But the shed was quite small, and they were all crammed together, like living in a caravan, and I think it must have been quite a suffocating existence in there. His mother was quite clingy. I can understand him wanting to break out on his own. Andrew was left there being mothered, while Bob escaped. But he did love that place, and later on when I helped Lindsey find that beach house in Sussex there was definitely a link for him with his childhood life.

Bob Carlos Clarke

1950s Southern Ireland was a fertile environment for the cultivation of sexual oddity, rife with papal propaganda, Protestant prudery, bigotry, hypocrisy and ignorance.

Early sexual encounters were tainted with the dread of disease, discovery, unwanted pregnancy, ruination and the wrath of God, all of which, except possibly the last, could have been prevented by the use of a condom. But contraception was illegal, and recreational sex a mortal sin, and many's the fair Colleen that got buggered both metaphorically and literally as a result.

In a triumph of optimism over opportunity, my dad continued to carry a condom right into his seventies. I knew this because its oval profile was embossed on to the face of his leather wallet.

He wanted to be Mick Jagger.

Eventually, in a moment of extreme need, I raided his wallet and stole the condom. It had OHMS and 'Use Before Sept 1948' printed on its military buff envelope, and the condom itself crumbled between my fingers like a perished rubber band.

A friend directed me to a notorious condom smuggler, a stout Canadian lad who reaped an unhealthy profit from the damned and the desperate. Behind O'Brien's pub he sold me a German 'rubber' called a Koralle for £1, an enormous amount to invest in what was usually an extremely brief encounter. It was washable and reusable, built with the durability of an all-terrain tyre, and the convenience of a rustproof drying rack. All it lacked was an emergency repair kit.

Lindsey Carlos Clarke

The idea of whether to conform or not presented a terrible conflict. There used to be this terrible fight within Bob all the time between rules and regulations and this other person he wanted to be, this person who liked rock 'n' roll. There was a parallel with my own father. He was bought up with lots of rules and regulations and a sort of upper-middle-class background but just sort of hated it and said, 'Bugger off, I'm not doing it any more.' From then on he became grown up, and just lived life absolutely the way he wanted to.

Bob Carlos Clarke

Smuggling contraceptives seemed like a worthy and easy way to a quick buck, so, on my return to England, I ordered a gross of Durex condoms from Pellen Personal Products, a mail order company who guaranteed discreet 'plain brown envelope' deliveries. Within days a bulky brown parcel arrived at my school address, and on my next flight from Heathrow to Cork, I taped the contents to the inside of my battered acoustic guitar. Unfortunately they shook loose en route, and were noticed by a ferret-faced customs officer. Triumphantly he waved my guitar aloft, until the little grey packets began cascading out of the sound-hole and on to his wooden counter.

Glancing away from my mound of contraband, I glimpsed my

parents peering anxiously through the arrivals window, and wished I were smuggling something, anything, different.

Lindsey Carlos Clarke

Bob's father was almost like a grandfather. He was an amazing cricket player, played for Eton, and he played at Wellington when they used to have Parents' Day. Everyone would ask Bob, 'God, is that your dad or your grandad?', so obviously he had a real phobia about this 'old' thing. But his father could bowl them out every time: even though he was very slow, he knew exactly how to do it. I think there was total admiration from Bob, but also a wish that his father was younger.

Bob's father died basically of old age, at 76. Not that old, but he was old-fashioned. I think Andrew was 12, so Bob would have been 20. Bob was already working.

I think he had a good relationship with his father at the end. There are sweet pictures of them on the boat in Ireland with Bob having cereal in his pyjamas with his arms round his dad.

Bob Carlos Clarke

The smirking ferret scribbled me a receipt for one hundred and forty-three Durex and took them away in a plastic carrier bag. For a moment I imagined the stench of burning rubber and a pall of black smoke over O'Connell Street. Maybe it was at this time I sensed the connection between sex and the forbidden fruit of the rubber tree.

The climax of my miserable years at public school was the day my extravagantly camp cousin, Timothy, arrived to collect me in his midnight-blue Rolls-Royce. The stately automobile drew admiring glances as it crunched across the gravel crescent. When the voluptuous young actress Diana Dors slid from the passenger seat, such an intense silence gripped my schoolmates that I felt I could hear the thunder of their combined heartbeat above the rattle of my own. To us term-time orphans, prematurely ripped from the maternal breast, she was an awesome Aphrodite in a lace mini-dress and cream buckskin thigh boots.

Back at Timothy's 'villa', Diana would lounge on his ivory-white grand piano, and smoke and swear most seductively while I sprawled on the carpet, and gazed up her skirt.

I could rant on for ever on the subject of school brutality, but I prefer to recount the only two pleasant memories that remain from that bleak era: Sonia and Susan.

Sonia was a housemaid at the school, a voluptuous, raven-haired 18-year-old, a goddess in polyester. On Friday nights, after lights-out, she'd take her weekly bath in the brightly lit bathroom adjacent to the spartan dormitory I shared with a dozen of my fellow prisoners, and every Friday night, in striped pyjamas and plaid dressing gowns, we'd queue at her bathroom door. Hushed with anticipation and a quickening pulse, each small, beslippered boy would shuffle forwards for his moment at the keyhole.

Statuesque and slippery in the blaze of a bare 100-watt bulb, Sonia's perfect body was a vision of pure delight in our ugly, love-less little world, where cold comfort was the snivelling of homesick boys sobbing themselves to sleep.

Now, forty years on, when I peer through my viewfinder at some thoroughbred beauty, I return to the keyhole. Sonia, if she is still alive, must be well into her sixties, but, for me, her loveliness remains as sharp and unfaded as a well-fixed photograph.

The other pleasant memory is of Susan, the teenage sister of one of my junior schoolmates. Sometimes she dropped by the school to collect her little brother, and several hundred small boys would rise to the occasion. With her sex-kitten pout and tousled blonde hair, she was the first model that ever impinged upon my consciousness, as she writhed on an acre of white shagpile in a TV commercial for Youghal Carpets.

Lindsey Carlos Clarke
He was at Wellington at the end of the 1960s and everyone used to return from the holidays with their hair long and the school would cut it all off. He said that practically everything he ever had was confiscated.

Bob Carlos Clarke
At half-term my skeletal old aunt Jessie, Marchioness of Ormonde, announced during tea to my mother, 'Sadly, I can envisage nothing for Robert but prison.'

Evidently I'd let the 'old school' down: never elected a prefect, a most unsporting sportsman, and, according to my school reports, a thoroughly subversive influence on the established order of things. My trousers were too tight, my ties too thin, my hair too long and my tongue too sharp. In time I was banned from wearing button-down collars and Chelsea boots, and sentenced to having a haircut every Friday for a term.

In 1968, as my last public school term expired, my housemaster, James Wort, wrote to my father: 'Robert is not a clever boy, and has not made the best of his time at Wellington. He would do well to put more thought into goals and waste less time on girls and guitars. He must see that he does not abuse any local privileges or he may find himself in deep water.'

'Local privileges' referred to Carol, the pretty 14-year-old girl-friend I had acquired in the nearby village of Crowthorne. She *was* genuinely pretty, although at the time I would have made do with almost anything with working female parts.

My schoolmates returned from school holidays bragging of improbable conquests, and got the occasional scent-drenched love letter, but mine was tangibly blonde and buxom, and lived by the school gate. I had love-bites and stray golden strands as proof. We would meet at every opportunity, in the surrounding woods or her late grandmother's musty little caravan.

My lover gave me her bra and white cotton panties, which I proudly pinned to my bedroom wall, along with her photograph and a lock of hair. Before long a cleaner complained, and the author-ities visited my room to dismantle my shrine, and confiscate a quantity of 'disagreeable reading matter'. On my final day, in the summer of 1968, Wort summoned me to his office, and handed me a crumpled paper bag containing some dog-eared reading matter: *Fanny Hill – The Unexpurgated Memoirs of a Woman of Pleasure, The Carpetbaggers* by Harold Robbins and my tattered copy of *Parade*.

Lindsey Carlos Clarke

In his last year, Bob and a friend decided to stage an alternative open day at the school, and so they typed out an ad to go in *It* magazine to say something like, 'Come one, come all, hippies and everything blessed, fabulous love-in, at Wellington School'. This also happened to be Parents' Day. An enormous quantity of hippies, dregs and goodness knows what else started to appear at Wellington and there was a huge hoo-hah and the fraud squad were called in to find out who had placed the ad. Bob says he found out about the investigation and rushed into his friend's room, woke him up and said, 'Quick, quick, where's your typewriter?', and they had to throw it in the lake so that they weren't caught. I think the machine was brand new.

Bob Carlos Clarke

Suddenly, after ten miserable years, I was free.

Henceforth there were just two options: obscurity or notoriety, and the former was unconscionable.

Mick Jagger and David Bailey were ideal role models: rock and photography, fashionably classless professions where bad behaviour and promiscuity were compulsory.

Basically, they fucked the best girls, made loads of money and got famous for it.

I packed my mother's Fiat 500 to the sunroof, and set off for Belfast to report on the rioting. I rented a room in a terraced house off the Falls Road close to the notorious Divis flats, a shabby tower block favoured by IRA snipers. The windows of my tiny bedroom were blanked with sheets of corrugated iron, and the oily stink of burning cars and the sporadic crackle of gunfire kept me awake and on edge.

From the cries and thumps, I guessed the young couple next door drank, fought and copulated in rota. There was nothing much else to do in such a place, and I wanted to get away as fast as possible.

I soon learned that a camera is a good excuse for anything. A person with a camera can make stuff happen. When I started my career as a photojournalist in Belfast in 1969, I quickly realised that the sight of a professional-looking cameraman was a red rag to rioters.

Everyone wants to be a movie star, and, in certain high-octane situations, the line between fantasy and reality gets very blurred.

I first met Mick in 1970, at the urinals at the Royal Dublin Horse Show. Later he passed through the crowd with Marianne Faithfull floating along beside him – two delicate, ephemeral, exotic aliens, sweeping through the sea of ruddy country faces and sludge-coloured Harris tweed. That evening I attended a ball at Castletown, a stately Georgian pile on the outskirts of Dublin. Briefly I danced with Marianne, or, more accurately, clung to her, choked with adolescent adoration, and my father's ever tightening black tie. Marianne! My ideal ex-convent girl angel-slut, in my arms.

All evening my feckless bubble-haired date dogged Mick's cloven-hoof steps, eagerly gathering his discarded cigarette butts. Much later, when we had to make do with each other on a friend's floor, she unclasped her brassiere and dumped a cascade of stinking ash and filters into our sleeping bag.

Around this time the Stones released *Beggars Banquet*, and I hung on every note. Tracks like 'Stray Cat Blues' and 'Parachute Woman' reeked of unspeakable depravity. But what really got to me was Michael Joseph's inner-sleeve photograph of the band, sprawled in the aftermath of a debauched banquet. Dutifully I pinned it up, next to my glossy publicity shots of Marianne in her black leather biker suit.

Jane Chesterton

Bob wrote some songs on his guitar, and they were not always good. He wanted to be a rock star, but everyone told him: stick to the photography. He absolutely loved Mick Jagger. I remember once he came back from some event and he said, 'I've kissed Marianne Faithfull!'

Bob Carlos Clarke

I passed an inauspicious year in Dublin doing this and that: a few months as tea boy at an advertising agency, and a few more as a trainee journalist with Express Newspapers. The training element mostly involved learning how to get drunk before lunch, before getting legless at lunchtime.

I can't recall much of what went on at that time, apart from a birthday when I drank most of a bottle of Irish whiskey and rode my Bultaco motorbike through the passenger door of a Ford Cortina. The collision caused considerable distress to the car, my pillion passenger, and myself. It was a good time to emigrate.

Lindsey Carlos Clarke

His mother discovered that Worthing College of Art would take him, because he wanted to go to art school, and then when he went there he started a photography course and that was it, he knew immediately: this is what I'm going to do.

• • •

School Reports for Robert Loraine Carlos Clarke

Rochelle School, Old Blackrock Road, Cork
Summer Term, 1955 (RLCC aged 5)
Geography/Nature Lesson: Much of the class discussions are above his head, but he is reasonably attentive.
Conduct: Good. Robert is obedient and reasonably quiet considering his age.

Autumn Term, 1955 (aged 6)
Writing: Excellent progress. Letters are firm and well formed.
Handwork/Painting: Excellent progress. Robert has good control over his hands. His pictures are full of interesting details and show sense of humour.

Spring Term, 1956 (aged 6)
Writing: Still confined to capitals, which are clear and firm.
Handwork/Painting: His delightful sense of humour shows in his pictures, which usually illustrate some dramatic happening or domestic tragedy!

Junior Department, Cork Grammar School, December 1957 (number of pupils in form: 6; RLCC aged 7)
Writing: Is neat and well formed.
Poetry: Finds this subject difficult.
Drawing and Brushwork: Enjoys these classes very much.

April 1958 (number of pupils in form: 5)
Literature: An appreciative pupil.
Irish: Finds it difficult to concentrate.

Conduct: Sometimes very good indeed, sometimes only fair.
Nature Study: Takes a keen and intelligent interest.

June 1958 (number of pupils in form: 4)
Religion: Robert is a very interested member of the class.
Writing: This term's results were not quite so good.
Handwork: Always very keen.
Drill and Games: 4th place.

Castle Park Primary School, South County Dublin, October 1958 (aged 8)
Mathematics: Tables are poor. He must try to be more independent.
Conduct in School: Good.
Conduct Out of School: Possibly a little too afraid of doing the wrong thing.

Winter Term, 1961 (aged 11)
French: Asks dozens of stupid questions, sometimes about French.
Conduct in School: He is interested, has some intelligence and ability, but refuses to think for himself. He must be more sensible because he can be good.

Winter Term, 1963 (aged 13)
Headmaster's Report: All credit to him for pulling it off. He should do well with growing self-confidence. We're sorry to lose him.

Wellington College, Michaelmas Term, 1964 (aged 14)
Tutor's Report: He has worked hard and deserves a high place in this lowish form. Languages remain rather weak. In the house he has been helpful and has tried hard at his rugger, and so improved quite a lot. As his talents are limited he needs to go flat out at everything.

Summer Term, 1965 (aged 15)
Tutor's Report: His efforts have flagged a bit, and this is a luxury he cannot really afford. He is not a clever boy, therefore anything less than his best is playing with fire.

O level results:
Elementary Mathematics: Pass
English Language: Pass
English Literature: Pass
General Classics: Pass
French: Pass

Summer Term, 1967 (aged 17)
Tutor's Report: As a technician he is still lacking, but it is good to hear of his keenness and lively writing. As a potential journalist he must master the craft of writing as well as the art, and the development of style is also a must. His talent in obvious things like games is extremely limited, but in one way and another he shows that service to the community is something which he regards as an essential and pleasant duty.

In all ways he is a far cry from the original common entrance failure type of boy he was.

Winter Term, 1967 (aged 17)
Tutor's Report: He is in with a chance in all three subjects. I have every hope that he will get his History of Art.

We have been generous in our treatment of him and given him various relaxations of routine, particularly in the matter of games. He must see that he does not abuse any local privileges he has been given, for this would be the quickest way to their withdrawal.

He edited our *Wall Magazine* last term with skill and enthusiasm. He must not do it again next term…

Summer Term, 1968 (final Summer Term, aged 18)
Tutor's Report: He has been a very interesting boy, original in his outlook and essentially an individualist. We have 'played him on a loose rein' as far as possible, for he was always a boy with limited interests in the routine schoolboy activities, but by and large he has not taken advantage of this.

If he can get started in the right part of the newspaper world to suit his talents he could be very successful. We all join in wishing him happiness and success.

Headmaster's Letter, 6 August 1968

I do hope that good news will come through for Bob and that he will have got at least two of his A levels. He has not been an easy boy to get through Wellington, for he basically has not enjoyed many of the obvious pleasures which most boys like. But we have helped him to enjoy life in the spheres in which he does excel, and by and large we have made him reasonably happy here.

Yours ever,

James

A level results:

English: D

Ancient History: E

Economics: O

Art History: D

8. eventually i said yes, said sue frame

Sam Chesterton

Bob had that wild side to him, but he was partly also a very old man. He liked everything just so. His eggs and bacon and whatever – it had to be done just his way. He also had his snobbish side where he revelled in his ancestry. Being a gentleman was very important to him, but at the same time he wanted to shock gentlemen.

Every Saturday we'd go to Worthing, to the Beach Hotel and art deco place on the front. We'd get cocktails and read the *Worthing Gazette*, and then we'd go to all its jumble sales. We'd get strange ties and winklepickers and old vases, which I've still got. All these things that people leave behind when they die.

Worthing was where he met Sue. She was a great beauty, incredibly so. And she was biddable. She was naïve, and we used to tell her all these outrageous stories which she'd believe. That made her huge fun too. But Bob had such a cruel streak to him. He did terrible things to his brother Andrew. And he was incredibly cruel to Sue. It began with nagging, and then he bashed her into a pulp of submission. No, not physically – mentally. She became very, very insecure.

Bob Carlos Clarke

I rented a bright, bow-windowed first-floor flat on the Worthing seafront above Stax, a fusty old drinking club. I got a big stereo and a small girlfriend who managed a boutique in Brighton. A generous cousin lent me his ancient scooter, and the most pleasant year of my life sped past in celebration of my first taste of freedom and West Sussex weed.

At this point my most vital source of visual inspiration was album sleeves. I can't recall much of the music but the covers are with me for ever. *Trout Mask Replica*, *Houses of the Holy*, *King Crimson*, *Sticky Fingers*. I had such fond memories of The Incredible String Band that I scoured the internet to buy three of their CDs, but, unstoned, the music was unbearable.

In Worthing two local dramas were unfolding. First, the controversy over whether the Bardot-esque teenage actress Susan Penhaligon should show her bum in the Connaught Theatre's production of *Romeo and Juliet*. (She did, but no one could actually see it without infra-red goggles.)

And, secondly, there was this girl student called Sue, unapproachably beautiful, in the year above me. I heard she did part-time photographic modelling, and realised that the only way to reach her was to become a photographer. The college had just installed a cupboard-sized darkroom and the rudiments of a photographic course, and so eventually I summoned up the courage to persuade her to pose for me on a sparkling 650cc Triumph Bonneville. We shot on the beach, the sun was bright and hazy, and the gentle sea breeze lifted her hair. Later that evening, when I processed the film, the negatives emerged crisp and sharp from the developing tank. And some years later Sue and I were married at Kensington Register Office. We had some great times, but marrying one's first model is a bit beyond the call of duty.

Sue Frame (née Green)

I was very innocent, a very protected girl, you know.

I was born in Lusaka (northern Rhodesia, it's now Zambia) and I was raised there, two British parents, English father and a Welsh mother, and I was there until just before my fourteenth birthday when I went off to a boarding school in England. I have to say that the teaching was pretty appalling, the emphasis really was on the arts, the ballet, the theatre, that sort of thing, and the teachers were all retired. I had an English teacher of 83 at one stage.

I can't say that I flourished academically there; I was out of my depth when I arrived from Africa. My parents were living in Worthing. My father was very academic and my mother was a very bright woman, but she didn't have the education that she deserved. I was a little bit of a hot potato because I liked art and all things pertaining to it, so it was decided that I would go to the West Sussex College of Art. I did textile design, and in my second year Bob came to Worthing to do his foundation course. I think he was vacillating a little bit about what he was going to do, and he was sort of fiddling around a bit with photography.

A few of the students had just asked me to model for them, the ones that were doing photography. The head of the photography department had somehow homed in on me and asked me to model for him. I was flattered by it. Apparently Bob saw my picture floating in a development tray, and I heard from one of the students that he had sort of taken a fancy to what he saw and wanted to get to know me better. He was certainly different from most of the students. He had a very, how can I put it, a sort of androgynous look about him, the way he dressed. He was dressed often in black and he used to wear these flowing scarves and I know that quite a few of the more butch students felt that he was a pretty boy. He always had the prettier girls in his company, and that didn't always go down well with the rugby bugger types. Anyway, I then heard somewhere along the line that he had picked me out and wanted to get to know me better but didn't know how. He asked questions about me and he said later that he even came and sat next to me because he wanted to hear what I sounded like. I have to say he was a dreadful snob.

This was 1969 I think. He was three months older than me, he was a June baby and I was a September one, both 1950. So anyway, a friend came up to me and said Bob Carlos Clarke is dying to photograph you and I was thinking, oh, I don't know, I'm not sure about this. So he approached me and said he needed something for the portfolio and would I comply and eventually I said yes, and that was just the beginning of it.

He was staying in a Victorian seafront flat at the time, and I went along and I was quite intrigued by him. As time went on I thought he was really different and he had all these stories to tell. He said he was sharing the flat at the time with this girl whom he had had an affair with, but it was over and they were friends and it was just a convenience thing.

In a way I became his muse. He photographed me all over the place, and I became more and more enthralled by him. I always remember the very first date: he came out with a box of Sobranie cigarettes. He said to me afterwards, 'When I saw you and heard you I thought you could only eat lobster for breakfast...' It was so far from the truth, but he was trying to impress me and he did. For me it was all quite innocent. I was so unexposed to the world. I became intrigued.

So we became involved and we spent an incredible first term at that college. He had a little purple scooter and in the end I ended up spending more time on the back of it, going to Brighton and sitting on the beach with him and being photographed, and just getting more and more intense.

The first photographs we ever did were – he had a motorbike from somebody and he had me posing on the motorbike. Then it was more just sort of general photographs. I suppose he was always trying to get me more and more scantily clad. It was that sort of thing really.

• • •

He invited me to Ireland that summer holiday. I'd been off to Spain with my family, but arranged that I would fly over to Ireland, and he was absolutely sweet, he was so excited that I was coming. I met his mother and I met Andrew. There was an eight-year gap between him and Bob, and I think Andrew was very much dwarfed by him.

His mother had a lovely, very comfortable little home in Cork, and we ended up going to her summer house at Ballyquin, which was further along the coast. That was absolutely lovely, it was idyllic. I had to stay in the summer house and I remember they had a copper kettle and Bob would spend hours polishing it for me, and making sure that everything was comfortable and just nice for me.

I met his father Charlie in the last years of his life, and although the poor old man was suffering from angina he still had his very lucid moments. Myra used to say that his eyes lit up when he saw me, and he would say, 'Just come and sit by the sea with me,' and he would hold my hand and just talk. I think Bob was affected by the fact that his father was so old. But he also had this legacy, and I think that Bob always felt he had to live up to it in some strange way. Charlie died when Bob must have been 19 or 20 and I know that he went to Ireland at the time of his death and took photographs of his father on his deathbed. You know, I didn't go with him but I heard all about it. I often think it had a profound effect on him. It was this thing, this legend that he felt he must emulate.

Also, he had a step-brother and a step-sister who were born to Charlie's first or second wife. Sandy and Diana. He didn't talk much about Sandy, but Diana, the daughter, was a great beauty and she made a huge splash wherever she went. She drove fabulous cars and was courted all over, and then she had a dreadful accident on a bobsleigh. She was on the sleigh with three or four men, and I think the sleigh went across her back, and it was broken, and she was put on heavy doses of morphine that she was never properly weaned off. But there was always a sort of glamour attached to her. Apparently if she went to the races she would arrive in this beautiful convertible and would just demand a good parking place. All these things seemed terribly glamorous to Bob, and I think he really loved the idea of it so much, and also wanted to have this glamorous life.

Sandy died recently. And Diana died before that. The morphine and everything else in the end, it killed her. Bob had all these snippets of stories that came back to him. I even remember him, or Myra, having a beautiful set of leather suitcases and vanity bags that were all actually tailor-made to fit into the back of a Bentley or a Rolls-Royce; actually curved and hand-stitched and all this kind of thing, and he loved that, he absolutely loved it.

Bob found it difficult with his brother, though. Andrew was still

A PORTRAIT OF COMPOSURE: BOB CARLOS CLARKE WITH HIS FIRST CAMERA ON THE BEACH IN IRELAND

THE WIVES: SUE FRAME ON WORTHING SANDS...

…LINDSEY CARLOS CLARKE IN *THE BLACK PATH*.

JILLY JOHNSON POSES IN *DAS SCHWIMMBAD* (LEFT); A MODEL NAMED ANDREA IS *KEEPING UP WITH THE JONESES* (ABOVE).

MARCO PIERRE WHITE WITH A MEAT CLEAVER AT HARVEYS, AND SERVED UP ON A SLAB IN BROMPTON
CEMETERY. THE CHEF FIGHTING IN THE TOP-LEFT CORNER IS GORDON RAMSAY.

HUGH LAURIE AND MODEL KAJA WUNDER.

quite a young boy when I met him, about 11. He used to hang about me in Ireland, and then I'll always remember being down on the beach with him and he telling me he hated me. Yet he was a sweet boy, and I think having the old father didn't help. He had quite a troubled time at school. By the time I actually married Bob, Andrew was very supportive of me, very protective. But Andrew was always also the butt of Bob's jokes. Bob would tease him mercilessly. I think poor Andrew just felt that he would never, never measure up to Bob in a way and I can believe that he could easily have gone off the rails.

So: this really idyllic holiday together – it further sealed my feelings about him. I mean, I was absolutely lock, stock and sinker. I was his.

• • •

Bob Carlos Clarke

I felt very blue as I closed down my Worthing flat at the end of that summer. I hired a van to take my stereo and me to the grime of Elephant and Castle, host to my new school, the London College of Printing. I set up home in a mouldy basement in Brixton.

Funds were in short supply, but a solution soon presented itself. Some of my fellow students were female, and a few of them quite pretty. With them as models and myself as photographer, we shot nude sets for the Paul Raymond publications *Men Only* and *Club International*. Fees were around £350 per session, which we split 50/50.

Before long I had exhausted the college's pool of beauty, and began to look further afield, placing advertisements in local newsagents and registering with model agencies.

The newsagents produced some spectacularly horrifying applicants. I only ever shot one, a feisty fast-food waitress from Croydon, who looked like a cross between Miss Piggy and a pit-bull terrier, but still contrived to be quite desirable.

The model agencies were less challenging, but more fruitful. It was a joy to discover that beautiful females could be selected and ordered from a catalogue. Many of the new models needed 'tests', photographs especially taken to build their portfolios and prove their talent. I could flick through a magazine, spot a girl, call her agent and have her delivered like a pizza, and the first girl I ordered came with a case of her own lingerie. We shot a couple of films and finished off in bed. I felt like I'd struck oil.

Sue Frame

Then I realised he wasn't being totally truthful about the girl he was sharing the flat with.

I suppose now it's actually pretty obvious, and when one looks back on the whole thing it was very much his modus operandi. She was older than him. I don't want to sound unkind but she was a very ordinary looking girl, but absolutely adored him and was obviously doing everything for him. And me, in my stupidity and naivety, and because I had fallen under his thrall, I just believed everything he said. And then to my horror I realised that she was still very attached to him, and that he was using her because she provided a comfortable home, she was earning a salary, she was secure whereas I was just a student, you know, with no particular future mapped out or anything at that stage.

Sam Chesterton

What Sue put up with to be with Bob…They lived in all these extraordinary places. When they lived in Brixton it was so awful, this squat they'd got from Timothy Tufnell, his uncle. One night a man came round and pissed against a wall, and Bob came down in his ill-cut dressing gown and hit him over the head with a hammer. Bob was hyper-tense. I remember going round there and sitting on orange crates and eating by candlelight. Sue used to cook. Probably spag bol.

Sue Frame

When he was at the London College of Printing in Elephant and Castle I was still down in Worthing and that was very difficult. He kept begging me to come up to London, to jack in my course and come up and be there, but I said, 'But you're still with Lucinda,' who was his other girl [name changed], 'and I can't do that.' He said, 'No, no, no, she's going, the relationship's finished, she knows that and I want you up here.'

So like a little fool I eventually went to my parents and left a very comfortable home. I got a job in London with a jewellery firm and I told my parents I had found a bedsit and I was going up to London. They were fairly horrified, but there wasn't much they could do. They eventually helped to take some of belongings up there. I ended up in a bedsit at the Oval, and Bob was living some-where close by like Stockwell. But he was still with this girl and I was desperately unhappy. Our meetings became very clandestine, and I was desperately homesick. But I kept thinking, if I go home now that'll be it, I'll never leave again, I've got to stick it out. And he was incredibly jealous if he ever thought I'd gone out with anyone else, or was seeing anyone else. He just wouldn't tolerate that. So we split up, because it was just sort of unbearable.

Simon Garfield
Did Lucinda know about you at all?

Sue Frame
Yes, I think she must have had an inkling and it was just awful. Some months went by. I went on holiday to Yugoslavia and I had a holiday romance there with someone very nice. I came back to London and thought this is all hopeless. Out of the blue I got a phone call from Bob and he said, 'Didn't you get my gift?' Because I was approaching my twenty-first birthday. I said I didn't know what he was talking about. He said he had sent me a bracelet to go with a tiger's eye ring he had made for me. And then he said, 'I actually really want to see you again.' I was very hesitant, but he really meant a lot to me. And by this time he was living in Brixton, in a row of old Victorian houses that were terribly run down. What had happened was that Lucinda had attempted to commit suicide; she'd taken an overdose and I think he'd just caught her in time. She'd been taken to hospital and had her stomach pumped, and that was basically the end of that. So that was not very…it was terrible.

Simon Garfield
Do you know the cause of her suicide attempt?

Sue Frame

Yes. I think he had said to her, 'This is it, the relationship really is dead, it's not going anywhere.' I don't know whether he'd ever said to her, 'I want to go back to Sue.' But she was distraught and that was what happened. I ended up moving into the flat that he had in Brixton.

He was going off to college every day and I was working with this jewellery firm in the West End, and life jogged along. We used to meet for lunch, and one day we went into Liberty and saw this lovely velvet that we both thought would make a beautiful jacket for him. A few days later he told me that he went back to Liberty and had begun to cut a large amount of this velvet from the roll, but he then saw two men in hats looking at him from the gallery. He thought they were store detectives. He left the velvet, but he said he stole a kids' book just to show he could do it. I wasn't sure I believed him, but the next day I went in myself and found the roll, and there was a large cut in it. He loved the bravado of it.

He had a little Fiat 500 to begin with and then he got a little blue Mini and he drove like a bat out of hell. It was quite frightening. I used to say he was like a pilot fish; he'd see these big juggernauts and I used to think my God, we're going to end up going under the thing, because he was a real devil in the car. And there were always escapades going on with his photography. He met up with the Road Rats, the motorcycle gang, and he would chat them up. We had a whole thing where somebody had been imprisoned in Canvey Island, and we drove down with all the gangs who were going to meet this man coming out of prison. I had to drive the car, it was early, early morning, before the sun came up, and Bob was hanging out of the sunroof, shouting at me to drive faster as he tried to photograph this whole cavalcade of bikers.

Bob Carlos Clarke

I stayed for a while in Stockwell with a big, tousle-haired socialist called Bea. She hated everything I stood for, but felt I could be 'saved'. I found her somewhat intimidating, but she fed me well and let me drive her car.

One afternoon, while she was at work, I photographed a Jamaican

On a mission with the Road Rats.

girl I'd met in Brixton Market. Unfortunately she found Bea's favourite antique oriental silk dressing gown, and wore it between shots. After she'd gone, I found it on the bathroom floor, with a prominent cigarette burn, a ripped hem, and a pungent aroma of coconut oil and sweat. By now Bea was on the short walk home from the underground station, so with seconds to spare I snatched up the gown, raced outside and stuffed it into our neighbour's dustbin.

Everything went fine for a few days – so well, in fact, that I began to think I was safe. Until one memorable summer's evening when she exploded through the front door shrieking, 'You're not going to fucking believe this. Mr Barnes is out front pruning his fucking roses in my fucking dressing gown.'

By nightfall I had found alternative lodgings. I found myself back in Brixton in a first-floor flat that would have been a bargain at £4.50 a week if it hadn't been in the terminal stages of collapse. After a few days the front door fell off and was, according to a vigilant neighbour, borne triumphantly away by four small boys with a larger one riding on top. Drunks took to relieving themselves in the hall, and a local vagrant settled in on the ground floor. Every night, for peace of mind, I braced my bedroom door shut with a scaffold pole, slept with a hammer under my pillow and pissed in the en-suite kitchen sink.

Sue Frame

He went off to Ireland one Christmas and left me in Brixton alone. By this time the tenement block was deserted, everyone had gone except me, and I had to stay there because I was still working. And he left me with a baseball bat because somebody had already tried to break into the flat. I thought, this is really chivalrous of you. In the end I stayed over the road with this woman whose father had been the Lord Mayor of London.

Bob Carlos Clarke

Under pressure from a local authority order condemning the property as uninhabitable, the landlord paid me £2,000 pounds to leave. With this as a deposit I paid £9,500 for half a house of my own in Balham.

My classmates ribbed me mercilessly about my bourgeois aspirations, but with stripped pine floors, chenille cushions and black and gold Biba wallpaper I felt quietly superior. But my grand apartment was short on space for photography. To frame a head and shoulders I had to crush myself into a corner and shoot diagonally through a doorway from the hall to the living room. I gave up on any idea of getting the whole picture in one take, and began to use photomontage to create home-made fantasies. Visitors to my new place had to tiptoe around a labyrinth of cut-up scraps of photographs, pots of glue and scattered scalpels.

Everywhere I went I shot skylines, doorways, highways, rocks, ruins, rivers, anything I might use later in a composition. I saved up and bought a DeVilbiss airbrush to spray inks and chemicals. My darkroom doubled as a bedroom with trestle tables and a blackout curtain. It didn't occur to me that spraying toxic stuff like selenium toner and potassium ferricyanide in a confined, unventilated space was potentially lethal, but the fumes had some mellow side effects.

Sam Chesterton

My father organised a mortgage for them at a time when it was very hard to get one, and they moved to Balham. My father did that for a lot of people – he was eventually Chairman of the Woolwich and then President when he retired. He was a great one for helping people he perceived to have talent.

Bob started earning his first real money by taking pictures for *Penthouse*, and I used to write the accompanying articles. This was in the early 1970s. He'd ring me up and say, 'Ooh, I've got this redhead and she's sitting in front of this bamboo screen and there's a cat...' I'd write a bit of crap and get £50. I was starting to write a novel, so the money came in handy. I had moved out of London and was living in Sussex, a deerkeeper's cottage on the Uppark Estate. At weekends there would always be this gang that came down, and Bob took lots of pictures that Jane and I have still got. He was very interested in solarising images, and he took a picture of me in an old barn with round windows, and he had me in front of it so it looked like a halo, and he solarised that.

He was getting commissions from teenage magazines, probably *Honey*, and he had to illustrate articles called things like 'Jealousy!'.

I also used to model for him in rather seedy circumstances. We went round to Celia Birtwell's, and he took these two girls, and they were doing a sort of lesbian thing, and I was sitting on the arm of the sofa supposedly looking completely uninterested. It was on the famous white brocade sofa in Celia's house.

Sue Frame

He started to earn a bit when he was at the Elephant and Castle because he did get the odd commission from various people who wanted portraits done. And then he took up with Bob Guccione and started doing *Men Only* and *Penthouse*. I hated it, but I was cajoled into posing in those pictures. They were very sedate compared to what one sees now, but I loathed doing it. He kept saying to me, 'We'll make money from it, we need money, come on, you've got to do it,' and of course, my lord and master, yes I would do it. I was always absolutely terrified and horrified that my family would see it.

Jane Chesterton

Bob was actually very good at writing. He did all those ghastly *Men Only* fantasy stories. And he had an absolutely brilliant ability to pick up on your weaknesses and exploit them. He called me Mrs Tiggywinkle. When I was younger I was very scared of the dark, so he would always be waiting to leap out at me from bushes.

Sam and Bob spent a time together shooting rats with crossbows and ridiculous things, and setting up strange photographs which helped him to get into the Royal College. But when Sam got married he sort of disappeared from Bob's life. Bob loved it when Sam was on his own because they did all sorts of exciting and daring things. Any sniff of domestic boredom made him run. But the truth was, there was a bit of Bob that was like that, a bit of cocoa and slippers, although he wouldn't admit it.

Sue Frame

He was a total dichotomy. He could be so sweet and so tender and he could be an absolute devil. I experienced that in my time. He was

With Sue and peg bag in a Worthing garden.

a Svengali; he would make me feel that I was the prettiest thing on two feet and at other times that I was something that had stuck to the bottom of his shoe.

Simon Garfield

Jane brought me more photos from those days, experiments with sepia and collage and hand-colouring that he did at Worthing. One photo showed Jane holding dolls in a wood and looking stoned. Lots of their friends were dressed up in Victorian gear with painted faces. Then there were pictures of Jane taken at Kensal Green cemetery when she was 17, dressed in a ghostly white net curtain, with an angel figure in the background. There were lots of pictures of Bob and Sue.

Lindsey Carlos Clarke

One of Bob's favourite sayings when he was looking through old snapshots of people was always, 'It's so fake, that smile. No matter how they're feeling, people always smile for the camera.' If you look at most pictures of Bob, he's not smiling.

Bob did a lecture one day in which he pointed out that nobody takes pictures when you're having an argument. You know, the con of the photograph, the glamorous life.

Sue Frame

In Balham we ended up with a parrot. I had been walking home from work one day and I saw a parrot in a pet shop and I looked at him and I thought he had eyes like a teddy bear. I went home and I said to Bob, 'I've seen the sweetest parrot and he's just so adorable.' And this was the really lovely side of Bob – the next day I came home and the parrot was in the flat. He became Beano, who I believe is now with Lindsey and Scarlett.

He was my first child and I'm actually still very angry that he's not with me. He's mine! And he adored me. Bob had a black VW Beetle which he studded with silver stars down the side, and very often at weekends we would drive down to Worthing to my parents' home. One morning we saw Bob out in the front garden with a Black and Decker and he decided to put a sunroof on this car so he literally cut it off like it was a tin, a sardine tin, he just cut through it and then he built a sort of crate lid made of wood and bolts and fixed that on the top of the car. And then he put a perch inside the car, which was Beano's perch, and that was our sort of Batmobile. Beano desecrated the inside of the car, you can imagine. He pulled the light fitting down, so that was hanging down on wires, and he crapped everywhere and we were always cleaning it out. That was really something.

Sam Chesterton

I had a parrot, an African grey, and that's how Bob got into them. Before they got Beano they used to have a crow, when they lived in Wimbledon. It had a broken foot, and they nursed it back to health and it used to hop about the flat. That was when the black and silver look was starting, and the crow was part of it. It could untie your bootlaces.

Sue Frame

We used to go to jumble sales at weekends and pick up – well, my thing was to get 1930s clothes, which were all the rage then, and he would pick up bits and pieces, silk scarves. We were really living on a shoestring and yet we would get invited to things like the Butterfly Ball in Grosvenor Square or to some incredibly wealthy person living in the Boltons and we'd get dressed up in our glad rags and go on his little purple scooter. It was huge fun really. I remember going to the party thrown by Nicky Kerman, the restaurateur who owned Drones. He had a huge social wedding and I had this little dress that I had picked up in a jumble sale and pressed and washed. It was like a silk chiffon thing, and they're dressed in Zandra Rhodes and David Morris jewellery, and there was Bob and I in our old outfits, yet somehow we got away with it.

Bob Carlos Clarke

A mutual friend called to warn me that a new muse was spreading the word that I'd tied her up and forced her to have sex. It was an outrageous distortion of the truth, but I envisaged my imminent arrest. In desperation I called her agent who laughed at my protestations, and explained that the model's tale of violent seduction had fired up his stable of beauties to such a degree that there was now a waiting list for my attention. He said he hoped I could handle it.

Sue Frame

Do you know Jordan? She had platinum blonde hair that was done up in a sort of cockatoo hairdo, and later she became one of the Sex Pistols' entourage.

I'd go out to do my day's work and come home with the shopping to cook the supper and there would be Jordan in her rubber or leather outfit. Or I'd come home and find Jilly Johnson and Nina Carter, déshabillé, no clothes on, being photographed and all that sort of thing. I just got on with it, and I thought, well, it's his work.

Bob also got a job taking photographs for Janet Reger, and I posed in them with a girl from Pan's People, the very beautiful Oriental girl. I was still working at the jewellery firm, and one day a very slimy young man who worked there came sidling into my office and said, 'Hmmm, I know what you're doing in your spare time...' And I looked at him and said, 'What are you talking about?' He said, 'I see you're working down at some strip clubs in Soho.'

I was absolutely dumbfounded and horrified. Anyway, the long and the short of it was that some strip clubs had cut out some pictures of me and this other girl from the Janet Reger campaign and stuck them in their doorway saying that we were part of their entourage. I said to Bob, 'You've got to go in and get them down, this is really awful,' and the dancer was also absolutely horrified. We even thought of going to court, but we decided it wasn't a good idea because of the dancer saying, 'I just cannot be exposed – I'm well known on TV and this will just be disastrous.' Bob thought it was a huge joke, whereas I was just dying inside.

But Bob could also be so caring. I remember a time in Balham when it was snowing really badly and there was an old tramp who we used to see round the vicinity, and I was coming home one evening and I said to Bob, 'Oh God, that poor old man sitting by the telephone kiosk, and his beard is covered in snow and he really looks so down and out…' And the next thing Bob was out, down the road, with a packet of biscuits and a hot drink for him.

But there was always that other side. He had this BSA 650 bike, and he said that if he ever thought he was getting too old he would just ride it off a roof one day. He didn't just say that once. He kept repeating it.

9. it was the girls who were never perfect, said geraldine leale

Geraldine Leale

One day I got a call from an agent. 'There's this new guy just out from the Royal College of Art, he's just finished, I quite like his pictures, and he'd really like to take some pictures of you.'

I thought I'd meet him because you always need new photos for your portfolio. I liked him straight away, a breath of fresh air, because usually I was sent round to these very stuffy places, or to very successful photographers who were so into their ego that it was all 'I'm so-and-so, don't even look at me.'

That's how I met Bob, and it was years before he met Lindsey. How did I meet Lindsey? It was a million years ago. I shared a flat with three or four others, and one of my flatmates was at school with her then boyfriend Andrew. We went to the same parties and we clicked straight away. I must have been 18, and shortly after we met I discovered I was pregnant, and I went on to have a handicapped child. So our life education took shape in very different spaces.

Simon Garfield

Geraldine Leale was in the kitchen of the flat she shares with her husband David opposite Ascot race course. Most of the time they live in South Africa, but they come over quite often to sort things out and see old friends. She's in her early fifties. She said her last bit of modelling was a couple of years ago.

Geraldine Leale

It was Lindsey who suggested I should become a model, and thank goodness she did because I was able to keep body and soul together while dealing with all this other stuff, and very profitably. She introduced me to her agent, and from the following day I never stopped working. The first rush was six or seven years, then I had another child, and then I picked and chose more carefully. I didn't do that much fashion stuff because I'm not that tall, but I did a campaign for the fashion chain Richard Shops, Hugh Hudson directed those, a really big deal. I did a Gold Blend commercial, Harmony hairspray, another big thing. I did a lot of shampoo and hair products – very prestigious well-paid stuff.

But with Bob it was never just going to be just a case of taking some nice pictures, it had to be an obsession. I learned that very quickly. We had a bit of a fling that lasted ten days or two weeks, quite full-on. I was living with somebody else at the time, and I thought, 'Bob's amazing, but he's barking mad.' And energetically he was brain-damaged. It was a very needy energy. He would do things that were really charming and sweet, but then he'd give you a hard time if you didn't respond. He knew that I liked reading the *Beano*, so he used to get a copy of the *Beano* and leave it on my doorstep with a little bag of chocolate money. Terribly sweet, but at the same time he wanted your undivided attention. He was like a mad child.

I lived in a ground floor flat in Putney, a big house with a drive around it. Bob used to park and creep around, do the peeping Tom thing. He was a great voyeur, he used to watch through the window and then say things to people for effect: 'Oh, Geraldine June [that was my modelling name] puts all her underwear in the window so that people can see it.'

He loved photographing me, and I loved his pictures, so he would call me up on any pretext – he had a new idea he wanted to try out – so he'd take the pictures and sometimes we'd end up having sex afterwards. But he never turned me on – he wasn't my kind of lover.

Simon Garfield

But did he…what did you say to him when you ended it?

Geraldine Leale

I told him I lived with somebody else, and there was someone else who was interested in me at the time as well, an ex-public schoolboy coke dealer. God, I was 20 years old and absolutely drop-dead gorgeous and all sorts of men were sniffing around. Bob couldn't forgive that, he wanted my undivided attention. This was 1974, 1975.

Simon Garfield

He was with Sue at this time?

Geraldine Leale

Yes, but they weren't married yet. He used to lure me back to their tiny flat in Balham, and he'd sometimes take pictures there while Sue was away. He was very considerate. He'd make sure you had a nice cup of tea and were comfortable and warm enough, and really mother you, and at the same time he was trying to get your pants down. He knew that I loved biscuits, and Sue would then know that I'd been round because there would be no biscuits left. He always wanted to leave a little trace. He loved the idea of spinning people around him.

He would always go in sideways. 'Do you want to have a relationship with me? I'm not really clear what's going on. In the event, you are doing my head in, so I need to back away from this.' I had enough problems with an autistic child, let alone an autistic adult.

Bob then drew me in to his inner circle. He used to call us Woodland Folk, and he knew the bloke I lived with, so he and Paul and Sue and I used to do things together – that went on for a year. He was so lovely with Tabitha, very sensitive. But it triggered

Height
Collar
Chest
Waist
Hips
Inside Leg
Shoe
Glove
Hair

Carlos Clarke

ADDRESS

PHONE

A home-made modelling card, mid-1970s.

something – I could see this deep distress in him, again that neediness. It was that vulnerability that endeared him to me, the fact he was always battling himself.

After I split up with my boyfriend I bought my own flat, and it was a real dump so Bob came round to help me sort it out. He was hanging this dusty carpet out of the window and the dust blew back in his face, and he was furious. He absolutely hated people laughing at him. He always had to say something to insult you or to make you feel embarrassed, so he'd always have the upper hand.

I always liked the fact that they weren't straight photographs. He'd play with them, and put you in this fantasy. Always his fantasy, of course, but always intriguing. In one of the books I'm the girl in the goggles and the flying hat, and there's one called Tennis Shoes, me in a white T-shirt with a pair of Green Flash trainers on, my legs pulled up under me, you can't see anything. It became an Athena poster. I think the one with the girl scratching her bum came earlier, and Bob maybe tried to capitalise on that.

Simon Garfield

So in what way wasn't he your kind of lover?

Geraldine Leale

He was too nervous. His nervous energy spilled into everything, and he was constantly looking for approval. He was always trying to pit himself against somebody else, pit himself against Mick Jagger for God's sake. Bob just couldn't relax. Having sex with Bob was never an act of love. It always felt as if you were this thing on the Petri dish, being observed in some way, and all your reactions carefully tabulated to be thrown back at you a long time later.

Bob loved being the cuckoo in somebody else's nest. He loved the idea that he could creep into my flat or anyone else's flat when the husband or boyfriend was out. He loved the idea of illicit sex, and he would create that. Once it becomes comfortable he's not interested any more. He had to feel he was pulling one over on whoever the cuckold was. For anyone to maintain that type of chicanery takes a great amount of effort. And it spiralled; it got worse as he got older. It wasn't just the women in his life – it was the persona of his life, and that had to be fed and watered.

The überpattern in Bob's relationships – he was always looking for what I call the ultimate mother. If he had that he could then run off and be the errant enfant terrible, and come back and tell his mother all about it and she'd be 'Oh, how lovely'. And I think that's what happened with Lindsey – he found his comfort zone. We all want that, don't we? Run off and do our thing and find comfort at home.

. . .

About a year after I met Bob I showed Lindsey some of his photographs, and she said, 'Oh, they're amazing. I'd like to meet him.'

I don't remember having that many conversations with her about him. We were both out there and doing the London things and being models and having a wild time, and we used to do quite a lot of drugs, well, dope. And he wasn't the only photographer on the block, there were lots of others. But I do remember saying to her that I'd had a fling with him but he was hard work. But she likes hard work.

Simon Garfield

Yes, she had an idea of what she was taking on, in a way that perhaps Sue didn't.

Geraldine Leale

I'm not sure that Sue ever had the long-term objectives that Lindsey had. Lindsey is a businesswoman. Sue was extremely charming, very funny, very pretty, worked hard, but I'm not sure she was ambitious. She wasn't involved in the photography business, and perhaps didn't understand how far Bob could go in it.

Simon Garfield

Was he envious of other photographers?

Geraldine Leale

No, that was one thing that always struck me about Bob. Or if there was that side to him I never saw it. If he liked other people's work he would give credit.

Simon Garfield

He only wanted to be Mick Jagger.

Geraldine Leale

He was at this concert once in Ireland, and he stood next to Mick Jagger while he was having a pee. He was so excited. But given the generation, a lot of guys were obsessed with Mick Jagger. And who wouldn't be? He's gorgeous.

I don't think Bob had any stated ambition. He said to me once, 'I never wanted any of this, I never wanted this big house, I just wanted to take my pictures.' I once lived with an advertising copy-writer who used to say, 'I'm going to do this, I'm going to blow this person out of the water...' but Bob never came up with anything like that. I think the thing Bob never got to grips with is that there is no final endpoint in photography – you just go on.

His technical ability just got better and better, but I think he needed to stop taking pictures of girls and try something else.

Of course he always had another girl who was younger and prettier, but it wasn't the fact that the work was never perfect, it was the girls who were never perfect.

Simon Garfield

He would meet a new girl, she would become the one, maybe they'd fuck, but then he'd realise she wasn't the one and it wasn't enough.

Geraldine Leale

He realised she wouldn't have the magic key that would turn the magic door that he thought was there.

10. why didn't they twig? asked lindsey carlos clarke

Sue Frame

The marriage. We had moved from Balham to Wimbledon to a beautiful flat. It was actually overlooking the common, big marble fireplaces; it needed a lot of work doing to it, which we both did. It was still the early 1970s, and Bob loved to have his bit of dope, and it became more and more of a habit. Just about every evening he'd roll these joints that were like Winston Churchill's cigars, hash, big roach, and he said, 'You know, come on, you've got to do it too, it's no fun otherwise.' Of course, I went along with it and it actually didn't suit me at all. I don't know if I was feeling insecure as well, but I started to really have hallucinations and I know it can bring on psychosis in certain people and I really think that was the way I was heading.

Meanwhile I was losing weight like nothing on earth. I'm actually pretty small anyway and I was just skin and bone and I was really, really ill. I went to the doctor in the end; I thought I was dying, I was so thin. He said, 'You're having panic attacks which is not uncommon for a woman in her twenties,' and I was put on a lot of tranquillisers and sleeping pills. And I was still trying to hold down my job. It reached a point…My parents were very worried about me and Dad eventually took Bob into the potting shed one weekend when we were down and said, 'Look, you've been with Sue for seven years, what are your intentions? If you don't see a future I think your kindest thing would be to leave her but if you want to stay with her I think you should give her some more stability.'

I didn't actually know he'd done this until afterwards. My parents knew that Bob was a very mercurial person. This was in 1975, and people weren't so liberal about just living with your partner as they are today.

It was always in my mind that I wanted children, but I'd never have children out of wedlock. That was the way that most people thought, I suppose. But Bob said to me afterwards, 'You know, I'm very anti-marriage. Look at my father, he got married three times.' And he also didn't like the idea of being a married man; he liked to be glamorous, the man-about-town kind of thing. But he said to me, 'Look, if it's a case of losing you, then I love you and we'll get married.' We had a register office wedding in Kensington and it was a really kind of funny affair. I mean, my parents didn't come, as my father was ill at the time. Bob said he didn't want his mother to come but she said she would be coming regardless, and we actually drove to the wedding in our black Batmobile and he put a big ribbon on the front. We drove through Kensington and people were cheering and smiling at us. It looked really weird. But we got married and Sam Chesterton's mother, Lady Chesterton, laid on a little wedding breakfast for us and it was actually really nice.

Jane Chesterton
Sue and Bob got married in my parents' flat in Kensington Church Street, the big block of flats called York House.

Lindsey Carlos Clarke
I went to Bob's wedding reception. He married Sue not long after we met as friends. On the day, Bob said to me, 'I don't know what I'm doing, I don't feel right.' He said her father had said that he should do it.

Sue was sweet, a very nice girl, very ordinary, a perfectly intelligent girl next door. I don't think she was equipped to deal with him at all.

Sue Frame

Lindsey was married to Andrew Cleveland, who was an aspiring musician, but wasn't having a huge amount of luck. We often used to go and have dinner with them, or they'd come to us, or we'd go out together and it was all a sort of jolly palsy friends sort of thing.

Lindsey was a *Sun* Page 3 model. There was her and her good friend Geraldine. And Bob actually always used to say he absolutely fancied Geraldine, and Geraldine was quite a beauty, and Lindsey was always a lot of fun, quite up for jokes and always laughing, very loud.

I meanwhile was carrying on…I'd left the jewellery firm and I was working for a very prestigious group of shops at that time. I don't know if you ever remember the Elle shops? Well, I used to do all the windows and the merchandising. I'd just travel round and get the looks together and I think at this time Bob was at the Royal College, but was beginning to think, 'Well, what's going to happen when I leave?' And I know he very much wanted to have somebody who would help with the administration of his work and do all the practical things while he was doing the creative stuff. Lindsey was earning a lot of money then as a model and I wasn't earning anything like that. My plan was to get out of what I was doing and get back into illustration work, which was what I loved, but it was a question of being financially in a position to do it. Even when I was married to him, Bob always insisted I pay my way.

Sam Chesterton

Sue was probably more spunky at the beginning, and then I think he pulverised her by taking her for granted and then becoming sexually bored with her.

Sue Frame

Obviously around this time he and Lindsey started having an affair and it became more and more involved. Whatever I say…I'm not fond of her because I actually feel what she did was really unethical. Her husband was devastated because he absolutely adored her and she told Bob in the end that she was kicking him out, which she did, and Bob kept saying to me, 'Poor Lindsey, the marriage has gone wrong.' It was things like, 'Well, let's have her round for dinner because she's feeling lonely and sad.' And I remember on one occasion she came round and I was doing something, getting some food ready, and she was in another room with him and the next thing I knew she burst out of the flat and was running down the road hysterically, and Bob came to me and said, 'Oh poor Lindsey, she's so upset, she won't listen to me. Please go and bring her back.' So muggins went running down the road, put my arms round her, said, 'Come on, Lindsey, come back, you mustn't get so upset, it'll all work out.' I brought her back to the flat. And I found out afterwards that what she'd been saying to Bob was, 'For God's sake, when are you going to leave that girl and come with me?'

So you can imagine I was not happy about it, and my sister told me afterwards that we'd all been at a party and Lindsey had looked at me and said to my sister, 'I know some people call me a bitch but when I want something I'll walk over anything to get it.' Bob was obviously very receptive to it as well; she was doing well, she was well connected in the modelling world, she'd made quite a bit of money, and I had become a bit of a dead loss as far as promoting his ambitions.

We'd been married for two years by then. We had a huge party afterwards, a whole fancy dress thing that people talked about, they even talk about it now, it was so wild. But Bob wanted everything – he wanted it to be 'erotic or neurotic', and everybody had to come dressed in their wildest clothes and we had to line the whole flat with black bin liners and all get dressed in the most bizarre clothes and we had complaints from the neighbours for months afterwards.

Simon Garfield
Had he been unfaithful to you before, as far as you're aware?

Sue Frame

Simon, I think he was. When you look back on it I think he did have dalliances with one or two people. He just, I don't know, he just couldn't keep himself zipped up. And yet he used to say to me if you ever...'I will kill you first before you leave me.' And he was so jealous of anyone who paid attention to me. Adrian George wanted to do a portrait of me, he stopped it. Adele Rootstein, who made all the mannequin models, she met me and she said she wanted to model my head. I'm little, I'm not of model stature, I'm small, but she wanted to model my face to go on a mannequin and he stopped it. It was things like that.

Sam Chesterton

When Lindsey first came into their lives there was an element, and one has to be careful what one says, that Bob and Sue didn't take Lindsey and her husband seriously. Probably more Lindsey's husband.

But there was the element of ambition there with Bob, and this titillation with Lindsey.

Sue Frame

I don't know, you have your impressions of Lindsey, but she was a very different person to me. She's very ambitious, very much with her eyes on the bright lights as well. You know, I got the impression back then that she wanted to be in the spotlight, wanted money, wanted all those trappings and I mean, I don't know, obviously what I say to you – people could say that's just sour grapes.

Lindsey Carlos Clarke

That thing that Bob said, about a friend telling him to fuck me to get revenge on Geraldine, I've since realised was probably just something Bob made up. There was no friend – it was just something he wanted to do, but he had to justify it, had to lie about it. It was going to be a familiar pattern.

Anyway, things didn't work out quite as planned. What happened was, we became friends, and the affair started about four months in. We used to have terrible rows when we were having our affair. There'd be four of us out to dinner, his wife Sue and my husband, and he would always say something to me like, 'You spend too much money on something.' But I was the successful model and I was probably picking up the bill for the dinner, so I'd say, 'Don't be ridiculous.' Then he'd insult me and I'd announce to my husband, 'Andrew, we're leaving.' I'd get in the car and say, 'I never want to see or speak to Bob ever again,' and my husband would say, 'You must calm down, darling.' Why didn't they twig? We were in this terribly passionate affair, and we were having a row as if they weren't there. It was mad, and they're sitting there like that, wondering what the hell's going on.

In the end we got caught. It was getting to the edge of the rainbow. I got a terrible call from his wife. She said, 'You know, he never wants to see you again,' and I just decided that I wasn't going to do anything, I just quietly sat back and he then rang me about two days later and said, 'Sue's in a terrible state and I might have to stay with her.' Instead of getting hysterical, I thought, two hysterical women, not a good idea, just step back. Probably the first grown-up thing I ever did.

It was too much for my husband and he was really mad with me. Then about a week later Bob called and said, 'I'd like to see you.' I thought he was probably going to say, 'I've thought about this and I've been such a shit to my wife.' But he said, 'Would you like to see me tonight?' And he moved in that night, and that was it. Cemented, you know.

Jane Chesterton

Sue was absolutely devastated when it all ended. When she was chucked out, Sue turned up to stay with me. I remember saying to her, 'What a horrible person to have done this to you,' and now isn't it ironic that many years later Lindsey's turned out to be such a good friend.

Sue Frame

When the time came, he decided I was not beneficial to him any more, and that was it. At the time I know he was tearful and he was very torn, and Lindsey was pulling the one way and I was begging him to give us another chance, but in the end I think he thought she was a far better bet than I was, so off they went.

I was left with the parrot and a few of my possessions, and I was so distraught. I gave up my job, I didn't know what to do with myself, and a friend invited me to the US. I said to Bob, 'I'm going to New York, I've got to cool my heels and clear my head,' and he said we'd have to sell the flat. I said, okay, but don't do anything until I get back. Then when I was away he got an offer for the flat, and he said, 'If you don't come back and sign it now I am washing my hands of it.' I flew back; I found he'd sold a lot of my furniture without my permission, and dumped a whole lot of it in a damp garage.

Bob Carlos Clarke *(letter to Sue Frame's parents, 24 October 1978)*
I have started half a dozen letters to you, none of which makes much sense, and all pretty irrelevant anyway.

I realise that nothing I write is going to alter the facts or influence your opinions. I just want to say that whatever the outcome of this mess, no couple could have hoped for such kindness and support that Sue & I have had from you both.

I know that I have been mainly responsible for what has happened, but I also <u>know</u> that I love Sue & deeply regret the hurt that this has caused her. We have to make decisions now & they <u>must</u> be the right ones. We aren't 18 any more and a mistake now would be far more tragic later on.

I do not want to be responsible for changing Sue – she is more perfect than any other woman I know. It isn't a simple question of comparison (as Sue believes). I see <u>no</u> alternatives to her, but our relationship had deteriorated over 2 or 3 years from a lively, exciting, promising partnership to a dull contract with no advantages <u>whatsoever</u>.

It has been a depressing and confusing fortnight & I have now thought very constructively, but, apart from our problems, I bitterly regret the distress this has caused you. I know you must see it as a betrayal, and I am sorry for that.

There is much I want to say, but I know that you will have thought about everything almost as much as Sue and I.

I <u>never</u> wanted to hurt Sue or disappoint you – I may be a habitual pessimist about almost everything, but I <u>did</u> want things to work out.

Whichever way things go I hope it is the right way in the end.

I'm sorry I have taken so long to write.

Love

Bob

Sue Frame

He was living with Lindsey in her Parsons Green bijou love nest and I still had the parrot and a few bags of clothes and luckily a few friends took me in.

Bob Carlos Clarke *(letter to Sue Frame, October 1978)*

By now you'll be off & looking forward to something a bit less depressing than Dulwich and Elle and my telephone calls. You must feel very alone now.

I know that you think I have found myself an easy alternative to keep me from facing reality & to some extent you are right, but I swear to you that the piece of you that has been torn out of the centre of me will not be replaced quickly or easily – if at all.

Whatever happens <u>I will not</u> stop loving you. <u>Nobody</u> is going to replace the special, useless, lovable feelings which I have shared with you for so long. I know nothing, my stupid head is like a weathervane.

Something tells me that you may be getting away from me in good time. I feel rotten inside – I have never felt like this.

I think I'm going to learn what matters the hard way.

Don't blame yourself, don't try to forgive me – This would have happened to <u>anyone</u> who was crazy enough to want to live with me. The little things that you didn't do are not important.

Yet again my icicle seems to have got the better of me.

I <u>will</u> be thinking of you – I <u>do</u> love you. I hope you can read this – I should type it out for you but I'm wrecked.

Be as good (to yourself) as you can.

B xxx

Amy says 'the man who makes no mistakes does not make anything' – she is the only sane voice in all of this.

Sue Frame
Amy was the old woman who lived downstairs, and Bob would spend a lot of time with her listening to her stories.

Sam Chesterton
I saw Sue just after he kicked her out, and she just broke down completely. I took her up to Scotland with me for Christmas, we stayed in a castle near Inverness. Everyone thought she was the most terrible drag, frightfully wet, because she spent most of the time crying. She was like a soggy sponge, poor thing.

Sue Frame
The break-up was pretty acrimonious. I was just so devastated and hurt I just couldn't really – I actually thought London is too small for the two of us. I don't want to hear about what's going on with him and I just want to get as far away as I can because it'll be the only way I can get my life back together. I think Bob probably felt terrible in his heart about what he had done because we had had a great love at one time. I mean we really had, and for all that he would tease me and things would go on, he was so jealous of any other man looking at me or anything like that and he – I hope I'm not making this sound like he was a total bastard, but he did have a very sweet kind side as well, but it would appear in strange ways. His mother always used to say about him that he was like the boy from *The Snow Queen*. She said a splinter of glass or ice went into his heart when he was born because he could be this sweet but he had this cruel side. You know, jokes made always at the expense of other people. He had a way of homing in on their real weak points and making a joke about it and yet there was always so much fun going on with him; it was an exciting life.

After two years the divorce came through and that was the end of it, but for years I've been haunted by him because he was the sort of person – he was such a strong personality and he was such a one-off person that you don't end with someone like that without them leaving a huge mark on you.

We had no contact at all. His mother used to write to me occasionally and I spoke to her a few times on the phone. She seemed very fond of me and I was very fond of her.

And then I got an invitation to come to South Africa. I'd always said one day I'd love to go back to Africa, back to where I was born. So I had this opportunity and I remember sitting on a bus; it was a cold January morning and I thought I can either slit my wrists or I've got enough money left in my bank account and I think I'm going to ring up this friend and say, 'Is the offer still on?' So I came out to South Africa. I left Beano with my parents, and that was actually when I met my present husband.

So the years went by and I used to fantasise sometimes about meeting Bob again and I just wish we could lay the bad ghosts to rest and have some closure on this.

• • •

Sam Chesterton

You ought to get hold of someone called Susie Slack. Susie Slack was a great figure in Bob's life, probably persona non grata with Lindsey. I think she was at the London College of Printing. She was pre-punk, always wore lipstick on her eyelids. Bob brought her down to deerkeeper's and she was a great hit, with her boyfriend Melvin. Bob thought they were so eccentric and was riveted by them.

Bob Carlos Clarke

Antonioni's infamous 1960s film *Blow-Up* popularised the idea that photographers spend their lives clambering all over their models. This is one reason for the enduring popularity of glamour photography as a middle-aged man's pastime. Apart from doctoring, it's the only socially acceptable way of undressing total strangers.

When it comes to a permanent monogamous relationship, the heterosexual male who photographs naked women for a living has a problem: finding a woman who can handle his tiresome obsession with the woman at the next table. Focusing all your creative energy intensely and intimately on a female for a period of months or years is about as close to a love affair as a man can get without necessarily falling in love. When the spark eventually dies and the final picture is taken, it's like losing a lover.

Sam Chesterton

And then he and Lindsey met the Commander, and they went into this whole rubber world together.

11. i wasn't guilty of anything, said emma ford

Philippe Garner

I'm just trying to remember my first impressions of him. Certainly a very handsome man, a very intense man, a kind of look that could weave a web around people, a multi-faceted man who was hard really to seize, which I like about people. If all you're ever going to see is what you get presented with first time, you think, right, let's move on, but with Bob you knew there were parts you were never going to get to.

Helmut Newton was always one of my great passions. I met him in 1975, and that was the beginning of a very long and enjoyable friendship. I was always being drawn to the layers of the images, and with Bob it was the same. And I was fascinated by Bob because he had a very particular charm, very engaging, mischievous.

In common with many highly creative people he had a degree of self-obsession and selfishness. It never bothered me because I'm fascinated by such people and take a kind of vicarious pleasure in their company, but my wife Lucilla sees it as a sometimes unequal relationship where it's all give give and I get nothing in return. In fact I get plenty in return. Perhaps it's because I think I admire enormously the courage it takes to ultimately wear so many private aspects of your personality on your sleeve. I've always been much more contained, and discreet and reticent of expressing myself in so many ways, and I just think that somebody who can live their art, live their trauma, it shows a kind of integrity and honesty which I admire. And that selfish single-mindedness, it's part of the artistic psyche and it was very much a part of Bob.

Ghislain Pascal

Philippe wrote some of the introductions to Bob's books. He gave us some very good advice about managing Bob's estate, and I think he advised Helmut Newton's widow and advised the Robert Mapplethorpe Estate, and he is the biggest Bob fan. We had lunch with him after Bob's death, and he was saying to Lindsey, 'I don't think you realise how important Bob's work is to English photography. He will go down in history as being unique, and in 50 years' time he will be respected.' And he's always been respected. If you talk to any photography student they all studied Bob Carlos Clarke. This is the irony – every student studies Bob. But people in this country, and it sounds like a cliché, are rather nervous of sex.

I always see Bob's work as an art form. I put his pictures on my wall, and I can admire them for being an artwork. And I can see them being there for more than ten years. If Bob had shot Kate Moss, he would be deified. But he didn't want the models to be bigger than the pictures. He only wanted to shoot ordinary girls. Even the Caprice one with the mask he didn't call it 'Caprice'. He called it 'The Masked Blonde'. Bob's work will live on because it is an art form.

Philippe Garner

I especially loved those early images, the collages. He loved talking about the process. When there's the opportunity of hearing from somebody who doesn't just make polite sounds but seriously pulls apart what it is that makes a picture tick, it was of enormous value to him. He would have his moments of self-doubt and sometimes these were considerable, so he would get a great deal from that re-assurance that the pictures contained what he was seeking to express.

Yes, the intensive hours of collaging and colouring, which shows already the extent to which he was constructing something artificial. He was creating the building bricks of this imaginary universe of his and much of his early work was his most important. It ties him very strongly and specifically to certain of the surrealists and I'm thinking of somebody like Hans Bellmer. The photographic aspect of what they were piecing together was the link to the real world, the recognisable hook for their audience: this is the world of real flesh and real objects and real things and yet it has been subverted into another universe by artistic interventions. It was Photoshop before Photoshop existed, but it wasn't Photoshop to be lazy, it was Photoshop because it was specifically taking the real and contorting it into something beyond.

One has to remember how relatively thin and limited and unadventurous the world of British photography was at that time. Measuring Bob up against his contemporaries in the 1970s, when he was starting out. I'm just scratching my head now to think who and what was artistic photography in Britain at that time? Well, artistic photography was either still in a tradition of independent reportage, along the lines of a Tony Ray-Jones, influenced by the generation of Robert Frank and Garry Winogrand, or it was going to be maybe a very microscopic look at nature in a sort of Romantic English tradition. I think of a John Blakemore, very beautiful – aren't fine grasses delicious when you get in close. But there was nothing like Bob. There was absolutely nothing like Bob.

Simon Garfield

Occasionally I would see the ghost of Cecil Beaton in there – those very meticulously crafted portraits with lots of props and studied jokes.

Philippe Garner

There's an Englishness or Britishness in both of those, and Beaton was also – without the darkness but with plenty of mischief and occasional viciousness – constructing a journey through his own identity and sexuality. I left Sotheby's at just the wrong time and missed my opportunity, but I always wanted to curate a Beaton show called 'Portraits and Self-Portraits', and my thesis would have been that every photograph he ever took of anyone was actually a self-portrait. He managed to find the imagery to travel on a journey of self-discovery through time, history and gender, and looked at in that way Beaton's work is utterly riveting.

Beaton did it for the most part by elaborate construction in front of the camera so it was just one click, he wasn't dependent on collage, but there was a very constructed artifice in front of the camera. Bob would do it by cutting up and piecing together the bits and one question this particular comparison begs is to what extent did Bob wish that he could trade places with the people that he was photographing. Was there a side of him that would have loved to enter those bodies and act out the fantasies for himself, and maybe he didn't know, maybe he didn't ask himself that so specifically. I'm not saying that he's in the wrong skin but it is the nature of sexuality that it is far more complex than one often stops to think about, and the feminine forces within the male and vice versa are powerful and stimulate enormous curiosity about what it would be like to inhabit the other.

Bob Carlos Clarke

When I find myself on a motorway or a train, speeding through some bleak suburb with terraces and tower blocks flashing past, I imagine the lives behind the curtains, fresh and unspoiled, awaiting discovery.

Philippe Garner

I love some of the pictures where he would use images of quite extraordinary architecture and take them out of scale or out of context so it was as if he'd assimilated the work of the film set designer Ken Adam, who created those extraordinary futuristic fantastical villains' lairs in the early Bond movies. Some of Bob's early pictures went to the levels phantastic, a kind of science fiction. It was science fiction pre-digital age, or just on that cusp. He peopled this territory with his women, who would then become half-woman, half-mutant and suggest a desire actually not to inhabit this world.

Upstairs I've got what I think is one of the best of the pictures of that type, in its black silk surround and big antique gilt frame. Have I mentioned it to you? *Das Schwimmbad. The Swimming Bath.* The swimming bath is one picture, the landscape is another, and then there's the model Jilly Johnson, whom he did a lot of pictures with at that time. I was so pleased to get it from him. He did it in 1979 or 1980, and a couple of years later he was on the point of trading it with somebody for photographic equipment. He said they were going to give him X many pounds of equipment for it and I said, 'Don't do it, don't do it, let me come round.' I gave him not quite as much money as he would have had for the equipment, but it was good hard cash, and he was very pleased to get it, and I think very pleased also for me to have that picture.

Bob Carlos Clarke

Here are a few tips:

1. Before approaching your 'target' be certain you've made the right choice. Once your introduction is underway, it's difficult and embarrassing to abort. Discreetly try to ensure that your judgement is not the result of some illusory impression, lighting, artful make-up, and/or the flattering, soft-focus filters of alcohol and lust.

A well-designed business card, printed with an appropriately cool and seductive image, is an essential element of 'the approach'.

2. If your target is accompanied by a male, it may be wise to address your opening words to him, or at least include him in your introduction. Heterosexual males can be wary and aggressive in the company of desirable females. Keep calm and cool, and don't anticipate an immediate commitment, and don't expect a phone number. With luck both might be forthcoming, but, in most cases, patience pays off.

3. You may not be a matinee idol, but it helps to look reasonably stylish and successful. No one wants to drop his or her pants for a seedy-looking loser. In this predatory society, anyone young and beautiful suffers perpetual harassment and quickly learns to ignore it. It's likely that your target has already been approached by all manner of low-life, so her first impression of you is crucial and will probably determine the outcome.

4. Tell her who you are and what you do. If possible provide well-known names as reference for your good reputation, perhaps an established model agency or brand name client. Don't mumble or waffle, be polite, confident and direct. Not: 'Um, er, I couldn't help noticing your, er, lovely long legs up the escalator...' but perhaps more like: 'Please excuse me, but you have a great look. Are you with a model agency? I'm a photographer working on a new book/exhibition/whatever and I'd love to include you. You're probably very busy but, if you are at all interested and would like to discuss it, please call me on this number...' Hand over your card, and depart with dignity. Don't hang about looking shifty. Your target should be left feeling flattered and excited that she has been honoured with such a special opportunity, and not with the uncomfortable sensation that she has just had a chilling brush with a pervert.

Philippe Garner

Partly what intrigued me about the pictures is whether he is photographing what he desires or photographing what he fears, and I suspect the answer is both. The power of sexuality is terrifying, and photographing it is a way of subjugating it. It's not that he wants to – it goes beyond the kind of corniness of fetishism, sadism. There is such a kind of strength of lust and passion for these bodies, for these curves, for these volumes, for this mythology of women who are on the edges of being women and goddesses. He is creating a universe, isn't he? Curiously, even the way he renders skin, it's not skin as we know it in regular life, neither the colour or the perfection or the sense of it. So there is just a kind of relentless fixation with women who are bursting with a kind of implied or evident sexuality.

But I can't believe that he could get to the age of 50 and still be predicated on adolescent lust, because I think one's nature changes, it evolves, it's not like you're on heat all the time. It's a process of trying to unravel and understand something which has marked you all of your life, and which is the fundamental...the matrix of life. It's way, way beyond being a tit and arse photographer. It's banal to say so, but to many people who may come to the pictures for the first time: 'God, they're sexy pictures!' Well, yes, but keep looking, other things will emerge.

So what are those other things? I think what they're saying is, 'Be careful what you wish for, it might come true' – the possibility that he had been able, through his chosen career or through his artistic path, to do something that I think for many men might be the stuff of fantasy. 'My God, fancy photographing naked women, directing them, having them pose for you!' And yet it came true and he could do it. But then what? And what did that relationship mean for him?

It became a scenario that he would play out again and again and again. But again and again to a point where at times I imagine he must have wanted to escape it, because it became his prison, a world of existential end-games where there is no end. And he had a sense of humour, sure, but not enough of a sense of humour, not enough of a sense of humour as an integral part of his philosophical engagement with the world to manage these forces and these syndromes that he found himself in. You know, he had the dark humour that was necessary just to survive and engage, but it wasn't the ability to really laugh at himself and maybe have several selves – the principal one being a person who led a stable life.

Bob Carlos Clarke

5. Choose your moment. Don't attempt an introduction anywhere noisy or distracting like a dance floor. If this is your only opportunity, write a brief note and hand it over with a business card. If you're in a club or restaurant where you know a manager or member of the staff, it may help to get them to set up an introduction for you.

To build her confidence, encourage your 'target' to check you out. If you're dyslexic or illiterate, don't use a note.

6. Watch your words. Most women respond positively to sincere and appropriate compliments, but at the introductory stage it's wiser to keep to 'hypnotic eyes' rather than 'magnificent buttocks'. Obviously the circumstances can affect the approach. 'Stunning tits!' may be an acceptable greeting at a rock festival, but less so at a funeral.

7. Invite your prospective model to view your work either at a safe and convenient public place, other than a toilet, or at your studio if

you have one. Suggest she bring a friend for company. Some of my favourite models have arrived as 'friends'.

If you have a girlfriend, wife or sister, ask her to be present. If not, a dog, cat or budgerigar will help to make you seem normal. (Reptiles and fighting dogs exempted.)

If you live alone in a damp basement with your collection of Victorian medical instruments and dismembered dolls, rendezvous elsewhere.

8. Don't discuss nudity until you have won the confidence of your prospective model. Show her images that fill her with enthusiasm, not dread. Don't be over-specific. Once the model has agreed to shoot in principle, it's just a question of tactics to reach the required result.

9. Never try to con, coerce or intoxicate models into nudity. Gentle persuasion is okay, but an even-sided collaboration is best.

10. PND or post-naked depression happens when your model's initial euphoria at being photographed nude subsequently evaporates, and she threatens legal action and demands the destruction of the negatives.

This can be caused by a number of reasons: 'My parents are Mormons, my husband's a psychopath' and so on. The result is a lot of wasted effort and expense, and best avoided by taking time to assess your model's state of mind prior to shooting. If in any doubt, get a signed agreement before the session.

11. Discuss plans to sell or publish the results with the model prior to the shoot. Commercial model releases are wordy and intimidating, so I use a simple contract of my own, defining the terms of our agreement. It offers protection both to the model and myself. I often work with friends on a basis of mutual trust, but it's better for both sides to be protected by a written contract.

12. When in doubt, check that your model is over the age of consent.

• • •

Emma Ford

At the beginning, Bob just wouldn't leave me alone.

I first met him when I went to his studio in Battersea with a friend of mine, Vanessa Upton. I was a make-up artist, Vanessa was going to model, and she took me there as a test. I had just come out of the London College of Fashion and had been working a bit for Trevor Sorbie. Bob kept on saying he wanted to shoot me, but I had never done anything like that before. I was 'no, no no', and I think it took him about six months to persuade me. I was 22, so nearly 10 years ago.

I had heard of him through other models. He was very charismatic, and on that first day he was all over me, and didn't really take much notice of Vanessa. He was always talking about my hair, 'Look how fluffy it is, you're like Picachu.' That was his nickname for me – Picachu. He would comment on your hands, everything you wore, what your style was. He thought I was some sort of little creature, and he wanted to capture that. He kept on saying, 'Oh come on, come over, just a couple of shots,' and in the end I said okay. Initially I was a bit shy, but he had a make-up artist, and it turned out amazingly. And then I spent about two years with him solidly.

Bob Carlos Clarke

Ideally, for the best pictures, I'd need to live with a subject for three years, or maybe three months would be enough, and really get inside her, both literally and metaphorically. That's the way to take great erotic photographs. It's a great shame in my mind that Naomi Campbell has never lived with a photographer, because that's why Naomi's photos are all surface and no depth.

Lindsey Carlos Clarke

His obsessions would come and go, and we all got used to it. You know, he'd be ranting about how wonderful some girl was, the new muse of his life. You've got to be so sharp about sussing people out, and I'd nudge James, his assistant, in the darkroom and say, 'Have you seen this one!' and he'd say, 'Oh God,' so we'd let it pass. Three or four days would go past and he'd say, 'That girl's a complete

At home with Beano, Lindsey and Bob.

nightmare!' and I'd go, 'Oh, you don't say…' Not all of them were like that. Some of them, like Emma, were around for years, and became friends to all of us.

Emma Ford

Even if he wasn't shooting me, he would persuade me to hang around and help out, and pay me £30 or something. We were instantly friends, and he was very funny. He became obsessed with certain things, the way I would walk, and he would shoot a whole series of pictures with lilies all over me, and he would always say things like, 'What knickers are you wearing?' He loved the fact that I was always a bit scruffy and had holes in my knickers. He would say things like, 'I'd love to cut that bit of fat off you and slice it up and serve it as crackling.' I mean, we would shoot all the time. We did private work for him, work for magazines and commercial work. We did the Urban Stone campaign – that was the poster that was banned. There's a whole cupboard-full of pictures.

Simon Garfield

One of my favourites is the one of you lying on top of another model.

Emma Ford

That's Pat, Pat the Lamb.

Simon Garfield

How did your relationship change over time?

Emma Ford

Everyone thought we were having an affair, but we weren't. We were never lovers. I spent practically every day with Bob for two years. I lived in the studio for a little bit, in a glass room. Lindsey and I always got on, and I got on particularly well with Scarlett, and I went to stay with them at the beach house, and I felt I was part of the family.

Simon Garfield

I can understand how Lindsey would be jealous – you around all the time, 20 years younger than her.

Emma Ford

I think because nothing ever happened, and I was…I wasn't guilty of anything. But I often did wonder: she must think something's going on. I used to ask Bob, and he said, 'Oh no, Lindsey's fine.'

Simon Garfield

Do you think he wanted it to be more?

Emma Ford

I do, yes.

Simon Garfield

And you resisted that?

Emma Ford

Yes I did.

Simon Garfield

Did he ever use that line about how the only way to really take great photographs was to get to know his model intimately – by sleeping with them?

Emma Ford

He didn't actually, no! But he would say, 'When are you going to sleep with me? I'm going to be dead soon.'

• • •

Lindsey Carlos Clarke

The idea of him being with somebody who was nude all the time didn't bother me – that was always part of our life. But the idea that he was obsessed by somebody…I think it came very gradually and a lot of people he was obsessed by were not because he was sexually entranced by them. I think this is where people misunderstood him. In a way it would have been much simpler if, on the odd occasion, he'd gone and bonked the odd model in the studio. That almost would have had a normality to it. But it was much more multi-layered than that. It was much more to do with ownership, he wanted adoration, he wanted love and he wanted to own them and that didn't necessarily involve the sexual act, although the obsession could have just the same implications as if they'd been in a passionate relationship.

• • •

We had great fun with another girl called Debbie, and Bob loved going out with two girls, obviously. We cared about her and we loved her, but then of course it would be over because of the new, new thing. He'd want something else and they'd be dropped in a way that was shocking for them because they didn't know what had happened. For *The Dark Summer*, Charlotte was the big obsession. She's on the cover. She really was a discovery, and he introduced her to the modelling agency and did a great deal for her. But then I always had to pick up the pieces. I used to keep in touch with them and make sure they were okay, and help them with things. I became this great picker-upper of everybody. I said to him once, 'You have to understand, you must be responsible for people. I don't care whether they're a friend or a lover or your postman that you get involved with – you can't be really nice to them for a period and then that's that.'

Bob Carlos Clarke

I met Kadamba at a Vivienne Westwood show. She was dark and petite and radiantly beautiful, and her irrepressible charisma magnetised everyone. She joked that she'd arrived from another galaxy, and wasn't staying long. She said she'd die young, and made me promise I'd be there to immortalise her 'like Marilyn'.

So it was a shock but not a surprise to hear that, on a summer afternoon in June 1998, she was murdered by an insanely possessive lover. Her mother asked me to take her final portrait at a funeral parlour in Notting Hill, but I was committed to some advertising shoot. Looking back, I think I missed something very special, and let Kadamba down.

Lindsey Carlos Clarke

We used to get wonderful invitations to things, and I'd always know if he sat next to anyone well known because they'd take a picture. I'd be on the other side, but I knew that I'd be cut off and it would just be a picture of him and Koo, or him and whoever it was. I didn't mind any of that, it seemed like common sense. I don't think I wanted the light on me at all – I quite liked being in the background.

Bob Carlos Clarke

One Sunday afternoon in March '97, a friend dropped by the studio unexpectedly, and with him was Princess Diana. Mischievously, he skulked in the shadow, so that when I opened my front door, I was immediately face to face with this living goddess in a white cotton shirt and faded blue jeans. I was dishevelled and paint-splattered from painting a backdrop, and it felt quite surreal as she sat in the kitchen while I struggled to make tea.

'Who is that?' Diana asked, pointing to a framed photograph of a model's bottom and legs.

I told her who it was.

'Oh! I was at school with her. I must have recognised her bum.' Then she noticed a shot I'd taken of the model Paula Hamilton doing a very plausible Diana impersonation. 'Sooo naughty!' she exclaimed, 'but much prettier than me!' As she left, she suggested we meet up again soon, but the closest I ever came to her again was following the route of her funeral cortege.

Whatever she may have been, Princess Diana most purely symbolises the popular ideal of Mother, Mistress and Martyr – Love, Sex and Death.

Lindsey Carlos Clarke

But then at other times…we didn't really have arguments…it was really a problem of being invisible and being not cared for in any way. The classic thing, he would say, 'Look, I really want this model to work for us, let's take her to the restaurant down the road and we'll talk about it.' But his focus was only ever directed at this person, so I might as well not have been sitting there, I might as well have been the waitress. And as he went out of the restaurant he would walk off down the road with me running behind. I used to think he was focusing on his work and he can't see anything else, so I would let him off that. But it keeps happening, and what happens is that it chips away at you and you start to feel worthless as a person: 'I'm obviously a piece of junk,' and that's not a great feeling.

• • •

Philippe Garner

His craft is something that many of his peers – all of his peers – will acknowledge. They may not find it easy to come to terms with the subject matter, but they will all admire his absolute commitment to the medium and his phenomenal craft. I mean, he could coax things out of a negative, he had a unique touch, and it's very rare among photographers to have that degree of engagement with the process. I guess that the darkroom was again a metaphor for the place he liked to inhabit, so Bob could lose track of time and I guess lose himself, it was another universe. That last darkroom he created is where I took the picture of him. It was an extraordinary space and place. If I compare it with the darkroom of the guys who do my printing, which is just a kind of scruffy hole in the wall; they keep it as clean as it needs to be but it sort of smells of chemicals and there's stuff splashed and stained, you wonder how a beautiful print can come out of it. But Bob's was like an extraordinary science-fiction operating theatre and you knew that every pipe, every tap, every steel surface, everything that he'd constructed for that darkroom – it was the architecture of his whole world. It really symbolised so much more than being a practical work place and I remember being very struck by that, just another world. I wonder where that's all gone. I guess it has gone now, hasn't it?

Simon Garfield

One Sunday afternoon I went round to Philippe Garner's house in West Hampstead, which was a sensitively decorated, predominantly white place with many photographs on the walls, including some fine vintage 1960s prints by Bailey, Lichfield, Donovan and Parkinson. One wall displayed a picture of Marianne Faithfull on the first day of a Mick and Keith drugs trial. Close by was a photo of David Hemmings as Thomas in *Blow-Up* holding his Nikon F up to his eye, the kind of image that inspired so many fantasies. Just as interesting were photographs Philippe had taken himself, which he kept in those large Ilford boxes that once contained just plain paper.

Philippe Garner

I'll show you if you're curious to see. Albert Watson...Bruce Bernard...Annie Leibovitz...Eve Arnold.

Here is Bob. Gosh, that's pretty dark, isn't it? And this was taken 26 April 1995. That was in the new darkroom and I just wanted to get a sense of the taps and stuff; those dark brooding shadows around his eyes.

Then there's Richard Avedon, Peter Beard, Andrew Douglas. Over the years they go on and on. But you see I have to be very careful with these photographers, I'd never dream of showing them my pictures. I get my camera out and pretend I'm just a bumbling little old lady asking if I can take a snap of them and I do it very quickly but I know what I'm doing.

God, poor old Bob, eh, when one thinks about it. I don't feel guilty about it, because I feel I gave him plenty, but I wish I had sensed how dangerous a path he was on. I might have tried to give him more. But then again I might also, out of sheer instinctive self-preservation, have backed off him precisely in order not to be dragged into the vortex.

PART TWO

12. now the hair, much more, that's good, that's great, yes! said david hemmings in *blow-up*

Ghislain Pascal

My mum was a model, and my father was a very well-known French fashion photographer. He worked for *Vogue* here and in America. He moved to London to work in the 1960s. If you pick up any of those *Vogue* books you see his pictures in them. He's Maurice Pascal.

He was in that era of Terence Donovan and Bailey, but he was the outsider, the Frenchie, not quite as successful as them. And my mum was a model in the same period as Twiggy and Joanna Lumley. They met on a shoot in Israel. She's Anthea Coveney.

Bob Carlos Clarke

Helmut Newton hates the word 'erotic', and unless I'm buying a professional's time from an agency I don't like the word 'model': both words are inadequate in the face of so many possibilities. Like 'mannequin' or 'sitter', the word 'model' has wooden, inanimate connotations: a thing you mould out of clay, a dummy you dress up and bend into shape. Although I *have* shot some complete dummies, I go to great lengths to cast real 'performers'. Many of my subjects are not professional models and we develop a working partnership that initially has nothing to do with making money, although it might later.

Ghislain Pascal

Not long after I was born we moved to Connecticut. By then my father had switched from photography to advertising, working in New York. Then he lost jobs. My parents were married just under ten years, and I was maybe three when they divorced – they were just completely incompatible people. My father's very French – VERY French. His mother's Corsican, his father's from Marseille. Very temperamental.

Philippe Garner

I've only met Ghislain a few times. We've had a meal or two and just chatted, resolved certain little issues. So I have a certain sense of him but not a detailed sense of him. He strikes me as being, how old is he, I was about to say a very savvy young man.

Mid-thirties? Well, that's pretty young to be juggling the things he's doing and he strikes me as behaving very professionally in the sense that he's in it for the long game. He seizes his opportunities as he can, but he doesn't seem like a flash-in-the-pan kind of character. He comes across as somebody who values his clients, but he manages to care without caring so much that passion will distort his professional judgement. He keeps enough distance from it to ensure he doesn't get seduced by his clients and the products that he's marketing.

Simon Garfield

Ghislain told me that one day his father just gave up photography completely. He must have had a crisis of confidence, a moment of total disenchantment with his work, and he burnt everything, and now there are very few photos of his, and all the negatives are gone. What survives are a couple of nice photos of his wife. She was a 1960s London model, not as big as the famous ones, but not that far beneath, and she did *Vogue* and all those things.

Ghislain Pascal
My dad is dead now. He died maybe ten years ago. Literally the first year I set up Panic he died.

Simon Garfield
He died in a car crash, possibly suicide, drove into a tree so one doesn't really know the situation. Perhaps one shouldn't make too much of this, but I was beginning to understand something: no wonder Ghislain was drawn to Bob.

Ghislain Pascal
In retrospect now I do think of it, Bob was a – well, it seems awful to say a father figure, but he was quite a lot older. He reminded me of my father – not that I had ever seen my father work, but his temperament – he was a real moody up-and-down person.

Simon Garfield
Ghislain's father burning all his negatives and prints – I always thought that was a very violent act.

Ghislain Pascal
He was never a photographer while I was alive. I never lived with him, so I never saw him in a work capacity. I know he went to New York and worked with Revlon as a commercial director before he got fired.

He would come and pick us up from school, we would have one lunch with him in the holidays. I only went on one proper holiday with him, to the south of France to stay with some friends of his.

It was a very simple relationship. We rang, me and my brother, to talk to him every Sunday evening, but we never really…he kind of lived all over the place between here and America. But I consider we had quite a close relationship.

He was intrigued by the fact that I got into this business. Most people think I got into it because of them, a model and a photographer, but it was purely by chance. At the end of his life he was living in America, and he read the *Sunday Times* out there, and he found it amusing to recite back to me what my clients were doing.

• • •

Simon Garfield

It was time to watch *Blow-Up* again. I had seen it once before, about
a decade after it was made in the mid-1960s, and I remembered it
primarily for its suggestions of sex. The poster had David Hemmings
as Thomas capturing his prey, straddling a model, Veruschka I think,
from above to get his best shot. That was one of three abiding images
for me. The other two were the sex scene with Jane Birkin and a girlfriend in opaque tights, having a play fight with Hemmings as they
tried on clothes and ending up – it was understood – having sex with
him on his studio floor. And the scene in which Hemmings enlarges
his photos to discover that inadvertently he may have been witness
to a murder. This was the crux of Antonioni's film, but its legacy was
the vision of the 1960s photographer, as master of something that
seemed to matter, at the centre of a happening London. It signalled
the start of something, and if you were an ambitious teenager it was
a film that could stay with you for ever.

Hemmings's character was supposedly modelled on David
Bailey, and his patter subsequently became a cliché: 'That's good.
Hunch. Hunch more. That's good. And the hair back. That's great.
That's GREAT! Give it to me! That's very good. Now the hair, much
more, that's good, that's great, YES! On your back, go on, come on,
work, work, work, great, and again, arms back, go, go, that's it, no,
no, head up, yes! Yes! Yes!'

Watching it again, I wasn't sure the film worked as much more
than a period piece. It wasn't thrilling, but it was frequently preten-
tious. But then it started to nag away at me. The mystery at its core
– what you saw, what you created in your mind, the blurrings of
reality – had as much effect on the viewer as they did on Hemmings.
You could theorise about it as much as you wished, or you could
just skim its pleasurable surface, a life that is still vaguely appealing,
a casual life of creativity and mingling with beautiful girls.

The film was important to Hemmings's career: he would later
grow heavy and jowly, but the film set him in the public's eye
the way only a good 1960s photo can: Lewis Morley's Christine
Keeler on that Arne Jacobsen chair; Bailey on Jagger; Bert Stern with

Marilyn on the beach. The film had clearly been important for Philippe Garner – with David Mellor he had curated an exhibition about *Blow-Up* and its suggestive themes at the Photographers' Gallery, and they were writing a book about it. He had a nice framed Italian poster of the film in his house.

And the film must have been important to Bob, one of those decisive flashes that opened up a new free world.

Philippe Garner

I don't know how many people I've heard say, 'It was seeing *Blow-Up* that made me want to become a photographer.' I saw it when it came out in 1967, when I was 18, and it marked me profoundly. But it works on several levels, and I think the people who say 'it made me want to be a photographer' have selectively edited out about 80 per cent of the film and are just grabbing at a few of the more frivolous moments in it. Because actually it is very dark. The whole film is about the existential dilemma that a photographer lives – he's never sure whether he's living and working in a world of reality or imagination, and he's always trying to steer a path between those.

He's very disillusioned at the beginning. There are a couple of quotes: 'I've gone off London this week…'; 'I wish I had tons of money, *then* I'd be free.' And he's looking for his own identity, and looking for a worthwhile path through this maze which is a kind of hall of mirrors of the images that he's making. In that respect it is actually, you're right, a very bleak film at the end in which nothing is resolved. So if one looks at the film seriously, I'm not sure it makes the life of the photographer that attractive.

Simon Garfield

One assumes, but I don't know whether Antonioni ever said this, that the inspiration for Hemmings was David Bailey.

Philippe Garner

It really wasn't. There had been some talk of making a documentary on David Bailey in the previous year, but Bailey was busy and the idea was shelved. And then Antonioni decided to make a film based on a short story about a photographer. The timeliness of that moment – of what was emerging in London – made it the most natural city to turn to as a setting. Antonioni did a great deal of research to build a composite character, and the general assumption is that Bailey is the principal matrix for it. But as far as I'm aware, they never actually met. He took bits of Bailey, but second-hand. He visited and spent a lot of time with a number of other photographers, and he has grafted together some very specific details to make his picture.

Blow-Up is so much about the point where an image which at first might appear to contain a fragment of reality actually starts to disintegrate. And you can see that Bob was fascinated by that. I've heard him talk many times about grain, he loved grain, and I've heard so many people talk about Bob with real respect for his ability as a printer to coax things out of a negative that others couldn't. So there was his profound engagement with what went on in the darkroom, but also a realisation that the moment you put a little bit of emphasis on grain, you take a little picture up to a certain size, you are actually deconstructing it, from being reality into a pattern of speckles. And I think that intuitively perhaps, not necessarily verbalising it, Bob enjoyed and appreciated that inherent ambivalence between the image that would completely seduce by its power and its authority and its erotic moment, and the fact it's all a trick. It's actually just tone and grain and artifice, only happening on that chemical two-dimensional plane. And he enjoyed playing with that, which is why the lusciousness and texture of the printed image was so important to him.

Simon Garfield

When I first met Bob he did a very good impersonation of Hemmings as Thomas in *Blow-Up*: 'Lovely, good, that's it…' he said to the model Gaby Richens when I saw him take photographs of her a few years ago at the White House, a private members' club in Clapham. The White House could have featured in the film without a single change. 'Give me the look!' Bob told her. 'Yes, yes, beautiful! You're a professional!' When Richens took a bathroom break, Bob told me that he had known her for many years, and 'must have done her 220 times by now'.

Bob Carlos Clarke

I was giving a quick-fix photographic soiree for mature students and I needed a model. She was 15, jailbait, unbeknown to me, of course. In my studio in Tite Street. I thought she was amazingly attractive, a combination of all the things I like best – Sophia Loren, Brigitte Bardot, Claudia Cardinale and a barmaid all rolled into one. She was also fantastically lazy, like a big chinchilla. I'm bored with models who won't eat because they're going to get fat or won't eat because they're going to get wrinkled. But Gaby can eat like a horse some-times – enjoying herself. And I've seen a lot of miserable scared girls.

Simon Garfield

Blow-Up seemed to exemplify another side of Swinging London that wasn't just about fashion and music this time, but about manipula-tion and the problems of intrusive reality.

• • •

Ghislain Pascal

There was a phone call from this hospital in Connecticut saying he had been involved in a car accident, and he was on a machine, and could we get on the earliest plane? So me and my mother and brother got a flight that afternoon to America. They were keeping him alive for us, he wasn't breathing on his own.

There was no other car involved. He had had dinner and drove home, didn't have his seatbelt on, and drove into a tree. And that was it. There were no witnesses. It was pretty straightforward.

Simon Garfield

Were there any thoughts in your mind that it wasn't an accident?

Ghislain Pascal

No. I do think now that it wouldn't surprise me if he had driven into the tree. He was 67 when he died, this was ten years ago. He was ten years older than my mother. He was living with his mother and his stepfather, didn't have a job, so it wasn't a very exciting exis-tence. When we went over there the thing that was news to us was that he had a girlfriend. When she turned up we were not particularly nice to her, but I don't suppose you do when you just find these things out.

The other thing we found out was that he had had a drink, but it was an open and shut case to them. He died when I was 23/24. At that age you're just looking forward, everything's new. Now I think it would be great to see those pictures, and we've tried, but it is impossible to find them.

13. i totally understood bob's problem, said allen jones

Philippe Garner

The power of the images doesn't fade. It is the power of Bob's sickness. He was able to achieve what he did because he ended up knowing how the body functioned, how the muscles functioned.

I think some photographers who photograph naked women, they never look beyond certain very basic images which they keep repeating. But I always had the feeling with Bob that he was so obsessed with working with these figures. For him it was almost like a sculpture, modelling; he was fascinated by what was going on under the skin.

Ghislain Pascal

I think I just move forward. I was like that with Bob as well – I think I cried when I got the phone call, very briefly, but even at the funeral, there's no point looking back, it's happened, there's nothing you can do about it.

My father is buried near Henley. I've been three or four times since he died. I just don't see the point. It's a hole in the ground and a cross – what are you supposed to say? Chris said to me, 'Well, if you feel like that, fine.' We cremated him, and then brought the ashes on the plane.

Their first child died, who would have been my sister, and they're buried in the same plot. Dominique is on one side, and it's a very pretty little stone cross. We could have buried him with his mother in America, but we would never have visited.

Lindsey Carlos Clarke

I have worn a rubber catsuit and it's deeply uncomfortable. It's either freezing cold or boiling hot. You have to be serious to peel yourself into that stuff. But the point is that me and Bob were never rubber fetishists. Bob couldn't stand the thought of wearing it, but sometimes we would go to serious fetish clubs because Bob wanted to find something interesting. They had a serious dress code, but sometimes we would be allowed in if we just wore black clothes. They were full of waitresses who were 70-year-old men in little maid outfits. I said, 'Oh my God, don't laugh, pretend we're having a great time and we're really cool.'

On another occasion Bob said he couldn't find an assistant and would I carry his bag and be his assistant? I think it was the Rubber Ball in the 1990s. I couldn't be bothered to put on the full outfit, so I went in a head mask, beautifully made in Japanese kid with a hole in the back for a ponytail. So in we go, and Bob goes off to photograph people, and I'm suddenly aware that there's someone standing right next to me in a full rubber red catsuit, head, hands, legs and willy all outlined in rubber, and he edges towards me and says in a very aristocratic accent, 'That's a most marvellous mask, who made it?' I tell him. He says, 'Oh God, they're marvellous, I got some marvellous gloves from them.' As the evening wore on I got more and more men with masks, and one had no mouthpiece and I see him blinking, and I'm thinking, 'I mustn't blink – I'm giving him a code.'

Philippe Garner

He was in denial of what one might call the real world because he was, very systematically, constructing his own. And at one level it might appear to be a world at which all desires could be fulfilled, you know, sexy and fantastic and exotic, but actually it was a night-mare, I mean quite literally I think. It was the sort of territory where, it was like Bob spent most of his working life exorcising demons and it's the kind of darkness and territory where you could wake up in the middle of the night shaking and think, oh, thank God, the world's all right after all.

Lindsey Carlos Clarke

I used to have lots of women ask me, 'How can you live with a man who photographs women like that?' I'd be thinking, well, he's always been like that. I mean, if you don't want to be with someone who photographs sex then you just don't choose to be. You marry a bank manager or something.

Simon Garfield

Bob liked quoting famous photographers he found inspiring, partic-ularly those sayings that conformed with his own view of his work. One of these was Man Ray in praise of iconoclasm: 'When I took photos, when I was in the darkroom, I deliberately dodged all the rules, I mixed the most insane products together...I committed heinous crimes against chemistry and photography, and you can't see any of it.'

Bob Carlos Clarke

Working in such confined and ill-equipped spaces was mostly hell-ish. One of my 'darkrooms' was a tiny bedroom adjacent to a railway, and I soon learned to time my exposures to avoid the vibration of passing trains. I became a human mole, rarely exposed to daylight, as days merged into nights, and weeks turned into months. Mostly it was a battle with collapsing trestle-tables, overheating enlargers and rogue hosepipes. This was how I discovered chemical abuse – flinging chemicals across prints to distress the image. I've always felt limited by the two-dimensional homogenised gloss of photographic prints, and gained great satisfaction from brutalising and distress-ing them.

After driving myself half mad, I learned that it was important to be able to maintain a certain distance and detachment from work in progress. I had become a neurotic and obsessive printer, making the same print over and over again, convinced that it could be improved. Often I worked until I collapsed, and would wake up the following day to find my apartment festooned with dozens of drying prints – all virtually identical.

Lindsey Carlos Clarke

Sometimes he'd print in the darkroom all night and come up at 5 o'clock in the morning and throw the contacts on the bed and say, 'It's crap, it's crap, it's crap,' and I'd say, 'Okay, honey…' I'd be, 'God, these are amazing, I think you should print this one.' He was too close to it, you know. What I didn't realise was how far he always felt it was from getting there. You know what I mean? I think he was…nothing was ever enough.

Bob Carlos Clarke

Towards the end of my studies at the London College of Printing I was contacted by the Commander, an impeccable silver-haired gentleman in his sixties, who published a quarterly magazine for devotees of rubber-wear. According to a few indistinct black and white photographs, the Commander had seen active service as a frogman in the Royal Navy, during which time he had developed a strong attachment to his diving suit. Now he wanted me to shoot for his peculiar pocket-sized publication.

Urgently in need of work, I went to meet him at his mews house in Paddington where he lived with some sort of psychotic Egyptian guard dog and an elegant cardigan 'n' pearls wife. She presided over the day-to-day administration of an adjoining garage-cum-dungeon packed with 'pleasure-wear' and an unsettling array of rubber tubes and valves.

We arranged a photo shoot for the following week, and on the day he drove me in his ancient silver-grey Bentley to a penthouse on a modern block in Roehampton. We stopped en route to collect our model, a pretty brunette called Angela. From her frayed mini-skirt and laddered tights, she looked like she needed the £50 fee even more desperately than I.

On arrival the Commander spread out his latest range of

skin-tight dresses and catsuits and showed Angie how to pull them on by dusting herself with Johnson's Baby Powder. Then with a lot of vigorous grunting, he buffed her suit to a high shine with Mr Sheen furniture polish, devoting particular attention, I noticed, to her taut buttocks. Finally satisfied, he winked at me conspiratorially, bade us good luck and disappeared.

Relieved to be rid of 'the client', Angie lounged on the sunlit terrace rolling a joint while I loaded a camera. We shot a couple of frames and gently succumbed to the warmth of the afternoon and the mellow grass.

Before long we were more involved with each other than the shoot.

Despite a certain reputation to the contrary, this was the first and only time to date that I have experienced an intimate encounter with a woman in latex, and, to be honest, it was quite a struggle. By the time I'd established that the zippered crotch was several crucial centimetres out of alignment with my model's, the black sun-baked suit had raised her temperature to such a point that sweat was hissing out of the seams in a fine spray.

Suddenly Angie snapped out of her steamy rapture, and sat bolt upright, staring over my shoulder. Unnoticed, the Commander had reappeared minus his immaculate Savile Row pinstripe, and now stood, partly concealed by the plate-glass patio doors, in a voluminous pair of off-white Y-fronts, brown sandals and a state of very evident arousal. Passion instantly evaporated.

Philippe Garner

I'm by nature a diplomat, and I didn't want to phrase anything in critical terms, so in constructive terms I would ask Bob questions about how far he could creatively and effectively repeat himself with a certain kind of imagery. Particularly, there was a period where he was so locked into the world of rubber and fetishism and there was a point where it was like, 'Bob, you've been there, you've done that, surely you've got all the skills, all the mastery of the medium and the mastery of your visual language, but you can use it in a broader way.' And he did to a certain extent, but he could have done so much more. I'm just thinking that in his portraiture, in his celebrity pictures, he could have done more fashion work, a sort of hybrid celebrity fashion, he could have tried to break the shackles of the studio more than he did. He did break out occasionally, but there was something fundamentally secure for Bob in working in the studio, because it was the ultimate controlled environment where he had mastery. Of course, he took some of his early photographs outside in a graveyard, in Brompton Cemetery. Where he was buried.

Bob Carlos Clarke

In those days, before leather and rubber hit the high street, the fetish scene seemed much more weird and avant-garde. In the early 1960s Honor Blackman and Diana Rigg lent a certain respectability to leatherwear, but rubber remained the preserve of 'perverts'. Magazines like *Atomage*, a pocket glossy, featured enthusiasts in gas masks and galoshes trudging about in bogs.

The man who did most to 'legitimise' rubber fetishism was the artist Allen Jones. His early work drew heavily on the 'sub-culture' of fetishism, and his famous woman-on-all-fours coffee table was the 'bête noire' of feminists. Allen became a good friend, and strongly advised me to lay off the fetish thing, which had attracted so much feminist approbation in the 1970s.

Undaunted, I devoted the following decade to shooting women in high heels, and got myself thoroughly rubber-stamped with a reputation that became something of an embarrassment when, a decade later, pink rubber party dresses became synonymous with bottle-blonde bimbos and provincial sex shops.

Lindsey Carlos Clarke

Allen used to come round and look at Bob's work in the darkroom. Bob used to spend hours and hours just trying to get the perfect print of his work, and of course he wanted approval and praise from Allen. On one occasion Allen just crushed him when he said, 'These are interesting. Very useful *reference* material,' as if Bob was Allen's researcher. It made Bob furious, that comment.

Allen Jones

I'm not sure, but I think I first met Bob at some party which Philippe had organised. Perhaps at a party for Helmut Newton. We had something superficially in common, although the photographic/ model scene was a world I didn't really know. Or the first time may have been just Bob calling up one day and saying, 'I want to crib your work,' or one of those pithy things he said. He always came on with 'Our revered master, let me see your latest ideas that I can use or look at,' in the most affectionate way.

He didn't teach me anything, but I loved his work. He would give me things that were lying around the studio. I have a very large file in my studio, all aspects of the figure used in advertising and fashion photography, and I would sometimes say to him, 'I'd like that for the files.' So he would occasionally send me pictures with a note saying 'for the files' – making a joke out of the fact that I didn't want it because it turns me on.

Bob Carlos Clarke *(posing as Leslie Waddington of Waddington Galleries, Cork Street, in a letter to Allen Jones, August 1998)*
Dear Allen,

Sadly the response to your exhibition opening has been less than enthusiastic. So far only four have accepted. The poor turnout is, I suggest, not so much due to your declining popularity as to the bad weather. Nonetheless I think we have to cancel the show.

Now to the problem of catering. I have managed to cancel the wine, but Searcys will not accept our cancellation at such short notice. This leaves us with a lot of canapés. I have already received a huge case of Hula Hoops, 300 lb of Philadelphia cheese, 6 vats of gherkins and, more significantly, 700 cans of Del Monte pineapple chunks. I can but hope that you can find a useful (or creative!) application for 3,500 cocktail bangers on 'harlequin' sticks.

I'm sorry about all of this – I know how much you were looking forward to the party afterwards. Why don't you have another go at some of those sexy rubber pictures? People really loved those.

Signed on behalf of
Leslie Waddington

Allen Jones

It was always a very affectionate relationship. I was intrigued by him, because he obviously lived first-hand in a world that I mined occasionally. I did take photographs of my wives and the odd friend in tight shiny clothing, and I would have shown Bob and he would have been very solicitous about it, because quite obviously they were amateur photographs. I was taking them for information. I liked to see how latex creased when it went around the body. It wasn't a big part of my arsenal, but that was our connection.

Simon Garfield

After a while it seemed to me that this was partly a story about boundaries and borders – what you could get away with, how you could shock and push people but still keep them with you.

Bob Carlos Clarke

What I liked about rubber and vinyl was the way it contained and perfected a body, concealing imperfections and defining contours beneath a gleaming synthetic skin. Once they'd mastered the technique of getting it on, the models loved it. It became an exciting ritual and a new way of simultaneously being exposed and impenetrable.

At first the outfits were crudely made from heavy gauge rubber constructed to withstand the rigours of practical pervery, but in the early 1980s I was browsing in Boy, on the Kings Road, when I noticed some particularly well-made clothing labelled 'Daniel James of London'.

It was the start of a five-year collaboration between Daniel and myself. He was a perfectionist who would make and remake outfits until they fitted like a second skin. We worked together to create his first mail-order catalogue, 'Maid in London', which I sold through my own mail-order company Strict Editions. It all sounded pretty high-powered, but in reality, it was just Lindsey and I, working through the night, packing up orders on the living-room floor. The best part was collecting envelopes stuffed with cheques and cash from PO Box 606.

Daniel also made costumes, like the mermaid's tail, specifically to my design, and his work became thematic to my second book,

The Dark Summer. Later, designers like Thierry Mugler and Jean Paul Gaultier embraced the fetish scene.

Philippe Garner

Bob had to earn a crust. Lindsey had organised a sort of mail-order business, and was selling quite a lot of prints under plain brown envelopes to the wrong kind of buyer. I guess it was easy money and irresistible. And at the same time, on a higher level, they were working with Hamiltons, who were trying to give them really classy shows and get high-end people looking and buying and collecting. One of the big buyers of the time was Alistair McAlpine. He's a true collector, and when he gets curious about something he just goes for it. He went big, big on photography and for a while around that time in the early 1980s he was probably Hamiltons' major single client, and he bought a great deal of material. He would move on to other things and sell a lot on, and I think the last pictures sold of Bob's at auction came from him.

So there was that, and then Bob and Lindsey were running this little cottage industry, doing these easy sales into a sort of fetishist market.

Allen Jones

My particular problem...the attitude towards the female figure, which was politicised by the feminist movement.

I happened to make my furniture sculpture at that time, an image that was a gift to the feminists, objectifying the female figure in an unequivocal way, in the shape of a table. The tirade went on for about five years, and for about ten years it was the reason that I would never be in any official museum show. In the end I mainly showed and sold abroad. So I totally understood Bob's problem: the world would be divided into people who thought his work was terrific, and those who didn't. A lot of other photographers, including Bailey in his time, dressed it up. In the fine art world you could go down the road so it looked very Renoir-like. But that's not what it's about. Now I think the attitude of people under 30 towards sexual imagery has totally changed – they view the attitudes of the older generation as something from the dark ages.

14. i never argued with my dad, said scarlett carlos clarke

Philippe Garner

Bob and I are about the same age, aren't we? I'm 58. But I think it would be fair to say that when I first met him I was somewhat in awe because of the big and courageous steps he'd taken to express himself, to explore the path of his very curious destiny and to live that artist's life – he was kind of throwing the dice and he was going to go with them. I'm somebody who's much more prudent, you know, step by step, moving forward, building my career and so on, so I just thought my God, to me there was an aspect to living the way he lived which I found very attractive and engaging. I was building slowly and steadily, and putting enormous importance on maintaining a kind of strength and an inner core of keeping grounded and secure. But gradually over the years I saw Bob losing the plot and getting so caught in a sort of negative vortex of his own obsessions. It was a downward and inward spiral that was not going, and could not go, to a healthy place.

Allen Jones

He did have a kind of a crisis, maybe one of many. I did feel that he was a terrific photographer with a tunnel vision on the latest Page 3 girl that he could get into rubber and photograph. I thought that demi-monde was quite exciting to dip into, but my conversation with him was that I thought he should broaden his image base. We only had one conversation about it, but I think that his anxiety to try to make something that legitimised him in some way, or gave him another audience, was a problem which ultimately he never solved.

The fact of the matter is, if you're dealing with very strong imagery – and anything to do with sex is contentious, particularly in the UK – you just have to reconcile yourself to the fact that the imagery will get in the way of people seeing how good a photographer, or in my case painter, you are. In that way we have a similar problem. I'm totally aware that my imagery will cut me off from a certain kind of acceptance. It would be easier if that imagery was gentler or different.

Philippe Garner

There was this curious kind of tipping of the balance in our relationship. As a youngish man I was envious of this kind of bohemian sophisticated freedom which this character was carving out for himself, but 20 years later I have a position where I have a sort of strength in knowing who I am and knowing what I've got. I don't mean materially, successfully, I mean my inner self managing all the demons and confusions, and actually coming out calm and more open. But I was seeing Bob become ever more neurotic, anxious, frustrated, inhibited. Because while he seemed to have opened up every possibility at a certain stage, he couldn't break out of a psychological prison he'd created for himself. To some extent it was also a geographical prison.

Lindsey Carlos Clarke

Did I tell you about the first time Philippe came round for dinner? Bob was very excited that he had agreed to come, this big London photography man who knew everyone. He had this plan that he would serve him a special pudding. So we had a pleasant evening,

I cooked the main course, and then Bob went off to prepare the dessert. The plan had been to use mostly felt from the tumble dryer, and before Philippe arrived he had gone to the machine and gathered layers of it, different colours from all our towels and whatever that had been in there. I never thought he'd go through with it, but he was in the kitchen putting layers of whipped cream between the felt and fluff and putting fruit on top.

He then came out of the kitchen with it piled high, and before he could serve it, Philippe, who is always so immaculate and considerate, said something like, 'The main course was delicious, but I'm not sure about this – what is it?' And then Bob and I just cracked up and told him, and we went straight to the coffee.

Philippe Garner

At different times we'd have the same basic conversation: how could he crank up his career, how could he extend the range of people who took him seriously, how could he up people's perceptions of him? I remember saying to him at one point that he was so locked into the world of fetishism and Fulham. I suppose I shouldn't compare him in the same breath as Helmut Newton, because I think Helmut had a far, far greater talent, but part of Helmut's talent was his brilliance in understanding how the world works and upping his game to the scale of the world, and Bob never quite knew how to break his boundaries. I mean, at the beginning, the plunge was going down paths of sexual aggressiveness – I won't say explicitness because others were more explicit but there wasn't the same shocking punch that Bob had. He was very bold, but then so often I would think, so, what next? How are you going to develop your curiosity about the world beyond the studio? It was all very internalised, it was all so self-reflective, self-referential. Personal fulfilment for him demanded that he break out of that, but how would he be able to do it?

Simon Garfield

Another of his favourite quotes was from Cartier-Bresson: 'Photography is a spontaneous impulse which comes from perpetually looking, and which seizes the instant and its eternity.' He believed in 'the decisive moment' like the rest of them, although he liked to increase the possibility of these moments by having as much control of his situations as possible. His early work was often outside, but as his career progressed he seemed to become frightened of leaving the studio. He often claimed the opposite was true.

Bob Carlos Clarke

In 1984 I shot 'Faithful Unto Death', a young 'widow' sobbing on the steps of a mausoleum in Putney Vale Cemetery. The autumn light was fading and my model was cold and unhappy in a skin-tight black rubber dress. That morning her lover had cancelled their wedding, and she didn't want to be photographed.

I asked her what she wanted to do.

'Cry!' she answered mournfully. So I gave her a tissue, and she began to cry.

Lindsey Carlos Clarke

He did get obsessed with people to a point of madness. One girl lived with us for a while when she wasn't in Manchester. She was lovely, Debbie, she's the girl crying on the steps in the rubber dress taken at Putney Vale Cemetery. He got her into the kit, and said to her, 'What do you feel like doing?' and she said, 'I feel like crying.' He said, 'Here's a handkerchief,' and that's the shot. She wasn't really crying.

Bob Carlos Clarke

The story had a happy ending. I got a great shot, and she earned a small fortune when, a few years later, the photograph was used for a national press campaign for a leading building society. The full-page advertisement provoked a flood of complaints: 'I am appalled by your gratuitous use of a high-heeled rubber-clad "lady" more suited to publications of a Continental nature than to a previously reputable financial institution.' And so on.

Happily the model soon wed a replacement husband, and I quickly got engaged to the magic of moral outrage.

• • •

Simon Garfield
Why did you want to get married?

Lindsey Carlos Clarke
It got complicated. By then we'd got three properties and Scarlett, and we then discovered that if we didn't get married and then we got killed in an accident together she becomes a ward of court. So suddenly it's chaos. We realised it was serious and we kept thinking, oh, we'll do it next year. You know, neither of us really wanted to. I just said to him, 'Let's do this for her, because you just can't beat the system.' So that's why we ran away and did it and we didn't really tell anybody.

His mother wasn't there, and my mother wasn't there either. In fact, my mother said to me, just before I went, she said, 'Have you got a ring?' I said, 'Oh God, no.' Anybody would think I hadn't been married before. We went to Wild Ones here on the Kings Road and I bought a ring for £10.50. They put it in *Tatler*: Bob and Lindsey spent £10.50, next to all these people who had spent thousands. What does it matter? It could have been an old bit of string, couldn't it? It doesn't make any difference. Scarlett was six, I think.

Simon Garfield
So what happened to his mother?

Lindsey Carlos Clarke
His mum died without knowing we were going to get married. Myra had a depressive illness which she'd had for years, and she finally had to go into a home although there didn't really appear to be anything wrong with her.

It was 1998. We'd done Christmas together in London, then we'd been over to see her, and I was going to tell her then. The problem was, she was in such a distressed condition that whatever you told her would just make more stress, nothing made her feel good, so I was worried that if I said we were getting married that she would start to, I don't know, I mean it was so difficult. I realise that this is somebody disconnecting, you know, everything made her worry. She used to make me phone up the bank all the time and check where all the money was. I'd speak to the bank and then when it was done I'd think great, that's done and she'd say, 'No, there's been a mistake, we'll have to start again.' The money issue became huge, like it did with Bob. We were married in Mustique about a month after she died. And of course Bob didn't want to tell anybody about the marriage because he thought it was utterly ghastly.

Simon Garfield
And how was he affected by his mother's death?

Lindsey Carlos Clarke
I think half of him was consumed with guilt. I used to say to him the year before, 'Look, your mum's going to get older, why don't we persuade her to come and live back here?' but I don't think he could cope with it really. I was very fond of his mother, she was rather amazing, and after she died he said to me, 'Those are just crocodile tears, you didn't like my mother.' I was thinking, God, that's quite a cruel thing to say, and it wasn't true.

I think I definitely became a mother figure to him. Without meaning to. Which of course means – who wants to sleep with their mother? I think that sort of ends the relationship really. You know, any disaster he's on the phone to me: it could be anything, 'My mother's been hit by a meteorite,' or, 'Where did you leave the chocolate?' It was all the same. If Bob had a list of ten things to deal with, he couldn't put them in any order of what was more important. He would just get hysterical about everything. I was probably doing the wrong thing in always picking up the pieces.

Scarlett Carlos Clarke
I never argued with my dad, but I used to get really pissed off with him. He used to play practical jokes on me, always winding me up, and I used to get really upset. Some of them were really dangerous. Whenever Mum went out he would invent a game and one of us would get really badly hurt. Building huge ramps in the garden, he strapped my feet on to the accelerator on a quad bike and just let me go on it. He forced the pedals down with wood so I couldn't stop. Then we had a really bad boat accident that Mum doesn't even

know about. And a motorbike accident, although that wasn't so bad. He would invent his own Olympic sports with people, like spitting, and bread shoes. Once he tied me to a fence with an elastic rope. He tied me round my waist, and there was a game where we had to pick up something really random like a wool clown. He was like, 'Don't worry, it won't break,' and I was saying, 'I bet it will.' He did it and showed me it didn't break, and then when I did it I turned around and the whole thing came at me at about 100 miles per hour and whipped me across the face. It made a dent, and the first thing he said was, 'Oh my God, don't tell Mum, don't tell Mum.' And he had it on film, with all the screams.

Simon Garfield
Scarlett was at home, on the sofa, petite and skinny, tousled brown hair and button nose, a very young and pretty face. That day she had taken GCSEs in English and Chemistry. Knowing of my interest in stamp collecting, she brings down some first-day covers to show me, but she didn't get much pleasure from them.

Scarlett Carlos Clarke
I'm 16 now. I go to boarding school in Croydon. I used to really like it. I want to go to art college, but when I'm older I want to do film. I used to make little films with my dad.

I went to his studio a lot. I didn't grow up thinking, oh, this is completely normal, everyone's parents photograph naked people, because I knew that other people thought it was odd. But it was always there, and it was never a big deal.

Geraldine Leale
Physically, Scarlett is very like Bob. He has cultivated in her a need and taste for constant action. Scarlett always wants things to be going on, and she's also learned how to entertain people. She's a brilliant mimic and very creatively minded. I hope she doesn't feel that she has to grow up in the shadow of Bob. I hope she's not over-awed by his legacy.

I thought he was an amazing father. Lindsey always wanted to have a child, but Bob always maintained he didn't want children. So

With Scarlett, late 1990s.

when she was pregnant with Scarlett, he was furious. All this child-hood rage…He used to call the foetus Little Cedric. In his mind this baby was the child he was when he was little. This cold-at-night, never fully looked after, miserable wretched child. He always used to call the foetus 'this miserable wretched child'. Little Cedric was this bedraggled…like something out of a Tim Burton book. He once got up and marched across the floor and kicked the sofa and said, 'Death to Little Cedric!' Lindsey and I looked at each other and we thought, this is posing a few difficulties…

Bob could take anything and convert it into a dark picture. As the arrival of Little Cedric came closer everyone was, 'Oh God…' He had the *Styx* exhibition at Hamiltons and then the party afterwards, 12 or 14 of his closest friends having a big dinner. Lindsey organised it, and then the next day she went off to have Scarlett by Caesarean.

The next day Bob pitched up at my house in the early evening, and it was the happiest I had ever seen Bob Carlos Clarke. He looked at me and said, 'It's a girl.' I flung my arms around him, and it was the first time ever I hugged Bob Carlos Clarke and actually felt I had made a total enveloping connection with him. There was always this brittleness and prickliness about him – he wasn't a person you could melt into. It was the first time I had ever seen his guard completely down, and he was so happy. It was a love affair from that day on, and having Scarlett really improved him. He mellowed. He was besotted with Scarlett, and she opened up a side of him that was totally unconditional. There was no expectation there. Little Cedric was never mentioned again.

15. why would anybody want me to do that? asked nicky barthorp

Philippe Garner

Okay, let's have a look at *Obsession*. This was 1981 and my God it seems like a lifetime. These are early collage, and Lindsey is on his bike, and virtually everything is artworked here. The opening pages we've got a few Polaroid SX 70s which are very much a homage to Allen Jones.

Either Bob or Lindsey asked me to do the introduction on the book because I guess there weren't that many people at that stage in their lives with whom he could engage who had a considerable knowledge of the medium. Perhaps there never were. Most of his clients and contacts were in the worlds of magazines, advertising, rock/pop, films and so on.

I came across some of these prints the other day and I realised they're not signed, and this just shows you how the world has changed. At the time none of us really knew what the protocols should be because they hadn't been invented yet, or if they were being invented by certain Americans we weren't really aware of it. Today a collector might think, oh, that's an unsigned print, to which my answer would be, 'This is a pre-signing print, so early and so special, before he would even think of making an edition.'

Simon Garfield

Bob did contribute to a book before *Obsession*, providing the photos for *The Illustrated Delta of Venus* by Anaïs Nin, but *Obsession* was his first proper large-scale collection.

Philippe Garner

This work emerged when there was this whole spate of album artwork being done for bands by the company Hipgnosis. It's wonderfully imaginative work – a kind of neo-Dadaist invention, like those photo montages by Paul Citroen from the 1920s of the cities of the future, anticipating Fitz Lang's *Metropolis*. So in Bob's early collage photographs you see this science-fiction, science-fantasy dimension to them, car crashes, the implosion of the American dream, often highly eroticised, wonderful but scary at the same time, post-apocalyptic stuff that also comes out of British punk and British anarchy. I think that Bob was always instinctively an anarchist. Here's some stuff that's very Vivienne Westwood, very Seditionaries, then these half-human half-mutant humanoids; you can imagine peeling off their skin and finding polished steel mechanisms behind it. This is a whole other universe from the later pictures where he gets much more into the carnality, the sensuality of the body. There was one which went through one of our sales, I wish I'd bought it, but one always forgets that there are a thousand other pulls on your limited resources, of the Concorde taking off against the extraordinary cityscape.

This one I did get: I love it. He'd given that to a benefit auction I conducted at Hamiltons. It's Jilly Johnson, ridiculously photogenic if you like that body type and body look because she's like, I don't know how to describe it, the muscles and sinews are just there, very visible and very elegant. Really elegant attenuation, this kind of thing I think is fantastic. Do you know how much of that's left in the archive?

So, *Obsession*: in the shops it wouldn't have been sitting next to books on Walker Evans! It really wasn't quite in the photography thing. Do you know this series which he did – She-an-me Fun Fashions? It was the tackiest mail lingerie catalogue. Bob had got some of his best girls in, and they must have had a great laugh doing it, Jilly Johnson, Nina Carter and some of the other top girls of the moment. He had to earn a crust, I guess.

In the introduction I think I was at pains to try and situate him in a continuum of photo history and that was where he wished to be situated. Today I'd be much more inclined to situate him as a cultural phenomenon within his own time but you know, for the first time being presented in a serious book, the type they call coffee-table books, it was the kind of credibility of there being a long-backed story to the strands of what he was doing which seemed to matter. Those Polaroids are lovely, aren't they?

Have you had a chance to look at Bob's books? The books on his shelf, his reference books? Assuming that Lindsey's kept everything, it's something you should do. Just thinking about Guy Bourdin, who's a quite different photographer, but Guy Bourdin's son has kept Bourdin's library and Bourdin had a kind of obsessive literary curiosity as well as artistic curiosity.

Lindsey Carlos Clarke

If you look through *Obsession*...I desperately wanted to be in one of those montages. In fact, the first picture he did of me, there's two of me on a motorbike. I mean I wish he were here now; we'd probably have an argument about it. People used to say to me, 'You were absolutely his dream doll girl,' but I don't actually think I was. I think I became much more useful on the other side. That's what really happened. I didn't find that. If one needed somebody in a photograph, you know, I could always do it, but we did some pictures, and he was like, oh God we need another model, and I was like, I'll do it, but in a funny way I wasn't really interested in doing that either. At that stage, David Bailey was still with Marie Helvin, and I didn't just want to be Bob's muse.

• • •

Nicky Barthorp

To me, their relationship was always incredibly solid, at least the mutual-need aspect was really solid. Neither of them did anything in their head without the other. He was always the more powerful person, but that was probably because she didn't allow herself to be. He needed to have the focus on him.

Simon Garfield

Nicky Barthorp was one of Bob and Lindsey's closest friends. Or at least she was one of Bob's closest friends until she did what Bob thought was an unforgivable act.

Nicky Barthorp

I met them because I had a studio apartment next door to where Oscar Wilde had lived in Tite Street, Chelsea, completely bohemian when I bought it, with no electricity. After a year or two Lindsey and Bob moved into the artist's studio below me. It must have been at the end of the 1980s, and I was 24. I wasn't there when they arrived, and a few weeks later I came back and found that the building had been souped up, and we had electricity. That was obviously Lindsey's doing. She immediately started organising meetings about the hallway carpeting.

We soon became a little family. I was an emotional wreck at the time. My fiancé had just died, and I was very low and had gone into hibernation. He was a drug addict, and I had been quite solitary for a while with him, and tried to help him but he sadly died. I had basically become a nun, and had decided I didn't want to be attractive to men, so I was very intimidated by their outgoing personalities and energy. I felt like a prude around them, and of course Bob seized on that and teased me.

When you know a couple that well, you're always aware of an undercurrent of unease, and that was always evident with the snide remarks they would make to each other.

Simon Garfield

That can sometimes be a healthy thing.

Nicky Barthorp

I always thought it was, until I knew more. It could be a mixture of wicked humour and cruelty, but from both. Cruelty veiled with humour, and much less veiled towards the end. Socially, Lindsey kept pretending that everything was fine, and I suppose she pretended to herself as well.

They were always my very cosy friends, always having supper on our knees and giggling, no pressure, a bit like *Friends*. I was an actress for a while, and he came along to the plays. I would then get these appalling letters from him pretending to be a really nerdy fan.

On one occasion I bought these rubber leggings, and he obviously found out about it, because a day or so later I got a phone call from someone who said there had been a mistake, and they were radioactive. I went running back to the store of course, where this man looked at me as if I was nuts.

Very soon after we met I started going out with Marco Pierre White. Bob and Lindsey already knew him by then, but I didn't meet him through them. Marco was married at the time, and we 'met' on the phone, but I don't really want to talk about that. I was working for Edina Ronay [the actress and fashion designer]. I was retail manager, organising the collections for the stores they had all over London. When I was with Marco there were endless problems – there was always fishing tackle and other things left down in the hall, a dog arrived…so the building meetings became a little bit more ferocious.

My relationship lasted two or three years. *White Heat*, Bob's book about Marco at Harveys, had already been finished I think, but not yet published. The book really made cooking fashionable and hip. Before then it was the Gavroche guys. Bob would be at Harveys until four in the morning, and we would sometimes all go there.

When I moved to France in 1995 he was very angry with me. He became quite babyish and turned his back on me for quite a while. We were such a little unit, and I broke that up. I know what it's like when great, great friends up and leave – you feel desperate. When I came back I would see him in the studio but he was always busy and there would always be sarcastic remarks about me leaving him.

That's when Lindsey and I became more girlfriends, rather than the threesome. I don't mean in a sexual way.

I always loved his work. It had this incredible textural quality, and it was a lot more interesting than the normal superficial stuff in that genre, much more depth. I was always in awe of him as an artist. Totally insecure brilliance, but brilliance.

Simon Garfield
Do you have any of his pictures?

Nicky Barthorp
Yes, I have my bottom – I modelled for him a lot. He gave me that bottom photo as a wedding present. I've got a Marco as well, lying on the granite.

It was a sort of brotherly/sisterly love that we had, he was very easy to be close to. He would often ask me to come up and help, and I would assist him with some glorious young girl, hold her in some strange position. I was never as young as any of them.

I would see all the daily goings on in the studio, so it became very natural to me. There was always naked girls in there, so it wasn't oh my God. So I suppose when he asked me to pose I was deeply flattered. Before I had thought, why would anybody want me to do that?

Bob Carlos Clarke
In time, the subjects you shoot will identify you. Newton, Mapple-thorpe, Witkin, have distinctly different erotic preoccupations as shown by their work. Some photographers live and die for sex, while others just skate about on the surface. Newton anticipated the current obsession with sex, wealth and power by decades, and estab-lished the currently fashionable style known as 'porno-chic'. Critics claim that he objectifies and degrades women. Newton says he makes them 'triumphant and dangerous'.

Nicky Barthorp
We would laugh – it would always be funny. But I didn't find it so easy. I can't imagine doing it now, in my mid-forties, but then I was

obviously quite a free spirit. This was quite soon after me wanting to be like a nun, I hasten to add. That was Bob and Lindsey's influence about the value of freedom of expression. Bob's spirit made that possible, and it was all very contagious. It was made okay: I thought, he does this every single day, this is an art form, and I saw it in another light. There was no taboo left. We would go off to those Rubber Ball things, often Lindsey didn't come, but I'd go with Bob and we'd dress up.

There was humour when we did the photos, but he was also serious, an artist. He wanted to get what he wanted to get. There was always flattery – I'm sure all those nubile young things adored him.

• • •

Simon Garfield

Emma, why did your closeness with Bob come to an end?

Emma Ford

He left the studio in Battersea and everything changed.

After Bob moved, I started working for Mick Jones, who needed a studio manager, and then he was producing Pete Doherty and The Libertines, and I started working as a TV presenter for Granada.

I kept in touch with Bob, and we were on the phone a lot. He got another studio in Clapham but I don't think he used it much. I remember him saying to me that he was sometimes fed up with things and wanted to change direction, but everyone has those doubts. I never thought too much about it. I remember saying to him, 'Why don't you do really edgy fashion or…'

I then got married and lived in New York for a year, and he got really annoyed and said he would delete my number from his phone.

Simon Garfield

This would become a familiar pattern. He would get very close to people and then he felt they would desert him. They were just getting on with their lives, but he would take it personally. He found that he didn't actually own them, no matter how charming he was, and how much attention he lavished on them. The fear of separation was clearly a big and real thing for him, a reminder of what he believed was the abandonment when he was sent away to school. And then of course his marriage was shaky, and Lindsey was deserting him too.

Emma Ford

He would go into sulks. I sent him a lot of cards from New York and he would ignore them.

16. yeah, a live alligator, said james betts

James Betts

I did a degree in photography, and when I finished I came down to London, with a view to assisting people. I'm from Birmingham but I went to Stoke-on-Trent University. Bob was always a hero of mine at college; his book *The Dark Summer* was a bit of a bible for us because, it was late 1980s, it was still kicking around the library, and it was, wow, this is great. I came down to London and called people and got sporadic bits of freelance. I didn't actually really want to be a full-time assistant to anybody.

I must have been 24, so that's 12 years ago. I saw an article in a professional magazine about Bob and the new studio he was building on Battersea Bridge Road, and at the time I was living on the west side of Clapham Common, so I thought that was very near. It had a phone number so I rang up. It was the usual Bob: 'Oh, I'm very busy at the moment, I've got several books on the go, I've got assistants at the minute. Call me in six weeks' time.' So I noted six weeks in my diary, not going to let this one go away. So then he said, 'Okay, come and see me.'

Bob Carlos Clarke

In the UK, good assistants are gold dust. Along with the photographer, they bear the most responsibility under extreme pressure for very low fees. The rest of the team get paid many times more to do far less, and are often credited for it, whereas the assistant must be a tea-maker, telephonist, technician, minder, gofer, pack mule and universal scapegoat for a fractional fee and little chance of acknowledgement. The perfect assistant is intelligent and reliable, with the discretion of a footman, the constitution of a pit pony and the perspicacity of a mind-reader, a clean driving licence, zero testosterone, and, if he can cook, print and retouch, so much the better.

James Betts

I went to see him in the Village in Battersea where he used to be, and it was daunting. You get in through these big gates, and I was standing there buzzing the intercom. Then somebody roars in on an old Triumph motorbike and it was him and I was easily impressed. He takes his helmet off, brushes his hair, says, 'Oh, James, oh brilliant, yeah, come on in.' I remember thinking that was pretty cool. I succumbed to that image a bit myself, and I learned to ride and got my own bike when I was working for him. That old cliché of photographers and motorbikes.

He was a very charismatic man, and he had this amazing studio. It was about 4,000 square foot, it was just white walls, bare floors like this, big windows down one side, you walk in you go, 'Wow!' And he said, 'Come and sit in the kitchen and show me your work,' so I did the usual thing, get your portfolio out, get explaining the history of the pictures.

It was all my college work and my degree work. I'd copied it all on to transparencies so I'd hold them up to the light. No one has transparency portfolios any more, that's how much it's changed. There are no transparencies with digital.

I'd done quite a lot of black and white. I'd done a thing about people with tattoos, quite atmospheric, harsh light. I never really thought I was much of a printer at that time, because I could see how difficult it was, but I was quite proud of those. I'd done some colourful landscapes as well, which I'm still proud of to this day, I still have them on my website.

Bob looked through and did his usual thing: 'Oh yeah, that's nice, you've got a pretty good eye.' So Bob thinks I've got a good eye – it was like Eric Clapton saying I think you're quite a good guitarist. Sporadically I'd call him. 'Oh no, no, no, nothing at the moment.' So I was doing whatever I could, often out of town on car shoots, usually two-week shoots. On a couple of occasions he called me and I was already booked. I thought, this is a nightmare: I can never work with him. But then there was one test for an advertising shoot that I could do and it went okay, and because I was local he often asked me to help out, but often it was a shelf that needed putting up, or a bit of painting or admin. One day he just said, 'You should probably come full time.' I was never PAYE or anything, I was always free-lance and he'd pay me a day's wage, and I didn't get holidays or anything like that. That lasted for about six and a half years.

Bob Carlos Clarke (*from his 'Essential Guide to Retaining Employment', a sheet he would give to each new assistant*)
Open studio at 9.30am.

Check bathroom for towels, soap, loo rolls, etc.

Ensure the fridge is stocked with fresh milk, bread and butter or Flora. Check heating and adjust as required.

Keep darkroom impeccable – clean trays, sinks, surfaces and floor.

Keep camera batteries charged.

You may use the studio for your personal work by prior arrange-ment. Please confine models and crew to studio area only, and away from kitchen, office, darkroom and galleries.

You may use my lighting, backdrops, reflectors, cables, clamps, etc but not cameras, lenses or materials.

When answering calls please do so promptly and politely. Try not to sound disgruntled, disorientated, disappointed, dyslexic, disenchanted, drunk or drugged.

Apathy: because this is one of the least demanding assistant's jobs in the history of photography, it is easy to become lethargic and prematurely aged. However, this is a big studio, and there is NEVER NOTHING TO DO.

Ghislain Pascal

I used Bob for every possible shoot that I could. There are very few good photographers in England – a handful – and for me he was one of the very best. He was partly responsible for Caprice's success – he helped create the image, and those leather pictures went around the world.

He came to my thirtieth birthday party, a private room at the White House, and someone rang up later and said, 'We were really upset by Bob and Lindsey, we thought they were so crude.' But to me he was always inoffensive. If he actually tried to come on to a girl they'd run a mile. Why would any of these young models sleep with Bob? He was married, an older guy, and any of these young models would...it was all just bravado from him. And with someone like Tamara, it would never happen.

I mean, I'm sure he must have...over the years. But in the early days he was absolutely...Lindsey and him were a team.

James Betts

As a second assistant you're there to move things, and put lights up and backgrounds up and tidy things away and keep an eye on everything. As a main assistant you'd be loading all the cameras and logging the film as well, you'd put your exposures down for every shot. You're generally there to be the right-hand man to the photographer and you're the eyes and ears to make sure all the technical side is okay, all the lights are firing okay, so the photographer can concentrate on whatever they're shooting.

When I started he'd say, 'Do you know how to process black and white film?' Of course I'd done it at college. Yeah, no problem. So I'd lock myself in the darkroom and go and process his film for him. Then he'd set me up with some contact sheets, and then, 'There's the enlarger, go and do some test prints.' I ended up doing all of his darkroom work, all of his printing. But he'd always be around. Very rarely I'd be locked away and just come out with loads of prints, I'd always be going backwards and forwards and going, 'What do you think?', and he'd tweak it this way and that.

That book in the college library – *The Dark Summer*. The questions people were asking were all, 'How does he do that?' There were a lot of montages, and it was quite different from anything anybody else was doing. We just used to pore over it at college and just wonder. His montage techniques by today's standards are very crude, just cutting things up and shading things in the darkroom. It's a lot of trial and error. I know he used to work for weeks on one print alone. They were quite Gothic. But it wasn't just me: to a lot of my friends as well he was a bit of a hero.

Bob Carlos Clarke *(from his poem 'The Immaculate Assistant')*

> Always place fresh paper rolls
> Adjacent to the toilet bowls
> Which should be clean and sweet of scent
> Devoid of models' excrement
>
> Assistants who are somewhat stoned
> Will soon forget the skills they've honed
> Abuse of drugs will dull their wits
> And turn them into useless gits
>
> He'll never stand and stare
> At supermodels' pubic hair
> Nor will he ever wince or whinge
> When metering an unkempt minge
>
> The wise assistant knows no lust
> His testicles are dry as dust
> And dust will be his main concern
> Whenever he has time to burn

James Betts

I don't think I knew a lot about him until I met him. Photography's one of those things, you don't tend to know the man behind the work, with the exception of maybe David Bailey. Now there are a few more than there used to be. I don't think I even knew his age or where he was from. He just had this quite exotic name.

That first test shoot he asked me to go on was a big advertising thing for Smirnoff and I helped him on the casting. We had hundreds of people through the studio – it was a party scene. We did two days, the party scene one day and then the idea of the campaign was whatever you saw through the bottle was different from the reality. So we had to shoot two girls ballroom dancing, and then you passed through the bottle and a face appeared in the background. We used a very young but not very well-known Alexander McQueen. He came across as brash, but not in a nice way. I thought he was rude. Bob and Lindsey are quite refined, nice polite people, and after he went away we said, 'What an awful man.' Of course, he ends up being one of the most famous designers in the world. Isabella Blow was styling it as well so that was a pretty memorable first big shoot.

We did the Powergen calendar for three years. He managed to turn it round because he got a charity on board, and if you get a charity involved then you can get celebrities and not have to pay them a huge amount. Black and white. The first few people we shot were Bryan Ferry, Jerry Hall and Ronnie Wood. It was amazing for me to be suddenly meeting these enormous stars. We shot Jerry Hall on an alligator. Yeah, a live alligator. It took six of us to carry it up the stairs in this enormous sort of coffin. It was about 12 foot long. We had to open all the windows in the studio to keep it cool, because if you keep them cool they're docile, and they tape up their mouths with Sellotape. Jerry Hall was petrified. She said she had once had a small pet one, but this was something else. She sat on it and just turned on this amazing smile for a couple of frames and she'd leap off.

Philippe Garner

He shied away from doing fashion or much celebrity work because I guess he felt that he was compromising his integrity, but I think it was also about staying in control. Just talking about it now I realise he needed to feel in control of events to feel at ease, and presumably there was enormous anxiety in a complex commission where there was input from art directors, and he was having to navigate other people's egos. It's easy enough for us to think that in theory he could have done it with the greatest of ease; he certainly had the technique, he certainly mathematically should have been able to, but psychologically it would have taken him way out of a zone where he felt secure and where he needed to be.

I wonder if Bob was capable of making photographs quickly, if he was capable of letting go of the need to pace things himself, if he could go with events – and I'm not sure that he could. I was thinking of that series of pictures he did of kids in clubs, one of relatively few very strong photo stories he made outside the studio, but they were kids and he was an adult, it was dark and he was pacing, prowling, selecting, he really was still in control of the situation. Also, nobody was going to judge it except himself, so it wasn't like he was there with an editor, an art director, there wasn't a team outside waiting to see what he'd got, so he wasn't putting himself on the line, was he, doing that?

He wasn't a great traveller. Bob and Lindsey would go off to Mustique, but again, to go there with Lord Lichfield is really to stay in a very particular London bubble and simply have it transposed to the sunshine for a little while. I simply can't visualise Bob travelling in strange cities, walking the streets and savouring the architecture and forgetting about himself and savouring the texture and ghosts of places and assimilating history in the broader sense. Actually if he had tried a little of that it might have helped him put his own issues in another perspective. I think that he led the life where the issues became the life to an all-devouring extent, and if I'd said to him, and I did on more than one occasion, 'How can you break out of that Fulham thing?', it really was a metaphor for saying: how can you break out of yourself?, which he kind of needed to do but simply wasn't able to.

James Betts

I've never worked for another photographer like him, because he would work on several different cameras at once, several different formats, and he'd go, '6-9, 6-4-5, 6-7, 6-8, give me that lens on that,' and you'd have to have loads of cameras loaded, whereas most people would shoot with one camera, with multiple backs, or a few lenses. But he'd shoot colour and black and white simultaneously, which not many people did. But when he was shooting his own stuff he often wanted to be left to his own devices; sometimes I'd help him if it was a bit complicated but he'd say, 'Go and do some printing, I'm going to do a shoot with this girl and be in the studio.' He liked that one-on-one, that intimacy.

He didn't have a great deal of male friends. He had male friends, but not close. He had loads of women friends. There was Kaja Wunder, a tall Estonian girl, who I ended up living with. Not in that way, she was my landlady for a little while. Obviously there have been countless ones over the years, and there would be an obsession there with them, and it wouldn't necessarily be a sexual thing, it would be an ownership. He'd shoot them and do everything with them, spend loads of time with them and sort of envelop himself in them. It was a weird sort of thing.

Bob Carlos Clarke *(in* Amateur Photographer*)*
The practical process of taking professional, set-up 'erotic' photographs is seldom arousing in itself. Encumbered by technical, commercial and legal considerations, the professional result rarely comes close to the candour and spontaneity of a private Polaroid. Hence the popularity of Readers' Wives – real women against real wallpaper.

17. he's really on the map, said philippe garner

Lindsey Carlos Clarke

We used to live on Stevenage Road, very near Putney Bridge. When the tide went out we used to walk along there and they used to throw things over the bridge – mostly guns, knives, spoons and forks, and then they would wash up. So we used to walk along the river collecting things. He'd pick up guns all the time. I used to open the front door, Bob would be covered in mud, and he'd go [holding up an imaginary bag with a huge grin on face].

The knives and forks in his pictures – we think that some of them came from the *Marchioness*. The photo of the fork and spoon twisted together – I think he gave that one an extra twist. We called that one 'Love', but it was a cross between love and suffocation.

Philippe Garner

He called that collection *Styx*.

They were virtually all salvaged items, and I think first he was going to photograph them in situ, where he found them in the mud, but then thought, well, why don't I just take them home and develop backgrounds on which to photograph them? Just a wonderful exercise. The ones he did do in situ just are electric, and I kind of wished

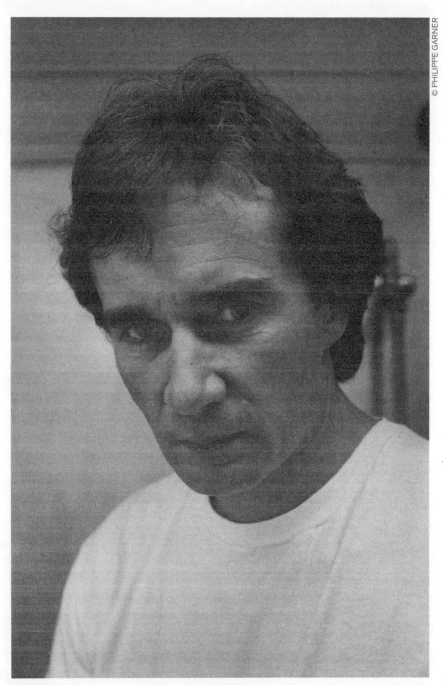

Photographed in his studio by Philippe Garner.

he'd stuck with that. It would have been a much more dogged task to actually photograph them in situ, but then it wouldn't have been Bob, I guess. He had to control the process more, and then he had to bring the erotic, you know, objects with erotic connotations into it. But I remember that was a hell of an exhibition at Hamiltons. Here it is [the catalogue], with an introduction by Bob. This wonderful photo of this glove – it just glows, doesn't it?

Simon Garfield

Styx, that show at Hamiltons, really seemed to represent some sort of pinnacle for him. He was suddenly famous in a way that he had never been. His art – his eye, his printing – was recognised as something worthy of wide attention. The show was widely reviewed, not all of it favourably, but it got the sort of attention that only usually came to the really big names. The launch was a social event.

Bob Carlos Clarke *(from the* Styx *catalogue)*

I have always lived close to water. The river Lea ran near by my childhood home, and our summer house in Waterford was a diminutive clapboard cabin perched 15 feet above the surf. I never go there now. But this shack still stands 35 years on, blasted by storms and bleached by summers, a mausoleum for my size 3 beach shoes and an archive for the flotsam I amassed as a tiny mud lark.

Now I have a home and studio both close to the Thames. In December 1990 I returned to the tide and the mysterious mud. It's a timeless place, isolated beneath the dank echoing bridges with the muffled drone of the city above, a cemetery for the distressed and discarded artefacts of a civilisation. Food, tools, bones and clothing encased in a uniform of grey effluent. Things that have been in, on and used by people, each item bearing the imprint of its provenance and the scars of its experience beneath the bridges: the spore of thieves, fractured pay meters, pillaged handbags, massive metal safes and discarded weapons. I planned to photograph these items where they lay, like the cruel record of an archaeological dig or a phonemic photograph, but the tides and the biting river wind drove me back to my studio with foul-smelling sacks of what I could carry: screws, cans and cutlery, sodden clothes and slabs of stone.

Under a lens, the uniqueness of each object became evident. Commonplace items displayed powerful and individual personalities, recorded with a minimum of interference by myself; they revealed a kind of monumental truth. The river came to represent the flow between birth and death, the inexorable process of creation and detrition, and a series developed. Historical and mythological associations and the complex circuitry that interconnects everything natural and man-made began to emerge.

Philippe Garner

You could say that the *Styx* show at Hamiltons was a pinnacle for him, but would he have recognised it? How would Bob have defined 'making it'? Nothing ever satisfied him in terms of having the kind of profile and credibility that he wanted for his work. And yet there were times where you felt that everything was going so right for him in quite concentrated moments. At Hamiltons the place was buzzing, heaving with paparazzi photographers. It was an event. And it was glamorous – some of the models were there. I remember Jilly Johnson was there. It was a sexy kind of electric evening where you felt, 'Bob's pulled it together, he's really on the map.' He's making it at a time when he was also getting some good advertising jobs and you associated him with all the accoutrements and appendages of a very successful lifestyle in that business.

That kind of evening would draw together the art directors, and the people who mattered in the media scene. His name was also carrying some resonance with the broader public and with keen amateur photographers. When he did a talk, they came in big numbers just to be in the presence of somebody who was to them a giant in the field. There was a moment where all that came together, and you might have imagined that Bob could have felt euphoric about it. He was entitled to. But that wasn't his way. Also, *Styx* had that extra flavour, because so much of it was not his usual erotic subject matter. It had an extra layer – it was making an artistic claim. So maybe he felt the crowd was there for the wrong reasons.

Simon Garfield

Philippe went off to find a box of Bob-related ephemera that would put a precise date on the *Styx* show and perhaps contain the catalogue. He put on a video for me that I had been keen to see for a while – a promotional film of Caprice. This contained interviews with the model, observations from Ghislain, and well as footage from a shoot that Bob did of her wearing a brunette bobbed wig. It was taken in 1997, and Bob looked very healthy on the film, and very keen on Caprice. Bob's photo on the video box is 'Masked Blonde', the same one with the latex leggings and gloves that appeared on the cover of *Esquire*. The blurb on the back read: 'Caprice's reputation as the world's hottest blonde is undisputed. In this video she increases the temperature past hot to scorching, with a display of steamy images. See Bob Carlos Clarke, photographer to the stars, persuade Caprice to take part in a shoot with a difference. The behind-the-scenes exposé at his studio culminates in a series of seductive, erotic images which leave little to the imagination.'

'Caprice is a supermodel,' Ghislain Pascal explained on the film, 'and that means she earns at least £10,000 a day for her work.'

'What I'd like to do today is shoot Caprice my way rather than her way,' Bob Carlos Clarke said. 'The most important thing is to be as graphically economical as you possibly can. When you look at photographers who are not so developed, they rely on props and sophisticated glamorous stuff to make the picture look like it's got some weight. But if you look at the best photographers they will be pared down to the bare minimum…Good, yes, both hands up…that's great…okay, beautiful, back to me with your eyes, good, good, good!'

'I was born in California…' Caprice said.

'Are her breasts her own?' Philippe Garner asked.

Philippe Garner

Here we are. The private view for *Styx* was Wednesday 8 January 1992. The invitation says it was supported by Olympus. And here are some reviews of the show, quite a serious review in the *Independent*. And…how interesting, *The Antique Collector*, 'Sex Lies and Cutlery' by Brett Gorvy, the same name as the person who's now worldwide head of contemporary art at Christie's.

Brett Gorvy (The Antique Collector, *February 1992*)

Although Britain's consumer magazines and poster hoardings are now awash with his recent campaigns for Bacardi and Vladimir Vodka, at the age of 40 Bob Carlos Clarke has become disgruntled with having to kowtow to the whims of advertising executives and their philistine clients. His primary motivation, he says, is no longer simply the money-making potential of any given project. Instead he has spent the last year striving to endow his work with a greater sense of integrity and lasting artistic value.

'The strength of any great photographer is his courage to be economical with his subject matter and technique,' he exclaims. 'The fact that I have wasted 20 years getting to this point just shows how slow a learner I am.'

Simon Garfield

Brett Gorvy admired his ambition, his desire to renew himself. He appreciated his skills in the darkroom, and he wrote what I felt was an honest appraisal of some of his earliest work: he detected the influences of both Allen Jones and the neo-classical nudes of Victorian painter Alma Tadema, and quoted Bob's confession that he was like a 'butterfly collector. I became obsessed with trying to capture the essence of these gorgeous creatures. But in the end it was a pointless and frustrating exercise. I was never able to retain on paper a sense of their timeless or absolute beauty.' Of his new work, Gorvy observed the way he managed to confer a monumental significance on his beachcombing finds, his tarnished knives and forks. Bob had depicted a tenderness rarely imagined to exist in such objects, but sometimes he pushed things too far, as in his 'contrived and corrupted' image of a spoon's handle entwined around a fork.

The *Independent* also assessed the show, but its critic Andrew Palmer was less generous. He wanted the beach finds – which also included shoes, scissors and a bra – to have been photographed in situ, in the slabs of mud and shingle from which they came. Apparently that had been Bob's original idea, but he was beaten back to the studio by harsh winds and tides. The critic found that the images were printed with the obsessive care of an Irving Penn, but were ultimately 'polished but pointless'.

Geraldine Leale

It was an absolutely damning review and he was very hurt. The pictures were beautiful, and he put a huge amount of work into them, and I couldn't believe that anyone could be so nasty. It was absolutely crushing to Bob.

Simon Garfield

So he went back to something that he knew and he found safe – his photographs of women.

Geraldine Leale

He knew that sex would always sell, despite the dour mood of the time. No matter how much we don't like the idea of it, if you want to sell something to somebody you create desire. We all want our desires fulfilled, and Bob understood that.

But by this time some of his pictures of women just looked dated. When I told my friend who was this advertising wunderkind that he should use Bob because he was doing really nice stuff, he said he wouldn't touch him. I said, 'But they're brilliant,' and he said, 'No, he does all those pictures of girls, they're smutty, we're not interested.' So I don't think Bob realised it, but he wasn't in fashion any more. Everyone started criticising Page 3 and the flaunting of women and sex in advertising, including me and I was a Page 3 girl, and it all became rather sombre and rigid-looking and sanitised.

Philippe Garner

With hindsight one realises what a house of cards it all was, how fragile it all was. One came away from that opening just being pleased and proud to know him, because there's the glow of success and achievement which is always very intoxicating, but there was an emptiness at the core of it for Bob – somehow it wasn't enough for him.

• • •

James Betts

At his height he had a massive fan base. At Focus on Imaging, which is a big trade show for photographers and the photography world at the NEC in Birmingham, they used to have these big lecture theatres and he'd do three talks a day for three days and he used to fill it. It was standing room only, 600 people at a time, and other photographers went along and got 20 or 30 people, but Bob would have 600. At the end everyone wanted to come and meet him, this enigma that was Bob, and they'd queue up and get posters signed, and buy books and it was like going on tour with a rock star. It was funny because I used to sit in the audience with Lindsey and he'd obviously tell stories and I'd get mentioned and Lindsey would get mentioned and he'd show slides and occasionally there'd be a Polaroid of me and at the end I'd have my own queue of people asking me, either students or wannabe assistants, asking how they could get to work with Bob and 'what a fantastic job you've got'. I'd get my own little fan club so he had a big following. He built up a big fan base through those photography magazines.

Lindsey Carlos Clarke
Oh God, terrible, terrible amount of fans, it was like an adoration society. When he used to do those lectures they used to line the walls and hang off the ceilings and talk to anybody they could possibly get, touch the hem of his robe sort of thing, quite ridiculous sometimes. That's why I don't understand why he felt sort of, so sort of inferior. People used to come to the door, you know, messengers, and they'd have a parcel and they'd say, 'I've just got to ask you, are you Bob Carlos Clarke?' He'd go yes, and they'd say, 'I've just got to shake your hand!' Lots of that used to go on. I don't think he was aware of it at all. He thought it was most peculiar. He'd think, well, that's a messenger, that's not important.

Simon Garfield
But of course there would be problems. *Styx* brought attention and sales, but it wasn't for the work that Bob had set his heart on for all those years, it wasn't about women. It was how Kenneth Williams felt about being hailed for his *Carry On* films rather than his serious work. So Bob went back to concentrate on his erotica, albeit with props attached. He would now shoot people like Rachel Weisz, and juxtapose their image against a bottle of washing-up liquid or a cup

of coffee. It was his take on Duchamp's ready-mades, and they received a similar sort of reception: outrage and disquiet drowning out the appreciation from his collectors and student fans. He did a whole series about domesticated goddesses, and he was particularly interested in issues of control and the manipulation of the sexes. He seemed to be asking the questions, 'Who's in charge here?' and 'Who's really in charge here?'

Ghislain Pascal

Like any person, he wanted the respect he was due. He wasn't seen in the same spectrum as Helmut Newton and Testino, but he never really did fashion, and so people only perceived him as an erotic photographer. Whereas Helmut Newton also shot for *Vogue* and got their credibility.

He wanted to do more editorial. The *Sunday Times* used him, but it was mostly him pushing his pictures to them rather than being commissioned. Like the teenage sex pictures which went all over the world. *Stern* bought them.

Simon Garfield

In October 1995 the *Sunday Times* magazine ran a big story about the sex lives of teenagers, and they used Bob's photos on the cover and throughout the piece. They were taken at Justin Etzin's teenage balls at Hammersmith Palais and the Astoria in Charing Cross Road, a dimly lit mass of snogging and groping for well-turned-out public school children who have paid £20 to attend. The photographs, all black and white, show tights and knickers but not much else, for the teens are patrolled by chaperones: 'Hands in pants is NOT acceptable,' the story explains. They are among the least explicit of Bob's pictures of couples, but among the most erotically charged.

In the little biographical sketch of Bob at the front of the magazine, he explained about his large-format Weegee-style camera technique, and said that at first, 'I felt like a cross between David Attenborough and a peeping Tom. But later my camera became a time machine, returning me to a place where my own experiences were just as tragicomic and passionate.'

Ghislain Pascal

Every artist needs a signature, a definable identity. Bob obviously found it very young. But the thing with Bob was moving him on.

He got lost in the 1990s, which is when we met and that's why we worked so well together. He'd become completely disillusioned with the business and alienated by it. The advertising agencies were just 'Bob Carlos Clarke – soft porn', so not getting it. And all these art directors were always trying to tell Bob how to take his pictures. They would all say, 'Bob, fantastic! I studied you at college!', and then ten minutes later they would be telling him how to change things. So when I came on the scene I was the barrier between that and Bob, and he was always much better when he didn't have anyone interfering.

That's why he had begun to shoot under a pseudonym, the Jackal, because he was shunned. Can you imagine that – Bob Carlos Clarke being reduced to that? He was never asked to shoot for *GQ*, and that was his natural home. He didn't shoot for *FHM*, because they always wanted to own the pictures and Bob would never give away his rights.

As it turned out he got a massive advertising job on the back of the pseudonym. He shot that famous Urban Stone campaign with the girls snogging, one of the filthiest advertising campaigns ever printed. But he came out of that, and towards the end we'd completely moved on, and he went back to doing his artistic work.

Lindsey Carlos Clarke

He needed to own his own props – not just the guns and the other things he found, but even shoes the models wore. If he didn't own the props, then he didn't feel he really owned the photograph. We've got hundreds of pairs of shoes.

He sort of felt he owned the girls as well. There was one girl he shot...We got the contacts, and we both knew which shot it was – she gave us this amazing picture. He said, 'Isn't it interesting – she's already older than when I shot her,' which was probably two days before. He said, 'She'll age and crumble, but I have her in my camera for ever.' He felt he owned them, but then he got bored with them.

He liked finding girls in clubs and bringing them to his studio –

he never quite knew what he had, and that excited him. The more dangerous the better. This girl here, Charlotte, he found in a club in a filthy old wig, and he cleaned her up and took her to an agency and then she was used commercially.

John Stoddart

I've taken a Sienna Miller picture where she's holding the gun that Bob gave me. A Webley First World War gun.

Bob was an influence to me a long time ago, without knowing who he was. He was this crazy guy on the extremes of photography, which was quite acceptable then. I wasn't even a photographer. I'd just left the British army. I used to see his stuff, alongside Bailey's. Bob had this European edge, and he always pulled it off, always made it look very sexy without ever being tacky.

But then…when we became friends he would call me up and say, 'I can't believe *Loaded* haven't called me up to do a job.' I was, 'What! Bob?' He literally got angry at *Loaded* magazine! I used to say to him, 'Why on earth would you be interested in what they thought of you?'

I think he just wanted volume. In the end he did do the *Loaded* calendar, and it was superb. I did three, and his was the best.

Ghislain Pascal

He was always supported by photography magazines, but he was never supported by…a magazine like *GQ*. You would think they'd be ringing Bob up every day.

John Stoddart

Yes, every day. But they're total charlatans. They're fucking cunts – their idea of sexuality was so fake.

I did say to him once, 'Bob, *Vogue* is not going to ring you up, because you're taking pornography.' He rang me one day to say, 'I can't believe this fucking Mario Testino – can you believe it, he's doing all the work.' And I said to him, 'Yeah, and you're doing tits and ass.'

Lindsey Carlos Clarke

He was fascinated by Cartier-Bresson and Steichen. In that era you had to be rather rich to be a photographer, and he loved the fact that Cartier-Bresson had class and a nanny, and money. Bob's father's first two wives were quite rich titled ladies, and he said, 'Isn't it a shame that I wasn't a product of that?'

Bob used to go out frequently without any money – not because he was ungenerous, but because he didn't think it was necessary. I used to get phone calls from restaurants we ate in a lot, saying, 'Just to let you know, Bob didn't pay the bill today.' It wasn't interesting to him. Sometimes he would wake me in the middle of the night and say, 'Have we got any money?' and I'd say, 'Yes, there's this and this.' I spent it all on property as you know. The moment I said yes, he went back to sleep.

Terence Donovan told him once, 'You never want to let her get hold of the wedge.' The wedge? Bob didn't even know where the bank was.

He was so controlling with everything in his life, except for money. But he loved cash. If rich people called at the house they might want a picture of their family for Christmas, but they'd say we don't want to go through Hamiltons Gallery. So he'd ask them to pay cash, and he'd come up to the bedroom with it in a big wad and wave it around.

He did some photographs for people who sold jacuzzis and one day they came to us and said, 'We know we owe you lots of money, but we can't afford to pay you, so would you like to come and choose a jacuzzi instead?' So we went along to the showroom and I wanted the ten-seater. It had to be craned in.

After people came for dinner and had a few drinks, they'd see the jacuzzi twinkling outside, and Bob would always say, 'You must go in.' They would say, 'But we haven't got our swimming costume.' So they went in naked: Bob found the jacuzzi was the most wonderful way to get people to get their clothes off. For him this was the most magic thing. Hysterical, because he had these beautiful women taking their clothes off every day in his studio, but what he wanted was to see his neighbours.

I remember my mother said to me, 'It always had to be full

tilt, it could never be calm.' Bob went out one day and bought some crosses with Jesus on them – four – and nailed them to our garden shed. He said, 'I'll call it *Le Manoir aux Quatre Jesus*.' I said, 'What, are we opening a restaurant now?' and he said, 'What a wonderful idea.'

He called Marco up and said, 'We're going to a new restaurant tonight,' and Marco said, 'Is it in the Michelin guide?' Bob said, 'Not yet.' Then we had four people round for dinner in this shed, which we lined with silk. We had a jacuzzi, they put their robes on, we took them in the car and then down the side entrance to our house blindfolded, and led them into the shed. The dress code was 'naked'. So they took their shoes and robes off and the six of us sat there eating in the nude.

We also had a big van which we drove around, and we'd ask people in for food in it, and I'd cook for them. Like a location van with a kitchen in it. We cooked for David Linley and Serena, before they got married, in Kensington Gardens.

And we used to have people who visited us – people who liked to be photographed with their mistresses and wives, rich people, very rich people. They would then want to buy the prints. Bob hated it if they had sex – said it made him feel sick.

• • •

James Betts

He wasn't that easy to learn from. He was instinctive. You'd never get a masterclass. I used to do my own test shots and show him and say, 'I've done this, what do you think?' and invariably he'd take the piss, more often than not, but he would occasionally say how he would have done things differently. You'd listen for what he doesn't say. He was a bugger to try and get information out of. There was more instruction when it came to printing. With his printing I was doing the leg work, whereas he was the brains, so that was much more about being taught.

A lot of people did see him as being stuck in the 1980s and stuck in his old style; actually, if you looked at what he was doing and how much his style changed, it wasn't, it didn't stay still at all, from his elaborate early *Obsession* stuff, the very elaborate montages, hand painted, whereas *Shooting Sex* stuff was much simpler, much starker, and much more about what's going on with the subject, so he didn't stand still.

He'd go off on some tangent but you realise that when someone is so creative they're creating so many ideas that some of them are going to fall by the wayside, some are going to be silly, but you have to keep going at them and try things and he was constantly doing that. Not reinventing himself, but pushing himself and trying different things and that's where his strength would really lie.

The reason he was always interested in the erotic side of things was not because he was a huge pervert or anything, it was more about pushing boundaries, making art out of something and finding that line and crossing it or pushing it, and pushing people's beliefs as well. The whole thing about nudes goes back to whenever, the twelfth or thirteenth century, but I suppose the way he was doing it was kind of interesting. Again the thing with Bob, people felt that he was unhappy with his reputation. Because if you don't know his work and you haven't been to the archive you sort of think, okay, rubber stuff, fetishism, that kind of stuff, and that was obviously – he didn't like just having that tag. That work was just a small amount of what he did.

The rubber was a purely aesthetic thing. The cat suits just made people's bodies look amazing. Yeah, if you say 'Bob Carlos Clarke' they immediately think rubber, but it was much more about the girls than the rubber.

He did try shooting men and he obviously did great portraits of Marco and Keith Richards and people like that, but he was not so interested in the male form. He didn't have a great many male friends. He had male friends, but not close. He shot men if he was interested in the man, whereas he was more interested in the female form; it's a classical thing where everyone is more interested in the female form really, and he definitely had his muses. Yes, Emma Ford was like that. You know, he did work like an artist in that way: he'd shoot one girl over and over again.

Bob Carlos Clarke *(in* Amateur Photographer*)*
In terms of prestige gallery sales, the market for contemporary images of the female nude barely exists, while similar images of men are selling like hot buns. There is a simple, albeit generalised explanation for all of this. Homosexuals have lashings of disposable income and lashings of boudoir adornment, whereas their exhausted hetero counterpart tends to be lumbered with at least one wife whose face does not light up when he brings home a £1,800 snapshot of some delectable Lolita in her birthday suit. And what about the children, and their friends, and that sensitive Norland nanny?

• • •

Bob Carlos Clarke *(from the first draft of* Shooting Sex*)*
I have heard that Helmut Newton doesn't make close friends with his models. He just gets them in, shoots them and ships them out. I like to go deeper than that. I try to find out what they want to do and what they want to express, and then we work together to achieve it.

When you photograph a model, it's a duet – a tango. When it goes well it's better than sex, and lasts for ever.

James Betts
Lindsey would always be there. She'd more often than not do the catering as well. We had a huge table we could sit about 12 people round and the lunches at Bob's shoots were infamous. Everyone used to come and say, I love coming to your shoots because lunch is so good; Lindsey used to do a great spread, you know, which is much nicer than getting caterers to bring a plate of sandwiches round. So she used to do all of that and I used to help her lay it all out, they were great, and Bob would hold court and tell loads of stories which I'd heard hundreds of times.

I suppose I left him about three years before the end. Half the reason I stayed there so long was because I was totally involved in *Shooting Sex*. I printed practically every shot in that book. I wanted to see it through and I'm very glad I did. I feel very privileged to have been involved with it, and I'm glad I'm mentioned in it. I'm mentioned obviously in the front but also in the text. I was his longest-standing assistant.

But I felt I had to get from underneath his shadow, and had to slightly distance myself from him as he was this all-encompassing figure. Because when my career was starting to take off he had this sort of controlling thing. He didn't make life easy for me; if I was saying to him, look, I've got a shoot on that day, I'm going to take the day off or the morning off, he would say, 'Well, what if I get a big shoot?' 'Well, you know, you're going to have to deal with that because I need to do this.' And he'd make things awkward and if I wanted to use the studio he'd let me use it for free, but of course it would always be, 'Ah, but if I get a proper studio booking, you're going to have to shift,' which isn't a great way to run your business.

I shouldn't have held on anywhere near as long as I did, but in some respects it was a cushy number. He never raised his voice to me once, and I fucked up as much as the rest of them. But there were some things he'd be brilliant in and some things you'd literally need to baby him through, you know the everyday things of life, constantly losing things. Even when I'd left him I'd still get phone calls saying, 'I can't find something, where is it?' Six months later. So I gradually weaned myself off him.

You want to be your own person, you don't always want to be referred to as Bob's assistant. In fact I'm much more comfortable about saying I was Bob's assistant now or in the last couple of years than when I first left him. After I'd left him and I was at a party, it might have been one of Ghislain's parties, and Bob and Lindsey were there. I was there with Shona my girlfriend, and someone said to me, 'Hi, where's Bob?' and I snapped and said, 'I'm not his keeper.' But now I'm fiercely proud of working with him.

Ghislain Pascal

When the first boxes of *Shooting Sex* arrived from the printers there was all this drama. Bob opened them up and the books inside were all blank pages. They had to go back.

Lindsey Carlos Clarke

We published it ourselves because Bob wanted control. We printed 6,500, with 3,000 for the UK. Whenever we had a meeting with publishers they always wanted a theme. They said, 'I know, Black Men, White Women.' But Bob would say, 'Don't be stupid – I'M the theme.'

He felt that once the photographs were in a book he could get on to the next thing. He felt it was the start of something, not the ending.

Simon Garfield

The book contained several hundred images spanning his career. His big muses were all in there – Kadamba, Caprice, Emma Ford, Gabrielle Richens – as were Nicky Barthorp, Sue Frame, Lindsey and Scarlett. There were portraits of the photographer too – with his parrot, with his bikes, bare-chested, upside down on his hands next to his VW Beetle on a beach. The text, which appeared in many different fonts, was an unreliable memoir, but it contained many salient and fitting observations.

Bob Carlos Clarke

Through hurricane and holocaust we cling to the images of our past and the ones we love as if to life itself. A photograph is the only physical proof that we really existed, that we were once strong and young, and maybe beautiful.

Simon Garfield

The book was launched in November 2002 at the Firehouse restaurant in Kensington. It was sponsored by Tia Lusso, a cream liqueur, and was attended by Tamara Beckwith, Patti Boyd, fashion designer Amanda Wakeley, the actor Oliver Tobias, and photographers John Stoddart, John Swannell and Barry Lategan. There were pole dancers.

Tamara Beckwith *(writing in* OK!*)*

Having known the divine Bob Carlos Clarke for ever and a day it was with a hop, skip and a jump that I got myself ready for the bound-to-be-beautiful launch party for his photographic book

Shooting Sex: The Definitive Guide to Undressing Beautiful Strangers. The Helmut Newton of Chelsea, Bob has had a penchant for shooting sexy girls for as long as I have known him. Mandy Smith, Amanda Smith, Amanda de Cadenet, Jerry Hall, Marie Helvin, Zoe Ball, Cat Deeley…the list of gorgeous creatures who have been happy to shed their inhibitions for him is endless.

His zany, blonde, ex-model wife Lindsey has been his dependable right arm for aeons, and is always on hand to lend a touch of genius styling to their loft studio in the Village, Battersea. A shoot with them is always full of laughter and absolutely guaranteed to have great catering…

I was escorted by my friend Andrew Wessall, who had the patience of a saint. I was then grabbed from behind and there was our glittering host, Bob Carlos Clarke. We had a quick kiss before I was abruptly abandoned for his muse, the six-foot-whatever Kaja Wunder, when she strode over. She is just awesome-looking, in that bold blonde Slavic way. I watched with relish as some of the girls who appear in Bob's book came to life in front of my eyes.

Lindsey Carlos Clarke

For himself he liked to read biographies. He liked to read about real people's real lives, especially if they were fucked up. He couldn't bear the ordinary. When we had people for dinner he always wanted to ask a fire-eater or someone who did something mad. I would just go to bed and leave them to it.

People did get worried about Scarlett. There were odd things around our house. One day they all had to do some colouring at school, and she came back with her picture of Pocahontas, and I noticed she had coloured the arms and legs black, as if they were wearing rubber. I was, 'Oh that's nice, darling.'

18. and some days it just felt sort of dark around him, said paul plews

Bob Carlos Clarke

When I first came to study in England, the buzz around photography was electrifying. Edgy new advertising agencies flourished, with clients who were keen and receptive to new ideas.

These days the best advertising has gone to the States, leaving UK photographers to battle each other for crumbs. Even the established UK publishing houses have become puppets of the US market, not daring to take a step without the funding of American co-editions. Almost all the best-known names in photography are now based in the US. Fortunately that wasn't so with Lartigue or Cartier-Bresson or most of the other truly great originals, and it's sad that the public perception of photography is now largely limited to celebrity and fashion, and kittens with balls of wool.

A UK photographer requires ten times the resilience and determination of his American counterpart. Like an Olympic swimmer training in a washbasin, an oak-tree growing in a thimble, a ballerina dancing on elephant dung, and all to the distant dinging of Herb Ritts's cash register, and the marching feet of Annie Leibovitz's ten thousand highly trained assistants who bear her between assignments on a gilded catafalque.

In the US, ancient masters are lionised and revered in proportion to their genius, while our own local legends fade like phantoms into obscurity and oblivion. Everything here is about being on the cutting edge, until one day it chops you up and feeds you to the sharks.

Paul Plews

One day, quite out of the blue, I got a call from Ghislain saying Bob was looking for a new assistant. It was an indirect connection: my other half, Sue, had a friend who was a partner of Ghislain's. I was 23, I had finished a photography degree up in Blackpool, and I was back home, not quite sure what I was going to do. James Betts had been working with Bob for years, but had decided to leave.

I certainly wasn't interested in the sort of erotic stuff that Bob was doing, I was more of a fan of Richard Avedon, his American West book, his portraits of workers. I'm probably very socially orientated in that way. I'd gone back to live with my parents in the north-east, a little place called Ashington, about 10 miles to the north of Newcastle, a big coal-mining town.

But the chance of working with Bob was something that was just too interesting and tempting to turn down. Also it was a chance to get into London and start learning about the industry with a view to getting photographic work myself. It was two weeks between getting the call and moving down to London, all very quick. I came down to meet Bob and Lindsey and I think we only met for about an hour. Something clicked somehow.

I came down early on this miserable day, so I spent a few hours in Clapham Junction, which is pretty grim at the best of times, and then you enter this massive studio in this big imposing school building with intercom and gates, a totally different atmosphere. I had no idea what to expect. Because of the name I had the preconception that he wasn't going to be English. I thought maybe, European, Spanish or something, but no, English as they come really.

Bob Carlos Clarke

At every level this business is riddled with bullshit and bigotry, and I reckoned that the only way I could tackle it was to turn its weaknesses to my advantage. So I changed my identity and began working under the pseudonym 'Jackal'. For the campaign for Urban Stone [three people, including Emma Ford, in a nightclub, increasingly enjoying each other's company and creating an erotic mood designed to sell the clothing company's denim and casual wear] I wanted to use people who were either friends of mine or were people that we could find on the street. But the client was insistent that we use models. We did our best, but the pictures looked set up, and lacked the intense realism required to make the whole thing appear believable. We had spent two days getting to this point, and I said to the client that we had spent a lot of money and perhaps we should give my idea a try. So we ditched the entire shoot, and I recast using a glamour girl, a club dancer and a handsome young guy we found on a West End street.

On the morning of the shoot my three new performers arrived looking wasted to perfection. One girl had been out drinking all night, the other had been brawling with her lover and had fluorescent bruises to prove it and the guy was completely wiped out from an all-night session as a podium dancer. We shot five ads over the next two days and it was so easy because the three of them knew exactly what to do. It's probably the best and most successful advertising series that I've done. I find that the more you try to stage-manage a situation the more artificial it tends to look. We started shooting at 10.30am in a club in the West End, and everyone involved thought that it was too early to start sex. Things didn't start getting interesting until after lunch, and my role was to move around and occasionally to offer them direction. I just told them the effect that I wanted to create and then tried to remain as unobtrusive as possible. My feeling is that you can create nothing that's more interesting than reality. The Urban Stone shoot helped me generate some very useful attention, and it was good to be involved in a campaign that broke new ground. All the tabloids wanted to use the shots to run with their story that asked, 'Are these the most explicit ads ever?'

Paul Plews

When I first walked in, Lindsey opened the door and Bob was sat behind his massive desk in his big black chair and it was all quite – I don't know, it was almost like going to meet a Mafioso boss. Afterwards, a few months down the line, Bob actually told me that during that hour that we met he didn't really understand much of what I said because my Geordie accent was still quite strong and he didn't have much experience of people from the north.

I found the work more intimidating than meeting him in real life. The sort of picture you have of people who shoot these glamour models…it can be totally wrong. It's like making a judgement on an artist by what paintings they make: one has no idea of the life.

There was enough stuff in *Shooting Sex* that I obviously admired and appreciated. His pictures of Marco I really liked, the stuff in the kitchen. And I also really liked the pictures he did at the debutantes' ball and those Urban Stone adverts. The prospect of the glamour world didn't really appeal to me at all – I mean, not in a red-blooded male sense, but in a sense that if I'm going to do something creative then I want to do social realism. I didn't cringe at the portraits, but I was always quite stand-offish when those jobs came in for him, and I used to step back a little bit and let him do his thing.

At college there's a certain amount of exercises in photography that you have to do. Still lifes or table tops, set in a studio, with the large-format camera. Then we'd have to do some beauty stuff, a nice white background with a well-lit model. It was all sort of quite naff stuff.

But now…are you familiar with William Eggleston's work? I really love that, the way that you can make an observation about society by taking a picture of some dustbins, or some railings. I'm really interested in seeing something that other people maybe don't see. But a lot of people looked at Bob's work and didn't see past the beautiful girl, but when you look at his other pictures you see that there was obviously another layer hidden.

Simon Garfield

Bob kind of got to the point in his late forties, early fifties, where the big issue for him became all about respect. He always felt that he was never fully taken into the arts fold and I know that he always wanted to be more highly regarded, and he never quite knew what success was. Was it selling at a show, was it taking the perfect photograph, or having pictures in the National Portrait Gallery? The art world was never going to welcome him in.

Paul Plews

There was always a real problem for him with the commercial work. We all have it to some extent, but how much do you do for the money, and how much for yourself or your art? Ghislain would always get Bob to shoot the Ann Summers thing, with Nancy Sorrell or whomever, and he was always grumbling. Ghislain would say, 'You're getting paid for it, it's all organised for you, we'll come to your studio, you just take the pictures.' I think there was always this sort of tussle between Ghislain and him. Ghislain knew it wasn't art, but that Bob had to do other things to pay for the art. You know, Ghislain was always 'Just fucking get on with it!', and Bob was always sort of digging his heels in, but he'd never pass it on to the model or the team around him. It was always a tussle just between the two of them.

And how far can you push your erotic work and still be regarded as an artist? We all know that Bob didn't attain the acclaim of Helmut Newton. You look at artists like Jeff Koons, who did what could be regarded as almost pornographic photos, but because he was already established in the art scene before he did that, it wasn't questioned. But I think possibly with Bob coming the other way, trying to get into the art market, it's regarded as some sort of smutty guy who takes these pictures and now who's trying to get respect. Which is such a fickle thing because it's a judgement based on what you've already seen, not on what you're actually looking at. But that's the way the art market is, isn't it?

Philippe Garner

I would say there's been a significant shift in the last ten years. The photography market has broadened out, the medium has become accepted as worthy of hanging on your wall and paying a big price for. The easy thing to say is that it's been accepted as an art form. It's such a sort of casual umbrella to describe it that way, but I think yes, modern photography, post-war photography and contemporary photography have become a kind of currency in the world of collecting and high-end luxury goods. In a sense that's what they are: luxury collectibles.

A number of factors have greatly reinforced that. Within the contemporary art community a significant number of artists have chosen the medium of photography and made it part of contemporary art culture. Indeed, photography is centre stage, while easel painting and drawing, the traditional skills, are currently marginalised. The fact that photographs have been given the blessing and endorsement of a broad contemporary art-collecting community and museum world has had a tremendous impact on the perceptions around the medium. Also, I think that the transition from chemical photography to digital photography has consciously or unconsciously created this sense that the kind of craft and skill that Bob was so great at is a kind of alchemy, all that masterly secret skill in the darkroom, and it is one that is now slipping away as a magic of another age.

And I think that the fact that we've turned not a decade, not a century, but a millennium, somehow makes everything and anything of the last millennium History with a capital H. It can be packaged and perceived as something remote even if it's only seven or eight years ago, something distant from the twentieth century.

In terms of the selling market, from the early 1970s it was a slow, incremental pulling out of the treasures, starting with 1840s, '50s, '60s, and gradually building the story. The first sale of photographs that I was charged with coordinating at Sotheby's was in December 1971. I don't think there'd been a major photography auction before that. I was 22, which is ridiculously young to be put in charge of coordinating that sale. It's significant that a decision was made by a major auction house to commit to the subject, and it was the first of what was to be an ongoing series. All of my instinctive interest in photography was in contemporary and modern photography, but professionally I plunged straight into the nineteenth century. We look at the first sale today and it seems very slight in its little red-covered catalogue. The top artists were Talbot and Cameron, absolute mainstays, and the most expensive lot was a copy of the

Pencil of Nature, Talbot's multi-part book, which I think made £2,600. It was the beginning of something.

• • •

Bob Carlos Clarke

As an exercise, it's worth trying to take a photograph in the style of a photographer you admire. By attempting to emulate the style of the brilliant New York paparazzo, Weegee, I discovered that shooting real life was far more interesting than anything I could cook up in my studio.

I developed my own approach – a fixed lens Fuji 6x9 camera fitted with a large, old-fashioned silver-dish flash. The experience left me with a bruised shoulder, from the heavy batteries, and considerable respect for the men who, in unfavourable conditions and with heavy, unwieldy plate cameras, managed to capture some of the most remarkable images of all time.

Like most teenagers, I thought I'd invented sex. The idea of fornicating forefathers, particularly my parents, was unthinkable. Eventually I had to accept that people had been doing it for quite some time, and realised that since anything that happens gets photographed, the chance of shooting something totally original was extremely slim. Helmut Newton is generally regarded as an innovator, but the influence of photographers such as Andre de Dienes and Brassaï is very evident.

I use books, magazines or any relevant reference to give my models some idea of what I want to achieve. Commercial models, who are often treated like cattle, appreciate a little respect and the opportunity to be involved in the creative process. I scour other photographers' work for inspiration, and in turn my own work is copied. Depending on my mood and the extent of the rip-off, it can be either flattering or infuriating. In fact, it's impossible to recreate truly great photographers like Lartigue or Leni Riefenstahl.

Scarlett Carlos Clarke

His talent? He was really original. He had his own ideas, and didn't really look at what other people were doing. His pictures show

how devoted he was to his work – he could spend hours developing to get a perfect print. But he probably didn't want to come across like that. Because he had this weird two-sided thing. He wanted to come across so rock and roll, so relaxed about everything, and he so wasn't that. Underneath he was really controlling, workaholic.

Bob Carlos Clarke

In the 1960s, Bailey, Donovan and Brian Duffy, dubbed 'the Triumvirate' by Norman Parkinson, got more fame and attention than any UK photographers have had since.

Now only Bailey survives as a photographer, like an endangered species sighted occasionally at openings with the myth of the 1960s swinging round his neck like a brandy barrel on a St Bernard.

In the early 1980s, according to popular legend, Duffy went a bit funny and fled into the countryside. In fact, he had gone very sane, saw the writing on the wall, and now enjoys life as one of Britain's leading antique furniture restorers.

Simon Garfield

And in 1996, after bouts of depression, Donovan hung himself in his study.

Philippe Garner

For me the beginnings of selling post-war twentieth-century work came in 1975 when I organised and conducted a benefit auction for the Photographers' Gallery and really that was a historic sale. It was a big step into the unknown to invite a lot of contemporary photographers to submit a work, and it was a great success. The top lot was a portrait of Colette by Irving Penn and it was the first time as far as I've been able to trace that a photograph by Irving Penn was offered at auction. That sale included the first time prints by Helmut Newton had ever been offered at auction, so there was some real historic firsts there.

This was when Bob was just starting to make a reputation. His was a byline that people such as myself were starting to recognise and become familiar with, but it would have been asking a great deal in that climate for Bob to have any realistic expectation for building a market for print sales. But then in the early 1980s when he was starting to have his first shows and making his first sales it all looked quite promising in a market that was still very much in its infancy. The fact that he was having any impact at all was something to be pleased with, but he didn't build it right.

Paul Plews

I don't know if you've ever been to the Photographers' Gallery, but Bob really hated the sort of stuffiness in there. But of course he would have loved to have had the chance to get in there for the seriousness with which it takes photography. He never felt like he was fully accepted or credited with anything. I think in a way that was probably a similar thing with the exhibitions as well. He did well in a commercial sense because he sold a lot of pictures, but it was never the money that Bob craved. He wanted the pat on the back, which in a way is what we all want.

Philippe Garner

It was some years before we ever had a print of Bob's in a sale and we did have one or two, probably late 1980s. He'd sold prints and original unique work, but it was too soon and it was too local as well. As I saw the market grow internationally, I came to realise that Bob was a local and essentially niche interest.

What he couldn't quite realise, I guess, is how to adapt his language to a broader audience. There were things in what he was doing, within the imagery, which potentially could strike more or less universal chords, certainly in our Western culture. But he wasn't very good at tempering them, at managing to weave in just enough distance, just enough humour, just enough other elements through which to make the pill palatable. I don't mean he should have popularised and debased, I actually mean he could have been savvy, been sophisticated. 'You're incredibly talented, you're doing something utterly fascinating, but you're limiting your audience because you don't know quite how to break out of the very sinister.' The overriding characteristic of so much of Bob's work is that it's actually quite spooky, it's scary, and people can enjoy the little frisson in passing but they don't...

I think ultimately a lot of people just sort of back off.

Bob Carlos Clarke

The fashion photographer Norman Parkinson preserved the impression of eternal youth, until he died in his seventies, by moving constantly across the world. Born Roland Parkinson-Smith in 1913, 'Parks' changed his name and presented himself as the ultimate-eccentric-English-gentleman-society-photographer.

He was in his seventies when I first met him, still elegant, six-foot-five tall, slender and lightly tanned from his home in Tobago, wearing a lilac shirt under a lime-green suit. He had a strange super-stition involving beaded Kashmiri hats, never commencing a shoot without one on. During the 1980s we shared an agent, and he became my favourite photographer-friend and mentor. He was the youngest old man I've ever known.

In the late 1980s he launched 'Porkinsons', his own special brand of pork sausages. I remember the launch party well because, on leaving the gallery, we were each presented with a pound of uncooked sausages. At traffic lights on the drive home a tipsy model who was travelling with me unwrapped her sausages and tossed them into the lap of an elegant woman in an open Jaguar. We left the poor woman shrieking in the dark.

To celebrate Parks's birthday we went for dinner to Marco Pierre White's first restaurant, Harveys in Wandsworth. Parks's date was the beautiful 17-year-old model Lisa Butcher, and he was on top form. He died on location on Valentine's Day 1990, a well-timed departure from a spectacular performance. After his death I bought a battered case of his camera equipment. It was touching to discover his favourite Kashmiri cap neatly folded into the lid.

Donovan's personal style was diametrically opposed to Parks. No peacock wardrobe, just rows of identical dark suits which he had tailored in batches to save time in deciding what to wear. He drove a sleek black Bentley to compliment his larger-than-life personality and proportions. Parks and Donovan didn't invent their style, it was just the way they were.

Parkinson teased me about my work: 'So *crude*, so *obvious*!'

Paul Plews

In a weird way, Bob wanted to be part of the establishment, but also didn't, and he couldn't quite measure the two up.

When I was with him, I won a prize at the NPG in 2004 for a picture that I took in Blackpool. This thing called the Schweppes Award, which started off as the John Kobal Award, and I won the prize for the under-25s section and Bob was really thrilled for me.

I think we had quite a strong relationship but it was never on a sit-down-and-talk-about-any-problems level. I like to think I'm fairly intuitive, and some days it just felt sort of dark around him. Brooding. I'd always make a bit of an effort to lighten the mood somewhat.

And Lindsey could see what I was doing, and that I needed support too. Moving to London for anyone is really difficult, but Bob and Lindsey took me in, they really looked after me. My girlfriend was in Australia and I missed her, and I was somewhere new, and Lindsey recognised someone who needed some support, because of course with Bob she was a master at that.

He said he never had any pictures of him working. So a few weeks later I took a photo of him with Katie, the girl. It was only me and him there working, and he built up a sort of relationship with Katie where they'd come to trust each other a bit.

Simon Garfield

That's such a great photo. It's included in one of the little catalogues produced for his last big show. It shows Bob in his large white studio, in a tight white T-shirt, white trousers and barefoot, with a large camera in his hand, prowling beneath a podium on which Katie stood looking down on him. It was jungle imagery.

Paul Plews

Bob always cared for these girls, not in a fatherly way because that might sound a bit creepy, but he was always concerned about their wellbeing, and that things were going well with their relationships, the work, whom they'd been working with. That is the only picture I've ever taken of Bob, and it was just literally a snap, I think I did two frames, and that was it. It's very strong, very direct. It's funny; it's like that thing that Helmut Newton does really well, that empowerment in the women he photographs. And with Bob I think he always felt that there was a respect thing there, an appreciation of their beauty, their strength. I think he just wanted to applaud.

• • •

Bob Carlos Clarke

Terence Donovan gave me two invaluable pieces of advice: never shoot on cameras that don't belong to you, and don't do weddings. The following week I agreed to shoot the wedding of the heavily pregnant 'Wild Child' Amanda de Cadenet to Duran Duran guitarist John Taylor, a celebrity event sponsored by *Hello!* magazine who had paid dearly for exclusive publication rights. At the time I didn't own a good 35mm camera, so I hired one for the day.

The marriage took place at Chelsea Register Office attended by a handful of relatives and friendly rock stars. I shot off a couple of rolls of 35mm colour transparency, and rushed them off to a lab for urgent processing. A few hours later the envelope of processed film landed on my desk. Out of 70 frames, 68 were unexposed. The final two frames of the second film featured the back of my assistant's head and a good shot of my feet. After a few seconds of blind despair, I took a deep breath and telephoned the newlyweds who were still carousing in a Chelsea restaurant.

Amanda answered: 'How are the shots?'

'Not great. Slight problem with the shutter. Can you get back to the Register Office immediately?'

'Oh shit! John!' I heard her shouting. 'Bob's fucked up...'

John Taylor

Yes, our wedding photographs. Ghastly, just ghastly. Amanda was six months' pregnant, and it was a *Hello!* magazine exclusive. We got married, and then we did the photos at Bob's studio. Then we went for lunch and Bob came running in saying there were big problems, and we had to go back and do them again, by which time it was, 'I don't want to see those fucking photographs.' But now I wish I had them.

He was a wonderful guy with a wonderful sense of humour, but he also had a kind of dark, fatalistic side to him. We had our children within weeks of each other. I've got a very cute picture of the two of us with our babies, both holding the bottles.

He believed that in order to have an edge you needed this rebellious streak. He was frightened of age, you know. You have to reconcile yourself between art and commerce, and between age and youth as well. They're the two great issues one has to face.

Simon Le Bon

He didn't just do John's wedding – he photographed the band. He had a very tough outlook on life – life was not sweet. Given what happened perhaps that sounds obvious. When he lived near Bishop's Park for a while he kept this beautiful restored 650 Triumph Bonneville, and he took me on the back of that. He told me some things I couldn't possibly repeat, as well. He had a great way with girls. He really did. Little girls as well as big girls.

What else? He used to go along the river at low tide. He did this porno shoot.

Simon Garfield

Really? How porno?

Simon Le Bon

Oh, everything.

• • •

Bob Carlos Clarke

Shooting sex should never be confused with *having* sex, which is far easier. Richard Avedon insists, 'You can't fuck and photograph at the same time,' which is forgivable at his age, and the late Terence Donovan advocated restraint: 'If you were going to photograph a cool glass of sparkling water with chinks of ice sweating down its sides, I think you'd be wise not to drink it before you took the picture. All the energy is in the anticipation.'

Eroticism relies upon a finely tuned conspiracy between the eye and the imagination. It's an entirely individual response. What excites one person may disgust another.

I interviewed Terence Donovan a few months before his death, and he summed it up: 'Eroticism is unquestionably something that slices into the viewer's psyche and touches a nerve. Something that is beyond what is there on the paper; it's never right there, it's much more about possibilities.'

Slaving over a writhing siren is hard work, and not always sexy, but there are times when lust intervenes. One especially libidinous glamour photographer told me he employed 'a pre-emptive strike' by masturbating ten minutes before working with his favourite girls. He claimed the advantages of this technique were twofold: the ability to remain cool and detached, or, should lust win the day, the ability to sustain a more prolonged and memorable performance.

Lindsey Carlos Clarke

It got to a point where he couldn't actually switch that part of his life off, and that's very difficult to deal with. It would have been nice to have said occasionally, 'Do you think we could sort of talk about something else for a second?' I would make an effort to take him to a film that everyone was talking about, and he would say, 'Okay then, but you organise it,' and then after I'd booked the tickets he wouldn't want to go because he wanted to work.

And then he would spend hours all night writing poems and cards to his new crushes, and I'd think, 'Oh come on, get over it.' He'd be terribly offended if these new crushes didn't answer the phone to him, or, you know, childlike, very childlike.

Simon Garfield

Were you not concerned at any time that it might turn into a different thing?

Lindsey Carlos Clarke

Of course, of course, and I made a conscious decision about that, and I just decided that I would not travel there. Because I didn't see the point.

Simon Garfield

Otherwise you'd go mad, if you couldn't contain it?

Lindsey Carlos Clarke

You'd go mad, you can't live your life like that. So I quietly took a knife to that part of my emotions and thought, I'll just cut this piece out.

Simon Garfield

How hard was that?

Lindsey Carlos Clarke

Very hard. Very very hard because, you know, it was an obsessive relationship and I was obsessed by him, mentally and physically. I had to distract and detach if I was to survive. And I was hurt, it was hurtful sometimes and he was very clever and very manipulative, and he could always argue his way out of anything. He could make something completely ridiculous sound absolutely fine; he had a marvellous way of doing that. So you'd think, oh, that has some logic to it, and afterwards think: I'm sure it doesn't. So, yes, I detached, but it's not really a great way to live. People afterwards said to me, 'Oh, you should have said something,' but the problem was there wasn't any point. There was always a reason.

He had a habit of doing this thing, which some people thought was completely despicable. You know, I'm actually quite a reasonable cook. I can cook a nice supper, even after we'd both been at the studio all day. I'd leave slightly earlier, and Scarlett would be in bed, although he did this before she was born as well. He'd potter around and watch a bit of TV, nothing really, what I'd call normal life, and then he'd disappear upstairs and I'd be thinking about what he was doing. He'd suddenly appear at the door dressed up, and he'd say, 'Look, I'm just popping out, Robert has got a new club opening and…' He hated clubs, he wasn't a club goer, but he was always hoping to find something, something interesting, something weird, an experience, always looking for an experience of some sort. Sometimes to photograph and sometimes not. He'd say, 'I'll only be an hour,' and I'd look at him and think, it's now 10 o'clock. How could you only be an hour? It's going to take you 25 minutes to get there, 25 minutes to get back, you're only going to be there for 10 minutes.

Plus I used to get fucked off, because I used to say to him, 'Look, I don't mind you doing that but surely you must have known before now and if you'd have told me I could have gone out too and seen Jane.' Like I didn't have a life, like I could just be glued in place and I wasn't allowed to move, and it took me quite a long time to suss out that I felt sort of suffocated and trapped by all that. You know what it's like: yes, very lonely.

And then he would come back at 3am, when I'd been asleep and been awake and God knows what, and he'd say, 'Oh God, it was awful tonight, so and so was there…', and he'd take me through the whole adventure which he obviously thought was riveting.

He once said to me, 'Lindsey, all your friends are so fat and ugly,' and I replied, 'But at least we talk, and they listen to me, and we share things and have a supportive relationship.'

Simon Garfield

Were you aware of sexual relationships, of him having sex with other models?

Lindsey Carlos Clarke

Only a couple of times, and sometimes it was not an issue. There were a couple of occasions that were more serious. I don't think he could really see what was wrong and what wasn't, so he used to cross boundaries and then be frightfully surprised that it wasn't a great idea and that everyone was terribly upset. There was one occasion…We were walking along the Thames one day when the tide was right out, and we talked about this person he had been with. What had happened was, she had a plan for him. I knew her, and I could have offered her advice: 'He's never going to leave me, you're just entertainment and that's fine but take it as that, don't look at it as something else.' But Bob just got bored, and she decided, 'I'm not going to let them disappear off, I'm going to fuck it up for them.'

And as we were walking along, he just said to me, 'Are you going to leave me?'

I don't think he ever really lived his life like he would have liked to have done. He would have been better not to have got into such a stable situation with me and he should have had a much wilder rock 'n' roll life. He should have had all the models, and done whatever he wanted to whenever he wanted to. He should have enjoyed the fact that when you get into some sort of sexual thing with somebody it's much easier to take the sort of pictures you want, the pictures you might not be able to take when they're just a cold stranger. It's funny, but I actually had more of a bohemian psyche than he ever had. I went to see a psychiatrist who said that he was partly self-invented. He became Bob Carlos Clarke in a sort of legendary way and started to live out what he thought that actually was, but the problem was he then wanted to run home to Mother.

Simon Garfield

Do you think he knew that? That perhaps he was a bit of an act?

Lindsey Carlos Clarke

He was in constant turmoil. We met Robert Mapplethorpe on several occasions, and he was actually living that life – he photographed it and he really went for it. And Don McCullin – he did it as well. But I know that people must have thought that Bob and I must have rubber fetishes, and nothing could be less true. It was only when we got very friendly with Allen Jones and his wife Deirdre that they too thought we were into it. But there was a big sort of visual trick in there. I think people did believe we were having some sort of absolutely wild life. I grant you that some of it was quite bizarre, but not nearly as much as other people wanted to believe.

It's the same thing we talked to Helmut Newton about: that line where you're trying to get the edge between pornography and art and sex all into one thing and you can't succeed every time but they're all going for the same thing, you know. Lovely nudes lying in green grass is very pretty maybe, but it doesn't give you anything, and Bob always sort of wanted that jolt, you know.

We knew Helmut because he used to photograph a friend of ours, Tanya Coleridge, a stunning-looking girl with dark hair. Helmut wanted to take pictures of her and I together; such a shame it never happened, because we were always in the wrong place, she was in America, I was here, he was in Monaco. But Helmut worked in a very different way. Helmut came from a fashion context. He used to get something all set up for his fashion shoot and then afterwards say, 'Come on, take off your dress, we'll do the shot without the dress.' Bob was not interested in fashion at all. It instantly dated something, it had a purity to it that Bob loathed. He said that fashion was the silliest thing you could do with a camera.

CAPRICE AS *MASKED BLONDE.*

EMMA FORD AND FRIEND; STONES FROM *STYX*.

LUST AND DESPAIR AT A TEENAGE BALL..

THE SHARK GIRL IN *ADULT FEMALES ATTACK WITHOUT PROVOCATION.*

LOVE, AS FOUND ENTWINED NEAR THE CARLOS CLARKE HOME BY THE THAMES.

THE PHOTOGRAPHER BY HIS DAUGHTER.

PART THREE

19. it changed so quickly – it was shocking, said crena watson

Bob Carlos Clarke

Terence Donovan's death was deeply troubled and upsetting.

In 1996 he dropped by my studio, but he was edgy and depressed. Five weeks later he took his own life. He was a good friend who taught me the importance of the wedge (fees, preferably in cash). He was also the only person who called to congratulate me on my exhibition *Styx*, which opened in London in January 1992 and sold nothing. He knew I'd invested all my energy in the shots, and consoled me with the news that Van Gogh had only sold one painting in his lifetime.

I still haven't reconciled myself to Donovan's death. There have been many explanations, but I feel sure that it had something to do with the process of 'fading away', which concerns every fashionable photographer.

Lindsey Carlos Clarke

I strove always to get him bigger and better studios, it was my dream. I suppose somewhere inside my dream was the fact that my father longed to get back to being just a painter. I knew my father had emphysema, and my longing for him was to make enough money to buy something in the south of France where he could just work and do what he wanted to do. But he died of motor neurone disease and none of it ever happened. I'm sure I put that desire into Bob.

Paul Plews

When Lindsey got the place in Putney, Bob hired another smaller unit in the Village, and the plan was that he would get things organised and then move to Putney, which obviously never happened. I wasn't there for the move from the studio, because I got my first real job in August, for Nottinghamshire County Council, to shoot 50 portraits for a new museum up in Ashington, where I'm from.

When I got back after the move, it just…something had changed, something had really changed in Bob.

Lindsey Carlos Clarke

Before he got really ill, he said to me, 'All my pictures – I think I've chosen the wrong ones off the contact sheets.' I said, 'Oh no. Oh no. We're not going down THAT road…'

Paul Plews

It must have been September when I came back. As soon as I met Bob, after I'd come back I gave him a call and told him I was here again, and I think he got me to come in and give him a hand in this new place he was using before he moved to Putney, and the whole atmosphere was different. I think part of the reason was the studio. Lindsey was looking for a fresh start, for Bob I think it was almost an admission that he wasn't at the height of his powers any more, that he wasn't the force he had been. It felt quite sad. That's how I always felt when I met him, like something had gone that he was never going to get back. I always used to have funny conversations with Bob. One day he'd been a bit down, and I'd asked him what was wrong. He told me that he'd always thought that he could do anything that he wanted to do, always the sort of person who thought why not, I'm fairly fit and I can do anything, and I think that on this one day he'd finally realised that he was never going to win gold in the 100 metres at the Olympics. Seems odd, but he really felt that up until then it was somehow still within his grasp. One day it was possible, and the next it had slipped away from him.

Crena Watson

I had the studio below him at The Village, that converted old school in Battersea. I had been there for six months when Lindsey and Bob got the studio above me, and I thought, 'Awful. Pornographic photographer moving here, Lindsey with her tits out etc.' I thought I would dislike them immensely.

It was about 14 years ago. Our first proper conversation was when we went to a pub for lunch, and I thought, these two are crazy. Lindsey did most of the talking. Together they were mocking me a bit, sussing me out. At the beginning I felt there was a side of him that wasn't very kind, but as I got to know him more he was kinder than I had thought. He would always find your weak spot and exploit it. My biggest fear was one day ending up living in a bedsit with a bare light bulb and a dripping tap, and so he used that. But in a way I was stronger than him. He said I reminded him of his first girlfriend who was very bossy and very scary. He was scared of you if you were blunt and strict.

Scarlett Carlos Clarke

Do you know Crena? She used to work in the studio below him. My dad called her boyfriend Ivan the Inseminator, and one day Dad stole his clothes, and wore all his suits. And then there were the door handles. Ivan had ordered some really expensive door handles for about £300, and we found out about this, and we bought the crappiest little wooden door handles and wrapped them individually before sending them to him, and he went absolutely mad.

Crena Watson

Bob and Scarlett had the most beautiful relationship I've ever seen between a father and daughter. They're quite similar. He adored her to pieces, he really did. He brought out a lot of artistic things in her. People say he kept on treating her like a little child, but that's lovely isn't it?

I didn't like his work at all at first, but now I appreciate it. I always think I know exactly what's good when I first see it, but with Bob's work I misjudged it. I still don't really like the sex thing. He hated my fashion work and laughed at it, and I didn't like his women in rubber, because I felt it was dated. But when he did that story in the *Sunday Times* with the teenagers, I loved that. The boy, and the couple next to him kissing. That's when I started to realise what he was about. He used the same flash as Weegee, and I bought one and he told me how to do it. I love that social reportage – it's actually quite difficult to do, and he did it beautifully. He wrote so well too, and some of the little films he made for Scarlett are wonderful.

Most photographers are very secretive and jealous of other photographers, but Bob wasn't. Every time I did some new work I'd ask him to come down to have a look, and he'd advise me in the most honest way. I started on my abstract seascapes, and he really helped me with those.

Hopefully I helped him a bit with digital. When that came in he absolutely hated it. He was a printer, and overnight everything you've known goes. I introduced him to Danny Chau, the digital printer, and that changed his mind. He could see that things weren't that bad and he started to get his head round it.

When he was in a restaurant he was restless, always looking to leave, unable just to relax and have a few drinks. He always said things like, 'Oh, you youngsters…' and I'm 50 now, so I wasn't that much younger than him. He always felt that with photography changing so fast…

It changed so much even from when I started. You used to be respected and paid properly and appreciated for your skill and knowledge. And that just suddenly went. He was like a god, and that was just taken away. The big budgets didn't happen any more, there were all these younger art directors who didn't know who anyone was, or what was good and what was bad. It changed so quickly – it was shocking. Nothing to do with digital, actually. When people say, 'It was digital,' that's rubbish. That's just a tool.

It was in the early 1990s that things changed. They had the recession and stopped paying proper prices, and they found that young people would do it. They could use someone who's not so good and then retouch after, so I suppose digital played a small part. It just became tacky. I used to walk around in Paris and see beautiful posters, and now it's all just things that look like they're for ASDA. Those changes frightened him enormously, and he could see that it would never change back. It frightened me too. I was on the cusp of the good times, but he had had the good times all his career, and then suddenly things drop, and no one knew who he was or wanted him much. Quite apart from the worry about money, you'd feel that everything you had worked for your whole life – all your skills and talent – is now nothing. And a lot of photographers commit suicide. It's quite common.

Simon Garfield

Wikipedia has a separate category for 'Photographers Who Committed Suicide', and as well as Bob and Terence Donovan the list includes George Fiske, Diane Arbus and Kevin Carter. But the list is shorter than the one in the category 'Artists Who Committed Suicide' and 'Journalists Who Committed Suicide'.

John Stoddart

Our friend Patrick [Lichfield] embraced digital photography, spent a lot of money on it, but he later regretted it. He said he lost everything because of it. I'm sitting there with Barry Lategan and Patrick said, 'I regret it with all my heart. All of my photography has gone.' He said, 'I have no travel, no one wants to take me away.' But he opened it up for everyone else.

Lindsey Carlos Clarke

Bob saw people shooting digital and then looking at screens or the back of their cameras to see what they had, instantly. But Bob did Polaroids. Often he wouldn't let people see what he had. It was a power trip. It's like a gun.

John Stoddart

I think it's over for someone like me, truly it's over. I reckon I've got five years left. They don't care. Recently I was photographing Boris Becker, and his people had never worked with a photographer using film. He had never seen Polaroids. It was a Polaroid Land

Camera, and he was saying, 'Ooh wow – what's that?' At the end they were all gagging for a Polaroid, and of course I wouldn't let them have one. They go for £500 each, my Polaroids.

Film photographers are becoming artisans. I will end up as some broke fella, but when you'll get photographed by me it will be a true photograph. You'll pay for that – for the chemicals and the dark-room and people mixing it all with dirty nails. It's humanity.

Lindsey Carlos Clarke

Bob used to say, 'It's funny when people say that my pictures can be easily reproduced. It would have been easier for Constable to reproduce *The Hay Wain* than for me to reproduce this exact print.' He meant the depth of the photos, the feel of them – every one unique. The chemistry that went on…they never ever looked the same. How could they?

John Stoddart

Bob was very upset when Patrick died, wasn't he? [Lord Lichfield died of a stroke in November 2005, aged 66.]

Lindsey Carlos Clarke

No, he wasn't upset. You know what he said? He said, 'I envy him.'

• • •

Paul Plews

When I was working with him, especially in his last year, we didn't actually shoot that much, taking pictures once a week maximum. But Bob always managed to fill his time. We used to spend time dropping off signed books at the bookshops, and we used to come up with rather eccentric ways to fill the day. For instance, Bob was asked if he wanted to enter a go-kart race at Cowdray Park, organ-ised by Lord Cowdray. We spent about four weeks building this go-kart that he was going to race.

It wasn't actually like having a job. And he had the place down on the south coast, Bracklesham Bay, and some of the pictures and constructions he built down there I admired more than any of the glamour pictures he'd taken. It showed not so much craft, but more passion.

Crena Watson

At the beach house he was quite a different person. It reminded him of his youth. He would make sculptures. I have the picture he gave me of the robots taken down there, which I love.

Everyone thought he must be travelling to exciting countries all the time, but he was asleep by 9 o'clock in front of the television. Every bone in my body feels that was the real him.

I used to go down there a lot. When he tried to cook in the kitchen he was always overly fussy in case he left a mess. Lindsey didn't like him in the kitchen. She was very obsessive about keeping everything so clean.

Paul Plews

And this fear of growing old. There was always a slightly sarcastic way he had of saying it. There was always a constant tussle between us when he was trying to prove something. I was 23, 24 when I was working there, and he'd always propose a competition to see who could...There was this bar that used to hang across the stairs. It was a big old school place, and everything had been stripped back with exposed beams. He'd always propose a competition to see who could do the most chin-ups on the bar, because he really looked after himself very well and you know, he regularly beat me, although I wasn't particularly interested. He'd always take great pride when he beat me. I think he kept his feelings of inferiority about his age at bay by keeping up with someone who was younger all the time. He convinced himself that he was still valid. We'd be messing around, probably when we should have been working. We'd made these swords out of lengths of pipe insulation, and we'd manufactured them so they had a grip, and then we developed a set of rules. Because Bob hated going to the gym and I was sort of a bit too lazy, we said that every night when we'd finished work at the studio, we'd have half an hour when we'd have a joust. But after 15 minutes we were both knackered. There was always that sense of childish humour. The people who came to the studio must have thought we were bonkers. We used to make films. Scarlett got a camcorder, his daughter, and she would be making films of our friends, and we thought it'd be funny, you know, she'd left it one day in the studio when she'd gone back to boarding school, and we'd make videos with it dressed up in this little Napoleon hat with an eye patch.

He was a great documenter of things. He'd always have a Polaroid book in which he'd write down the various things he was doing. That's a normal photography thing, but he made it very artistic, using his pictures as a collage, suggesting to me that he was a really frustrated artist.

Lindsey Carlos Clarke

Then he used to do his music. For a short while at the end he thought he was going to be a pop star. That's when I really started to think he was going crazy. Not that I have any objection to anybody doing anything they want to do, but he really thought that he could definitely write a pop song and make it a big hit. He went to Barbados and stayed with some friends, and this chilled-out guy who owns a huge company, and likes to surround himself with lots of people in the music business. He had this recording engineer and Bob said, 'I want to play you my music.' I was thinking, oh no, let's not do this. The guy looked at him and said, 'Look, can I say something to you? You are Bob Carlos Clarke, you are a pretty cool hot photographer, you're number one to most people, but why on earth do you want to do this?'

• • •

Crena Watson

I'm very intuitive, I have good instincts about people, and I could never see him doing what he did. Never picked it up. So I got that wrong.

He loved Lindsey to bits. Couldn't show it. When they were thinking of breaking up before, he said to me, 'I can't imagine my life without her.' He said that the rejection from her was like the one he remembers when he was sent to boarding school. Someone's really there, and then they reject you. When he came back he found that his mother had had another child.

The last lunch I had with him was two weeks before he went into hospital. He knew they were breaking up. She couldn't handle it any more. Which is understandable, but I think they're both to blame. I don't think it was just Bob, it was both of them. She became too controlling and became indispensable, and then withdrew, and I think that's an unhealthy thing. And I told her that. I think they had a much better marriage than she actually realised.

He said to me, 'Oh, it's really over now, and I'm going to be in that studio alone.' I said to him 'But, Bob, you've got the beach house,' and it was 'Oh, it's got too many memories.'

I said, 'You'll always be close to Lindsey, you'll be best friends.' And he said, 'All I think about is driving my van into a brick wall.' And then he got tearful, which he would never ever do. So I put my arms around him, and he looked really embarrassed about showing that emotion. He said, 'I've been a very bad husband,' blaming himself.

I was with another friend at that lunch, and I said to him, 'You don't think he'd kill himself, do you?' But he was very English and just dismissed it.

When he was in the hospital I called him on his mobile, pretending I didn't know where he was. I said, 'Bob, let's go to the beach soon and have some fun,' and he said, 'I can't, I've sort of had a nervous breakdown.' He didn't tell me where he was, and that was that.

Simon Garfield

So all these things were happening to him at once: the work drying up; digital; Lindsey.

Crena Watson

It was because she was threatening to leave him. That was the major thing.

Lindsey thought they could still have a friendship, and they would each have their own lives. She obviously needed different things to him. It's very easy from the outside to say, 'They were right for each other,' but you never know the absolute feelings inside.

The studio in Putney may not have worked for him. She would have been living in the house in Chelsea with Scarlett, and he would have been cut off by himself in suburbia. He couldn't cook. He was talking about getting another studio for him in Chelsea near Theo Fennell, but he couldn't see how it would work.

Paul Plews

When I got back from Newcastle I quite vividly remember having dinner with my flatmate and saying that I didn't know if I could go to work for Bob any more because I just felt so strongly that sense of despair he had. You know, despair's not too strong a word; it got to where he couldn't see a point to it any more, in terms of photography. I think once the studio was gone he felt cut adrift, because he didn't have a base any more. You know, the studio was his place, his darkroom. I think he felt a lot that the house that they lived in in Chelsea, as much as he'd been involved with it, he felt that that was Lindsey's domain, and everything was how she'd wanted it to be. I think when the studio was gone it almost felt like he was less of a – not so much less of a man, but less, less of a creative force.

Simon Garfield

Did the new place not have a darkroom?

Paul Plews

No, the new place was actually an apartment really, but had enough space that you could do a small shoot in there, portraits and things, it had enough room.

Simon Garfield

That's interesting, because printing for him was half the work, wasn't it?

Paul Plews

Thing is, at the end I can only recall Bob printing for two days while I was there, throughout the whole year when I was full time. With the *Love Dolls* pictures there was a lot of retouching, a lot of manipulation. Photoshop work which was something he shied away from for a very long time.

Simon Garfield
So that was digital?

Paul Plews
Yes, a lot of it was filmed and then scanned, and then retouched and printed digitally. They're digital prints. For the idea of the show that was perfect, because it was the whole idea of the manipulation of women and that sort of thing, so it fitted perfectly, so he embraced it in that sense. But in a way you lose connection, because printing is such a physical thing – you really are connected: you're picking out the paper, you're putting it in the wash, you're bleaching it back, you're taking light out with your fingers. All these little things build up to the fact that you no longer feel so involved with your work any more. I've found that myself, because I'm now fully digital and it's not a satisfying process in the way that it used to be when you're loading film and you're more involved with the camera. It's almost like an artist uses a paintbrush. There's something material there. For me it was quite a swift transformation, but for someone who printed for 30 years, or 35 years, it was pretty hard.

Philippe Garner
The arrival of digital he made into an issue, but he didn't have to. He could rail against digital or the new generation that were using it, but I'm sure if Bob had applied himself he could have used digital, mixed digital and chemistry. But instead he tended to use that as another excuse for railing at the world: everyone's leaving him behind.

Simon Garfield
So you would just go in and there'd be a general feeling of gloom in the air?

Paul Plews
It wasn't gloom, it was almost like an acceptance that it had ended. In the old place there was a photographer below, Crena, who would end

up buying his beach house, and there was another one further down-stairs, and although there wasn't much communication between them, there was still the feeling that you're around other photogra-phers. Bob really needed that, you know, he was a very social person, he needed to be around people. But with all that, I can remember being really shocked when Lindsey said he'd gone into the Priory. I knew he'd been ill, and I knew he was slightly unwell, but then I'd been away in early March to New York to visit a friend, I'd been away for a week, and I'd come back and he was in there. Maybe I had an idea he was going to be going somewhere to try and get some sort of rest.

Towards the end I would probably do between a day and a half and two days a week for him, but quite often I'd just do a half-day. I'd pop in at 11 if I wasn't working, we'd have some lunch, talk about this and that, I'd do some things on the computer, a bit of filing, what-ever needed to be done. The new place always felt very temporary, not very homely. Bob had never made any attempt to unpack anything, to use the place as he wanted it, and everything was still in boxes. That was the real feeling I got from Bob, that sort of frantic, very sort of anxious feeling. Perhaps I was being a bit naïve, but you never realise how bad things are for someone when they're in that situation. Knowing Bob and knowing his sense of humour, it was almost like you wanted to turn round and say, 'Stop being so stupid, what's wrong with you, you having a mid-life crisis?'

• • •

Jane Chesterton

At the end I felt that I knew Lindsey better than Bob, because she'd tell me all her secrets about him.

Linds and he also used to come together and we'd go out for supper. Often he would try to shock me – tell lots of stories until he got a reaction.

But then Lindsey would also use me as a confidante, and they saw things very differently, so it was a tricky path to tread.

Bob was such a completely mixed person. Remarkably talented, very energetic, incredibly dark and introverted, very passionate. It was almost as if he deliberately cut himself off by looking through a lens. He didn't like being pigeonholed. There were large parts of his character that he didn't like, that he didn't want to recognise. The cosy, comfy conventional bit that was there – that was the bit he really despised in himself.

Lindsey was so important to him. She enabled him to do his work, and she was unbelievably lucky to be so unbelievably glamorous and sexy, and at the same time provide the cosy bit as well. So it should have all been wonderful, but of course life wasn't like that for them. Passionate and thorny all the time.

The age thing for Bob was a huge problem. He really minded about that. He would suddenly go, 'It's all going – my hair and my looks...' His jokes all had that edge, because those were the things he was really scared of. Incontinent old people with no memories fumbling through – he hated the idea of that.

Sam Chesterton

I think because he'd seen his father as an old man. He became absent-minded – the usual thing, and I think maybe that frightened him.

Jane Chesterton

He came round here just before he went into the Priory. He said to me, 'Please look after Lindsey.' I said, 'You silly bugger,' the way one does. One never quite knows – he had such a huge theatrical element to him. But he obviously had black thoughts all the time. And I think his mum definitely had that as well.

When Lindsey told me about him wandering outside and just freezing it was clear something wasn't right. I don't know how long he hadn't been well. But my experience of people who have these problems is that they're fiendishly clever, and very good at hiding things. When he was in the Priory...you know how you try to put yourself in other people's shoes?...when he was in there I couldn't really see a way out.

In the last year or so, whenever we went out, he found it almost impossible to sit still during a meal. He was never great at relaxing, he was always a bit like an elastic band, but he became like a really taut one. He was so impatient – move, move, move.

Sam Chesterton

I saw him briefly in his last year, when he had the *Love Dolls* exhibition in Madrid. I hadn't seen him for years, and he tentatively sent me an email, and I thought that was like a hand coming out. I wrote back saying, 'Wonderful, great that you're coming out, we'll definitely come to the show and do come down to stay with us afterwards.'

He wrote back: 'Oh, I don't know if I'll have time, so busy, and I'll have to spend all my time with Jacqueline Gold.'

So we went up to Madrid – my wife and I and my sister-in-law. We went to the show and Bob was being frantic, I hardly got to talk to him, and he said, 'Let's meet for breakfast.' So we waited for him in the morning and he didn't show up. We rang him and said, 'We've already had breakfast now, why don't we meet up later?' But then he was gone. He said, 'I'll come down to you because I want to photograph fighting bulls.'

But of course he didn't come – that show was only a few months before he died. I had no real idea about what was going on.

I sent him an email afterwards. I had a niece who wanted to become a photographer and was coming to London and I wrote, 'Bob, she doesn't know anything about photography, it would be very sweet if you could take her out to lunch and just put her off or put her on…'

He wrote me this rather pathetic email saying, 'Things aren't good, and I don't think I'll be able to help, I have no studio, I have no life' – that kind of an email.

Then I sent him the wrong sort of email really.

Simon Garfield

A pull-yourself-together kind of email?

Sam Chesterton

No, I didn't send that one, I sent one saying, 'It's not so great being 60…' Not very helpful. But I said, 'But it's okay, one gets on with it, but things are different.' But I had no idea that this was all going on.

• • •

Simon Garfield

Can you tell me a little bit more about what you were saying earlier about how you feel your work isn't valued much any more?

Bob Carlos Clarke *(conversation with author, 2001)*

What the magazines require these days is not art. It's just some sexy pictures of a sultry girl, a formula from which they rarely digress. If you're a guy at KwikFit who fits exhaust pipes there's no point getting clever and imaginative with exhaust because they won't work. It's the same with what I do – there's no point doing strange lighting or funny props because they won't run it. Basically, what I've been doing all these years has become redundant.

• • •

Bob Carlos Clarke *(from the first draft of* Shooting Sex*)*

When people flick through my earlier books and come across a portrait of a much younger me, I know what they're thinking:

'My God, is that *you*!' Or worse, 'How long ago was *that*?'

For the purpose of deification, an early death is essential.

If you want to qualify as a legend: get famous young, die tragically and dramatically, and never underestimate the importance of your iconic photographs.

When I met Robert Mapplethorpe at his final show at Hamiltons Gallery in London he was frail and wasted from AIDS, which was soon to kill him. I complimented him on his great new work, and he commented wryly on the steep rise in gallery prices for his photos since his demise had become public knowledge. As Helmut Newton accelerates into his eighties, you can almost hear the dealers smacking their lips.

Rupert Morris

Helmut Newton, a friend of Bob's, died in January 2004 at the age of 83 in a car crash on Sunset Boulevard in Hollywood. Bob said of him: 'If I could live that long and die in a Cadillac at the age of 83 coming out of Chateau Marmont – I can't think of anything cooler.'

Lindsey Carlos Clarke

He wanted to ride around like he was 19 on his motorbike. He still looked great. I mean most men of his age didn't look like that. But it wasn't enough. I tell you, I used to find him standing in front of the mirror and he was like, 'I can't believe it, I can't believe it.'

Scarlett Carlos Clarke

I remember thinking, I can't imagine him being old. But I never thought he'd kill himself. I did think he could be in an accident, because he was always doing things. I think he hated it…he saw me growing up, and that made him feel older. As I was getting older it meant that I was going to leave.

He hung out with a lot of young people, and people probably thought it was because he fancied them, but I don't think it was. He probably liked people thinking that, but he just liked being around the young. He didn't like Mum's friends.

Emma Ford

I had dinner with him a couple of days before he went into the Priory, in an Indian restaurant in west London. Just me and Bob. I remember saying to him, 'Are you okay?' And he had that look, very distant, and I was, 'Why are you looking at me like that?' He was very emotional, but I never analysed it at the time. Then he came to my boyfriend's studio, where he was recording, and gave everybody his book. And that was the last time I saw him.

Maybe a day or two before the end I was calling and calling, and he had never not returned my calls before. Then I called Lindsey, and she called back to say he was in the Priory. That in itself was – I couldn't believe it. She said he had a bit of a nervous breakdown. I wanted to go to see him, but I didn't want to interfere.

Lindsey Carlos Clarke

He couldn't be there for me because he could hardly be there for himself. He had become something so complex and so difficult that I had begun to mourn for him before he was dead.

20. shall we not do that today? asked lindsey carlos clarke

Rupert Morris *(at the graveside)*
Bob liked cemeteries. He published *The Dark Summer* 21 years ago, and wrote in the Foreword:

'In the city they form oases of silence and seclusion, and their shadowy monuments are full of form and texture. Graveyards exude a strange combination of peace and tension. The mood is unpredictable: they may be threatening in sunlight or tranquil under a thunderous sky. Immortalising a split second of beautiful, transitory youth holds a special irony in such a place.'

He took many of those photographs in this very cemetery. He felt at home here, and there could be no more appropriate place for him to be buried. But before we finally commit his body to the ground, would you all like to take a moment in silence to remember Bob in your own way, in thought or in prayer.

Ghislain Pascal
It was just all about moving Bob on. He did enjoy shooting the girls, obviously, so long as they were fun. If some miserable girl came along with big fat thighs that he had to retouch then he wouldn't

After a night in the clubs, circa 2000.

enjoy it. But he could do all that standing on his head, which is why he started doing the still lifes, and the *Love Dolls* series with Rachel Weisz and all the other ones in that show.

Simon Garfield

When I met him he was already working on the *Love Dolls* show, although he probably wasn't thinking in terms of an exhibition at that point. I think it was meant to be an exploration of women's power in the domestic situation, and there were little powerful jokes in most of the pictures. One of them featured a woman with a red switch on her arm. It was in the off position, but we were meant to believe that if it was turned on there might be some sort of explosive and uncontrollable situation. Another had the word 'Automatic' on her chest. One of them, festooned with a feather headdress, had a large metal key in her back. One of them was split into two halves: on the right was the actress Rachel Weisz, looking rather pissed off in a full latex bodysuit, while on the left was a large bottle of washing-up liquid with the word 'VICE' on it. Obviously it was a pun, but it was so obvious that it seemed to have something more hanging on it. Like most of these pictures, it made the viewer uneasy; they had menace to them.

Ghislain Pascal

It had been ten years since he had had an exhibition. The reason he didn't want to do one was because he was suspicious of galleries – he always felt they ripped him off. I think *Love Dolls Never Die* really moved his work on. There's no doubt that *Obsession* and *The Dark Summer* is dated, but the new stuff was modern. But we had another run-in with the gallery and it all went tits up. This was the cycle towards the end – constantly dealing with problems. A sign of success is getting the cheques, and he was getting the money, but perhaps not what he was due. Listen, he wasn't hard up. But if you do an exhibition you want it to be sold out.

But we got some good reviews, we took the exhibition to Spain, Madrid, in the beginning of 2006, a few weeks before he died. Jacqueline Gold of Ann Summers sponsored it because she wanted more publicity for her shop out there. It was a phenomenal success, we went out for dinner with Saatchis, Ann Summers's advertising company in Spain. Jacqueline was never sure about Bob, but when she came back from Spain she said, 'I got Bob so wrong – he's such a lovely guy. Intelligent, bright, entertaining, good company.' So people started to notice him again, but then it all went very rapidly downhill.

• • •

Lindsey Carlos Clarke

Obviously, in any situation like this you're always searching for answers. The last exhibition – that was when he really came to the edge of success and failure and I really thought he was leaving the planet.

The *Love Dolls* show, the last one, seemed to sum so much up. Before it opened [at London's Eyestorm Gallery] I said to him, 'Okay, success and failure.' I held up my two fists and said, 'This one is success and this one is failure: what does success mean to you?' He said, 'I sell all the pictures.' And I said, 'What's failure?' And he said, 'I sell no pictures.' So I said, 'What about the space in between?'

'Oh, I can't talk about that, can't talk about that.'

The guy from the gallery, Eyestorm, phoned up two days before it opened and said, 'I've got some news for you. Somebody in Switzerland has bought the whole set.' That was amazing, and worth something like £65,000. I told Bob and asked him, 'Where are you now, success or failure?' And he said, 'Oh, that's nothing to do with it really.'

I said, 'What are you expecting to happen, just tell me, the show opens on Thursday and you know, lots of publicity, but are you expecting the whole Kings Road to fill with people with flags and bells and go "Bob Carlos Clarke, oh-oh-oh"? Because unfortunately, unless you're Madonna or Princess Diana or Mother Teresa, you're not going to get that. As it is, you're a very skilled but quite specific, unusual photographer who happens to have been lucky enough to practically do what he's wanted most of his life.' I was worried at that point that he really was getting a sort of deluded sense of grandeur.

Simon Garfield

So he was half expecting that adulation?

Lindsey Carlos Clarke

He didn't say that, and he probably would have said something facetious like, 'Don't be ridiculous,' but in there I really got the sense that he was looking for some sort of monster adulation that just could never be.

I used to say, 'Why don't we just go out and have lunch and just go to the Tate, go and do something like in the old days, like normal people?' We always used to go off and have adventures and find weird locations or wonderful places or strange objects. Regarding work, he said, 'I only really want to take the pictures I want to take and I don't want to do any commercial work unless they offer me something that I really really want to do,' and I said, 'Fine, that's fine, let's do that.' Because I truly believed he was certainly at a stage in his career when he could have done that very successfully.

He was very disturbed by the time Christmas came, Christmas 2005, and my mother said to me, 'God, I'm worried about him, he seems confused,' and on Christmas day he went up to Brompton and made the most bizarre film, running in the cemetery, you could hear him breathing on the camera, jolting around, done deliberately, through the gravestones.

Allen Jones

At the opening of the show he had a kind of installation in the basement. There was a girl sitting on a chair with spotlights pointed at her. He wanted to see my reaction to her. It was done very beautifully. We'd had conversations about how realistic you could make an artificial figure. He had some brochures from Japan and the States of companies that were making sex dolls which…well, you see a photograph of it and you just think it's a real person sitting there. So there's this amazing scene downstairs at the opening, it took my breath away. He said to me, 'It's that [fake] surface, you can prod it, you know.' So rather gingerly I stepped forward and prodded her knee, and of course it was a real figure. He created this really mesmeric image. Something like that – it could have been a presentation at the Turner Prize.

I can't remember if it was that night or not long afterwards that we went out together. He was always saying that he'd take me to some clubs, so we went to a couple of those pole-dancing clubs that he'd taken photographs in, and it was a very sad image, like something out of decadent Berlin. At one of them there was this, just this poor-looking girl who was listlessly doing her stuff on stage, and apart from Bob and I there were two other couples there, one of them totally drunk, and the other totally ignoring the act. Not very glamorous, but interesting that that was our last encounter.

We ended up at 2.30 having a drink and coffee at Le Caprice. He was full of nervous vitality but I had no idea that he was in such a crisis.

Nicky Barthorp

The last time I saw him was at Christmas. I had dinner with them at the house, and I went away feeling extremely sad about him. I constantly write for myself, and I wrote that I had this sensation that he was like a ball of wool unravelling uncontrollably. I felt like he had lost…For me Bob had always lived in this wonderful fantasy land, and created that for other people as well, and I felt that completely unravelling. He was very sweet and dear and very vulnerable. The mood of the evening was that things weren't the same between them, and she was turning her back on him. All evening it was that, and more snide remarks without the humour directed at each other.

The following morning he texted me several times, which he had never done before. He used to call me Agent Orange, and he said, 'Please, please come back to London, it's empty without Agent Orange.' Bob had never ever shown me that vulnerability, and it was a complete alarm bell.

Lindsey Carlos Clarke

In January he just started to behave very oddly. He used to sleep downstairs in the basement. It was like an apartment down there, it was really wonderful, and the original idea was that all sorts of things could happen down there, for Scarlett, for my mother. But now he was down there and I used to come down in the morning and take him a cup of tea and he'd already be up and dressed and sitting absolutely rigid on the bed almost hyperventilating, and saying, 'I can't go on like this.' He'd say, 'I can't sleep, I can't eat, I can't breathe. I think I'm going to do something terrible.'

I knew exactly what he meant, and I'd say, 'Well, shall we not do that today, shall we do something else?'

I rang our doctor and said, 'Guy, look, would you do me a favour, would you call Bob in for a cholesterol test?' Bob had staggeringly high cholesterol, absolutely off the Richter scale, pumping adrenaline all the time. Guy said, 'What's wrong?' I said, 'He's just not right, and I am frightened.' Don't forget that at the weekends Scarlett was home from school, and I was desperate to keep her out of this loop. One night Bob picked her and some of her friends up from a dance, and she said to me afterwards, 'Something's wrong with Daddy,' and I said, 'Yes, I know, he's going to see a doctor.'

Guy said, 'Lindsey, he's having a down time and he's insecure,' and this and that. I said, 'Guy, he talks about killing himself every day. Every day I go downstairs and he'd tell me a new method he'd thought of to do it.'

It got worse and worse, and I got absolutely terrified. When Scarlett was here she used to get into my bed in the morning and say, 'Let's go and take Daddy a cup of tea,' and I used to think, oh God... So we'd go downstairs and I'd say, 'You just wait here, darling, because he might still be asleep,' because I was absolutely freaked out about what I was going to find.

I started to come down quite early in the morning and find the front door here open, and I didn't know where he was. I would remember things he said in the past, like he would ask, 'How fast would I have to drive my van into this wall in order to kill myself?' I'd be in my pyjamas, and I'd be racing round these streets thinking, where are you, where are you? I'd see the van and see him sitting in it and I'd tap on the window and he'd look at me absolutely like he didn't know who I was. 'Bob, what are you doing?'

'I don't know what I'm doing.'

'Let's have some breakfast.'

So finally we went back to see Guy and he said, 'I'm going to suggest you see a psychiatrist at the Priory.' So finally I persuaded Bob to go there, and on the way he kept saying, 'What am I doing here? There's no point, I'm not doing it.' I'd just say, 'Let's see.' You know, I started to really speak to him like a child.

Simon Garfield
When was this?

Lindsey Carlos Clarke
This is now January/February, and we went to see the psychiatrist at the Priory and he said, 'Do you want Lindsey here or do you want to talk to me on your own?' Bob said, 'I don't mind.'

I sat there absolutely silently, always hard for me, and he asked Bob, 'What do you feel?' and Bob then said: 'Look, the real problem is, I've done something absolutely terrible. I've done these pictures for this DVD, and it's all these models, and they haven't signed a release form, and they're all going to sue me. There's 15 models and they're all going to sue for a million pounds, and that's 15 million pounds, and I don't have 15 million pounds.'

And he went into an absolute tirade about this stupid DVD. I rang Ghislain who said there was nothing wrong. 'I promise you on my life, it's all fine, all those pictures have already been cleared.'

The psychiatrist then said to me, 'Lindsey, can you just fire off some words about Bob and what he's like as a person.' I said: 'He's clever, he's manipulative, he's magical, he's mercurial, he's dangerous, he's cruel.' I just went through it all. And he said, 'That's very interesting, you've given me an absolutely classic description of somebody who is very creative, but right on the edge.'

He said to Bob: 'You are a very sick man. You have three choices. First choice, you do nothing and I do not know what the consequences of that will be. Second thing is you come to me as a day patient and Lindsey brings you here every day and she picks you up at night, but that is incredibly difficult and stressful and dangerous for your family. Third option is you come into my hospital and you spend some time here and we try and help you.'

We went to him on a Friday, and he said we should think about it over the weekend and then call him on Monday morning. He said, 'The only way I ever lose patients like you is when they kill themselves.' And then he said, 'Do you ever, have you ever considered killing yourself ?' Bob said no, and at that point I said, 'That's not true, every day you tell me you're going to kill yourself.' So we left there, came back here for the weekend, Scarlett came and had a very hideous weekend with me feeling awful the whole time, and trying to make things normal and everything feel okay. All the time this was going on, Bob was sitting rigid at home, staring at a newspaper or at a wall.

On Monday morning very early I knew I couldn't make the call from here. I rang the secretary for the psychiatrist and I said, 'I have to bring him in, we are in serious trouble here, we are off the Richter scale and I'm frightened.' I said, 'We are insured by BUPA but I don't know whether this is covered,' and she said she was sure it was.

I said to Bob: 'I think we need to go back to the Priory, we need some help.' He said, 'I don't want to do that.' They'd given him various antidepressants and pills, but I don't think he was taking them. Guy had given him some as well. A little pill for this, a little pill for that, so he had a complete phobia about what somebody might be doing to him.

I said, 'Let's just pack a few things in a bag.' By now I'm shaking so badly trying to keep this together. I said, 'Look, we'll just get in the car, we'll just go and see them and have a chat.' Getting him into the car, absolutely terrifying, stood on the step, had him here for three-quarters of an hour, couldn't make him move, couldn't make him get in the car, finally got him in the car, and I'm thinking to myself, this really isn't happening, Lindsey, you are not doing this, you are somewhere else and you are looking through a glass somewhere. Please God, why is there nobody here to help me?

And who would you ask?

So: got him in the car, and then as we drove up the road I saw him reach for the door and I thought he was going to throw himself out of the car. So I quickly hit my switch and he looked at me and said, 'What did you do that for?' And I said, 'Oh, it's just a habit, I always lock myself in the car,' which I actually do, but…

Got up to the Priory, got out of the car, stood for another half an hour before he went up the steps, finally got him in there. We were there most of the day, and they found him a room. I mean, it's not a great place, whatever anybody thinks, it's quite depressing that place. Various people came to see him and I finally drove away at about 6 o'clock that evening and I was shaking so badly I could hardly drive the car. Jane rang up and said, 'What's going on?' and I just burst into tears and said, 'I don't know, I don't know.' She said, 'All right, don't drive, pull over, I'll come and get you.'

Scarlett Carlos Clarke

I try to remember what I was thinking at the time, and I can't. I went to see him in the Priory when he was really ill, and all I remember is him looking at me, and it was as if he was thinking, 'I know that this looks weird, but I don't know how to deal with it, I can't come out of it.' It was seeing someone who was the biggest thing in your life just deteriorate…someone who's got that character not being able to get it back and just turn into his worst nightmare.

I knew there was something wrong, because the night I went back to school I said to Mum, 'I think Dad's being really odd, really quiet, so not like him, hardly talking at all.' Then the next day, when Mum said he's gone into the Priory, I wasn't even that upset by it. I just thought, he's going to get better.

Lindsey Carlos Clarke

Then I went back to see him. I spoke to the psychiatrist who said, 'We are very worried about him, he's sort of psychotic, he's sort of burbling about.' He told me he thought the police were outside, he told me the *News of the World* were after his computer, he told me that he'd done terrible things although he couldn't tell me what they were, and he went on and on about this DVD again and how we were going to have to sell everything and how he was so sorry, and that my mother was going to have to sell her house and live in a cardboard box.

It was just agonising, but I had to put on a terrible British face – 'Marvellous, right, well, I'll bring you another pillow, and then we'll do this,' and he kept saying to me, 'I need more socks and under-pants,' and when I opened the cupboard when he'd been there about a week there must have been 30 pairs of underpants and 30 pairs of socks there, but still I was asked to bring more. And he said that everyone else was dressed in designer clothes. Not that I noticed – they looked like they were wearing filthy old tracksuits to me. He looked shocking in himself, absolutely shocking, like a ghost, absolutely drawn.

He said the food was awful in there, and I said I could come and eat with him one night. He said, 'No, you're not allowed to.' But of course you are, so we went to an incredibly nice sort of dining room with buffet food, seriously good food. He said he didn't speak to anybody in there but while we sat there on our own everybody came up and said, 'Hello, Bob.' Then he told me he was in terrible trouble because he wasn't going to the right classes, and I thought, you think you're at school.

And then he started to rub my cheek one night and said, 'Poor Mummy, poor Mummy.' And I thought, please don't do this, please don't do this, this is agonising, this is so painful, please don't do this. I mean, watching somebody go completely mad in front of your eyes is just terrifying. And then he'd have very lucid bits and he'd send me a very lucid text.

Geraldine Leale

Three days before Bob died I had this dream, and I only told Lindsey about it recently, because I didn't think she could cope with it before. I saw Bob as this Little Cedric-type character, and he was at a party with six women, I dare say the most important women in his life. Certainly I was there, and Lindsey was there, Nicky Barthorp was there, and I think Sue was there. He looked at me and held his fingers to his lips, making me know he didn't want to talk. I looked at him and I said, 'What's wrong with your legs?' He just had this look of pain.

It bothered me so much that I got up and drew a picture of what I'd seen. I'll show you what it was…It was a body, like that, normal, his arms and head and torso, and then from the waist down these little spindly legs with those boots that kids wore when they had polio in the 1960s, with callipers. His feet were just dangling like a puppet. He was attached to this structure like this…

Simon Garfield

Geraldine drew a grid, parallel lines with metal. I said, 'Oh, a Zimmer frame,' and she said:

Geraldine Leale
No, a railway track.

Lindsey Carlos Clarke
After he'd been there about two weeks they said to me he was definitely responding to treatment, and he was going to be all right. It
was going to be a bit of a slow haul but he was getting there and I
sort of felt slightly relieved but I also felt my God, I'm in the middle
of buying this studio down the road here, selling this one up here,
trying to keep sane, trying to tell Scarlett…I had to tell Scarlett he
was in the Priory. And she said, 'Is Pete Doherty in there?' And I
said, 'Not at the moment, I don't think.'

I thought, I'm going to get this terribly damaged human being
out, and so my plan was get that studio on the road as fast as possible. I said to James we should get them to paint it as fast as
possible, get all his stuff laid out so it feels like home.

And then it was the last Friday night. I took him some food in,
and I said, 'Scarlett's coming home from school tomorrow and we'll
come and see you. We won't come in the afternoon but we'll come
in the evening, okay?' And I said goodbye to him. There's this corri-
dor where you walk down to this crossover point where the rooms
are. I remember standing at the end of it and looking back and
seeing him standing there, and I remember he said goodbye to me
and I just had that very odd feeling: I don't think he looks much
better to me.

And Saturday morning came and I got some lunch together and
picked Scarlett up from Clapham. She said she wanted to go shopping and what time are we going to see Daddy, dah dah dah. It was
about two o'clock and the doorbell went and there were three
policemen on the doorstep and I immediately thought, oh my God,
I've been caught, haven't I, putting on lipstick in the camera, oh
God, on the mobile. All the things we do in the car. Absolutely thinking it's me. I always think it's me because I was arrested when I was
17, so I always think, oh, they've come for me, my daughter's going
to see me arrested.

There were two men and a woman and they stood there for quite
some time and they said, 'Can we come in?' And I said, 'Absolutely.'

And I'm thinking, what's going on?, my brain going through everything, you know, and then she said what relation are you to Robert Carlos Clark and I knew immediately, I knew immediately. And then I looked and I realised they'd got London Transport Police here on their uniform. Scarlett was here and just burst into tears at the top of the stairs. And I said, 'Hang on a minute, you have to go now.' I just wanted them to leave. 'I don't want to know anything, just go away, I can't, I can't, you can't do this in front of her, you can't do this,' but they weren't going and she came down the stairs and she was absolutely, she just didn't, she couldn't couldn't assimilate it, it was fascinating, she went straight to the freezer and got out an ice cream.

I never forgot it. I just looked at her and thought, that's amazing. And they said, 'Look, we need to talk to you,' so one of them stayed downstairs with her and they came up here and they said to me that he'd jumped in front of a train.

21. we really have to manage this, said ghislain pascal

Lindsey Carlos Clarke

They said, 'Do you want to call somebody?' And I said, 'Who? Why?' So I picked up my phone and went through it, and all I could find was numbers for restaurants. I finally up came with Geraldine's number and I pressed the button and she came on and she said, 'Hi, darling.' I could hardly say it, I couldn't verbalise it, it was like none of this is happening, I'm somewhere else, aren't I?

I said: 'Bob's killed himself,' and she said, 'Oh fuck, okay, I'll be with you, I'm coming, I'm coming.' And then the police spoke to her and I don't know, it was like that weird film, *Picnic at Hanging Rock*, where everything goes into slow motion.

Geraldine Leale

Lindsey called me and said, 'Something's terrible happened. Bob's dead.' So I drove round immediately, driving crazily to get there, and it was like the car wasn't moving. When I got there Scarlett came out and her little face was heartbroken. I put my arms around her and the first thing I said was, 'Your daddy was so proud of you.'

The police had just left. We just sat there. I figured my role was not really to say anything, just to be a presence and support whatever happened. There was nothing to say. My sister had died two years before, leaving children roughly the same age as Scarlett, and I knew that all you could do was just sit there with them.

Scarlett Carlos Clarke

I remember the day it happened so well. I didn't even cry, I don't think. I had come back from school on the train that morning, we were having lunch at home and Mum said, 'Oh, Dad's getting better.' I think he'd already died by then, but she didn't know. She said, 'He's going to come out next week and check his emails.' It seemed so normal.

When the police arrived I was upstairs, and I thought, he's just been in a car accident. Then I looked at Mummy's face and I was, oh my God.

Then I went downstairs. It was like a dream. I was talking to a policeman about his family – I was interviewing him, loads of questions, 'Are you married?' I remember going to the fridge and getting ice cream to try to be as normal as possible.

That evening Mum went out, which annoys me. We had already arranged that this old nanny of mine that we hadn't seen for ages was coming round. I think Mum was trying to make it as normal as possible, like everything was going to carry on as before, but it still pisses me off.

Geraldine Leale

Lindsey went out later. I could tell from her face it just hadn't sunk in. I think if it had been me I would have stayed at home and probably gone hysterical, but I know that Lindsey always had a problem with the way her mother dealt with her own father's death – her mother went hysterical. Lindsey can't deal with hysteria. But she was so overwhelmed, she couldn't deal with her own feelings. I don't think it's something Scarlett will fully understand until she's older.

• • •

Philippe Garner

I'm trying to remember the last time I saw him. I think it was at the opening of his last show at Eyestorm in Maddox Street, and on that occasion, and on the few preceding occasions which were reasonably widely spaced, he had certainly appeared to me more and more, what's the word, there was a wild and deeply anxious look in his eye. There was a kind of…he was being eaten up by uncontrollable forces. I guess because it had perhaps always been a part of him and to some extent was incremental, it didn't shock me so much.

But on another occasion there was an opening at the Royal Academy where Allen Jones was previewing a new piece, and I guess I should have figured I'd see Bob there as he was a friend of Allen's. It was one of those moments where I turned round and he was there and it was like boom, I was shocked by the look on his face.

I'm trying to remember when I took that portrait of him in the darkroom, because I often look at that and think how there is something just so intense and dark going on in his gaze. He was not a happy man, I mean really tormented.

At Maddox Street he was on an up, it was his night, there'd be a kind of revved-up tension about him. He'd keep it going and it would be fine, but it was the sort of tension that ultimately was enormously draining on those around him. Maybe I felt, oh, I'm getting a little older and calmer and more cynical, I feel a bit of a disconnect with this need, this frenzy. Because even things that I'm intensely passionate about I can still talk about reasonably calmly and I don't necessarily need to lay them on other people. I just felt, fond as I was of Bob, that, phew, after a little while with him you felt the need to come up for air.

So I was conscious that Bob was not going in a healthy direction, but I guess I'd been conscious of that for a long, long time. That he'd boxed himself in psychologically to certain traumas, forces that were going to consume him. I just kind of figured, well, he'll balance things and just keep going, because that's what life is about, you just keep going, and actually hopefully he should be able to count his blessings, which were considerable, you know, although he never realised them: he didn't believe that he was materially secure, but he was; and although he may not have regarded family life as the central plank of his life, he had all the ingredients for a fulfilled family life if he'd known how to accept them, how to embrace them. And professionally there was always the need for reassurance and never the confidence to feel that he could say, 'I really have created something and I can be proud of it.' Nothing was good enough or right enough or got him where he wanted to be. And his circle of friends – it was probably a diminishing band of the faithful.

John Taylor

I loved Bob, and Amanda loved Bob too. What happened to him…We were both shocked, but not entirely shocked. For so many of us our children just pull us through. I get low sometimes, but I never get that low so that I wouldn't want to be around my kids.

They don't see life's riches.

James Betts

When he died I hadn't seen him for a good couple of months. I'd tried to see him, I'd phoned him a few times. I spoke to him a couple of weeks before he went into the hospital. I said, 'I'll pop in and see you.' He said, 'Oh, I'm not feeling very well, I've got pneumonia or something, come and see me soon.' And I said, 'Okay, no problem.' And that was the last time I spoke to him.

I didn't know he was suffering from depression, and when he died it was an enormous shock because I didn't even know he'd been in hospital. When he died I'd been away for the weekend, I'd been to Paris. On the Monday morning a friend of mine phoned me, another photographer who used to work for John Stoddart, and he said, 'Have you heard the news?' And I said, 'What news?' He said, 'Bob's died,' and at first I wouldn't believe it. I thought I can't phone Lindsey because if it's a prank or if it's real, if it's not true it's a terrible thing to call someone about and if it is true, you know, it's only just happened. So I called Ghislain and asked him and he confirmed it and he said there was an accident, he was hit by a train.

And at that stage obviously Ghislain wasn't really divulging what had gone on, he was kind of protecting Lindsey a bit and the family and so I was thinking, do you know what, originally I thought he must have been scavenging, because he was a terrible scavenger and I thought, I bet he was scavenging on a rail track, a terrible accident.

And I was in an absolute state, terrible shock and upset, and eventually when I called my friend back who told me I said, 'Just to let you know I've had it confirmed – yes it is true.' He said, 'I've found out a few more things since then, John Stoddart had bumped into Marco and Marco had said that Bob was depressed and had been in the Priory,' and then my head started spinning and I was thinking, what the hell's happening? Because I knew nothing of this and I couldn't take it in, and I was a mess for a couple of weeks after that, it was horrible. Eventually I took a few days before I did eventually call Lindsey and strangely enough that made things better, because I could see that she was dealing with it and she was okay and she and Scarlett were all right.

But for her, the way Ghislain describes it, it was not entirely unexpected. Obviously it is a shock, and especially such a horrendous way of doing it, but apparently, well, I'm sure Lindsey will tell you, he had threatened several times before.

Philippe Garner

He'd kind of figured that there was one sure way out, and sooner rather than later. There was this time where he just moved into the basement where she was surprised to see him alive in the morning. She would have to go down before Scarlett went down just to check that there wasn't anything awful waiting.

He wanted recognition. What recognition did he want that was so missing for him? The money wasn't a key, he didn't spend money on anything hugely significant. He had this old motorbike, he went on holidays, and she looked after all that anyway, she had a tremendous instinct for upgrading their properties. He was probably a bit like the queen with money.

But I guess that he just didn't get people discussing, engaging, acknowledging his photographs at the level at which he needed them to be read. To a great extent, the British don't do the dark intensity that he represented, so they'd pick at the surfaces of the pictures. In his mind they would kind of trash them or cheapen them, and this would infuriate him because it made him feel so completely misunderstood, and feel that all his effort was wasted. It's like railing in rage. It was a degree of rage at an uncomprehending world, which would only serve to reinforce the decision he'd made a long time ago to inhabit another one, the world of his imagination. But he needed some succour and companionship within it. Actually he needed more support helping him maintain one foot in each. But he couldn't get people to go the full journey into his world; they didn't know how, they didn't want to, they didn't need to. So I think he valued me as somebody who could be a knowledgeable and honest and constructive commentator on his work, but also as somebody who could truly connect to the issues. You might think, 'Well, that surprises me about Philippe, because he seems such a well-adjusted gentleman,' which I think on balance I am, but that doesn't mean I don't have areas which I am very happy to keep alive, because I don't want to shut down all the...I don't want to block out fears, anxieties and all these things, they're a part of you.

I knew that Bob and I were speaking the same language, the visual territory that he created is terrain I can make sense of. Not just as a voyeur unpicking it with elegant words, but I feel it, it troubles me, those are my...I've lived parts of it, mercifully not in the ultimately destructive way that he did.

And the concerns about growing old...The horror, the horror of his own mortality and decay. I just see that as such a kind of hopelessly negative way of reading things and again, a reflection of his inability to find perspective.

Scarlett Carlos Clarke

I remember the day of the funeral, and I remember planning it and saying, 'Play this music,' and planning black and red roses.

At the funeral I felt as though I was on my own in there. Mum said there were men sobbing at the back, and I never noticed that. I didn't feel sad that day at all. It didn't feel like anything.

When he died, things changed at school. I think before, people thought I had some sort of perfect life, and then when it happened they were really horrified, but it was a bad thing they could relate to, a problem.

James Betts

The funeral was quite surreal. In one way it was good because I saw a lot of people I hadn't seen for a while. There were a couple of other assistants and a couple of the girls and we ended up, we just went out and got really drunk and sort of drowning our sorrows with pints of Guinness in his honour.

Lindsey had made sure it was a cool day and he got a stylish coffin, and we had the Rolling Stones playing. She made sure that it was just fairly close friends, not that they had much family at that stage. I think there were about 80 people in all. It was a beautiful clear April day.

Ghislain Pascal

He never talked about suicide to me. Lindsey said he talked about it all the time. Never to me. It wouldn't have crossed my mind. He absolutely doted on Scarlett – they had such a fantastic relationship. He could spend the whole weekend with Scarlett on his own, and I don't think there are a lot of fathers that are that comfortable with girls of that age. She used to turn up and spend all day in the studio when he was photographing. He would photograph her all the time, and she photographed him – that one photo we used time and time again for all the obituaries. She took that picture. It would never have crossed my mind that he would...

I don't think he could ever realise, until it was about to happen, he couldn't imagine life without Lindsey. He thought he could, but he couldn't. I'm not saying that drove him to the end, but whatever it is that triggers depression, then the chemicals start moving in...it was all tied together. He couldn't imagine life on his own. He couldn't cope. He was completely dependent on her for everything.

Oh yes, they were living together until the end. It must have been incredibly hard for her. But in the end he pushed her away, and she didn't have any choice but to think about moving on. He realised what he was going to lose, and it sent him over the edge.

Simon Garfield

Did she blame herself at all?

Ghislain Pascal

No. She couldn't. Absolutely she couldn't. She stood by him until the end. Most women would just have said, 'Oh, fuck it.' But she's a fantastic mother, and she was a fantastic wife to Bob.

When he died, everybody wanted to talk to her, but I just forbade it. I don't think she would have been in any state. *Grazia* magazine fucking biked round a letter the day after he died asking her to do an interview. I rang them up and told them to fuck off – so insensitive.

Simon Garfield

How did you feel when you heard?

Ghislain Pascal

Obviously immediately I was very upset. But post that, I'm not very sentimental. Even when my own father died, I'm quite 'just move straight on and get on with it'.

The first thing obviously was dealing with it. It happened on a Saturday. I said to Lindsey, 'Do you want me to come round?' and she said, 'Don't bother.' So the first thing was, fuck, how's this going to get out? It's Saturday, so okay it's not going to make the Sunday papers because it was now 3 o'clock. By Sunday I was thinking, God, we have to manage this.

I spoke to a couple of people, and they said if you commit suicide it can affect your insurance and all that kind of stuff, so I rang Lindsey on Sunday and I said, 'We really have to manage this because it could affect you,' and she's: 'Let's just leave it for a while…' And then on Monday morning I said to her, 'Look, we have to release some kind of…we can't just ignore it because it's just going to come out on its own and it won't be pretty.'

So I sent a mass email out to everyone, all our contacts in the media and newspapers, saying that I was very sad to announce that Bob had died. I didn't say how. I think I said 'killed by a train'. It was worded to sound as though he had been involved in an accident. We made it sound like an accident. And then the first story appears in the *Evening Standard*, just a short news story saying he'd been killed in a train accident. And then of course the speculation started. We just denied it all. I said, 'We've got nothing to say.' And then slowly it all came out.

There was a whole lot of interest as well because he'd walked out of the Priory, and there was a whole lot of anti-Priory stories at that time.

We didn't acknowledge or confirm that he'd committed suicide until much later, and that was when he was buried. Lindsey wanted it in the eulogy, she wanted to tell the story. It was a fantastic eulogy, very honest.

And before then the obituaries, and I thought, he's getting exactly what he wanted – recognition at last. He was only going to get more and more famous. The response was phenomenal, all over the world.

And of course after his death he gets into the National Portrait Gallery, whereas before he never did. He was forever offering pictures to them. When I talk to people at the National Portrait Gallery now they're all Bob's fans, so maybe he did it in the wrong way.

After his death Scarlett said she wanted to enter the National Portrait Gallery Deliotte Portrait Award, so I spoke to a guy there, and they said, 'I'm really sorry, she's too young to enter, but we'd love to have her portrait in the gallery.' That great picture she took of her dad on the edge of the bed. She was just over the moon – she was the youngest person ever to get a picture in there. She was 15, but she'd taken it when she was about 13. And then they took out one of the pictures that Bob had given them but they had never exhibited – of Marco Pierre White, and they put it up.

Paul Plews

I tried to help, be positive about things in a different way. I would suggest things about maybe shooting this, or doing that. But all the time everything was still in the boxes, like he knew. It was weird. Everything was packed, everything was neat and it was bizarre. From September when he moved out of the studio, his photographic passion almost ended there. Because we did shoot some pictures, but nothing that he felt strongly about.

The last thing I shot with him was a picture of a girl on a motorbike, sort of lying over a motorbike, a girl called Cat.

Simon Garfield

Gosh. He took those famous pictures of Sue and then Lindsey on a motorbike, so it came full circle.

So you went to New York, and you were there for a week, and you came back and he was in the Priory?

Paul Plews

I think he may actually have been in before I went, but I made a fatal mistake, still not grasping the full reality and gravity of the situation. I would speak to Lindsey and Ghislain and ask how he was, but I never called him myself, which was a real regret, because I just got the impression that he should just be left to rest and it seemed like it might stress him out. I always sort of felt that maybe I should step back a bit and let things improve. But he was in the Priory for a week or so before I went away. I think it was the day after I got back from New York that I got the call from Lindsey in the morning to tell me what had happened. So yeah, that horrible feeling of: could you have done something? It was a big regret that I didn't go and see him.

Lindsey called me and I just knew before I answered the phone. I don't know what it was, but I just absolutely knew what she was going to tell me. God, yeah, I mean it destroyed me, I took it really badly. I didn't realise how much it had affected me, but you know, sort of months afterwards, it was a weird feeling that I'd been close to…We had more, it never felt like a working relationship, it was more like a friendship. It didn't really sink in until the funeral. I don't know if Lindsey's told you, but she asked me to take pictures at the funeral, so Lindsey's got the pictures somewhere. It helped me in a way, doing that, because it was something that focused me on other things, something practical.

I took people going into church, various things outside, and the burial service. I got the pictures developed and contacted and didn't even look at them and still haven't really seen them properly. Lindsey just took them and put them away. I think she only looked at them properly about a year later. She told me she saw something in them she hadn't seen before. I don't know what it is, but something very fitting about them.

It felt like a very heavy responsibility having to take those pictures. Like a wedding I suppose, you only get one shot at it. Taking them felt so wrong. You know, funerals are so…it's not something you want to forget, but it's a time to be with other people who are there, and in a way it separated me from that. I didn't feel like I could get close, not so much because I feared offending people, because everybody knew that Lindsey had asked me to do it, but it would still be an intrusion into grief, no matter that I was his friend. And there's that famous picture of that woman crying with her handkerchief.

The worst thing afterwards was that the official story was that it was an accident, and of course I get a phone call from someone at the *Daily Mail*, asking me for a comment. A lot of people knew that I'd worked for him, but I never had the conversation with Lindsey as to what the actual story was, or what I could say or what I couldn't say. It felt like a dirty secret.

It took me six months to feel I'd come out of something, like something had lifted. They say that bad luck comes in threes; I had a good friend that died a few months earlier, then Bob, then a family member a few months after. With the other two it was that cliché – you've just got to make the most of what you've got and the people that are around you. But the thing with Bob was, I could never take anything positive out of it. It always gave me a feeling of pointlessness, perhaps the same feeling that Bob had. He had a wife whom he seemed to have a great relationship with, he had a fantastic daughter, they had an amazing house, a place on the coast, and it just seemed on the surface of it, it seemed like such a waste. It didn't ever give me any feeling of appreciating life more, which sometimes in a perverse way can come out of death. But it did make me realise that in a photographic sense I should really pursue what I want to do, what I love doing, because Bob obviously felt he was doing things he didn't want to do quite a lot of the time. That's probably the one thing that came out of it.

• • •

Lindsey Carlos Clarke

They wouldn't let me see the body. I mean, my desire to see it was pretty high, I can assure you.

Simon Garfield

And they wouldn't let you because it was just too horrendous?

Lindsey Carlos Clarke

Apparently. But I think that because Bob was such a visual photographic person he would probably have wanted me to. I sort of felt that it was something I should have done. I didn't see my father after he died and my mother always said, 'When I'm dead, you must have a look, it's absolutely fascinating, dead bodies, quite extraordinary.'

I kept thinking, I just have to see him, and in my mind what's so strange is I think I remember it happening, like I was there, but of course I wasn't there. I have this whole view of the train and this thing and the train, and all the people, and the body on the track, I can see it. And all the commotion.

Simon Garfield

Crena told me that the police came round with several things in plastic bags, including his Nokia phone, which apparently was still working, and his broken glasses. I never even knew he wore glasses.

Lindsey Carlos Clarke

I have been to the railway crossing, another girlfriend took me and she got in a terrible state and burst into tears and I just felt absolutely nothing. She said to me, 'I thought you were going to jump.' What I realise is that he must have done it in a split second. Bob had fantastic timing, and he must have had split-second timing because you have to go over the barrier and then into the train: it's two jumps.

Simon Garfield

The decisive moment…

Lindsey Carlos Clarke

Scarlett was only 14, so I said, 'Well, the funny thing is, bodies are weird on impact because I once saw a dog that got hit head-on by a car and it looked completely whole but it was all jelly inside.'

I started to get this terrible thing in my stomach here, which just shook all the time, the most awful jelly-like feeling. I couldn't get it to stop. And I spoke to a friend of mine whose brother killed himself about two years before, and she said it's exactly what she had. She said, 'It went after we had the funeral.'

Simon Garfield

Did you still believe he would kill himself once he was in the Priory?

Lindsey Carlos Clarke

No, I didn't. I thought what was going to happen was that I was going to get a very damaged bird out of the Priory. I thought he's going to move into the studio, and there's this rather wonderful beam that hung in the middle of it, and I thought I was going to find him hanging from there one day.

But I sometimes think this was absolutely on the cards for a very long time. When I went to Isabella Blow's memorial, Geordie Greig [editor of *Tatler*] spoke, and he said, 'Isabella always talked about wanting to kill herself and normally Isabella got exactly what she wanted.' But of course there's a thousand unanswered questions. I do miss him in extraordinary ways. You know: 'Where are you?'

We both camped upstairs after it happened. Scarlett slept upstairs with me and we used to sit up and talk; she used to look at endless pictures, and that was when she came across that thing he had written: 'If you want to qualify as a legend: get famous young, die tragically and dramatically, and never underestimate the importance of your iconic photographs.'

And that was the point we really decided to go for it at the funeral, not to hide anything. When we were making the arrangements I could hear Bob's voice in my head all the time. The funeral people said, 'You can have mahogany...' but I could hear him saying, 'I want it fucking piano black.' I went to the cemetery with Scarlett just before the funeral, and we laid out all the chairs, and I said, 'Daddy's going to be in the coffin here…' We did the whole dance so that she wasn't freaked out when it happened. We went to talk to the grave diggers when they were digging the hole, and we made our choices about the music. I just had to let her feel the whole edge of it. I was so terrified of the day, of her falling apart and not wanting to fall apart.

At home people arrived all the time. Endless police here with fingerprints and forms to fill in, then suddenly they'd arrive with yet another plastic bag containing a wallet with a big gash through it.

And we got thousands of letters. Most of them from people I had never met in my life who were suddenly best friends of ours. I'm sure they thought they knew Princess Diana as well. Scarlett and I used to open them and say, 'Okay, what are they asking today? Do we want to go on their catamaran?' And people ring you up crying. If anybody dies, don't ring them up crying, ring them up and say, 'What can I do?'

On the day we had Ghislain here, and my friends Geraldine and Jane, and Nicky Barthorp was over from France and Sam Chesterton had come from Seville. We drank two bottles of very expensive champagne, I was completely ratted, and when I opened the door to the man in the hat, the funeral director, we all just fell about laughing. So off we went up the road, and the problem was that up until that time all the people I'd seen had been my close friends. Now it was all these others looking absolutely awful, what a miserable bunch. We were on another planet. Apart from the fact we were in terrible shock, I was absolutely out to lunch but absolutely determined I was going to take complete control of the situation. It was completely like a film set.

There was absolutely no crying on that day, couldn't do that, too much to do. It had to work, it had to fit together, it had to be absolutely as he would have wanted it. I also made a decision it was better for me, or I thought that I might just go up and over the edge.

Bob couldn't bear crying women, so we had sobbing men. In the past if I felt very unhappy, I would go out and get in the car and drive away, there was a special place where I used to park where I could go and cry, and sort myself out and come back. I had various places, I had the place in Fulham, round the back where we used to live. Then I had a place just as you go through the cut through Hyde Park, and I had…there were all sorts of locations that would be suitable for this particular mission, and it's quite an addictive behaviour because I still have it.

22. my heart just turned over, said sue frame

Sue Frame

You know, when I heard about his death, a lot of thoughts and feelings sort of carried me back to my years with him, and our time on the beach in Ireland. When I wrote to Sam Chesterton and I was kind of mulling over the whole thing, I said something I perceived happened to Bob was that in a sense all the family values had been ingrained in him and he actually loved them, and yet in his quest to be this very successful photographer, and to mingle with the rich and famous, I think he actually lost his way. I think he lost his integrity in a sense, because in many ways he still wanted all those family things, but he couldn't meld the two together.

Scarlett Carlos Clarke

What was Sue like? Was she dull? Apparently she's quite nice. Obviously Dad liked her because she was pretty. He did horrid things to her. She probably has an ideal image of him, which if their relationship had gone on he could never have lived up to.

Sue Frame

About six months before Bob died I was in England, and I'd seen this book he'd produced, and I just thought, you know, maybe if I did see him again it would just be nice. I could just take some good memories to finish our story. I'd gone up to London with my sister and we'd actually gone to the little bookshop in Charing Cross Road where I believe he sold a lot of his books, and there was nothing there, but the man who ran the shop said, 'Actually he might be in this afternoon because I think he's bringing in a new consignment.' My heart just turned over, and I thought, I don't think I've actually got the nerve to go through with this. What if he's disdainful, what if he's…?

I had imagined that he was on the pig's back, that he was having a wonderful life, and little did I know that he was going through hell. Anyway, my nerve failed me and I said to Al, 'Come on, I actually don't think I can do this… I couldn't bear it if he rejected me now.' And we walked out of the shop and we were walking down the road and Al said to me, 'Oh come on, Sue, this is a chance, take it.' We walked back again, and I got to the door and I said, 'I can't, I actually can't do it.' And that was that.

That was September 2005. And then the following March I got the news that he had killed himself and that he was desperately unhappy, that he and Lindsey had basically parted.

I had no contact with him at all after our divorce. I just thought I've got to make a clean break because if I don't I won't stand a chance of rehabilitating myself. I was in a shocking state when he left me; I'd had my heart torn out.

My cousin in England read about it in the newspaper. He didn't have my email address so he emailed my sister, who had also known Bob very well and been really fond of him in the time that we were together, and she rang me from Barbados. She just said, 'Look, Sue, sit down, I've got something to tell you.' It came as a dreadful shock. I was very shattered. I am so sorry that I never took that last chance to make peace with him. I mean, I don't know if he actually really cared or not, but for me I really felt I needed to do that.

Simon Garfield

It sounds as if there's still a part of you that loves him. Clearly you have such strong feelings towards him even now.

Sue Frame

Yes, I think because of the type of person he was he left an indelible mark on me and I have carried it through the years. When his mother died he never told me about it, but I think I had a sixth sense about it. It's that kind of silence you feel when someone isn't there.

I was talking to a friend this morning, saying that this thing had come up with you and that I'd be speaking to you and she said to me, 'Oh, Sue, I think this is the best thing you could do.' She said hopefully it will be cathartic.

A lot of his work I don't like that much. I can see the genius in him, and I think I can look at it and think, yeah, that's pretty amazing, but some of it doesn't appeal to me. But the pictures of the forks and knives he did, those sort of things, they're beautiful. You can really look at them. His print work was so incredible.

For nine years I was his muse and I was his model and I went through all the rough years with him, all the times when we didn't have money and I was there for him. Look, whoever he was with, he would still have gone on to be the great photographer that he was, but I believe I played a big part in it. He used to say to me, this was one of the mean things he'd say, he'd say, 'Oh God, it's such a pity you don't have bigger boobs and longer legs. I could have made a fortune out of you.' You bastard.

Simon Garfield

Would you have attended his funeral had you heard about it in time?

Sue Frame

If I'd been in England? I might have. I would have found it difficult seeing Lindsey because, well, I just would have. I don't know if you can understand that. Did Lindsey ever mention me to you?

Simon Garfield

She did. All she said was that you were very sweet and very good for Bob but he, as you said, he wanted something that was going to take him to another level. I'm not sure she'd say it in these words but I think the temptation for him was too strong. She hasn't said anything uncomplimentary about you, but why would she?

Sue Frame

I'm not trying to put her down but I'm trying to tell the truth. I feel if something's going to be written, it doesn't matter who it's about, one must tell the true story.

• • •

Jane Chesterton

Oh, I miss him a great deal.

Lindsey called me. I was stuck, I was down looking after my parents. She rang up and said, 'The police have just come round.' Luckily her friend Geraldine was on her way. I remember being deeply shocked.

Afterwards Lindsey spoke to me every day – she used her friends very well. At the funeral I actually saw my own grave – another woman with my name. It was all rather photographic. It was wonderfully lit, and great music, a lot of light overhead, stylish. I think he would have approved. He'd taken a lot of photographs in that graveyard. But it was all rather wonderful. I was with Scarlett, and Lindsey was brilliant, kept herself completely together, probably floating through in shock. She was very professional about it.

Sam Chesterton

I was really shocked when it happened. I think Janey must have told me. He always used to joke about it, or at least I always thought it was a joke.

Sue Frame

After it happened, Sam said to me that to die like that in front of a commuter train at Barnes…how domesticated. He said you would have thought he would have at least chosen the *Orient Express*.

Sam Chesterton

At his last show in Madrid there were a lot of new images, but also some familiar ones from those cemetery days, and the one used for Scottish Widows. Of course we used to have this cemetery life, going for picnics in Kensal Green and Highgate. Very beautiful – the nicest thing on a lovely day, to go a cemetery with a white starched tablecloth and put it over somebody's grave and have a bottle of champagne.

Nicky Barthorp

I wasn't aware that things were so bad at the end. I heard about his death through a friend of mine. I rang Lindsey immediately and she said, 'I want you to come now,' so I flew over, and stayed with her for a week. She was hyper, and sometimes I would sit with Scarlett as Lindsey went off alone organising everything. She was in control most of the time, but there would be moments when she broke down. She's not a natural blubberer, but I have this image of her sitting with her head between my legs, uncontrollably sobbing. She was dealing with everything in a slightly robotic fashion, 'under control, under control, under control' was her main thing, particularly for Scarlett, and I said to her, 'The shock is going to hit you.' And then when the funeral was over she flew over to me in France with Scarlett for a couple of weeks. She spent a lot of time trying to understand what had happened.

Emma Ford

Somebody called me, I think it was Vanessa, and told me that he'd committed suicide, and I didn't believe it. I thought maybe he'd done a runner, one of his pranks. I'd completely dismissed it – I thought maybe he'd gone to Brazil or somewhere. Then James Betts called me and I knew it was true.

I was completely crushed. I felt guilt. I still feel guilty that I didn't go to see him, because I'm convinced I would have been able to stop him. I felt as if I'd lost my arm. I still feel like that.

I think of him every day. Yes, every day. I moved to LA shortly after he died – it was one of the factors that prompted my move, leaving everything behind in London. I miss our friendship. Things would happen in the day that would remind me of him, or that I'd want to tell him about. If I had any problem, he'd be the one I would call.

Allen Jones
I had no idea that Bob had killed himself. I was away. It must have been a couple of weeks afterwards that Lindsey rang up, and said, 'You heard what he did?' I didn't know what she was talking about, and I thought, oh no, what's he done this time?

She said he was dead. I felt very sad. What an awful situation.

• • •

Remembering Bob Carlos Clarke (*from Coilhouse website*)
You were one of the greatest fetish photographers that ever lived, and it's not the same without you.

What passes for fetish photography these days is a joke, and you were one of the only people who got it: you understood that it was more about clothes staying on than taking them off, that it was all about contour and personality. The girls in your pictures didn't make stupid faces while holding their boobs, and you could bring sexuality to any object you photographed, even if it was a stone or a fork.

Wish you were still with us.

Six Responses to 'Remembering Bob Carlos Clarke'
December 30th, 2007 at 10.01am
Kevin Says:
Amen.

December 30th, 2007 at 11.57am
Io Says:
Wow, I never realised that the album cover of *Phantasmagoria* by The Damned (one of my faves of all time) was one of his photographs. I'm so glad that someone else also sees that the allure of fetish photography lies more in creating an erotic sensation with lighting, movement, the gloss of a latex gown,

and the threatening point of a stiletto – rather than an obvious *Maxim* (or *Penthouse*) image where the end culminates in REMOVING the very thing which is fetishised (the latex, the corset…and so on) or using the item(s) merely as peripheral props. I have so often been deterred from typical fetish photography because the photographer seemed most interested in how I was going to get naked. Nudity can indeed accent some images very nicely, and I have nothing against being the subject of an erotic image, but my idea of eroticism doesn't lie in spreading my asscheeks. An image that stimulates mentally as well as visually is always the most erotic – Bob knew that, and with his death went a great artist.

December 30th, 2007 at 5.37pm
Zoetica Says:
That last image – glorious!

December 31st, 2007 at 12.03am
Buny Says:
I absolutely adore the last image. I had a Damned poster of that image in high school. Something about the light breaking through the clouds and the goth lady – it is just Neat Neat Neat! Thanks for finally letting me put a name to that image!!

January 9th, 2008 at 9.29am
Andrew Carlos Clarke Says:
Think about you all the time – always love you. Andrew c c.

January 29th, 2008 at 3.03pm
Andrew Carlos Clarke Says:
Truly great man – he just didnt know it.

• • •

Sue Frame
I've got boxes and envelopes full of stuff from him, from our time together. Mostly pictures he took mostly of me before he had really

hit the big time. Snapshots, out at parties, more informal things. I put them away in envelopes and hadn't looked at them for donkey's years, and some of them I thought maybe I should burn because I don't want my children to see them. On the other hand I've been very open and honest with my kids on the most part. I've got one son at home, he's 17, my eldest son is doing a design course, and my daughter is working for a house and leisure magazine.

Simon Garfield

Are they interested in him at all?

Sue Frame

I think there is an interest. They say that in a way they would have liked to have met him, but then sometimes they're quite derogatory and say they'd like to punch him and get that parrot back for you and silly things like that. They think he sounds different, and it's something they hadn't been exposed to, and they're intrigued.

Me? I'm making jewellery. We do sometimes talk of coming back to England. We're having turbulent times in South Africa at the moment – I don't know whether you're heard about all the xeno-phobia? I've been backwards and forwards to England because my darling father passed away recently and my mother had a stroke, so it's been a terrible year.

I tried to get in touch with his brother Andrew several times, but I've found him very elusive. I know he was working with an estate agent at one point, but I just couldn't seem to penetrate the barrier, and in the end I gave up.

Simon Garfield

I met Sue a few months after we had spoken on the phone. She was over from Johannesburg for a month, staying in her mother's bunga-low in Goring-by-Sea, West Sussex, and visiting her daily in a nearby nursing home. She made tea as she told me about her three children, and then she showed me photograph albums of Bob and her from the 1970s. There were photos from their wedding and wedding reception, from their time in Worthing and London, and from trips to Sam Chesterton's deerkeeper's cottage. They looked happy, and there was much clowning around in crazy clothes and masks.

She had also brought over two letters, the one Bob sent to her parents when they split, and the one he sent to her a few days later. ('Something tells me that you may be getting away from me in good time.') Sue asked me about Lindsey, Scarlett, Sam and Geraldine, and said she had found the experience of reliving her time with Bob both painful and cathartic. As she spoke she played with her ring, which Bob had bought for her more than thirty years before.

epilogue

23. sometimes i don't really think he's gone at all, said scarlett carlos clarke

Simon Garfield

I had been waiting at Luciano for about an hour before Marco Pierre White actually turned up. It was a Saturday morning, and we were there for the hanging of the last 20 or so of Bob's pictures. Marco owned Luciano with Rocco Forte – it was his upmarket trattoria in St James's Street, Piccadilly. He'd probably hate the idea of it being called a trattoria, but it did provide unpretentious comfort food. It was clearly Marco's idea to cover almost every inch of the walls with Bob's photographs. There were the famous pictures of Caprice and Jerry Hall, and some lesser-known models too, all in various stages of kit off or wearing rubber. There was that early classic picture of a girl dressed as a mermaid. It wasn't all girls – there were those still lifes of knives and forks that Bob had found by the Thames, and a pair of shoes with stiletto heels, and a close-up portrait of voluptuous roses with dew on them that his wife Lindsey had stolen from a nearby garden. But even the roses and stilettos and the entwined forks were sexually charged. Many of the pictures featured in his last *Love Dolls Never Die* show and now also featured in a pamphlet-sized catalogue with a black cover called *Dark Genius*.

Philippe Garner had written a brief introduction, the first piece of Bob criticism he had written since his death.

Philippe Garner *(from the* Dark Genius *booklet)*
Bob's constant obsession was to make photographs, and he did so at full intensity. He succeeded in creating on paper a compelling vivid universe drawn from the deep, dark well of perverse imagination. His was an unnerving world of sinister eroticism, of goddesses, warrior queens and avenging angels, a strange territory of carnal icons, of myth and phantasm. Bob's pictures – loving, skilfully and meticulously crafted – were always profoundly imbued with the complexities of his morbid, often melancholic perceptions. They are filled with tension and a mood of anxiety, their frequently aggressive sexual elements coloured with a diabolical sense of mischief and ambivalence. Bob's pictures have a powerful, often disquieting presence. They have a forceful integrity and effectively reveal the conflicts and the creative single-mindedness that defined his spirit. These photographs will ensure their author's longevity.

Ghislain Pascal
The first thing we did after Bob died was the permanent display at Luciano, a living exhibition of 50 of Bob's pictures, and we sell them off the wall and we get lots of enquiries. When Marco first opened Luciano it was full of old gold-framed pictures with ornate country scenes. Now the restaurant looks so modern. George, the maître d', is always telling Marco that people are complaining, but I think Marco likes that.

The more people eat there, the more we sell. It's where all the hedge funders go for lunch. And we don't have to pay Marco commission, so the money goes straight to Lindsey.

Marco was amazing when Bob died – he was one of several people who offered Lindsey money. And he paid for the reception at Frankie's after the memorial service.

Simon Garfield
There were already about 30 large prints on the walls, and a couple of guys were hanging the final 20. They were introduced to me as

'the finest picture-hangers in London'. Bob's wife Lindsey sat at a table telling stories about her husband's photos. She mentioned that what surrounded us now were 'really just posters. They're still beautiful, but they're not like the ones I've got in the archive, the ones Bob printed himself. They just breathe. They have such depth and they shine.'

Lindsey said she was used to waiting for Marco; occasionally he wouldn't turn up at all. Her phone rang: the ringtone was 'Gimme Shelter' by the Rolling Stones. Bob loved the Stones – they played 'You Can't Always Get What You Want' at the start of his funeral and 'Sympathy for the Devil' at the end. He photographed the Stones on several occasions. And as she was saying this there was a commotion by the door, and Marco appeared with a small entourage, including his girlfriend and the man in charge of food at Selfridges.

Marco was wearing baggy cords and wellingtons, and he'd just come in from the country. He put three boxes of ammunition on one of the white tablecloths, and began to enthuse about hunting deer, and how he liked to shoot at things from the window of his car. Then he looked around and announced that he wanted to paint all the walls 'fucking red'. There wasn't much you could see of the walls between Bob's pictures, but I think he meant he wanted red on the ceiling as well. 'Fucking red,' he said to any waiter who was straightening the knives ready for the lunch crowd. 'What do you think? Red! Fucking red everywhere!' No one was in a mood to mess with him; I got the impression that no one ever was. If you questioned him, questioned his red, he would take you to pieces.

He ordered drinks for everyone, and began talking about his divorce case. He was called over to the private dining room where there was a problem with the size of one of the new pictures. The plan was to hang it on the door leading to the disabled lavatory, but the door frame was just a little too small to accommodate it. The main loos were downstairs – to pass them you passed those famous Bob photos of Marco that had helped launch him as a celebrity, with sweat and a meat cleaver – but the disabled one had to be upstairs because there wasn't a ramp. The obvious solution was to choose a slimmer picture to go on the door, perhaps the one nearby of a woman with an intricately tied paper bag over her head, but Marco had another way forward. 'Just raise the handle a bit.' This would have been a good idea had the door led to the kitchens, but someone immediately pointed out that if you raised the handle, a person in a wheelchair wouldn't be able to reach it. Marco realised this would be a problem, and then said, 'Fuck 'em! Terrible thing to say, but fuck 'em!'

Bob Carlos Clarke

I shot Marco when he was starting out with his first restaurant, Harveys. He was pushing himself and his chefs right to the limit of their endurance, and, at the end of a gruelling, sweltering, swearing shift, he'd crash out under a restaurant table and sleep there until dawn. Marco wanted to do a book, and I was intrigued by the contrasting worlds of his infernal kitchen, and the effete gentility of the restaurant, separated only by a sliding door. On one side, the muted buzz of gourmets and gastronomes punctuated only by the chink of cut glass and fine china, and the other, like the worst corner of an Hieronymus Bosch. Lindsey encouraged the idea of a book collaboration, and came up with a title: *White Heat*. For a year or so, I hung out at Harveys, shooting for the first time on 35mm Polapan, the film that gave the book its characteristic gritty, damaged charisma.

After Marco and *White Heat*, chefs and cookbooks were changed for ever.

Simon Garfield

Marco then moved back into the main dining room and talked a little about how much he missed Bob, and how much fun they'd had. Bob had been his best man at his first wedding, with Lindsey the only other witness. He said that he thought Bob was one of the few people who understood him – he called him his 'prop' – and even though they could go months without seeing each other, they would pick up a lovely conversation as if they met every day. Marco said he liked getting drunk with him. Some people, he said, were aggressive and vile when they were drunk, and Bob could get very moody. Marco, on the other hand, said that he became like a Labrador, unaggressive. 'I would take my cock out and it would be funny. You know, I'd take you along with me.'

'Got a name for your book yet, Simon?' he asked me.

'I was thinking about "Exposure".'

'Yes – fucking great. Call it "Exposure". You know I don't mean what I said about the disabled, don't you?'

He said a few nice words to Lindsey and Scarlett, who had turned up after Saturday shopping. And all the while, the two picture-hangers were going round the room filling in the gaps, until there was just one picture left. It was an old one, from the 1980s, a girl with blonde bubble hair a bit like Tina Turner's. Bob had titled it *Girl In Stockings,* and Lindsey said it was one of the key pictures that had inspired Bob in his theme for his second book, *The Dark Summer.* The woman's waist was in a corset, and you couldn't see her face at all, only her hair, this corset, her stocking tops, one bare arm apparently cupping a breast, and her naked back. It reminded me of a photo taken in Paris in 1939 by Horst P Horst, but Marco didn't make the same link. 'Wait a minute,' Marco said, squinting at the photo. 'I thought I recognised that girl.' He paused for effect. 'I FUCKED her!'

No one was in the least bit surprised. 'Years later,' Marco explained, 'she did a kiss-and-tell with one of the papers. I didn't mind at all. It was elegant. She said I was great.'

Lindsey Carlos Clarke

In a funny way they were fairly similar, Bob and Marco, they both were so special and so talented and you'd always have to be walking on eggshells with them because you never quite knew what they were going to do.

I do remember, and I don't know if he's like this any more, but Marco hates bald people. A designer came to see him for the book he was doing with Bob, and Bob just knew he was trying to say to the publisher 'you've got to get this man out', and Marco suddenly stood up and said, 'I'm not doing it, I'm not doing this book,' and he just walked out of the meeting. They were all these very grown-up, rather silent sort of publishing types, all rather horrified. And then on another occasion he did have an interior designer turn up at Harveys who was bald and I think he threw him physically through the door. A long time ago Marco said to me, 'I never wash my hair – you never see a bald tramp.' I don't know what he meant by that, but it's true.

What happened was, we met Marco when he was dating a girl we knew. We went to her flat and she said, 'I've met a mad chef, I want you to meet him.' So off we went for supper, Bob and I, and Marco told me all about how he was going to make this thing with this pudding, and then he was going to get this bull's bladder and fill it with meat and then it was going to explode with flavours on your plate. I listened to all this and I thought, either he is seriously talented or he's bonkers.

Then he opened Harveys and he was living all over the place and working 25 hours a day, and he came and he said to us, 'Somebody has offered me £2,000 to do a book and I don't know what to do,' and at this point we'd done quite a lot of publishing. Bob said, 'Be very careful because you need to know what you're doing and you need an agent.' He asked Bob to do the pictures, but Bob said he wouldn't take pictures of food. Then one day Bob suddenly said to me, 'I've got an idea. What I'd really like to do is Marco absolutely rock 'n' roll in the kitchen.' Nobody had ever done that.

Marco was already getting a reputation, but what Bob did was to put it into photographs, which nobody had ever done before. Before that it was always chefs in chef's whites, and precious food on plates. But Bob wanted to do the image of the chef – all the sweat and work. Bob used this special technique, this special film which gives the pictures that sort of ripped-away feeling. They did that project over nearly two years. It was a nightmare, thousands of photographs just to pull out the bits that you're interested in. The first publishers we approached said, 'Well, we think it's quite an interesting idea but it would probably only sell a few copies in London.' Then the publishers who agreed to it lost their nerve and decided they also had to have proper food photographs. Don't get me wrong, the food and recipes are amazing, but if we redesigned it today we would do it differently.

Simon Garfield

Someone told me that *White Heat* was the first modern cookery book to sell over a million copies, the first to treat the chef as a hard-living celebrity whose sweat was an integral part of your supper. You see that everywhere now, most obviously in Gordon Ramsay, one of Bob's protégés. Lindsey told me that Ramsay desperately wanted Bob to photograph him, which he did on a couple of occasions, but apparently it was a difficult situation. She said that Bob felt he'd just be repeating himself.

Philippe Garner

I remember the last exhibition in Maddox Street. I got into a conversation with somebody on the opening night, sort of explaining to him what I found so extraordinary about Bob's pictures. In some of the pictures he'd posed the girls as if they were those renaissance *figures écorchées*, where the skin's removed and you see every twist and turn and every muscle and contortion, not in exaggerated contortions, just to direct and guide the poses to create this sense of energy under the skin, a kind of dynamic within the body, and that to me was the level of mastery which I had enormous respect for. It might be the equivalent in another era of the kind of fabulous draughtsmanship that could reveal these nuances, just a little shift of relief in the body that would explain its dynamic. Bob had that kind of skill: he developed through his career a tremendous refined eye and engagement with his subject matter. But I fear that I'm describing subtleties which, while they're certainly present, were missed by many who were distracted by the more obvious symbols of the accoutrements of sexuality.

• • •

I had lunch with Lindsey on Tuesday. I just think they're trying to get their head around how to build the basis of a market at another level of prices because the material's finite and is a long-term source of revenue for Lindsey and for Scarlett, and they want to raise the bar now rather than later so that they start to get a decent return for things and have a strategy for the sale of material. I mean we were talking about various aspects of it, whether it's time to put an important piece up at auction, and I'm not sure that it is, yet, because the only things that have been at auction, and there's been relatively little at auction, and the price reference points are lower than they deserve to be, so to then go in with a piece at a much higher price, even though one would try to explain why one was thinking bigger, is, it's perhaps asking too much of the marketplace and possibly what's needed is some gallery presentation at much higher prices with red stickers so revive the primary market and the secondary auction market will follow naturally and inevitably.

It's tricky, because for Bob to make a really strong price at auction you have to put up something really good, which is why I think it would be better to do it having built a little momentum through other means. You know, I get this all the time, people who have a stock of something and they want to test the market and they just want to put a mediocre thing out to test the market and I say that won't test anything, that'll show you that people don't get excited by the secondary things. And yet they're not in a rush to sell a really great piece because they're not replaceable and I think that by a really great piece would mean either one of the really top early artworks or a just killer later print made by Bob, a big silver print, where there may be just two or three examples of that particular image and so on. Those giclee prints and editions are a part of the fodder but it's not those that are going to make the running to set any benchmarks.

We had lunch at Luciano. It's kind of wallpapered with Bob's pictures; it's a frieze, terrific.

Curiously, we noticed when we were there the other day, it wasn't designed that way but it's a very male place for lunch. I guess St James's is such a male territory, so different from 100 yards up in Bond Street and Fenwick's and all that strip which is really ladies-who-lunch area. When you're south of Piccadilly, the clothes, the shops in Jermyn Street, it's all male stuff, St James's is the wine, the hat, the shoes, the hunting gear, the whole business, and it's the area of choice for so many fund managers, it's a relatively recent thing, dense with those guys who all have power breakfasts in The Wolseley, which is great, and if they get a moment from their busy day they pop in and see what's on the walls at Christie's. They constitute a significant client base. We went in at one; at 2.15 they're all gone, back to their desks, back to making money. It wasn't one of those leisurely sequences of people.

And one thing we touched on was the phenomenon we've seen in the last few sales of the incredible value attached to certain celebrity subjects and wild prices we got for Kate Moss pictures and others. There's just a huge appetite: I guess it's just totally civilised and victimless trophy hunting. You don't have to go out and shoot wild tigers or whatever and stuff them and put them on the wall. You just go to Christie's and buy a picture of someone and hook it on your wall and there is that kind of kudos attached to it. I did tactfully say to Lindsey that maybe there are some pictures where it's the combination of a great photographer and a very high-value subject that one might sell, and Lindsey rightly said, 'You're right, but Bob hated that whole thing.'

Ghislain Pascal

Philippe also said to Lindsey, and it was great advice, 'You mustn't let Bob's past life consume your new life. You mustn't get involved in the day-to-day sale of his pictures and running his estate, or else you'll never move on.'

So that's where I come in. We're constantly selling his pictures. And just pushing the prices up. If we sell something and then get another enquiry about the same or similar work we push the price up a bit further. And we have a number of galleries that sell his work that I work with. Some bloke came along recently and bought four pictures for forty grand. And last week we sold £110,000 of Bob's pictures. About 20 of them – all the *Love Dolls*. Just as well. Lindsey is a compulsive property purchaser.

There are three ways we make money. There's the direct print sales: Lindsey gets 50 per cent, and the dealer gets 50, and then I take a cut from their share, usually 10 per cent. Then there's the picture syndication, which splits 50/50 between me and Lindsey, and then there's his photo books, for which I take 10 per cent.

You can imagine: after Bob died, all of his pictures have gone through the roof. There was one price before he died, and another one now, obviously. We do sell new ones printed after he died, but they're still in the editions, stamped and signed by Lindsey. The largest editions are 100, but some are nine. We have also started some new editions after he died, and some of those are in Luciano as well.

They're cheaper. Philippe Garner from Christie's has helped me with that, because otherwise I'd flog everything. He said that basically you can do whatever you want, but the most important thing is to have absolute control and transparency. And don't flood the market.

In terms of prices: the signed giclee editions, when Bob was alive they were £500. We're now selling them for £10,000–£12,000. If they're not signed they're £2,000. The silver gelatins that were £800–£900 when Bob was alive, a little 12x16, they're now £25,000. Those are the ones that people really want, and we haven't released any more of those. But you've seen the archive: there are cupboards full of beautiful silver gelatins we haven't released in any edition.

Simon Garfield

Ghislain had developed a sideline to accompany his sale of Bob's prints. This involved ensuring that no one else could sell them without his permission. He had solicitors who were suing people in America for selling unauthorised digital copies of his pictures, and there were also people who he believed had used ideas in Bob's pictures and were passing them off as their own. He needed commercial lawyers and intellectual property lawyers. One current case involved going after a soft drinks company for what he thought was a blatant use of one of Bob's trademark images: a woman licking her lips. Caprice had posed this way in the photos accompanying my *Esquire* article all those years ago. And a close-up of Kadamba's lips and tongue featured on the cover of the *Shooting Sex* book. A similar close-up image appeared on a recent advertising campaign, and Ghislain wasn't impressed.

Ghislain Pascal

It's pure Kadamba! She was the girl who dated Noel Gallagher, and the fact she was murdered – that's why it made the news. I think Kadamba was her real name.

Anyway, we're suing them. My boyfriend Chris saw this image all over London. That tongue is so specific. That tongue is very erotic and specific. That's such a Bob thing…and look at the lips and the teeth. Anyway, we've gone for them: £50,000 we're asking for. We're on it. We'll get it. Or we'll get something, there's no doubt in my mind. Next we'll go to the papers, give them a bit of a scare. They'll go into crisis mode. It's the sort of thing Ann Summers would love, a bit of controversy, but it's not how this big drinks company will look at it. They're saying they never heard of Bob Carlos Clarke, but in our next lawyer's letter we're going to ask who the photographer is, and wouldn't it be funny if it was one of Bob's old assistants? Bob had loads of assistants who are now very successful photographers. Or if the photographer is under 40 they would have inevitably studied Bob at college. That would put a hole in their argument straight away. The one thing about Bob is, you go to any ad agency and you'll find all his books – *Obsession*, *The Dark Summer*, *Shooting Sex*. And even if it doesn't get any money, it's good PR for Bob, isn't it?

Paul Plews

It's hard to know about what will happen to the value of his work. It's difficult, because Bob made a real effort not to shoot celebrities. But you look at the National Portrait Gallery and what they do; they collect pictures of notable people. I can't ever see his work getting past that cult following that he's got, but of course I'd love to be proved wrong, because I'd like it to be seen by more people.

Every time I see Lindsey, she keeps asking me – because I haven't got any of Bob's pictures – she said straight away after he died, which one would I like? I've never been able to pick one, but now it's past the time of being too painful.

I really like the picture of the girl with the bag over her head, I think it's quite extreme, but it was one of the first ones I worked on with him. Bob had seen some Japanese pictures he had liked, and so we found this girl and a guy who was experienced in doing the tying, because it's a real art in itself. And it was such a charged atmosphere because the girl was really getting off on the whole experience. She had this bag on her head, and as more and more time went on you could almost feel the atmosphere she was so engrossed in it. It was really sort of captivating to watch.

Simon Garfield

Was that a sexual charge?

Paul Plews

Yeah, absolutely. I think Bob shot ten rolls of film, so she maybe stood there for ten minutes or so, and the atmosphere…you can imagine, coming from working in an estate agent's and then it was sort of, 'Oh my God, what have I let myself in for here?' I've got a fantastic Polaroid of the whole scene. The woman looks amazing, just a fantastic shot, just one of those things we were so lucky to capture.

Simon Garfield

Arriving at Lindsey's house in Chelsea for our last interview, there is artificial turf on a ledge outside where she plans to put her pots.

She gives me a large scrapbook with many of Bob's love letters and notes to or about her from the early days – a memoir of a courtship with lots of nicknames and rude jokes. There are also many humorously doctored photographs and collages with Lindsey in various states of undress.

She also unfurls a very large family tree: at the top of it, the Clark name is missing the 'e'. She says: 'They managed to trace the Clarke family all the way back to Cromwell. They found they were related to Joshua Reynolds…'

She then drives me a mile or so to the apartment where she has stored all of Bob's photographs, negatives and artefacts. It is part archive, part home for her builder Arthur, who sleeps among some of Bob's most famous framed pictures. It occupies the ground floor of a large house consisting of several studios, originally built by a father who hoped his children would all become artists. The ground floor is occupied by a large table, several easels, a sink and a newly installed bathroom, with the walls full of Carlos Clarke prints and props – the crown of thorns, detritus from the beach, scissors. His 12-string guitar leans in one corner, above a wooden model of a horse. Upstairs is a galley bedroom and many Ilford photographic paper boxes containing his original prints. In one box are pictures of the photographer.

Lindsey Carlos Clarke

Look how long his hair was. Well I took those…Oh my God we were like children. Fucking hell. These pictures are how I remember him best.

Look at these ones, recent. Look how mad he looked…that's terrifying, definitely frightening. There's something disturbed going on there. But when he was relaxed he looked amazing. There he is with his father, so sweet. He loved his dad. Having his cereal, with Molly, his maid. And that's at Ballyquin…

• • •

Isn't it funny what happens to mouths? If you look at his mouth here, when he was still pretty good-looking…Oh my God, Mr Angry on his motorbike, I'm trying to date the coat…Bob in drag, Bob and me, a long time ago in St Tropez. I was pregnant with Scarlett when these were taken. This is Pippa – she was a child model. Bob would never let us go on holiday on our own, we always had to have another woman to entertain him, so he could take pictures or what-ever…These are in a cemetery – his two favourites were Brompton and Kensal. This is Marrakesh somewhere…another one in the cemetery…His bubble car…smiling, look how happy and young he was there. Ah, now we're getting somewhere: this is Bob in Ireland with his first real girlfriend, his first lover, Carol. And that's Sam and Jane, Uncle Andrew, that's Paddy the dog.

These are interesting – this is Sue and him. These are the pictures that made me so angry and jealous [self-portraits, with Bob hold-ing Sue, and Sue naked]. He did one as a Christmas card, and he put it through my letterbox. We were already having an affair, and I was so angry. Poor Sue, still, it wasn't her fault, and anyway she was saved.

Simon Garfield

The archive also has two long shelves of books. These contain the photographer's inspirations and heroes, some 60 volumes. We pull some from the shelves and flick through them: Hans Bellmer, Sally Mann, Weegee, Avedon, Allen Jones, Andre de Dienes, *Hollywood Babylon* by Kenneth Anger. There are many more, and Lindsey takes another one down: *Scene of the Crime: Photographs from the Los Angeles Police Department Archive*, a heavy volume with black and white photos of murder scenes and bloodshot victims from the first half of the last century, havoc of a Bonnie and Clyde and gangland variety. The introduction is by crime writer James Ellroy, who observes, 'You'll get intimate with victims, perpetrators, cops with game-face stoicism and cops in plain duress...the dead-body interiors say we all die alone. The march of death continues. There are bodies inside and outside, in cheap hotel rooms, on plank saloon floors, in semi-rural dump sites, draped over cement steps, spread across railroad tracks...'

'This was one of his absolute favourites,' Lindsey says. 'He used to pore over it. You can borrow it if you want.'

A light came into her blue eyes as they fell upon an image of a man with half his body smashed and spattered across the frame; a black and white photo, but you could smell the blood. 'I think Bob would have really loved it if I had photographed him on the train tracks like this...'

I asked: Did you ever see the police photographs of his death?
No.
Do you have the coroner's report?
No. I remember the horrible phrase 'death by multiple injuries'.

Lindsey Carlos Clarke

The thing is, my friend said to me, the thing is you have this terrible feeling of guilt with suicide, because you believe you could have done something. So I keep thinking I could have gone there that morning, could have stopped it, we could have done this, we could have done that.

I still wait for him to pitch up. We had this plan. He used to say to me, 'I'm not famous enough,' and I would say, 'Come on, why don't you fake your own death and we'll go to Brazil or somewhere?' Maybe that's why I needed to see the body, I don't know.

And then I went on some sort of adrenaline high. Scarlett and I laughed so much over certain things, we just got side-splitting laughter. It's the same as crying I think, but I couldn't really cry at all. It's like feeling the edge of something – it's so big I can't do it.

My main big concern thing is to do with Scarlett. All I know is, this is for ever, this damage is for ever now. So one can only repair the damage as much as one can. My father died when I was 17 and I miss him every day. A friend of mine, whose father also killed himself when she was 14, always said her question was, 'How could you leave me?' But I think Scarlett knows that that wasn't quite the case here. Nothing was a consideration, his own anxiety was too much for him. If he could have logic'd it out he wouldn't have done it. I said to Scarlett, 'You know when I think about my father I sometimes think, terrible things happen in the world and at least he's missing them.'

Simon Garfield

But you must feel this great kind of anger as well?

Lindsey Carlos Clarke

Anger? Anger like you can't believe. I sort of think everybody failed him, we all failed him somehow. And then this terrible empty feeling of sadness and remorse and a feeling of how vulnerable he was. That's why I protected him, because I knew I was stronger than he was, always. I'll never love anyone like I loved him. I think there's a piece of me that's gone, that doesn't exist. It's still a jolt. Sometimes I wake up in the morning and I think, oh what a lovely day, and I look out and think, oh no, it isn't a lovely day at all…

The funny thing is, I think it's worse now than it was then. We must have lived in total shock for the first year. Scarlett and I went on a sort of wild rampage, and just got on aeroplanes and flew first class and we just did all sorts of strange things. Lots of retail therapy, which has never really been my thing. Everyone's coming out to dinner, everyone! We're all going to lunch, right, I'm paying, let's drink champagne, oh let's drink cocktails.

Simon Garfield

What's the situation at the cemetery now?

Lindsey Carlos Clarke

No headstone, nothing. It's time to do it now, but I'm absolutely glued to the spot. I shall probably put the family crest with its motto 'nevertheless bravely', with a broken arm, an arrow with a broken arm. But what I've always really wanted for Bob was to have two marble figures, two girls, and they'd have marble bodies and then they'd have black marble arms, like long fetish gloves. It'd probably get defaced up there.

• • •

Simon Garfield

To what extent were you separated at the end?

Lindsey Carlos Clarke

Well, we weren't. The fact of the matter was, he was living in the basement.

All I said to him was, 'I can't live like this.' And he just said, 'Don't bully me.' I could never get any communication...I said to him, 'Bob, I cannot go to my grave like this.'

Simon Garfield

'Like this' meaning what?

Lindsey Carlos Clarke

Unloved, unfucked, unspoken to, un...just robotic. I said to him, 'What do I do in your life that you couldn't pay somebody to do?'

He said, 'Oh, don't be ridiculous. People our age don't have sex.' I looked at him and I said, 'That's not quite what I mean.' I found it very difficult to have a conversation with him on anything at all. It was always, 'I'll come back in a minute...' He could never address anything.

We sold our big studio, the 4,000-square-foot one. I didn't want to sell the studio, because I didn't see what the point was. But I found the studio in Putney and I said to him, 'Look, do you just want to do your art? We have enough money for you just to do the work you want.' He said yes, and we spent a huge amount of money doing it up. The Putney studio had a courtyard, so he could do his arty-farty stuff and then when he got bored he could sit out there and have a beer. And then he said, 'I don't want to be in Putney.' So I wonder if the real fuck-up didn't come when we sold the studio. We moved out in September 2005, seven months before the end, although he still had the final shows to come.

He did some very odd things, getting rid of a lot of equipment. As if he was getting ready for the end. He was a master of the darkroom, so when that went...People would say to him, 'Why don't you do more colour?' and he would say, 'I haven't even finished black and white.' Packing up that darkroom was something very final for him. Because there wasn't space in Putney he was going to rebuild the darkroom at the beach. But then I think he just looked at it in the box and thought, no. He thought his equipment looked like space junk. He thought, this is over. And then he thought, everything is over.

I also said to him, 'Why do you envy photographers and artists who fuck their models? Why don't you have it? Why don't you just do it? If that will give you the picture you think you really want. Do it.' It was something he wanted to do, but then he also wanted to run home. It was like living with a cross between a Victorian school-teacher and a delinquent teenager.

And then we decided to sell Putney, and I found him this wonderful studio in Chelsea, bang in the middle, next to Emma Sargeant. You get a huge space at the bottom and a studio at the top, fab. Not an aircraft hangar but certainly wonderful portraits you could do there. I went with Jane Chesterton and Scarlett, and it was £1.1 million and I offered them a million. You have to be termed an artist to buy one, they won't let you otherwise, but of course it was no problem with Bob, and it was really exciting. I even said to him, 'Why don't you absolutely have the life you want? Go to lunch when you want...pick up the models you want.'

The personal side was also majorly important, but it wasn't something that had suddenly happened. It was something we had discussed five years previously. I had said to him, 'Why do we have everything? Why do we have a fabulous studio and great house, and a house by the seaside and a beautiful daughter – and why are we so unhappy?' I said, 'I'm lonely. I'm lonely because you're not in the room with me ever.' He could never disconnect from what he was doing. Quite near the end we went to a party near Charing Cross, and a girl hung around his neck all night. I felt sick, I thought, I can't do this any more. I felt like an idiot.

I said to him once, not long after moving into this [current, Chelsea] house, 'You can have your girls in your studio but don't you ever, ever bring one of them back here.' The beach house was supposed to be pure as well, but that didn't last long. So, 'No girls at my house, I want it uncontaminated,' but now of course it's been contaminated by the police showing up at the door.

When I tried to get out five years previously…My whole reason wasn't that I really wanted to leave him. I loved him, I was obsessed by him. But I got no love from him. Yes, he used to ring people up and say, 'Tell Lindsey I love her,' but that wasn't much use to me. Even people we hardly knew.

There was a day his motorbike got stolen when he was with somebody else who shall remain nameless. He said he'd gone to see her to help her hang some photographs…Now, as a great male friend of mine said to me, if he fucked lots of models at his studio, one would almost say, whatever…is that that exciting? But it was much more complex than that. It was about secrecy. He said to me, 'I don't enjoy sex unless it's secret.' I said, 'Well, if I leave you it won't be secret any more, so will you then have to find another secret?'

I said to him, 'I want to change the shape of how we operate.' Loads of people change their lives. He said to me, 'But I'm not a drunk, and I'm not violent and I don't take drugs…' I said, 'Well, that's three of the addictions, what about the addiction to other people? To the degree where you practically sleep outside their front door and endlessly surround them with poems and presents? Because that's what he did with me, and I'm sure he did it with Sue. And now he was doing it with others. I think he was amoral – I don't think he understood. He would have made a fantastic criminal, a fantastic robber. Everything had to be a risk. He took terrible risks with Scarlett when she was little. My mother used to freak out.

Simon Garfield

Was he into coke as well?

Lindsey Carlos Clarke

No! He hated drugs. He used to smoke a little bit of dope, which was very good for him, because he used to go to sleep then. Always a relief.

I didn't want to disappear out of the loop. All I wanted was to be with him. The problem was, all I was was a dogsbody.

Simon Garfield

Were you unfaithful to him?

Lindsey Carlos Clarke

Um, no. Not until very close to the end.

Simon Garfield

Did he find out about it?

Lindsey Carlos Clarke

He was suspicious a couple of times. The thing was, I thought I was going to be very clever. I made a decision with a girlfriend of mine. I said, 'I'm going to pick up a man I don't fancy. I'm going to pick up a man I don't fancy and I'm going to have sex with him. And if I don't fancy him I won't fall in love with him, and that'll be really easy.' I did manage to achieve this, strangely enough, which was quite intriguing. I totally understand how people…if you get into the right frame of mind you can have sex with anybody. It's just never been where I've been at.

I never set out to be totally faithful, because I've never thought about it like that. It so happened that the person I was in love with, I was with. It was very bad being in a bed with somebody, dreaming about having sex with the man I'm most in love with. And then realise he's asleep next to me, but actually not have any sex or warmth with this person. For a long time. Ten years. Twelve years. Fifteen years maybe.

So I found this strange gentleman five years before the end. Crena used to call him the Briefcase. This very dreary man. We met in Barbados. He was quite a good listener. He was an English psychologist who lived in America, which was seriously convenient. He'd come over and stay in a hotel, and I loved the idea of the Whore and the Hotel thing – that Belle de Jour fantasy. My husband's photographing these amazing women in all sorts of positions, but I'm actually doing sex for real in this strange hotel down the road. Is this not a weird thing to do? He used to really irritate me, this man. I always used to order really expensive wine just to annoy him. He was obsessed by me. He used to say how much he was looking forward to staying at my house. I thought, you must be joking. I used to come out of the hotel, get into my car, put the stereo on really loud and think, this is going to pad my life. I'm going to make two pieces of the jigsaw fit together.

Of course it didn't work. It lasted about six months. Then what happened was, Mr Stupid sent me a text. Bob and I each had a mobile phone number that only had one digit difference. Mr Stupid sent the text to Bob. And not a very interesting text. Some dreary thing about some dreary music he once played bass guitar on. But Bob, with special radar, got alerted. Then he got into my phone…Bob was fantastic on secrets, and I wasn't. He got into my phone and found a much more interesting text, sent it to his phone, and then went into a blind rage. He charged into the bedroom in the middle of the night and said, 'I don't want you taking my child to America!' Why would I do that? He said, 'I need to know who this man is.' No you don't. You've never told me anything you've done in your whole life – why would you need to know this?

The fact of the matter was, I was right over it anyway. He did lots of pleading. He would come into the bedroom in the middle of the night and say, 'I want us to stay together.'

I said, 'Fine, but you've got to change something. Go see some-one.' So he went to see a therapist. For a while things were better. Not amazing, but better. But then he decided not to go again, because he felt, 'Lindsey's here and everything's fine.' He probably thought, 'So long as my life is being run okay, I can get on and pick up another girl, and photograph her at the beach, and then prob-ably sleep with her. Because my life's okay now.'

I wish I could just ask him now: This girl, what happened there? And what about that one? And that other one?

• • •

Philippe Garner

I like to feel that Bob's work deserves a place, and a not insignificant place, in the annals of British photography. But I think there is quite a lot of work to be done to situate him as a significant artist in an ongoing artistic British tradition. I don't mean finding the right fancy art-speak, but finding a way in plain English.

Curiously since his death nothing has come up in the big auction houses. I gather a few bits and pieces have come up in secondary sale rooms. Ghislain told me he'd bought one or two things in Bloomsbury because they were estimated low and went even cheaper; they weren't on the radar.

In many respects, Bob's work satisfies many criteria for being a highly marketable product. Sorry to use such a word for it, but it's high, high quality, sufficiently rare, there's a finite amount, many of the prints are unique. It is quite tough, but a lot of it just manages to be about the right side of the line in a marketplace which is actually increasingly broadminded. And now he's dead, and we know there's an extraordinary story around him, so I think all the ingredients are in place for it to become something which is really collected and sought after.

John Windsor (*writing in the* Observer, *May 2006*)
Best tip in affordable contemporary erotic photography is Irish-born Bob Carlos Clarke...

Clarke never matched Helmut Newton's ultra-stylish *Sie Kommen* – four sassy-looking nude women marching in line towards camera, which is worth at least £30,000 at auction – but his fetishistic, often rubber-clad women of the 1980s and 1990s are already iconic. Two fetched £476 and £547 in the February sale and his more famous Tanya Catsuit – bare breasts, rubber pants – fetched £881 at Bloomsbury three years ago.

Philippe Garner

But it will be a tough job to resituate him in the marketplace without the collaboration of a really strong gallery with good national ties that can pitch him not just in Britain but internationally, a gallery with real connections that might stage exhibitions in the US, in

Europe, in the Far East. And I think it needs the benefit of a little bit of curatorial credibility; where are our British museums giving some sort of respect to what Bob achieved? There is a wall of silence from the V&A, from Tate Britain, the museum at Bradford. They should systematically be spotlighting work of real substance. I'll make a comparison, I don't know, I'm not trying for one moment to suggest that Bob is an equivalent artist to Francis Bacon, though in some ways there are parallels in their psychology; but why isn't Bob represented in major British collections? They're both engaged, it's a sort of fight to the death with death, darkness, the primordial forces of sexuality. I think it's a tragedy and actually shameful that he's not represented.

Ghislain Pascal

I invested a lot of time and money in him. Setting up Panic Pictures and the website – it cost tens of thousands. In a sense I'm annoyed that Bob did kill himself, because the reason I set it up was so that I would have other strings to my bow, not just dealing with individual clients all day long. The Bob stuff was good fun, it was different, and now I don't have that.

Philippe Garner

When I went to the archive with Lindsey after his death there were all those extraordinary pictures that he had scribbled over, defaced them, where he'd got into a fight with his own pictures. I was quite unfamiliar with those until then. I thought of the Baconesque wrestling with your medium, and this extraordinary controlled rage that was funnelled into the moment of creativity. I found them kind of scary because you just felt the force of his personality there, wrestling with his own pictures.

• • •

Ghislain Pascal

The reason he called me Squirrel was because he had this theory that I was hiding all my nuts, getting all the money and just hiding it. The greatest thing that Bob could have said was that he trusted

291

me. I've never ripped off anybody, it's just not in my nature, and he knew that. And the reason our relationship worked was because it was based on trust.

Lindsey Carlos Clarke

No he didn't. He didn't trust anybody. But I trusted you.

Ghislain Pascal

He was always convinced that I was making an absolute fortune from him. When he came round to my old house in Clapham, he said, 'How did you pay for this?' Like, Bob, shut up. You've got a £2 million house in Chelsea and a studio and a beach house. He never appreciated what he had.

Lindsey Carlos Clarke

I sold the beach house last year. It just sat there, it's a responsibility because it's right on the sea. I talked about it with Scarlett, and we just didn't really know what to do, because we didn't really want to go there any more.

I went down with Plews not long after Bob died. We drove down on this very windy day and it was very spooky, and all his things were there, and the wind sort of howled through the house and it was like a film set. I suddenly thought I'd like to close the book on this really. And then Crena said she wanted to buy it. Scarlett said she'd really like Crena to have it because then she could still go down there.

After Myra died, both Bob and Andrew inherited some money. Not a huge amount but enough, and I said to him, 'What are you going to do with it, because whether we're married or not it's not my money, it's from your family.' He said he couldn't think about it, so I remembered the beach hut he loved as a child in Ballyquin. You know that photo he shot of the girl on the stones – that's in Ballyquin, that's Sue. So basically I recreated that idea of the beach thing for him and for Scarlett. I used to drive down every week on a Friday with Jane Chesterton, and we'd go along the coast everywhere looking for a beach house, and then somebody tipped us off and said there's a house that's come up for sale, right on the beach, and there it was, a shell, and we looked through the letterbox and I just rang the agent and said, 'What do you want for it?' Unfortunately, everyone else wanted it too, so I had to go to sealed bids, which was absolutely terrifying, but I got it.

And then last year, after about nine years, I brought back his stuff. We used to collect stones with holes in them and we had a big loop of them and Bob used to call it 'your mother's migraine necklace', because my mother's always got a migraine, and we were convinced it was so heavy it would definitely bring one on. He really used to play down there, and make beautiful things.

Jane Chesterton

This is Bob and me on the beach in Ireland…this is the same, Bob and me. When he had no money I lent him enough to buy his first camera and he was very grateful, so he always called me his sweet benefactress. He did all the shots at my twenty-first birthday. Scarlett has asked to have some of these.

Simon Garfield

She showed me a collage in rainbow colours, printed on fabric: three people dressed as sad clowns, Sam Chesterton and Lucy, a friend, with Bob in green paint looking envious. And she showed me a handmade collaged postcard, with Jane dressed in a Guides uniform. It was inscribed: 'My Sweet Benefactress. To Jolly old Janey, with love and best wishes for a spiffing Christmas and a Wizard New Year.' It was signed Sob and Boo, which was Sue and Bob.

Paul Plews

I went down to the beach house maybe half a dozen times. It always felt like Bob's retreat and his moods changed. Whatever pressure he felt, whatever weight he carried around when he was in London, probably about acceptance, to be seen to be doing things, I think when he went down there it was just – all that went. He would spend so much time collecting the driftwood, making lamps and other strange things. It was almost taking refuge in smaller, mundane aspects of life, just the tactile beauty of small pieces of wood. It's like an obsession, building something and looking for the perfect piece that'll fit. I suppose we all have our obsessions.

Lindsey Carlos Clarke

I always thought he was going to die down there. I thought he was going to drown himself. I thought he was going to wait until it got really rough in the sea because he wasn't a great swimmer, and I thought that's what he's going to do. He's going to go out one day and not come back.

Ghislain Pascal

Lindsey's moved on. She loved him, for God's sake, there's no doubt about that, but she's moved on.

And Scarlett has coped very well. Obviously it's still early, so it's very difficult to tell.

Crena Watson

It never entered my mind that I'd buy his beach house. It was on the market for a year after he died. I sold my studio, and I was looking for a long time for a new place. I used to get so claustrophobic in London, but I couldn't find anything that would satisfy my need for nature and my need for work. Then one day I got a big tax bill and I thought I can't afford anywhere in London, so I just said to Lindsey, 'I want to buy the beach house.' Someone else was just about to sign for it, but of course I got it. It's been a challenge living down there alone. I had a boyfriend who lives in Hong Kong and it was just too difficult.

I've had the builders in, changed it a bit, and I feel I can be creative there. The waves come right up to the edge of the garden. I don't feel Bob's presence there at all now, or at least not in a morbid way. When Scarlett came there after I had moved in, and something fell over, she thought maybe it was a sign. On the beach, after he had died, I once saw her setting fire to a letter she had written.

Simon Garfield

A letter to him?

Crena Watson

Yeah. She didn't see me watching.

• • •

Simon Garfield

I went down to the beach house for the first time in August 2008. It was called 'Starfish'. Crena picked me up in her black Beetle from Chichester train station, and I thought it funny that it was the same type of car that Bob had once cartwheeled against on a beach, but this didn't really have any significance.

As we were driving through some quiet and respectable areas, heavy with the elderly, Crena asked me what I thought the beach house would look like, and I could tell it was a loaded question. I said: 'Wild, isolated, very near the sea, ramshackle...'

She said, 'That's what Bob would have wanted you to say.'

After 15 minutes we pulled up in Bracklesham Bay, and there it was: a house in a suburban street, with neighbouring houses on either side. There was a builder's van outside and bags of stuff either going in or out.

Crena showed me the studio she had converted and extended from a garage, a place she would soon use to take, manipulate and print her imaginative photographs.

It was a nice clean space with interesting ceiling lamps, but it didn't look like anything special. Unlike the house itself.

It was one of those enviable houses in which you can see right through the ground floor from the front door, in this case to the sea. There was a copy of *Elle Decoration* on a side-table, and the house would have looked right at home in it: elaborate wooden lamp sculptures that Bob had made, Italian floor lamps, some fine modern art, furniture from modernist shops on the King's Road. But the real wonder was at the back, the deck and terrace that led to a garden that led to the sea. The shingle on the edge of the garden contained more sculptures that Bob had assembled from driftwood, and the terrace also had a little bath in it, that Crena told me was occasionally used by Scarlett when the weather was fine.

In the kitchen we had an idea: Crena would take photographs of some of the main characters in this book. Because she was a friend of Bob's, her subjects would trust her and relax. For her it seemed like another way of saying goodbye to Bob.

Crena Watson

Did I tell you about the time Scarlett went to get his bag? The Priory wouldn't just send it round to their house, someone had to go and pick it up. Lindsey didn't have time while she was organising the funeral, or she couldn't face it, so Scarlett went by herself, which was very brave. When she got there they said she was under 18 and they couldn't give her the bag, so she went home, forged Lindsey's signature on a letter authorising it all, and then went back to get it. It was mostly socks – lots and lots of pairs of socks.

• • •

Andrew Carlos Clarke

Our relationship ended very well, and we were good friends before he died.

Simon Garfield

Andrew Carlos Clarke was on the phone from Ireland. He was recovering from drug addiction, and had recently come out of a clinic. He was keen to help as best he could.

Andrew Carlos Clarke

I'm not that well at the moment, but I'm okay. I don't know what you know about him or what I can tell you.

I'm eight years younger than him. He used to put me in go-karts and let me go flying off down the hill. He tied me on the back of his bicycle and went as fast as he could. He always said this thing about coming home and finding a younger child in the nest. I don't think it really affected him that much, but I think he liked to say it. But I think Bob was much closer to my father, and I would be much closer to my mother.

My father was 66 when I was born and 75 when he died. He was very aristocratic, hung around with all the right sort of people. As a young man he worked for the Duke of Marlborough. I used to love the stories he told of the war. He was in the First World War – in the Black Watch. He fought at Gallipoli. Out of his battalion only two came home. My mother's first husband, Rob Watson, was shot down and killed over North Africa in the Second World War. She always wanted to go to North Africa to see the memorial there, but she never did.

He was older than most people's grandads. It was a bit embarrassing at school when the parents came to play cricket and he wasn't really up to it and had to have runners. He was a very wild man, always chasing women. He had a couple of illegitimate children too I think. In fact, I know one of their names but I don't know if I should say.

I went to Marlborough College. A desperate experience – like a prison. It was the done thing – people thought it was good for you. I was there until I was 16. I failed all my O levels, I think the first person there in 50 years to do so. I went on to a crammer, which turned out to be even worse.

Bob once got stabbed. He was in the woods and he got stabbed, but I don't know the details. I remember him being constantly in trouble with motorbikes. When we had our house on the beach he drove my father's car one night and he sank it in the sea. You've heard the story of the condoms? When he brought 200 or something into the country when he came over for his holidays. He was allowed something like five for his stay of two weeks. He would have been about 18. He brought back quite a few girls. He married this girl called Sue Green, and I think he was having an affair with Lindsey before they got married. I'm trying to think of what sort of things I can tell you that you want to know. After school he worked for the *Daily Express* in Dublin for a short while.

I first got into farming, and then I was a mechanic. I never really stuck to any work properly. I had a drug problem for a good few years, which didn't help my relationship with Bob at all. He wasn't really into drugs but I was, and that strained our relationship. I was at his first wedding, to Sue. I lost my virginity at that one. With a top London model, who had also been a girlfriend of Bob and was done as a sort of jealousy thing.

Sue was a very gentle person, just probably not strong enough for him. But she was a really beautiful girl.

Over the last five years I got on much better with Bob. We were emailing each other every week. And we would be calling each other on the phone. It wasn't bad – we just didn't see very much of each other.

We sent each other songs from our childhood – Irish songs, that kind of stuff. He would send me funny pictures. I was a great admirer of his work, although I didn't find the pictures sexy, like most people would. Maybe that was just because it was done by my family. Mum was very proud of his work. She wasn't embarrassed by it, she was a fairly open person. We were both at her funeral, but I didn't attend Bob's funeral because I was sick and couldn't get over to England. I had pneumonia.

I heard of his death – a guy who was working with me came and told me. I was in bed, I was sick. Lindsey called, I think. I knew he was in the Priory. I was talking to him all the time. I was probably the last person he spoke to. I got a lovely text from him just before he died, saying it was a pity we hadn't got on better and that really we loved each other – that sort of thing.

Simon Garfield
That sounds like it has an air of finality about it.

Andrew Carlos Clarke
Yeah.

Simon Garfield
He didn't talk about killing himself, did he?

Andrew Carlos Clarke
Well, I'd arranged for the police in England to pick him up, because I knew he was going to do something. It was through a friend who was in the CID. Bob had agreed to come over to Ireland a few days before he killed himself. I was pretty much aware he was going to kill himself.

They were going to put him on a train to Heathrow and get him over to me. Because I was too sick to travel. He was aware of it. He had a mobile phone when he was in the clinic, which I don't think he was allowed to have.

Simon Garfield
And did you feel that you could have somehow pulled him out of it all?

Andrew Carlos Clarke
Yes. He and Lindsey were splitting up at the time. You knew that, obviously. He was very mixed up and sad over Lindsey – he died of a broken heart. It was one of the main factors. There was this threat made to him as well that he was terribly worried about.

Simon Garfield
I heard about that from Ghislain Pascal, his agent, but I was never sure how real that was.

Andrew Carlos Clarke
It was really real.

Simon Garfield
He was being threatened by people for some copyright screw-up?

Andrew Carlos Clarke
He wouldn't tell me exactly who was threatening him, but he certainly told me it was very serious. He wanted to get hold of this gentleman who looked after our affairs and would have given him proper advice on it.

As far as I know it was related to a woman – he might have crossed somebody. He certainly seemed to think it was very serious.

Simon Garfield
You were too ill to come to the funeral, but you came over afterwards?

Andrew Carlos Clarke
Yeah. I get on all right with Lindsey but I get on very well with Scarlett.

Simon Garfield
Can you see much of Bob in her?

Andrew Carlos Clarke

Oh, an awful lot. The way she talks. She looks like him. And she'll be an artist as well one day.

Simon Garfield

What do you miss most about Bob?

Andrew Carlos Clarke

I hold him in very high regard. And I really miss not having him around. I am always thinking about him.

• • •

Simon Garfield

And so, after all that, I had written my Bob Carlos Clarke book. Mostly, it was just a group of his friends sitting around talking, although some of them never knew each other and some were separated by half the world. I hope it's been a seductive tapestry; I hope it's got the man. I found the experience fascinating and moving, and what began as a vague interest soon turned into a more passionate quest.

Do I like Bob? Do I like the portrait of Bob I uncovered? It's much more involved than that: I began to see myself in him. Not the extremes, but what man doesn't hold some of his obsessions and desires? Who wouldn't want a bit of his life a bit of the time? And who wouldn't share his disappointments of middle age?

I am so grateful for the way everyone was so open and had such insights. And how great were Philippe, Geraldine and Lindsey in particular? Ghislain Pascal seemed to have no problem giving up his role as the prime subject, although obviously he was happy that one of his clients was being written about in such detail. It might even increase the value of his photographs. I just hope that it will increase people's appreciation of them.

Since I had first started talking about doing a book with him, Ghislain had parted company with Emma B and Jacqueline Gold, and Bob had become even more of a focus for him. As the autumn of 2008 began, he and Lindsey were doing all sorts of small projects

Bob with his brother Andrew, Ireland 1964.

together – including choosing prints for a bedroom at Marco Pierre White's Yew Tree Inn in Berkshire – and some big ones as well, including the possible opening of a gallery selling Bob's prints. And Lindsey was talking vaguely of moving abroad – getting the whole of Bob's estate running smoothly and then somehow putting more distance between her past and her future.

It was clear that more than two years after he died, her former husband's presence still dominated her life. There had been another relationship with another, younger, man, but always there would be comparisons, and the inevitable sense that she would never find anyone else quite as alive as Bob was. Or as Bob is.

Andrew Carlos Clarke believed he could have saved his brother's life had he got to him in time. I'm not so sure – I think the path was fairly set. And I think that anyone who had tried to save him from himself would not have emerged unscathed; those who had tried in the past had been deeply scarred by him, and by remembering him with love had tried valiantly to erase the pain he had caused them.

It's a shame that Bob couldn't have read this book, as that may have changed his impression of how highly his work was regarded, and how much people cared for him. And he could have seen himself as others truly saw him, which may possibly be as he really was.

Perhaps this book is finally the recognition he felt he deserved. Would that have made much difference to the end of the story? Probably not. It wouldn't have been like *It's A Wonderful Life*, where James Stewart gets down off the bridge.

Lindsey Carlos Clarke

Probably not. But I also have a funny feeling: we saw Terence Donovan about a month before he killed himself, and they'd given me all sorts of reasons of what they think happened there. But Terence Donovan had also come to the edge of a situation where he was no longer the young happening photographer who could dance with girls, not that he ever did probably very much. But the idea – it's a power thing. But Bob could have really been the grand master. I remember Scarlett saying, 'If only Daddy would calm down, he could be so cool.'

Simon Garfield

Because not all artists are obsessed like that.

Lindsey Carlos Clarke

No! Allen Jones isn't like that, thank God.

Simon Garfield

But even geniuses like Picasso, they live a long life, they change, they adapt, they have different periods, they go in and out, they fuck up their lives.

Lindsey Carlos Clarke

Picasso was a complete bastard as well.

Simon Garfield

They fuck up their personal lives for the sake of their art, but somehow their art sees them through. But for Bob, the art wasn't enough.

Lindsey Carlos Clarke

The great divide – he couldn't somehow join his personal life with his work life. I know we weren't blissfully happy, but there was a big area of our lives where we were fantastically good together. We had the same visual thing. He could say anything to me about his work, I wasn't put out by anything, and if he'd come back with a body in the car I wouldn't have been terribly surprised. But I think my personality was all about repair. I always believe I can fix everything, that's something inside me. You do what you're best at, but no matter what I did, it wasn't enough.

• • •

Simon Garfield

I had been keen to buy one of Bob's prints for months, and I knew Ghislain and Lindsey would do me a deal. But the choice was difficult. I wanted to get something representative, and something on a large scale. I couldn't afford one of the early collages, and would be pushed to get one of the limited-edition signed prints. I reasoned

I'd be just as happy with a large digital print, and although I loved a great many of his pictures of women I feared they might cause offence. This was in 2008! Astonishingly, my reaction to Bob's work was the same one he had faced so frequently over 30 years, the same one that had held him back: I was nervous of it, it was potent, it had the power to confound and upset.

There were many pictures of alluring women I liked, but in the end I went for *Roses*, the safest of choices, a huge black and white study of four roses dripping with dew. Lindsey told me she had stolen them one morning from a neighbour's garden. But of course these aren't just roses. They were probably on their last day before the petals began to fall, a study of decay. And the furl of buds and petals suggest nothing so much as vaginal folds. It is a luscious photograph, vibrant and dying at once. It cost me £1,000, and it excites me each time I look at it, and I never have enough of it – so many layers.

Oddly enough, I had learned my lesson about this from the work of Allen Jones. Not long before I had met my ex-wife in the early 1980s I had bought an Allen Jones print called *Beach Scene* from a shop in the King's Road. This depicted the outline of a woman in a figure-hugging bathing costume lying on her back on a beach, a huge expanse of blue sky behind her, and she was being brought a book by what I assumed to be a man in a dark suit – perhaps a butler, but as you only saw the outstretched sleeve of the jacket, who knows? The print cost me a few hundred pounds, and I loved the luxuriousness of it, the way it took you to St Tropez or similar.

Allen Jones

The image is very lyrical, and the woman is hardly depicted in a chauvinistic way.

Simon Garfield

It seemed to me the woman was in charge, the dominant force being served by a male, but my ex-wife didn't like it at all, judging it – I guess, as this was the decade that the word took off – sexist. So we took it to Waddington Graphics in Cork Street and swapped it for a John Hoyland print now worth half the price. And after our divorce, she got to keep it.

• • •

Scarlett Carlos Clarke

Sometimes I don't really think he's gone at all. And then some days I think: he really has.

Sometimes what I've learned about Dad in the past two years makes me feel as though I didn't actually know him when he was alive. It makes me feel as though he was acting all his life, covering his real feelings. He probably wouldn't have been able to share them. It makes me feel I didn't really know him. Now I know him so much better. I'm not angry with him. I think I understand what it would be like to be in his skin. It would have been very difficult, not being happy with himself. At least, I hope I understand him now.

Lindsey Carlos Clarke

After Bob died, Scarlett said that she was worried that people were only friends with her only because of what had happened. There's a real double-edge thing going on there, deep insecurity being 16 and also a sort of inner peace and emotional maturity. Girlfriends of mine come round and have a drink and say, 'Oh, bloody hell, my boyfriend's pissing me off,' and Scarlett goes, 'I don't think he's really suitable for you,' or, 'I think you're being unfair...'

I'm pretty cool with her about school and things. If my daughter's not pregnant or on drugs, I really don't care. I mean after what's happened, I never forget reading an article after John Lennon was shot, and Yoko said they'd been so precious about their diet, and they'd been so careful about not drinking and smoking, and being so careful with themselves, and they had Sean, the boy, and were so careful with him, and Yoko said to Sean after John was shot, do whatever you like – so I do understand that.

They do this thing at school where they ascertain what job you'd be suitable for. You spend a whole day doing this career guidance thing, and they concluded she'd be best as a cross between a prison wardress and a long-distance lorry driver. She rang me up straight away and we were splitting our sides. You know, I just want her to go to art school, because she'll really enjoy it, and because that's where you do your most interesting part of growing up. You're partly an adult but you're still being looked after. For me, art school was the best bit. I remember my father said to me, 'There are creative people and then there's everybody else.'

Scarlett Carlos Clarke

That photo of him that I took? It was just this perfect moment.

Simon Garfield

Scarlett was leafing through some of her father's books, and an album that she had made of old family pictures, and the page fell on the famous photo she had taken of her father. It is a sad shot, his head on the palm of his hand. He looks weary, bare-chested, the edge of an unmade bed working as a nice metaphor for a turmoiled mind. We may see too much in it, knowing what we now do. But he is looking at the lens as if to say, 'No artifice here.' After he died, it was hung at the National Portrait Gallery. As Ghislain had told me, Scarlett was the youngest photographer ever to make it in there.

Scarlett Carlos Clarke

They always say I was older than I was when I took it. I must have been younger than 14. It wasn't a planned thing – he wasn't posing. He was just sitting on the bed in Mum and Dad's bedroom in Stevenage Road. He developed it and said, 'Oh, this is a really good photo,' but I couldn't really tell. He said, 'It's the only photo that someone's taken of me that I like.'

One of the photos he did of Marco went up next to it.

I put this album together after he died. That's my uncle Andrew in Ireland. My dad's mum was a really good photographer as well. That's their dad when he was really old. That's the dog he was given when he was really ill. Dad hated Uncle Andrew – he was horrid to him.

That's Mum and him. That's me. This is Mum and Dad playing games with people he knew. Even if he hardly knew them he'd get them roped in. That's him and Patrick Lichfield, and that's Patrick's daughter. That's Mustique. When Dad first gave me this book he ripped out some of the pages, some of the rude bits. This is Mum's best friend, Geraldine. He went out with her. These ones in Havana are my favourite ones. Oh no, these are – these ones in the club. And that's him and Sue together, and that's Sue on the bike. That's me drunk at a New Year's thing. And these are recent, after the funeral at Frankie's.

That's the one of me that was on the cover of a photography magazine, the hat is made of black feathers. I hate it. I never wanted to do it, so he said, 'Okay, we'll make a deal, I'll give you money...' so it became a job. The photo's not natural, make-up on when you're six years old, not normal. I like the photos he did of me that are just normal, normal black and white pictures, just playing.

So there we are, all these photos, and I'm getting more.

Did you ever meet my dad?

Simon Garfield

A couple of times, yes.

Scarlett Carlos Clarke

He would have wound you up if he met you.

Simon Garfield

I'm in his *Shooting Sex* book, right at the very end. I'm the journalist from the *Observer* he mentions. Your dad was sitting at Bar Italia in Soho in the early morning, feeling frayed from working late. 'I catch my reflection behind the bar,' he wrote, 'and I'm reminded of the words of a journalist who interviewed me recently for the *Observer*. He couldn't decide whether I was glamorous or sleazy. I'm not sure which is worse, but from this perspective glamour is keeping a very low profile.'

Scarlett Carlos Clarke

I'm not sure he would have liked you.

Simon Garfield

Well, the times that I met him I always thought, I should like to talk to him more, and I assumed there would be opportunities to do that.

Anyway, thanks for all your time, you've been very open with me.

Scarlett Carlos Clarke

Is that it for now? I'm sure there must be lots of things I haven't thought of. You can join us for dinner tonight if you want and we can talk some more.

afterword

Andrew Carlos Clarke died of a heart attack in October 2008.

He had been unwell for a while, and suffered from emphysema, but his death was a great shock to all who knew him. When I talked to Lindsey about it she said, 'Andrew told you that Bob died of a broken heart, and I think it was probably the same for him.' Andrew missed his mother greatly, and when Bob committed suicide he believed he would never recover.

Lindsey described a bleak, well-attended funeral in Ireland, with Scarlett brave through it all despite her grief. In his will, Andrew left Scarlett his coveted purple Porsche, the car in which they had driven around Ireland on her last visit.

The Little Black Gallery, a partnership between Lindsey Carlos Clarke, Ghislain Pascal and Tamara Beckwith, opened in Chelsea in November 2008. The first show was a great success, featuring photographs by Bob Carlos Clarke, Crena Watson, Paul Plews and John Stoddart, alongside Terry O'Neill, Norman Eales and Barry Lategan. The second exhibition, entitled Kiss, featured embracing couples from all perspectives.

The third show, planned for May to July 2009, will be a Bob Carlos Clarke solo exhibition, featuring several of the photographs in this book and some unique early work. It will be Bob's first retrospective. Everything will be for sale.

SG, February 2009

acknowledgements, and a note on sources

I wish to thank everyone who helped me with this book, particularly those who agreed to be interviewed and offered both hospitality and trust. They had no knowledge or approval of the way I would treat their thoughts and words, and I hope I have been true to their intentions. The quotes from Bob Carlos Clarke come from my own interview with him and a few photography magazines and exhibition catalogues, but the majority are from the first draft of the self-published *Shooting Sex*, used with permission from Lindsey Carlos Clarke and the Estate of Bob Carlos Clarke.

www.bobcarlosclarke.com
www.simongarfield.com